Oracle Press™

Oracle9*i* for Windows® 2000 Tips & Techniques

Oracle Press™

Oracle9*i* for Windows® 2000 Tips & Techniques

Scott Jesse
Matthew Hart
Mike Sale

McGraw-Hill/Osborne

New York Chicago San Francisco
Lisbon London Madrid Mexico City Milan
New Delhi San Juan Seoul Singapore Sydney Toronto

McGraw-Hill/Osborne
2600 Tenth Street
Berkeley, California 94710
U.S.A.

To arrange bulk purchase discounts for sales promotions, premiums, or fund-raisers, please contact **McGraw-Hill/Osborne** at the above address. For information on translations or book distributors outside the U.S.A., please see the International Contact Information page immediately following the index of this book.

Oracle9*i* for Windows® 2000 Tips & Techniques

1234567890 CUS CUS 01987654321

ISBN 0-07-219462-6

Publisher
Brandon A. Nordin

Vice President & Associate Publisher
Scott Rogers

Acquisitions Editor
Lisa McClain

Project Editors
Ami Knox & Carolyn Welch

Acquisitions Coordinator
Athena Honore

Technical Editors
Ray Hachem & Soumendra Paik

Copy Editor
Ami Knox

Proofreader
Linda Medoff

Indexer
Valerie Robbins

Computer Designers
George Toma Charbak & Michelle Galicia

Illustrators
Michael Mueller & Lyssa Wald

Series Design
Jani Beckwith

Cover Series Design
Damore Johann Design, Inc.

This book was composed with Corel VENTURA™ Publisher.

We would like to dedicate this book to the memory of the victims of September 11, 2001. One of the victims, turned hero, was an Oracle employee named Todd Beamer. Todd's heroics and the heroics of his fellow passengers on United Flight 93 saved countless innocent lives that day. For the ultimate sacrifice made by the passengers on that flight, a grateful nation is forever indebted to you. In recognition of these sacrifices, we have asked the publisher to direct a portion of all future author royalties from the sale of this book to the Todd M. Beamer Foundation: http://www.beamerfoundation.org/.

Scott, Matt, and Mike

About the Authors

Matthew Hart has been assured that this author blurb would not list any incriminating information about his inability to stay on a bike or ski a straight line. He was told the words "accident prone" would not be used. He has also been assured that no one would possibly mention any surprise at his ability to keep a job for over three years at Oracle. Matthew also insisted on mentioning that he has a both a wife and a daughter, which proves, he insists, that he is a healthy, balanced individual. His wife refused to comment on any and all claims of health and/or balance by the author.

Scott Jesse is a full-time father of three and a part-time husband (aspiring for a full-time position). Scott has been an avid Denver Broncos fan for his entire life, and an avid Colorado Rockies and Colorado Avalanche fan for their entire lives. He has also been known to occasionally hit a golf ball past the ladies' tees (at least once per 18 holes). Aside from these endeavors, Scott has moonlighted as an Oracle Support Professional for the past 5+ years, where he currently holds the title of Senior Technical Specialist and Oracle Certified Professional.

Mike Sale is the husband of Laurie and soon-to-be father. He enjoys his guitar, rollerblading, and antiques. Mike has been a hopeless geek since discovering 6502 assembly language programming as a teenager. Mike has been at working with Oracle since version 6 and is an Oracle Certified Professional DBA. He has done extensive work with the Oracle Database, OAS, 9iAS, and Oracle Portal. Mike currently works as a Consulting Technical Specialist and Team Lead on the Product Line Bug Diagnosis and Escalations (PLBDE) team and is the Oracle NT/Windows 2000 representative for the Compaq/Oracle Joint Escalation Center.

Contents at a Glance

PART V

Appendices

Contents

PART III

Windows 2000: The Premiere Enterprise Management Platform

PART IV
Clustering and High Availability

PART V
Appendices

Foreword

In recent years, the Windows operating system has become an increasingly popular platform for the deployment of Internet applications. During that time, the Oracle database has grown into the market-leading database for the Windows platform.

From the outset, Oracle's goal has been to provide the highest performing and most tightly integrated database on Windows. As a result, Oracle invested early to move its market-leading database technology to the Windows platform. In 1993, Oracle was the first company to provide a database for Windows NT. Initially, Oracle's development efforts were concentrated on improving the performance and optimizing the architecture of the database on Windows. Oracle7 for Windows NT was redesigned to take advantage of several features unique to the Windows platform, including native thread support and integration with some of the Windows NT administrative tools, such as the Performance Monitor and the Event Viewer.

Because the Internet has revolutionized the way organizations conduct business with customers, partners, and employees, Oracle*9i* for Windows has evolved to enable organizations to thrive in this new business environment. With solutions based on Oracle*9i*, any organization, large or small, can seize the new opportunities presented by the Internet while simultaneously reducing technology costs.

With the release of Oracle*9i* for Windows, the database has evolved from a basic operating system level integration to more advanced service integration on the Windows platform. As always, Oracle continues to innovate and to leverage new Windows and Internet technologies. Oracle*9i* provides an environment where Internet applications can experience high levels of performance, reliability, and scalability, all at a low total cost of ownership. This book provides key inside knowledge on how to take advantage of these capabilities and optimize Oracle for the Windows platform. It is written by some of the key experts in Oracle databases on Windows. It is an invaluable resource for any type of Oracle deployment on the Windows platform.

As readers will learn, Oracle*9i* for Windows provides an extensive set of tools and features sufficient to run almost any business operation, whether for departmental use or enterprise deployment. Simply stated, it allows customers to take advantage of the ease of use of Windows, while delivering the power of Oracle.

Enjoy!

Alex Keh
Senior Product Manager
Oracle Corporation

Acknowledgments

It's hard for me to believe that this book is finally finished. For a time there, I wasn't sure it would ever happen. My wife Tricia likened me to the Jack Nicholson character, who kept typing the same sentence over and over in *The Shining*. There were times when she wondered if there was ever going to be an end result other than a stack of paper with the same sentence typed over and over. To that end, I have to express my undying gratitude to her for her enduring patience and support, and acknowledge that she truly is an incredible individual, wife, and mother. My greatest accomplishment in life was convincing her to marry me. I also must say thank you to my three children—Erica (6), Amanda (5), and Mitchell (3)—for their bright smiles and patience with me during the last several months. Thank you for not growing up too fast yet. Please accept my apologies for working late nights and missing too many bedtime stories, and know that I will make it up to you. Finally, acknowledging the contributions of my family could not be complete without also acknowledging my parents and the incredible role models they have been for me. Thank you for everything.

In addition to my wonderful family, I want to express my gratitude to my co-authors Matt Hart and Mike Sale. Each of them has provided tireless dedication and unique expertise to help make this book a well-rounded project, and it would not have been possible without their input. In addition, I must thank their wives for the sacrifices they have made and for letting me steal their husbands away for a time. I also want to wish them all the best, as each of my co-authors and their wives embark on the incredible journey of parenthood. I assure you, it is a journey without parallel. Thanks also go to Ray Hachem and Soumendra Paik for their contributions in the technical editing of the book and invaluable input in ensuring the accuracy and validity of the content.

Aside from these cohorts, so many other co-workers deserve thanks for their assistance and encouragement. In particular, I want to express my deep gratitude to my director, Chip Brown, for his support and encouragement from the very beginning of this project. Aside from Chip, I would like to thank Alex Keh, the Product Manager for NT, for his constant and ongoing participation in keeping the support staff in the loop on changes and features involving Oracle on the NT product line. Also, other members of the support management staff, including my managers Andy Taylor and Martin Ingram, deserve thanks and credit for their help in providing time and resources to complete this book. In addition, I want to acknowledge all of the assistance of my support co-workers, from whom I learn more on a daily basis than I ever could by reading a book. In particular, my thanks go to my buddies Joe Donnelly, Steve Correia, and Peter Trent for always helping me keep things in perspective, and always keeping me in my place.

Behind the scenes at McGraw-Hill/Osborne, I still know very little about what it takes to publish a book, but I know it is a daunting task. Everyone there has been so patient with us first-timers, in particular Lisa McClain, whom I especially want to thank for her patience and support, and for sticking with me through the initial rocky beginning. In addition, Athena Honore and Ami Knox have been invaluable in keeping us on track and ensuring that all goes smoothly and the final product is readable. Thanks to all for all of your support.

Scott Jesse

How can you properly acknowledge all of those people who have made this book happen? It has been a unique opportunity that would not have been possible without the publisher and their editorial staff. In particular I would like to thank Lisa McClain and Athena Honore for their enduring patience and assistance. I would also like to thank Ami Knox for her very hard work through material that really needed her hard work.

Working at Oracle has long been a dream job for me. I always found Oracle able to balance the need to absolutely assure data availability with the desire for those really cool features. I seem to be one of those folks who are blessed with the gift of a job they love. I would like to thank all of those nameless Oracle employees who grind away at the products to make them what they are. I stand on the shoulders of giants.

I would like to specifically thank Scott Jesse for his efforts that made this project happen. Scott is an amazing resource of experience at Oracle. He knows the Oracle RDBMS on the Windows platform down to the minute details and, even better, he can explain it to people right at their level. Scott really had the vision to push this book from a possibility into a reality. He put up with my travel induced periods of unavailability with grace and patience. Thank you, Scott.

When I first met Matt Hart, he occupied the cube across from mine for a while. We have had many engaging discussions that have nothing to do with Oracle but have made me a more reflective and observant human being. Matt is an amazing sponge that soaks up new features and capabilities at an amazing rate. I see much bigger things for Matt in the future. Thank you for being a friend and a colleague who continually challenges me to grow in many ways.

I would like to thank Chip Brown and the other managers at Oracle who have continually given me the opportunity to excel. They have believed in my ability again and again to take on projects of importance and bring them to the next level. My current manager, Zahra Afrookhteh, has been particularly supportive near the end of the book. Thank you all for your support.

I would like to thank those people at Oracle who have taken the time and exercised extreme patience when confronted with my obnoxious and seemingly endless questions. Thank you GP Gongloor, Kevin Reardon, Emmett Price, Pete Baker, and Roderick Manalac for your help with specific questions I needed to answer with the definitiveness that only you could provide. I would also like to thank the various team members from Oracle who have assisted me to understand more about their specialties. I remember my first few days at Oracle and one person in particular who reached out to me and became my model for work at Oracle; I attribute much of my success at Oracle to Paul Hood and his heads-down dedication to the work at hand and customer focused approach. He shines like a light in a cynical world.

A group within Oracle works the tough specialty of bug fixes on the popular but challenging Microsoft platforms. These people have made the work that Scott and I started on a small crack team a success. My thanks go out to the NT DDR team and in particular to Venkat Subramanian, Ruben Becker, Scott Nye, Sanjay Somnali, Nagendra Ramaiah, and Rudresh Vadrahalli.

Finally, I would like to acknowledge my wife Laurie for her enduring love and support. Without her I do not see how I could have finished this project. She is my best friend and true love. Even when my laptop appeared to be an appendage she made sure I had the time and support needed to finish this project. Our marriage is one founded on our commitment to God; from this commitment grows our love. I thank Laurie for trusting in God when things became trying. From this trust I have been able to experience more love and joy than I can imagine. During this project we have begun the unique journey into parenthood. Our unborn child lies in her womb kicking as I write. I suspect that as this project draws to an end I enter into the most challenging and rewarding time spent as a parent. Thank you, Laurie. I love you.

Michael P. Sale

Who reads the acknowledgments? In the history of the book dating back to the middle ages, the space we now call the acknowledgments would be the spot from which the author could grant all glory and gratitude to whichever rich patron had funded the thing. So it was common that no one would read the lengthy acknowledgments except those who expected to be mentioned.

With all due respect then, I must first extend my thanks to the McGraw-Hill/Osborne team, who believed in a rag-tag collection of unproven authors and gave us the opportunity to show the world what we collectively know. In particular, Lisa McLain and Athena Honore have played an integral role in getting us from idea to completion. Ami Knox, our copy editor, has turned my trying prose into something both readable and engaging, and I can only sit back and wonder how. I also want to thank our two dedicated technical editors Ray Hachem and Soumendra Paik. They waded through a disparate pile of chapters and managed to keep us honest and focused.

I have known Scott Jesse since two weeks into my tenure at Oracle Corporation and learned most of my work habits from him. Our relationship has been the most rewarding of my professional career, and I want to thank him for putting me in a position to be able to write about what I'm good at.

I met Michael Sale during a brief tour of duty through the war zone of late night Oracle Support nearly two years ago. From the day I met him, I have been continually surprised by just how deep his knowledge goes. I haven't seen the bottom yet. I thank the vagaries of fate that allowed me to put my name next to his on a book. I can only look better by the association.

Finally, I must thank my wife Beth for banishing me to the dungeon of my office when the twinkle of inspiration faded from my eyes. She labored through her third trimester while I labored through the bulk of this book, and never blinked when she told me yes, I'm fine, go finish your chapters. She has been my strength and my inspiration. To call this book a labor of love would do egregious disservice to the labor she so recently undertook; in comparison, this book was merely a pastime. Thanks for tolerating it, Beth. You are my patron, and all glory and gratitude are yours.

Matthew Hart

Introduction

Oracle9*i* for Windows 2000 Tips & Techniques. This is quite a mouthful. This book, as we mention in the first chapter, is dedicated to the core products of the two largest software companies in the world—Microsoft's flagship operating system, Windows 2000, and Oracle's flagship database, Oracle9*i*. These two companies are such fierce competitors that neither one likes to acknowledge the other, yet somehow they seem to be able to coexist. We have embarked upon this project because we have, for several years, been caught in the middle of this situation—supporting the Oracle RDBMS on a platform that we often do not want to acknowledge as viable competition to more traditional Unix-based RDBMS systems. Partly for this reason, there has always been a dearth of good information for Oracle on Windows NT, so we hope this book will somewhat fill this void.

Who This Book Is For

This book is meant primarily for DBAs who are looking to maximize the performance of the Oracle RDBMS on the Windows 2000 platform, increase the availability and reliability of the RDBMS, and get the latest information on the new features in the 9*i* release.

The Scope of This Book

This book focuses primarily on the Oracle 9*i* RDBMS on Windows 2000. The core of the book will be aimed at maximizing the utility of the RDBMS and getting as much out of your database as possible. We cover issues central to database administration, and highlight issues specific to Windows 2000. This includes essential features such as tuning, backup, and recovery, as well as high-end features such as clustering and standby databases, which focus on high availability. In addition, we provide current information on new features in 9*i*. When necessary, we point out differences between the 9*i* release and the previous 8*i* releases. We also discuss centralizing and simplifying database administration using Enterprise Manager, and developing a usable strategy for upgrades and migration, which will allow the DBA to stay on top of current releases and patches while still maintaining stability of the system. Finally, we discuss Oracle's interaction with various tools and applications and how best to integrate these tools with Oracle 9*i* on Windows 2000.

How This Book Is Organized

The book is organized into five parts.

Part I: Overview

The overview in Part I has two chapters that briefly introduce Windows 2000 and the Oracle 9*i* database. These chapters provide some essential tips on setting up the Win2K environment, and also introduce the 9*i* database and show how it is specifically implemented on the Windows platform.

Part II: Implementing the Oracle RDBMS on Windows 2000

Part II is where we begin to go in depth with new features of 9*i* and essential administrative tasks for a Sysadmin on a Windows 2000 system running Oracle, and, of course, for any database administrator. We discuss the Windows 2000 environment, presenting techniques useful to the Oracle DBA, and then begin with essentials of database management. In addition, we provide troubleshooting tips specific to the Windows 2000 platform. This section concludes with a rousing discussion of backups, with an emphasis on the wave of the future—Server Managed Recovery, a.k.a. RMAN.

Part III: Window 2000: The Premier Enterprise Management Platform

This section begins with a focus on client software, which is useful even if the database itself is not on Windows 2000 (most shops still have Windows clients). We next move on to using Enterprise Manager on Windows 2000 to centralize administration of the Oracle RDBMS. This too can apply even to shops with databases on other platforms. We then discuss additional tools and methodologies for monitoring and optimizing administration, and conclude with a chapter on managing upgrades and migrations of the database and the operating system.

Part IV: Clustering and High Availability

This section focuses on one of the hotter areas of growth in the RDBMS arena: clustering and high availability. In this section, we relate these issues directly to the Windows 2000 platform. We demonstrate how to achieve high availability on a low budget with Oracle Failsafe and MSCS, and discuss how to increase performance and scalability with Real Application Clusters. We also discuss replication and introduce the newest innovations in the standby database arena. We conclude with a final chapter aimed at combining these features to achieve maximum availability and performance. This last chapter introduces a new product for Oracle9*i* called Real Application Clusters Guard, and then discuss a combination RAC database and Standby setup, with RMAN as the go-between.

Part V: Appendices

Part V contains two appendices—Appendix A, Media Management Configuration for RMAN Backups to Tape, and Appendix B, Generating and Finding Diagnostic Information for Oracle9*i*.

PART I

Overview

TIPS & TECHNIQUES

CHAPTER 1

Windows 2000

As mentioned in the introduction, this book encompasses the core products of the two largest software companies in the world—the Oracle9*i* RDBMS and Microsoft's Windows 2000 operating system. While this is by no means a comprehensive discussion, we introduce the architecture of Windows 2000 and lay the groundwork for understanding Oracle's implementation of Oracle9*i* on Windows 2000. The following topics are discussed:

- Different flavors of Windows NT/2000
- Processes and threads
- Memory
- CPU
- Disk subsystem and I/O
- Networking
- Security
- Microsoft Management Console
- Computer Management Console
- The Windows 2000 Registry

Oracle and Microsoft

This book provides an interesting juxtaposition, encompassing the confluence of the core products of the two largest software companies in the world—the Oracle9*i* RDBMS and Microsoft's Windows 2000 operating system. Although the two companies are fierce competitors, it is impossible for one to ignore the other. Not so many years ago, it seemed inconceivable within Oracle that anyone would actually try to run a production system on Windows NT. However, as Windows NT exploded into the small- to mid-size server market place, it became apparent that more and more Oracle customers were doing just that. Oracle on Windows NT has since matured into a mainstream product, garnering attention within Oracle once reserved exclusively for the higher-end Unix and VMS operating systems. As Microsoft attempts to edge into the enterprise server arena, Oracle stands poised with Release 9i to deliver the best possible database solution for Windows 2000 and beyond.

Windows 2000

Even though the initial release of Oracle9*i* will support both Windows NT 4.0 and Windows 2000, we have chosen to focus this book primarily on the latter. Windows 2000 has been shown to have certain advantages over its predecessor. Here are the three main reasons for this book's focus on Windows 2000:

- **Reliability/stability** It seemed that Windows NT 4.0 required a reboot with even the most minor configuration change. There are far fewer reboots required with Windows 2000—basic administration tasks can be accomplished and take effect while the machine is up and running.
- **Scalability** Database applications stand to reap great benefits from this feature. Windows 2000 offers support for more CPUs, more RAM, and more nodes in a cluster.
- **Inevitability** In the due process of evolution, a time will come when fixes for Windows NT will no longer be available. Similarly, device drivers for new hardware will cease to be written for NT 4.0. Eventually, new applications will not run on Windows NT 4.0. That is just the way the world works. In addition, any thoughts of moving into the 64-bit Wintel world will necessarily require Windows 2000. (Current versions are of course 32-bit, but future 64-bit releases will have the Windows 2000 look and feel, plus support for 64-bit hardware.)

Flavors of Windows 2000

Before we get started, we should discuss the various flavors of Windows 2000 and what they are meant for. There are four different versions, with the following specs for each:

- **Windows 2000 Professional** This version of Windows 2000, meant for laptops, home use, or client desktops, is equivalent to Windows NT 4.0 Workstation. Windows 2000 Professional supports two processors and up to 4GB of RAM.
- **Windows 2000 Standard Server** Equivalent to Windows NT 4.0 Server, this version is the basic server platform, which supports up to 4 processors and up to 4GB of RAM.

- **Windows 2000 Advanced Server** With support for 8GB of RAM and 8 processors, as well as 2-node clustering capability, this is the upgrade equivalent to Windows NT 4.0 Enterprise Edition.
- **Windows 2000 Datacenter Server** This version has support for up to 32 processors, 64GB of RAM, and 4-node clusters. There is no NT 4.0 equivalent. Datacenter Server is the Windows 2000 product aimed at entry into the high-end market. Windows 2000 Datacenter Server can only be purchased when preinstalled by hardware vendors who have passed certain certification tests from Microsoft. Therefore, the Windows 2000 Datacenter Server has limited device driver support as compared to, say, Windows 2000 Professional, which must be able to run on just about any platform. This allows for streamlining of some of the operating system code on the Datacenter edition, and should theoretically lead to better performance and stability.

The preceding specifications are not hard and fast rules, but give you a general idea of what the parameters are. Certain OEM versions of the Windows 2000 Operating System (OEM in this case stands for *original equipment manufacturer*) may support additional numbers of processors, or more memory, as long as the OS is preinstalled at the factory, or installed from the specific media that was shipped with the server. Microsoft maintains a *Hardware Compatibility List* (*HCL*), which is available on their web site or on the CD-ROM as a .txt file, listing hardware certified to run the various versions of the Windows 2000 operating system.

Future Releases

The next release of Windows 2000 is called *Windows XP*. Oracle9*i* will be certified to run on Windows XP as well as Windows 2000 and NT 4.0. Windows XP is meant to consolidate all of the Windows operating systems under one masthead, so the so-called consumer versions of Windows— Windows 95, Windows 98, and Windows ME (Millennium Edition)—will go the way of the dodo, and be rolled into one product line with the current code path for Windows 2000/XP. To accomplish this, Windows XP will need to have even greater device driver support and the ability to run on an even wider variety of hardware.

In addition, the future holds a 64-bit version of Windows 2000 and Windows XP, which will run on the recently announced 64-bit Intel hardware. Although it will take some time before this hardware becomes affordable and widely used, once it takes hold, the 64-bit OS will change the competitive landscape for the Windows 2000/XP line by dramatically increasing the limitations of the current 32-bit OS. We discuss some of those limitations later on in this chapter.

Suffice it to say that Windows 2000 gives you much more flexibility than Windows NT in terms of the ability to add additional processing power and/or memory to your system and, therefore, get the most from the Oracle9*i* RDBMS. While Oracle9*i* will run on any flavor of Windows 2000, from Professional to

Datacenter, we recommend that for production systems, you run Windows 2000 Standard Server or Advanced Server (unless you have need for Datacenter Server, for high-end, mission-critical applications and multinode clustering). Advanced Server enables you to take full advantage of the memory and other resources available, and also allows you to utilize the clustering features, even on a single node. We discuss in later sections of the book how to best take advantage of these resources; we turn to advanced tuning and administration of the Oracle9i RDBMS in Chapter 5, and we discuss clustering in Part IV.

A Brief Look Inside Windows 2000

Before we go into more detail on navigating the interface, we begin with a brief discussion of the Windows 2000 architecture, including these topics:

- Processes and threads
- Memory
- CPU
- Disk subsystem and I/O
- Networking

Thread-Based Architecture

Windows 2000 is primarily a *thread-based architecture*, as opposed to Unix operating systems, which are *process based*. This means that most applications on Windows 2000 (including Oracle) are implemented as a single *process* with multiple *threads*. This thread-based architecture gives Windows 2000 certain advantages, in that it is much easier to share memory. Memory space is addressed on a per-process basis. Sharing memory between processes can be clunky, and leads to additional coding. In addition, a thread, which is a subset of a process, uses less memory than a process would. This gives thread-based applications the advantage of being more efficient, since all threads of a given process share the same process memory space. It is much more efficient, and an easier implementation, to share memory between threads within the same process than it is to share memory between distinct processes. This leads to more efficient memory usage and faster communication between threads.

One disadvantage of a thread-based architecture is the very fact that all memory is so easily accessible to other threads. If a given thread begins to spin out of control for any reason, it can overwrite the memory space for all threads and cause the entire process to crash. Under a process-based architecture, a single process spinning out of control is far less likely to bring down other processes with it.

Services and Processes
Windows 2000 runs many of the processes needed for the system operation in the form of a *service*. Simply put, a service is a way to kick off a background process at startup time. If you are familiar with Unix, services can be thought of as being similar to a daemon. Services can be configured to start up a process at boot time, and can also be configured to log on with a specific ID. This allows a process to start up automatically, even if nobody logs on to the machine. Oracle9*i* uses services to start the process for the database, as well as the Listener, Intelligent Agent, and numerous other processes. The Oracle9*i*-specific services are discussed in more detail in Chapter 4.

Types of Threads There are two types of threads on Windows 2000—*user* threads and *kernel* threads. User threads cannot directly access the hardware layer, whereas kernel threads do. All Oracle threads are *user-mode* threads. Therefore, Oracle never has direct access to the hardware layer. Device drivers, which by nature must access hardware, will run in *kernel mode*. User-mode threads are also referred to as *nonprivileged* threads because they do not have direct access to memory, and are restricted to operating within their own address space. Kernel-mode threads would, of course, be considered *privileged* threads.

Since all Oracle threads are user-mode or nonprivileged threads, Oracle must use specific APIs for requesting system services from the kernel. When this happens, a thread will transition to kernel mode, execute whatever operation needs to be accomplished (for example, an I/O operation), and then the thread will switch back to user mode before control is returned to the application. Therefore, even though we say that all Oracle threads are user-mode threads, you may observe an Oracle thread spending time running in kernel mode.

Memory

With this thread-based architecture come certain limitations, the foremost of which is memory. Because the architecture consists of threads in a single process, the process address space is limited, and there is less room to maneuver. Since Windows 2000 is still a 32-bit operating system, a single process is limited to 4GB of address space, half of which is reserved for the operating system. This 2GB of system memory that is reserved for the OS is also referred to as the *system address space*. It contains OS kernel code, *Hardware Abstraction Layer* (*HAL*) code, and various other structures needed to manage the interaction of the process with the OS. This 2GB of system address space is off limits to the application process. Therefore, with Windows 2000

Blue Screen of Death

If you have worked with Windows NT for any length of time, you are undoubtedly familiar with the *Blue Screen of Death* (*BSOD*). This is the lovely blue screen that displays nonsensical hex numbers and OS functions when something very bad happens to your server. Generally, you are left with no options other than punching the power button and praying the system comes back up. The infamous Blue Screen of Death can have various causes, but threads running in user mode should never be able to cause BSODs, because they do not have access to the hardware layer. Often, it may seem that an application is causing a BSOD, because the application is making system calls that uncover a problem. The application is simply the bearer of bad tidings, resulting from a call that was made to an OS routine or device driver, which, in turn, resulted in a switch to kernel mode. The reality is that only kernel-mode functions can cause a BSOD. Therefore, the ultimate culprit is a device driver, an operating system function, or a simple case of bad hardware.

Standard Server, a single application process can address a total of 2GB of memory. With Windows 2000 Advanced Server, using the /3GB switch in the boot.ini file, you can change this balance to 3GB for the process versus 1GB for the OS. This is known as *4-gigabyte tuning*, or *4GT*, which we discuss in more detail in Chapter 5.

On 32-bit Unix-based operating systems, where applications are implemented as processes, each given process still has a 2GB limit of addressable memory. However, since there are multiple processes for a single application, the total amount of memory that can be used by the application is vastly higher. If more memory is needed, it is simply a matter of spawning additional processes and, if necessary, adding more memory. Applications on Windows 2000 must be viewed in the context of a much more finite limit, since every thread is using memory that comes out of the address space for a single process. Once that ceiling is reached, more threads cannot be allocated.

Going Beyond 4GB

Given this limitation, one might wonder what the point of having 8GB or 16GB of RAM in a single server would be. Keep in mind that this limitation is still on a per-process basis. Therefore, if you have multiple applications or multiple instances of the same application, then each individual instance, running as a separate process, can address its own individual process space. In the case of Oracle,

a single database *instance* runs as a single process, consisting of multiple threads. However, a second database instance on the same machine would run as a separate process, with its own separate memory space. So, it is conceivable that one could have two instances using 3GB of RAM apiece.

In addition, there are ways to allow a single process or application to address more memory than would be allotted in a 32-bit address space. To accomplish this, Windows 2000 uses something called a *physical address extension* (*PAE*). PAE essentially increases your address space to 36 bits from 32 bits, but you must have a Pentium Pro processor or later to take advantage of this. Under Windows NT 4.0, an additional driver from Intel called the *PSE36* driver is required to take advantage of a full 36-bit address space; but this is no longer the case with Windows 2000 Advanced Server—the support is now built into the operating system. A given application must still be written using the *Address Windowing Extensions* (*AWE*) API. All Oracle 8*i* releases (8.1.5–8.1.7) support AWE. However, the first 9*i* Release (Release 1) will not support AWE. Oracle will likely reimplement AWE support in 9*i* Release 2. We discuss memory issues such as 4GT, AWE, and other issues in more detail in Chapter 5.

This issue will become a moot point once the 64-bit chip becomes widely available. Microsoft has a 64-bit version of Windows 2000 ready to run on the 64-bit hardware, and Oracle is also prepared to deliver a 64-bit version of the database on the new 64-bit OS. Once in a 64-bit environment, the per-process address space leaps into the terabytes, and a given process will be able to use as much memory as you can throw at it.

Reserved vs. Committed Memory *Reserved memory* is memory that a thread addresses and reserves for future use, but does not actually commit. Since it is not committed, it is memory that is still available for use by other processes. However, since it is addressed, it still comes out of the total memory limit for the process that owns the thread. Therefore, reserved memory counts against the 2GB or 3GB limit, and the combined total of reserved and *committed memory* of a process cannot exceed these limits, as noted previously.

Virtual Memory and Paging Windows 2000 takes advantage of *virtual memory* by *paging* memory to disk. Therefore, it is not necessary to have a full 4GB of RAM in order for a process to address that much space. If enough physical memory is not available, then the memory pages of a particular process will be transferred to disk, and be stored in the *page file*. If the process references that address later on and finds that it is on disk, then that page will be read into memory and another page may be moved to disk. Obviously, the additional I/O incurred by this type of operation has performance implications, and you should strive to avoid paging as much as possible.

CPU

As noted previously, Windows 2000 can support as many as 32 CPUs in a single system. However, the kernel is slightly different for a *single-processor* system versus a *multiprocessor,* or *symmetric multiprocessing* (SMP), system. If Windows 2000 is installed on a single-processor system, about a half-dozen kernel files will be slightly different. The reason for this is that a single processor system can suffer unnecessary performance degradation if using the multiprocessor kernel.

A quick check to verify that your system correctly recognizes all installed processors is to take a peek at *Task Manager.* Right-click the taskbar across the bottom, and choose the Task Manager option. Click the Performance tab. This gives you an overall view of the system memory and CPU usage as a whole. On multiprocessor systems, you should see a separate graph for each CPU.

No special setup is required for Oracle9*i* to take advantage of SMP systems, as long as the OS correctly sees all processors. If you have multiple CPUs in your system, but you see only one graph on the Performance tab (see Figure 1-1), then your OS is not correctly configured for SMP. This may happen if you installed additional processors after the OS was installed. If a second processor is added after the initial installation, the kernel files will not recognize the second processor. The kernel must be upgraded or

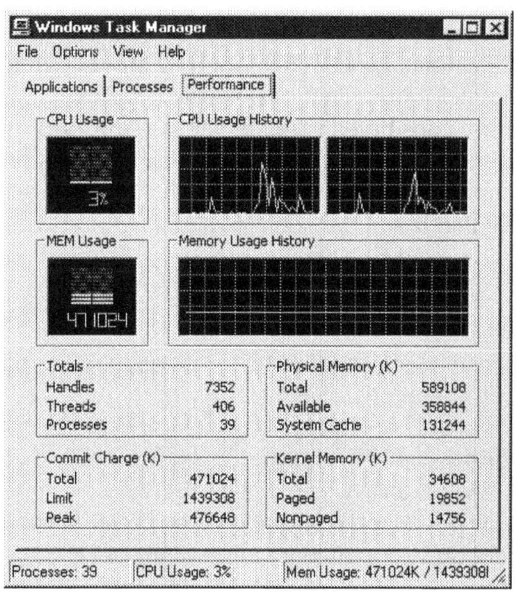

FIGURE 1-1. *Task Manager*

the OS reinstalled in order to recognize the second processor. Under NT 4.0, this could be a painful proposition—you would have to use a utility called UPTOMP.EXE, which is available from the Windows NT Resource Kit, in order to upgrade the kernel to a multiprocessor kernel. However, with Windows 2000, it is a simpler matter. The kernel can be upgraded via the Computer Management Console, simply by updating the device drivers for the processor.

It is important to note that if Windows 2000 is installed on a multiprocessor system to begin with, the multiprocessor kernel files will be copied in place during the installation. Adding a third or fourth processor or more to a system that already has multiple processors does NOT require a kernel upgrade or a reinstallation. We go into more detail on the Computer Management Console later in this chapter, and we discuss the specific process of upgrading the kernel to support multiple processors in Chapter 3.

CPU and Threads Once the system has been successfully set up to recognize multiple processors, Windows 2000 will automatically load balance threads across all of the CPUs in the system. There are no default processor affinities, nor is there a single master CPU. By default, any thread can run on any CPU. However, the *processor affinity* for given threads can be manually altered. Oracle allows this to be done via a Registry parameter, ORACLE_AFFINITY, which we discuss in Chapter 5.

If all CPUs are in use, then CPU time given to threads is managed via the priorities assigned to the threads. Priorities range from 0 to 31, with higher priority translating to more CPU time. Levels 16 through 31 are real time and are generally reserved for system/kernel-mode functions. Levels 1 through 15 are generally used by applications, and are considered variable because this priority can change, depending on the operations in which the thread is engaged. For example, after an I/O operation completes, a thread waiting for that I/O will get a priority boost, increasing the chance that it will run sooner. Manually modifying priorities for Oracle threads is discussed in Chapter 5.

Disk Subsystem

In this section, we give an overview of the file systems supported on Windows 2000, hardware, and I/O considerations.

File Systems on Windows 2000 Under Windows 2000, there are three options for file systems: FAT, FAT32, and NTFS. Support for FAT32 is new to Windows 2000. FAT (which stands for *File Allocation Table*) is a holdover from the 16-bit DOS/ Windows environment. It is supported by all versions of DOS, Windows 3.1, and Windows 95. If you want to access partitions from a combination of these operating systems (for example, to configure a dual-boot system), FAT is the best choice since partitions are visible from either DOS, Windows 3.1, Windows 95, or Windows NT. However, the FAT file system does not provide full *C2 security* (discussed in the sidebar "C2 Security," later in this chapter), and the maximum file size on a FAT partition is 2GB, with a maximum volume size of only 4GB.

FAT32 is primarily used for Windows 98 operating systems, and the only reason it should be used on Windows 2000 is if you need to dual-boot to Windows 98 (since Windows 98 cannot read NTFS partitions). The only real advantage of FAT32 over FAT is that it provides support for larger files and volumes (4GB and 32GB, respectively).

NTFS (short for *New Technology File System*) was developed especially for the Windows NT operating system. The NTFS file system offers the ability to place permissions on files and directories, as well as support for much larger files and volumes, providing better performance. The theoretical limit on volumes/files is 16 exabytes for NTFS; but the practical limit on a volume is 2 terabytes, with the file size being limited only by the volume size.

Windows 2000 includes the latest version of NTFS, NTFS 5.0, which provides additional features such as mounting volumes to folders. This allows a new disk volume to be mounted as a directory on an already existing drive, similar to the mount command on a Unix system. This feature provides flexibility by letting you get around the limitation of 26 drive letters. In addition, mounted drives provide a way to add additional storage to a system, without having to change drive letters. New drives must be mounted to empty folders, as we discuss in Chapter 3.

For these reasons, on any true production system, the only real file system choice is NTFS. FAT or FAT32 volumes can be converted to NTFS by running the convert command. For example:

```
C:\>convert E: /FS:NTFS
```

The next time the system is rebooted, the file system on the specified volume will be upgraded to NTFS. For more information on this, enter **convert /?** from a command window.

Asynchronous I/O *Asynchronous I/O* simply means that an I/O function returns execution back to the calling thread immediately, so that the thread can continue on with other processing. Using *synchronous I/O*, an I/O function does not return control to the caller until the write operation has been completed. On some platforms, asynchronous I/O must be enabled via special operating system configuration. If asynchronous I/O is not enabled, Oracle can be configured to use multiple DB Writer (DBWR) processes to simulate asynchronous writes (DBWR is discussed in detail in Chapter 2). However, on Windows 2000 there is no special configuration required. Asynchronous I/O is always enabled, and most Windows applications, including Oracle, are written to take advantage of this. Therefore, Oracle on Windows 2000 will write to disk asynchronously, without any special configuration (such as multiple DBWR processes). Even so, the OS may run certain

write operations synchronously if it deems necessary, so while we normally do not recommend multiple Oracle DBWR processes on Windows 2000, you *may* observe some small gains in write performance by enabling this feature.

Hardware

Windows 2000 supports various types of hard drives and hard drive configurations. The most common types are *Enhanced Integrated Device Electronics* (*EIDE*) and *Small Computer System Interface* (*SCSI*). SCSI drives are the most commonly used and recommended drives in a server built for database applications, because SCSI provides faster data transfer and support for more drives. In addition, when running in a clustered environment where shared access to drives is necessary, SCSI drives are a must. Most hardware platforms also support *fibre-channel* connections between the server and external disk cabinets, which also requires SCSI drives. Although Windows 2000 supports the ability to stripe data and create volumes using software RAID capabilities, this is not as efficient as a hardware RAID. Whenever possible, volumes should be set up using the hardware configuration utilities. We discuss the mechanics of viewing and setting up the disk configuration in Chapter 3, when we discuss the Disk Management applet in the Computer Management Console.

Networking

All Windows 2000 machines, regardless of the flavor, have the ability to act as both a client and a server on the network. The *Workstation Service* is the process that allows the machine to participate on a network and access network resources. The *Server Service* allows the machine on which it is running to serve up network resources to be accessed by other machines.

In addition, a machine may be a member of either a *domain* or a *workgroup*. A workgroup is a loosely coupled group of computers, which may or may not share resources amongst themselves. In fact, a workgroup may have only one member—your computer. A domain, on the other hand, is a more tightly controlled association of computers. Accounts, rights, and resources are controlled from a *domain controller*. A user on a machine that is a member of a domain may log on either to the domain itself or to the local machine. Note that while a domain account and a local account may have the same names, they are two different accounts, and therefore will have different rights and privileges. We discuss this in the section "Security" later in this chapter.

Investigating the Current Network Setup Networking properties can be viewed in Windows 2000 by right-clicking My Network Places and selecting Properties, or by choosing Network and Dial-up Connections from Start | Settings. Once you are into the Networking Properties window, you will see a separate icon, or network connection, for each network adapter that you have in the machine. Windows 2000 supports various networking *protocols*, primarily TCP/IP, NetBEUI, and NWLink.

The only protocol installed by default on Windows 2000 is the TCP/IP protocol. TCP/IP is used extensively by Oracle for networking connections, the Intelligent Agent, and the Oracle HTTP Server. In some cases, such as on a laptop or home computer, if TCP/IP is not installed or configured, the Oracle database may not start up due to networking parameters in the init.ora file. We discuss Oracle networking in more detail in Chapter 7.

To view installed protocols and IP information on a Windows 2000 machine, double-click the network connection associated with a given card, and then click the Properties button. Here, you will see the description of the network card and the networking software that is installed. Double-click the Internet Protocol (TCP/IP) line. This will display the IP address of the machine you are on, along with the subnet mask, gateway, and DNS servers. If the box next to Obtain an IP Address Automatically is checked, this means that you are receiving an IP address from a DHCP server. This IP address would be subject to change once the lease from the server expires. Oracle recommends using static (permanent) IP addresses, so that tools such as the Intelligent Agent and the Listener work properly. This information can also be viewed from the command line by entering **ipconfig** at a command window. By default, **ipconfig** displays the IP address, subnet mask, and default gateway for each adapter card. Additional info is available by entering **ipconfig /?**.

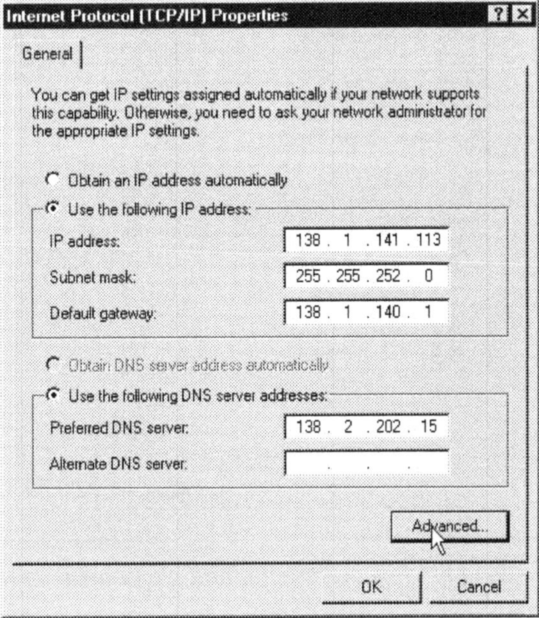

Clicking the Advanced button on this screen allows you to see more detail on DNS and WINS servers. DNS and WINS are two different ways to resolve host names to IP addresses. WINS is specific to Windows platforms, whereas DNS is a standard that works across platforms. DNS is the most common standard, and you will find that when using such options as clustering and Oracle failsafe, DNS is the preferred method to resolve host names. Windows 2000 supports the dynamic registration of clients with a DNS server, thus on the DNS tab you have the option to register the connection's information with DNS. You can also determine which suffixes to append to your computer name (for example, MYMACHINE.<MYFORPROFITCOMPANY.COM>). These settings here can have an impact on Oracle 9i networking connections, which we discuss in Chapter 7.

Next, let's take a look at *bindings* on Windows 2000. Go back to the Main Network and Dial-up Connections box. From here, go to the Advanced menu and choose Advanced Settings. This allows you to specify the order in which multiple adapters or multiple networking cards are bound. If you have only one protocol and one card, then this is not of interest to you. However, if you intend to do any clustering, you will likely have multiple cards, as shown in Figure 1-2, and the bindings will need to be checked from here. In a cluster, cards that talk to the outside, or public, network

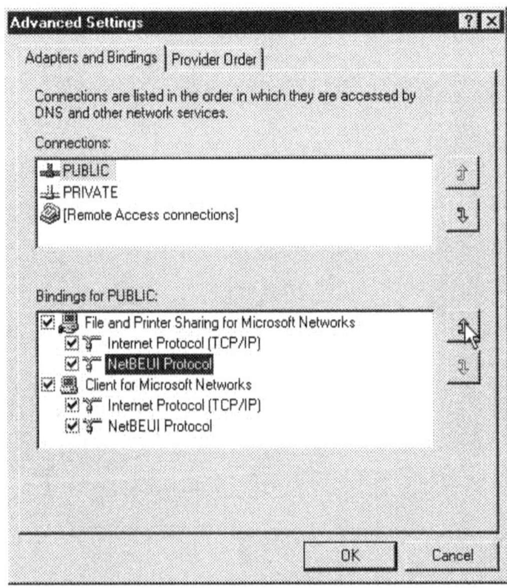

FIGURE 1-2. *Viewing binding order with multiple network cards*

should be bound first, and cards used for internal cluster communications should be bound last. We discuss this in further detail in Chapters 8 and 9.

Sharing Folders Folders can be shared by right-clicking the desired folder, either through the Windows Explorer or in My Computer and choosing the Sharing option. This will take you into the Folder Properties page, with the Sharing tab already selected. Click the Share this folder radio button option, and assign a share name to the folder that is unique on that machine. Security can be set up on the shared folder by clicking the Permissions button. Current shares on the system can be viewed by entering **net share** at the command line. For additional options, enter **net help share**.

Mapping Drives Once a folder has been shared, you connect to it by mapping a drive using the *Universal Naming Convention* (*UNC*) or full name of the resource. The UNC comprises the server name and the share name, in the form *servername*\ *sharename*. So, if you shared the C:\ORACLE\ADMIN folder using a share name of ORCLADMIN, on a server called ORACLE1, the full UNC would be \\ORACLE1\ ORCLADMIN. To connect to this share remotely, right-click the My Computer icon and choose Map Network Drive. Pick a drive letter to assign, and then for the Folder box, type in the full UNC: \\ORACLE1\ORCLADMIN. You can also accomplish this from the command line via the **net use** command. The following command will map drive Q on a client machine to the associated share on the server:

```
C:\>net use Q: \\oracle1\orcladmin
The command completed successfully.
```

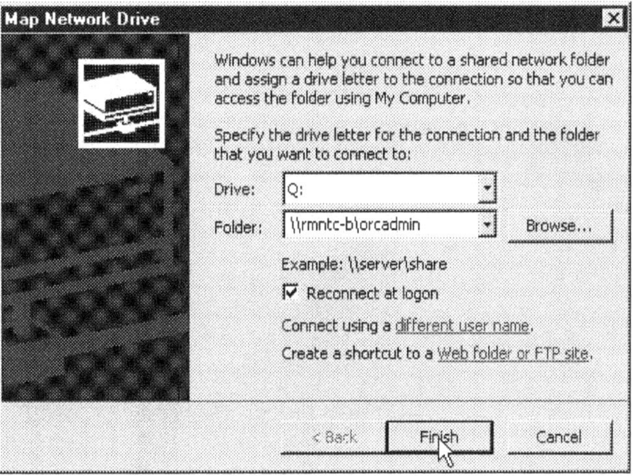

In addition to mapping drives for administrative purposes, you may find it useful to map a drive to a remote machine from your database server for archiving purposes. This allows you to have Oracle automatically write archive logs to a separate machine. In order to accomplish this, you must configure the Oracle service to log on as an account that has network access (we discuss this further in Chapter 4).

Security

Security is always a big concern on any operating system. Windows 2000 provides C2-level security as defined by the National Computer Security Center (NCSC). Security is controlled at various levels using rights and privileges. A *right* typically applies to an object—for example, access to a file—while *privileges* apply to operations on the system. The privilege to load a device driver is a good example. System-level security ensures that the Windows 2000 Registry is protected from malicious users. Application-level security is easily implemented on Windows 2000. Windows 2000 also provides support for domains and groups. These features allow administrators to control security for a large group of users.

User Rights Assignment

Users and *groups* are discussed in the next section, when we discuss the Computer Management Console. This section outlines assigning certain rights to users, such as the ability to log on as a service or log on as a batch job. This has been separated under Windows 2000 from the actual task of creating user accounts. There is now a separate icon in Administrative Tools labeled the Local Security Policy. Access this

C2 Security

Windows NT 4.0 has been officially placed on the Evaluated Products List by the U.S. Government, whereas Windows 2000 is still officially under evaluation. Since this process takes several years, the official evaluations are not yet complete. (Source: *Inside Microsoft Windows 2000, Third Edition*, Microsoft Press.) Note also that a C2 security rating does not mean that by installing Windows 2000 your site is automatically C2 certified. Certification applies to an entire site, including hardware, software, and the environment that the system is in. Essentially, not only must you have the correct software in place, but you also have to use it correctly. It is up to an individual site to become C2 certified.

by clicking Start | Programs | Administrative Tools | Local Security Policy. Once in this window, you will see folders for Account Policies and Local Policies.

Under Account Policies, you will be able to define defaults for password life, password history, password complexity, and other options. When creating a user under Local Users and Groups, if you specify Password Never Expires, then these settings will not take effect. Account Lockout under Account Policies determines how failed logon attempts affect the ability to continue logging on.

Through Local Policies, you will be able to audit certain actions via the Audit Policy folder, and assign certain rights to users or groups via the User Rights Assignment folder. Auditing information will be written to the Security Log in the Event Viewer, as discussed in Chapter 3. User Rights Assignment allows you to assign the privileges mentioned previously (for example, log on as a batch job). Note in Figure 1-3 that under the User Rights Assignment heading, there are columns defining the local setting and the effective setting. With Windows 2000, if you are in an Active Directory Domain environment, rights assigned at the Domain Controller take precedence over rights assigned on the local system. Therefore, if you assign rights to a user on the local system, they may not necessarily take effect, depending on what the effective setting is. Observe also that the right to log on as a batch job has been granted to RMDTLAB\Administrator. This is an account on the domain RMDTLAB. If this were an account on the local machine, the local machine name would precede the username. In addition, be aware that

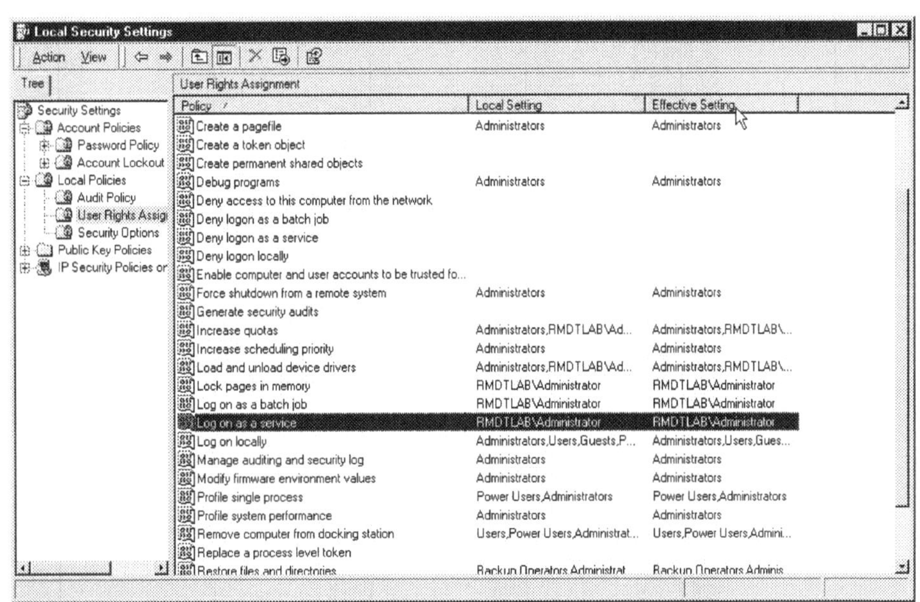

FIGURE 1-3. *User Rights Assignment view in the Local Security Settings window*

Administrator (singular) is a single user, whereas Administrators (plural) denotes an entire group of users.

Although it is not required on Windows 2000 to create a specific group for the Oracle installation (for example, a dba group, similar to what you would create for installations on a Unix system), the account doing the installation must be a member of the Local Administrators group, and you must be logged on to the local machine (as opposed to being logged on to a domain account). In addition, the Oracle9*i* installation does create a group called ORA_DBA on the local Windows 2000 system where the installation is done. The installer's account is added to the ORA_DBA group automatically. Members of this group will have the ability to connect internally to the database without any further authentication required. We discuss this in more detail in Chapter 4.

File Permissions on Windows 2000

In the section "File Systems in Windows 2000" earlier in this chapter, you learned that there are three choices for file systems on Windows 2000—FAT, FAT32, and NTFS. Only NTFS gives you the ability to set permissions at the file level. To set or view permissions, right-click a file or folder in the Explorer and select Properties. From here, go to the Security tab (see Figure 1-4). By default, new folders or files will inherit the permissions set on the parent folder, and files/folders at the root level

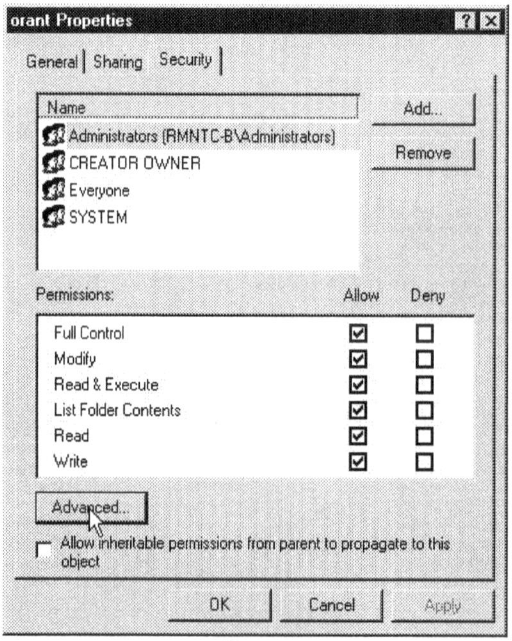

FIGURE 1-4. *Folder security properties*

inherit permissions set on the drive itself. If you desire to change this, uncheck the box beside the option Allow inheritable permissions from parent. This will allow you to set permissions on a folder or file that are different from those of the parent.

Next, click the Advanced button. The Permissions tab allows you to see more detailed permissions than the previous screen. The Auditing tab allows you to set up auditing on files, and the Owner tab allows you to take ownership of the files or directories. (Note that auditing requires additional setup to be done in the Local Policy Editor. We discuss auditing and the Local Policy editor in more detail in Chapter 3.)

Enhanced Security Features on Windows 2000

Windows 2000 provides additional security enhancements not available on Windows NT 4.0, which we list here. Some of these features are beyond the scope of this book; however, we discuss single sign-on features in Chapter 3 and Chapter 4, when Active Directory and OS authentication are explained.

- **Encrypted file systems** Encrypts files on your hard drive so that no one can access them without using the correct password. This is not a feature you want to use for Oracle files, but it may be convenient for tracking passwords, or for other types of files. Attempting to encrypt files associated with Oracle will render them inaccessible to the database.
- **Kerberos 5** Supports a single logon for faster authentication and network response. Kerberos 5 is the primary security protocol for domains in Windows 2000. Native authentication uses Kerberos security protocols in Windows 2000, and allows the operating system to perform user identification for Oracle databases. With native authentication enabled, users can leverage single sign-on to access Oracle applications simply by logging into Windows. This is discussed in more detail in Chapter 7, where we explain client connectivity and LDAP authentication.
- **Internet Protocol Security (IPSec)** Supports TCP/IP encryption and virtual private network (VPN) traffic across the Internet.

The Windows 2000 Interface

Now that we have discussed some of the underlying structures in Windows 2000, let's take a look at the hallmark of the OS—the interface. One of the new features in Windows 2000 is the Microsoft Management Console (MMC). The MMC is a console that provides a central location to host tools that a system administrator or a user accesses most frequently. These tools, called snap-ins, may come from Microsoft to assist in managing the hardware and software on the system, or they may be third-party snap-ins such as the Oracle snap-in for the MMC, which allows management of

certain database functionality from the console. The MMC is a way to centrally locate management of the OS, a server, or your network, in that you can customize the console with whichever applications you need to run most often, and save the console to the desktop for easy access. Entering **mmc** from the Start menu or from a command window gives you access to the base console.

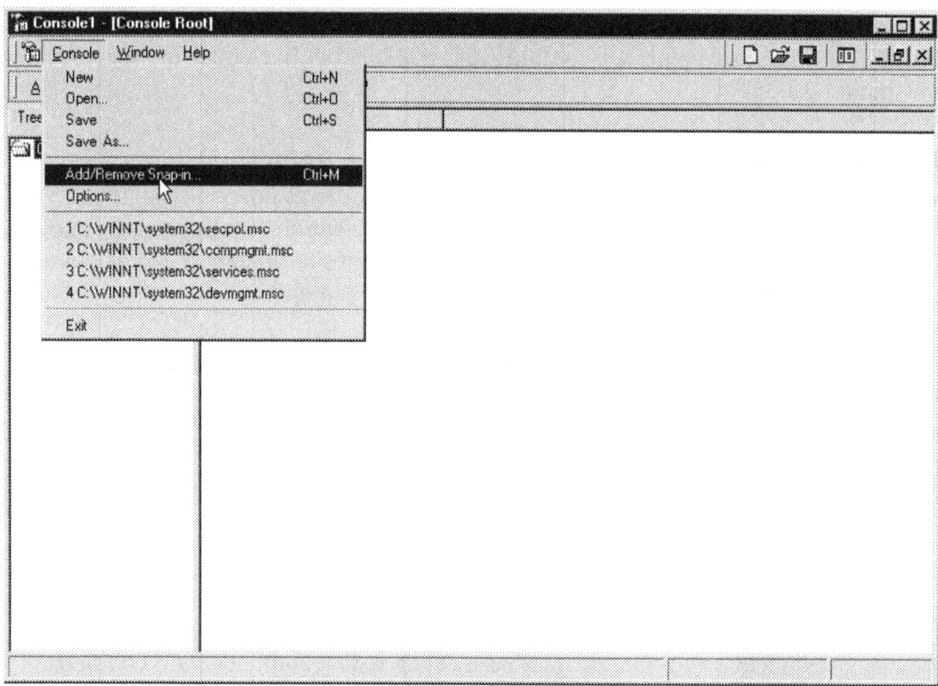

Computer Management Console

The management of the operating system in Windows NT was done largely through disparate programs and applets in the Control Panel. So, while you can customize a Microsoft Management Console to host the applications you run most frequently, Windows 2000 has also centralized computer management for you into a single, preconfigured console called the Computer Management Console. From a single location you can view and control services, manage disks and users, view the Event Log, create performance logs, and much more. You will find the Computer Management Console in the Administrative Tools program group by clicking Start | Programs | Administrative Tools | Computer Management. Figure 1-5 shows this console. We discuss most of the tools available in the Computer Management Console and how they are used in Chapter 3. These are the tools that you will need access to on a regular basis when managing a Windows 2000 Server running Oracle9*i*.

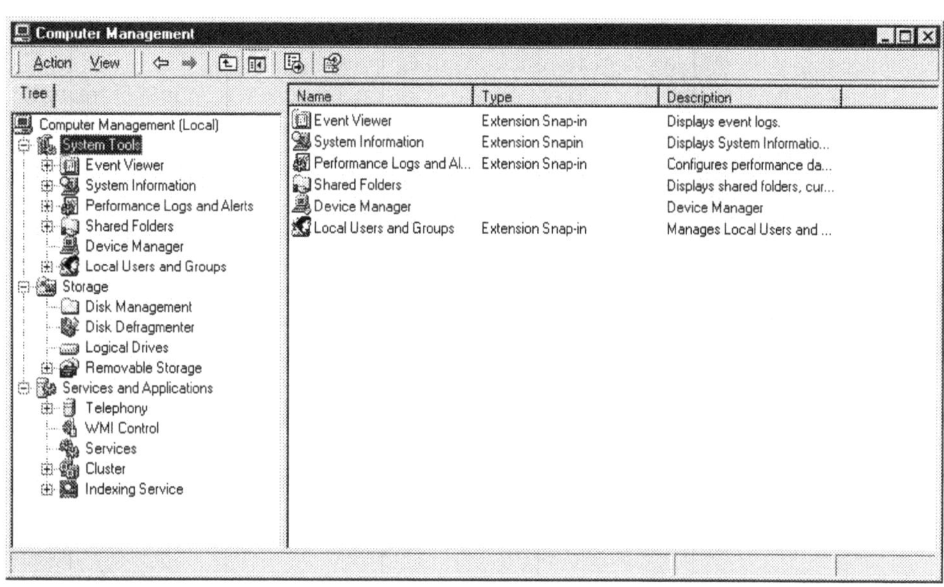

FIGURE 1-5. *The Computer Management Console*

The Registry and the Environment

One of the things that make Windows unique among its compatriots is the Registry. Although any modern-day Windows user is familiar with the term, it often evokes fear in the hearts of less-experienced users, and rightly so. The Windows 2000 Registry can be considered the nerve center of the operating system. Simply put, the Registry is a database that contains system information pertaining to the OS, the hardware, and any installed software. It is the primary place for environment settings for most users and applications (as opposed to a .profile or .cshrc file on Unix), and contains information vital to booting and configuring the system.

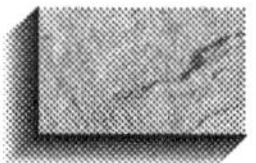

CAUTION

Since this is the central repository for the operation of the Windows 2000 operating system, you should use extreme caution when viewing or making changes to the Registry. Changes to values in the Registry take effect immediately. There is no Save or Discard option when closing out the Registry after a change. Any missteps when viewing or editing the Registry, such as deleting the wrong key or changing the wrong value, can lead to disabling of installed applications or corrupting your operating system installation.

Given the preceding caution, you should immediately make a backup of your Registry before making any changes, or even before you just start poking around. We discuss tips on making Registry backups in Chapter 3.

Once you have made a backup of your Registry, take a look at a couple of the main sections. As mentioned previously, users and applications, including Oracle, get their environment information primarily from the Registry. It is organized hierarchically, in hives, keys, subkeys, and values. To access the Registry, click Start | Run, and enter **regedit**.

NOTE
You can actually access the Registry in two different ways. By running regedit, you have greater search capabilities, and it is easier to back up and restore keys. However, security on a key or value can only be viewed or changed by running regedt32 and selecting Permissions from the Security menu. In addition, regedt32 gives you a wider range of data types to specify when adding values to the Registry.

Once into the Registry, you will see the five main components: HKEY_CLASSES_ROOT, HKEY_CURRENT_USER, HKEY_LOCAL_MACHINE, HKEY_USERS, and HKEY_CURRENT_CONFIG. For the most part, applications, including Oracle, write primarily to HKEY_LOCAL_MACHINE, with some information written to HKEY_CURRENT_USER. Therefore, we will not concern ourselves with any of the other keys. For convenience sake, these keys will be referred to as HKLM and HKCU throughout the rest of this book.

As mentioned in the preceding text, we will primarily concern ourselves with the HKLM key. This appears as a folder in the left-hand pane when running regedit. Click the + (plus) sign next to this key to expand it. Here you will see a SOFTWARE key, a SYSTEM key, a HARDWARE key, and perhaps a Cluster key, if you are running Microsoft Cluster Server. We talk more about the Cluster key in Chapter 10. Applications such as Oracle will generally create subkeys within the SOFTWARE key for their application-specific information. The other area of interest for Oracle users is the SYSTEM key. Navigate to HKLM/SYSTEM/CurrentControlSet/Services. This is where information is stored on the services that are defined on the system. Since the Oracle database and Listener and many other Oracle processes run as a service on Windows 2000, you may want to add this key, along with the Oracle key under HKLM/SOFTWARE, to a Favorites list for quick access. Do this by highlighting the key in the Registry Editor window, and choosing Favorites | Add To Favorites from the menu bar (this is only available in Windows 2000). Next time you need to access one of these keys, simply select it from the Favorites menu, and you will be taken there directly.

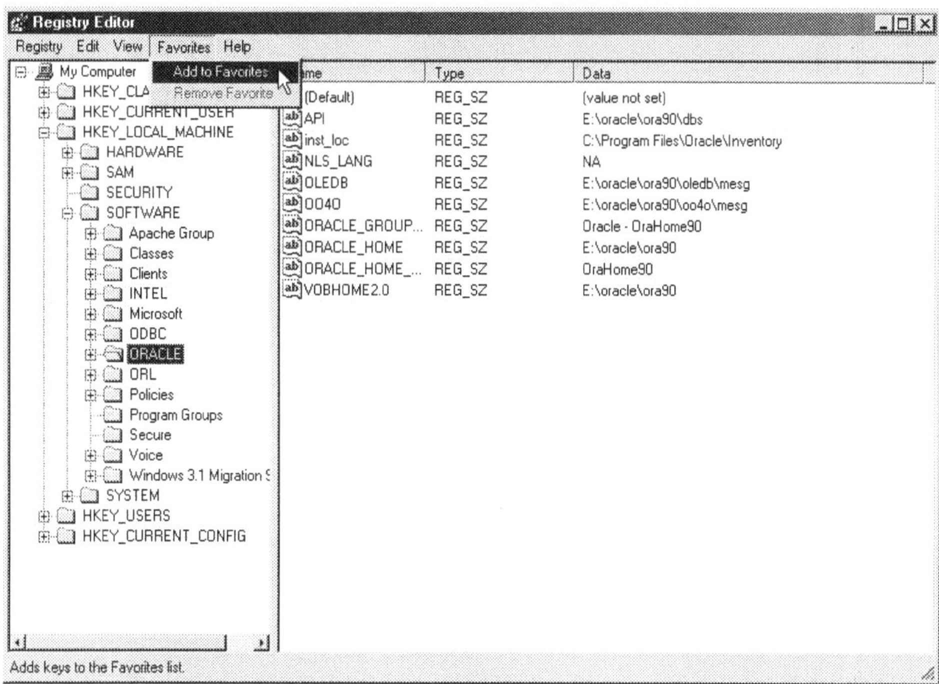

It is under the HKLM\SOFTWARE\ORACLE key that you will find settings for the various homes on the machine, and within these, the ORACLE_HOME, ORACLE_SID, NLS_LANG settings, and so on. These settings are discussed in more detail in Chapter 4, when we delve into the installation of Oracle on Windows 2000. If you already have Oracle installed, you may want to look around at the various settings here now, and also make a backup of this key, as demonstrated previously. Otherwise, go ahead and exit from the Registry Editor. As mentioned before, any changes that you make in the Registry Editor take effect right way; so when exiting, there is no prompt asking whether or not you want to save your work—any damage has already been done.

Defining Environment Variables in My Computer

Although the Registry is the primary repository for environment settings, it is not the ONLY place where environment variables are set. Certain variables can also be set in the System Properties window. To see this, right-click the My Computer icon on your desktop. On Windows 2000, there are five tabs, titled General, Network Identification, Hardware, User Profiles, and Advanced. Click the Advanced tab. Here you have three options—Performance Options, Environment Variables, and Startup and Recovery. Click the Environment Variables button on this screen to see the settings available. Under User Variables, you will see environment settings for the specific OS user that is currently logged on. Usually, there is not much more than settings for

the TEMP folder. System Variable is where you will see settings for the majority of items that affect Oracle. Here, you will see the path, classpath, windir, and other system-wide environment variables. User variables and system variables can be added, modified, or deleted here by selecting the appropriate variable and the corresponding button (New, Modify, or Delete).

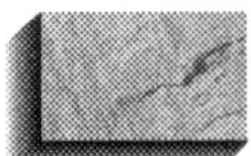

CAUTION
For the most part, you should not set environment variables for Oracle in this location. Particularly, do NOT set ORACLE_HOME. This is taken care of in the Registry, as discussed earlier in this chapter, and in Chapter 4 on installation of Oracle. Other Oracle settings, such as LOCAL and ORACLE_SID, can be set here, but can lead to confusion and can cause you to connect to the wrong instance.

Defining Environment Variables from a Command Window

Finally, to complete our discussion on the environment settings, open up a command window. Here, you can set environment variables that will override other variables that are set in the Registry or in System Properties. Variables set here only affect applications launched from within the window itself. To view any currently set variables, simply enter **set** at the command window (similar to entering **env** in a Unix environment). Although the set command does not give you a complete listing of all environment settings, it will show some useful information, such as the current username, user domain, computer name, path, class path, and so on. It will also display any variables that have been set previously from within that particular command window session. Variables can be changed or set by the following command:

```
set <variable_name>=<new_value>
```

For example, you can see in the following example how to change the ORACLE_SID environment variable to a new SID called PROD90 from within a command window session:

```
set oracle_sid=PROD90
```

This setting will last as long as you are in that particular command window, and will override the current ORACLE_SID setting in the Registry, or a setting in System Properties. Note that there are never any spaces around the equal sign (=). Also, environment variables set from here are generally not case sensitive.

Summary

In this chapter, we have discussed some of the basic features of Windows 2000 and the architecture of the OS, including thread-based architecture, memory issues and limitations, CPU, disk subsystems, file systems, I/O, and networking. In addition, we covered security briefly, and navigated through some of the basic components of the interface, introducing the primary features that you will need to become familiar with to run Oracle9*i* on Windows 2000. Finally, we discussed where the environment is defined—in the Registry, System Properties, and command windows. Chapter 3 discusses these issues in more depth, and there we go into detail on configuring, monitoring, and troubleshooting Windows 2000 in order to allow you to get the most from the Oracle9*i* database.

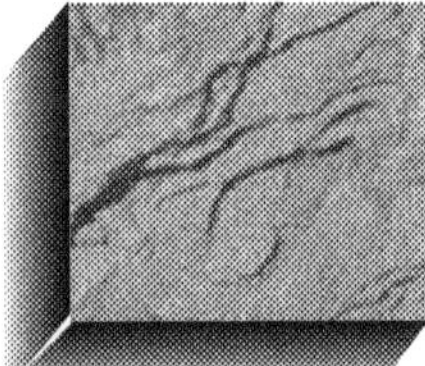

CHAPTER 2

Overview of Oracle9*i* RDBMS

Oracle Corporation's commitment to platform independence met its match when it came time to write RDBMS code for Windows. The first implementation of the Oracle RDBMS came on version 7.1, nearly two decades into the database business, and Oracle had to rethink many of the architectural precepts in place up to that point. Today, after ten full product revisions and countless tweaks and fixes, Oracle9*i* emerges with the best of both worlds: the strength and reliability of Oracle RDBMS and the ease of use and robust management features of the Windows operating system.

This chapter briefly explains the essential pieces and parts of the Oracle9*i* RDBMS as it operates on Windows 2000. It is by no means a full explanation; having fought the temptation to compose entire doctoral dissertations on the life span of an Oracle data block, we instead offer only the highlight reel. For the purposes of this book, all we need is an overview of the Oracle architecture to set the stage for the following chapters. If the principles are clear, then all tips and techniques forthwith can be seen as the logical outcome of a system that was built to be the best data storage system to date.

If you are already familiar with the Oracle RDBMS on Unix platforms, we go to great lengths here to put the architecture together from a Windows perspective so that the differences between the two are clear. If you have picked up this book because you know Windows like the back of your Palm Pilot but are new to Oracle, we still keep the discussion of the database in the vernacular. If you have worked with Oracle on Windows for some time now, and you're looking through this book for the juicy nuggets we've assembled to make your life easier, well, we recommend this chapter anyway. Repetition breeds mastery. In this chapter, we discuss the following topics:

- Oracle process architecture
- The Oracle9*i* instance, and its memory structures
- Oracle database file layout and mechanics
- Internal database management
- Database integrity checking

Process Architecture

When a user opens a Windows 2000 console and clicks the Microsoft Word icon, the operating system spawns a process that coordinates the work that the word processing application will do. This process is known as an *application process,*

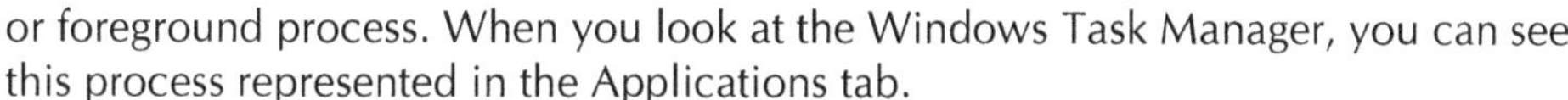

or foreground process. When you look at the Windows Task Manager, you can see this process represented in the Applications tab.

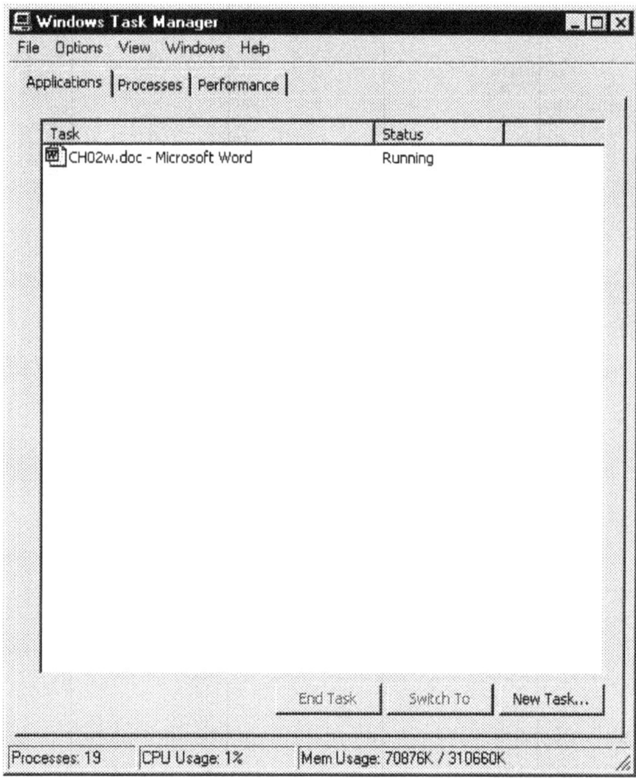

However, this screen does not represent all the processes running. If you move to the Processes tab of the Task Manager, you now see dozens of processes running. What gives? Well, the Processes window is showing not just application processes, but any background processes. These are processes set up to run in the background of the operating system, behind the scenes and invisible to the user (for the most part). These background processes often contend with applications, or foreground applications, for resources (see Chapter 3 for more information).

Oracle runs as a background process on Windows 2000, and can be started and stopped using Services in the Computer Management Console, as described in Chapter 1. More specifically, there is a corresponding process at the operating system level for every database running on the machine. For instance, the following illustration shows two Oracle databases running.

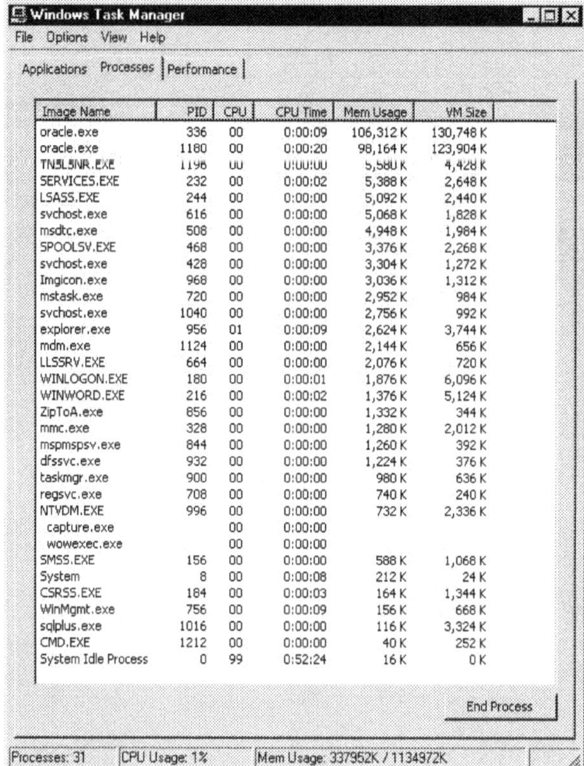

Image Name	PID	CPU	CPU Time	Mem Usage	VM Size
oracle.exe	336	00	0:00:09	106,312 K	130,748 K
oracle.exe	1180	00	0:00:20	98,164 K	123,904 K
TNSLSNR.EXE	1196	00	0:00:00	5,580 K	4,428 K
SERVICES.EXE	232	00	0:00:02	5,388 K	2,648 K
LSASS.EXE	244	00	0:00:00	5,092 K	2,440 K
svchost.exe	616	00	0:00:00	5,068 K	1,828 K
msdtc.exe	508	00	0:00:00	4,948 K	1,984 K
SPOOLSV.EXE	468	00	0:00:00	3,376 K	2,268 K
svchost.exe	428	00	0:00:00	3,304 K	1,272 K
Imgicon.exe	968	00	0:00:00	3,036 K	1,312 K
mstask.exe	720	00	0:00:00	2,952 K	984 K
svchost.exe	1040	00	0:00:00	2,756 K	992 K
explorer.exe	956	01	0:00:09	2,624 K	3,744 K
mdm.exe	1124	00	0:00:00	2,144 K	656 K
LLSSRV.EXE	664	00	0:00:00	2,076 K	720 K
WINLOGON.EXE	180	00	0:00:01	1,876 K	6,096 K
WINWORD.EXE	216	00	0:00:02	1,376 K	5,124 K
ZipToA.exe	856	00	0:00:00	1,332 K	344 K
mmc.exe	328	00	0:00:00	1,280 K	2,012 K
mspmspsv.exe	844	00	0:00:00	1,260 K	392 K
dfssvc.exe	932	00	0:00:00	1,224 K	376 K
taskmgr.exe	900	00	0:00:00	980 K	636 K
regsvc.exe	708	00	0:00:00	740 K	240 K
NTVDM.EXE	996	00	0:00:00	732 K	2,336 K
capture.exe		00	0:00:00		
wowexec.exe		00	0:00:00		
SMSS.EXE	156	00	0:00:00	588 K	1,068 K
System	8	00	0:00:08	212 K	24 K
CSRSS.EXE	184	00	0:00:03	164 K	1,344 K
WinMgmt.exe	756	00	0:00:09	156 K	668 K
sqlplus.exe	1016	00	0:00:00	116 K	3,324 K
CMD.EXE	1212	00	0:00:00	40 K	252 K
System Idle Process	0	99	0:52:24	16 K	0 K

As mentioned in Chapter 1, on Unix platforms, the various background processes of the RDBMS truly are separate *processes*. By running a **grep** command, you can see this:

```
$ps -ef | grep ora
oracle  2226    1  0 16:43:34 ?      0:00 ora_reco_prod90
oracle  2224    1  0 16:43:34 ?      0:16 ora_smon_prod90
oracle  2220    1  0 16:43:34 ?      0:03 ora_lgwr_prod90
oracle  2230    1  0 16:43:34 ?      0:00 ora_d000_prod90
oracle  2234    1  0 16:43:35 ?      0:00 ora_d002_prod90
oracle  2228    1  0 16:43:34 ?      0:00 ora_s000_prod90
oracle  2218    1  0 16:43:33 ?      0:02 ora_dbw0_prod90
oracle  2222    1  1 16:43:34 ?     10:42 ora_ckpt_prod90
```

On Windows, however, the operating system shows only the single Oracle process for a given database. Within that Oracle.exe process, Oracle utilizes threads to manage the work of the database. We discuss in Chapter 5 how to monitor Oracle threads, but here it is important only to know that Oracle takes advantage of Windows' threaded architecture for performance gains. The first iteration of Oracle on NT did in fact have separate processes for each background process, but memory sharing became difficult, and the switch to a threaded architecture improved performance by roughly 25 percent.

In a Unix environment, the background processes would be started by the act of connecting as a sysdba user and starting the database. In Windows, however, it is important to realize that a process must already exist *before* we can ever connect to the database and issue a startup command. That process is started by the service that corresponds to the database in the Services Console. The service is created via the **oradim** command, an Oracle command specific to the Windows 2000 platform. We demonstrate the creation and starting of this service, and use of the **oradim** command in Chapter 4.

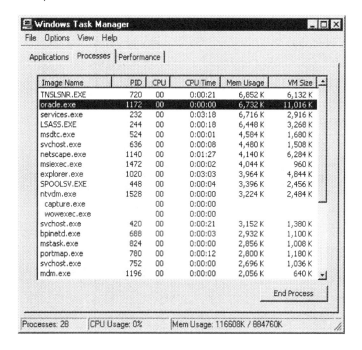

Windows Task Manager

File Options View Help

Applications Processes Performance

Image Name	PID	CPU	CPU Time	Mem Usage	VM Size
TNSLSNR.EXE	720	00	0:00:21	6,852 K	6,132 K
oracle.exe	1172	00	0:00:00	6,732 K	11,016 K
services.exe	232	00	0:03:18	6,716 K	2,916 K
LSASS.EXE	244	00	0:00:18	6,448 K	3,268 K
msdtc.exe	524	00	0:00:01	4,584 K	1,680 K
svchost.exe	636	00	0:00:08	4,480 K	1,508 K
netscape.exe	1140	00	0:01:27	4,140 K	6,284 K
msiexec.exe	1472	00	0:00:02	4,044 K	960 K
explorer.exe	1020	00	0:03:03	3,964 K	4,844 K
SPOOLSV.EXE	448	00	0:00:04	3,396 K	2,456 K
ntvdm.exe	1528	00	0:00:00	3,224 K	2,484 K
capture.exe		00	0:00:00		
wowexec.exe		00	0:00:00		
svchost.exe	420	00	0:00:21	3,152 K	1,380 K
bpinetd.exe	688	00	0:00:03	2,932 K	1,100 K
mstask.exe	824	00	0:00:00	2,856 K	1,008 K
portmap.exe	780	00	0:00:12	2,800 K	1,180 K
svchost.exe	752	00	0:00:00	2,696 K	1,036 K
mdm.exe	1196	00	0:00:00	2,056 K	640 K

End Process

Processes: 28 CPU Usage: 0% Mem Usage: 116608K / 884760K

The Parameter File

So, we have a single process started for our database, Oracle.exe. Now what? With a process started, we can map memory pages for Oracle use by starting the instance itself. The parameter file, or init.ora, defines your memory allocation when starting the database instance. It also defines the location for the control files, which will not exist yet if you have not yet created the database. When the database is started, Oracle uses the parameters in the init.ora file to allocate memory on the computer. In the Task Manager, the amount of physical and virtual memory will increase dramatically for Oracle.exe after issuing a **startup** command for the database. We discuss specific parameters and parameter types in more detail in Chapter 4.

The Background Threads

After the database has been started, several important threads do the bulk of database management work. The following list describes briefly the function of each background thread.

- **SMON** The System Monitor process performs system management duties in the background, such as extent cleanup. SMON also coalesces free space within Oracle datafiles, and is responsible for instance crash recovery.
- **PMON** The Process Monitor performs process management tasks, such as freeing up resources after server processes crash. Remember, on Windows 2000, we say "process" but we mean "thread."
- **DBWR** The Database Writer writes database changes to Oracle datafiles on disk.
- **LGWR** Oracle keeps a chronological journal of every change that occurs in the database by writing them to a log file. The Log Writer process coordinates and writes all log information.
- **CKPT** Oracle keeps datafiles and log files up to date with each other by occasionally writing a checkpoint to datafile headers. The Checkpoint process writes the current system change number (SCN) to each file header when a checkpoint event occurs
- **ARC*n*** When a database is running in archivelog mode, every redo log that fills up with system change information is copied to an archive location for safekeeping. Oracle calls these files *archive logs*. Introduced in 8*i* was the ability of multiple archive processes to start up if redo log switching occurs too often. The first process would be named ARC0, the next ARC1, and so on.

The Oracle Instance

It is useful to consider the memory area used by Oracle as the *instance*. The instance refers to the place in memory where Oracle manages data, user connections, and all the locks, latches, buffers, pools, and buckets that make up the RDBMS. When we refer to the instance, we are not necessarily referring to the database itself, which essentially consists of the physical files on disk. Rather, the instance is the staging area in memory where users access the database.

The instance is divided into different structures that operate differently based on their individual function. Figure 2-1 shows a diagram of the different structures. Understanding these is critical when a DBA is maximizing the Oracle implementation on Windows 2000. Let's spend a few moments looking at each piece.

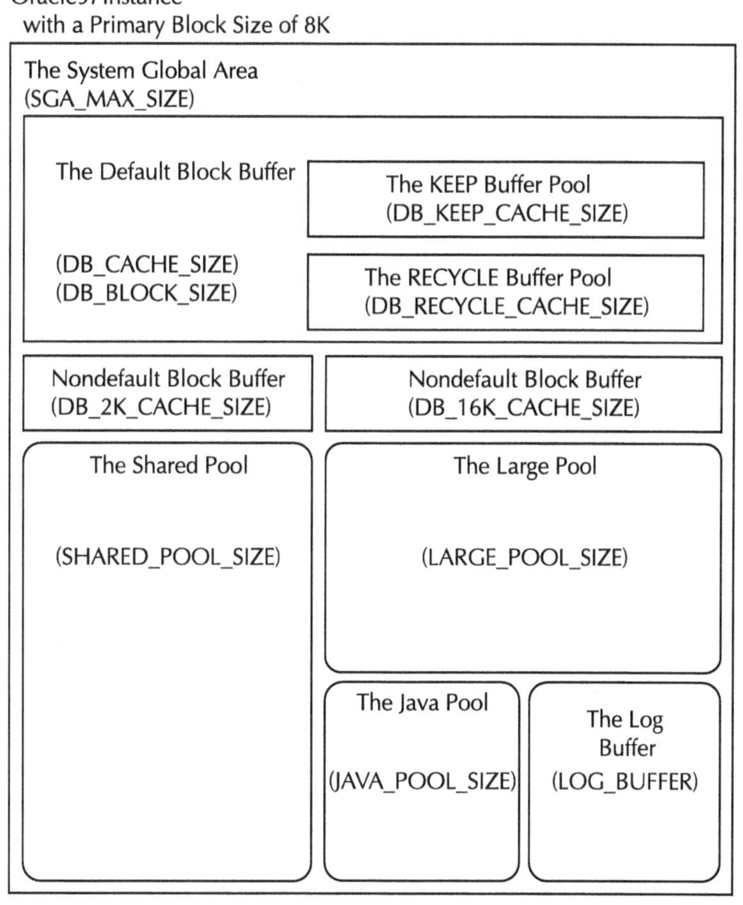

FIGURE 2-1. *The architectural features of the Oracle9i instance*

The Buffer Cache

The buffer cache is the section in memory that literally acts as the staging area for data in the database. When a user runs a SQL statement that requests a certain amount of data be returned, the data must be pulled from the datafile and put into the buffer cache. The working unit of data that Oracle pulls into memory is known as a *data block*. Every row of data in a table, every index leaf, and every piece of system information exists in a data block. When a table row is updated, for instance, Oracle pulls the entire block into memory from its datafile, makes the change in memory, and then writes the block back down to disk.

If a row is simply requested on a SELECT operation for a report, the block is read into memory from its datafile and the user process gathers the selected information from memory. As this row will not be modified in memory and then rewritten, the block is put on a list to be aged out of memory. As more blocks are read from disk, older blocks are slowly aged out.

The size of the data block is configured at database creation time in Oracle8*i* and lower. This value was set for the life span of the entire database and could not be modified. In version 9.0.1, Oracle significantly changed the rules concerning data block sizes, forever altering the landscape of the database. Now, a database can be configured with multiple block sizes; and, therefore, the buffer cache is divided in memory into multiple areas where different-sized blocks are manipulated. We discuss this at great length in Chapter 4.

New Feature in Oracle9i

How important is block size? In a database that is used primarily for online transaction processing (OLTP), most transactions are very small updates and inserts of single rows. If we set the size to 2KB per block, we can imagine that most transactions will require 2KB of the buffer cache to complete. If, on the other hand, we configured the block size to 16KB, every transaction, no matter how small, will eat up 16KB of memory. So on an update operation that updates a salary field for an employee, we may only be changing 20 bytes of data, but we've wasted 16,364 bytes of memory along the way.

Block size decisions are driven by the data. If the data is usually manipulated in small chunks, small sizes should prevail. If the data is usually manipulated in large chunks, then a large block size will yield better results. Before 9*i*, complicated (and expensive) strategies were implemented in attempts to segregate "small" data and "large" data into separate databases due to single-block size limitations. Now, multiple block sizes can be integrated into a single database. This not only provides for better utilization of the buffer cache, but it also allows for the use of transportable tablespaces across databases that may have been originally implemented with different block sizes (see Chapter 4 for more on transportable tablespaces).

OLTP, DSS, and Hybrid: A Brief Discussion

Online transaction processing, or OLTP, refers to the most common type of database, and the type that Oracle brags about when it discusses how many transactions per second it can handle. OLTP refers to databases that have anywhere from 100 to 100,000 simultaneous transactions constantly updating, inserting, and deleting data. Online retailers are perhaps the most famous OLTP databases, processing thousands of hits every minute as users browse the site and then place orders for products. From the DBA's perspective, these databases must be equipped to handle thousands of minute transactions, many of which are identical to each other.

Decision support systems (DSS), which are just as important as OLTP databases, refer to the type of database used for operations collectively known as *data mining*. In this type of database, the primary operations are long ad hoc queries that look at trends in the data, from the average amount of money every consumer spent at a retail site to the exact number of sales each region was responsible for generating in a specified amount of time. DSS systems drive business intelligence. This type of database must be equipped to handle large queries that select millions of rows at the same time, and then sort through the rows, organizing them for the user who needs to make business decisions based on the output.

More and more, these two very different database types are converging. Business intelligence is being reported in real time, even as the data is being updated by end users. A database that must function as both OLTP and DSS is usually referred to as a *hybrid database*. This database must be configured to satisfy the needs of OLTP users as well as DSS users, two very different uses that contend for resources.

Shared Pool

The interface language for an Oracle database is SQL and, programmatically, PL/SQL. Commands that are entered by users must be parsed into usable system calls to manipulate data. This parsing occurs in the *Shared Pool*. The Shared Pool provides useful cost gains by parsing all SQL and PL/SQL in a shared memory area for all users. Therefore, if the same SQL statement has been previously parsed by a different user, we can simply reuse the parsed statement instead of parsing it again.

Large Pool

The Large Pool came into existence when Oracle developers found the Shared Pool being overused for purposes that fell outside the scope of its original design. So those new purposes were given their own memory pool to fight over, therefore keeping them separate from SQL and PL/SQL parsing.

Multithreaded Server The multithreaded server (MTS) is the primary Large Pool occupant. MTS is the default configuration for all databases in Oracle9*i*. In non-MTS environments, every client that connects to the database spawns a corresponding server thread. These server threads have approximately 1MB to 2MB of memory resources allocated to them. This can lead to a quick consumption of system resources simply due to user connections.

MTS instead pre-spawns shared server threads that can be used by multiple client threads. This optimizes resource utilization by accounting for "dead-time" from clients—those periods of time when client processes sit idle. These pre-spawned "dispatcher" servers use the Large Pool for memory resources.

Backup and Restore Buffers Backup and Restore buffers utilized by Oracle's Recovery Manager are drawn from the large pool as well. Recovery Manager, or RMAN, allows the Oracle database to manage its own backup and restore operations, and includes an API interface for backing up directly to tape devices. RMAN, as an integrated piece of the RDBMS, reads the database at the data block level and loads the blocks into special memory buffers before streaming them to the backup location. These buffers are created in the Large Pool if we establish backup I/O slaves. This is discussed thoroughly in Chapter 6.

Java Pool

This is the fixed size portion of the SGA that is allocated for use by the database's *Java Virtual Machine* (*JVM*). The JVM uses this chunk of memory for all session-specific Java code and data. It is used differently when the listener and database are configured for dedicated connections versus MTS.

If the database is configured for a dedicated server connection, then the *java_pool* contains the read-only pieces of each Java class that is used by sessions. Typically, these pieces are about 4KB to 8KB per class. In this configuration, all Java session state information is kept in the User Global Area (UGA), which is part of the Process Global Area (PGA)—and thus is not found in the SGA, but in dedicated server threads on Windows 2000.

If the database is configured for MTS, then the read-only pieces are also kept in the java_pool, as with a dedicated server setup, but the UGA data is not kept in the PGA but instead in the java_pool. This portion of UGA code grows and shrinks with usage, but you must evaluate the largest possible size and multiply that by the maximum number of concurrent sessions that will use Java stored procedures and set the java_pool accordingly.

The Database Files

So far, this discussion has focused on the memory components of the Oracle instance. Let's turn our focus now to the physical components, that make up the database itself. An instance would sit idle and unemployed if no storage area existed on disk for data. The place on disk where Oracle stores data is called the datafile.

The Oracle Datafile

Oracle builds datafiles at the time of tablespace creation, and every datafile is logically associated with only one tablespace. Files can also be manually added to existing tablespaces. The location and size of the file must be specified by the administrator, as in this example:

```
Sqlplus>create tablespace users datafile 'd:\oracle\oradata\prod\
user01.dbf' size 200m;
Sqlplus>alter tablespace users add datafile
'd:\oracle\oradata\prod\user02.dbf' size 50m;
```

However, Oracle9*i* introduces Oracle Managed Files (OMF) to simplify this. OMF allows you to specify new file locations in the init.ora, and have the names automatically generated. We discuss Oracle Managed Files in more detail in Chapter 5.

New Feature in Oracle9i

Different datafiles serve different purposes, but the underlying structure is identical. Upon creation, a datafile is mapped out as a series of data blocks, which are given specific block IDs to identify them as unique storage areas in the database. This block ID, called a *data block address* (*DBA*), is the primary means by which Oracle identifies and accesses data throughout the database. When a user requests data from a table, Oracle checks block mapping information in the system tablespace, and then retrieves the block from disk based on the DBA. Oracle copies the block from disk into the buffer cache, where the user process can read it, or modify it and wait for the DBWR process to write the changed block back to disk. Without the data block address given to each block at the time of datafile creation, this entire process would lack the speed and grace of data retrieval that Oracle has built its reputation upon.

This also explains why datafile creation can often take some time to complete. If the database has been created with a block size of 2KB, and we create a datafile of 4GB, Oracle must put headers on over two million blocks. Back in Oracle7, block formatting did not occur at the time of file creation, making file creation a breeze but costing users valuable processing time when they began to actually use the datafile. Instead, Oracle now eats the performance time of formatting blocks at the time of datafile creation, ostensibly before the file must be used.

Maximum Datafile Size

An Oracle datafile on Windows 2000 can contain a maximum of 4 million database blocks (to be more precise, 4,194,304 blocks). Therefore, the maximum datafile size depends on the block size. With a 2KB block size, your maximum datafile size would be 8GB. On the other hand, a 16KB block size allows a maximum file size of 64GB, provided of course that you are using NTFS for your file system.

Information about the datafiles in a database can be viewed using SQL statements run against data dictionary views. The most important view is V$DATAFILE, which shows the file number, filename, each file's size and status, and other information about the file pertaining to its integrity and usage. To associate a datafile with its tablespace, use the view DBA_DATA_FILES, which gives not just the filename, but also the associated tablespace.

Segments and Extents

A tablespace keeps track of the logical organizational unit called a *segment*. A segment is the organizing unit within a tablespace that differentiates between different database objects. A table is a single segment. An index is another segment. Each segment acts as a bucket for *extents*. Extents are sets of data blocks that are grouped together so that segment growth is not required to grab physical space one data block at a time. Although segment size is based on the overall size of the object it represents, extent size is set at the time of object creation. If a table will grow very quickly due to thousands of row inserts every day, setting a large extent size is preferable, as extent allocation will happen less often. However, if a table grows slowly, a larger extent size may simply waste space as it grabs megabytes at a time, even though it grows by only a few bytes every day.

Roughly speaking, segments and extents are logical working units for space management on disk, tying logical objects such as tablespaces, tables, and indices to physical space within datafiles. But the extent is ungainly for manipulation in memory, so the data block remains the working unit for data modification in the buffer cache.

The Control File

The RDBMS handles the relationship between the different logical units of a database (tablespaces, segments, extents, and blocks) in the SYS base tables in the system tablespace. But how do we identify and control the physical datafiles? When we add a new datafile to a tablespace, where is storage information held?

To keep track of datafiles (and, as you'll see, log files), Oracle uses the *control file*. The control file contains a series of structures that track where the datafiles are, how big they are, and any checkpoint information contained for each. While the control file has taken on a larger and larger role with each release of the Oracle RDBMS, its primary role continues to be file location and identification. In a nutshell, think of the control file as containing a copy of the datafile header information, and therefore knowing as much about each datafile as they know about themselves.

The control file is aptly named for its role in database administration. It contains control information about where on disk datafiles and log files must exist in order for the database to operate. If a datafile or log file needs to be relocated, the control file must be modified to point to the new location. However, since the control file is a binary file, it cannot be edited. It must be modified via an **Alter Database** command.

Due to its role as a sort of traffic controller for the database, the control file contains plenty of information about the database that is useful to database administrators. Oracle built many of the often-used V$ views on top of structures within the control file to provide a window for inquiring minds into the information contained therein. The view V$DATAFILE, discussed previously, provides pertinent information about each datafile associated with the database. Next, in our discussion of Oracle log files, we introduce you to V$LOGFILE and V$LOG.

The Log Files

When a database is created, we specify a certain number of redo log files that will be used to record all database changes. The default database has three log files divided into three groups. A log file *group* is any number of log files that contain the same information. Think of them as mirrored copies of each other, used in case one of the files goes corrupt or is lost due to media failure. A log file *member* is any log file that has been specified to belong to a group, as illustrated in the following diagram.

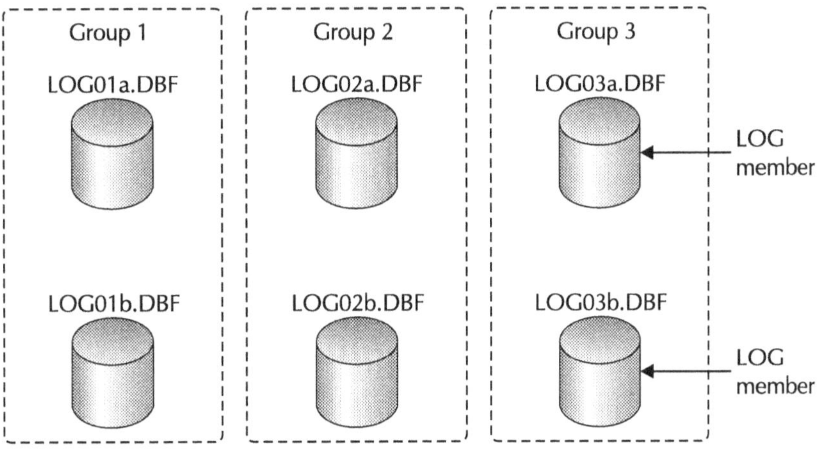

Think of the log file as the port of entry for the database: every change that comes in must be accounted for. Every DML statement in a database is given a system change number (SCN). When the change occurs, an SCN is logged for that change, and both the SCN and the change it represents are written to the current redo log file. Every database change is written sequentially to the redo log. (An exception to this is when a table is altered with the NOLOGGING keyword. This allows certain types of writes to the table, referred to as *direct writes,* to go directly to the datafiles, bypassing the redo logs. This option is discussed in more detail in Chapter 5.) When the current log file fills up, Oracle switches to the next log file, and so on, until all redo log files are full. When the last log is full, the log writer process (LGWR) goes back to the first one and overwrites the previous entries. This round-robin process continues, time after time, for the entire life span of the database.

The continuous stream of change information, simply called *redo* in Oracle vernacular, is used by the database for instance and media recovery. If a transaction is updating a block, the change is first written to the log file and then to the datafile. Therefore, it is possible for committed data to exist in an online log file, but not yet exist in a datafile. If the database crashes while in this state, Oracle can use the log file for *automatic instance recovery* on a restart, replaying the transactions that were complete, but unwritten to the datafiles, and reapplying the change. This process is automatic, with no user intervention required.

Because Oracle reuses online log files in a round-robin fashion, automatic instance recovery using log files is limited to the size and number of online redo files associated with the database. But the redo stream can be preserved for the entire life span of the database by enabling archivelog mode for the database.

Archived Redo Log Files

When a database runs in archivelog mode, every time a log switch occurs, the ARC*n* process wakes up and makes a copy of the log file that was just completed. It copies the file to the location specified by the parameter LOG_ARCHIVE_DEST in the init.ora file for the database. By doing this, you essentially save a copy of every change that has ever occurred to the database.

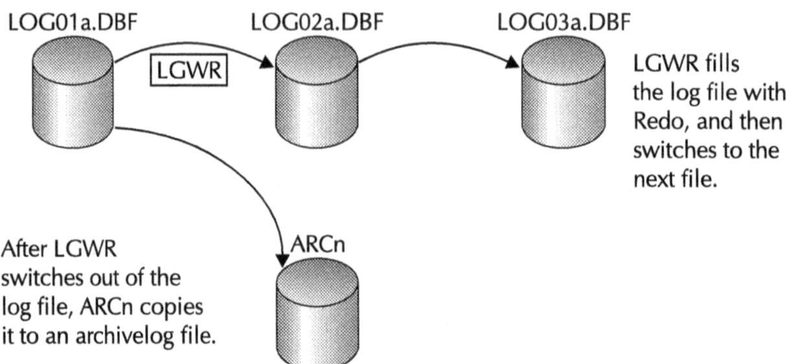

If you lose the database to some disaster or another, the database—or a given datafile—can be restored from the last good backup, and then you can apply the changes in the archived redo log files from the time of backup to the time of disaster, and achieve zero data loss. As opposed to the automatic instance recovery that occurs if the database goes down ungracefully, this type of recovery is referred to as *media recovery*, and requires manual intervention.

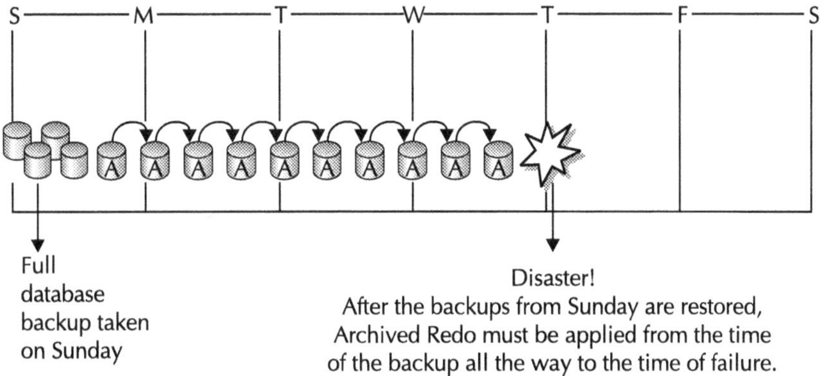
S M T W T F S
A A A A A A A A A A
Full database backup taken on Sunday
Disaster!
After the backups from Sunday are restored, Archived Redo must be applied from the time of the backup all the way to the time of failure.

Discovering whether your database currently operates in archivelog mode simply requires running the following command from sqlplus (you must have sysdba privileges):

```
SQL> connect / as sysdba
SQL> archive log list;
Database log mode              No Archive Mode
Automatic archival             Disabled
Archive destination            e:\oracle\oradata\prod90\arch
Oldest online log sequence     39204
Current log sequence           39207
```

To Archive or Not to Archive?

Making the decision to run in archivelog mode seems easy to support analysts like us, who have spent the majority of our careers here at Oracle recovering damaged databases. What seems to be the best way to determine whether archivelog mode is right for you is how you answer this question: If the database is lost to a disaster, can you manually rebuild all new data that has been created since the last backup? If the answer is yes, then archivelog mode may simply be an administrative headache you can avoid. However, if you do not have the means to easily rebuild data, then you must run in archivelog mode so that all data entry is protected. We discuss enabling archive logs when we discuss database installation and creation in Chapter 4. Using archived logs for recovering from disasters is covered in detail in Chapter 6.

Internal Database Management

Neglected so far, we must discuss the internal management components that exist in every database. A lot of work must take place in the background to keep track of millions of independent pieces of data, data that usually grows in size every hour of every day.

Merely keeping track of data obviously isn't the only function an Oracle database provides. Especially in new versions such as 9*i*, many internal components make up a massive toolkit of data manipulation utilities and time-saving management tools. At length this book will uncover many of these features, but a few pertinent ones will be mentioned here, especially if they have been introduced in 9*i*. But first, let's talk about the primary components of database management.

Tablespaces

What is this tablespace thing we keep talking about? A *tablespace* is the logical container for different objects in the database. If you are migrating from SQL Server to Oracle, you may be familiar with SQL Server's use of the term *database*. SQL Server refers to a database in the same vein that Oracle uses a tablespace. In Oracle, a database comprises one or more tablespaces, and a tablespace comprises one or more physical datafiles. Compare the logical container, the tablespace, to the physical container, the datafile. A datafile is attached to a tablespace so that the objects that are internally organized by tablespaces can be written to physical locations on disk. But Oracle does not logically map objects to specific datafiles, but rather to specific tablespaces. Put another way, a database table knows which tablespace it belongs to, but not which datafile it physically resides in; objects in the database have *tablespace affinity*, but not *datafile affinity*.

Different tablespaces are created for storing different types of data. The system tablespace, of course, holds the data dictionary. In addition, Oracle recommends creating separate tablespaces for user data, indexes, temporary (sort) segments, and rollback or undo segments. Depending on what you use the database for, you will likely have several different user data tablespaces, to hold different types of data for different applications. If you use Oracle Database Configuration Assistant (DBCA) to create the database, you will likely have additional tool tablespaces, acting as repositories for holding data specific to certain Oracle features, such as Intermedia. In this section, we provide an overview of the system tablespace, temporary tablespace, and rollback/undo tablespace.

The System Tablespace In a nutshell, the system tablespace is the place where the software magic happens: ask the database to do something for you, the system tablespace grinds away, and voila! It's done. Of course, if you pull back the curtain, the wizard turns out to be an old man pulling on cords and flipping switches madly.

More realistically, the wizard of this particular Oz happens to be hundreds of database objects busy every nanosecond of a database's life happily exchanging bits of data, writing new data, and deleting useless data. These *base tables*, as they are known in the vernacular, have odd and unintuitive names that make them hard to remember and tough to reference. This is done on purpose, and here's a tip: if you are not exactly sure what you are doing, never muck around inside the system tablespace. A random delete from a base table, and suddenly all your data has disappeared into the ether.

Next, allow us to briefly touch upon the major components in the system tablespace that you should be familiar with.

The SYS Schema Two separate schemas exist after creation for managing the database and objects in the system tablespace: SYS and SYSTEM. To SYS go all the critical objects that dictate the life and time of a database. Objects in the system tablespace should belong to only these two users. If you find any objects that belong to other users in this tablespace, you need to get them removed as soon as possible. Are they damaging anything just being there? Not exactly. But there exists the possibility of problems coming from nowhere if you start building custom views for the DBA as the user system, or if application tables are in this tablespace. A good rule of thumb is to use the system built views, but keep all DML out of the system tablespace.

The system tablespace is populated with physical objects at database creation time via the script SQL.BSQ. Here, the base tables are created from which you will find information on used extents and free extents, what the type of each object is, what its name is, where to find it, and how big it is (how many extents it comprises). Perhaps more importantly, tables in the SYS schema control the sizing of extents, where extents exist, and where to find free space to write new extents. The SYS user also owns tables that track performance information about how many blocks are read into memory each second, how many are written back, and much, much more.

Obviously, all of this information can prove vital to the database administrator, but you do not want to look for it directly in these SYS user's base tables. To make this cryptic information more readable, and as a means of protecting the actual wheels and cogs of the database from inadvertent modifications that could prove fatal to the database, the data dictionary creation is rounded out by running the catalog.sql and catproc.sql scripts. These scripts are required with every database creation, and must be run as user SYS. Additional scripts may need to be run to further populate the data dictionary with information needed for certain optional features (such as catrep.sql to take advantage of advanced replication, as discussed in Chapter 9).

The SYSTEM Schema If logged in as the SYSTEM user, or any other DBA account, you have access to the views that describe nearly every important piece of the SYS schema. These views tend to be named DBA_*, such as DBA_OBJECTS, which gives pertinent information about every object in the database. The "DBA" identifier tends to name objects that a database administrator (that means you) needs to have access to in order to properly manage a database.

Each user built in a database has access to views about his or her own objects; these views are prefixed with USER_*. So it follows that a DBA can see all objects using DBA_OBJECTS, but a single user can see only its own objects using USER_OBJECTS. A third set of views are available for users who have been granted privileges on other user's objects. This set of views are prefixed by ALL_*. So a development user named DEV might be granted privileges on application user APP's tables; these would show up in DEV's view ALL_OBJECTS but not in DEV's view USER_OBJECTS.

To describe the structure of these views, use the **describe** command in sqlplus:

```
SQL> describe dba_objects;
 Name                                      Null?    Type
 ----------------------------------------- -------- ------------------
 OWNER                                              VARCHAR2(30)
 OBJECT_NAME                                        VARCHAR2(128)
 SUBOBJECT_NAME                                     VARCHAR2(30)
 OBJECT_ID                                          NUMBER
 DATA_OBJECT_ID                                     NUMBER
 OBJECT_TYPE                                        VARCHAR2(18)
 CREATED                                            DATE
 LAST_DDL_TIME                                      DATE
 TIMESTAMP                                          VARCHAR2(19)
 STATUS                                             VARCHAR2(7)
 TEMPORARY                                          VARCHAR2(1)
 GENERATED                                          VARCHAR2(1)
 SECONDARY                                          VARCHAR2(1)
```

In this way, administrators can look at free space in a tablespace, or how large a particular table is (by number of data blocks or bytes), or which objects belong to which database user.

System Rollback Segment Oracle also builds the system rollback segment at the time of database creation, and it serves a critical purpose for the life span of the database. This rollback segment is used exclusively to hold undo information for objects in the SYS schema, and cannot be used for any other purpose.

Temporary Tablespace The temporary tablespace is the tablespace where sort segments will be written to for a sort operation that overflows from memory (see the discussion on SORT_AREA_SIZE in Chapter 4). A temporary tablespace should be defined at creation time as a TRUE temporary tablespace, and when new users are created, they should be assigned to the designated temporary tablespace. Otherwise, sort segments will end up being allocated in the system tablespace.

Default Temporary Tablespace Oracle9*i* simplifies the process of creating users and assigning them a temporary tablespace by introducing the concept of a *default temporary tablespace*. When a default temporary tablespace is defined in the database, all newly created users are automatically assigned to that designated tablespace for sort segment overflow. This avoids the common problem in previous versions of forgetting or neglecting to assign a temporary tablespace to a new user, and having sort segments go into the system tablespace by default. We discuss details in setting up and defining a default temporary tablespace in Chapter 4.

New Feature in Oracle9i

A tablespace that is being used as a temporary tablespace, but actually allows permanent objects (such as the system tablespace), will not use temporary segments efficiently. Temporary segments in a tablespace with contents defined as permanent will need to be deleted and re-created each time they are needed. On the other hand, temporary segments in a true temporary tablespace are not removed after an individual sort operation. Instead, sort segments in a temporary tablespace remain allocated, so that they can be reused by the next sort operation that comes along, saving the cost of having to constantly allocate and deallocate segments. Thus, it may appear that your temporary tablespace is full, when, in fact, it simply has empty segments waiting to be reused by the next sort operation. This is perfectly normal, and these segments will still be cleaned up whenever the database is shut down. You can check whether a tablespace is defined as a true temporary tablespace by querying the CONTENTS column in the DBA_TABLESPACES view.

Rollback Segment or Undo Tablespace In addition to a temporary tablespace meant for holding temporary segments, Oracle also recommends creating a rollback segment tablespace, or an undo tablespace, meant solely for holding undo segments. So, what are undo segments, and why do you need them? What is the difference between an undo tablespace and a rollback segment tablespace? These are all valid questions, with equally valid answers. In the next sections we discuss transactions, rollback segments, and undo, and the role they play in an Oracle9*i* database.

The Oracle Transaction The *transaction* is the lifeblood of a database. A transaction defines how you use a database, from updates to inserts to deletes. All of these activities have an atomic size that we refer to as a transaction. But when does a transaction begin? When does it end?

When a user issues a SQL statement to insert a row, he or she has begun a transaction. That transaction lasts until the first explicit commit or explicit rollback occurs, the session ends and an implicit commit occurs, or a DDL statement is executed. To be specific, a transaction is the length of time between commits. Good application code generally attempts to keep this length of time as small

as possible; but for conceptual purposes, the size of a transaction isn't as important as the fact that it is atomic in nature, a self-contained thing. In fact, Oracle names every transaction that occurs in a database; the SCN is simply a number that is incremented for every transaction, so every transaction has a unique SCN associated with it.

Rollback Segments and Undo Every transaction in the database can be undone by the user. Say a user updates everyone's salary in the EMP table to multiply the current value by 1.05 to give a 5 percent cost-of-living increase in wages. After doing so, the user selects the salary of a particular user, prior to committing, and notices that Tom Jones, who used to make $50,000 per year, is now making $75,000! Oops, the user has accidentally multiplied the value by 1.5 instead of 1.05. Instead of running another update statement, the user can simply type **rollback**, and all DML in the current session gets undone.

Oracle facilitates this element of transaction processing by taking a snapshot of every row being updated in the EMP table and placing this "before" image in an object called a *rollback segment*. This snapshot is kept around in a rollback segment until the user either commits or rolls back the transaction. All uncommitted DML is implicitly committed when a user exits from a session gracefully (by issuing an explicit EXIT command).

The accumulation of all these "before" images of every DML statement is collectively referred to as *rollback* in the vernacular. Managing a system's rollback can consume plenty of time in a database administrator's life. For every long-running transaction, like a massive update of everyone's salary in a company or the repricing of every retail item in a company's warehouse due to inflation, every single row is stored in a rollback segment. This not only costs you disk space, where you write the rollback to, it also costs you disk contention. By far the worst possible side effect of all this rollback creation is transactional failure. During a long-running transaction, if the database runs out of datafile space in the rollback tablespace, Oracle aborts the transaction and begins to, well, roll it back. The error message you see in such a situation is ORA-1562: "Unable to extend rollback segment *name* by *n*," where *n* specifies a value in bytes that Oracle could not find in the rollback tablespace. So, configuring adequate space for rollback segments, and making sure you have enough of them, is no insignificant task.

Oracle holds a copy of the snapshot of a row that is modified because of one fact that defines Oracle transactions: the Oracle RDBMS is an optimistic writer. Based on database usage, it is more likely that a change a user makes will be permanent rather than be rolled back. So, instead of keeping a list of all changed rows and leaving the unchanged rows alone until the commit occurs, Oracle makes all changes nearly as they happen. Then, in the unlikely case of a rollback, it rewrites the changes to their unchanged state at the **rollback** command. This means that Oracle is optimized for the change, but will take the performance hit if it must roll back.

Notice we stated that Oracle makes the changes "nearly" as they occur. As we explain in the next section, a changed block in memory is considered "dirty," and is put on a list in memory to be flushed at the next explicit commit or every three seconds, whichever comes first. In this way, disk writes occur in batch jobs so that writes to disk aren't happening nonstop.

Rollback Segments and Read Consistency If Oracle writes a changed block back to disk, and that block has not been committed and therefore doesn't exist yet, how do other users access the block for information? When the request for a block is made, Oracle finds the block is "fuzzy," or in between two states of existence: it has a new value, but that value is locked because the user who made the change has not committed the change, so other users are prohibited from seeing it. In addition, Oracle *must* return the data as it existed *at the time the query began*, not as it exists now. But the block does not have the pre-change value; what the block does have is a pointer to the rollback segment that contains the unchanged values of the block. So Oracle looks up the rollback segment, finds the snapshots of the requested rows, and returns those values to the user asking for them.

Obviously, there are performance hits for all this excess work, which is why it is recommended that rollback segments be kept in their own tablespace, preferably on separate disks. This is also why application development for Oracle transaction processing will often be focused on keeping the size of every transaction small, and avoid allowing a user to leave a change uncommitted for even a brief period of time. If it is necessary for a user to think about a change before committing it, try keeping that commit time on the application's dime, not the database's.

An Explanation of the Infamous ORA-1555

If you have worked for a number of years with an Oracle database and have never seen the ORA-1555, consider yourself in the fortunate minority, and make sure your application developers get a big bonus check. The ORA-1555 has plagued the life of DBAs for years. Oddly enough, it remains relatively misunderstood. So we have decided to give it a good once-over before moving on, as an explanation of this error not only demystifies the cause of ORA-1555, it also gives you a good case study for how rollback is used.

Let us set our scene: Imagine, if you will, a large table that holds a listing of every possible kind of wood screw a hardware store can order from its supplier, along with the wholesale price. This table is very large, but every row must be changed very frequently; often, a small set of rows are changed at a time, but it could be that every row must be changed at the same time. Humor us: We have no idea how often the price of wood screws changes, but for our example let's say it happens a lot. A hardware store manager's nightmare, these wood screws.

At 9:00 A.M. Monday morning, a long-running query begins. A manager at the store is running a report that looks at the price of every wood screw so he can make

his weekly price changes on the floor. The query begins at the first row and loads each value into memory, doing a full table scan. There are over a million rows to look at, so this is going to take some time. At 9:05, a transaction updates the price of a single wood screw, and then another. This is caused by a data entry employee who must update the prices of certain wood screws every Monday morning based on the volatility of wood screw prices nationwide. This employee updates the price, commits it, and then moves to the next price to update. The application he uses commits often in an attempt to keep transaction size low.

The manager's corresponding process in the database is using no rollback segment, as he is only doing a select. The data entry employee, however, is using rollback for each transaction. In fact, Oracle chooses which rollback segment to use based on the current database load, so it could be that the employee is using a different rollback segment for each price update.

Here's where we get to the critical facts: *the "before" image of the price of the wood screw is held in the rollback segment only as long as the update statement is uncommitted.* As soon as the transaction is committed, the snapshot is released and can be overwritten by another transaction. Rollback information for a transaction may not be overwritten immediately, and Oracle certainly does not waste its time actually deleting the rollback information from the rollback segment. So rollback for a transaction is often available long after the transaction has been committed.

Okay, so the select statement reaches a row that has been updated. However, due to read consistency rules in the database, the process wants a consistent picture of the entire table as it looked at 9:00 A.M. So, if a row is changed at 9:05, the process goes looking for that row's rollback information in the rollback segment. But that rollback segment has already been overwritten, and therefore the manager's process has no way of discovering what the row looked like at 9:00 A.M. The rollback segment doesn't know, and the table doesn't know. Without read consistency, the transaction aborts with the error ORA-1555: "Snapshot too old." This is a meaningless error statement, of course, but here's what it means: there is no way to return a read-consistent image of the data you have selected in your transaction.

What remains so confusing about this error is that the manager gets the error, but it is not because of something he did. The data entry employee is not to blame either; his transaction simply updated the row and then committed the work, leaving a picture behind in a rollback segment of what the row used to look like, in case anyone cares. The real culprit is the third transaction, which could be modifying data in a completely different area of the database, but requests a rollback segment extent when it just so happens that the next one available holds the snapshot of the price of a single wood screw at 9:00 A.M. When it fills that rollback segment with its information, it has single-handedly sabotaged the manager's Monday morning wood screw price report.

What is to be done, then? The "action" section of the error report tells us the rollback segments are too small; however, increasing the size of rollback segments only helps if all updates are large. If there are a series of small updates in a row, it is possible that the same rollback segment extent will be used over and over. So there is some wisdom, if you have a lot of small transactions running at the same time as a few very large transactions, to instead increase the total number of rollback segments so there is less likelihood that a transaction will have to reuse any rollback segment for the expected duration of any one long-running transaction. Still, it's a crapshoot. Even better is to try to offload long-running transactions to a time when there is low traffic; if the manager had a job that automatically ran his reports Sunday night so they were complete before the data entry employees came Monday morning, then the problem would not exist.

System Managed Undo

Due to the numerous pitfalls and errors associated with rollback segments, and therefore the amount of time database administrators must spend tuning them, Oracle9*i* has introduced a new way to handle undo. This is referred to now as *system managed undo* (*SMU*).

System managed undo may be new to Oracle9*i*, but those who used Oracle in version 6 and lower remember a time before rollback segments. The new implementation of system managed undo takes the best of rollback segments and combines it with a series of system-controlled algorithms that provide all the necessary elements of having undo available to transactions without all the headaches of tuning them yourself.

Not that you can turn SMU on and simply walk away; while this is the main reason for the implementation, Oracle couldn't resist adding configurable elements to SMU that give advanced DBAs new tools for data manipulation. Even if you prefer to turn SMU on and ignore it, the basic architecture is worth becoming familiar with.

Enabling System Managed Undo For SMU to be enabled, an undo tablespace must exist within the database. This tablespace would be created in lieu of a rollback segment tablespace. An undo tablespace is created by default if the database is created using the Oracle9*i* Database Configuration Assistant. Alternatively, an undo tablespace can be created at any time after database creation. Oracle allows only a single undo tablespace to be in use at any one point in time, so make sure you create a large enough tablespace to handle all undo creation for the entire database. Once SMU has been enabled, and the undo tablespace built, Oracle will manage undo for all transactions in the database without further user intervention. In addition, creation or manipulation of rollback segments, as it used to be known (for example, via SET TRANSACTION or ALTER ROLLBACK SEGMENT), is no longer allowed. These commands will error out when SMU is enabled. Here's how it works.

Undo Segments If you are familiar with the architecture of a rollback segment, don't worry too much about Oracle changing the game. Within the undo tablespace, the rollback segment is alive and well. Oracle simply renamed it to be an undo segment. This serves the primary purpose of making sure that DBAs do not confuse the two, as there is one very important difference: you can mess with rollback segments, but you cannot mess with undo segments.

The first time an undo tablespace comes online for use, Oracle creates a certain number of undo segments and brings them online. By default, Oracle creates ten undo segments in an undo tablespace. The total number of undo segments then grows based on usage. After there are many undo segments, the next time the instance is bounced, Oracle brings only a certain number of them back online using the calculation of the initialization parameter SESSIONS * 1.1.

Now the first rule that SMU applies is simple: one transaction per undo segment. This may fly in the face of common wisdom, which dictates that rollback segments are wasted if there aren't four or five transactions concurrently using the same one. But this wisdom is based on the fact that rollback segments usually have large extent sizes to compensate for a large array of different transactions, and that they grow to be very large. Therefore, if only one transaction used a rollback segment that was over 100MB in size, that would truly be wasteful. But the new architecture ensures that even if a single transaction grows a particular undo segment to be 100MB in size, other undo segment can reuse the extents from that undo segment if necessary. So a single undo segment's size is unimportant.

When a transaction requests space for undo storage, the request first hits the header block of the undo tablespace to find a free undo segment. If all undo segments are busy with active transactions, the undo tablespace will create a new undo segment. The initial extent of every undo segment is 64KB, and the next extent is based on the total size of the undo tablespace. Typically, this remains 64KB: tests with the default undo tablespace (210MB) and a nondefault undo tablespace of 500MB gave us uniform 64KB extents. Every undo segment is at least two extents in size to begin with, and then grows one extent at a time until the transaction is complete.

If during the allocation of a new extent the undo segment finds no more free extents in the undo tablespace, it first steals extents from offline undo segments. Any undo segments without active transactions are considered offline. If all undo segments are online, and therefore there are no offline segments, the extending segment steals an extent from an online segment that has free, unused extents. If there are no free extents in any online undo segments, then the undo tablespace extends the size of its datafile into free space on disk. If this is not possible due to file size constraints placed by the DBA, then the undo segment steals unexpired extents in its own segment. If there are no unexpired extents in its own segment, it will use unexpired extents from another undo segment. If this final step fails, then the RDBMS finally gives up and signals the "out of undo space" error.

An *unexpired extent* refers to an extent that has not aged out of the *retention policy* instituted by the DBA for the undo tablespace. At any point, the DBA can specify how long he or she wants every extent to be unusable by another transaction in order to keep the "before" image of a transaction available for read consistency. Here we have a new solution to the ORA-1555 error discussed previously. If it is known that there will be hour-long transactions running, you can set your UNDO_RETENTION to 3600 seconds (this parameter is specified in the init.ora), meaning that no undo segment extent will be reused for an hour. Although this is good for read consistency, these extents are used last by the algorithms we've been describing, so you must compensate by having plenty of space available for new extents. We discuss specifics on enabling system managed undo in Chapter 4

Database Integrity Checks

Oracle's relational database management system must continually strike a balance between storage efficiency and user accessibility. Storage efficiency drives data to exist only once within a database, and then allows all users access to the same data. But how can you make sure that thousands of users can simultaneously read and write to the same database objects? This capability requires a system that guarantees data integrity. This system can be roughly divided into two categories: logical integrity for reads/writes, and physical consistency for datafiles and data blocks.

Read/Write Safeguards

To guarantee access to data without sacrificing the integrity of the data itself, Oracle employs a system of cascading object locks. Locks are held by users and are identified based on the type of lock. Table 2-1 describes the different levels of locking.

Lock Level	Type	Description
0	None	No lock
1	Null (NULL)	No lock
2	Row S (SS)	Row Select lock: no blocking
3	Row X (SX)	Row Exclusive lock: blocks other writers
4	Share (S)	Shared lock, usually held by nonuser resources
5	S/Row X (SSX)	Row Exclusive, Object Shared lock
6	Exclusive (X)	Object Exclusive lock (usually DDL)

TABLE 2-1. *Oracle's Six Levels of Locking*

Here is the simple, dogmatic breakdown that you should burn into your long-term memory for instant recall whenever you are looking at locking issues:

- Readers cannot block readers.
- Readers cannot block writers.
- Writers cannot block readers.
- Writers do block writers.

Even simpler, the only time a user is blocked from an operation is when that user attempts to write to a data block that is currently being written by another user.

This modern wonder is accomplished by usage of the buffer cache, as described earlier. Because a block is read into memory before it is modified, the unmodified block still exists on disk. So a second user can therefore read the unmodified block into memory even as the same block is being written by a different user. However, if the second user wants to modify the same block as the first user, he or she must wait for the first user to commit his or her work and therefore allow the "dirty" block to be written to disk before he or she can load the block into memory for his or her own modifications. The block that has been modified by the first user only appears in its modified state to the user who modified it. Every other user sees the block as it appeared before the modification; upon commit, however, the modified block appears in its modified state to all users who request that block after the commit point. Refer to the earlier section, "Rollback Segment or Undo Tablespace," for more detail regarding how Oracle contends with long-running transactions and data mutation.

The importance of the "logical working unit of commit" cannot be overstated at this point. If a user process is allowed by application logic to run amok, modifying thousands of blocks over a span of hours without issuing a commit, all other users expecting access to those blocks for write operations will be blocked. There are application trade-offs that have to be considered when making decisions concerning commit intervals, the most obvious of which is the ORA-1555: "Snapshot too old" error (discussed earlier in this chapter).

Deadlocks

Because writers block other writers, its possible for writers to block each other, causing an unfixable lock called a *deadlock*. Here's how it works: User Tom updates Row A of a table but does not commit the change. User Harry updates Row B of the same table and does not commit the change. Tom then requests Row B for an update. Because Harry has Row B locked, Tom waits for Row B to become unlocked. Harry in turn requests Row A for an update. However, Tom has Row A locked, so Harry waits for Row A to become unlocked. But neither lock will ever be released, as each is waiting for the other lock to be released first. This results in a deadlock, and Oracle will abort the second transaction with an ORA-60: "Deadlock detected" error.

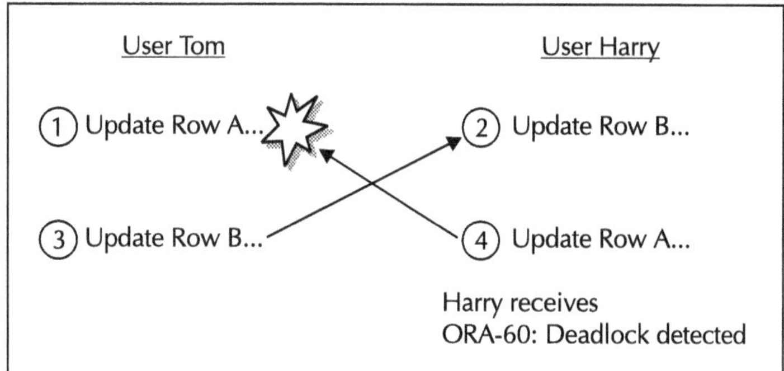

Physical File Safeguards

With so much simultaneous writing to files occurring, Oracle must be able to guarantee that writes complete and do not contradict information in the system tablespace or other dependent tablespaces. This requires that all files be up to date based on a timestamp. The CKPT process gives the database this timestamp by having the control file increment a sequence number by a count of one, associating the most recent SCN with that sequence number, and then broadcasting that SCN and log sequence number (LSN) to every datafile, which then records the LSN and SCN in the file header. This event is known as a *checkpoint*. CKPT forces the DBWR to flush all dirty buffers from the buffer cache before creating the new LSN, thereby guaranteeing that with the timestamp of the checkpoint, all blocks have been written and all files are in sync.

A checkpoint can occur for a number of different reasons. The most common checkpoint event is a log switch. When a redo log is full, the LGWR signals a log switch and begins writing to the next redo log. CKPT wakes up and performs a checkpoint at this time.

Log switches as well as checkpoints can be forced by a user with dba privileges:

```
sqlplus>alter system switch logfile;
sqlplus>alter system checkpoint;
```

Besides user commands, a checkpoint can be configured based on system parameters (issued dynamically with an **alter system** command, or specified in the init.ora file). LOG_CHECKPOINT_INTERVAL can be set to a number of redo log blocks that, when filled, cause a checkpoint. Do not confuse log block size with data block size; log blocks refer to the operating system blocks that make up all system I/O. On Windows 2000, the block size default depends on the size of the disk partition, as listed in Table 2-2.

Disk Partition Size	Corresponding Default Block Size
512MB or less	512 bytes
513MB to 1024MB	1024 bytes
1025MB to 2048MB	2048 bytes
Greater than 2048MB	4096 bytes

TABLE 2-2. *Default Block Sizes*

The other system parameter for checkpoints, LOG_CHECKPOINT_TIMEOUT, changed its behavior in 8i from previous releases. Now, the value for this parameter will ensure that a checkpoint event will occur *nnn* seconds after the last write to the redo log. This ensures that if there is low activity on the database, and therefore more common checkpoint events are not happening often enough to ensure speedy recovery, Oracle will force a checkpoint at a specified time after the last redo log write. Previously, LOG_CHECKPOINT_TIMEOUT simply specified a time in seconds that a checkpoint would occur following the last checkpoint, regardless of any database activity. The new behavior prohibits excessive checkpoints by only activating one if there is log activity.

All of this stuff is pretty expensive, internally, but these kinds of integrity checks are the backbone of reliability that Oracle boasts about year after year.

Summary

Oracle uses Windows native thread architecture for managing processes, which provides performance gains but costs memory mapping capabilities. Oracle divides its memory area into different regions that handle data blocks, system management information, SQL parsing, and connection pooling using the buffer cache, dictionary cache, Shared Pool, and Large Pool. All database information, from dictionary data to user data, resides in the datafiles, which are associated with logical containers called tablespaces. Log files contain all redo information, a journalized history of every database change. These files are archived for media recovery to the archive logs. The Oracle control file maps out where all datafiles, log files, and archive logs exist on disk, as well as keeping track of integrity checking mechanisms, called checkpoints. Integrity checking occurs in order to protect data from concurrent users, using cascading locking mechanisms to ensure that all users see current and correct versions of each data block. The Checkpoint process keeps all datafiles current by broadcasting the current system change number and log sequence number to every datafile header each time a checkpoint event occurs. Oracle performs internal database management within the system tablespace, using objects in the SYS schema. The SYS schema provides database administrators with views that can be used to monitor database mechanisms. Prior to 9i, Oracle used rollback segments to manage transaction undo. In 9i, system managed undo has been introduced to decrease the amount of time database administrators must spend tuning undo segments.

PART II

Implementing the Oracle RDBMS on Windows 2000

TIPS

&

TECHNIQUES

CHAPTER 3

Configuring Windows 2000

There are three basic configurations of Oracle on Windows 2000: as a management platform, as an Oracle client, and as a database server.

The first configuration is the platform from which you will manage Oracle installations across various machines on various operating systems. Most system and database administrators are given a desktop PC to perform day-to-day tasks that are not DBA specific (such as reading e-mail). From this desktop, you can also manage Oracle components installed on other operating systems (for example, Solaris, Linux, and HP-UX). Even so, you will want to configure Windows 2000 to make your system and database administrative tasks quick and easy.

The Oracle client software configuration is used in more configurations than you might first suspect:

- Web applications that connect to an Oracle database:
  - IIS 5 ASPs that use ADO to connect to an Oracle database
  - Perl DBI application running on Apache that connects to an Oracle database
  - Any J2EE application server that uses the thick JDBC driver
- Client/server applications:
  - Desktop Visual Basic application that uses OLEDB or ODBC to connect to an Oracle Database
  - Desktop Java application that uses the thick JDBC to connect to Oracle

In any of these configurations, at least an Oracle client installation is required. In some cases, software vendors may hide this fact from the user; but the Oracle client libraries are necessary to connect to the database *unless* you use the JDBC thin driver.

Operating system configuration offers the greatest return on investment in cases where Windows 2000 hosts the Oracle database. In this chapter, we will review some key things you can do to optimize Windows 2000 configuration to interact with Oracle. Here are the tips and techniques we offer in this arena:

- Optimizing Windows 2000 for Oracle
- Upgrading to multiple processors
- Working with the Computer Management Console
- Building custom MMC consoles
- Using the Windows 2000 shell
- Integrating Windows 2000 and Unix
- Using the Resource Kit appropriately

- Using tools from the Sysinternals web site
- Using the Event Viewer
- Managing disks
- Using the Task Scheduler Service
- Understanding and controlling the Windows 2000 environment
- Understanding Active Directory
- Remote Administration with MMC
- Remote Administration with VNC
- Remote Administration with the Windows 2000 Telnet Server
- Remote Administration with pcAnywhere and other commercial tools
- Locating other resources
- Contemplating the future of Windows

The Oracle RDBMS on Windows 2000 should usually run alone on its own server-class machine. In order to best ensure reliability and performance, you will need to configure the version of Windows 2000 you are running to best work with Oracle.

Tuning Windows for Oracle

One of the more common issues that Oracle database administrators face is how to configure the operating system to optimize it for database usage. In this section, we give you a number of quick tips you can implement to improve your operating system configuration for Oracle.

Optimize Windows 2000 for Oracle

Below are a number of tips you can implement right away to improve performance, availability, and manageability.

Know When Rebooting Is Required

In Windows 2000, there are far fewer tasks that require you to reboot. Here is a list of some that still do require you to reboot:

- Making changes to the configuration of an ISA card

- Adding or removing communication ports
- Installing a service pack or hotfix
- Changing the computer name
- Changing the system font
- Promoting a server to a domain controller
- Changing the DNS suffix
- Changing the IP address of a DNS server
- Installing Terminal Services
- Changing the system's locale

Use a Wallpaper to Identify Your System's Key Information

Create a JPEG file that identifies key information about the system such as node name, CPUs, memory, network cards, disk, and Oracle installation details (for example, Oracle home location and default Oracle SID). You can do this easily with MS Paint or any other graphics tool. This handy identifier keeps you from running commands on the wrong remote system, a common problem when many GUI remote desktops are running at one time. The JPEG also makes it easier to determine if you have connected to the correct remote computer. Check out the free bginfo tool from Sysinternals that makes getting this information even simpler.

Optimize Use of Device Drivers

Make sure that you are using a stable device driver and configure the device optimally to best serve a dedicated Oracle server. A bad device driver can make an otherwise rock solid system randomly transform into a blue screen generator. With the next generation of the Windows OS there will be a higher level of device driver certification. Windows 2000 Datacenter already requires a level of certification to allow for the new features and to ensure overall system integrity. Follow that trend and stick with heavily integrated systems from vendors like Compaq and others (see the Oracle Technology Network web site mentioned in the section "Resources" later in this chapter).

Many device drivers have configuration screens or Registry settings that allow you to optimize use of the device for your application. Become familiar with these settings and learn the effect of setting changes on your applications through the use of performance baselines and controlled testing.

Optimize CPU Usage and Configuration

Before running out to get that new 64 CPU Datacenter server, you may want to try some of the following suggestions to improve CPU utilization.

Upgrade Kernel to Multiprocessor When Adding Second CPU In Chapter 1, we alluded to a simpler process on Windows 2000 for upgrading the OS kernel when going from a single processor to multiple processors. As promised, here are the steps:

1. Go into the Computer Management Console (see Figure 1-5 in Chapter 1 for a depiction of the Computer Management Console). Under System Tools, select the Device Manager.
2. Click the plus sign (+) next to the computer name to expand the list of devices, and then expand the device called Computer. You should see a display similar to Figure 3-1. As you can see in the figure, this machine already has the multiprocessor driver installed.
3. To upgrade your kernel, simply right-click, choose Properties, and then select the Driver tab in the dialog box that appears. Click the Update Driver button.
4. The Upgrade Device Driver Wizard appears and walks you through the steps for upgrading the processor device driver.

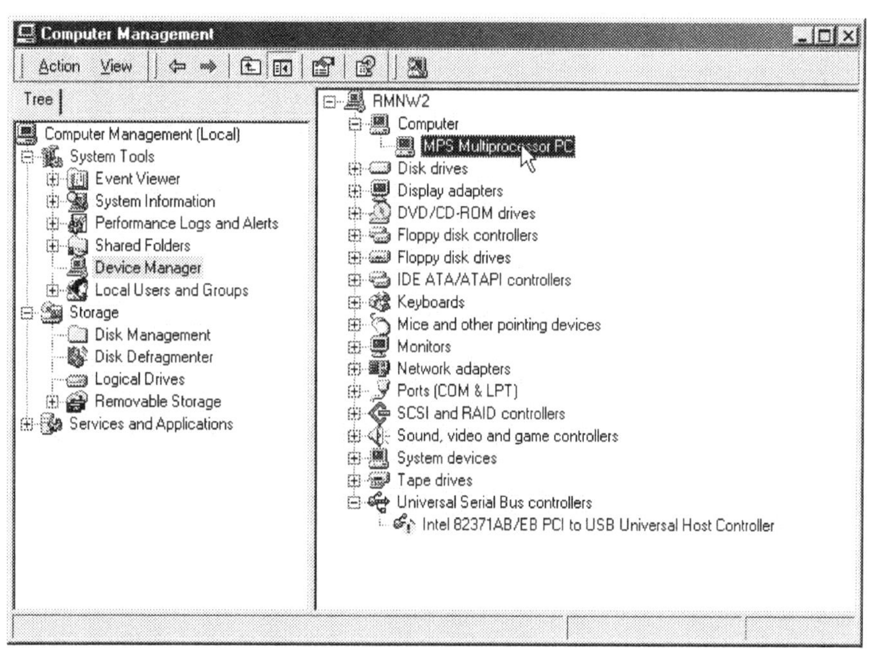

FIGURE 3-1. *Computer Management Console multiprocessor device driver*

Disable Screensavers A screensaver can suck an amazing amount of CPU and provide no useful purpose to a database server. In particular, disable the 3GL screensavers. Screensavers can grab valuable CPU from the OS and Oracle. If you must use a screensaver, use the Blank Screen screensaver to minimize CPU usage.

Log Out Log out of your system when you are not doing something that requires you to remain logged on to the console. This will help minimize running applications.

Configure the System as an Application Server Set Performance Options to Background Services on the Advanced tab of the System applet in the Control Panel (or right-click My Computer and then select Properties). This gives priority to applications running as services, such as the Oracle Services, as opposed to programs a user starts when logged in to the GUI desktop.

Monitor the System for Highly Interruptive Hardware Hardware that consumes CPU interrupts and time should be avoided. Often, inexpensive hardware is cheaper because it offloads work onto the CPU. Higher quality hardware will handle calculations on the peripheral's own resources. As an example, try to maintain the following options for disk controllers and network cards:

- Network cards that support DMA, as opposed to PIO-supported bus mastering
- 64-bit PCI disk controllers kept on a PCI bus separate from network controllers

Use Performance Monitor to track the Processor Object's % Interrupt Time counter. Baseline and benchmark this counter, and then monitor it regularly to spot possible problems. You can experience immediate performance gains where I/O is a bottleneck by switching to a good hardware RAID controller from the Windows 2000–supplied software RAID feature.

Keep Security Auditing to a Minimum The more layers of security auditing that are implemented, the more that the CPU has to spend cycles on this operation. Audit when and where necessary, and only to the level that is appropriate to your environment.

Optimize Network Configuration

Network configuration is an important performance piece that can easily become the hidden performance bottleneck. Try the following tips to avoid problems and tune your system.

Configure Network Cards to Use the Fastest Speed and Mode Available
This is, as opposed to "auto detection," the default setup for most NICs. If it is optimal and possible, enable the Full Duplex setting and manually set the maximum line speed.

Remove Unneeded Network Protocols Try to keep TCP/IP the sole protocol stack if you can. If you must include NetBEUI, understand that it is a chatty protocol that can hamper your network capabilities. NetBEUI was implemented by Microsoft as a protocol for small workgroup networks and is largely discouraged even by Microsoft now. If you do not have a specific need for SPX (for example, you are using Netware), then make sure you remove SPX as well.

Optimize Net Protocol Bind Order Set the primary protocol, typically TCP/IP, to be at the top of the list of protocols in the Advanced Settings dialog box, accessible through the Advanced file pull-down menu in Network and Dial-up Connections. Make sure to do this for each NIC.

Disable or Optimize File Sharing for Oracle Ideally, you should disable the Microsoft "share" functionality to minimize security exposure and network traffic. If you need to use the File and Printer Sharing for Microsoft Windows feature, enable the option Maximize data throughput for network applications from the Connection Properties dialog box for each network card installed on your system.

Optimize Disk Configuration

Oracle can be a very I/O-intensive application. Make sure that you properly configure and tune the disk and file system. Here are a few tips to help you begin your journey.

Distribute File System Activity Across Disks and Controllers Proper distribution of I/O is one of the first rules a database administrator learns. It is often one of the first performance axioms a database administrator will remember. Identify hot Oracle files using Stats Pack (see Chapter 9, or refer to the comprehensive Oracle Press book *Oracle High-Performance Tuning with STATSPACK*) and OS tools like Perfmon. Alter your disk configuration and file layout to spread I/O across disks and controllers.

Ultimately, you should stripe activity to evenly spread activity properly across volumes, according to the type of disk access for particular files, and at the same time meet your fault tolerance goals. Review the section "Disk Management" in this chapter for more information on fault-tolerant configuration suggestions.

Defragment Disks Prior to Creating or Placing Data Files on a Disk The fragmentation state of an Oracle datafile remains the same from the time of creation until the file is resized either manually or through autoextend. To *safely* defragment a datafile, the instance should be shut down. Oracle documentation actually indicates that the service should also be stopped in order to ensure safe defragmenting, although our investigations with Sysinternals utilities such as Process Explorer and Filemon do not show that the service holds any handle on datafiles once the instance has been shut down. At any rate, you can avoid having to deal with defragmentation if your file system has enough contiguous free space to ensure that the datafile will not be fragmented when created. More tips on defragmenting and working with Oracle datafiles appear in Chapter 5.

Don't Use Disk Compression Oracle database files don't support disk compression. Avoid it like the plague when dealing with Oracle files. There are certain situations on user workstations where disk compression can be useful. We find it useful for our collection of scripts and source code used for database and system administration.

Don't Use Disk Encryption Encryption, like disk compression, adds a layer of processing that slows disk reads and writes. If you are worried about encrypting your data, then use the DBMS_OBFUSCATION package and Label security to selectively encrypt sensitive portions of data instead.

Do Not Use More Than 70 Percent of Free Disk Space To maintain optimal disk performance, it is important that you don't use the whole disk. This limit pertains to seek speed, space for the OS file system (NTFS) to do its work, the ability to maintain a defragmented disk, and concentration of disk head movement to the faster inner tracks of the platters. If you have disk space to burn, then you may see performance gains on some disk subsystems when you avoid using more than 50 percent of disk capacity to minimize seek distance and keep data on the inner tracks of the platters.

Use More Disks Rather Than Large Disks You can help distribute I/O, maintain greater throughput, and decrease response times by using smaller disks of at least the same seek time and rotational speeds. For example, four 9GB 9ms seek time 10K rotational speed drives will offer you better performance than one 36GB 9ms seek time 10K rotational speed drive. This configuration also provides more flexibility in layout and faster recovery times for hardware failure.

Optimize Memory Usage

Because Oracle 9i now requires 512MB of RAM for a database installation, we likely do not have to prompt you to avoid wasting memory. Do not forget to include the memory used by your connections as well as the SGA in your memory usage estimates for the oracle.exe process.

Run Oracle on a Dedicated Server Oracle can be a memory hog. In particular, do *not* run an Oracle database on a system that performs the following functions:

- Primary or backup domain controller (or a domain controller, if in a Windows 2000–only domain)
- File server
- Print server
- Remote Access Server
- Router, proxy, or firewall of any kind

Don't Use Fancy Wallpapers If you have a valid use for wallpaper, keep the size of the file to a minimum.

Disable Unnecessary Services Do the best you can to disable services that you will not need to run your system. If you need a service's functionality intermittently, then set the startup type to Manual. The first thing to do is check with your network and system administrators to verify the requirement to run a specific service in your enterprise. In particular, consider the following suggestions:

- If your system doesn't need to print regularly, then stop the Print Spooler service and set its start type to Manual.
- Stop the License Logging Service unless you specifically require it.
- You should not use a dynamically assigned IP address (DHCP) on a database server, nor should a database server act as a DHCP server. Make sure the DHCP Client and DHCP Server Services are disabled.

Learn the services you need for your environment and use them sparingly. Keep a list of the services you will expect to see running on your system to identify possible hacks and cracks as well.

Do Not Automatically Start Programs You Don't Need Check the contents of your Startup menu (Start | Programs | Startup). If the contents include anything that is not absolutely necessary, then remove the unnecessary items. Be aware that you may have a Startup menu for the current user and one for the default user. Check both.

Span Paging Files Across Physical Volumes Create at least two paging files across two physical disks. You can create up to four paging files and still experience performance benefits. Make sure that the total size of your paging files is at least two times your physical memory. Ideally, you should not have a page file on the same drive as your OS, but doing this disables crash dump creation when the system fails. You may want to keep it off the system drive on very stable certified systems. The ideal configuration is four page files located on four stripped volumes spread across multiple disk controllers.

Properly Size Your Paging Files Make sure that your paging file is at least two times the size of your physical memory. We often see problems when people upgrade machine memory, but make no changes to their page file configuration. Monitor page file usage from Perfmon via the Paging File Object's % Usage Peak counter. Make sure that your paging file is always sized greater than or equal to peak usage. This will avoid the expensive process of growing the paging file.

Do Not Create Databases with Options You Do Not Need If you do not need options like the Oracle JVM in the database, do not install them. You can drastically reduce memory usage if you don't use the Java option. Be sure that you need the buffer cache, shared pool, large pool, and java pool initial allocations. Resize these pools to match your needs.

Microsoft Management Console

As we mentioned in Chapter 1, the Microsoft Management Console is a framework that can be customized with various predefined Windows 2000 and third-party snap-ins. This framework makes centralized management through a single console easier than ever. In this section, we will first discuss the Computer Management Console that comes with the OS and follow with tips on customizing your own MMC.

Computer Management Console

The management of the operating system in Windows NT was done largely through disparate, unrelated programs and applets in the Control Panel. Windows 2000 has centralized and "componentized" computer management through the use of various incarnations of the Microsoft Management Console (MMC). From a single location, you can view and control services, manage disks and users, view the Event Log, create Performance Log views, and much more (see Figure 1-5 back in Chapter 1). You will find the Computer Management Console in the Administrative Tools program group along with other useful MMC incarnations, such as dedicated performance and services consoles.

In this section, we will discuss the key information and snap-ins available from the Computer Management Console. These include the System Summary section, Disk Management, Event Logs, Services, Local Users & Groups, and the Performance

Monitor. We will also provide some tips on using the Computer Management Console for managing remote machines.

System Summary

The System Summary can be found by expanding the plus sign (+) next to System Information. Highlight the System Summary folder in the left pane to view information about your machine in the right pane. Here you will see the full OS version, the name of the machine (system name), total physical memory (RAM), and total virtual memory, among other tidbits of information. Total virtual memory is the total amount of memory available to the system, including physical RAM plus the page file. This summary can be saved to a text file or to a System Information file by right-clicking the System Summary folder.

NOTE

This same information can be found by entering ***winmsd*** *at a command prompt. Although the System Summary and the Computer Management Console are specific to Windows 2000,* ***winmsd*** *and* ***winver*** *can be run on a Windows NT 4.0 machine to display similar information.*

Services

We briefly described services in the architecture section of Chapter 1. In this chapter, we will examine where service information is stored and viewed. Services can be accessed from the Computer Management icon (under Services and Applications), and can also be viewed by going to Start | Programs | Administrative Tools | Services.

Once into the services, you can view the service name, an optional description you can modify to your delight, current run status, the startup type (Manual, Automatic, or Disabled), and which account the service uses to Log on as. You can sort on each of these columns by clicking the column heading. For example, click the Startup Type column heading to view all services that will start at boot time grouped together.

To change or view more service detail, right-click the service and select Properties. Under the General tab, you will see what executable the service calls and the Startup type. Under the Log On tab, the account that runs the service is displayed. As noted previously, a service will log on and start up its associated process whether or not anyone has actually logged on to the machine. Most services log on as the Local System account by default. This is a Windows 2000 operating system account that exists on every machine, yet each machine's System account is unique to the machine on which it exists. We will discuss how the logon account affects Oracle Services in more detail in Chapter 4.

Services can be stopped or started by right-clicking and selecting the appropriate option, and they can also be managed at the command prompt by issuing either **net stop <servicename>** or **net start <servicename>** (for example, **net stop oracleserviceorcl**). Entering **net start** by itself will give a complete list of all currently running services.

The Recovery tab allows you to determine actions that take place if a service fails for some reason. This allows a service to be automatically restarted if it fails, run a job upon failure, or even reboot the machine if this service fails. This is a rather basic way to provide a modicum of high availability for certain processes. We will discuss more robust methods of achieving high availability, such as clustering and the Oracle Failsafe feature, in Chapter 11. The final tab is the Dependencies tab. This tab allows you to view other services that must be running before this service can be started.

Disk Management

Expand the Storage node of the Computer Management Console and select Disk Management (aka Disk Administrator). From this console, you can partition new drives, repartition existing drives, format drives, and assign or unassign drive letters.

The Disk Management display will show you the logical drives on the top half, including the drive capacity, the amount of free space, and the file system for existing logical volumes. The lower half of the display will show you the physical layout of the disks, starting with Disk 0. In this area of the display, logical drives will be shown as a part of whichever physical disk they actually belong to. You will also see each volume's file system type. To learn more about the new features of Windows 2000's volume management, check out the section "Managing Disks" later in this chapter.

Event Viewer

Event Viewer is the logging mechanism for events on Windows 2000. Operating system errors and informational messages will be written to the System Log. Applications running on the system, including Oracle9i Server, will write informational and error-related messages to the Application Log. In order for this to occur, the Event Log Service must be running.

You can also save log information by right-clicking and choosing Save As. If you save the file as type *.evt*, you must open this file from within the Event Viewer. Saving it as a text file will allow the data to be viewed from any text editor. You can send a saved version of your Event Log to Oracle Support for analysis that might help solve your problem. The binary-formatted .evt log files will change their timestamps on events to sync up with the computer on which they are opened. Therefore, if you save the file from a computer running in the Eastern time zone, and open it on a system running in the Mountain time zone, the timestamps will be off by two hours. For more details on using the Event Logs for system administration, check out the section "Using the Event Viewer" later in this chapter.

Managing Users and Groups

User and Group management is now done via the Local Users and Groups snap-in, under System Tools in the Computer Management Console. From here, you can add, modify, and delete users and groups on the local system, or simply view which users are part of which groups.

There are two types of users on Windows 2000: domain users and local users. A group is simply a logical association of users with like needs and purposes, and grouping users simplifies the tasks of granting access to certain resources on the system. Although it is beyond the scope of this book to give a complete description of Windows 2000 domains and managing accounts in a domain environment, it is important to understand certain differences. Domain users are authenticated on a remote machine called a *domain controller,* and many of the privileges for a domain account are set on the domain controller, rather than on the local machine. A user account may be a member of the Domain Administrators group, yet not have any privileges on the local system because the account is not part of the Local Administrators group. A domain account and a local account may even have the same names; however, they are treated as entirely separate entities. Permissions assigned to the domain account will not translate to the local account, and vice versa. Also, be aware that passwords on Windows 2000 are case sensitive, but usernames are not.

To view whom you are currently logged on as, simply press the CTRL-ALT-DEL keys simultaneously. This will clear your screen and display a Windows Security dialog box with a Logon Information section that tells you the username under which you are logged in the format of *COMPUTERNAME\Username* (see Figure 3-2). Check this against the system name on the System Summary page, as described earlier in this chapter. If the computer name displayed in the Windows Security dialog box is *not* your local system name, then you are logged on to the domain. You will see the importance of this in Chapter 4, as Oracle9i Server requires that installations be done while logged on to the local computer as a member of the Local Administrators group.

Remotely Managing Servers Using the Computer Management Console

You can connect to other Windows 2000 nodes to monitor and manage them remotely via the Computer Management Console by right-clicking the Computer Management root of the tree of items and browsing to the node you want to manage

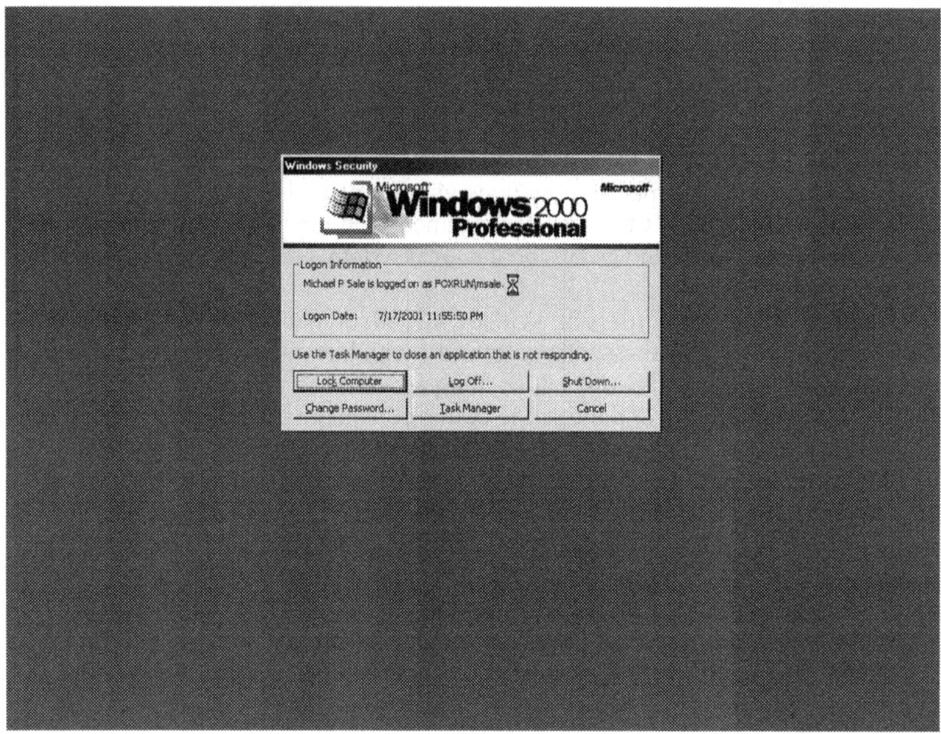

FIGURE 3-2. *Find the computer name and username.*

or entering the node name directly. If you want to manage disks from a remote node, you must upgrade from the volume management tool installed with Windows 2000 to the VERITAS Volume Manager for Windows 2000 (see Figure 3-3). With this upgrade you also gain much more flexibility and manageability in disk management. Check out the section "Managing Disks" later in this chapter.

You can also send a pop-up message to the console of various computers from the Management Console by right-clicking the root of the tree again, navigating to the All Tasks menu, and selecting Send Console Message (see Figure 3-4). From here, enter the recipient node names and the message. Note that these nodes need to have the Messenger Service running to allow the pop up message to appear. This feature is useful in a shop with numerous database or system administrators who may be working on the same machine at the same time.

Make Your Own Snap-Ins

The MMC is a framework that is available for independent software developers to develop their own snap-ins that allow administrators to better centralize and customize system administration. Developers interested should review the Platform

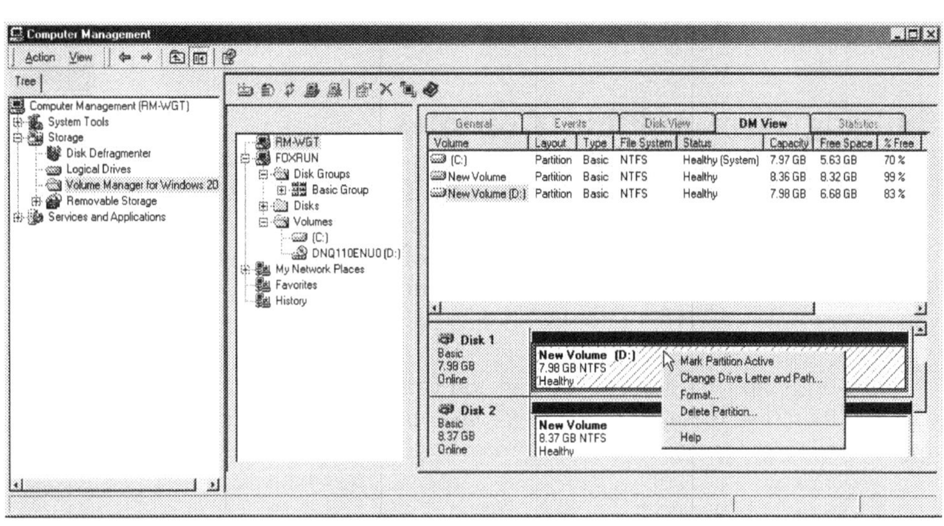

FIGURE 3-3. *Manage remote nodes and disks via the Computer Management Console.*

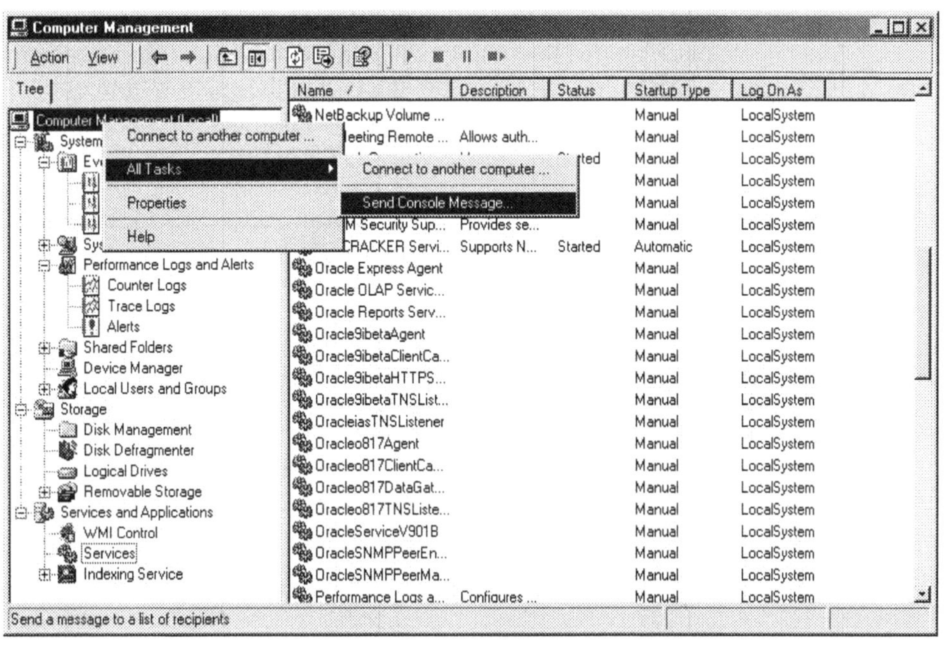

FIGURE 3-4. *Send pop-up messages from the Computer Management Console.*

SDK's MMC start page at http://msdn.microsoft.com/library/en-us/mmc/hh/mmc/mmcstart_1dph.asp, as well as the WMI sections of the Platform SDK.

Building Custom MMC Consoles

The MMC is a useful tool in and of itself because it lets you customize and build your own version of the Computer Management Console for DBA-related activities.

You will not find the MMC itself anywhere within the Start menu because it is only a framework. You start your own version of the MMC via a command line, run prompt, or shortcut you create that executes **mmc**. If you have a Windows keyboard, you can press WINDOWS LOGO KEY–R to bring up the run prompt (see Figure 3-5), type **mmc**, and press ENTER.

From this empty framework you can add various snap-ins that are of interest to you, and then save these as .msc files for later use. To add your own counters of interest, follow these steps:

1. With a blank MMC up, press CTRL-M.
2. From the Add/Remove Snap-In dialog box, click the Add button on the Standalone tab.
3. From the Add/Remove Standalone Snap-in dialog box, select the snap-in of interest to you, and then click Add (see Figure 3-6).
4. For some snap-ins, you will be prompted to select either the local computer or a remote machine that the snap-in will connect to. If you select a remote node, you will be able to perform the function of the snap-in from one machine upon another. Select as appropriate for your needs. For snap-ins that do not offer the option to control remote nodes, you will be immediately

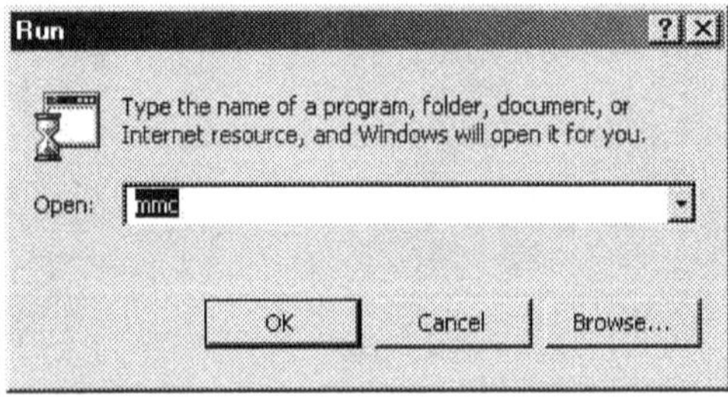

FIGURE 3-5. *Standard Windows 2000 run prompt*

returned to the Add/Remove Standalone Snap-In dialog box. Repeat step 3 for each snap-in you are interested in.

5. On the File pull-down menu select Save As, and save the configuration to the standard location for your system management files.

There is a special snap-in type named **ActiveX Control**. The Performance Monitor chart in the Performance MMC console, found in the Administrative Tools program group, is an ActiveX Control that you can add as a snap-in to your custom console. You can create custom real-time monitoring of systems to identify current problems or bottlenecks. Add the computer management snap-ins or the individual snap-ins that you are interested in, and then add the ActiveX Control named System Monitor for each view you would like to see of system resources. To add a System Monitor control, follow the first two steps given previously for adding snap-ins. Select ActiveX Control in the Add Standalone Snap-In dialog box and click Add. The Insert ActiveX Control Wizard will appear. Click the Next button to advance to the next step. Scroll down the list of available controls and select System Monitor Control. Click the Next button, name your new System Monitor view to match the collection of counters and charts you will add to the control, and click Finish.

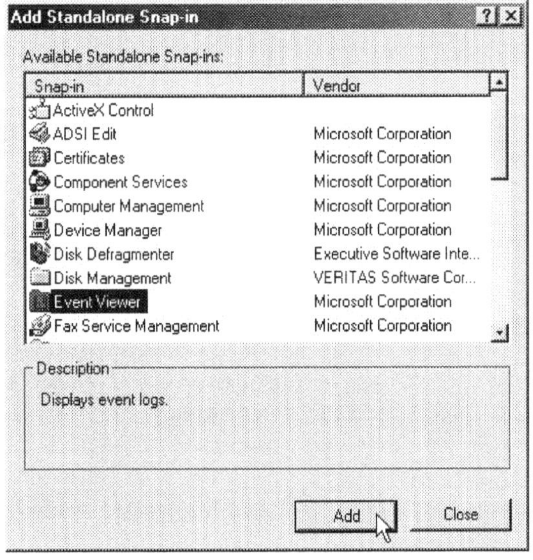

FIGURE 3-6. *Add a stand-alone snap-in to an instance of the MMC.*

The following are examples of System Monitor views you can create in your customized MMC:

- CPU Monitor
- Disk Monitor
- Network Monitor
- Memory Monitor
- Database Process Monitor

Once you have a System Monitor control for each of these areas of interest, you can add the appropriate counters. Learn more about each counter by using the Help file from the Resource Kit (RK), which is discussed in the section "Using the Resource Kit Appropriately" later in this chapter. For example, you might add the following counters to your CPU monitor view:

- System Object: Processor Queue Length
- Processor Object: % Processor Time for each processor and the _Total
- Processor Object: % User Time for each processor and the _Total
- Processor Object: % Interrupt Time for each processor and the _Total
- Processor Object: % Privileged Time for each processor and the _Total

If you have a system with a large number of counters you wish to display all at once, then you will want to change your view from Chart to Histogram or Report view. You may instead decide to format the view to create distinctive lines for the _Total instance of the processor objects and the % Processor Time counter, the key counter for aggregate understanding of CPU usage. While you are getting familiar with the various counters and are in the process of identifying bottlenecks, we suggest that you develop a number of views and adjust scales to help identify issues. If you are a numbers person only, then try the Report view. This view shows you the numbers as a snapshot is taken. Report viewing is most useful with counters that simply do not belong on the same scale but need to be evaluated together. Over time you will find that there are certain key views that help you identify problems with your system and/or your database.

The real-time monitoring is a reactive and immediate approach that will help you become familiar with what to do in an emergency or when a problem only occurs for a short defined time. In order to get a bigger picture view over a longer period of time, you will want to use the Performance Logs and Alerts functionality.

Performance alerts allow you to capture an event and react to it by doing one or more of the following:

- Log an entry in the Event Log (default action).
- Send a network message to a machine.
- Start a Performance Log.
- Run a program and pass it pieces of the alert's components for processing.

For example, you might want to set an alert that fires if the oracle.exe process's working set of memory grows larger than 80MB or the amount of available memory drops below 5MB. When that alert fires, you automatically send an e-mail to the database administrator's pager with the details of the alert, and start a predefined log that keeps extensive track of the system's CPU, process, and memory activity.

NOTE

For performance alerts and logs to work you must have the Performance Logs and Alerts Service started. You can also use various features of Oracle Enterprise Manager to perform these functions from a central location; and in that case, you will need to have the Oracle 9i Agent Service running. We suggest that you are familiar with both methods to ensure that you have and know how to use the right tools at the right time.

Command-Line Management

There was a time when almost all Oracle administration had to be done from the command line. With the improvements in Oracle Enterprise Manager and other GUI tools such as Net Manager, management of Oracle can be done from either a GUI tool or the command line. Still, the command line offers some advantages that the GUI cannot. You can do remote operating system and database administration without incurring a large overhead. On a system that is not responsive at the desktop level, you can often be very successful at the command line. The command line offers many benefits to those that know how to use it successfully. This section helps you use the command line to make database and system administration more effective and efficient.

Using the Windows 2000 Shell

The Windows NT/2000 shell is a friend to those that are familiar with the command line from DOS and anyone that has a Unix background. Although a good argument can be made that the Unix command-line tools and utilities are superior to those that come with Windows 2000, the Windows 2000 command line is very useful. This is particularly true once you add command-line utilities from various resources to your path.

The first thing you need to do is customize the command prompt to allow for your particular needs as an Oracle user. After doing this, you can easily copy and paste using the mouse, navigate back over the results of your commands, and make the command prompt more readable for yourself.

You may want to make changes to your command prompt for just your current session or be able to save a variety of configurations for specific classes of tasks. Windows 2000 no longer displays the command prompt in the Programs menu. Instead, the default shortcut command prompt is now buried in the Accessories menu.

Start by creating a shortcut based on the default shortcut, titled Command Prompt, found in Start | Programs | Accessories. To create your own copy to edit to your liking, follow these steps:

1. Select Start | Programs |Accessories.
2. The list shown should contain the Command Prompt shortcut. Right-click the shortcut and select Send To | Desktop. This will create a copy of the default shortcut on your desktop to use as a template from which to work (see Figure 3-7).
3. Make a copy of the new Command Prompt shortcut that is now on your desktop. This will be your first custom configuration.
4. Right-click the shortcut and select Properties. This will bring up the Properties dialog box, in which you specify various properties for your shortcut. Change the name and other values to suit your needs, save your changes, and close the dialog box. We use a shortcut called dbadmin for administration that starts in our scripts directory and has a screen buffer size height of 300, a window size height of 40, and Quick Edit and Insert modes turned on.
5. Click OK to save the shortcut and put it in a location that is convenient for you—for example, on the Quick Launch toolbar or on you desktop.

You may want to change the default command prompt shortcut. If so, then navigate back to the Accessories menu, right-click over the top of the Command Prompt shortcut, and click Properties. Make your changes and save them.

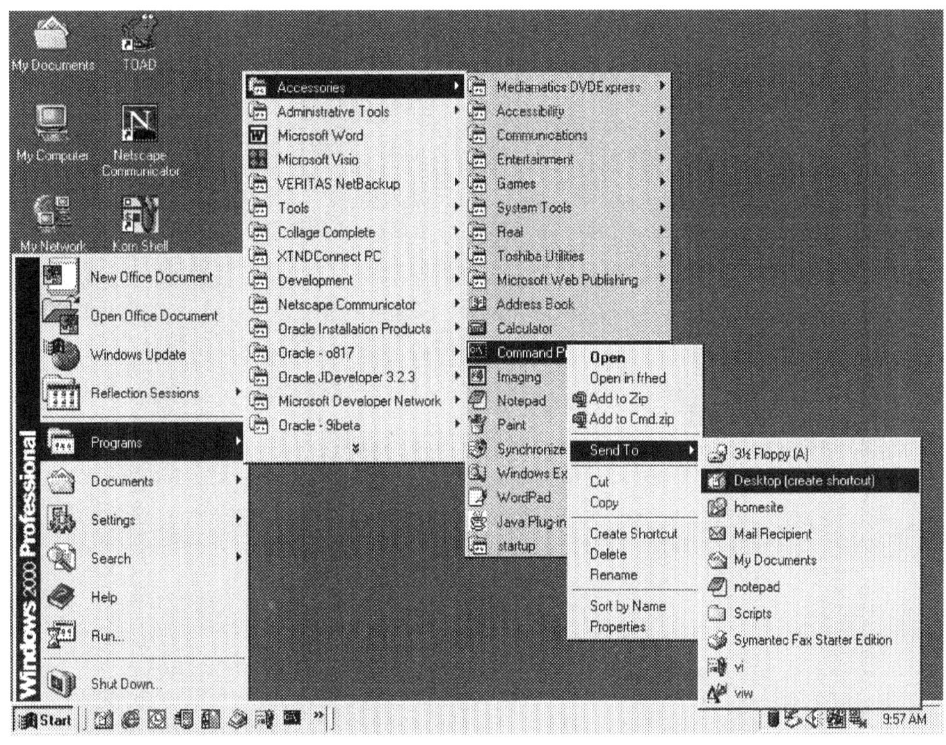

FIGURE 3-7. *Copy the Command Prompt shortcut to the desktop.*

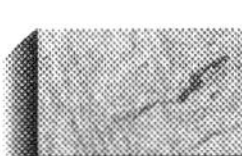

NOTE
Because many people often start a command prompt from the run prompt (see Figure 3-7), we suggest that you also make the changes to a command prompt window that has been started at the run prompt. Save the setting for the shortcut, and these settings will be maintained for future run prompt uses.

If you want to save the changes just for your session, edit the command prompt once it is started by pressing ALT-SPACEBAR, clicking Properties, and making the changes you want for your session. Once you've finished making your changes, click OK and take the default for Apply Properties. This will keep your changes for the life of that command prompt.

In the sections that follow, you will find descriptions of the most relevant elements for each tab of the Shortcut Properties dialog box.

General Properties

This tab contains the essentials of any shortcut, including the times last accessed, modified, and created.

- **Title** Specify a title to your liking for simple identification.
- **Read-Only** Enable this check box if you want to keep yourself and others from accidentally making permanent changes to the shortcut. This enforces editing of the shortcut directly, as opposed to editing on-the-fly.

Shortcut Properties

This tab is used to set the action behavior of the shortcut.

- **Target** The cmd.exe has a number of useful command-line options that you can use to your advantage. To display these options, enter the following at a command prompt:

  ```
  C:\> cmd /?
  ```

  You might want to start up a command-line SQL*Plus that does not prompt you right away for username and password, and when finished with SQL*Plus exits to a C\:> prompt. You can accomplish this with the following target:

  ```
  %SystemRoot%\system32\cmd.exe /K sqlplus.exe /nolog
  ```

  Unless you use the command-line option /D, the commands found in the Registry (see Figure 3-8) at HKEY_LOCAL_MACHINE\Software\Microsoft\Command Processor\AutoRun and HKEY_CURRENT_USER\Software\ Microsoft\Command Processor\AutoRun will execute when you start the command line. Make sure you check these Registry entries when troubleshooting a problem unique to the command line. You can also use the AutoRun Registry entry to run a script to configure your environment. In Figure 3-8, you can see how we have created the Registry entry to set the Oracle environment whenever we start a command prompt. If you want the program only for the Oracle user, then make sure you are logged in as oracle (or whatever user you have created to install the Oracle software), and add or change the AutoRun entry under the HKEY_CURRENT_USER Registry tree. Once again, to troubleshoot environment issues, use the /D command-line option to turn off the execution of any **AutoRun** command found.

- **Start In** Change this setting if you would like to start on a particular drive in a particular directory. For instance, you can set this property to your scripts directory for database administration work and to your source directory for development work.
- **Shortcut Key** Use this to set a key combination that is not used in any applications you would like to be able to start the shortcut from if you are a command-line junkie. Be aware that overly complicated key combinations may be difficult to reproduce.
- **Run** Typically, you will want to use a normal window, but there may be times where you would like the prompt to run full screen. In those cases, set this property to Maximized. You can toggle to a Maximized command prompt window any time while the prompt is in the current window via the key combination ALT-ENTER.
- **Change Icon** This button brings up a dialog box that allows you to select the icon you will display for the shortcut. If you plan to create a shortcut specifically for running SQL*Plus, then you may want to browse to the sqlplusw.exe file and select its icon.
- **Comment** You can include a description that will be displayed as the tool tip when hovering over the icon.

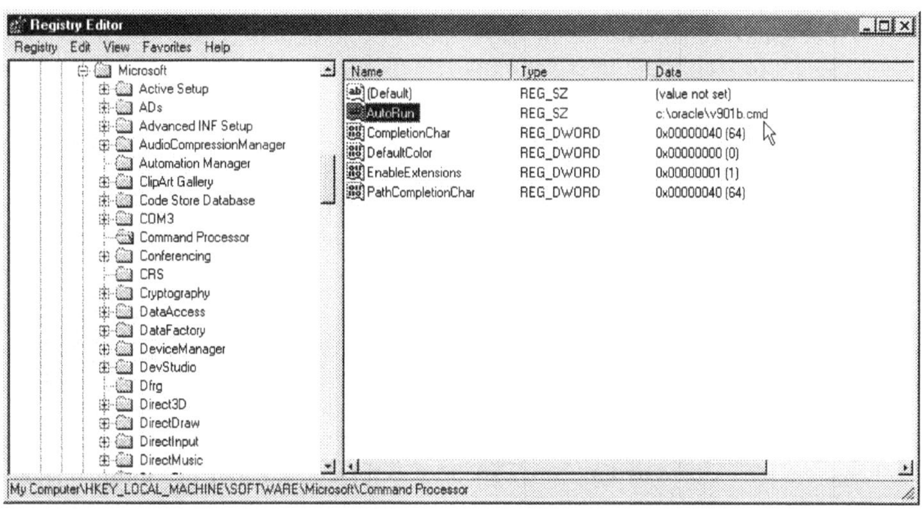

FIGURE 3-8. *AutoRun a command file on command-line startup.*

Options Properties

This tab is unique to the command-line shortcut. Use its values to change how you can interact with the command line and some look and feel options.

- **Cursor Size** We keep this at the default setting, Small; but according to your eyes' ability to spot the blinking cursor, you may want to select Medium. Be aware that if you set this property to Large, the cursor will then look like the one used to indicate Insert mode.
- **Command History** You can use the up and down arrows to navigate the history of this cmd.exe process. The Buffer size property sets the number of commands to keep in the history. The Number of buffers property indicates the number of cmd.exe processes that are able to have their own history buffers. Finally, the Discard old duplicates property allows you to eliminate duplicate entries of the same command in your history. Set this property to fit your preference.
- **Quick Edit Mode** We always have this option turned on. It allows us to use the mouse to select areas of the command prompt screen—it works slightly different from a word processor selection via the mouse, but is very useful for coming up with quick lists for pasting of a column of output from a command into a document or script.

  With this property set, select the area of interest, and then press ENTER to actually copy the area to the Windows Clipboard. If you wish to paste directly back into the command line, just right-click immediately after you make your selection to paste it in. To summarize: paste via right mouse click, and copy via mouse click-and-drag.

Font Properties

Do you find that the command prompt text is too small to see? Do you think that the command prompt default fonts are obnoxiously large? You can change the font selection and size to meet your needs from this tab.

Layout Properties

The key elements to adjust here are buffer screen size and window size.

Window size allows you to determine how many lines you want to view at a time and how many characters across you want to be able to see. The default is 80 characters across, assigned as the width, and 25 lines down, assigned as the height.

The Buffer Screen Size setting assigns the size of the buffer that the command prompt will keep in memory. SQL*Plus queries usually have column widths that extend beyond the default width of the command line in SQL*Plus. You can specify the effective width of the command line by setting the buffer screen size width to a value greater than the sum of the column widths you wish to display. You also need to change the SQL*Plus setting for *linesize* to an equivalent value (for example, SET LINES 9999). You can then use the command-line horizontal scroll bar to navigate the results. You can now spool the output of a SQL statement, otherwise useless in the default configuration, to a file, and then import the resulting file into Microsoft Excel as a delimited-by-space file.

Changing buffer screen size height allows you to review the history of your commands. Set this value to an appropriate size to meet your needs. We use 300 as a default, and have used a setting as high as 9000 to ensure navigation for results that would otherwise never be seen again.

NOTE

Setting the buffer size and some of the other properties affects the size of the executable in memory. Verify that the memory usage for your configuration is acceptable by looking at the memory used by cmd.exe via the Task Manager (start with the key combination CTRL-SHIFT-ESC*) on the Process tab in the Mem Usage column. Be aware that multiple command prompts will show up as multiple processes with the same name. We have also found that very large buffer and history property changes tend to drain CPU resources and cause paging as well.*

Colors Properties

You may wish to set these to increase readability. Many people prefer black text on a white background. You may want to set up a prompt that has a background to distinguish it as a potentially dangerous command prompt for administrative or long-running tasks.

Unix Integration Tools

The previous sections have demonstrated how to create a command prompt that is much more productive than the default prompt, but Windows NT and Windows 2000 both lack the command-line tools and daemons that Unix offers. To integrate Windows 2000 into a Unix network, you need to know about the key services that Windows 2000 does not normally provide:

- X server
- NIS or NIS+

MKS Toolkit

We highly recommend the MKS Toolkit as a replacement for the command prompt and a development environment for Unix lovers stuck on a PC. Here is a list of only a few of the native Unix utilities that come with the MKS Toolkit: alias, awk, sed, xargs, cat, chmod, chown, ls, grep, egrep, env, find, head, tail, cmp, cut, cp, vi, who, tar, compress, uncompress, diff, df, dircmp, du, id, umask, tee, ipcs, ipcrm, kill, od, mv, and ps.

The MKS Toolkit comes in a variety of flavors at a variety of prices. You can find the package that is right for integration with your Unix network at http://www.mks.com.

Microsoft Services for Unix

Microsoft Services for Unix (SFU) is an add-on package for Windows NT and Windows 2000. It includes a special version of the MKS korn shell and a selection of the utilities from MKS as well. We were surprised and disappointed that it didn't include sed and therefore doesn't really qualify as a command shell replacement, but instead serves as a supplement to enable better integration with Unix systems. It includes these services:

- Client and server software for NFS with a variety of other services that allow integration of your systems with Unix environments that heavily use NFS.
- NIS tools to enable migration and integration with NIS security environments (a needed complement to the NFS utilities).
- A version of the MKS korn shell with over 60 utilities such as grep, ls, ps, cat, and vi. If you want full shell capability, get MKS to complement SFU.

At under $200, this package ultimately gives you the services you will need to do most integration with Unix networks, and a little shell scripting functionality. It may or may not meet your needs. If you need to mount NFS volumes, it is a nice, less expensive alternative to other more full-featured NFS clients, such as Hummingbird.

For more information on services for Unix, and a great variety of white papers on how to integrate Windows 2000 environments with Unix, check out http://www. microsoft.com/microsoft/sfu.

Cygwin

For those who are not able or willing to fork out hundreds of dollars for a toolkit and don't need many of the daemons, check out Cygwin (http://www.cygwin.com). The Cygwin project is the combination of a DLL written by Cygnus that allows a developer to use Unix system calls. This capacity enables porting of the GNU development tools and utilities. Once installed, you can use the tools and utilities from the Bash shell provided, or you can use the tools and utilities from the Windows command shell (cmd.exe.)

Hummingbird's Maestro and Exceed

Hummingbird provides Maestro as an NFS suite for the PC, and Exceed as a connectivity suite for the PC, including an X server. These are popular tools for doing Oracle installations from PCs now that Oracle's installer requires X. Check out the installation documentation for Solaris and other Unix platforms for specifics at http://docs.oracle.com. You can also read more about Hummingbird's product line at http://www.hummingbird.com.

Using the Resource Kit Appropriately

The various Windows 2000 Resource Kits are made up of key references, printed books that can also be found online, as well as tools and utilities. Many of these utilities could be considered indispensable. On the other hand, many of the included utilities give hackers a variety of tools they can use to manipulate your system and others on the network. In the right security context, the Resource Kit should be installed at least in part to help you with system administration and provide utilities you can use to write useful DBA scripts. In the wrong security context (for example, outside your firewall or on systems where a variety of users might have access), the Resource Kit can be used to gain access to all kinds of juicy information.

One of the things you can do to avoid security problems is to install only particular executables that are useful and leave off the rest. Also keep these executables out of the normal environment, and instead use an environment-setting script to alter the path to include the utilities when needed. To ensure even greater safety, you can rename some of the utilities to your liking in order to hide them from users who may be looking for them by name. Here is an example of a script you might put somewhere in your path to add the Resource Kit utilities to your path for administration activities for this session:

```
SET PATH=%PATH%;D:\PROGS\RK
```

Key Resource Kit Online Sites

The Resource Kit is much more than what gets installed on a disk. Some of its most useful elements are its published documentation. These online resources will help

you keep up with changes in the Resource Kit and access electronic versions of the printed materials.

- **Windows 2000 Resource Kit** The indispensable set of toolkits' home on the Web.

  http://www.microsoft.com/windows2000/techinfo/reskit/default.asp

- **Windows 2000 Online Resource Kit Books** The online version of the printed materials in a searchable and indexed form on the Web.

  http://www.microsoft.com/windows2000/techinfo/reskit/en/default.asp

- **Windows 2000 Server Resource Kit Tools** A list of all the utilities with a description, and a link for some to deeper descriptions and downloads.

  http://www.microsoft.com/windows2000/techinfo/reskit/rktour/server/S_tools.asp

- **Windows 2000 Resource Kit Web Resources** Resources that are listed in the printed materials and found on the Web.

  http://www.microsoft.com/windows2000/techinfo/reskit/WebResources

- **Windows 2000 Resource Kit Free Tool Downloads** A selection of the tools that are included on the Resource Kit CD-ROM.

  http://www.microsoft.com/windows2000/techinfo/reskit/tools

Some of the must-have free utilities are described in the following table:

Free Tool	Description
Kill	Kills processes from the command line. The unique function of this tool is its ability to force the killing of the process with the -f command-line option.
Dumpel	Dumps the content of the Event Log to a tab-delimited file. Use this utility in the command line.
Installation Monitor	Tracks the changes made by setup programs to the Registry.
Now	Echoes the current date and time along with arguments passed to the utility. Use this utility in the command line or in batch files.
Qslice	Shows the CPU usage of a process that lets you drill down to the thread level. You can use this tool along with queries to V$SESSION, V$PROCESS (use SPID = THREAD ID in decimal—you'll need to convert the result to hex), and V$BGPROCESS to differentiate between the various background processes.

Support Tools

If you cannot justify the cost of the Resource Kit for each machine, then you can still take advantage of the support-oriented tools of the Resource Kit that Microsoft includes on the operating system installation media. You can find them on the Windows 2000 CD-ROM in the directory \Support\Tools. Here are some of the important executables installed with the support tools: kill, netdiag, pmon, poolmon, pviewer, reg, logtime, logevent, ntimer, timethis, typeperf, and tlist. For details on each of these, try the command followed by /? or take a look at the Help file that is installed with the support tools.

Tool	Description
diruse	Determines disk space usage in a directory if used in your batch files. **diruse /M .** will show the number of megabytes in use for the current directory.
forfiles	Cycles through a list of files in a directory or files in a directory tree. Use in your batch files.
freedisk	Checks for disk space and returns 0 if an operation is possible; otherwise, returns 1. Use this tool in batch files to avoid running out of disk space.
logevent	Writes to the Event Log from your batch file to log results into the OS facility. Use this tool in the command line.
mcast	Sends or listens for multicast packets. Use for examining network characteristics and for testing reactions to multicast packets.
netset	Views and configures the network from the command line.
ntimer	Shows elapsed time to complete a command line and breaks down CPU time for the command (User/Kernel/Idle/Total).
pathman	Adds and removes elements to and from the path environment variable.
pmon	Provides a command-line view of processes such as the GUI Task Manager's Process tab.
pviewer	Examines process details from this GUI tool. Also sets process and thread priorities.
reg	Finds, reads, and manipulates Registry entries.
setx	Sets user- and system-level variables into the Registry at the command line.
scanreg	Finds Registry entries that match a pattern from the command line.

Tool	Description
timethis	Times the response of a command line. For example, **timethis lsnrctl status** runs the command and shows timing. Elapsed time is usually the most interesting.
typeperf	Displays performance counters on the command line until a key is pressed. The command **typeperf 3 "\Processor(0)\% processor time" > ptime.csv** will write processor usage on the first processor with a timestamp and value to the file ptime.csv. You can open this file in Microsoft Excel.
tlist	Lists the currently running processes on a machine. If a process ID number is passed as a parameter, then details of the process memory usage, including loaded DLLs, are sent to stdout.
Counters.chm	Performance Counter Reference Help File

Sysinternals

Winternals maintains a freeware site named Sysinternals (http://www.sysinternals.com) that has a number of utilities you can use to diagnose problems and help get you out of a jam. In many cases, existing Microsoft tools do not exist to address the problems these freeware tools address. This site is best known for the NTFS hack that allowed the DOS OS to read and work with files on NTFS. If you happen to have the need to understand certain internal features of the Windows NT/2000 kernel, then many of the utilities come with source code.

In particular, you will find the tools useful for examining and troubleshooting problems in which you might need to monitor low-level OS activity. Use Regmon if you want to see exactly what is being read from the Registry. If you need to see what files are being accessed, try Filemon. The following sections discuss some of the utilities from this site:

Process Explorer

Get a good look at what is happening within a process on your system through the Process Explorer (see Figure 3-9). You can see what files this process is using, what Registry entries it is accessing, what devices are being used, and more. You can filter

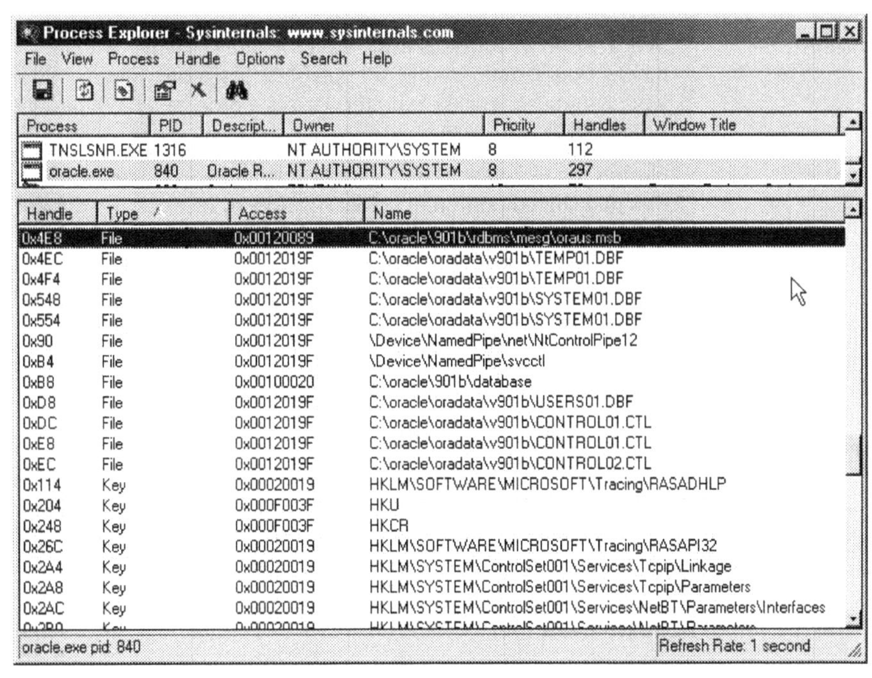

FIGURE 3-9. *Sysinternals.com Process Explorer*

and highlight according to simple rules you provide. Use this tool to answer questions such as, "What is this process doing?"

Tool	Description
PsUtilities	A collection of command-line utilities you can use to monitor and work with the system.
Regmon, Filemon, Diskmon	Monitors activity on the Registry, file system, and disk volumes in real time. All have the capability to easily filter and highlight to focus your view. These tools are useful for understanding and diagnosing the behavior of the system and applications.
DebugView	Intercepts debug print output by device drivers. It can be used in place of a debugger on your system because it is lightweight and simple to use.

Tool	Description
Listdlls	Indicates what process is using the Oracle DLLs when you are having trouble uninstalling or applying a patch on a system where you cannot use Process Explorer. Passes a process ID as a parameter to get details for just that process.
Sync	Flushes the file system caches to disk. Windows caches access to files in a shared portion of kernel memory to increase performance. This cache is one of the reasons you never want to shut down a Windows 2000 or NT system by just turning off the power. This executable enables you to command the system to flush this cache to disk, thus reducing the risk of problems if power is lost or the system must be improperly shut down.

System Administration

This section addresses three key areas of system administration that are of concern to Oracle database administrators: the Event Viewer, disk management, and scheduled tasks. These elements of administration are essential to understanding the life of a system, managing IO and availability, and completing regular tasks that can be performed without human interaction.

Using the Event Viewer

The Event Viewer on Windows NT and Windows 2000 systems is the repository for warnings, failures, and information logged by the operating system, the auditing mechanism of the domain and/or the local security database, and application-maintained logging. There are three basic logs that are populated:

- System Log
- Security Log
- Application Log

Always check the System Log first if you have any problems with Oracle. This is where you will find problems with disks, controllers, and other hardware, and device drivers, service startup, memory errors, and other system problems.

The Security Log

The Security Log requires some setup to get interesting information. Configure security auditing through policies. A thorough discussion and instructions on how to set up Windows 2000 security policies for your environment is beyond the scope of this book, and we do not feel that we can avoid giving you enough information to be safe. Become very familiar with group policies, security templates, and more security features to design your security infrastructure on Windows 2000. With that said, we will show you how you can track failed local login attempts on a stand-alone server that doesn't participate in a domain:

1. Start the Local Security Policy MMC console found in the Start | Programs | Administrative Tools folder.
2. Expand the Local Policies node, and then click Audit Policy.
3. Right-click Audit logon events and select Security.
4. Click the Failure option in order to log failed logon attempts to the security Event Log, including attempted logons over the network

See Figure 3-10 for an example of a logon failure event.

The Application Log

Oracle uses the Application Log extensively to report on the background process activity, instance status, and a number of other events related to the Oracle database and listener. Be sure to look out for warnings and errors related to Oracle. To simplify instance monitoring, create an Application Log view with a filter on the event source that corresponds to your database SID. For example, oracle.orcl would show up for the ORCL SID (see Figure 3-11 for an example).

Event Log Filtered Views

You can now filter on a variety of aspects of the log. For example, you can create an instance of the MMC with a filtered view of the Application Log to show you *just* the entries for the source of your database instance (see Figure 3-11). For instructions on creating your view, see the section "Building Custom MMC Consoles" earlier in this chapter. Once you have an MMC with the standard Event Log views, right-click the Event Log of your choice and select New Log File View. Rename the new view and adjust the properties to filter appropriately.

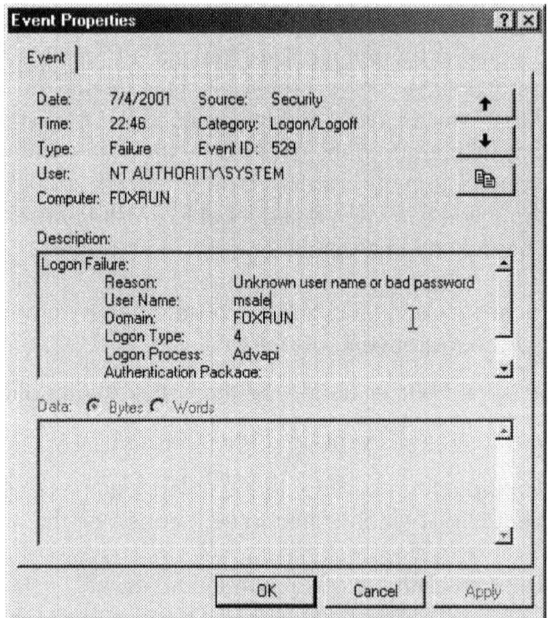

FIGURE 3-10. *Security Event Log logon failure event*

On Windows NT the Event Logs were not as easy to manipulate and use for administration based on historical trends. You had to use utilities to extract textual data for analysis and reporting outside of the Event Viewer, and the log would become full and prove an annoyance. Much of that has changed in Windows 2000. The Event Viewer has been drastically improved from an administrator's view in Windows 2000. Here is a list of some of the key features of the logs and the viewer to help simplify database and system administration.

Oracle Auditing to the Application Log You can set up the Application Log to enable auditing of logins to the Oracle database as opposed to the OS. Here are the steps you need to take in order to enable the Oracle auditing feature to log on to the Windows 2000 Application Event Log:

1. Set the init.ora parameter AUDIT_TRAIL = OS for the instances you want to audit.
2. Use SQL*Plus to connect to the database as SYS and run the script cataudit.sql found in %ORACLE_HOME%\rdbms\admin.
3. Bounce the database.

From this point forward, the Application Log will show a record for default actions such as connecting as sysdba. See an example of this event in Figure 3-12. You can add additional auditing of particular events via the database. To manage auditing on more actions and objects, see the Oracle documentation.

Circular Logging Avoid those irritating Application Log Full error messages by setting the Log Size parameters for each log. You can set the maximum log size and even log the system's reaction when the maximum size is reached. The three reaction options are as follows:

- Do not overwrite the same activity as in NT.
- Overwrite only events *x* number of days old.
- Overwrite events as needed.

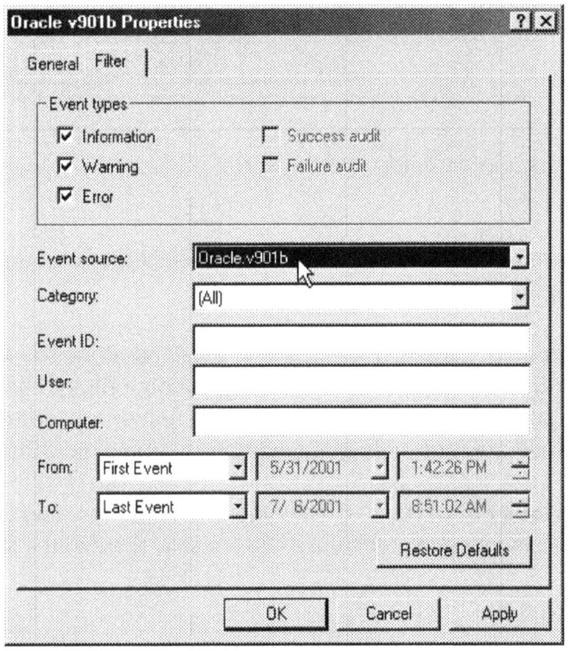

FIGURE 3-11. *Filter the Application Log for an Oracle database instance.*

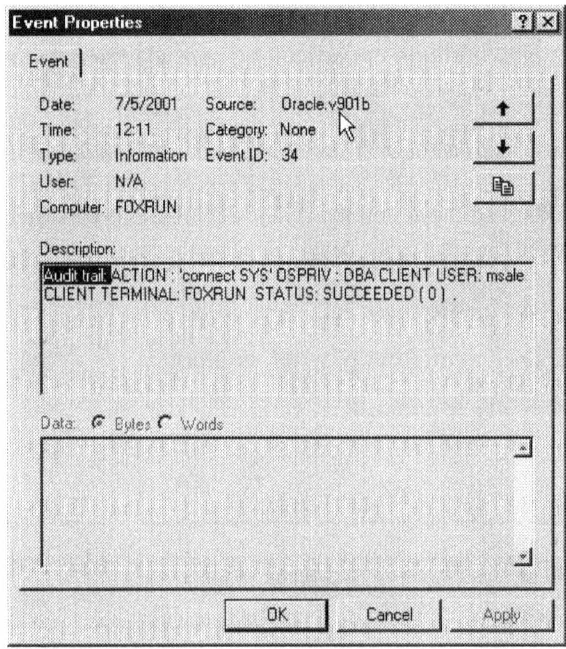

FIGURE 3-12. *Example Oracle audit event*

Return to defaults at any time via the Restore Defaults button on the Configuration dialog box (see Figure 3-13).

MMC Integration Because the Event View is a stand-alone snap-in for the MMC, you can create valuable custom consoles that give you a filtered and focused view of the history of your system and its applications. Creation of additional filtered log views that are named appropriately grants you incredible flexibility and power.

Save Logs in Various Formats Create your own custom views of the various logs with filters in place, and then export them as text or save them in the following formats:

- Binary .evt event file format
- Tab delimited
- Comma delimited

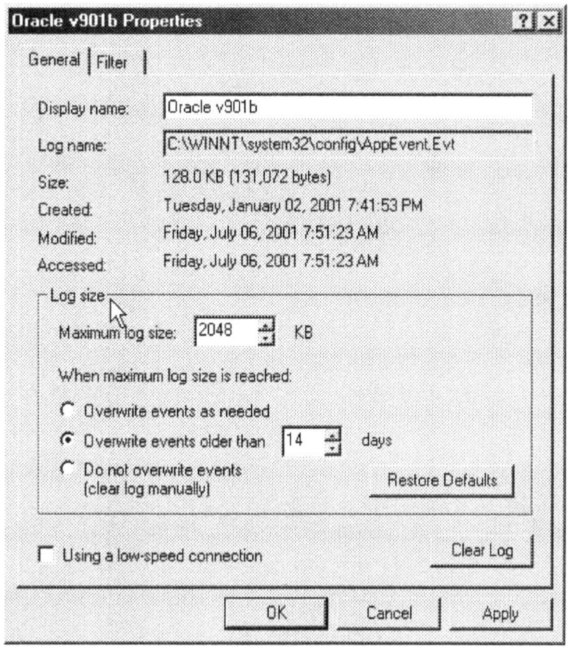

FIGURE 3-13. *Configure Event Log properties*

You can use an .evt file to analyze historical data or to send out support to an organization. With the tab- and comma-delimited formats, you can import data into a database using SQL*Loader or the new Oracle9i feature of external tables for an administrative web site, or analyze and transform the files using Perl or another scripting language. You can also just import the data into MS Excel, and chart the occurrence of events that might affect availability or show activity levels.

Managing Disks

Disk management in Windows 2000 has changed more under the covers than from a user perspective. VERITAS, in cooperation with Microsoft, has provided a piece of its volume management experience in the Windows 2000 Volume Management tools. If you intend to have more than 20 volumes, we strongly suggest that you upgrade to the VERITAS Volume Manager. The flexibility it provides, along with the remote management capabilities and performance tools, make it a worthwhile investment for server farms with large disk arrays. The key user interface difference

for basic disk management is the movement of the tools into the Computer Management console (see the "Computer Management Console" section earlier in this chapter).

Online Disk Management

You can now make most changes to disks and raid configurations without rebooting. You can even add new disks without rebooting if your hardware supports it. If you upgrade to VERITAS Volume Manager, you gain even greater flexibility.

Remote Disk Administration

You can manage disks on remote systems in which you are a member of either the Local Administrators group or the Server Operators group. If you upgrade to VERITAS Volume Manager, your remote management capabilities are far superior. If you need to do remote management, invest in the VERITAS Volume Manager.

Dynamic Disks and Volumes

Dynamic disks and volumes are new to Windows 2000. Basic disks and volumes that were found in Windows NT are still in Windows 2000, but they no longer support certain advanced functionality. Basic disks use partitions, whereas dynamic disks use dynamic volumes. Dynamic disks allow you to have an unlimited number of volumes per disk, as opposed to four partitions per basic disk.

The key change is that in order to create OS-managed RAID sets, you are required to use dynamic disks and volumes. Even though you cannot create Windows 2000 RAID sets on basic disks, you can still manage and upgrade existing volume sets created previously in NT.

If you have a large number of volumes to manage, you can use VERITAS Volume Manager to move subdisks around in order to alleviate performance issues or take slower disks out of a volume and replace them with fast disks on separate controllers—all while the volume is online and without rebooting! You can also take dynamic disks and migrate them to different boxes without data loss when using VERITAS.

Mount Points

You can now mount an NTFS volume or partition to an existing folder. This can help you avoid the limitation of 26-lettered disks and help maintain a more logical structure.

Windows 2000 now provides a defragmenter based on the Diskeeper defragmentation tool (http://w2k.diskeeper.com) for manual analysis and defragmenting of a local file system. The full-featured version allows you to schedule defragmenting or even let it decide when to defragment. It can also defragment remote systems that have Diskeeper installed on them, and defragment more than one volume at a time, an essential for very large systems with terabytes of files to maintain.

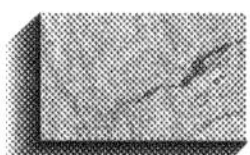

NOTE
For more on defragmenting from Microsoft, check out the article "Disk Defragmenter in Windows 2000: Maintaining Peak Performance Through Defragmentation," at http://www.microsoft.com/windows2000/techinfo/administration/fileandprint/defrag.asp. Microsoft documents the packaged defragmenter limitations at http://support.microsoft.com/support/kb/articles/Q227/4/63.ASP.

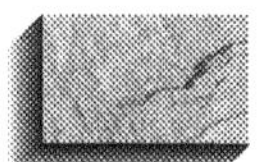

NOTE
If your datafile systems are properly isolated and implemented at datafile creation time, you should never have to defragment them. You will have to pay attention to fragmenting your Oracle home file system, and the file system or systems where your log and trace files exist.

RAID

Although we won't go into the details of the various permutations of RAID configurations, here we give some key tips to point out the best way to implement (or not) RAID for an Oracle environment.

- Choose hardware RAID over software implementations.
- With hardware RAID controllers, make sure that your controller cache has a battery backup.
- Stay away from RAID 5 for files that need fast writes to disk because RAID 5 performs four physical I/Os for each single logical I/O. Keep at least your redo logs off of RAID 5 volumes.
- RAID 0+1 (striping mirrored sets) gives you fault tolerance without quite as much hit on performance as straight mirroring.
- Stripe (RAID 0) across controllers as well as disks to increase performance.
- Put redo logs and archive logs on a separate disk subsystem than control files and datafiles because logs are accessed sequentially as opposed to datafiles, which are typically accessed randomly.

- If you are going to use Windows 2000 software RAID, buy and use VERITAS Volume Manager for Windows 2000. This is an upgrade to the Disk Manager and allows much greater flexibility and capability. With the VERITAS Volume Manager you can create 0+1 RAID and multiple mirrored volume sets (for example, four volumes mirroring each other as opposed to two volumes mirroring each other) and monitor volumes for hot spots.

File Systems

Windows 2000 supports a number of different file systems, but there is really only one you should use for almost every situation: NTFS. NTFS allows for the combination of large file size, security, optimization for large file performance, and simple recoverability of the system volume via the Recovery Console. On a developer's machine where you might need to duplicate the environment of a client, you may be forced to boot into Windows 98 or some other flavor of the consumer OS. If so, then try and stick with FAT32 and keep all Windows 2000–specific software off of that volume.

Cooked vs. Raw

Oracle already bypasses the file system cache for the most important operations, but it still writes to disk using the file system driver. By moving to raw partitions, you remove the intelligent layers in NTFS and you also lose the benefits that the file system offers, such as security and journaling for recovery. Raw partitions are also quite complex to manage on Windows 2000 and require planning and keeping records. That said, raw partitions can give you a 10 to 15 percent performance gain and are required for Oracle Parallel Server. Take into account the various aspects of your system, your database, and your performance and availability goals, and select raw or formatted file systems appropriately. If you have a system that writes massive amounts of redo entries, you may want to create raw partitions just for your redo logs.

Be Aware of the Number of Drive Letters

The 26 letters for drive assignment can be a serious limitation on a large box. Windows 2000 offers the following workarounds:

- Raw partitions with renamed symbolic links
- Mount points

Be careful when reinstalling Windows 2000 on a system that has more than 26 raw partitions. The installation process assigns these partitions drive letters if you do not delete them before installation, thus forcing you to install on a volume you may not wish to install on.

Defragment Disks

Keeping your disks defragmented improves performance for sequential disk access. When a file is laid down on the disk, it is not altered unless it is autoextended or resized by hand. This means that when you create a datafile, you want a contiguous amount of space big enough to hold the datafile in one chunk. Make sure that you have at least 30 percent of the disk space available after you lay down a datafile to ensure speed and allow for defragmentation tools to work most efficiently after you have created the datafiles.

The Task Scheduler Service

You can schedule operating system jobs with Task Scheduler, accessible from the Control Panel by clicking Scheduled Tasks. The Task Scheduler is the Windows equivalent of the Unix **at** command, but with a nice little GUI interface for creating and managing tasks. You can create tasks that will be run based on a time interval (for example, every hour or every week), one time only, when the system is idle, when the computer starts, or when you log on. The job is run as a particular user and requires a password to log on. You can add multiple schedules for the task that combine any of the schedule elements. If you set the task to run when the system is idle, you can qualify what that means through advanced properties of the task.

The problem with the task scheduler is the lack of ability to schedule tasks to occur more often than once a day, as you can with the Unix cron daemon. To get around this, you can add multiple schedules, but this method has manageability limitations. There are third-party tools that provide very capable scheduling features, but Oracle offers a solution that is OS agnostic and very flexible—the Job functionality of Oracle Enterprise Manager.

The Operating System Environment

One of the keys to successfully running Oracle on Windows is understanding the key elements of the environment that Oracle interacts with. This section will help you to manage Oracle in the unique environment on the Windows operating system.

Understanding and Controlling the Environment on Windows 2000

The Windows 2000 environment can be rather complex if you delve down into the various layers and options available. In this section, we will take a look at underlying structures and the various ways you might be affected by interaction with the environment.

The Oracle environment is not so simple that you can get a comprehensive overview by running the **set** command and reviewing the variables that are currently set on the system. The system and your applications, including Oracle, will also read persistently stored environment settings from the Registry. In order to best administer and troubleshoot your systems, you must also understand how to interact with this environment. For example, when you start the default command line and examine the environment via the **set** command, you will find that the ORACLE_HOME and ORACLE_SID variables are not set. Even so, you can start SQL*Plus and connect to the database. Why? Because Oracle reads these variables from the Registry. To monitor the Registry in real time, you can use the Sysinternals tool Regmon, as described in the "Sysinternals" section earlier in this chapter.

The Windows 2000 Registry is the hierarchical database used to store persistent variables, user information, and system information for both the OS and applications. It is a key component in the Windows OS implementation of the Oracle database and should not be altered without a clear understanding of the edit. You can functionally equate the Registry to an Oracle system datafile, the data dictionary. In the same way that Oracle strongly advises you not to muck around in the SYS schema's tables, Microsoft does not want the unknowledgeable user mucking around in the Registry. Even so, Microsoft exposes the Registry to administrators through tools such as regedit, and to developers through the API. This access is needed for manageability of the system and organized, manageable storage of persistent system and application variables. To facilitate accurate and flexible Registry management, Microsoft has provided the Resource Kit with a Registry reference (see the section "Using the Resource Kit Appropriately" for more details on the Resource Kit). You can find this reference as part of the online kit resources at http://www.microsoft.com/windows2000/techinfo/reskit/en/default.asp. This site features a relatively exhaustive reference to the keys that the OS writes as well as a good overview and explanation of what the Registry is and the structure of the data.

A hierarchical database stores objects in a parent, child, grandchild (and so on) structure. You might be thinking that you don't know what the structure of a hierarchical database looks like. Our bet is that you have already been working with files and folders in Windows Explorer. Directory hierarchies are conceptually the same structure as a hierarchical database. Some other examples would be Active Directory structures and Oracle's LDAP information store, OID. The Registry has a few base keys that you will primarily be concerned with. From these keys you will navigate down the tree to the values stored in an element of the tree down the hierarchy. For our purposes, these keys are as follows:

- HKEY_LOCAL_MACHINE (HKLM)
- HKEY_CURRENT_USER (HKCU)

You will be primarily interested in structures beneath these keys that store information about Oracle installations, services, and environment settings that are inherited from the Registry.

Registry and Home Keys

Oracle on Windows systems keeps information regarding Oracle-installed software in the HKLM/Software/Oracle tree of the Registry. Beneath this key are keys that correspond to each Oracle home's individual Registry settings starting with HOME0 and incremented up. In this key you should set variables used by Oracle executables in this home. If you ever wonder what Oracle home is currently being accessed, you can start SQL*Plus at a command line and try to run a script using the environment variable for the Oracle home followed by a file that doesn't exist.

```
SQL> @%ORACLE_HOME%\WHATISIT
SP2-0310: unable to open file "c:\oracle\901\WHATISIT.sql"
```

Notice the error message tells you where it looked for the file, thus giving away the location of the Oracle home. You can repeat this with the various environment variables that are stored in the Registry by replacing ORACLE_HOME with variables such as ORACLE_SID or ORACLE_BASE. For more detail on the Oracle keys in the Registry, see Chapter 4.

Setting Environment Variables at the System or User Level

When you start a program, what are the environment variables that it has access to? Through the Win32 API, a program can obtain a value stored in the Registry, but what about the values that are set by default and available by querying the environment? The User and System environment variables provide name-value pairs accessible via the environment. From the command line, you can add, change, and delete these values. To view these variable settings for the system and for the current user, follow these steps:

1. From your desktop, right-click My Computer and select Properties.
2. Click the Advanced tab.
3. Click the Environment Variables button.

You can view, alter, add, and delete variables for the local user profile (under the HKCU tree in the Registry) and for the system (under the HKLM tree in the Registry).

If your system and user environments have the same variable set to different values, then the value of the user environment variable overrides the system environment variable on the command line.

System environment variables can be found in the Registry at HKLM\SYSTEM\CurrentControlSet\Control\Session Manager\Environment. User environment variables can be found in the Registry at HKCU\Environment.

Setting Environment Variables at a Command Prompt

In order to best ensure that your environment is set the way you need it to be set, you should go to a command line and set your environment there. You can do this via the **set** command either directly at the command line or in a batch file. We suggest that you create a batch file for the different environments you would like to set and put these in your path. You may even want to put them in a directory you create just for batch files you would like to be able to run from a command prompt at any time. This allows you to centralize the location and allows for quick implementation across your server farm. Here is an example of a collection of **set** statements and startup of key services you might have in order to properly create an environment in which to run Oracle utilities:

```
c:\oracle>SET ORACLE_SID=v901b
c:\oracle>SET PATH=%ORACLE_HOME%\BIN\;%PATH%
c:\oracle>net start OracleServicev901b
c:\oracle>lsnrctl start
```

If the service has already been started, then the **net start** command will return a harmless error message indicating that the service is already started. Instead of entering all these commands at the command line one at a time, create a text file with the extension .cmd and store it in your path with the following content:

```
SET ORACLE_SID=v901b
SET PATH=%ORACLE_HOME%\BIN\;%PATH%
net start OracleServicev901b
lsnrctl start
```

Some Interesting Keys

Here are some interesting keys that are not prominently documented:

- **ORA_XCPT** Use this key to stop the generation of the core files. The small core file generated on Windows NT/2000 is not normally a problem; but if you have a problem that generates a massive number of the core files, then you can use this parameter to turn their generation off.

  Put this one in HKLM/Software/Oracle/HOME*X*, where *X* is the number of the Oracle home where you want to turn off core dumps.

- **ORA_*SID*_XCPT** Functions the same way as the ORA_XCPT, but stops the core file generation for just the SID indicated in the key.

- **SQLPATH** This key, kept in each home hive under HKLM/Software/Oracle/HOME*X*, acts like the path variable for the command line, but in SQL*Plus. Add directory entries separated by a semicolon.

Setting Permissions on Files/Folders: Oracle Considerations

In order to ensure security, system administrators will often lock down files and directories by removing permissions that are there by default. When working with Oracle on a system, it is important to remember that you will need to perform an installation as the local administrator, and that the account that runs the service for the database instance will need to have full access to Oracle-related files and folders. Here are the details of what you should change to ensure security:

- The user account that installed Oracle needs full control over files and folders in the Oracle home directory structure.
- The account that runs the Oracle Services (the system account, by default) needs full control over the files and directories that hold all Oracle datafiles, control files, password files, archive locations, dump directories (for example, bdump and udump), and other directories that may be used by an instance (for example, directories indicated in init.ora for the parameter UTL_FILE).
- The account that runs the Oracle Services also needs full control over much of the Oracle home directory tree. We suggest that you just give full control to this account, but you may have need to narrow it down further. If so, then make absolutely sure that you grant full control over the %ORACLE_HOME%\bin directory to the account.
- Users who need to run Oracle utilities such as SQL*Plus, Import, Export, and SQL*Loader will need to have read and execute permissions on those executable files.

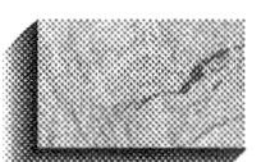

NOTE
If Oracle will be using any resources that need to be accessed via the network (for example, a mapped drive), then you need to change the account that starts the service to an account you can add the appropriate rights to on the machine that holds the networked resource. This can also be more secure because a hacker could create a service that automatically has the rights of the system account without ever knowing a password.

Active Directory

Active Directory is Microsoft's next-generation hierarchical database for storing objects of interest. Typical objects of interest include users, printers, machines, and many other objects; you can also design and create your own objects. Oracle offers integration for Oracle user authentication and instance connectivity information to be stored in Active Directory and authenticated via the Kerberos package used in Windows 2000 domains.

Net Naming with Active Directory

There are a number of ways to resolve the connection information for a database. The typical method is to set up a tnsnames.ora file for each client. This can become unwieldy, and in an environment with a large number of instances, you will run into a character limitation on the size of the tnsnames.ora file as well as a performance problem.

Integration with Active Directory allows Windows 2000 domain administrators to set up Active Directory to store connection details that would otherwise be kept in the tnsnames.ora file. This centralizes administration of instance connectivity information and in a large environment can drastically reduce time spent troubleshooting connection problems.

Remote Administration

Remote administration tools are an essential element to efficiently managing systems. This section talks about some solutions and the key issues in remote computing on the Windows platform. For those of you that are managing Oracle on Unix systems, you should try and use the same solutions for both platforms. Due to the nature of Windows 2000, you will need at least one GUI remote administration tool no matter what.

Remote Administration with MMC

In the earlier section "Computer Management Console," you learned how to use the Windows 2000 Computer Management Console to remotely administer other Windows 2000 servers. It is important to note that some of the computer management tools do not work remotely, and other means of remote administration are likely needed in combination with MMC-managed remote administration.

Here is a brief review of the method we discussed for connecting to a remote computer with the Computer Management Console:

1. Open the local version of the Computer Management Console.
2. Right-click the node in the left pane titled Computer Management (Local) and select Connect to another computer.
3. Either enter the name of the computer directly or browse to the computer you are looking to manage. Click OK once you have selected the node you wish to manage with your mouse.

From this point, you can manage many of the facilities on the remote computer. In accordance with your network and domain setup, you might be more limited than you think. The best methodology is to try to use the various functions to see what works in your environment.

See the "Computer Management Console" section, earlier, for instructions on how to save a console connecting to a remote computer for later use.

Remote Administration with VNC

Virtual Network Computing (VNC) is a remote administration tool that allows you to access the GUI desktops of both Windows and Unix systems. The key advantages of this tool are that it is free, it works across operating systems, and the client is lightweight. It seems to be slightly slower and lacks many of the other features that tools such as pcAnywhere have, but free is alluring!

One of the little-known features of VNC is that you don't *need* the client software to access the remote desktop. You can use your browser instead. Just form the URL in the address bar of your browser like so: http://*hostname.domainname*:5800. This access method does appear to be slightly slower and even more sensitive to network configuration, but it is great for access on-the-fly where you don't have the VNC client installed.

VNC can be downloaded at http://www.uk.research.att.com/vnc/ for various operating systems. We use a Linux system to administer various Windows computers at work because we can set it up to do automatic authentication and we don't get the VNC desktop confused with the Linux desktop. A handy tool!

Remote Administration with the Windows 2000 Telnet Server

The Windows 2000 Server product line now comes with a Telnet Service that allows you to get a command line on a remote Windows 2000 Server from any OS. The Telnet Service should *not* be used on nodes outside of your firewall or if you are in any way concerned for security of the passwords used in the Telnet process into

the computer. Why? Because even when using NT Lan Manager (NTLM) authentication, you pass the password in a form that can be recombined and hacked with a software utility quite easily. For a much more secure remote command line, review the commercial version of the SSH daemon for Windows NT/2000 at http://www.ssh.com.

For further information on setting up the Telnet Service, check the standard Windows Help file (Start | Help) by searching on the term "telnet." If you do plan on using this service, we suggest that you set it up for initial NTLM authentication, and then if that fails, try the standard username/password challenge you see when using Telnet to get into a Unix system. You set this option in the Registry by running a command-line setup utility as follows:

1. Navigate to Start | Programs | Administrative Tools | Telnet Server Administration.
2. Select the option Display/change Registry settings.
3. Select the option NTLM.
4. Continue through the prompts and set the NTLM value to 2.

Once you have started the service, you use Telnet to access the Unix system directly using NTLM authentication; if you happen to not be able to authenticate via NTLM, you will then be prompted for the username/password combination. If you want to tighten up security to deny even that, you should set the NTLM value to 1 to enable *only* NTLM authentication. Please do note that even with only NTLM authentication, we were able to use a network sniffer and a brute password cracker for NTLM passwords to break into our own setup. Due to the nature of this vulnerability, we suggest that you avoid even NTLM authentication outside your firewall and go directly to the commercial SSH daemon for Windows NT/2000 mentioned previously.

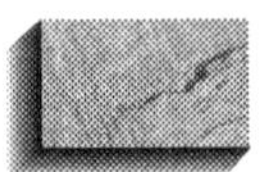

NOTE
The NTLM authentication method has been around since before the inception of Windows NT. Over the years this method has been found to be lacking, and in Windows 2000 a Microsoft implementation of Kerberos authentication has been introduced.

Remote Administration with pcAnywhere and Other Commercial Tools

Most administration of your Windows 2000 server farm can be done via a command line with proper setup, but the easiest and quickest way to complete many tasks is via a GUI desktop. When we say "easiest and quickest reference," we are assuming that you have the capacity to work with a GUI tool over the network to manage your computers. If you are working over a slow network (for example, WAN or dial-up network), then we suggest that you do all you can via a command-line interface and use the GUI only when needed and to verify that there are no error notifications that require interaction to continue. Most businesses have already standardized on a particular remote access tool. If your business has not yet found a tool or is not satisfied with what you have, you might want to take a look at these tools.

pcAnywhere

This is the most popular remote administration tool on the market. It has been around for years and works quite well. Over time, pcAnywhere and other remote access tools have become more friendly to enterprise management instead of single-user remote control. We use pcAnywhere at Oracle to manage and support Oracle on Windows and have been happy with the tool. We have also seen other tools at client sites that have features that made management of a large number of systems much easier. Here is a short list of other software packages you can use for remote access:

- Tarentella (the up-and-coming tool for remote access to Windows and X for Unix boxes)
- Timbuktu
- LANTastic
- Remotely Possible
- Carbon Copy
- ReachOut
- NetBus

Resources

To deal with particular challenges you will face, you need to have a number of resources you can turn to for help. This section provides some of the essentials.

Microsoft Resources

Next you will find a number of resources to help you with getting and staying up to speed with the Windows platform in general.

- **Microsoft Developer's Network (http://msdn.microsoft.com)** A great resource for understanding the internals of the OS and keeping up to date with the latest.
- **Microsoft's Support Site (http://support.microsoft.com)** One of the most thorough online support sites, although you may have to wade through unrelated articles. You will find lots of Oracle-specific documents for developers as well as administrators. We recommend you start here for unknown OS problems, next try the MSDN site, and then go to the *Windows 2000 Magazine* site.
- **Microsoft Technet (http://www.technet.com)** This is the IT professional's web site by Microsoft. A good resource to check in on regularly for tips and new features. You will also find a variety of articles that can help you configure the OS to your needs and troubleshoot common problems.
- ***Windows 2000 Magazine* and its web sites** This is a never-ending resource of excellent tips and techniques that are refreshed on a monthly basis. We strongly suggest subscribing to the magazine, formerly *Windows NT Magazine*, and using the web site. Some of the interesting web sites managed by the magazine are noted here:
- http://www.win2000mag.com
- http://www.windows2000faq.com
- http://www.windowsitlibrary.com
- http://www.winscriptingsolutions.com

Oracle Resources

These resources contain the latest in Oracle technology and reference materials you will need to manage your personal growth in understanding Oracle.

- **Oracle Documentation Center (http://docs.oracle.com)** This site has Oracle documentation freely available under the license agreement. If you want to research new products or learn more about installation requirements, check here first.
- **Oracle Technology Network (http://otn.oracle.com)** Check out the Windows Technology Section at http://otn.oracle.com/tech/nt/ for white papers, Oracle software information and downloads, and CD-ROM order forms.
- **ssh.com** This is the source of the commercial SSH version for Windows servers. You will be interested in this package if you need remote administrative capability on boxes that are in an unsecure environment.

Looking Ahead

Today, Oracle on Windows is a very stable, available, and high-performing product. The one area where Oracle is not allowed to shine on Windows 2000 is on very large systems. This is in part due to the fact that Unix is typically chosen over Windows for such systems. The 64-bit future of Windows .NET Server will change all that. Windows will be able to compete with systems and clusters in a way that it never could before. Already, existing changes made between Windows NT and Windows 2000 and proposed improvements in Windows .NET Server make the manageability future of Windows a bright proposition. Oracle is ready and waiting to implement changes that take advantage of this future. This section peers into that future to give you a base for planning and hope for growth and efficiency without having to sacrifice platforms.

The Future of Windows

The future of Windows is headed for enterprise super-server capability and capacity, with the 64-bit versions of the server operating system and continuing domination of corporate and home desktops. Upcoming Microsoft operating systems will have an impact on Oracle's capabilities to use more memory and handle more connections.

Windows XP

Windows XP is the replacement for Windows 2000 Professional. It will have some improvements that are not really relevant to database administrators or even stand-alone server administrators. Even so, it will be one of the first 64-bit Microsoft operating systems available. Despite this fact, it is in no way a server operating system designed to run an Oracle database in a production environment for many users.

The 64-bit version of XP is directed toward workstation users. It is likely that no 64-bit specific software will be available at the time of release. XP will have a number of expanded capabilities that allow power users to upgrade to their hearts delight. At release time, XP will support up to 16 gigabytes of physical memory and up to 8 terabytes of virtual memory. Utilizing 64-bit XP to its fullest will be difficult because 32-bit software usually runs better on 32-bit hardware and slower on 64-bit hardware. Don't use 64-bit XP unless you have software that needs the 64-bit capabilities. Why? XP 64-bit has a minimum physical memory requirement of 1 gigabyte. Ouch!

From a domain management perspective, XP fits right in with the Windows 2000 domain model. Here are some features that might help push corporate PC support for the rollout of XP:

- Improved Plug and Play

- System Restore
- Device driver verifier and rollback
- Built-in firewall
- Built-in remote administration tool

Many of these features, if rolled out as a corporate standard, can drastically reduce the load on a company's PC support department.

From an Oracle perspective, there is no compelling reason to upgrade for the majority of applications that use a database because the client tier of older client/server applications work just fine on Windows 20000 or Windows NT, and the newer n-tier application architecture essentially requires a server operating system. That said, the 32-bit version of XP is an improvement over the initial version of Windows 2000 Professional for end users and for domain administrators working with users whose desktops may still be as old as Windows 95.

Windows Advanced Server Limited Edition 64-Bit

Microsoft has announced a server class version of Windows 2000 that will sport a 64-bit API that developers of large server applications, such as the Oracle RDBMS, can take advantage of. Much of this has been waiting on the release and general commercial availability of the Itanium 64 processor from Intel. Depending upon your needs, this may be the first OS move to consider for development and testing. This version of the OS is tagged "Limited Edition" because it is designed as an interim step to Windows .NET as a 64-bit platform. Microsoft only expects limited use of this OS due to the cost and the eminent release of .NET Server.

Windows .NET

.NET Server is the next version of the Windows OS for the server product line. The beta name was Whistler, and it shares a code base with the XP beta. At the time of this writing, this version is scheduled to be released in early 2002 (in fact, its previous marketing version name was Windows 2002 Server). The name of the OS indicates the push of the development by Microsoft to component or software services offered up by the OS. .NET Server will more than likely be released as a 64-bit version out of the box. This alone will be a boon to Oracle running with a much larger process space, making it capable of handling greater loads and doing more data warehousing work with room to spare.

Like XP, .NET Server will integrate with your existing domain's administrative infrastructure. These are some of the interesting features listed in the design goals for .NET Server:

- Remote support for "headless" servers—servers that have no monitor, keyboard, or mouse.
- Support for NUMA memory access and 64-bit processors

Oracle and the Future of Windows

Oracle has already been in the process of preparing for a 64-bit Microsoft OS release for some time; in fact, Oracle has a beta release of 8.1.6 64-bit, built on top of Whistler Build 2267, available on OTN. But don't get too excited—this release is also built on a special Intel IA64 chip that isn't readily available (unless your company can successfully negotiate with Intel directly to obtain this chip). Once the 64-bit processors from Intel and the server OS from Microsoft go into general availability, Oracle will respond with a 64-bit release as soon as it is possible to ensure its stability and interoperability with the OS.

Summary

There are many things that you can do to improve the interoperability of Oracle and Windows 2000. This chapter has given you some key information that you can use to configure your system today, as well as resources that can be used now and in the future to dig deeper into what you can do to improve manageability, availability, and performance of Oracle on Windows 2000.

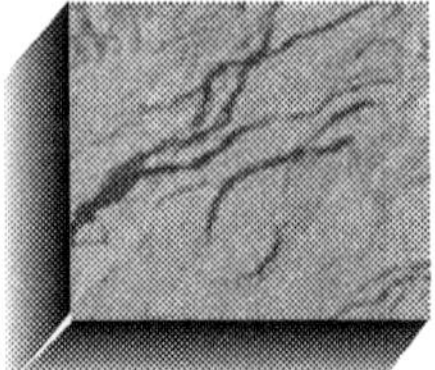

CHAPTER 4

Installing and Configuring the Oracle RDBMS

In this chapter, we focus on the installation of the RDBMS. We go into more depth about the specific considerations for an Oracle database on Windows platforms, including setting up the environment and understanding how Oracle interacts with the Windows 2000 Registry. We discuss the mechanics of creating a database, including details of what the Database Configuration Assistant does and tips for building a custom database. In addition, we introduce many new features of the Oracle9*i* database, including system parameter files, database templates, multiple block-size support, and system managed undo. Tips covered in this chapter include the following:

- Naming conventions in previous Oracle releases
- Understanding and implementing multiple Oracle homes on Windows 2000
- Navigating the Registry and the environment
- Using the Oracle Home Selector
- Realistic requirements for an Oracle9*i* installation
- Implementing Optimal Flexible Architecture on Windows 2000
- Using and troubleshooting the Oracle Universal Installer
- How and why to use the ORADIM utility
- Setting automatic startup/shutdown of the database
- Deleting services
- Troubleshooting ORA-12560 and ORA-24314 errors
- Defining the structures of the database
- Using multiple block sizes
- Enabling archiving—specific issues on Windows 2000
- Easing administration by setting up a default temporary tablespace
- Taking advantage of system managed undo
- Replacing Connect Internal and Server Manager
- Setting up OS authentication for sysdba connections on Windows 2000
- Deleting an ORACLE_HOME
- Removing Oracle altogether from a Windows 2000 machine

History of Oracle on Windows NT

When Oracle7 was first released on Windows NT, the concept of *multiple homes*, or multiple versions of Oracle installed in different directories, was foreign. Although multiple homes have always been standard in a Unix environment, the Registry on Windows NT made this more difficult. On Unix, you simply change the environment by setting variables at the command line, or running a new .profile or .login, and so on. However, on NT, it is not so simple to change the environment, because it is defined primarily in the Registry. Therefore, the first releases of Oracle7 on NT were implemented as single home products—that is, once you created your ORACLE_HOME, all products had to be installed in the same home directory.

File Naming on Previous Versions

This single home requirement did not prevent a user from having multiple versions installed—it simply meant that later versions had to be installed in the same directory as the older versions. To facilitate this, version numbers were appended to the DLLs, executables, and other files that needed to be unique for each version. So if one were to install 7.2 and 7.3 in the same home, the installation would work because you would have two versions of each executable—imp72.exe and imp73.exe, exp72.exe and exp73.exe, and so on. The database executable would be either oracle72.exe or oracle73.exe. Complicating matters further was the fact that not all utilities had a version that matched the database version. So the Server Manager that came with 7.3 was really 2.3.x, giving us an executable name of svrmgr23.exe, and the Server Manager version that came with 8.0.x was 3.0.x, giving us an executable name of svrmgr30.exe. This naming convention was carried through to 8.0.6, even though 8.0.4 and higher supported multiple ORACLE_HOMEs. Thus, the database executable on 8.0.6 was oracle80.exe, import was imp80.exe, and Server Manager was svrmgr30.exe. As you can see, this convention allowed releases that had differing first two digits to coexist in the same home. So 7.3.x and 8.0.x could coexist in the same home, but 8.0.4 and 8.0.6 could not.

Multiple Oracle Homes on Windows NT/2000

As noted, release 8.0.4 of the RDBMS on Windows NT was the first release to support multiple Oracle homes. So, while you could still install 8.0.4 in the same home as a 7.3 release if you so desired, you also had the choice of installing it in its own home. This was accomplished by adding separate subkeys for additional homes under the main ORACLE key in the Registry. Recall from Chapter 1 that Oracle creates its key under HKLM\SOFTWARE\ORACLE. Releases prior to 8.0.4 looked directly to this key for necessary environment variables. Starting with release 8.0.4, however, Oracle began creating subkeys during the installation for each home titled, appropriately enough, HOMEx, where *x* is the number assigned to the home, beginning with 0. Therefore, products in the first ORACLE_HOME created get their environment information from HKLM\SOFTWARE\ORACLE\HOME0, as seen in Figure 4-1. The next home created gets its information from HKLM\SOFTWARE\ORACLE\HOME1, and so on.

If the first product that was installed was a pre-8.0.4 product (for example, 7.3.4), then the installer for that earlier product would not have created a HOME0 key. However, when the newer product is installed, it will create an empty HOME0 key as a placeholder for the older version's home. The products installed in the older version's home will still get their environment information from the main HKLM\SOFTWARE\ORACLE key, but the new home, now defined as HOME1 during the installation, will read HKLM\SOFTWARE\ORACLE\HOME1 for its environmental roadmap. This is true for all releases from 8.0.4 onward, up to and including Oracle9*i*. So, if you were to install Oracle9*i* on a machine that already had 7.3.4, for example, the 9i installation would create an empty HOME0 key as a placeholder for the 7.3.4 home, and then create a HOME1 subkey for the 9i installation. If you plan to run older products on the same system as Oracle8i

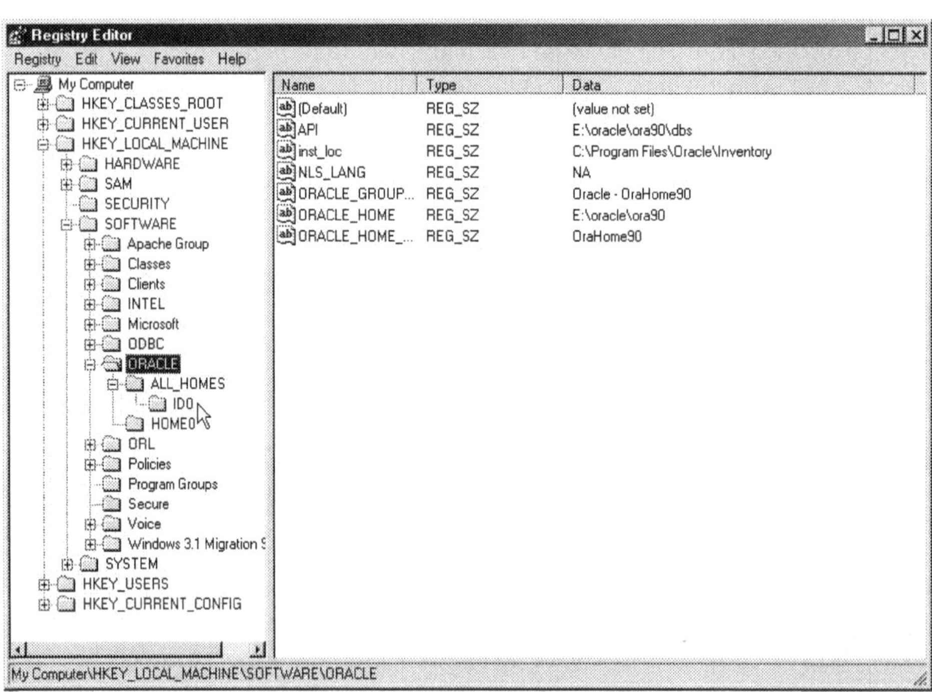

FIGURE 4-1. *Registry showing Oracle and HOME0 structure*

or Oracle9i, you should make sure that the older release is always the first to be installed. Installing 7.3.4 after Oracle9i has already been installed will end up with neither release working correctly.

Starting with Oracle8i, it was decided that this should be simplified, and brought more in line with how Oracle operates on other platforms. Each version of the product is now *required* to be installed in its own home. You cannot install release 8.1.x into a home that already has 8.0.x installed—you *must* create a separate home for the 8i installation. Therefore, Oracle8i is the first release on NT to drop the convention of appending versions to the files. The executable for the database is now just oracle.exe. Likewise, import and export are imp.exe and exp.exe, and so on and so forth. This convention carries forward to Oracle9*i*.

If you attempt to install either Oracle8i or Oracle9*i* in an 8.0.x home, the Installer will give you a warning message and will not let you proceed. If you attempt to install Oracle9*i* in an Oracle8i home, you will get the same warning. However, installing a later 8.1.x release in an older 8.1.x home—for example, installing 8.1.7 into an 8.1.6 home—is allowed. In this instance, the older release (8.1.6) is automatically uninstalled prior to the 8.1.7 installation. The same will hold true for later 9.x releases. We will discuss upgrades, migration, and change management in Chapter 10 of this book.

How Oracle Interacts with the Registry

If you have multiple homes on the machine, to determine which key is being read for products in a particular ORACLE_HOME, simply navigate to the bin directory in that ORACLE_HOME, and open up the file called oracle.key. This is a simple text file with only one line that will read something like this:

```
Software\ORACLE\HOME0
```

Since all Oracle executables are run out of the bin directory, when an Oracle executable is run, it will read the oracle.key file in its current bin directory to determine which key contains the environment information pertaining to its particular ORACLE_HOME. In the preceding example, it would look to HKLM\Software\ORACLE\HOME0, as we see in Figure 4-1. Next, any environment variables set in System Properties (as discussed in Chapter 3) are evaluated. If these settings are different from the Registry, settings from System Properties are used. Finally, if an executable is being run from a command window, any environment variables set within that particular command window will be evaluated and taken into account; in most cases, these settings should take ultimate precedence. For this reason, you should never set the ORACLE_HOME from a command prompt or in System Properties. Always let the setting in the Registry be the only setting for ORACLE_HOME. Otherwise, an executable can become lost and not know which home it belongs to.

The Oracle Home Selector

The Oracle Home Selector is a utility used to select which home you want to be the primary Oracle home. However, this does *not* change which key is being read by an executable. All the Home Selector does is change the order of the different ORACLE_HOMEs in the path. By selecting a given home as the primary home, you are simply placing that home's bin directory first in the path. This is important if you have multiple versions installed in different homes, with the same names for executables.

For example, assume that you have release 8.1.7 and release 9.0.1 installed in separate homes on the same machine. You want to run an export of your 8.1.7 database, but the executable for each release is just exp.exe (remember, no more version numbers are being appended to executables). If you just type **exp** from a command prompt, which version will be run? On Unix, you would set up your environment so that only one ORACLE_HOME\bin directory is in the path. However, on Windows 2000, all ORACLE_HOME\bin directories are placed in the path under System Properties. Therefore, whichever one is first in the path is the one that will be run.

To ensure that the correct version of exp is run, you can use the Oracle Home Selector utility, accessed by clicking Start | Programs | Oracle Installation Products | Home Selector. Select the release 8.1.7 home as the primary home, and it will be first in the path for any subsequent command prompt sessions (you must start a new session in order for this path change to take effect). Other ways to deal with this are by changing into the correct ORACLE_HOME\bin directory prior to running exp.exe, since the current directory is always first in the path search. You can also explicitly set the path from a command prompt window or within any scripts being run, or specify the full path to the file whenever it is typed in, as shown here:

```
D:\Oracle\Ora817\bin\exp.exe
```

The Oracle Home Selector is useful primarily when running executables from a command prompt. GUI tools, which are run from a given Oracle program group, have shortcuts that specify the full path to the executable, so the Home Selector should not have an effect on applications run from a program group.

The Oracle Universal Installer

Having laid the groundwork by discussing previous releases, let's now look at the installation of the Oracle9*i* database. The first thing to note about the installation of Oracle on Windows 2000 is that Oracle does not use any of the standard Windows Install routines that most other programs use (for example, InstallShield). Oracle has always used its own installer for the purpose of being able to standardize the installation of Oracle across multiple platforms. Starting with Oracle8i, the decision was made to make the installer a Java-based program, with the ability to do a GUI installation on all platforms. Hence, the evolution of the Oracle Universal Installer (OUI).

Java-Based Installer

Since the OUI is a Java-based application, there are certain display requirements that must be met in order for the installer to fire off. First, you must have a *minimum* screen resolution of 800×600 pixels and a display setting of at least 256 colors. You can have more colors, but avoid using the True Color setting, because that can have a tendency to throw off Java applications. Though rare, there are still some servers out there that have video cards that do not support a combination of 256 colors and 800×600 pixels. If that is the case on the server where you are installing, you must plan to upgrade the video card to support better resolution. (Note that this could also happen if you are using the wrong video driver, so be sure that you have the correct video driver for your display adapter.) There are times when, for whatever reason, the setup.exe on the root of the CD-ROM does not kick off. We have experienced this problem primarily when installing from a staging area across the network. If you encounter this problem, try navigating to the \WIN32\INSTALL directory on the first disk of the CD-ROM set. The setup.exe in that directory should always work. If you encounter problems, go to the Task Manager and kill any setup.exe programs that are running, and then try again.

Group Requirements

If you are used to installing in a Unix environment, you may be wondering why you are not prompted for a group name such as "dba" for the OS account. The reason is that you must do the installation as an account that has local administrator privileges on the target machine. This will ensure that the Registry and path are properly updated with information needed for Oracle to operate. In addition, since the installation is done with administrator privileges, a group called ORA_DBA can be created by the installer during the installation. The account doing the installation will be added to the ORA_DBA group, thus giving that account sysdba privileges on any databases on the machine. We discuss sysdba connections in more detail later in this chapter, and we discuss OS groups and authentication in Chapter 5.

Space Requirements

The Summary page, displayed after you have picked all the install options and just before the installation actually begins (that is, when the file copy of the CD-ROM begins), will list the selected options, give you space requirements for the installation,

and indicate how much free space is actually available. This report can be somewhat misleading for two reasons:

- It does not take into account the space required to create a database.
- The Summary page does not take into account the need to uncompress files from the CD-ROM or staging area.

During the installation, Oracle copies several compressed .jar files to the ORACLE_HOME\jar directory. These files are deleted once the installation is complete, so while the Summary page may give us an accurate count of space used when all is said and done, during the installation itself, you will find that you actually need more space. Therefore, if you are right on the cusp of having enough space for the installation, the installation may actually fail because there is not enough space to copy and uncompress all of the files.

In addition, Oracle will create an Orainstall directory in your TEMP folder. To view this, right-click My Computer, choose Properties, and go to the Advanced tab. From here, choose Environment Variables. Check the user variables section. Although there is a TEMP set as a system variable, Oracle is writing to the TEMP directory assigned under User Variables. By default, this is C:\Documents and Settings\Administrator\Local Settings\Temp. If your computer has minimal space on drive C:, the installation might fail because the TEMP directory is also used for extraction of files during the installation. Also, if any Oracle-related jar files already exist in CLASSPATH under System Variables, they should be temporarily removed prior to installing.

Based on this, we would recommend a *minimum* of 3GB of free space on the drive where you are making the ORACLE_HOME, in addition to any space required for the database. Ideally, the database should be on a different drive altogether from the ORACLE_HOME. For drive C: (or whichever drive contains the program files and TEMP directories), we would recommend at least 300MB of free space.

Memory Requirements

Officially, the Oracle-recommended minimum requirements for RAM are good only for the purpose of actually running the installer. Anyone who thinks that they can actually run a decent database with the minimum recommended memory requirements needs to reevaluate their career choice. Realistically, we recommend that you put as much memory into the machine as you can afford, or as much as the machine will take, whichever is less. Seriously, though—even if Oracle will successfully install on a machine with 128MB of RAM, you should not be attempting to run Oracle9*i* on a machine that has only 128MB of RAM. If you intend to use it for anything other than the most basic testing, we recommend that you have *at least* 512MB of RAM. If we had our druthers, the minimum would be 4GB for any production machine. In Chapter 5, we will go into more detail on determining memory requirements for a given database configuration.

Service Pack Requirements

Oracle9*i*, when installed on NT 4.0, will check that you are running at least Service Pack 5. If not, the installation will not continue. There are no Service Pack requirements to install on Windows 2000. However, Oracle recommends that you run on the latest stable Service Pack whenever possible. We discuss Windows 2000 Service Pack issues in more detail in Chapter 10.

Stopping Services Prior to Installing

If you are installing in an existing ORACLE_HOME, as you might be if you are patching or upgrading, or if you are simply adding additional product options, you should make sure that you stop any Oracle Services that are running from that particular home. By the same token, close any Oracle applications (for example, SQL*Plus) that are running from the home to which you are installing. It should not be necessary to stop services that are running from a different ORACLE_HOME. So, for example, if you are currently running 8.1.7 in HOME0, and plan to install 9.0.1 in HOME1, you can leave the 8.1.7 database in HOME0 up and running during the installation.

If you receive write errors on certain files during the installation, the first item to check is that all Oracle Services in that home are stopped. A write error occurs because Oracle is trying to copy over a new version of a file, but the old version is already in use. If all Oracle Services are truly stopped and you still receive the error, then check third-party services that may have a handle open on an Oracle file. Some known culprits include Compaq Insight Manager and Microsoft's SMS service, or any service that uses SNMP protocols. You can nail this down for certain with the tlist utility (discussed in Chapter 5) or by downloading the Process Explorer GUI utility from http://www.sysinternals.com (as discussed in Chapter 3). When run in DLL mode, as seen in Figure 4-2, this utility allows you to search on the name of the DLL (as reported in the error on your installer screen) on which you are getting the write error, and find any programs that have a handle open on that DLL. This should help you catch the culprit red-handed. Kill the offending process and continue with the install.

Beginning the Installation

Let's go through the installation of Oracle9*i* and look at the various options of note. When you first run the setup program, whether from a staging area or from the disk

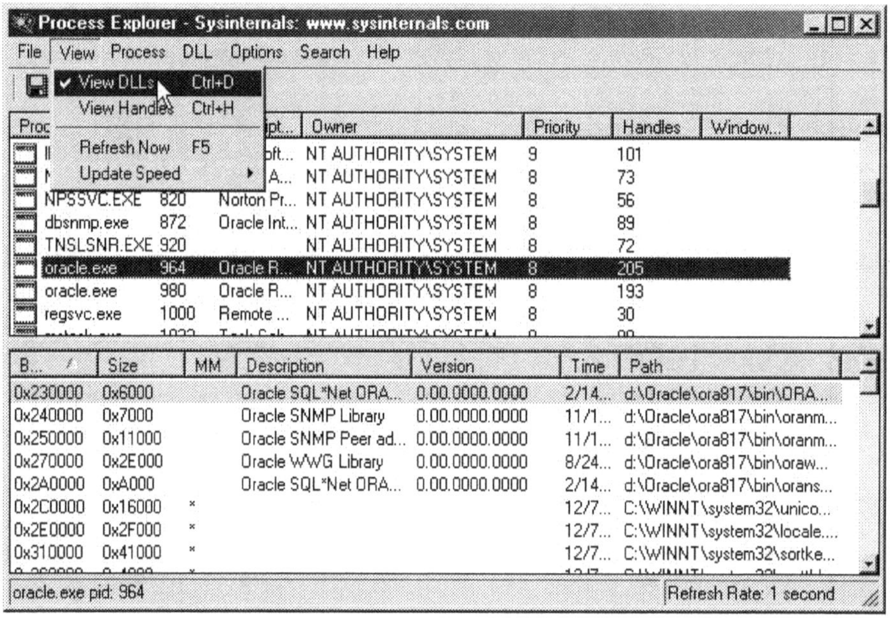

FIGURE 4-2. *Using Process Explorer to find handles on Oracle files*

itself, you will see the initial Welcome screen. On this screen, you can choose to view currently installed products, and you can also choose to deinstall products. We will discuss removing and deinstalling products toward the end of this chapter in the section "Deinstalling Oracle Products." For now, our focus is on the installation itself.

Viewing Installed Products

Back in the good old days (before Oracle8i), one could readily view a simple text file called NT.RGS (or Unix.rgs or netware.rgs), which existed in the ORACLE_HOME\orainst directory, to tell you what products had been installed on your system. Now, though, in addition to copying files to the ORACLE_HOME, the installer will create an Oracle directory on your system drive in the Program Files subdirectory (usually this is going to be C:\Program Files\oracle). This is where the installer logs its actions and keeps track of installed products. Installed products are maintained in the directory C:\Program Files\Oracle\Inventory\Components—this is not as easy to decipher as the original text file was. This directory will have individual folders for each component installed. Drilling down through each folder will give you an idea as to the component to which the folder belongs, but the only way to effectively decipher what has been installed is to run the OUI and click the Installed Products button on this initial Welcome screen.

The installation itself will be logged to a file called InstallActions.log, which will exist in the directory C:\Program Files\Oracle\Inventory\logs. Each subsequent installation will rename the existing log file with a name including the date and time, and a new InstallActions.log file will be created to track the current installation.

Defining the Current Installation

The first screen after the Welcome screen is the File Locations screen (Figure 4-3). This screen gives you the opportunity to define the name of your ORACLE_HOME and the directory where you want it to be created. Note the Source directory across the top. If you are running the installer directly from the CD-ROM, the source will be automatically populated. However, if you are running the installer as a stand-alone, when installing a patch, for example, you will need to click the Browse button in the Source area of the screen; navigate to the appropriate staging area; and select a file called products.jar, which the Installer will read to display the installation options.

In the Destinations section, you will select a home name and a directory for the installation to go to. On a fresh machine (one with no prior Oracle products installed), the installer will pick a local drive that has the largest amount of free space available as the location for the ORACLE_HOME. So, if drive E: has the most free space, the OUI will suggest a path of E:\Oracle\Ora90. You can change this to whatever you want on this initial screen. Refer back to Figure 4-1, which shows the Registry. Once you click Next to proceed past this File Locations screen, the Windows 2000 Registry is immediately updated with this information. With a brand new installation, the ORACLE key will be created under HKLM\SOFTWARE. If there are already existing Oracle products, the installer will create the HOME*x* key for the appropriate home number. If you make a mistake on this screen and need to go back, you must clean up the Registry yourself. To do this, delete the most recently created HOME*x* key under HKLM/SOFTWARE/ORACLE. In addition, you will need to delete the corresponding ID*x* key under HKLM\SOFTWARE\ORACLE\ALL_HOMES. Again, we will discuss removing an ORACLE_HOME in the section "Deinstalling Oracle Products."

FIGURE 4-3. *File Locations page—defining locations for the Oracle installation*

Installing Oracle8i on a Pentium 4 Machine

Though this book's main focus is Oracle9i, it bears mentioning that if you attempt to install any Oracle8i software (including client software) on a box with a Pentium 4 processor, the Oracle Universal Installer will fail to initialize. This is actually not the fault of the OUI, but rather one of the components of the Java Runtime Environment (JRE). Specifically, the Just-In-Time (JIT) compiler does not recognize the Pentium 4 processor and therefore no Java applets using the JIT compiler will initialize.

To work around this problem, you have two choices. First, you can contact Oracle Support and obtain the patched version of the OUI (reference patch #1507768). This will require that you run the patched version of the OUI, and then on the File Locations screen you will need to choose the source by navigating to the \STAGE directory on the CD-ROM. Open the file called products.jar and proceed with the installation.

Alternatively, you can copy the contents of the 8.1.x CD-ROM to a staging area on the hard drive or network, and then rename or delete all copies of the file called symcjit.dll from the staging area. This will force the installer to run in nojit mode (meaning the JIT compiler is not used), and the installation should proceed as normal.

This problem only affects Oracle8i releases—it is not an issue with Oracle9i. However, we mention it here because of the potential impact, due to the fact that even client machines running on Intel Pentium 4 processors, regardless of the OS, can be affected. Thus, even if you are running an Oracle9i database, you may encounter this problem if you have 8i client installations.

Understanding Optimal Flexible Architecture

Before we proceed further, let's briefly discuss Oracle's Optimal Flexible Architecture (OFA). This is a standard for Oracle installations that eases administration and encourages separation of data files for performance reasons. In the path suggested previously—E:\Oracle\ora90—the first directory is the ORACLE_BASE, and the second directory is the actual ORACLE_HOME. Releases of Oracle on Windows NT prior to 8.1.x (that is, 8.0.6 and below) do not use the concept of an ORACLE_BASE. The default directory for Oracle installations in those earlier releases would have been E:\ORANT—this would be the ORACLE_HOME, with no thought of an ORACLE_BASE directory. What the ORACLE_BASE directory provides is a top-level directory, which will become a container for the ORACLE_HOME, an admin directory and an ORADATA directory. Refer to the right-hand side of Figure 4-4, to get an idea of what the ORACLE_BASE directory structure looks like.

The installation of the files necessary to run Oracle will go into the directory E:\oracle\ora90. This is the ORACLE_HOME, which contains replaceable files, all coming off the media during the installation. Some of the notable subdirectories in the ORACLE_HOME include the aforementioned bin directory, which contains the executables and DLLs required for Oracle. In addition, the RDBMS\admin directory contains the scripts and other files needed to create your database and populate the data dictionary. One other directory of note within the ORACLE_HOME is

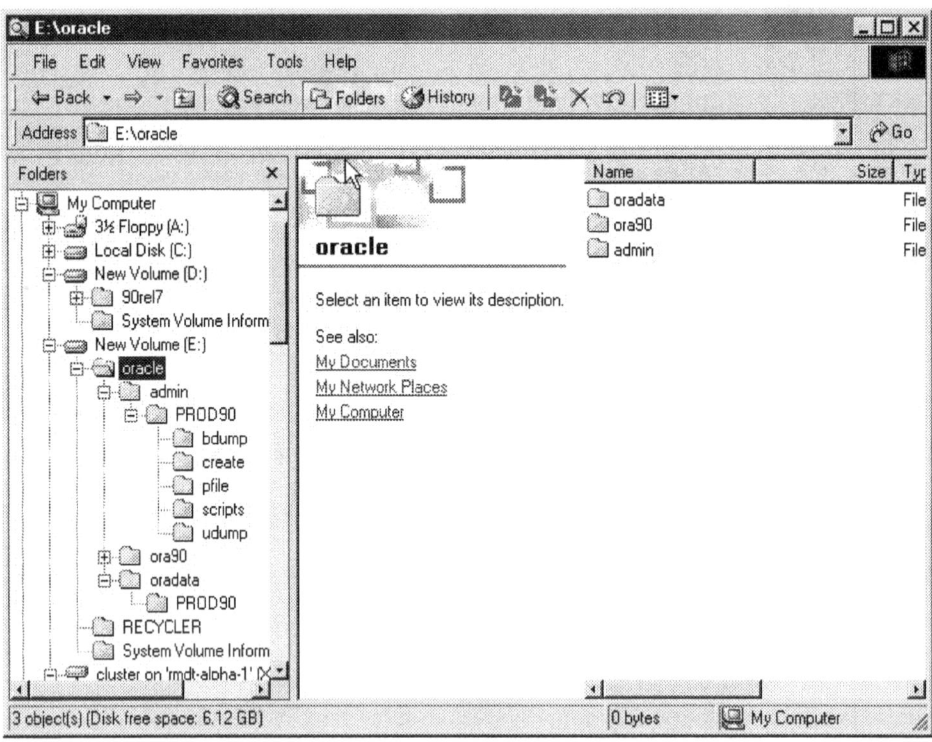

FIGURE 4-4. *ORACLE_BASE and admin directory views*

the Database directory. On Unix systems, the password file and parameter file will be kept in ORACLE_HOME/dbs, and there is *no* Database directory. On the Windows 2000 platform, the Database directory is where the parameter file and password file are kept. Although there is a DBS directory on Windows 2000, it is not used.

In addition to the ORACLE_HOME directory, Oracle recommends creating the admin directory within the ORACLE_BASE, as a container for the parameter file and trace files. The ORACLE_BASE\admin directory should contain a separate subdirectory with each instance name, and then subdirectories within there for the pfile, bdump and udump, and script locations (refer to the left-hand side of Figure 4-4).

Finally, the ORACLE_BASE\ORADATA directory is the container for the database files themselves. Again, the ORADATA directory should have subdirectories within it with each instance name, in case you have multiple instances. Since you will likely want to spread datafiles across multiple drives, we recommend that you create an \Oracle\ORADATA directory at the root of each drive where you have datafiles, and place the files here according to the instance names. Adherence to these principles will allow you to achieve better redundancy and performance by providing a structure for duplicating control files and log files, and distributing different datafiles across multiple drives for i/o performance gains. In addition, these standards will enforce a structure that is easier for multiple database administrators to maintain and support, because everyone involved can use the same standards and practices.

NOTE
If selecting one of the preconfigured databases, the Database Configuration Assistant will by default want to place the files within the ORACLE_HOME. When prompted for the location, we recommend that you choose ORACLE_BASE\ORADATA as the directory for database file location (for example, D:\oracle\oradata). It is not necessary to specify the SID name—the Database Configuration Assistant will always create a subdirectory with the SID name for you.

Products Installed Outside of the ORACLE_HOME The Oracle Universal Installer is installed outside of the ORACLE_HOME. This installation directory is determined by a Registry variable called INST_LOC, which is in the base Oracle key HKLM\Software\Oracle. The default location is C:\Program Files\Oracle\ Inventory. The Java Runtime Environment (JRE), necessary for running certain Java-based utilities and programs, is also installed in C:\Program Files\oracle. Although you can select alternative locations for these products, we recommend that you stick with the defaults. We also recommend that you do install the installer itself, so that it can be run by itself later on, either to install patches or to deinstall products. Otherwise, you will need to have access to the CD-ROM.

Wrapping Up the Installation Choices As you proceed through the installation screens, you will be given the following options for available products:

- Oracle 9i Database
- Oracle 9i Client
- Oracle 9i Management and Integration

Select the appropriate option here (choose Oracle 9i Database, since this is a book on the database). You will then be given the following options for installation types:

- Enterprise
- Standard
- Personal
- Custom

The primary differences here are how the product is licensed. Enterprise includes just about every possible option, whereas Standard requires you to separately license the options you want to use. Personal is meant as a stand-alone installation for testing purposes.

Finally, you will get to the database configuration screen, where you will be able to pick if you want a preconfigured database. If you choose one of the following database options,

- General Purpose
- Transaction Processing
- Data Warehousing

you will be prompted for the instance name, and a preconfigured database will be laid down at the end of the installation, with the instance name and location for the datafiles that you specify. If you choose Custom, you will again be prompted for the instance name, and then given the opportunity to customize your own database and create database templates at the end of the installation. We will discuss this in more detail in the next section.

After providing the database name and the database character set you wish to use, proceed to the Summary page. Although there is not an option to print this information, it will be captured to the InstallActions.log file mentioned previously. You will be able to refer to this log file later on for details on the installation type and products that were chosen. From here, click Install, and go grab some lunch—this will take awhile.

Creating the Database

Depending on the options that you choose, the Oracle Database Configuration Assistant (DBCA) will kick off after the installation completes and walk you through the steps to create a database. This product has matured considerably through the various releases, and it now gives you the flexibility to create files anywhere, create multiple tablespaces, and define all init parameters prior to the actual database creation. In addition, the Oracle9*i* DBCA adds the ability to create and use database templates to further simplify the creation and copying of databases. We will discuss database templates in more detail in Chapter 5.

It is not necessary to run the DBCA immediately after the installation. If you chose a Software Only option on the Database Configuration screen during the installation, the Assistant can be kicked off any time later by simply firing up the icon from the Database Administration folder in the Oracle9*i* program group. If the Assistant fails for some reason at the end of an installation, chances are that the installation itself has still completed successfully. You can correct whatever problems the Assistant encountered and then simply rerun it at any time later, without needing to reinstall from scratch. Because of its flexibility and interface, we strongly recommend that you take advantage of using the DBCA to create your databases. However, it also helps to understand what it is that the DBCA is actually doing; so in the following section, we will walk through the process of manually creating a database, and relate that to various screens in the DBCA.

Behind the Scenes with the Oracle Database Configuration Assistant

Figure 4-5 gives you an idea of the various steps that the Database Configuration Assistant goes through to create a database. But what is the Assistant *really* doing?

To create a database, the DBCA goes through several steps. In a nutshell, these steps are as follows:

1. Define the database name.
2. Create the service.
3. Create the parameter file.
4. Execute the actual create database statement.
5. Create additional tablespaces.
6. Populate the data dictionary with scripts.
7. Run scripts for adding options.

Here, we will go through these steps and discuss what is going on behind the scenes at each point. If you choose an existing database template in the second screen of the DBCA, many of these choices, including parameters and options selected, are made for you based on generic principles of various data processing models. You can view these selections by highlighting the desired template on the second screen of the DBCA and clicking the Show Details button. If you select the New Database template, you will have more control over defining different parameters and options. If you have

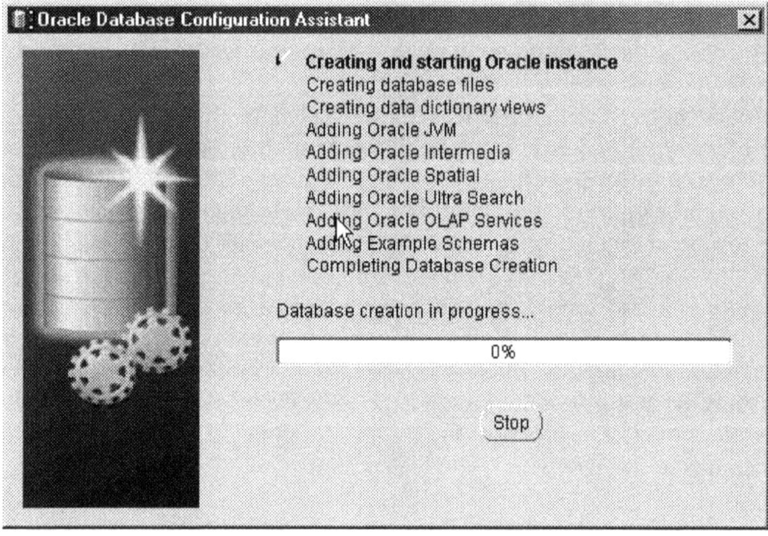

FIGURE 4-5. *Database Configuration Assistant creating a database*

selected one of the preconfigured databases, the DBCA will only copy existing database files off the CD, essentially do some configuration and then start that database, therefore some of the steps in the procedure will not be necessary.

Naming the Database

The database name and the instance name are not necessarily synonymous. The database name, also called the global database name, will normally include your organization's domain name. In prior releases, Oracle would default to using a domain name of .WORLD; however, starting with the 8i release, Oracle began defaulting to a domain name already defined on the system. Refer back to Chapter 1, where we discussed the domain name in the networking setup, and you will find the domain name that Oracle will use as the default domain name. If we were to create a database called PROD90, in the domain US.ORACLE.COM, the full global database name would be PROD90.US.ORACLE.COM. However, the instance name would be just PROD90.

The global database name is important to know when connecting to the database and/or creating database links. The domain will be defined as an init.ora parameter called DB_DOMAIN, or it may also be defined in the sqlnet.ora file with a parameter called NAMES.DEFAULT_DOMAIN. You should make sure that these parameters are set correctly to match your organization's domain name.

Using the ORADIM Utility

We know now that in order to create a database on Windows 2000, there must first be a process to attach to. As we discussed in the previous chapters, this process is started by way of a service called OracleService<sidname>. How is this service created, though? The answer is a utility called ORADIM.EXE. The basic syntax of the **oradim** command for creating a new service is as follows:

```
oradim -new -sid <sidname> -intpwd <password> -startmode AUTO/MANUAL
-pfile <full path to the parameter file>
```

Of course, when using the DBCA, this command is executed for you automatically in the background. However, the **oradim** command is a constant in the life of an Oracle database administrator on the Windows platform. Even after the database has been created, you will likely need to use this command for various reasons throughout the life of your database. Therefore, we will devote the next portion of this chapter to a discussion of the **oradim** command and its various uses. For a full list of parameters, simply type **oradim** at a command prompt, with no arguments. Here is an example of the actual command, which would be run from a command prompt:

```
C:\>oradim -new -sid PROD90 -intpwd elway1_b2b -startmode AUTO -pfile
D:\oracle\admin\prod90\pfile\init.ora
```


Understanding ORADIM Parameters

Here, we are creating a SID called PROD90. The SID name is synonymous with the instance name, and can be up to 15 characters long. A service called OracleServicePROD90 will be created in the Services Console. Services are created in the Registry under HKLM\System\CurrentControlSet\Services. By default, the service will be set to Logon As the LocalSystem account, which is the operating system account specific to this machine, as discussed in Chapter 1. Do not confuse this account with the Oracle system account in the database.

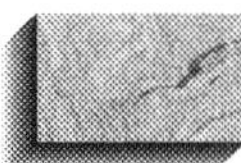

NOTE

You may see indications in some documents that a SID name can be longer than 15 characters (some say up to 64 characters), but this does not actually work. While ORADIM will successfully create and start a service with an instance name of 16 characters or more, you will not be able to attach to the service. Your connect attempt will fail, generating the error message ORA-24314: "Service handle not initialized."

The password for sysdba (the artist formerly known as "internal") connections in our example is elway1_b2b, and the password is stored in a file outside the database called pwd<sidname>.ora. As noted earlier in this chapter, the password file will be found in the ORACLE_HOME\Database directory. We will discuss how this is used for authentication in the section "Authenticating Using the Password File," later in this chapter.

Automatic Startup of the Database

The service itself (meaning the oracle.exe process) will always be defined after creation to start automatically when the machine boots up. However, specifying AUTO as the -startmode option of ORADIM signifies that the database is also set to start and open automatically whenever the service starts.

In releases prior to 8i, the automatic startup of a database was managed by creating a second service called OracleStartPROD90, whose sole function was to start up the database. However, this is now handled by way of two Registry entries in the appropriate HOME*x* key. Thus, the **oradim** command in releases 8i and 9i will only create the one service—OracleServicePROD90. The Registry values in question are found in the appropriate HOME*x* key, under HKLM/Software/ORACLE. The first value name is ORA_PROD90_AUTOSTART. Because we specified -startmode AUTO on the command line, this value will be set to TRUE. The second value name will be ORA_PROD90_PFILE, and the value will be the path to the parameter file, which will be used to automatically start the instance—in this case, D:\Oracle\admin\prod90\pfile\init.ora. When troubleshooting problems with automatically starting the database, these two parameters are the first place to start—make sure that they are set correctly for each SID on the machine.

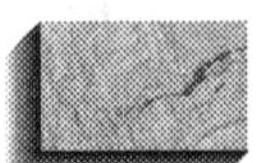

TIP

There are times when you do not want the database to start up automatically with the service. For example, if you are restoring a backup in a recovery scenario, you will likely do so with the service stopped. In order to mount the database for recovery, you will need to start the service back up before you can connect. In this situation, you do not want the database to be started automatically. Prior to starting the service, you can edit it using the ***oradim*** *command* ***C:\>oradim -edit -sid PROD90 -startmode manual****. You can accomplish the same thing by going into the Registry and setting the value of ORA_<sidname>_AUTOSTART to FALSE for the appropriate SID.*

Automatic Shutdown of the Database

In addition to these startup parameters, ORADIM adds three additional parameters for shutting down:

```
ORA_<sidname>_SHUTDOWN - Defaults to TRUE
ORA_<sidname>_SHUTDOWN_TIMEOUT - Defaults to 30 (seconds)
ORA_<sidname>_SHUTDOWNTYPE - Defaults to I (Immediate)
```

These Registry values tell Oracle how to treat the database if the service is stopped while the database is still running. If you just kill the process with the database running, Oracle has to perform crash recovery on a restart, similar to a shutdown abort operation. However, killing the process is worse than a shutdown abort, because Oracle cannot even do the minimal housekeeping required to guarantee that instance recovery will succeed on the subsequent restart. Sometimes this cannot be avoided. However, when possible, you should always attempt to shut down cleanly prior to killing the service or the process.

With the default settings as shown previously, when the service for an instance is stopped, Oracle attempts to perform a shutdown immediate operation on the database. The timeout specifies how long to wait for this operation to succeed. If the shutdown immediate does not complete within the 30 seconds specified, a shutdown abort is performed, and the service is allowed to stop. These same settings should apply to a shutdown of the entire server, as well as just stopping the individual service. However, our testing has had mixed results in the case of a server shutdown. Test this in your own environment, and heed the mantra from Oracle Support—"Have you tried this with the latest patch?" To be absolutely certain the database comes down cleanly, shut it down manually before stopping the service or rebooting the server. One additional note on shutdowns—unlike on Unix platforms, a shutdown of the database on Windows 2000 does not clean up all of the memory associated with various threads, because the process is still running. After a shutdown immediate operation, stop the OracleService<sid> to ensure that all memory is cleaned up and released after a shutdown.

Deleting Services

To delete services for cleanup purposes or troubleshooting, you again use ORADIM, but with different command line parameters:

```
oradim -delete -sid <sidname>
```

In our example, we would use the following command:

```
C:\>oradim -delete -sid PROD90
```

As noted previously, ORADIM is only dealing with the services, so this command only deletes the service itself and the instance-specific Registry values. The parameter file and datafiles are left untouched. Therefore, it is common to use this command to quickly re-create services when troubleshooting authentication problems or problems with the automatic startup. Although the password file should be deleted by the **oradim** command as well, this is often not the case. You should check the ORACLE_HOME\Database directory after running the command and make sure the password file is gone. If not, delete it or rename it prior to re-creating the service.

CAUTION
*The **oradim** command will delete services without touching the database files, but if you use the Database Configuration Assistant to delete a database, you are truly deleting the database—including files and the whole nine yards.*

There are also times when the **oradim** command may not clean up the services correctly. If this happens, you can delete the services directly from HKLM\System\CurrentControlSet\Services. Simply highlight the appropriate Oracle Service and delete it. Note that you should stop the service prior to deleting it. If you do not, the service may still show up in the Services Console, but the status will display as DISABLED. If this occurs, you will need to reboot the machine to clear it up.

The oradim.log File

A delightful feature of the **oradim** command is that it provides very minimal feedback at the command prompt. However, it does write a log file in the ORACLE_HOME\Database directory called, appropriately enough, oradim.log. In Oracle9*i*, this log is more useful than it was in previous releases in that it appends new entries instead of always overwriting itself, and it now includes timestamps—perish the thought. If you are having trouble with ORADIM, or having trouble autostarting, check the oradim.log for possible clues.

Setting the ORACLE_SID

Once the service is created, this will give you the means to start a process, which you can now connect to. In order to accomplish this feat from the command line, you should set the ORACLE_SID first:

```
C:\>set oracle_sid=prod90
```

Unlike Unix, these commands are not case sensitive. Be aware, though, that there can be no spaces around the equal sign; so while the following command will never give you an error, your SID will not be set correctly, and you may end up connecting to the wrong instance:

```
C:\>set oracle_sid = prod90 (wrong-there should be no spaces
around the '=')
```

When setting the SID and making a connection without a connect string, this is what is referred to as a *bequeath* connection, or a connection local to the box, using no networking protocols. The DBCA will always make a bequeath connection. When attempting to make a bequeath connection, you may see an error message such as ORA-12560: "TNS Protocol Adapter error," or ORA-24314: "Service handle not initialized." If you encounter one of these errors, there are several possible causes:

- Check that the SID is set correctly—no typos and no spaces around the equal sign (as noted previously).
- Check that the service for the instance is actually running.
- Make sure that there are no special or illegal characters in the SID name. Stick with alphanumeric characters.
- Make sure that you have 15 characters or less for the instance name.
- Ensure that you are local to the machine. If using remote access software, make sure that it behaves as if you are local on the machine. Windows 2000 Terminal Services is an example of a remote program that does *not* give you true local access, and bequeath connections are *not* allowed when using Windows 2000 Terminal Services.

Creating a Parameter File

To continue on with the path the database creation takes, we must have a parameter file, or pfile. Note that there is a pfile in two places. When an instance is started with no pfile specified, Oracle looks for a pfile in ORACLE_HOME\Database called INIT<sidname>.ora, depending on what the environment variable ORACLE_SID is set to. You will find that the standard is to simply create an IFILE entry in here, which points to the true parameter file, in the ORACLE_BASE\admin\<sidname>\ pfile directory.

New Feature in Oracle9i

A new feature in Oracle9*i* is the ability to also create a system parameter file, or an SPFILE. This is a persistent file that allows parameters changed via an **alter system** command (as determined by the SCOPE argument) to be written out to the

SPFILE. The next time the database is started, the SPFILE is read as well as the normal initialization file, so the parameters become "persistent." The SPFILE defaults to the ORACLE_HOME\Database directory. We will discuss this in more detail in Chapter 5.

The DBCA breaks the parameter file down into four main categories: File Locations, Db Sizing, Memory, and Archiving. Refer again to the section "Understanding Optimal Flexible Architecture" earlier in this chapter. We will take a look at each type in the following sections.

File Location Parameters

Recall in Chapter 2 that we described the control file as the roadmap to the rest of the database. The control file will be created at the time you create the database, and any subsequent file creations/modifications will be duly noted by the control file. Where the control file gets created will be determined by the init.ora parameter CONTROL_FILES. Oracle can be told to look for a control file somewhere else by simply shutting the database down, moving the file, and modifying the CONTROL_FILES parameter. By the same token, control files can be added or removed from the Oracle database's radar by again simply shutting down and modifying the init.ora, and copying the files to the appropriate locations prior to starting back up.

Other file location parameters in the init.ora include destination information for certain functions. System trace files such as the alert log, and trace files for pmon, smon, dbwr, and so on, are written to the directory defined by the parameter BACKGROUND_DUMP_DEST. User trace files are written to USER_DUMP_DEST. (Refer back to the section "Understanding Optimal Flexible Architecture" earlier in this chapter.) The background and user dump destinations should be directories within the \Oracle\admin\<sidname> structure—for example, D:\Oracle\admin\prod90\bdump. LOG_ARCHIVE_DEST should be a directory within \Oracle\Oradata\<sidname>.

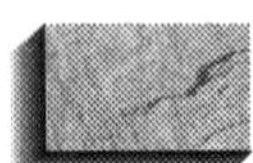

NOTE

Be certain that the operating system account under which the Oracle service logs on has permissions on these directories. Recall that the OracleService<sid> logs on as the LocalSystem account by default. Whether you leave this as is or change this to another account, you must ensure that this account has full control of all directories within the ORACLE_BASE, and on all drives where datafiles exist.

DB Sizing Parameters

One of the most critical physical parameters that we define *prior* to database creation is the size of the physical blocks, which make up the datafiles. This is defined with the parameter DB_BLOCK_SIZE. While the DBCA will allow you to change this in 1KB increments, don't. Acceptable values in Windows 2000 are 2KB (2048), 4KB (4096), 8KB (8192) or 16KB (16384) block sizes

As discussed in Chapter 2, you generally want a smaller block size for OLTP databases and a larger block size for DSS or Data Warehouse systems. It is important to set this value appropriately prior to the creation of the database, because while other parameters can be changed easily enough later on, you only get one crack at setting DB_BLOCK_SIZE. Well, er, uh—okay, that used to be true. Oracle9*i* now enhances flexibility in this area by supporting files with multiple block sizes in a single database. So, setting the parameter DB_BLOCK_SIZE will define what will come to be known as the *standard* or *default block size*. This is the block size that will be used when the system tablespace is created. Additional tablespaces can be created with a different block size by specifying the BLOCKSIZE argument on a **create tablespace** command (provided the proper cache area has been allocated in the SGA—this is explained in the next section of this chapter):

```
SQL> create tablespace bs_test
datafile 'D:\Oracle\oradata\PROD90\bs_test2k.dbf'
size 10m blocksize 2048;
```

If you do not specify a block size when creating a tablespace, the default size defined by the parameter DB_BLOCK_SIZE will be used. Therefore, you should still put some thought into setting this parameter, and try to set it to the block size you expect to be most commonly used.

You can view the block size of an existing file by querying a new column called BLOCK_SIZE in V$DATAFILE. However, since all datafiles within a single tablespace must have the same block size, there is no corresponding column in DBA_DATA_FILES. Instead, you must query BLOCK_SIZE from DBA_TABLESPACES. You cannot specify a block size when adding an additional datafile to an existing tablespace—only on the initial **create tablespace** command. When adding a datafile to an existing tablespace, the block size will come from the tablespace. In addition, valid block sizes must be configured with their own cache area in the init.ora file, as you will see momentarily.

Although the DBCA has SORT_AREA_SIZE defined under DB sizing parameters, we felt that it made more sense to include a discussion of that parameter in the section "Memory Parameters," because it is truly an area of memory, and can be modified at any time after the database creation.

Memory Parameters

Memory parameters deal primarily with structures in memory. We will just touch on a couple of the main ones here. We discussed in Chapter 2 the different areas of memory within an Oracle database, and what each one does. Here, we will discuss what the actual parameters are, and how to determine some initial values.

The Buffer Cache We begin with the parameter that defines how most of your memory is consumed. The DBCA displays this on the screen as "Buffer Cache," but the corresponding parameter is actually DB_CACHE_SIZE. DB_CACHE_SIZE defines how much memory is used for holding the default-size database blocks. Per our discussion of the buffer cache in Chapter 2, the larger this cache is, the more blocks that are kept in memory, and the less likely we are to have to go to disk to reread a block. In releases prior to 9i, this area in memory was defined by the parameter DB_BLOCK_BUFFERS. This parameter actually referred to the number of database blocks to keep in the buffer cache, so in order to determine how large the buffer cache was, you would have had to multiply DB_BLOCK_BUFFERS by DB_BLOCK_SIZE. The DB_CACHE_SIZE parameter simplifies this by allowing you to just specify the total size of the buffer cache.

Defining the Buffer Cache for Multiple Block Sizes

DB_CACHE_SIZE defines the cache size for database blocks of default size. To use multiple block sizes, you must specify a separate buffer cache for *each* block size that you intend to use (yes, perhaps you *should* buy more RAM, now that you mention it). Assuming that your default block size is 8KB (DB_BLOCK_SIZE=8192), and you wanted to create additional files with either a 16KB block size or a 2KB block size, you would add the following to the init.ora file:

```
db_2k_cache_size = (value in bytes or Megabytes)
db_16k_cache_size = (value in bytes or Megabytes)
db_cache_size = (value in bytes or Megabytes)
```

In our example, it is not necessary to specify db_8k_cache_size, nor could you if you wanted to, because this is the default block size. This cache is defined only by DB_CACHE_SIZE. These values must be set and in place *before* you can create a tablespace with a nondefault block size. Otherwise, the command will generate an error:

```
SQL> create tablespace bs_test2
datafile 'D:\Oracle\oradata\PROD90\bs_test4k.dbf'
size 10m blocksize 4096;

create tablespace bs_test2
```

```
*
ERROR at line 1:
ORA-29339: tablespace block size 4096 does not match configured block sizes
```

It is possible to dynamically set these parameters via an **alter system** command. However, this still requires planning ahead. You cannot create a buffer cache on-the-fly unless you have already set the parameter SGA_MAX_SIZE to a value that is greater than the current SGA size. By default, these values are the same. As you can see from the example, you may end up needing to restart the database in order to effect this change. We will discuss setting SGA_MAX_SIZE, and its impact, in greater detail in Chapter 5.

```
SQL> alter system set db_2k_cache_size=10240000 scope=both;
alter system set db_2k_cache_size=10240000 scope=both
*
ERROR at line 1:
ORA-02097: parameter cannot be modified because specified value is invalid
ORA-00384: Insufficient memory to grow cache

SQL> alter system set sga_max_size = 402141568 scope=both;
alter system set sga_max_size = 402141568 scope=both
*
ERROR at line 1:
ORA-02095: specified initialization parameter cannot be modified
```

Shared Pool, Large Pool, and Java Pool

Refer back to Chapter 2 for definitions of what the Shared Pool, Large Pool and Java Pool are used for. The SHARED_POOL_SIZE parameter determines how much memory to reserve for the Shared Pool. You should set this initially to at least 50MB. If you are using RMAN and the multithreaded server (MTS), both of which we recommend, then you will want to set LARGE_POOL_SIZE initially to at least 50MB as well. Finally, if you are intending to run a Java-enabled database, set JAVA_POOL_SIZE to at least 50MB. Again, these parameters are defined in bytes or megabytes. We will discuss tuning these parameters in Chapter 5.

SORT_AREA_SIZE

Memory is allocated on a per-user basis for sort operations. The size of this space in memory is determined by the parameter SORT_AREA_SIZE. Data will always be sorted first in memory no matter what, and it will always be sorted in chunks equal to SORT_AREA_SIZE. When a sort set does not fit entirely in memory, Oracle will sort first in memory in a chunk of size equal to SORT_AREA_SIZE. Then it will dump

that sorted chunk out to the user's defined temporary tablespace, and read in more data until SORT_AREA_SIZE is reached again. As each chunk is sorted, Oracle will write the individually sorted piece out to disk, read another set of data into memory, and sort that chunk and write it out to disk as well. Once all of the data has been read, you will end up with a number of individually sorted segments on disk in your temporary tablespace. Each of these segments must then be merged to provide one large, sorted chunk.

Therefore, even if you know that most sort operations are not going to fit into memory, it may still behoove you to make SORT_AREA_SIZE larger, because this will result in fewer chunks that need to be merged at the end of the process. Remember, though, that SORT_AREA_SIZE is allocated on a per-user basis, so having multiple users doing concurrent sorts may result in excessive memory consumption if this parameter is set too high. In addition, SORT_AREA_SIZE should fit evenly into the extent sizes that are allocated for the temporary tablespace. We will discuss the temporary tablespace and storage options in more detail later in this chapter.

Archiving Parameters

Recall our discussion in Chapter 2 on determining whether to archive or not. If you have made the decision to archive, the database can be created in archivelog mode, or archivelog mode can be enabled later on. Before you enable archivelog mode, you must define the following parameters in the parameter file:

```
log_archive_start=TRUE
log_archive_dest_1 = "location=E:\Oracle\Oradata\PROD90\archive"
log_archive_format = PROD90%t%s.arc
```

If you enable archivelog mode for a database, but fail to set LOG_ARCHIVE_START=TRUE, you must manually archive online log files before Oracle can begin overwriting current redo entries in its round-robin fashion. This will manifest itself as a database hang, as no activity can occur if Oracle is unable to write to the log file.

Note the parameter LOG_ARCHIVE_DEST_x. This tells Oracle where to write the archived logs. In Oracle9*i*, you can specify up to ten *different* destinations, indicating the importance of having a good copy of these archived redo logs for recovery purposes. It makes sense to want at least one of these destinations to be a remote mapped drive. However, if the service for the instance (for example, OracleServicePROD90) is left at the default setting of logging on as the LocalSystem account on the OS, you will not be able to access a shared drive. The LocalSystem account *only* has privileges on the *local system*, oddly enough. Unless you change the service to log on as another account, attempts to archive remotely will fail with an OS access denied error (OS 5). For this reason, we recommend that you define a standard OS user other than LocalSystem to start up services for any instances running on your Windows 2000 systems. Make sure that this OS account has full control on any local drives *and* has access to any remote shares where you want to archive (including a standby database destination, which we will discuss in Chapter 13).

The LOG_ARCHIVE_FORMAT parameter simply defines the format that the name of the archived logs take—%t will insert the thread number (usually 1, unless running OPS or RAC) and %s will insert the sequence number.

CAUTION

Do not specify an uppercase S (%S) in your LOG_ARCHIVE_FORMAT parameter on the Windows 2000 platform. This will limit the number of digits in the sequence number to five digits, leading to the possibility of overwriting archived logs. Using a lowercase s (%s) will avoid this problem. See Oracle Alert #60514.1 for more details on this.

The Database Storage Page

The Database Storage page in the ODBCA will allow you to specify the locations of files created when the database is created (see Figure 4-6). You will be able to see each tablespace created and which file belongs to which tablespace. In addition, you will be able to see the control file locations and locations of the online redo logs. In the next sections, we will discuss the details on creating the database and various types of tablespaces you should have within an Oracle9*i* database. Refer to back to Chapter 2 for definitions of these files and tablespace types.

The Create Database Command

The **create database** command is issued from a nomount state. An example of a basic **create database** command follows shortly. You can also find a sample script in the ORACLE_HOME\rdbms\admin directory called build_db.sql. In your **create database** command, you specify the file(s) for the system tablespace, as well as the files for the online redo logs. Note that you do not specify a block size when issuing the **create database** command, as the default DB_BLOCK_SIZE will be used here.

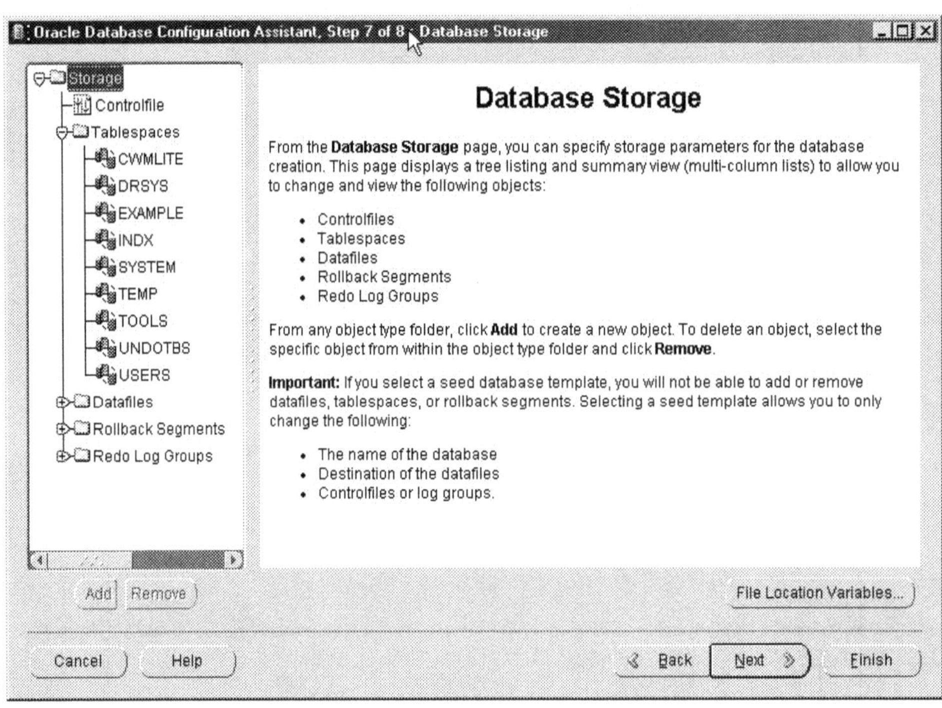

FIGURE 4-6. *The Database Storage page*

Of course, any directories must be created beforehand when creating the database manually. If using the DBCA, the Assistant will create directories for you.

```
C:\>Set oracle_sid=prod90
C:\>sqlplus
SQL*Plus: Release 9.0.1.0.1 - Production on Tue Sep 11 08:48:00 2001
(c) Copyright 2001 Oracle Corporation. All rights reserved.
Enter user-name: / as sysdba
Connected to an idle instance.
SQL>startup nomount
ORACLE instance started.
Total System Global Area 57124108 bytes
Fixed Size 70924 bytes
Variable Size 40198144 bytes
Database Buffers 16777216 bytes
```

```
Redo Buffers 77824 bytes
SQL>create database PROD90
      controlfile reuse
      logfile 'D:\oracle\oradata\prod90\redo01.log' size 50M reuse,
      'D:\oracle\oradata\prod90\redo02.log' size 50M reuse,
      'D:\oracle\oradata\prod90\redo03.log' size 50M reuse,
      'D:\oracle\oradata\prod90\redo04.log' size 50M reuse
      datafile 'D:\oracle\oradata\prod90\system01.dbf' size 500M reuse
autoextend on next 100M maxsize 1000M
 character set WE8ISO8859P1;
```

Note that you do not specify the name or location of the control file in your **create database** command. This is pulled from the parameter file, based on what you specified in the parameter CONTROL_FILES.

The preceding statement will create just one tablespace—the system tablespace. As mentioned in Chapter 2, you can see how the system tablespace is created and populated by viewing a read-only file called sql.bsq in the ORACLE_HOME\rdbms\admin directory. (This is done implicitly by the **create database** command, and you must never attempt to run this script yourself.) Here, you can see the tables and indexes that are created to store the metadata that is the data dictionary. And, of course, if you are creating the database manually, once the database has been created, you must run catalog.sql and catproc.sql to create the views and packages and procedures with which you manage your database.

Setting the Default Temporary Tablespace

We mentioned in Chapter 2 that Oracle9*i* introduces a new feature that allows you to set the default temporary tablespace for any new users who get created. Recall that, in previous releases, if a user was created and no temporary tablespace was specified, the default value for the temporary tablespace was SYSTEM. This was based on the logic that the system tablespace was the only tablespace guaranteed to exist. Starting with Oracle9*i*, however, a database administrator can define *any* tablespace to be the default temporary tablespace. Therefore, if a user is created without specifying the temporary tablespace for this user, then the default temporary tablespace setting will automatically be used.

You define an existing tablespace to become the default temporary tablespace via an **alter database** command, and it can be queried via a new view called DATABASE_PROPERTIES:

```
SQL> alter database default temporary tablespace temp2;
Database altered.
SQL> select property_value from database_properties
where property_name = 'DEFAULT_TEMP_TABLESPACE';
```

```
PROPERTY_VALUE
--------------------------------------------------------------------

TEMP2

SQL>create user humphrey identified by bogart;
SQL> column username format a20
SQL> column default_tablespace format a20
SQL> column temporary_tablespace format a20
SQL> select username, default_tablespace, temporary_tablespace
from dba_users where username = 'HUMPHREY';

USERNAME             DEFAULT_TABLESPACE   TEMPORARY_TABLESPACE
-------------------- -------------------- --------------------
HUMPHREY             SYSTEM               TEMP2
```

The column format lines are included to make the output more readable. As you can see, the default tablespace for the user's permanent objects is still the system tablespace, but the temporary tablespace was set to TEMP2, even though it was not specified on the Create User statement. This is due to the fact that TEMP2 had previously been set up as the default temporary tablespace. A database can have only one default temporary tablespace.

Enabling System Managed Undo

As discussed in Chapter 2, for system managed undo (SMU) to be enabled, an undo tablespace must exist within the database. An undo tablespace can be created at any time after database creation:

```
CREATE UNDO TABLESPACE UNDO_01
DATAFILE 'E:\ORACLE\ORADATA\PROD90\UNDO_01.DBF'
SIZE 10M REUSE AUTOEXTEND ON;
```

As with the default temporary tablespace, Oracle9*i* allows only a single undo tablespace to be in use at any one point in time, so make sure you create a large enough tablespace to handle all undo creation for the entire database. The tablespace can be changed dynamically without shutting down the database using the SQL statement:

```
ALTER SYSTEM SET UNDO_TABLESPACE= UNDO_01;
```

Additional Parameters to Support System Managed Undo Oracle uses init.ora parameters to enable and configure SMU. The parameter that starts SMU for a database is UNDO_MANAGEMENT=AUTO. If this value is left to MANUAL (the default), then rollback segments behave exactly the same as in Oracle7 through Oracle8i. A database *cannot* be run using both system managed undo and rollback segments; you must configure for one or the other. Which tablespace will be used by SMU is controlled by the system parameter UNDO_TABLESPACE = *<tablespace name>*.

The most intriguing new parameter is the UNDO_RETENTION parameter. This parameter defines the period of time (in seconds) that Oracle9*i* will retain undo information, regardless of whether it has been committed. Recall the heartrending story about wood screws and the ORA-1555 error from Chapter 2. The problem with an ORA-1555 error usually surfaces due to a long-running query occurring while other transactions are being processed. The "before" image can be lost due to updates from other sessions that have been committed, and then the read consistent image is overwritten by new data in the rollback segment. By setting UNDO_RETENTION, you have a certain degree of control over how long that information is retained. So, if you have reports with queries that consistently take about 25 minutes to complete, and these reports occasionally fail due to an ORA-1555 error, you can avoid this problem by setting UNDO_RETENTION = 1800, or approximately 30 minutes (the default value is 900 seconds). This parameter can also be set dynamically via the following command:

```
SQL>alter system set undo_retention=1800
```

Note that this will *not* guarantee that undo operations for committed transactions will be retained for that time period. Other transactions in the database will take precedence; so if we run out of space in the undo tablespace, then Oracle9*i* will still reclaim space by freeing up undo segments that hold committed data, just as in previous versions. The alternative would be to allow these ongoing transactions to fail or hang. Therefore, to guarantee that UNDO_RETENTION works as desired, you must make sure that you have adequate space in the undo tablespace to retain all of the information for the specified time. This parameter also has a significant bearing on how much benefit can be garnered by using the Oracle Flashback feature—another new 9i feature, which we will discuss in Chapter 9. You can use a new view called V$UNDOSTAT to help determine how much space is needed. Each row in V$UNDOSTAT displays statistics on the number of undo blocks used over a ten-minute interval, so this will give you a rough idea of the space needed, depending on the workload at the time it is queried.

One final parameter to discuss in regard to SMU is the UNDO_SUPPRESS_ERRORS parameter. Suppose you have an application that is coded with many **set transaction** commands or **alter rollback segment** commands, yet you want to take advantage of SMU. We already know from Chapter 2 that with SMU enabled, these commands will error out. If your application has error handling built in, (as any

good application should), then these statements may cause the application to abort. Rather than rewriting the application, you can set UNDO_SUPPRESS_ERRORS= TRUE (yes, it can be done dynamically). This way, instead of the error being returned to the application, a message will be written to the alert log only.

You can see the current undo settings by issuing the SQL*Plus command **show parameter undo**. This will show you the values for UNDO_MANAGEMENT, UNDO_TABLESPACE, UNDO_RETENTION, and UNDO_SUPPRESS_ERRORS.

Additional Create Database Options New clauses have been added to the **create database** command, so that if you script database creation, you can specify the undo tablespace and default temporary tablespace both at database creation time. Therefore, our **create database** command from earlier in this section would evolve to look something like this:

```
SQL>create database PROD90
    controlfile reuse
    logfile 'D:\oracle\oradata\prod90\redo01.log' size 50M reuse,
    'E:\oracle\oradata\prod90\redo02.log' size 50M reuse,
    'F:\oracle\oradata\prod90\redo03.log' size 50M reuse,
    'G:\oracle\oradata\prod90\redo04.log' size 50M reuse
 datafile 'E:\oracle\oradata\prod90\system01.dbf' size 500M reuse
autoextend on next 100M maxsize 1000M
UNDO TABLESPACE "UNDOTBS" DATAFILE
'F:\oracle\ora90\PROD90\undotbs01.dbf' SIZE 200M
DEFAULT TEMPORARY TABLESPACE TEMP2
TEMPFILE 'G:\oracle\ora90\PROD90\TEMP2.DBF'
character set WE8MSWIN1252
;
```

Finalizing the Database Creation

The preceding discussion of database creation should give you an understanding of just what it is that the DBCA is doing behind the scenes. Again, we recommend that you use the DBCA to create your database whenever possible. If you wish to generate scripts for your database creation, you can have the DBCA do this for you on the final screen. Conveniently, in Oracle9*i* the DBCA now gives you the ability to create the database *and* create scripts all in one fell swoop (see Figure 4-7). We recommend that you take advantage of this, so that you can refer back to how the database was created should questions arise or if components need to be rebuilt in

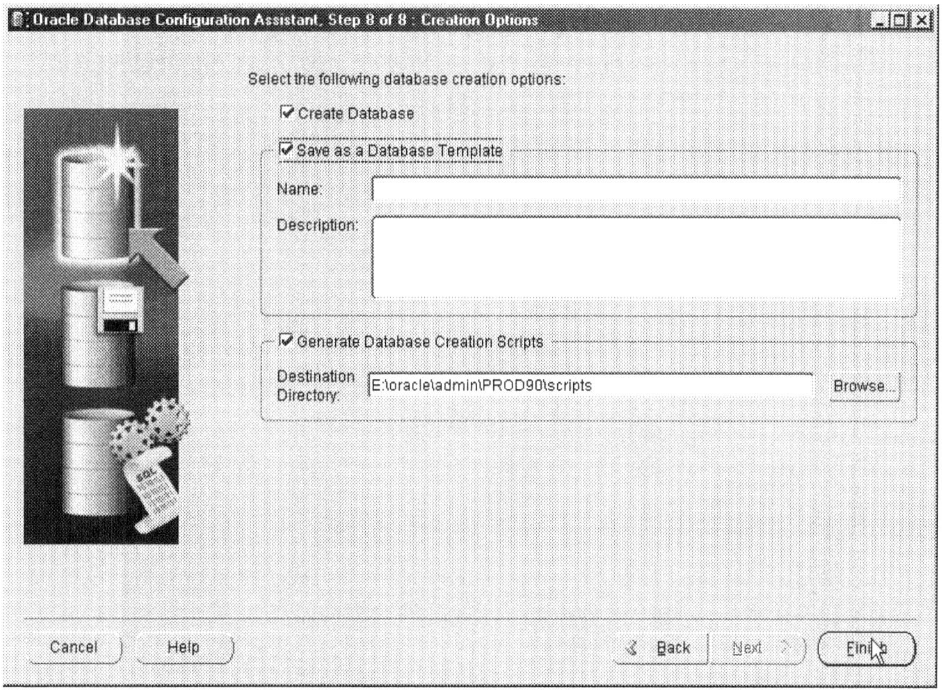

FIGURE 4-7. *Generating scripts for your database*

the future. Yet to be discussed is the use of database templates from within the Oracle9*i* DBCA. We will defer that discussion to Chapter 5, along with many other juicy topics.

Configuring Database Options

One final note on options in the database: if you choose to create a new database, the fourth screen of the DBCA will allow you to choose the options and sample schemas that you want to have installed. Options selected here will determine what additional schemas and tablespaces are created, and what scripts are run at the end of the installation to populate those schemas. If you neglect to select these options when the database is created, you can run the DBCA at a later time, and from the first screen choose Configure Database Options In A Database.

The Demise of Connect Internal and SVRMGRL

For those of you who did not believe that Server Manager and Connect Internal would ever go away, behold:

```
C:\>svrmgrl
'svrmgrl' is not recognized as an internal or external command,
operable program or batch file.

C:\>sqlplus

SQL*Plus: Release 9.0.1.0.1 - Production on Tue Sep 11 08:48:00 2001

(c) Copyright 2001 Oracle Corporation.  All rights reserved.

Enter user-name: internal
Enter password:
ERROR:
ORA-09275: CONNECT INTERNAL is not a valid DBA connection
```

Alas, it is so. Server Manager and Connect Internal have indeed received their last rites in release 9i. Long live SQL*Plus and "Connect / as SYSDBA" (not very catchy, is it?). Fortunately, everything that you could do in Server Manager can now be done in SQL*Plus. You can start up and shut down the database; you can issue a **show parameter** command; and, if you do not like to be prompted for a login right away, try using **sqlplus /nolog**. If you want to script a connection by calling SQL*Plus and connecting in one shot, you need to use double quotes as follows:

```
D:\>sqlplus "/ as sysdba"
```

In fact, we feel that it is much simpler now to have everything consolidated into one tool. One benefit—there is no more confusion about which tool to use to run scripts from.

Authenticating sysdba Connections to the Database

Where the confusion will come into play is likely going to be in regard to authentication. Without Connect Internal, how will I connect to the database? There are two ways to answer this. First, using OS authentication. During the installation of the database on Windows NT or 2000, the Oracle Universal Installer will create an operating system group called ORA_DBA. The OS account that is doing the installation (that is, Administrator) is then placed in the ORA_DBA group. In addition, a line is added to the sqlnet.ora file (found in ORACLE_HOME\ Network\admin):

```
SQLNET.AUTHENTICATION_SERVICES=(NTS)
```

If attempting to make a connection from a client, this value must be set on both the client machine and the server. This combination allows any OS account in the ORA_DBA group to connect to ANY instance on the machine, using the following syntax:

```
SQL> connect / as sysdba
Connected.
SQL>
```

This is equivalent to a connect internal statement. To reiterate, the ORA_DBA group allows users in this group to connect to *any* instance on the machine. After installing, the installer's account is added to this group. If you want additional users to be able to connect in this fashion, you will need to add them to the group yourself later on. If you want to restrict access on a per-instance basis, you can create an OS group with the instance name embedded—for example, ORA_PROD90_DBA. User accounts in this group can *only* connect to the PROD90 instance using "/ as sysdba". Refer to the discussion in Chapter 3 on creating local groups for details on how to create and delete groups for this purpose.

Authenticating Using the Password File

The other way to authenticate yourself is by using the password file. As noted previously, the password file is created when you run the **oradim** command and pass -intpwd. In the preceding example, the password for sysdba connections is elway1_b2b. You can also create or re-create a password file by running the **orapwd** command as in the example here:

```
D:\Oracle\Ora90\database>orapwd file=pwdPROD90.ora password= Elway1_b2b
```

Note that when running the ORAPWD utility, the password file must be called pwd<sidname>.ora, and it must be placed in the ORACLE_HOME\Database directory. To ensure this, either specify the full path in the FILE= portion of the command, or navigate to the correct directory before running the command (as we did in our example).

Specifically, this is the SYS password that we are creating. Regardless of what the SYS password may have been prior to running the **oradim** command or the **orapwd** command, if you re-create the password file, the SYS password will change. Again, this command is *not* case sensitive, nor is the password. You can now connect as follows:

```
SQL>connect sys/elway1_b2b as sysdba
```

Granting sysdba Privileges to Other Users One of the parameters that we did not discussed for the **oradim** command is MAXUSERS. The default value for this parameter is 5. Similarly, the **orapwd** command has a parameter called ENTRIES, which has the same meaning and also defaults to 5. You can grant sysdba privileges to additional accounts in the database, depending on how many entries are specified by either MAXUSERS or ENTRIES (which, in turn, depends on how the password file was created). For example, assume user Scott has a password of TIGER. First, connect as a user who already has sysdba privileges, and then grant the privilege to Scott:

```
SQL> connect sys/elway1_b2b as sysdba
Connected.
SQL> grant sysdba to scott;
Grant succeeded.
SQL> connect scott/tiger as sysdba;
Connected.
SQL>
```

This grant statement adds the user Scott to the password file, allowing him to make SYSBDA connections. Note that he connects with his own password, rather than the SYS password. If the password file is ever deleted and re-created, any grants of sysdba privileges must be reissued. Remember, if the user is logged on as a member of the ORA_DBA group or ORA_<SID>_DBA group, you will always get connected, regardless of what password you specify.

NOTE
Re-creating the password file using the ORAPWD utility requires that the service be restarted before the new password takes effect. Adding yourself to the local ORA_DBA group will allow you to connect immediately. However, if SQLNET.AUTHENTICATION_SERVICES is not already set to NTS in sqlnet.ora, you will need to add it and restart the Listener service.

Additional User Accounts Created When the database is created with the DBCA, several accounts within the database are created as well. You can view these accounts and change their passwords by clicking the Password Management button once the database creation is complete. Most of these accounts are locked. In order to use some features, you will need to unlock the accounts for the schema associated with those features. You can choose to unlock them here, or you can unlock them later via OEM or SQL*Plus. For more information, choose Help in the

Password Management window, or refer to the documentation for the specific features you are using.

Deinstalling Oracle Products

We mentioned briefly at the beginning that the Oracle Universal Installer offers the ability to remove or deinstall products. This works fine for individual products. However, if you want to completely remove an ORACLE_HOME—or better yet, completely remove Oracle altogether and get a fresh start—the Oracle Universal Installer does not provide a facility to do this, because the Registry entries associated with an ORACLE_HOME are not removed by the installer. Therefore, we will outline steps here to accomplish these feats.

Removing an ORACLE_HOME

To remove an ORACLE_HOME, you should start by deleting any databases in that home. Do this by running the DBCA and choosing the option to delete a database. This option will delete the services associated with a database, and also delete the directory with the instance name (including the datafiles) from ORACLE_BASE\ORADATA and ORACLE_BASE\admin.

Next, run the Oracle Universal Installer to uninstall all of the products from the ORACLE_HOME. On the Welcome screen (the first screen of the installer), choose Deinstall Products. You will be given an Inventory screen that shows the existing ORACLE_HOMES. You can remove all products from an existing 8.1.x or higher ORACLE_HOME, or you can remove just individual components. Note, however, that if you specify the removal of all of the products from an ORACLE_HOME, the installer will still leave the Registry keys intact. Select the appropriate home from which you want to remove products and click the plus sign (+) to expand the home. Place a check mark in the box next to the products you want to uninstall, and then click the Remove button. If you do not want to remove all products in a home, click the plus sign (+) again to expand the list further.

If you do proceed to remove all products within a home, that home will no longer display in the main inventory list. However, there will still be environmental settings pointing to that home in the path, in the Registry, and in the Programs folder. To remove these entries, you must run regedit and delete the corresponding HOME*x* key under HKLM/SOFTWARE/ORACLE. In addition, you will need to delete the corresponding ID*x* key under HKLM\SOFTWARE\ORACLE\ALL_HOMES. Note that if this is not the last HOME created on the machine, this deletion may have some negative consequences down the road when additional products are installed. For example, if you have HOME0, HOME1, and HOME2 on a machine, attempting to delete HOME0 or HOME1 may cause problems with later installations.

Once you have deleted the appropriate Registry keys under HKLM\SOFTWARE\Oracle, you should also navigate to HKLM\System\CurrentControlSet\Services and delete any Oracle services that were specific to that particular home.

Next, edit the path (as described earlier in this chapter) and remove any references to directories in this particular home. You should also physically delete the ORACLE_HOME subdirectory under ORACLE_BASE. Finally, you will want to delete the program group associated with the ORACLE_HOME. Do this by changing to the following directory in the Windows Explorer:

```
C:\Documents and Settings\All Users\Start Menu\Programs
```

Find the particular group for your home (the home name should be part of the group name) and delete it.

Removing Oracle Altogether

The steps for completely removing Oracle are similar. We still recommend deleting any databases and uninstalling products, but this is not absolutely necessary, and in some cases may not be possible. If the environment on a machine is damaged beyond repair—due to a botched installation or some ill-advised Registry hacking, for example—then you may not be able to get the OUI to even run. This may be why you are trying to remove Oracle to begin with—so that you can get a fresh start.

1. Begin by stopping all of your running Oracle Services and closing any Oracle applications.
2. Run regedit, and this time delete the entire Oracle key under HKLM\Software. Do the same under HKEY_CURRENT_USER\Software.
3. Next, go to HKLM\System\CurrentControlSet\Services and delete *all* services that begin with "Oracle."
4. Do the same under the key HKLM\System\CurrentControlSet\Services\Eventlog\Application—be especially careful when deleting items under services, as deleting non-Oracle services can have catastrophic consequences.
5. Remove all references to Oracle directories from the path.
6. Remove any environment variables that have been set in the System Or Local Variables section.
7. Remove *all* Oracle program groups under the directory C:\Documents And Settings\All Users\Start Menu\Programs.

8. Reboot the machine to ensure no Oracle files are left in memory.
9. Delete the ORACLE_BASE directory on all drives.
10. Delete the directory C:\Program Files\Oracle.

Following these steps should give you a clean slate to start over with a fresh Oracle installation.

Summary

In this chapter, you have seen how the Oracle installation on Windows platforms has evolved over time to become more like the standard you are probably accustomed to on other platforms. We have given tips for making sure that you have an adequate system to handle an Oracle9*i* installation, and tips for using and troubleshooting the Oracle Universal Installer. Hints on getting the database creation right the first time included information on new features such as the system parameter file, multiple block sizes, system managed undo, and the default temporary tablespace. Finally, we wrapped everything up by discussing some of the vagaries of removing Oracle from a Windows 2000 system. In the next chapter, we will delve into more advanced topics, which will help you truly take the most advantage of Oracle9*i*'s power and flexibility on the Windows 2000 platform.

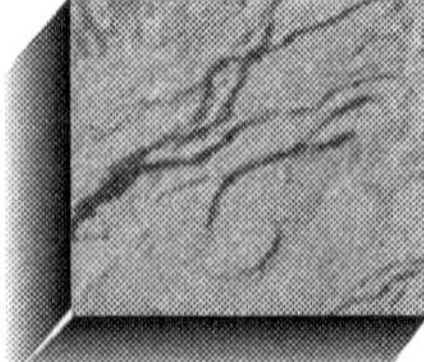

CHAPTER 5

Advanced Database Administration for Windows 2000

In this chapter, we discuss and explain the specific administration tasks associated with the Oracle database, and how to get the most out of each minute spent on these tasks. Although not meant to be definitive, this chapter dives into the specific administration tools provided on Windows 2000 as well as generic Oracle tools, with tips for using them effectively. We will go into detail on some of the uses for database templates in the Database Configuration Assistant, and other features such as the system parameter file. In addition, we will take a look at Oracle's implementation in the Windows memory architecture, discussing how to manage and monitor threads and get the most out of the memory available. We will give tips on using the Performance Monitor to tune and diagnose problems, as well as tips on using other utilities to accomplish the same ends. Finally, we end up with discussion of some of the more interesting new features in Oracle9i that are generic to all platforms. Tips in this chapter cover the following topics:

- Using database templates on Windows 2000
- Local extent management
- Using Oracle Managed Files
- What is an SPFILE?
- Understanding SGA_MAX_SIZE and the dynamic SGA
- Understanding memory usage on Windows 2000
- Memory per connection
- Monitoring memory usage within the database
- Monitoring memory usage at the OS
- Troubleshooting memory errors
- Making the most of the memory available
- Why use orastack?
- Tuning the SGA
- Going beyond 3GB (Oracle 8i only)
- Identifying and viewing threads
- Killing threads within the database
- Adding Oracle-specific counters to the Performance Monitor
- Using pviewer and tlist

- Monitoring CPU utilization
- Monitoring disk performance
- Viewing threads with Oracle Administration Assistant
- Configuring operating system authentication
- Reorganizing tables with DBMS_REDEFINITION
- Using transportable tablespaces with differing block sizes

Advanced Database Creation and Management

In the previous chapter, we discussed the basics of creating a database on Oracle9*i* for Windows 2000. We begin this chapter by going into more detail on some of the new features in Oracle9*i*—database templates, the SPFILE, dynamic resizing of the SGA, and Oracle Managed Files.

Using Database Templates on Windows 2000

New Feature in Oracle9*i*

As mentioned in Chapter 4, database templates are a new feature of Oracle9i. The primary purpose of database templates is to ease the creation of multiple similar databases, and transition databases from one system to another. Database templates are managed via the Database Configuration Assistant, but the templates themselves consist of files in the directory ORACLE_HOME\Assistants\dbca\templates. When you choose to create a new database from the first screen of the Database Assistant, the list of templates that shows up is based on the files in this directory.

In this directory, you will find files of three types: .dbc, .dbt, and .dfj. Files with the extensions .dbc and .dbt can be edited and viewed via Wordpad. The .dbt files are configuration files that do not have datafiles associated with them—they are simply a guide to the creation of a new database, and files will be created via the execution of the **create database** command. On the other hand, the .dbc files are also configuration files, but they are associated with a set of jarred (compressed) datafiles in a .dfj file. Creating a database with one of these templates will result in the actual datafiles being uncompressed from the associated .dfj file and copied to a location specified by the roadmap provided in the .dbc file.

Why Use Database Templates?

So, why would one need database templates? Several reasons come to mind. First, a template can be used to duplicate your database structure and create similar databases on numerous machines. To do this, simply choose Manage Templates from the first screen of the DBCA, and create a database template that includes the structure of an existing database. If the directory structure on other machines will be different, select the option Convert File Locations to use OFA Structure. This will convert the file locations using the environment variables for ORACLE_BASE and ORACLE_HOME on the target machine, regardless of where those variables actually point. Once the template is created, copy the appropriate .dbt file over to the target machine, placing the file in the ORACLE_HOME\Assistants\dbca\templates directory. Now, when the Database Configuration Assistant is run on the target, choose to create a new database. You will see your template on the new machine as one of the choices. This is a very handy way to mass-produce databases on multiple machines with the same structure.

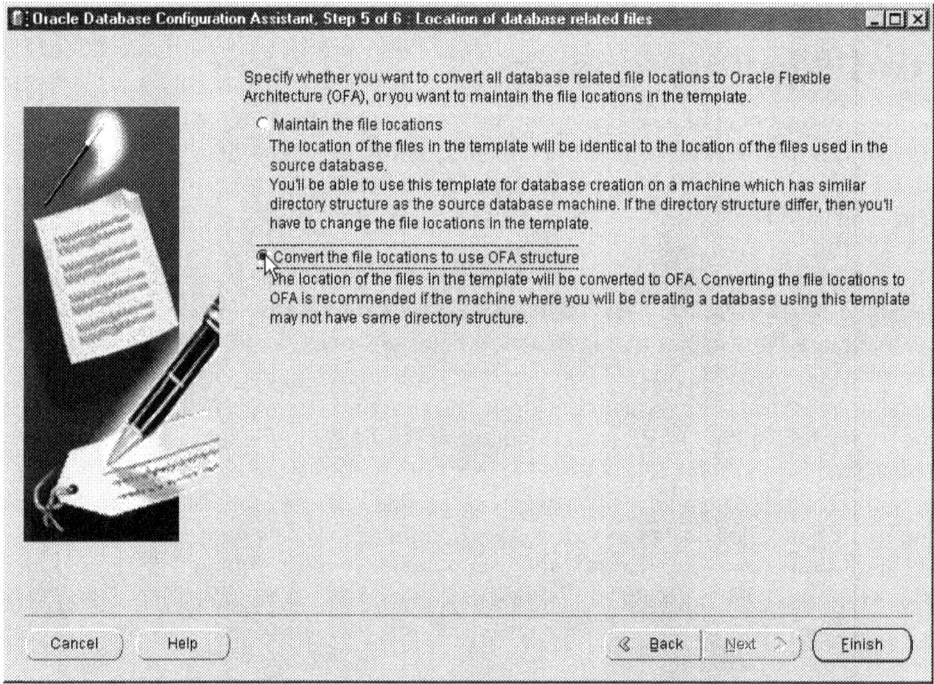

Copying Your Database via Database Templates

Another option when creating the template is to choose structure as well as data. This will actually jar (compress) all of the datafiles for your database and put them in one large file with the .dfj (datafile jar) extension. You can then copy this file, along with the associated config file (.dbc), over to a new machine, and have your data move with it. This is ideal for moving from a test to a production environment, or back again, when you want to test on live data. However, the usefulness of this depends on the size of your database, as the .dfj files for a very large database can become unwieldy to manage, and depends on free space available on the drive containing the ORACLE_HOME.

TIP

If you choose to convert the file locations using OFA structure, the locations are all defined using environment variables. This allows a template file with a .dbt extension to be used on any platform to create the structure of a database. However, since the actual datafiles themselves are platform specific, you cannot use the .dbc and .dfj files to move the actual database itself from one platform to another—you can only move a database and its associated files if the target is the same platform as the original database. For purposes of moving datafiles, Windows NT and Windows 2000 are considered the same platform, so copying datafiles from a Windows NT system to a Windows 2000 system, and vice versa, is supported and will work.

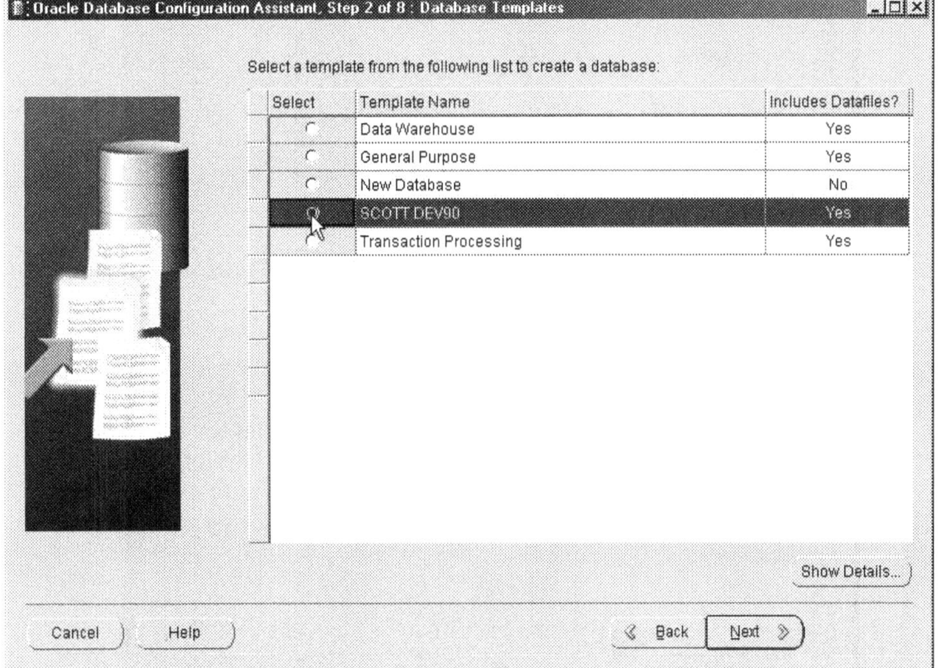

Local Extent Management

Local extent management refers to how extents are allocated and managed in a given tablespace. The choices are dictionary managed versus locally managed.

Dictionary managed extents are tracked through the data dictionary in tables such as SYS.FET$ (Free Extent Table) and SYS.UET$ (Used Extent Table). Therefore, any time new segments are allocated or released, we must engage in DML (inserts, updates, and deletes) against these tables in the data dictionary. If extent sizes are poorly tuned, or if we have a case like a temporary tablespace, where many segments are being allocated and deallocated, excessive DML can occur against the data dictionary. This, in turn, can result in a space transaction (ST) enqueue wait, as other processes may need to engage in the same type of operations.

Locally managed extents are managed within the datafile itself, eliminating the need to access the data dictionary for this information. The default for extents is AUTOALLOCATE, which means that Oracle determines the size of the extents for you using bitmaps in the headers of the files themselves. If you specify a storage clause for an object created in a locally managed tablespace, Oracle will take the values of INITIAL, NEXT, and MINEXTENTS and use those values to calculate the initial size of the object's segment. On the other hand, you can specify uniform extent sizes for the tablespace, in which case all extents in the tablespace will be of the same size:

```
SQL> create tablespace TEST_LOCAL
   datafile 'D:\ORACLE\ORADATA\PROD90\TEST_LOCAL.DBF' size 10M
   EXTENT MANAGEMENT LOCAL UNIFORM SIZE 2M;
```

The key thing to note is that starting with Oracle9i, tablespaces default to locally managed; whereas in previous releases, the default was dictionary managed. A tablespace can be moved from local to dictionary managed, or vice versa, using the DBMS_SPACE_ADMIN package:

```
SQL> execute dbms_space_admin.tablespace_migrate_to_local('USERS');
PL/SQL procedure successfully completed.
SQL> execute dbms_space_admin.tablespace_migrate_from_local('USERS');
PL/SQL procedure successfully completed.
SQL>
```

Views used for tracking extent usage in a locally managed tablespace are DBA_LMT_FREE_SPACE (free extents in all locally managed tablespaces) and DBA_LMT_USED_EXTENTS (all extents in the locally managed tablespaces). These are useful in particular for locally managed temporary tablespaces to track sort extent usage and availability.

Oracle Managed Files

Another new feature in 9i is the concept of Oracle Managed Files, or OMF. As an overview, OMF allows you to define the location of new datafiles that are added to the database via an init.ora parameter. This allows you to simplify the creation of tablespaces by leaving off the filename. So, for example, you could create a tablespace by simply saying:

```
SQL> Create tablespace omftest;
```

Locating and Naming Oracle Managed Files

By default, the command above will create a datafile that is 100MB in size, set to automatically extend, with a maximum size equal to the maximum number of blocks allowed in a datafile. But where will it put the file? This is determined by the init.ora parameter DB_CREATE_FILE_DEST, which can be modified on-the-fly via an **alter system** or an **alter session** command. Set this equal to a directory on the server that you have access to, making sure that the directory exists (otherwise the command will fail). Then, when a tablespace is created or a datafile is added to the tablespace, the file will be placed in this directory.

The same can be accomplished for log files via the parameter DB_CREATE_ONLINE_LOG_DEST_*n*, where *n* is the number assigned to the destination, ranging from 1 to 5. You can specify multiple online log destinations in the init.ora file, as well as a destination for datafiles, as follows:

```
DB_CREATE_FILE_DEST=D:\Oracle\oradata\prod90
DB_CREATE_ONLINE_LOG_DEST_1=D:\Oracle\oradata\prod90
DB_CREATE_ONLINE_LOG_DEST_2=E:\Oracle\oradata\prod90
DB_CREATE_ONLINE_LOG_DEST_3=F:\Oracle\oradata\prod90
```

Then a subsequent command to add a log file group does not need to have multiple members specified:

```
SQL>alter database add logfile group 3;
```

Instead, the preceding command will simply place one log member in each destination defined. Again, the default size is 100MB. The default size of the file for either command can be changed by adding the size keyword and a file size (for datafiles, you must also use the DATAFILE keyword) as shown in this example:

```
SQL>alter database add logfile group 4 size 50m;
```

or

```
SQL>create tablespace omftest2 datafile size 50m;
```

By leaving the filename off, the filenames themselves are determined by Oracle. You do not have say so in the name of a file. The filename will start with ORA_, include the TABLESPACE_NAME, and end with an 8-character, unique string,

determined by the RDBMS. Thus, in our example, a datafile will end up being named something like this:

```
D:\ORACLE\ORADATA\PROD90\ORA_OMFTEST2_ZR09SH00.DBF
```

Note that if you specify a name for the file but do not specify a directory, the file is not considered an Oracle Managed File, and you *must* specify a size. The file will *not* be placed in the directory defined by DB_CREATE_FILE_DEST—instead, the file will be put in the ORACLE_HOME\Database directory.

Dropping Oracle Managed Files

One of the features of OMF is that when the tablespace is dropped, Oracle Managed Files are automatically deleted from the operating system. With regular files, a **drop tablespace** command will leave the file on the operating system, to be deleted later. When a tablespace created with Oracle Managed Files is dropped, the files will always be deleted from the operating system, with no special syntax required. If a tablespace is comprised of both types of files (regular and OMF), then only the OMF files are deleted. In addition, dropping a log file group that was created using OMF will also result in the log files being deleted from the operating system.

You can accomplish this same behavior on *any* tablespace by using new syntax to include datafiles on a drop:

```
SQL> drop tablespace TOOLS including contents and datafiles;
```

Note that you must specify "including contents and datafiles"—you cannot just say "including datafiles." Thus, it is not possible to drop the files without also dropping the metadata about the objects from the data dictionary. Dropping a single datafile from the database via the command **alter database datafile xxxx offline drop;** will not cause the datafile to be deleted from the OS because Oracle still maintains metadata about objects in that file, and the file can still be recovered, even after an offline drop.

SPFILE

Oracle9i allows you to change more parameters than ever on-the-fly, without the need to restart the database; but this leaves the database administrator in a situation of needing to remember to change the parameter file before the next time the database is restarted. The *system parameter file* (*SPFILE*) is a way to allow parameters that have been changed dynamically to be written out to the parameter file at the same time so that they become permanent. This is accomplished via the new SCOPE argument in the **alter system** command. If this argument is left off an **alter system** command, and the database was started with a PFILE, then SCOPE will default to

MEMORY ONLY, meaning the value will take effect immediately, but the next restart will revert to the value in the PFILE.

Alternatively, if the database was started with an SPFILE, you can specify a scope of SPFILE, or a scope of BOTH. For example, say we issue the following command:

```
SQL>alter system set db_create_file_dest='E:\oracle\oradata\PROD90'
SCOPE = BOTH;
```

This is an indication that we want the parameter to take effect immediately (memory), and we also want it written to the SPFILE so that the next time we restart the system; it will remain in place. If the database was actually started with an SPFILE as opposed to a regular parameter file, and if you leave the SCOPE argument off, then the default value of SCOPE for an **alter system** command switches to BOTH.

In order for the SPFILE to be specified as part of the SCOPE argument in an **alter session** command, the database must have been started with an SPFILE. You can determine if this is the case by issuing the **show parameter** command. If the value column is blank, then a regular PFILE was used to start the instance:

```
SQL>show parameter spfile
NAME            TYPE     VALUE
-------------- -------- -----------------------------------------
spfile          string  %ORACLE_HOME%\DATABASE\SPFILE%ORACLE_SID%.ORA
```

As you can see, another advantage of the SPFILE is that it provides the ability to see from within the database what parameter file was used, making it more a part of the database than in previous releases. If you start up the database with just the regular init<sid>.ora file, then once the database has been started up, information on which parameter file was used is gone. On the other hand, with the SPFILE, that information can be checked with the **show parameter** command for as long as the instance is up.

When Is the SPFILE Used?

The SPFILE presents an opportunity for confusion as to which file is actually used to start up the database. A **startup** command from SQL*Plus, with no parameters, looks first in the ORACLE_HOME\Database directory for spfile<sid>.ora. Next, it looks for a file simply called spfile.ora. Finally, if neither of these files exists, the **startup** command will look for the init<sid>.ora, as was always the case in previous versions. So, if you specify startup by itself, the SPFILE will be used if it exists, and init<sid>.ora will be ignored.

On the other hand, if you specify STARTUP PFILE=xxxx;, then whatever parameter file you specify will be used, and the SPFILE will be ignored. Having the database automatically started by setting the ORA_<sidname>_AUTOSTART=TRUE and ORA_<sidname>_PFILE=<full path to the PFILE> values in the Registry is the equivalent to specifying STARTUP PFILE=xxxx from the command line. Therefore, when the database is automatically started via the parameters in the Registry, the SPFILE will not be used. Thus, if you allow the database to be automatically started, it could very well give you different parameters than you would get by specifying a simple startup from the command line, depending on whether or not the SPFILE exists.

Eliminating Confusion on the SPFILE

If you want to use an SPFILE, you need to develop a strategy to eliminate confusion on which file is used to start up the database. Unfortunately, you cannot specify the SPFILE itself in the AUTOSTART section of the Registry. Attempting to do so will result in the error message ORA-1078: "Failure in processing system parameters." This will be seen in the ORADIM.LOG, as discussed in Chapter 4. Thus, the simplest way to accomplish this is to create an init<sidname>.ora file in the ORACLE_HOME\Database directory. This file should contain *only* an SPFILE= entry, as shown in the following example, which in turn points to the system parameter file:

```
###Contents of D:\Oracle\ora90\database\initprod90.ora
SPFILE=D:\oracle\ora90\database\SPFILEPROD90.ORA
```

Now you can specify the init<sid>.ora in the Registry, guaranteeing that the AUTOSTART will read the SPFILE, and you will get the same results from the command line with a normal **startup** command in SQL*Plus. Any time that values are changed via the **alter system** command, if you specify SCOPE=SPFILE, the value will now be preserved in the SPFILE used to start up the database.

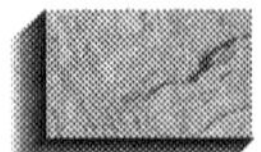

NOTE
The SPFILE can be viewed by using Wordpad, but it is a binary file. You should not attempt to edit the SPFILE manually—only change values by issuing the ***alter system*** *command, with SCOPE=SPFILE or SCOPE=BOTH. As such, it is important to make a backup of this file and/or have a normal parameter file handy to use for startup. That way, if something goes wrong with the SPFILE, you can still start the database up and then re-create the SPFILE.*

Creating an SPFILE After Database Creation

The Database Configuration Assistant gives you the opportunity to create the SPFILE under the File Locations tab, as discussed in Chapter 4. By default, the box beside the "Create persistent initialization parameters file (spfile)" option will be checked.

If you do not choose to do this at database creation time, you can create an SPFILE later by issuing the **create SPFILE** command, as seen here:

```
SQL>CREATE SPFILE ='d:\oracle\ora90\database\SPFILEPROD90.ORA'
FROM PFILE='d:\oracle\ora90\database\initPROD90.ora';
```

If you do not specify the name of the SPFILE, it will be placed in the default location of ORACLE_HOME\Database, and will be called spfile<sidname>.ora.

New Feature in Oracle9i

Using SGA_MAX_SIZE and the Dynamic SGA

As mentioned in Chapter 4, components of the SGA can be dynamically resized via the **alter system** command. However, you are still constrained by the fact that your total SGA size cannot go beyond the value set for SGA_MAX_SIZE, a new parameter introduced in Oracle9i. If you do not set this parameter at startup, SGA_MAX_SIZE will default to the total value of your SGA, and this parameter *cannot* be altered dynamically. Therefore, you cannot initially increase any component of the SGA (for example, DB_CACHE_SIZE) without first shrinking another component (for example, SHARED_POOL_SIZE). As noted in Chapter 4, if you want to define a buffer cache for a nondefault block size, you must first ensure that you have room to fit the new buffer cache within the free memory available under SGA_MAX_SIZE.

Modifying SGA_MAX_SIZE

You can only change the size of SGA_MAX_SIZE by modifying the init.ora file and restarting the instance. If you are using an SPFILE, you should alter the parameter as such:

```
SQL>alter system set sga_max_size = 3021414568 SCOPE=SPFILE;
```

This will write the new value out to the SPFILE so that it will take effect the next time the instance is restarted. If you try to specify a SCOPE of MEMORY or BOTH, you will receive an ORA-2095 error indicating that the parameter cannot be changed on-the-fly.

Note that on Windows NT and 2000, if you set a higher value for SGA_MAX_SIZE than what you are currently using for the total SGA, this memory is still reserved by the OS at startup time and will still count against the total memory that can be addressed by the process, regardless of whether it is being used. We will discuss this in more detail in the next section, "Oracle Memory Usage on Windows 2000." This can lead to wasting of memory resources. Therefore, you may want to avoid setting this in your production environment unless you intend to expand the SGA soon. On the other hand, it can be useful in a test environment where you want to measure performance and hit ratios with different values set, prior to settling on final numbers that are best for your environment.

NOTE
Even though some documents say that LARGE_POOL_SIZE and JAVA_POOL_SIZE can be dynamically changed, in the initial release of Oracle9i, this is not the case. Other values, such as SHARED_POOL_SIZE, DB_CACHE_SIZE, and so on, can be modified dynamically; but LARGE_POOL_SIZE and JAVA_POOL_SIZE cannot. This may change in later 9i releases.

Oracle Memory Usage on Windows 2000

Memory so often seems to be the main constraint when trying to increase the performance of any application, but particularly a database. So often the answer to improving performance is, "You need to add more RAM." If only it were that simple. Just how much RAM can you add, and how do you make the most of the memory that you have? The next section will be invaluable in answering these questions.

Oracle in the Windows Memory Architecture

As we have mentioned several times in earlier chapters, a single process on the Windows 2000 platform can address a total of 4GB, and, by default, half of this is reserved for the OS. This means that a single Oracle instance, running as a single process, can address 2GB of RAM. Once you have hit this limit, you oftens seem to hit a brick wall. As mentioned in earlier chapters, when 64-bit Oracle on Windows arrives, this will cease to be a problem. Until this occurs, though, this limitation of the 32-bit Windows world is one of the most crucial to understand for users on the Windows 2000 platform. Thus, we will devote the next section to strategies for coaxing, cursing, and cajoling as much as possible from your Oracle database, given the constraints of today's world.

Give Oracle All the Memory You've Got

In Chapter 1, we recommend running Windows 2000 Advanced Server for several reasons, but one of the primary reasons is the ability to increase the memory available to the process from 2GB to 3GB. This is referred to as 4GT, or 4-gigabyte tuning, because it changes the distribution of memory within the 4GB process address space, giving only 1GB to the OS, and leaving the rest for the process. The feat is accomplished by adding a switch to the boot.ini file (as mentioned in Chapter 1).

This switch works *only* on machines running Windows 2000 Advanced Server or Windows 2000 Datacenter Server. It will have no effect on machines running Windows 2000 Standard Server or Windows 2000 Professional. (Note that this switch *can* also be used on Windows NT 4.0 Enterprise Edition.)

To make this change, you will first need to be able to view the boot.ini file. To see the file, choose Folder Options from the Tools menu in Explorer, and navigate to the View tab. Uncheck the box next to Hide protected operating system files to deselect the option. This will make the boot.ini file visible in Explorer. The file can be found at the root of your boot partition, normally drive C:. Make a backup of the file, and then add the following switch (defined in **bold**) under the [operating systems] section of the boot.ini file:

```
[boot loader]
timeout=30
default=multi(0)disk(0)rdisk(0)partition(2)\WINNT
[operating systems]
multi(0)disk(0)rdisk(0)partition(2)\WINNT="Microsoft Windows 2000
Advanced Server" /fastdetect /3GB /PAE
```

For the rest of this chapter, we will assume that you have made this change, and thus assume that your address space limit for the process is 3GB. If you have not or cannot change this value (because you are not on Advanced Server, for example), then please be aware that whenever we refer to the 3GB memory limit, you must substitute 2GB in its place.

Configuring Applications for 3GB

In order to take advantage of this switch, an executable must have the bit IMAGE_FILE_LARGE_ADDRESS_AWARE set in the image header of the executable. Running the imagecfg.exe utility, which is available from the Windows 2000 Resource Kit, sets this bit:

```
C:\>imagecfg -l oracle.exe
```

The executable for Oracle9i (oracle.exe) should have this bit set already. However, since patches to the RDBMS generally involve copying a new image of oracle.exe, there have been times when the bit was not set correctly at the factory. If it appears that Oracle is not fully utilizing the memory available, it will not hurt to rerun this utility. (Of course, all databases need to be shut down when doing so.)

Where Did All of That Memory Go?

After having set the /3GB switch, you have increased addressable memory by 50 percent, from 2GB to 3GB. But what does this mean? What is using this memory?

Memory Usage at Startup To begin with, just the very act of starting OracleService<sid> will consume a certain amount of process overhead for the executable itself. With each release of Oracle, this number goes up. On Oracle8i, the process alone used about 35MB of RAM, but on Oracle9i, we have observed this to be around 65MB, without even starting the instance.

Once the instance is started, you must allocate memory for the SGA, of course. As noted previously, this total value is equivalent to SGA_MAX_SIZE. If you have not set SGA_MAX_SIZE, it is calculated by adding the values for all buffer caches for the various block sizes in use in your database, LARGE_POOL, SHARED_POOL, JAVA_POOL, and LOG_BUFFERS. You can find the size of the SGA by querying the view V$SGA, like so:

```
SQL>select sum(value) from v$sga;
SUM(VALUE)
----------
202141568
```

Next, you need to account for threads in the database. When the database is started up, as we discussed in Chapter 2, several threads are allocated at the outset, such as threads for SMON, PMON, DBWR, LGWR, and so on. In addition, depending on various init.ora settings, you may see an ARCH thread for archiving, an SNP*x* thread for each JOB_QUEUE_PROCESSES value, and EMN*x* threads for AQ_TM_PROCESSES values. Therefore, it would not be unusual to see an Oracle instance that is just started up with an SGA of, say, 200MB, yet is using over 300MB in total memory address space due to the process overhead and the various background threads awakened during startup.

Stack Space for User Connections Finally, you need to account for users who will connect to the database once it has opened. Again, each user connection is a thread of the main oracle.exe process. How much memory does each thread consume? A quick answer to that question is about 3MB per connection. However, that does not really do justice to reality. This number is variable and includes stack space (both reserved and committed), as well as PGA and UGA memory.

Refer back to Chapter 1 and the discussion about reserved and committed memory. Reserved space is the amount of virtual address space that is reserved for the thread to grow. The committed space is that amount of the reserved space that is actually backed by physical memory (or page file) when the thread is created. By default, on Windows 2000, each thread that is created within the Oracle executable allocates 1MB of stack space. Only 4KB of this stack space is actually committed memory, so the rest of the stack has no physical backing. However, the entire stack space of each thread still counts against the 3GB limit for the oracle.exe process.

PGA Memory In addition to the stack space, each thread consumes space for the PGA, or Program Global Area, which is an area within the memory address space of the Oracle executable used exclusively for that particular connection. This is a variable portion of memory and will likely be the largest chunk of memory allocated for a given thread using dedicated connections (rather than MTS). How much memory is allocated depends primarily on the following parameters:

- SORT_AREA_SIZE
- HASH_AREA_SIZE
- CREATE_BITMAP_AREA_SIZE
- BITMAP_MERGE_AREA_SIZE

These parameters define how much memory is allocated on a per-session basis for dedicated sessions. Note that the memory is not actually allocated, however, unless the operations take place, so if you set CREATE_BITMAP_AREA_SIZE to 20MB, but you only have one user who is creating bitmapped indices, then only that user is allocating that memory.

Monitoring PGA and UGA Memory Usage

The views V$SYSSTAT and V$SESSTAT contain statistical information on connected sessions. V$SYSSTAT serves two purposes. First, it contains the key values, with the name column telling you which statistic numbers do what:

```
SQL> column name format a35
SQL> select * from v$sysstat where name like '%pga%';
STATISTIC# NAME                                     CLASS      VALUE
---------- ----------------------------------- ---------- ----------
        20 session pga memory                           1   16452980
        21 session pga memory max                       1   16452980
```

Second, the value column gives you the overall system-wide total for that particular statistic. If you want to monitor PGA memory on a per-session basis, you would query V$SESSTAT and look at statistic #20 or #21:

```
SQL> select * from v$sesstat where statistic# in (20,21) order by value;
```

By the same token, statistics 15 and 16 show UGA memory:

```
SQL> select statistic#, name from v$sysstat where name like '%uga%';
STATISTIC# NAME
---------- ----------------------------------------------------------------
        15 session uga memory
        16 session uga memory max
```

Starting with Oracle9i, additional columns have been added to the V$PROCESS view to allow you to see PGA memory usage directly, without the need to join to

V$SESSION. The columns are PGA_USED_MEM, PGA_ALLOC_MEM, and PGA_MAX_MEM. Although not an exact match, these columns should give you similar values to what you would see in V$SESSTAT.

Monitor Memory Usage from Outside the Database

So, how do you monitor the memory usage on a Windows 2000 system? There are a couple of different ways. The most common method is to use the Performance Monitor, which comes with Windows 2000.

Monitoring Memory Using Windows 2000 Performance Monitor

Access this via Start | Programs | Administrative Tools | Performance. Be sure that you have the System Monitor highlighted on the left-hand side. To monitor memory, first click the plus sign (+) across the top. This will open the dialog box to add counters to the chart. As you can see, you can monitor a remote computer or a local computer. (We will go into more detail about the Performance Monitor in the section "Using the Performance Monitor" later in this chapter).

Under Performance Object, select Process, and from the list of counters choose Virtual Bytes. On the right-hand side, select Oracle from the list of (process) instances, and click the Add button to begin charting the virtual bytes for the process (see Figure 5-1). This value, Virtual Bytes, gives you the accurate count of all memory being addressed by the oracle.exe process. If you look at the Mem Usage column

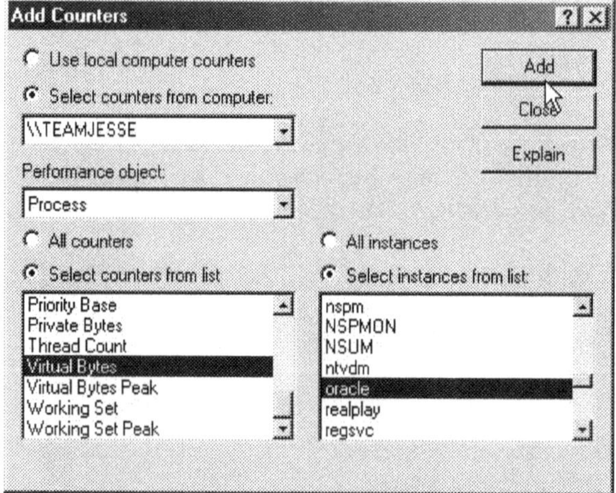

FIGURE 5-1. *Monitoring virtual bytes for oracle.exe*

in Task Manager, you will only see the working set, or the amount of main memory currently in use. On the other hand, the VM Size column in Task Manager still does not give you the full picture, because it shows only committed memory. The Virtual Bytes counter in Performance Monitor is the true picture of all memory consumption, including reserved and committed memory being used by the process. This is the number to monitor for accuracy as you are approaching the 3GB- per- process limit on Windows 2000.

Monitoring Memory with pviewer

Recall from Chapter 3 that pviewer is one of the utilities available by installing tools from the \SUPPORT folder on the Windows 2000 CD-ROM. The pviewer utility will give you an accurate count of total virtual bytes, if you highlight the oracle process and choose Memory Detail. This will give you a snapshot of various components of memory usage, including committed memory. Under Virtual Memory Counts, Virtual Size will show the total memory that has been addressed by the process. This number should match the Virtual Bytes value in the Performance Monitor (see Figure 5-2). The drawback of pviewer is that it is not a dynamic look at memory. To get the most current information, you must go back to the main page and choose Refresh.

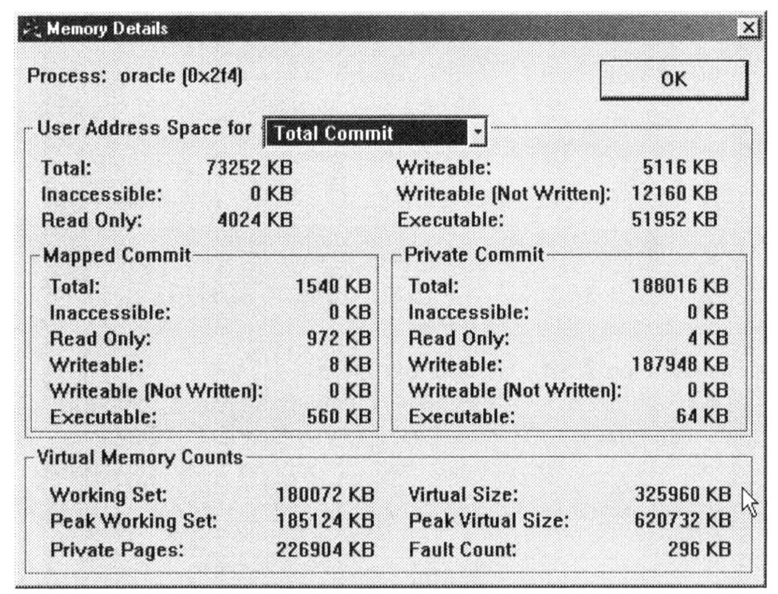

FIGURE 5-2. *Memory details in pviewer*

Diagnosing Memory Errors: ORA-12500, ORA-12540, ORA-4030, and ORA-4031

As you approach the per-process limit, new connections are likely to fail with an ORA-12500 or an ORA-12540 error. These errors are usually an indication that you are running out of process address space, and no more connections can be made due to a lack of resources. Note that due to memory fragmentation, it is likely that you will start to receive these errors before you have reached the true maximum memory usage for the process (that is, it may be possible to start seeing ORA-12500 errors when the Virtual Bytes value is around 2.7GB, or even a bit lower). If you do not have enough physical memory (combining RAM and page file) to provide a full 3GB address space, then you will start to see errors whenever the total memory available to the OS has been maxed out.

An ORA-4030 error is another indicator that the process has run out of operating system memory to address. Do not confuse the ORA-4030 error with an ORA-4031 error, which is usually an indication that you are running low on SHARED_POOL memory within the database's SGA.

Use Your Memory Wisely

If you are running into the preceding errors, you will need to evaluate the overall memory usage of the instance. To reduce memory usage or fit it to your needs, you have a few choices:

- Reduce the number of connections to the database by using a multithreaded server (also referred to as Shared Servers, as described in Chapter 7).
- Reduce the stack size of each connection.
- Reduce the PGA usage of each session.
- Reduce the size of the SGA.
- Use AWE Windows Memory for DB_BLOCK_BUFFERS (8.1.x only).

Using orastack to Reduce the Stack Size

To view the current stack size of a given executable, you can run the orastack utility, which comes with Oracle9i. The orastack utility will be in the ORACLE_HOME\bin directory, which should be part of your path. Simply run orastack and pass the executable name:

```
D:\oracle\ora90\bin>orastack tnslsnr.exe

Dump of file tnslsnr.exe

Current Reserved Memory per Thread  = 1048576
Current Committed Memory per Thread = 4096
```

The orastack utility's true merit comes into play when it is used to change the stack size. Note that the process must be stopped in order for the stack size to be changed:

```
D:\>net stop oracleorahome90tnslistener
The OracleOraHome90TNSListener service is stopping.
The OracleOraHome90TNSListener service was stopped successfully.

D:\>orastack D:\oracle\ora90\bin\tnslsnr.exe 500000
Dump of file D:\oracle\ora90\bin\tnslsnr.exe

Current Reserved Memory per Thread  = 1048576
Current Committed Memory per Thread = 4096

New Reserved Memory per Thread = 500000

D:\>
```


Which Executables Should You Reduce the Stack Size For? Usually, if you are bumping up against the process memory limit, it is because you are attempting to make user connections numbering in the hundreds or even thousands. Since most of these threads are created by the Listener via incoming net connections, running orastack on the tnslsnr.exe executable will give you the most bang for your buck. Running orastack against the Oracle executable itself will change the stack for background threads (SMON, PMON, and so on), parallel query slaves, and MTS (Shared Server) dispatchers and servers. However, if you are using MTS, be aware that by running orastack on the actual oracle.exe itself, you will reduce the stack size of each of these shared servers and dispatchers. Finally, you can run orastack against any executables that connect directly via a bequeath connection. SQL*Plus is one example. This may be worthwhile if you are generating lots of connections locally with SQL*Plus.

Determining an Appropriate Stack Size As a general rule, even though Oracle reserves 1MB of stack space, less than 500KB is needed for normal, day-to-day operations. You may be able to reduce the stack size to as low as 300KB without any impact. However, there are times when certain recursive operations, such as inserts or updates that fire off several nested triggers, may require more stack space. If you lower the stack too much, you may end up with a stack overrun, which will result in an ORA-3113 error. Therefore, you should thoroughly test different values of stack size before implementing a change in production. And, yes, orastack can be used to *increase* the stack size if needed.

Reducing PGA Memory Used

Recall the parameters that affect the size of the PGA from our discussion in the section "PGA Memory." Of these, SORT_AREA_SIZE is probably the best candidate for tuning.

Monitoring Sort Activity You can monitor sort activity on your system with the following query:

```
SQL> select name, value from v$sysstat where name like '%sorts%';
NAME                                                                  VALUE
---------------------------------------------------------------- ----------
sorts (memory)                                                        13203
sorts (disk)                                                           1910
sorts (rows)                                                       32504307
```

If you observe that a significant number of sorts are already being done in memory, you may be able to reduce SORT_AREA_SIZE. On the other hand, you may find that your SORT_AREA_SIZE is too small, and needs to be increased if too many sorts are going to disk. In many cases, a large reduction or large increase in SORT_AREA_SIZE may have little impact on how many sorts occur on disk because the majority of sorts may be very small, whereas larger sorts are so large that they will never fully fit into memory. You should monitor sort activity on an ongoing basis, with a variety of different values for SORT_AREA_SIZE, in order to settle on the best value for your system.

PGA_AGGREGATE_TARGET Oracle9i introduces a new parameter called PGA_AGGREGATE_TARGET, which enables you to avoid having to tune individual parameters associated with the PGA. The theory behind this parameter is that the DBA can define the total maximum PGA being used by all sessions, instance-wide. When this value is set in the init.ora file, WORKAREA_SIZE_POLICY defaults to AUTO, meaning Oracle automatically sizes the xxx_AREA_SIZE parameters listed in the earlier section on PGA memory, based on the load of the database. This automatic memory management should theoretically be more efficient than a shotgun approach of saying *all* users need *x* amount of SORT_AREA_SIZE or HASH_AREA_SIZE, and so on, since not all users behave the same. In addition, this provides the additional benefit of allowing the database administrator to know for certain the maximum PGA memory used within an instance, making it easier to determine how much memory can be used by other structures. The total PGA memory used may be less than, but should not exceed, the total defined by PGA_AGGREGATE_TARGET.

The following query from the *Oracle9i Performance Guide and Reference* will help you determine if you have set PGA_AGGREGATE_TARGET high enough, or if it is too high:

```
SQL> column profile format a40
SQL> column percentage format 9999
SQL> column cnt format 99999999
SQL> select name profile, cnt, decode(total, 0, 0, round(cnt*100/total))
  2  percentage from (SELECT name, value cnt, (sum(value) over ())
  3  total from v$sysstat where name like 'workarea exec%');
```

Here's a sample of the output you may see:

```
PROFILE                                        CNT PERCENTAGE
---------------------------------------- --------- ----------
workarea executions - optimal                17513         95
workarea executions - onepass                  922          5
workarea executions - multipass                  0          0
```

This output tells you if you need to change the setting of PGA_AGGREGATE_TARGET. You want to shoot for zero multipass executions and a low percentage of one-pass executions. If these numbers are too great, you may want to increase PGA_AGGREGATE_TARGET. If optimal work executions is 100 percent, then this is an indication that you can afford to reduce this value.

Additional new views in Oracle9i have been added to further assist in tuning PGA_AGGREGATE_TARGET:

- V$PGASTAT
- V$SQL_WORKAREA_ACTIVE
- V$SQL_WORKAREA

Refer to the *Oracle9i Database Performance Guide and Reference* for more information on tuning PGA_AGGREGATE_TARGET.

Reducing the SGA Size

Although reducing the SGA size is not the ideal solution, there may be times when it is appropriate. With monitoring of the correct information, you may find that your SGA is over allocated, and you can actually make better use of some of that memory by leaving it for PGA or stack space for connections. While this is not a comprehensive

section on tuning by any stretch of the imagination, here are some tips on monitoring various components of the SGA.

Monitoring POOL_SIZE Parameters During peak times, you want to see few reloads in V$LIBRARYCACHE, but you also want to see as little free memory as possible in V$SGASTAT:

```
SQL> select * from v$sgastat where name like '%free mem%';
POOL        NAME                            BYTES
----------- -------------------------- ----------
shared pool free memory                  58205868
java pool   free memory                  52916224
```

If you see high amounts of free memory during *peak* usage times, consider lowering the appropriate POOL_SIZE. However, you need to avoid excessive reloads, as seen in V$LIBRARYCACHE:

```
SQL> select namespace, gethitratio, reloads from v$librarycache;
```

Striking this balance is key to ensuring that you are getting the most out of your memory.

Tuning Redo Log Buffers Redo log buffers are a relatively small piece of the SGA. It is not likely you will conserve much memory by reducing the size of these buffers. On the other hand, a small increase can give you a large bang for your buck. To do so, use this query:

```
SQL> select name, value from v$sysstat where name like 'redo log space%';
NAME                                                                  VALUE
---------------------------------------------------------------- ----------
redo log space requests                                                   3
redo log space wait time                                                 39
```

A nonzero value for these parameters is normal, but they should be close to zero. High or increasing values could signify a problem. If this is observed, consider increasing the LOG_BUFFERS parameter.

Tuning the Buffer Cache Release 9i introduces the DB_CACHE_ADVICE parameter to assist in tuning the buffer cache. This parameter can be set dynamically to a value of ON or READY. This will populate values in the view V$DB_CACHE_ADVICE, but you must enable this parameter and run with a representative workload for a time in order for the view to be populated with useful data. Be aware that this will cause a slight performance hit and also increase the memory used in the SHARED_POOL, so do not leave the parameter set any longer than necessary. Also, do not attempt to tune the shared_pool_size while this parameter is enabled, as these SHARED_POOL results will be skewed.

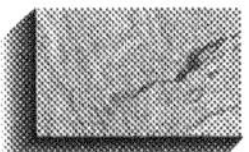

CAUTION

We do not recommend attempting to dynamically resize any SGA parameters with DB_CACHE_ADVICE turned on. This combination has been known to result in an ORA-600 error in early 9i releases. In addition, when it works as documented, you will still be gathering statistics for the original values of any BUFFER_CACHE parameters, so there is no sense in dynamically resizing the buffer cache while cache advice is turned on. Before dynamically changing the SGA, be sure to set DB_CACHE_ADVICE=OFF, and keep up on the latest 9i patches.

Here is a sample query that can be run against the V$DB_CACHE_ADVICE view to glean advice on sizing buffer caches. Note that we include the BLOCK_SIZE column, implying that there are multiple block sizes in use. V$DB_CACHE_ADVICE will show estimated read values for each block size that is in use in the database (defined by DB_nk_CACHE_SIZE, as noted in Chapter 4).

```
SQL>  SELECT size_for_estimate, buffers_for_estimate,
block_size, estd_physical_read_factor, estd_physical_reads
FROM V$DB_CACHE_ADVICE;
```

The output from this query will show the theoretical cache size (SIZE_FOR_ESTIMATE), how many buffers that equates to (BUFFERS_FOR_ESTIMATE), the block size (of course), and the estimated factor and actual number of reads that would occur with the various cache size estimates. We recommend formatting the columns as noted in the Oracle9i Performance Guide as such, to make it more readable:

```
column size_for_estimate    format 999,999,999,999 heading 'Cache Size (m)'
column buffers_for_estimate      format 999,999,999 heading 'Buffers'
column block_size                format 99999 heading 'Blk Size'
column estd_physical_read_factor format 999.90 heading 'Estd Phys|Read
Factor'
column estd_physical_reads       format 999,999,999 heading 'Estd Phys|
Reads'
```

Using Memory Efficiently

Thus, a portion of the output might look something like this:

```
                                            Estd Phys    Estd Phys
  Cache Size (m)      Buffers Blk Size Read Factor         Reads
---------------- ----------- -------- ----------- ------------
               7       3,402     2048        1.12       16,569
               7       3,780     2048        1.00       14,771
               8       4,158     2048         .98       14,471
               9       4,536     2048         .96       14,167
              10       4,914     2048         .94       13,864
```

Note the read factor on the line for 7M and 3780 buffers is 1.0, indicating this is the current value for DB_2K_CACHE_SIZE. (This is denoted by the fact that the Blk Size column is 2048—thus, we know this is for the 2KB cache.) This output indicates that with the current size of the 2KB buffer cache, the physical reads are 14,471. If you were to increase this cache to 10MB, physical reads would go down to 13,864, and if you decreased this cache by a mere 378 buffers, physical reads would go up by nearly 2000. The full output will show a larger range of estimated values, ranging from 10 percent of the current size to 200 percent of the current size, giving you a wide range of estimated values to choose from.

Trust but Verify Once you have settled on values for the various cache sizes, you can monitor their efficacy by querying V$SYSSTAT, with this query from Metalink Note #98891.1:

```
SQL> select 1 - (phy.value / (cur.value + con.value)) "HIT RATIO"
from v$sysstat cur, v$sysstat con, v$sysstat phy
where cur.name = 'db block gets'
and con.name = 'consistent gets'
and phy.name = 'physical reads';

HIT RATIO
----------
972280606
```

If the ratio is below 90 percent, you should consider increasing BUFFER_CACHE values and/or gathering more info with DB_CACHE_ADVICE enabled. A value in the high 90 percent range indicates that you may have room to reduce buffer cache memory without adversely affecting performance.

Going Beyond 3GB

So far our discussion has focused on maximizing the use of memory up to the 3GB limit provided under Windows 2000. However, as we alluded to in Chapter 1, it is possible to go beyond this limit. This is done by taking advantage of the Address Windowing Extensions API on Windows 2000. An application must be specifically coded to make use of this API. This support is *not* included in the first release of Oracle9i for Windows 2000 (plans are to reintroduce VLM support in 9i Release 2); however, it is possible to take advantage of this additional memory using release 8.1.6 or 8.1.7 on Windows 2000. Oracle currently recommends that if you require this additional memory, you stick with release 8.1.7 until such time as additional options become available on later releases of Oracle9i. Therefore, we will give a brief description of enabling AWE in 8.1.7 and what exactly this means.

AWE and Windows 2000

AWE allows you to use any additional RAM that you have on your system beyond 4GB. In order to take advantage of this, you *must* have more than 4GB of RAM, you must have an Intel Pentium Pro or later processor, and you must be running Windows 2000 Advanced Server or Windows 2000 Datacenter Server. As noted in Chapter 1, there are no special drivers needed for Windows 2000 to take advantage of AWE—the support is built into the OS.

To take advantage of this support, you must first boot the Windows 2000 machine with the /PAE switch placed in the boot.ini file. (Refer to the earlier example of boot.ini in this chapter in the section "Give Oracle All the Memory You've Got.") You must also ensure that the user account under which the Oracle8i Service runs has the privilege to lock pages in memory. Check this by going to Start | Programs | Administrative Tools | Local Security Policy. Under Local Policies, choose User Rights Assignment, double-click the privilege option Lock Pages in Memory, and add the appropriate account. If the service logon has not changed from the default, the account will be SYSTEM. Otherwise, select the appropriate logon ID and add the privilege. The OracleService<sid> will then need to be restarted.

AWE and Oracle

Specifically, the Oracle8i releases will allow you to configure space above the 4GB barrier for database block buffers *only*, thereby freeing up memory in the standard process address space (below the 3GB line) for user connections, PGA memory, and the various memory pools that make up the SGA.

In the init.ora file, you will need to set the parameter USE_INDIRECT_DATA_BUFFERS=TRUE. Without this parameter, Oracle will not address any memory above 4GB. Next determine the *total* amount of memory that you will require for the buffer cache, and set the values for DB_BLOCK_SIZE and DB_BLOCK_BUFFERS appropriately. So, for example, if you determine that you need a buffer cache that is 6GB in total size, and you have a DB_BLOCK_SIZE of 16,384, you would set DB_BLOCK_BUFFERS to approximately 250,000. Therefore, your total buffer cache would be 16,384×375,000 = 6,144,000,000, or approximately 6GB. (Remember,

AWE only applies in 8.1.x at this time, and we must define the buffer cache using the number of DB_BLOCK_BUFFERS in releases prior to 9i.)

Next, you will need to set the Registry parameter AWE_WINDOW_MEMORY in the appropriate key for your ORACLE_HOME—that is, HKLM\Software\Oracle\HOME0. This parameter is specified in bytes and, if not set, will default to 1GB. What you are doing by setting this value is determining how much of the total buffer cache should be treated as normal memory, coming from the 3GB process address space. Continuing with the preceding example, by taking the default of 1GB for AWE_WINDOW_MEMORY, you are saying that out of the 6GB of total buffer cache space, you want 1GB to be treated as normal memory and the remaining 5GB of the buffer cache to come from the address space above the 4GB barrier. You will want as many buffers as possible to be kept in the normal address space, since accessing buffers beyond 4GB is slower than accessing virtual address space buffers (though still faster than incurring a disk I/O operation).

Troubleshooting Memory Problems Related to AWE Window Memory

You should be aware that every block buffer *above* the 4GB barrier requires a header in the normal address space of approximately 200 bytes. So, in our example, we would have around 312,000 buffer headers, pointing to buffers in the extended address space, each taking up about 200 bytes, or roughly 80MB of memory. With a smaller block size, this number could be significantly higher. Thus, you must ensure that these headers; the value for AWE_WINDOW_MEMORY; and all of the other memory requirements for the oracle.exe process, including the code, the rest of the SGA components, all PGA memory, and the stack for each user connection, will fit into the normal 3GB virtual address space for the process.

Be sure that you have enough physical memory to handle the remainder of DB_BLOCK_BUFFERS beyond AWE_WINDOW_MEMORY. In our example, we defined a buffer cache of 6GB, with 1GB coming out of the normal address space. The remaining 5GB must come out of memory above and beyond the 4GB of system and process address space available to the process as a whole. Therefore, this example would only work on a machine with at least 9GB of RAM. You should also leave some room to account for fragmentation and other processes using memory. Only one process can access this additional memory at a time.

As mentioned, the /PAE switch can only be used with more than 4GB of RAM, but you can simulate this behavior with less memory by setting the value of MAXMEM in boot.ini. Setting this value to 2GB, as demonstrated here, will imply that any memory above 2GB is to be reserved for AWE memory:

```
multi(0)disk(0)rdisk(0)partition(1)\WINNT="Microsoft Windows 2000 Advanced
Server" /fastdetect /PAE /MAXMEM:2048
```

The focus of these tips is to help ensure that you are not only using all of the memory available to you, but also using it in the most efficient manner. Resources are always scarce in the real world, and memory can sometimes be the scarcest of all. Not wasting it is as important as making sure that you have enough, and the preceding section should give you a head start in dealing with the necessary choices and tradeoffs to make the most of what you have. In the next section, we will look at tips for monitoring and tuning other aspects of your system.

Using the Performance Monitor

We mentioned the Performance Monitor briefly in the section "Monitoring Memory Using Windows 2000 Performance Monitor," and also in Chapter 3. Aside from monitoring memory usage, the Performance Monitor can be used to monitor and log most of the essential performance information needed to tune your system. Here, we will briefly describe the essentials of understanding the Performance Monitor, and how to use it to your advantage with your Oracle database.

Understanding and Using the Performance Monitor

The System Monitor is the tool that allows you to view what is currently happening on a system. Counters are added by clicking the plus sign (+) on the toolbar (see Figure 5-3). This brings up the Add Counters dialog box, which allows you to choose objects you want to monitor (process, thread, disk, processor, and so on) on a particular computer. The Add Counters dialog box, shown earlier in Figure 5-1, lets you choose what you specifically want to monitor in regard to that object. Clicking the Explain button will give you more detail on what is monitored by a particular counter. Finally, the list of instances in the Add Counters dialog box will allow you to choose which specific object you are monitoring. In the case of threads of a process, there may be several choices. You can select all of them to be monitored by holding down the SHIFT key and adding them all to the chart at once. A separate graph will be created for each.

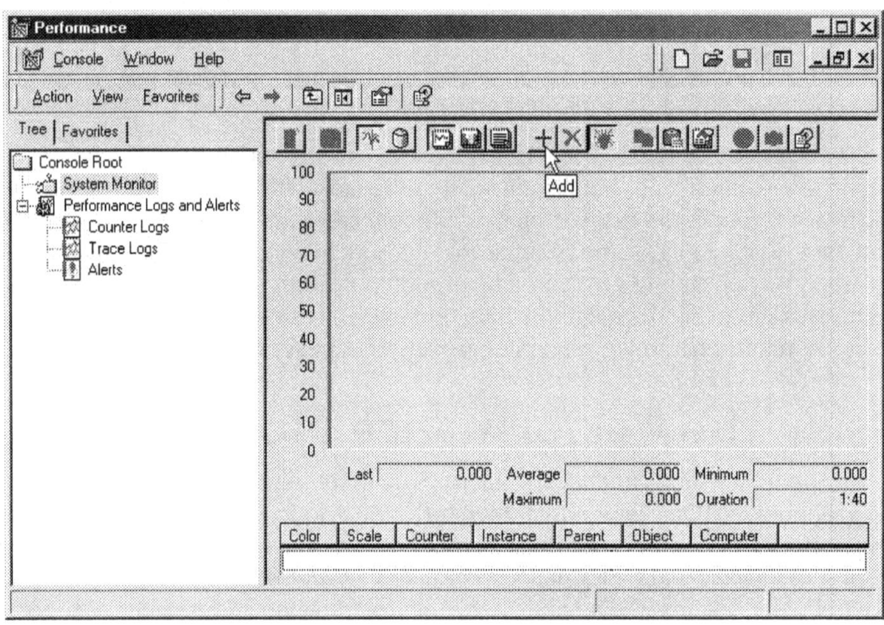

FIGURE 5-3. *Adding counters to a chart in the Performance Monitor*

It is important to note that when looking at multiple instances of an object, Windows assigns a number to each object of the same name, based on its order of creation. This number can change, depending on if an earlier instance of an object goes away. Let us take the example of a thread. A process such as oracle.exe may have 100 threads. Initially each thread is numbered from 0 to 99, but this is not the true thread ID—this is just the number you see assigned to each instance of the object-called thread. If thread #50 disconnects, all of the thread instances with higher numbers shift down, so thread #51 becomes thread #50, and so on. The actual ID of the thread will never change during its life. We will discuss thread IDs later in this section.

Logging Information Using the Performance Monitor

You can choose to continually monitor certain counters by creating a performance log. To do this, expand Performance Logs and Alerts in the Performance Console. Right-click Counter Logs and choose New Log Settings. Give the file a name, but do not specify an extension—an extension will automatically be appended, depending on the file type you choose later. On the General tab, choose which counters you want to monitor and how frequently. From the Log Files tab, you will choose what file types you want and how they are named (the default file type is .blg, or binary log file). Finally, on the Schedule tab you will specify when you want to start and stop the monitoring for this log. Log files can be opened later for viewing from within the System Monitor by clicking on the Disk icon (View Log File Data) in the System Monitor toolbar. Note that you must still add the counter(s) by clicking the plus sign (+) and adding the information to the chart in order to see the logged information.

Under Performance Logs and Alerts, you can also set up an alert, designed to kick off when a certain threshold of a particular counter is reached. For example, you may want to set up an alert to have a certain machine notified with a Net Send message when virtual bytes for oracle.exe reaches a certain limit. Right-click Alerts and choose New Alert Settings. Provide a name for the alert, and then select the appropriate counter (for example, virtual bytes for the Oracle process, as shown in Figure 5-4) and determine the limit at which you want to be notified. Under the Action tab, choose Send a Network Message to: and enter the computer name of the message recipient. Figure 5-4 shows an example of what the alert looks like.

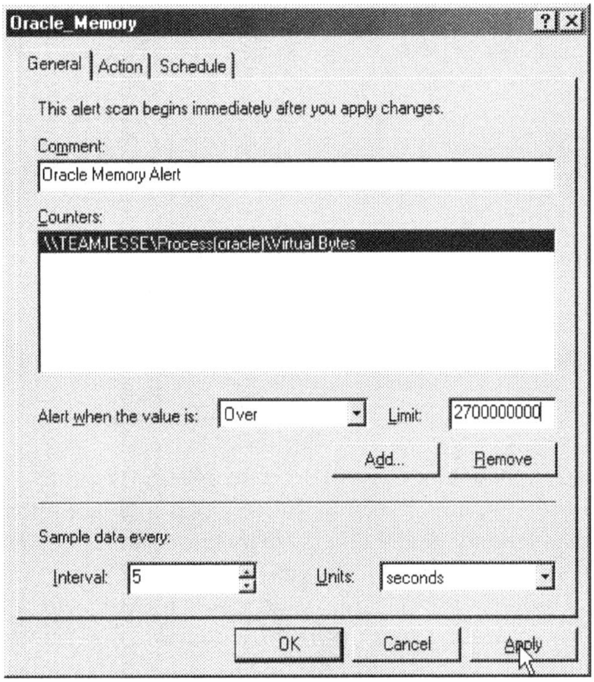

FIGURE 5-4. *Alert for virtual bytes limit*

Adding Performance Counters Specific to Oracle

Oracle provides counters to integrate with the Performance Monitor on Windows NT/2000. These are not installed by default, so you must do a custom installation. Scroll to the bottom of the products to select and expand Oracle Products for Windows. Here you will see the Oracle Performance Monitor for Windows NT. Once installed, an Oracle9 Registry key will be created under HKLM\System\CurrentControlSet\Services. There will be a subkey of Oracle9 called Performance, which contains logon information to the database. Here you will see values for username, password, and hostname.

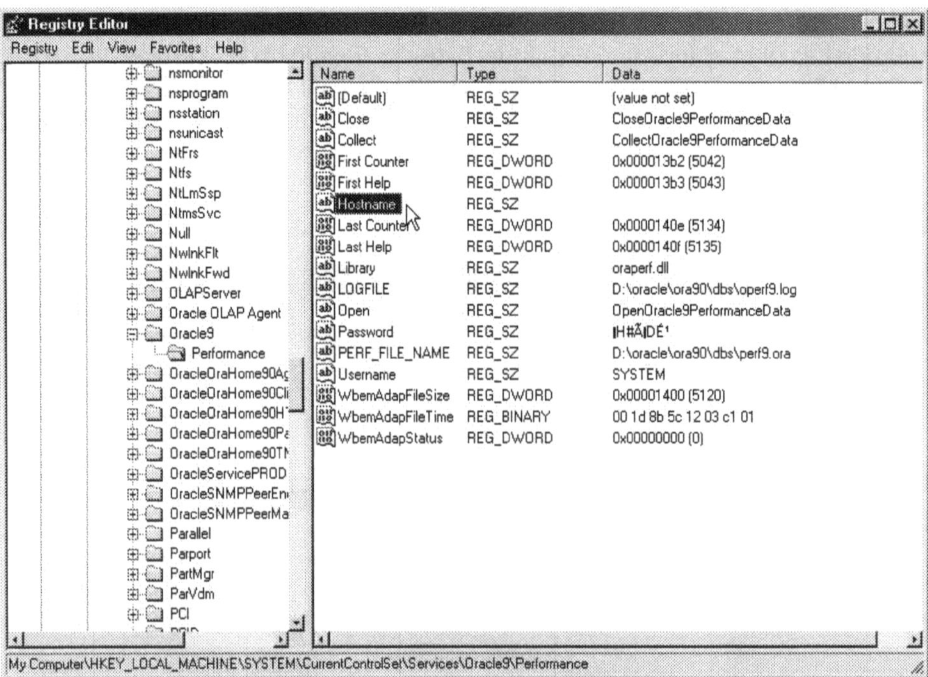

Only one Oracle instance can be monitored at a time. The instance to be monitored is determined by the hostname. If blank, this will default to the instance defined by ORACLE_SID in the home where the Performance Monitor is installed. (The utility is a single home product, meaning it can only be installed in one ORACLE_HOME.) Once installed, you will see a list of counters as shown in the Figure 5-5. If the counters in Figure 5-5 do not show up, check the log file defined in the Performance key in the Registry (by default, ORACLE_HOME\dbs\operf9.log). Chances are that the username, password, or hostname are invalid.

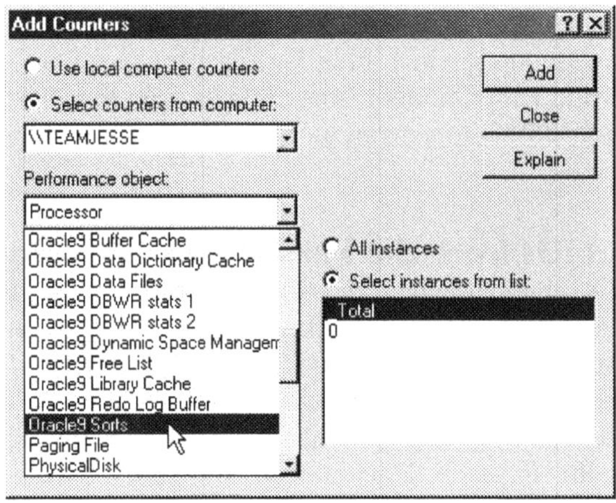

FIGURE 5-5. *Oracle-specific performance counters*

These are queries run by the Oracle performance utility to gather information for the Oracle-specific counters in the Performance Monitor:

```
select count from v$waitstat where class = 'free list'
select name, phyrds, phywrts from v$datafile df, v$filestat fs where
df.file# = fs.file
select value from v$sysstat where name = 'redo log space requests'
select value from v$sysstat where NAME = 'sorts (memory)'
select value from v$sysstat where NAME = 'sorts (disk)'
select value from v$sysstat where NAME = 'recursive calls'
select value from v$sysstat where NAME = 'DBWR timeouts'
select value from v$sysstat where NAME = 'DBWR lru scans'
select value from v$sysstat where NAME = 'DBWR checkpoints'
select value from v$sysstat where NAME = 'DBWR buffers scanned'
select sum(reloads) from v$librarycache
select sum(pins) from v$librarycache
select sum(gets) from v$rowcache
select sum(getmisses) from v$rowcache
select null from seg$ where ts#=:1 and type# != 9
select name from v$datafile
```

Identifying and Viewing Threads Within the RDBMS

How do you match a thread within the database to a thread that you can see in pviewer or the Performance Monitor? The SPID column in the V$PROCESS view

will give you the OS thread ID of each thread. It is not necessary to do any conversion of this number. In Oracle 8.0 and earlier versions, this value was a hex number, which then had to be converted to decimal in order to get the true OS thread ID. This is no longer the case starting with Oracle8i—the SPID as seen in V$PROCESS is given in decimal. Matching that SPID to a given thread in the Performance Monitor, though, can be tricky.

Getting Thread IDs from the Performance Monitor

As noted previously, when viewing threads in the Performance Monitor, (or even when viewing threads through pviewer), the threads are simply shown in numerical order of creation, starting with 0. The true thread ID can be found by choosing Thread from the Performance Object drop-down list in Performance Monitor, and then choosing ID Thread from the counters list. In the Instances list box, you will now see a separate line for each Oracle thread, showing the instance number of the thread (indicating its order of creation). You can select *all* threads by holding down the SHIFT key and then choosing Add. Now the value in the Performance Monitor will show you the actual thread ID that you can match up to the SPID column in V$PROCESS.

How might you use this? Let's say for example that you have an Oracle session spinning out of control, consuming all of the CPU on a system. Initially, you will likely just see this as the oracle.exe process taking all of the CPU in Task Manager. To find out what is going on, though, you need to figure out which specific thread(s) is hogging all of the CPU. This can be accomplished in the Performance Monitor by choosing Thread as the Performance Object and %Processor Time as the counter. Highlight all instances of threads within Oracle and add them to the chart to determine which thread(s) is consuming the CPU. Let us assume, for example, that thread Oracle/20 is consuming most of the CPU. Follow this up by identifying the true thread ID for that particular instance of the thread by following the steps outlined previously. As you can see in Figure 5-6, Oracle/20 gives us a true Thread ID of 2496.

Next, query V$PROCESS and join it to V$SESSION to determine the OS user in question. The query that follows will tell you the terminal, program, and OS user name of the user with thread ID 2496:

```
SQL> column osuser format a30
SQL> column program format a20
SQL> column terminal format a20
SQL> select s.osuser, s.program, s.terminal
from v$session s, v$process p
where p.spid='2496' and p.addr=s.paddr;

OSUSER                         PROGRAM              TERMINAL
------------------------------ -------------------- --------------------
RMNTOPS2\Administrator         sqlplusw.exe         RMNTOPS2

SQL>
```

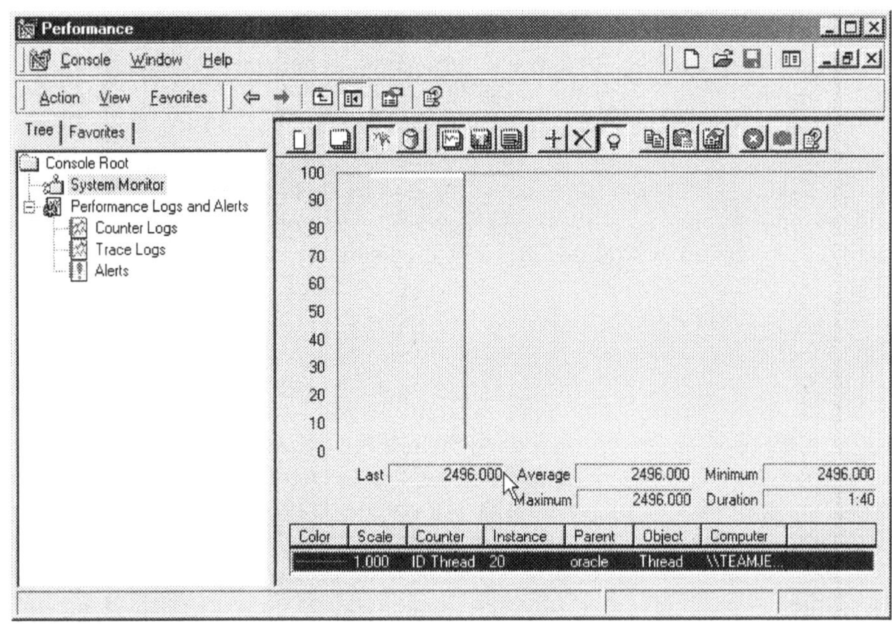

FIGURE 5-6. *Identifying threads with the Performance Monitor*

Alternatively, you can work backward by querying from the database as follows:

```
select sid,b.value from v$sysstat a, v$sesstat b where
a.statistic#=b.statistic# and name='CPU used by this session'
order by b.value;
```

This query will order sessions by the SID using the most CPU resources. You then need to join this SID with V$SESSION and V$PROCESS to get the SPID:

```
select a.sid, b.spid from v$session a, v$process b
 where a.paddr=b.addr;
```

Using pviewer

The pviewer utility can be simpler to use than Performance Monitor, though the scope of what can be monitored is more limited. For example, in the preceding scenario, which showed a single thread consuming 100 percent of the CPU, this can easily be determined using pviewer by simply highlighting the oracle.exe process and looking at the CPU time for each thread. This is a cumulative total, so it is likely that if you

are experiencing a problem, the thread with the highest cumulative total is the culprit. Knowing this allows you to view threads that were consuming CPU, even after the problem has gone away (as long as the thread is still connected to the database). The pviewer utility still shows threads as they are seen in the Performance Monitor—numbered in the order created. So, in our example, you will still see the culprit as thread #20, not the true thread ID. You can identify the thread as shown previously using the Performance Monitor. A better method of identifying a thread is to use the Oracle Administration Assistant for Windows NT. We will discuss this later in this chapter in the section "Using the Oracle Administration Assistant."

Using tlist

Another utility available by installing the support tools from your Windows 2000 CD-ROM is the command-line utility called tlist. The tlist utility, run by itself, will give you a list of all processes on the machine, similar to what you would see in the Processes tab in Task Manager. However, tlist's real value comes by giving it a process name, or PID. If you pass the PID of an Oracle process to tlist, it will return information regarding the process, including the instance name, number of threads, virtual size (yes, the true total), working set, and so on. In addition, tlist will display a list of threads in the process, with their thread IDS and the state of each thread. Finally, you will see all DLLs used by that process.

Identifying the Correct Process When There Are Multiple Oracle Instances

Observe the output that follows, which is just the first few lines of output after running tlist against the process with a PID of 2048:

```
C:\>tlist 2048
2048 oracle.exe
   CWD:       D:\oracle\ora90\DATABASE\
   CmdLine: d:\oracle\ora90\bin\ORACLE.EXE TEST90
   VirtualSize:    309480 KB   PeakVirtualSize:    309480 KB
   WorkingSetSize:170460 KB   PeakWorkingSetSize:170460 KB
   NumberOfThreads: 16
   1528 Win32StartAddr:0x01328d70 LastErr:0x000003e5 State:Waiting
   2040 Win32StartAddr:0x77dc95c5 LastErr:0x000003e5 State:Waiting
(Repeating thread information removed)
        0.0.0.0 shp  0x00400000  ORACLE.EXE
     5.0.2163.1 shp  0x77f80000  ntdll.dll
        0.0.0.0 shp  0x60600000  oraclient9.dll
        0.0.0.0 shp  0x610a0000  oracore9.dll
.(etc)..
```

Notice the third line of output:

```
CmdLine: d:\oracle\ora90\bin\ORACLE.EXE TEST90
```

This tells you that the SID name associated with PID 2048 is TEST90. If you are running multiple Oracle database instances, this is an invaluable way to match the SID to the PID for each instance.

Identifying Processes Holding Oracle DLLs

The tlist utility can also be used to determine what processes have a handle open on a particular DLL, by using the -m switch and giving it the name of a DLL. The command shown here lists all processes using the file called ORACORE9.DLL:

```
C:\>tlist -m oracore9.dll
oracore9.dll - 1068 agntsrvc.exe
oracore9.dll - 1148 Apache.exe
oracore9.dll - 1172 TNSLSNR.EXE
oracore9.dll - 1192 dbsnmp.exe
oracore9.dll - 1656 Apache.exe
oracore9.dll - 2048 oracle.exe
oracore9.dll - 2188 sqlplus.exe
```

In this example, all of the processes are Oracle processes. However, this is a useful way to determine what third-party processes may be holding onto a particular Oracle DLL and thereby preventing an installation from completing (as we discussed in Chapter 4). Note that in order to get feedback, you must give the full name of the DLL, including the .dll extension. For a full list of parameters to use with tlist, enter **tlist /?** from a command prompt.

The orakill Utility: Disposing of Troublesome Threads

Once you have identified a problem thread within the database, the session can be killed via the command **alter system kill session(SID, SERIAL#)**. However, this does not always clear up the problem. The thread may be too far gone to be terminated cleanly, or the system may be CPU bound, and may take too long to respond. On a Unix system, it is common to just kill a user process with a **kill -9** command. A process on Windows 2000 can be killed as well, in several different ways. The kill utility comes with the Windows 2000 Support Tools. Observe also that there is an option to kill the process from within pviewer. Likewise, you can simply right-click a process in Task Manager, and choose End Process.

But this does not answer the question of how to kill a single stuck thread within a process. We do not want to kill the entire process if we don't have to—remember that this process is the entire instance. The orakill utility is provided by Oracle to

terminate a thread quickly and cleanly, and still leave the rest of the instance intact. Run orakill stand-alone from a command prompt for usage:

```
C:\>orakill

Usage:  orakill sid thread

  where sid    = the Oracle instance to target
        thread = the thread id of the thread to kill

  The thread id should be retrieved from the spid column of a query such as:

        select spid, osuser, s.program from
        v$process p, v$session s where p.addr=s.paddr

C:\>
```

So, to kill the thread with SPID of 1488 in instance TEST90, you would issue the following command:

```
C:\>orakill TEST90 1488

Kill of thread id 1488 in instance TEST90 successfully signalled.
```

Ramifications of Using orakill

When running orakill, Oracle uses the Windows 2000 call TerminateThread(). This call is also used in the case of a shutdown abort operation. Because of the nature of the TerminateThread() call, the stack space used by the thread is not freed, but remains allocated for the life of the owning process (oracle.exe). If you are only terminating threads occasionally due to runaway or hung processes and the like, this should not be a big problem. However, in the case of a shutdown abort operation occurring when many sessions are connected, this can result in a severe resource problem if this stack space is left hanging around in the process address space. Therefore, it is imperative after issuing a **shutdown abort** command that you also stop the service prior to restarting. This will terminate the process and free up all memory associated, allowing a clean restart of the process and the database.

Monitoring CPU Usage

Until now, we have focused primarily on memory issues related to Oracle on Windows 2000. We now shift our focus to other activities, starting with CPU activity. To monitor CPU, Task Manager will give you a quick glance at how the overall CPU utilization on the system is doing through the Performance tab. The Processes tab will give you even more info on which process is using the most CPU. However, to get down to the thread level and determine which thread within a process is consuming the most CPU, you must use something like the Performance Monitor or Process Viewer, as we have demonstrated in the previous section.

On the main page of the pviewer tool, you have the ability to give a process a priority boost under the Priority section, or you can provide a given thread within a process a boost in priority. It is not normally necessary to boost the process priority unless it is contending with another process on the server. If that is the case, you may be better off just killing the other process. On the other hand, boosting a thread's priority may provide some benefits—for example, if SMON is cleaning up temporary segments and is fighting for CPU time with other threads in the database. However, if SMON already has 100 percent of the CPU, or close to it, a priority boost is not likely to make any difference.

Oracle gives you the ability to assign an affinity of a given thread to a given CPU in a multiprocessor system. Again, this is rarely used, but you may decide that you want to assign all background threads to have an affinity to a particular CPU. Remember that, by default, there is no processor affinity—all threads can run on any CPU. To set an affinity, you must set Registry entries for ORACLE_AFFINITY in the appropriate HOME key. We recommend that you not tie a thread to a particular CPU in this fashion, but if you see the need to do so, refer to Metalink Note #108512.1.

Disk Usage on Windows 2000

Eliminating bottlenecks with the disk and I/O subsystem is another area crucial to good performance of your database. Preventing and/or discovering bottlenecks is key to smooth operation. The following section gives you a brief look at getting started in the direction of boosting I/O performance on your Oracle/Windows 2000 server.

Defragmenting Disks

Disks should be defragmented prior to putting any Oracle datafiles on them. We recommend using extreme caution when defragmenting disks that already contain Oracle files. You should never defragment disks with Oracle files while the database is open. Defragmenting disks with the database shut down is likely safe, but you should always make a backup just in case.

Disk Compression

Likewise, do *not* compress drives with Oracle datafiles. Oracle does not support datafiles for an active, running database on compressed drives, nor should you compress the drive containing the ORACLE_HOME or an archive destination. At the very least, this will result in poor performance, and in the worst case can result in corruption of data. Using compressed drives to store backups of datafiles or archived logs is outside of the span of control of Oracle. As long as the files

are fully uncompressed and restored to their previous state before they are needed by Oracle for a recovery, this would not pose a problem, since backups are offline and not being accessed by the database unless a recovery is performed.

Monitoring Disk Usage

By default, the Performance Monitor on Windows 2000 does *not* have disk performance counters enabled. This has to be done from a command prompt by running **diskperf -y**. You can see if disk counters are enabled by running **diskperf** by itself:

```
D:\oracle\ora90\BIN>diskperf
Both Logical and Physical Disk Performance counters on this system
        are currently set to never start.
```

Running **diskperf** with the -y switch will enable disk counters, but requires a reboot for them to be started. Once you have enabled disk counters and rebooted, you can check disk I/O activity by choosing PhysicalDisk from the Performance Object box in the Performance Monitor console. You will then have several counters to choose from, including the following:

- % Disk Time
- Avg. Disk Bytes Transfer
- Current Disk Queue Length
- Disk Transfers/Sec
- Split IO/Sec

To get details on what these counters monitor, highlight the counter in the Add Counters dialog box and choose Explain. You can then choose which specific disks you want to monitor from the instances on the right-hand side. This can be used in conjunction with the V$FILESTAT view to identify I/O bottlenecks, such as slow disks, or disks that need to have files moved elsewhere to reduce contention.

Using the Oracle Administration Assistant

We mentioned the Oracle Administration Assistant for Windows NT earlier in the section "Using pviewer." The Oracle Administration Assistant (ORAADM) is a tool provided by Oracle to manage many of the tasks we have discussed specific to the Windows NT/2000 platform. It is a snap-in to the MMC that gives you the ability to view databases on local or remote computers, configure the startup and shutdown options of the service (as discussed in Chapter 4), configure which account the service logs on as, and even stop and start the service itself. Perhaps the most valuable information this tool provides, though, is the process information; this interface does the work for you in identifying threads in the database and displaying true thread IDs, indicating whether a thread is a background or foreground thread, and showing the CPU usage of each thread. It also gives you the ability to kill a thread (it actually makes a call to orakill, as discussed previously). Last, the Administration Assistant gives you the ability to create and manage operating system authenticated accounts to the Oracle database.

Getting Started with the Oracle Administration Assistant

The Administration Assistant is accessed by clicking Start | Programs | Oracle <homename> | Configuration and Migration Tools | Administration Assistant for Windows NT. Once in the console, you will see the local machine always listed under Computers. You can choose a remote computer to manage via a right-click on Computers.

Configuring Operating System Authentication with ORAADM

Once a computer has been added, you can add users who have privileges to start and stop the database (database administrators and database operators), or you can add a normal OS authenticated user to the database. In this section, we will discuss the creation of operating system authenticated users via the Oracle Administration Assistant for Windows NT.

Adding sysdba Privileges to an OS Account

You can see what users are members of the ORA_DBA group on a given machine by highlighting OS Database Administrators—Computer. Remember that the ORA_DBA group contains users that have privileges to *all* databases on that machine. As mentioned in Chapter 4, this group should be created automatically during the installation, and the account from which the installation was done should already be a member of this group.

On the other hand, you can drill down to the individual databases to select a given database. You'll have to first right-click the database you want and select Connect Database from the pop-up menu. Once into the database, you will see another console simply titled OS Database Administrators. This lists users who are in the ORA_<sidname>_DBA group. OS users who are members of the group for

this particular database can *only* connect as sysdba to *this* instance. If you right-click either of these applets and choose Add/Remove, you will be walked through the process of adding an OS account to the given group. If the group does not yet exist (for example, ORA_PROD90_DBA), then it will be created automatically.

Configuring a Standard OS Authenticated User

A normal user can be added to the database via the External OS Users applet, as shown in Figure 5-7. Here, you'll have to right-click the applet name and choose Create, and then you will be walked through the process of selecting an operating system user account. This applet will actually create a database user via the **create user** command within the database. You will be prompted to choose a default profile, as well as a default and temporary tablespace. You can also determine quotas for this database account for each tablespace (the default is unlimited quota). Finally, you will be given the opportunity to assign database roles to the user account.

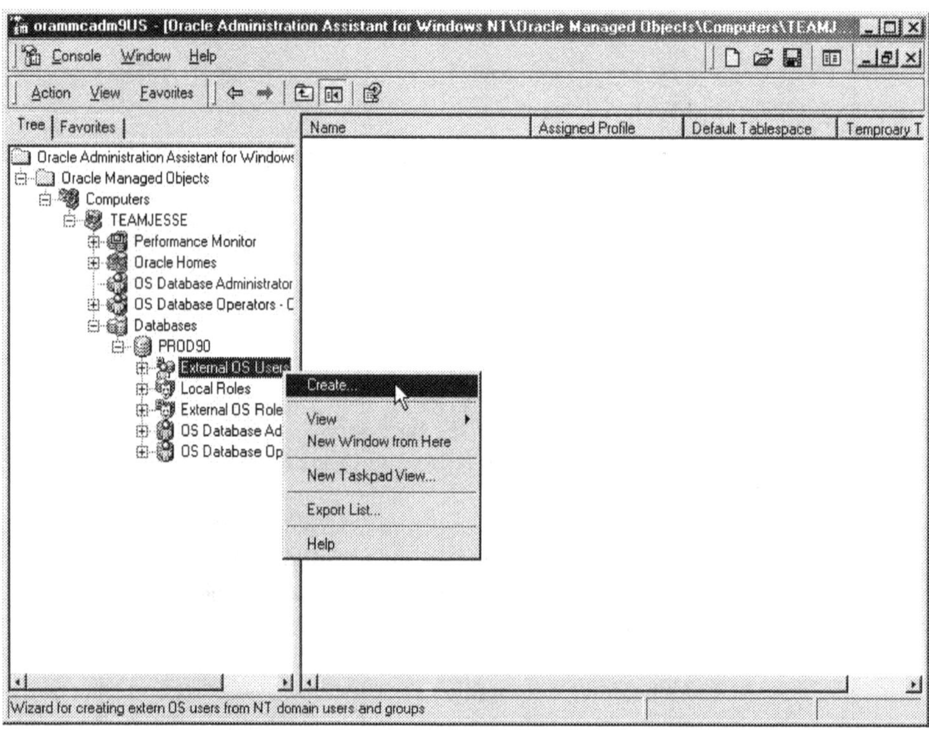

FIGURE 5-7. *Creating a database user authenticated at the OS*

One of the keys for any type of OS authentication to work correctly is the setting of SQLNET.AUTHENTICATION_SERVICES=(NTS) in the sqlnet.ora file (found in ORACLE_HOME\Network\Admin). This must be set on the server and on all clients requiring OS authentication. Another key issue to note here is that the actual username in the database will be prefaced with both OS_AUTHENT_PREFIX and the domain name. If you are not a member of a domain, the local machine name will be used for the prefix. By default, OS_AUTHENT_PREFIX is set to OPS$, so an OS user named JANET in the domain RMDT2000 would actually have a username in the database of OPS$RMDT2000\JANET. If you want a null string for the prefix instead of OPS$, you must set the init parameter OS_AUTHENT_PREFIX to two sets of double quotes prior to creating the users in the database:

```
OS_AUTHENT_PREFIX=""
```

This parameter cannot be modified dynamically.

Once the database user is created in the database, the OS user must be authenticated by logging into the domain specified. Then, just use a / (slash) in place of username/password when logging on:

```
SQL>connect /@prod90.rmdt2000.oracle.com
Connected.
```

If you do not want the domain to be prefixed to the username, you cannot create the user through the Oracle Administration Assistant—the Assistant will always prefix the domain name. To create a user manually in the database, issue a command similar to the following:

```
SQL>create user JANET identified externally;
User created.
```

This example assumes that the OS_AUTHENT_PREFIX is set to null (""). Otherwise, you must preface the account name with your prefix:

```
SQL>create user OPS$JANET identified externally;
User created.
```

Also, you *must* set the Registry parameter OSAUTH_PREFIX_DOMAIN to FALSE in the appropriate HOME key in the Registry (it will not be there at the outset, and by default this value is set to TRUE). Otherwise, any connections will result in an ORA-1031 error, because by default it will check for a database account called OPS$<domainname>\JANET, when in fact the database account name that you created is simply OPS$JANET. By default, OSAUTH_PREFIX_DOMAIN is TRUE, and all accounts created using ORAADM will prefix a domain name.

Viewing Thread Information Using ORAADM

The Administration Assistant can also be used to view all threads, along with the actual thread IDs, of sessions connected to the database. To see this, right-click an instance and choose Process Information from the pop-up menu. This will give you a window listing the type of each thread (foreground or background) and each thread's ID. If a thread is a background thread, the name of the background thread (PMON, SMON, and so on) will be shown.

This same information can be seen from the command line by joining V$BGPROCESS with V$PROCESS and V$SESSION:

```
SQL> column "Name" format a15
SQL> column spid format 9999
SQL> column schemaname format a10
SQL> column type format a15
SQL> select a.spid, nvl(b.name,s.program) "Name", s.schemaname,
  2    decode(a.background,1,'Background','Foreground') "Type"
  3     from v$process a, v$bgprocess b, v$session s
  4     where a.username<>'PSEUDO'
  5     and a.addr=b.paddr(+)
  6     and a.addr=s.paddr;

SPID      Name            SCHEMANAME Type
--------- --------------- ---------- ---------------
211       PMON            SYS        Background
212       DBW0            SYS        Background
213       LGWR            SYS        Background
215       CKPT            SYS        Background
217       SMON            SYS        Background
285       RECO            SYS        Background
365       sqlplus.exe     SYS        Foreground
7 rows selected.
```

The Process Information window in ORAADM will also show you CPU utilization of each thread, and give you the opportunity to kill a thread with a Kill Thread button that calls orakill and passes the SID name and thread ID for you (see Figure 5-8). Clicking the Help button will give you information on all of the various aspects of the Administration Assistant.

If thread information does not show up in this window, this is likely due to the fact that OS authentication is not properly configured. As noted previously, you must set SQLNET.AUTHENTICATION_SERVICES=(NTS) in the sqlnet.ora. If it is not set, you must add it and restart *both* the service for the Listener and the service for the database, in order for the change to be recognized by the Administration Assistant.

If you do not want to use OS authentication, you will need to manually configure a username and password. The username and password that the ORAADM console logs on with are stored in the following location:

```
\\HKEY_LOCAL_MACHINE\System\CurrentControlSet\Services\OracleOraconfig.
```

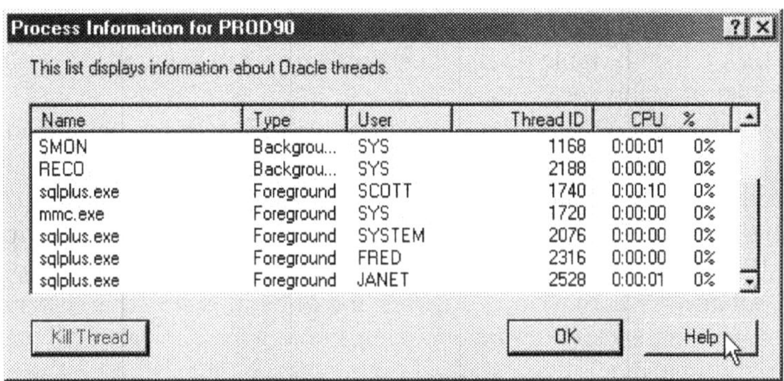

FIGURE 5-8. *Process (thread) information viewed from the Administration Assistant*

Starting with 8.1.7, a utility called ocfgutil.exe was implemented to set the username and password. If the preceding Registry key does not exist, the utility will create it. You will find this utility in C:\Program Files\Oracle\Oraconfig. The syntax is as follows:

```
ocfgutil <username> <password>
```

Running this utility will update the information in the Registry with the logon name and password provided (the password field will be encrypted when you view it in the Registry). This method should only be used if native OS authentication is not configured. If using native OS authentication now or at any time in the future, this should work whether or not you have run ocfgutil.exe.

Additional 9*i* Features

Much of the focus of this chapter so far has been on matters specific to Windows 2000. Let us not forget, though, that the beauty of Oracle is its portability across so many different platforms. Having said this, we will now shift our focus to some of the new 9i features that have nothing to do with integration with the OS, but rather are features generic to the database and that work the same on any platform.

New Feature in Oracle9*i*

Reorganizing Using Oracle9i DBMS_REDEFINITION

The issues regarding how to organize and time the reorganization of Oracle tables may become a debate of the past, depending on how well you trust new features. Oracle9i introduces a supplied package that allows tables to be reorganized without pulling them from production and making them unavailable. DBMS_REDEFINITION is a series of packages that can be used together to rebuild a table with different extent sizes, in a different tablespace, with new columns or combined columns, and so on. The trick is that the table does not become unavailable during the reorganization process, except near the very end.

To accomplish this, DBMS_REDEFINITION uses Oracle's materialized view architecture to keep a log of all transactions that occur to the original table while the second, reorganized table is being built. Therefore, you start the process of building a clone table based on a select operation from the original. As this is a simple select operation, there is no locking on the original table (except, of course, a lock against any DDL). All new DML that occurs against the original is stored in a snapshot log after the initiation of the rebuild. After the completion of the new table, all transactions recorded in the snapshot log are applied to the interim table, thus bringing the table up to date with the original. During this final step, the original is locked momentarily in order to confirm that no new transactions occur. After all transactions have been applied, the interim table becomes the original table, and vice versa. The original table is still accessible for testing, but has the name of the interim table. The interim table, now with the name of the original, is available for production updates with no difference to users.

This procedure, which involves three or four simple PL/SQL procedures to be executed, is extremely flexible in its application by database administrators. Although the principle is simple, the usage could be for nearly any operation that may sacrifice usability of a data table. Index rebuilds, column additions, trigger additions, space defragmentation operations, tablespace moves, and almost any other data reorganization that could affect production can now be done without availability sacrifices.

The genius of the system lies in its openness. The interim table can be predefined with any number of changes in column names, column sizes, indexes, primary keys, constraints, and space parameters. The DBMS_REDEFINITION is called, and you map the columns from the original to the interim, and the materialized view operations then take care of data movement without interrupting any DML against the original. This simplicity in design might seem daunting, as there are behaviors that have been bred into database administrators over the years concerning the troublesome amount of work that must go into table redefinition. This breeding means you usually tell application developers, system administrators, managers, and pretty much anyone else that will listen, "Once the tables are designed, that's it. We can't go back and rebuild after we are in production." This is still a good principle to stick to—in fact, we gave a disclaimer at the beginning of this section: "reorganization of tables may become a debate of the past." You might want to keep this a secret; it can lead to lazy testing and development, which we never condone.

The good news is that very few who might take advantage of this little piece of code need ever hear of it. It can be our little secret. Here's how it works.

Identify and Confirm Candidates for Reorganization

First, identify tables that could possibly benefit from being rebuilt. This could be an obvious piece of advice: if you're reading this, you probably know the table or tables already. Significant performance gains can sometimes be found in reorganizing fragmented tables. Other candidates may include tables that need to be partitioned, have their indexes renamed and rebuilt, or have constraints changed. No data conversion can be employed during the reorganization, so exclude any candidates where data needs to be changed. The utility is for DDL reorganization, and cannot perform any DML operations against data being moved from the original table to the interim table.

After identifying possible candidates, verify that the utility can be used against them using the procedure DBMS_REDEFINITION.CAN_REDEF_TABLE. There are only two arguments that need to be passed: the username of the owner of the table and the table name. Execute the following as SYS:

```
EXECUTE DBMS_REDEFINITION.CAN_REDEF_TABLE ('SCOTT', 'EMP');
PL/SQL procedure successfully completed.
```

If the table fails to meet any of the restrictions on reorganization, this returns an error:

```
SQL> EXECUTE DBMS_REDEFINITION.CAN_REDEF_TABLE ('SCOTT', 'NEW_EMP');
BEGIN DBMS_REDEFINITION.CAN_REDEF_TABLE ('SCOTT', 'NEW_EMP'); END;
*
ERROR at line 1:
ORA-12089: cannot online redefine table "SCOTT"."NEW_EMP" with no primary
key
ORA-06512: at "SYS.DBMS_REDEFINITION", line 8
ORA-06512: at "SYS.DBMS_REDEFINITION", line 236
ORA-06512: at line 1
```

The restrictions are as follows:

- The candidate table must have a primary key.
- The candidate table cannot have any materialized views or materialized view logs defined on it.
- Advanced queuing (AQ) tables and materialized view base tables cannot be reorganized with DBMS_REDEFINITION.
- Overflow tables of index organized tables (IOT) cannot be reorganized online.

It is important these restrictions be met; otherwise, the CAN_REDEF_TABLE procedure will fail, and you will receive an error message.

Create a Test Table and Make a Dry Run

After identifying the table for an online reorganization, don't blaze ahead into the following steps. Although there is no underlying damage done by an abortive online reorganization, there are definitely a lot of headaches that can be avoided by making a dry run first. All this requires is creating a small test table and reorganizing it first, recording all your steps in an output file. You can then work out all the kinks of the entire process before moving ahead.

Determining how big to make the test table depends on the size of the real table you want reorganized. A five percent sample can be sufficient. To create the test table, run the DDL for the original table in a test user's schema. Be sure to include all keys, constraints, indices, and triggers from the original. If such a DDL is not readily available, do the work to make sure you get the environment as close as possible to the original. A primary key is essential at the very least. Next, load a subset of data from the original:

```
Insert into test.emp select * from scott.emp
where rownum < 5000;
```

The rownum qualifier is a handy little way to get just a certain number of rows from a table with little fanfare or advanced programming. After loading some data, commit the transaction and then run CAN_REDEF_TABLE against your test. If any errors occur, make sure you created a primary key.

Next, build a test interim table. This table should reflect any changes you need to make to the original. This could be as simple as changing the storage clause to reflect a larger extent size. Perhaps you want a new column. Make the changes to the interim table, but do not add any indices, triggers, or constraints. We will do this after the data is loaded from the original.

Start the Reorganization

Before starting the reorganization, get a row count of the original, as demonstrated in the following example. You can use this to determine when the first phase of reorganization is complete.

```
Select count(*) from test.emp;
count(*)
-------
5000
```

To begin the process of reorganization, use the procedure START_REDEF_TABLE. This procedure builds a materialized view log on the original table to log any changes, and then begins to refresh a prebuilt materialized view with data from the original table. The interim table functions as the container table for the materialized view being used; so all changes go directly into the interim table using the mechanism of a materialized view. We pass the table owner, original table name, interim table name, and column mapping information to START_REDEF_TABLE.

```
SQL> EXECUTE DBMS_REDEFINITION.START_REDEF_TABLE -
> ('TEST', 'EMP', 'EMPLOYEE');

PL/SQL procedure successfully completed.
```

If you forget to build the interim table EMPLOYEE, this command will fail with the error ORA-942: "Table or view does not exist."

You can check the progress of the interim table by querying for the row count. When the row count matches the original table, the first phase of the reorganization is complete.

Add Indices, Triggers, and Constraints to the Interim Table

After the first phase is complete, you can add indices, constraints, and triggers to the interim table. This can be done at any point during the first phase of reorganization, but it makes more sense, particularly for indices, to wait until the majority of data is loaded into the new table. Usually, the performance of a b*tree index is much better if most of the data exists before it is built, as the b*tree will be balanced on a new index. Once the index exists, DML against the rows will start to skew the index.

All triggers and constraints must be created as disabled and deferred, and they will be enabled after the interim and original tables switch identities.

Synchronize the Interim with the Original Table Occasionally

After the first phase of reorganization is complete, and you are busy building new indices on the interim table, it makes sense to refresh the interim with any new data that may have appeared in the original since the beginning of the reorganization process. To this end, use the SYNC_INTERIM_TABLE procedure. This simply flushes any entries in the materialized view on the original table and enters them into your interim table, thereby decreasing the total amount of refreshing that must take place at the completion of reorganization.

```
SQL> Execute DBMS_REDEFINITION.SYNC_INTERIM_TABLE -
> ('TEST', 'EMP', 'EMPLOYEE');
PL/SQL procedure successfully completed.
```

Finish Reorganization

After all indices, triggers, and constraints have been built, you are ready for the final stage of reorganization. The procedure FINISH_REDEF_TABLE is called, which does a final refresh of the interim table and then switches the identities of the original

and interim tables so that the interim table now has the name of the original table, and the original now has the name of the interim. In our example, that means we renamed the EMPLOYEE table as EMP, and vice versa. All the new attributes we gave to interim table now exist for our original.

```
SQL> EXECUTE DBMS_REDEFINITION.FINISH_REDEF_TABLE -
> ('TEST', 'EMP', 'EMPLOYEE');

PL/SQL procedure successfully completed.
```

The original table is locked in exclusive mode at the very end of this procedure, as the actual switch between the two occurs. This downtime window is small and independent of the amount of data in the table. All of the materialized view mechanics that were built for the reorganization are dropped at this point. The original table, now called EMPLOYEE, can be either dropped or used for testing purposes.

Transportable Tablespaces

With the use of the transportable tablespace feature, movement of data between two databases has never been easier. This feature allows tablespaces to literally be moved from one database to another, without using export and import to complete the transition. Instead, you utilize a copy of the datafiles associated with the tablespace and a special form of export that only contains metadata about the tablespace. By moving the files to the server of the new database, you simply run an **import** command that points out the copied datafiles, and that's it: the tablespace is now a part of the new database. Of course, the datafiles cannot be moved between different platforms, so this functionality only works between two databases on the Windows NT or Windows 2000 platform (yes, files can be moved from Windows NT to Windows 2000, and vice versa).

This feature is not new to 9i, but it's useful to be familiar with this powerful tool. This allows an efficient way to archive old data from an OLTP environment to a data warehouse or a means of moving data from a production environment to a test environment. This is also a fast way to perform offline instantiation for advanced replication (prior to setting up any replication triggers, that is).

Transportable Tablespaces and Disparate Block Sizes

Perhaps the biggest hindrance to using transportable tablespace in Oracle8i was the inability to merge tablespaces from databases with disparate block sizes. What is new to release 9i is the ability to transport tablespaces between databases, regardless of block size. In fact, though we have discussed the ability to use multiple buffer cache sizes in 9i as a performance feature, this feature arose primarily from the desire to use transportable tablespaces, rather than being viewed as a performance objective by itself.

Of course, if you have a default block size of 4KB, and you will be transporting a tablespace with a 16KB block size, you will need to set the DB_16K_CACHE_SIZE parameter in your PFILE or SPFILE to an appropriate size. Here's how it works. In this example, let's say you want to move the tablespace FOR16K from the database PROD90 to the database TEST90, both of which reside on the same computer. TEST90 has a default block size of 4KB. First, you need to determine if a tablespace qualifies for transportation. The following initial restrictions apply:

- The two databases involved must be on the same hardware/operating system configuration. You cannot transport a tablespace from a Unix platform to a database running on Windows 2000.
- The character set of both databases must be the same.
- If a tablespace of the same name already exists on the new database, you will not be able to transport the tablespace.
- No materialized views or function-based indices can exist in the tablespace.

For a full list of restrictions, see the reference *Oracle9i Administrator's Guide* from Oracle Corporation.

Check the Tablespace for Portability

After checking the restrictions list, you next confirm that the objects in your tablespace set are self-contained. This means that if you have primary key indices in a different tablespace than the object they reference, you will need to move both tablespaces together. To check for self-containment, use the package DBMS_TTS. This package will determine if the tablespace meets the minimum requirements to be moved. It can be run as the user SYS from SQL*Plus:

```
SQL> execute sys.dbms_tts.transport_set_check('FOR16K', TRUE);
```

This populates the view TRANSPORT_SET_VIOLATIONS with any violations that need to be fixed prior to transportation. In the test environment, there is only one table, MATT.TRANSJUNK, in the tablespace FOR16K, so no rows are seen in the view.

Preparing the Tablespace for Transport

Next, you have to prepare the TEST90 database for a 16KB block-size tablespace. To change this, you must create a DB_CACHE for 16KB blocks in the initTEST90.ora file, and then bounce the TEST90 instance (or you can use the SPFILE, as outlined previously in this chapter):

```
db_16k_cache_size=2097152
```

After making appropriate changes to the TEST90 instance, turn back to the originating database, PROD90. You must place the tablespace in read-only mode for the duration of the export and copy operations.

```
SQL> connect system/manager@prod90
SQL> alter tablespace FOR16K read only;
```

Next, you begin the OS copy of the necessary datafiles associated with the tablespace users.

```
C:>copy d:\oracle\oradata\prod90\for16k01.dbf
   d:\oracle\oradata\TEST90\for16k01.dbf
```

Beam Me Up, Scotty

After beginning this copy, you can run your metadata export:

```
C:\>set oracle_sid=prod90
C:\>exp transport_tablespace=y tablespaces=(for16k)
tts_full_check=y file=c:\stage\transdump.dmp
```

This will prompt for a username and password. Use sys/password as sysdba, as shown here:

```
Export: Release 9.0.1.1.1 - Production on Mon Sep 17 12:57:55 2001
(c) Copyright 2001 Oracle Corporation. All rights reserved.
Username: sys/oracle as sysdba
Connected to: Oracle9i Enterprise Edition Release 9.0.1.1.1 - Production
With the Partitioning and Real Application Clusters options
JServer Release 9.0.1.1.1 - Production
Export done in WE8MSWIN1252 character set and AL16UTF16 NCHAR character set
Note: table data (rows) will not be exported
About to export transportable tablespace metadata...
For tablespace FOR16K ...
. exporting cluster definitions
. exporting table definitions
. . exporting table                      TRANSJUNK
. exporting referential integrity constraints
. exporting triggers
. end transportable tablespace metadata export
Export terminated successfully without warnings.
```

And that, as they say, is that. On the production database, put the FOR16K tablespace back in read/write mode after the **copy** command completes. The production tablespace downtime is over.

```
SQL>connect sys/oracle@prod90 as sysdba
SQL>alter tablespace FOR16K read write
```

You then set your environment to the new database and simply run the import. All the footwork has been completed by the **copy** command. Notice in the import statement that you need to specify the datafile associated with your tablespace. This parameter is necessary, as it allows you to specify the new location of the datafile as it will appear in the V$DATAFILE view of the TEST90 database. Even if the datafile location will not be different on the new machine, you still must specify the datafile location in the **import** command.

```
C:\>set oracle_sid=TEST90
C:\>imp transport_tablespace=y file=c:\stage\transdump.dmp
datafiles=('d:\oracle\oradata\prod90\for16k01.dbf')
tablespaces=(for16k) tts_owners=(matt)
Import: Release 9.0.1.1.1 - Production on Mon Sep 17 12:59:58 2001
(c) Copyright 2001 Oracle Corporation. All rights reserved.
Username: sys/oracle as sysdba
Connected to: Oracle9i Enterprise Edition Release 9.0.1.1.1 - Production
With the Partitioning and Real Application Clusters options
JServer Release 9.0.1.1.1 - Production

Export file created by EXPORT:V09.00.01 via conventional path
About to import transportable tablespace(s) metadata...
import done in WE8MSWIN1252 character set and AL16UTF16 NCHAR character set
. importing SYS's objects into SYS
. importing MATT's objects into MATT
. . importing table                    "TRANSJUNK"
Import terminated successfully without warnings.
```

You complete the transportation by logging into the TEST90 database and bring the transported tablespace into read/write mode.

```
SQL> connect system/manager@TEST90
SQL> alter tablespace for16k read write;
```

Summary

This chapter is meant to provide insight into the inner workings of Oracle9i, with much of the focus on Oracle's integration on the Windows 2000 platform. The difficulty in this chapter was not in determining what to put in, but in deciding what to leave out. This chapter only scratches the surface of what can and should be done to get the most out of the RDBMS on Windows 2000, but it provides useful and essential insights, with a huge jump start in the right direction. We discussed new features in 9i such as database templates, the system parameter file, and Oracle Managed Files. We also gave platform-specific details on tuning Oracle on Windows 2000, covering areas such as memory, disk I/O, and CPU utilization, as well as the vagaries of thread identification. Finally, we wrapped up with more new features in Release 9i: online table reorganizations and a new twist on transportable tablespaces, with the inclusion of support for multiple block sizes. In the next chapter, we will move on to discuss backup and recovery considerations.

CHAPTER 6

Backup and Recovery Considerations

Backups—the collective sigh hangs heavy over the heads of database administrators and system administrators alike. Thinking about backups wastes valuable time that could be used tuning the database, testing the next version, or golfing. The negative psychology runs deeper when you consider that, typically, we think the most about backups after something has gone wrong, and suddenly we need to know everything about them: it's suddenly hour thirty-seven of a nonstop, job-on-the-line, weekend data recovery binge. But, more than anything else, deep down in our guts, we are all thinking the same thing: if all this hardware, all this software, worked the way it should, the entire concept of backups would just go away.

Despite all this, we'll say it again: disasters happen. Mistakes happen. Bugs happen. So, are backups important? No one really argues this point. But we have a saying around here: everyone has a backup strategy, but few have a recovery strategy. The point behind the pithy one-liner is that a backup strategy gets put into place, and then forgotten. Forgotten until crunch time, and then valuable minutes pass by as entire IT departments struggle to track down this or that tape, and trying to remember what exactly gets backed up. Suddenly, a clustered, redundant, high-availability data system is brought to its knees, unavailable for hours as recovery takes place.

Backups must be considered in a broader light than simply a copy of data in case of a disaster. Understanding and maintaining backups throughout the entire life cycle of a database is an integral piece of any serious high-availability solution. When a disaster occurs, we need to know one thing: not that we have a backup, but rather how fast can we get the database back into production?

When it comes to backups, the most important tips we can provide are simple, and reflect a database administrator's operating principles more than anything else. Plan for disasters before they happen. Keep a trained eye on the strategy you implement. Remain flexible. Test backups frequently. But you've made it past the first page of this chapter, so we assume you're looking for ways to put these principles into practice. So, in this chapter, we discuss the following tips and techniques:

- Basing the backup strategy on business needs
- Aligning backups with your company's business before agreeing to a service level agreement
- Using cold backups to make your life simple
- Using Windows 2000 Backup
- Using third-party backup products
- Understanding and implementing hot backups
- Leveraging server managed recovery

- Understanding the benefits of Oracle9*i* Recovery Manager (RMAN)
- Understanding RMAN configuration
- Integrating RMAN with media management software to maximize backup power
- Understanding the benefits of an RMAN implementation
- Comprehending RMAN backups: syntax and usage
- Establishing persistent backup parameters
- Understanding RMAN restore and recovery
- Comprehending RMAN recovery: syntax and usage
- Understanding and using incomplete recovery, or point-in-time recovery (PITR)
- Using tablespace point-in-time recovery (TSPITR)
- Using RMAN backups to create clone copies of production databases
- Testing backups for recoverability

Base Your Backup Strategy on Your Business Needs

When you set out to plan your backup strategy, the first thing to look at is the business needs of the database you are backing up. All business needs can be interpreted as system parameters for a database, and likewise business needs can be transformed into parameters for backups. To do so, we look at the business from two different perspectives: what is the nature of data going into the database, and how frequently is that data accessed?

The Nature of Data

A database administrator by definition must be familiar with the type of data being stored in his or her database, but setting up a backup strategy changes the perspective of what we need to know about the data. The question you should first ask: how is the data in this database generated? For instance, do you run nightly batch jobs generated by an application, or do you have twenty data entry employees transcribing data from other sources into the database? Is the database populated with data from

web designers for real-time access by web site visitors, or does it store information created by customers in real time?

Essentially, you can divide data into two types. The first kind of data is generated outside the database, and then inserted into the database for storage and manipulation. If an application stores all user input until a daily job inserts the entirety into the database with a single run, then the batch job can be run again. If web designers build graphics and text for display on a web site, these can be reinserted into the database. The important characteristic of this type of data is that the database is not the only copy.

The second type of data is data that exists only in the database. For instance, an online customer orders a book. That order, along with the thousand other orders that occurred at roughly the same time on the web site, do not exist outside the database. If these transactions are lost, they are lost forever. No external list can be reinserted into the database.

These two types of data set your recovery priorities because they set the level of external recoverability. *External recoverability* is the level to which your data can be salvaged without database backups. For instance, if you have a week's worth of data stored simultaneously in the database and in batch files on the application server, you can relax a little. A weekly full database backup should be sufficient—you can simply rerun any batch file inserts that happened since the backup. Most data warehouse environments tend to have a high level of external recoverability, as they receive their data primarily from other databases.

However, if the database is the single repository for your data, then you must act a little more carefully. If the database is lost at any moment, you're only as good as your last database backup. Your priority for backup strategy must focus on internal recoverability. *Internal recoverability* is the level of reliance we have on the internal architecture of our database for salvaging any lost data. Most OLTP databases have a high level of internal recoverability, as the data cannot be tracked externally in any reasonable way.

As you may remember from Chapter 2, we mentioned that the decision to run in archivelog mode versus noarchivelog mode came down to how the data was loaded. Here you see the same decision to be made: if you have a high level of external recoverability, then archivelog mode may be unnecessary. However, if your internal recoverability is very high, archivelog mode is essential to data integrity.

Frequency of Data Usage

From the perspective of the business, you must next define how available the data in this particular database must be. More than any other rule, availability defines a backup and recovery strategy. If a database crashes, for whatever reason, the data is unavailable until you can restore the backups and bring the data back online.

The period of time between the crash and restored data availability is referred to as the *mean time to recovery*, or *MTTR*. Reducing the MTTR must be a considered a top priority in all high-availability environments.

Define availability based on business needs. If a database receives all of its data during normal business hours, Monday through Friday, then don't break your back running backups while the database is up. Take it down on Sunday and back up everything, guilt free. If, on the other hand, your database receives product orders twenty-four hours a day, seven days a week, then you must plan the backups carefully to ensure they minimally affect regular database operations.

Align Backup Strategies with Business Needs Before Agreeing to a Service Level Agreement

Because you are conscientiously planning a backup strategy that takes advantage of and/or must compensate for the business needs placed on the database, make sure that the planning process includes any management personnel that must sign off on strategy implementations. In this way, realistic expectations can be built into the service-level agreement (SLA).

The SLA is the document that defines the relationship between the database administrator and the company he or she works for. It defines the parameters for database availability, such as its hours of operation, who has access to which database objects, how long various application implementations will take, and (most important for this chapter) how long it will take to recover in case of disaster. In the best situation, the SLA is a physical document that all sides have agreed to; but, in the absence of a physical document, think of the SLA as the implicit expectations your management has for the livelihood of the database. Often unrealistic, these expectations are based on what the salesperson told them about the product, or even what you promised to accomplish (gulp) during your job interview. Whatever the reasons for the expectations placed on the database administrator's back, whether realistic or not, it is the responsibility of the database administrator to come clean about how prepared the database is for catastrophe.

Critical to placing realistic parameters in the SLA is having an understanding with all parties concerning what it takes to be extremely available. Database availability can be an expensive prospect, and if the CIO won't put up the money to help a database administrator guarantee the database's stability, then that CIO must accept that the database may go down and stay down until backups are restored. This balance between the cost of managing the database and the database's availability must be understood and acceptable to all parties. Obviously, this is easier said than done, but that does not diminish the importance of this principle.

So, after reading this chapter and looking at the business needs of your database, we encourage you to approach the interested parties and have a frank discussion about how backup and recovery strategies affect overall database cost and overall database availability. Remember, both of these come back to single factor: the company's bottom line. What is more expensive: database outages or backup and recovery resources?

Cold Backups Make Your Life Easier

The importance of data availability helps define an important backup decision: whether you should take the database down for the backup. A backup of the database when it is shut down is referred to as a *cold backup*, and a *hot backup* refers to a backup operation that occurs when the database is up and operational.

Cold backups are a reliable piece of any backup strategy. If your database can be shut down for a period long enough to make a cold backup, by all means take advantage of this situation. This cannot be emphasized enough: cold backups make your administrative life easier. If a complete server failure occurs, and you must restore the entire database from a backup, the most reliable backup is the cold one. If a database is shut down, then you know that Oracle has flushed all dirty buffers to disk, rolled back any incomplete transactions, and sent a checkpoint to all datafile headers. In essence, you can trust that the files that are backed up are clean and in no way fuzzy.

This only holds true if the database is shut down cleanly, meaning using a **shutdown normal** or a **shutdown immediate** method. A normal shutdown waits patiently for all pending transactions to commit or roll back while denying any new transactions from starting. This can take quite some time, depending on how many users are connected and how many active transactions exist. If there is even one ad hoc user connected who has inserted a single row but forgot to commit it before going to lunch, a **shutdown normal** will wait for this user indefinitely.

For this reason, the best shutdown method for a cold backup is the **shutdown immediate** method. An immediate shutdown terminates all active transactions, forces them to roll back, and then closes the database. Although quite authoritarian in nature, this method lets the database administrator guarantee that the database closes in a reasonable time frame before the cold backup begins.

Under no circumstances should you ever use **shutdown abort** before a cold backup. A **shutdown abort**, to an Oracle database, is in most ways the same as simply pulling the plug on the server (or stopping the service, as mentioned in Chapter 4). The database shuts down no matter what sort of activity is occurring, including active disk writes and active log writes. All of this must be cleaned up when the database is started and opened again, at which point instance recovery rolls back any uncommitted transactions. However, the database, although shut down, is in an inconsistent state, and therefore the backup that is taken after a **shutdown abort** will also be inconsistent and thus unreliable.

An old trick of the trade is to use the following commands to ensure the database is in a consistent state before a backup:

```
shutdown abort;
startup restrict;
shutdown normal;
```

Although this is generally acceptable, a **shutdown immediate** will ensure the database is in the same state as the database using the three commands in our example, while avoiding the mess of restarting the database to get a clean shutdown.

After the database is shut down, an OS utility must then be used to copy the Oracle files to the backup location. If the backup location is simply another drive or a network drive, then the Windows copy utility can be used. If all datafiles exist in the same directory, this is a simple command:

```
copy d:\Oracle\Ora90\oradata\*.dbf        z:\backup
```

Otherwise, each file must be named specifically and, therefore, updated whenever a new datafile is added to the database. Other than the datafiles, a cold backup should include a backup of the control files, redo log files, a copy of the init.ora, and the password file (if one exists). With all of these files, a cold backup can simply be restored from backup and a **startup** command can be issued with no further database administrator interference. Thus, the simplicity of the cold backup.

When Shutdown Immediate Hangs

There are times when a **shutdown immediate** will hang for an excessively long time. Usually, this is because of rollback. If the **shutdown** command came at the tail end of a transaction that had been updating tables for over five hours, then that entire transaction must be rolled back completely before a clean shutdown can occur. There is no way to avoid this. If a **shutdown abort** is issued and then the database is started, the rollback simply picks back up where it left off, and the subsequent **shutdown normal** or **shutdown immediate** will hang again until the rollback completes. To avoid this behavior, you must be familiar enough with the database to ensure that a clean shutdown is not required at the same time that a large DML statement is running.

Bear in mind, of course, that the database opens from the time the backup was taken, and any subsequent data entry is lost.

To ensure that all necessary files are backed up, use the database and its V$VIEWS to dynamically build the backup script each time a backup is run. So, instead of creating a .BAT file that issues a **copy** command, use SQL to generate a new .bat file each time it is run:

```
connect system/manager
set echo off pages 0 feed off sqlp #
spool c:\stage\cold_bkup.bat
select 'copy '||name||' c:\backup ' from v$datafile;
select 'copy '||name||' c:\backup ' from v$controlfile;
select 'copy '||member||' c:\backup ' from v$logfile;
spool off;
exit;
```

The file c:\backupscripts\cold_bkup.bat will look like this:

```
#select 'copy '||name||' c:\backup ' from v$datafile;
copy C:\ORACLE\ORADATA\REPO\SYSTEM01.DBF c:\backup
copy C:\ORACLE\ORADATA\REPO\UNDOTBS01.DBF c:\backup
copy C:\ORACLE\ORADATA\REPO\CWMLITE01.DBF c:\backup
copy C:\ORACLE\ORADATA\REPO\DRSYS01.DBF c:\backup
copy C:\ORACLE\ORADATA\REPO\EXAMPLE01.DBF c:\backup
copy C:\ORACLE\ORADATA\REPO\INDX01.DBF c:\backup
copy C:\ORACLE\ORADATA\REPO\TOOLS01.DBF c:\backup
copy C:\ORACLE\ORADATA\REPO\USERS01.DBF c:\backup
copy C:\ORACLE\ORADATA\REPO\OEM_REPOSITORY.DBF c:\backup
copy C:\ORACLE\ORADATA\REPO\TRANS_REPTEST01.DBF c:\backup
#select 'copy '||name||' c:\backup ' from v$controlfile;
copy C:\ORACLE\ORADATA\REPO\CONTROL01.CTL c:\backup
copy C:\ORACLE\ORADATA\REPO\CONTROL02.CTL c:\backup
copy C:\ORACLE\ORADATA\REPO\CONTROL03.CTL c:\backup
#select 'copy '||member||' c:\backup ' from v$logfile;
copy C:\ORACLE\ORADATA\REPO\REDO03.LOG c:\backup
copy C:\ORACLE\ORADATA\REPO\REDO02.LOG c:\backup
copy C:\ORACLE\ORADATA\REPO\REDO01.LOG c:\backup
#spool off;
```

Using Windows 2000 Backup Utility

If you would like to offload backups to tape or other media, Windows 2000 provides a basic interface for scheduling backups of files to these devices. You can access Backup.exe from Start | Programs | Accessories | System Tool | Backup. This backup utility can be used to handle backup, as well as restore operations.

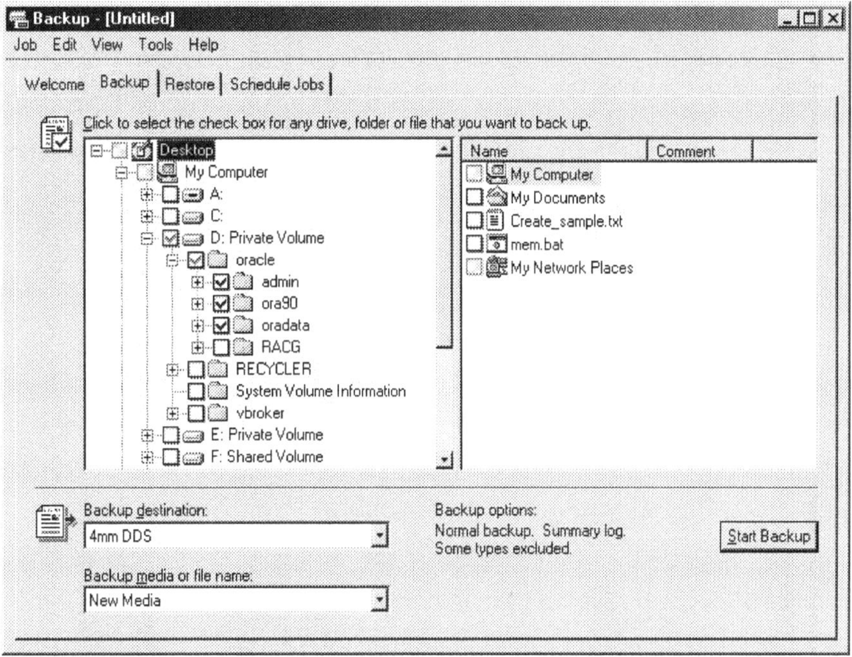

Third-Party Backup Products

A host of vendor products exist to provide further functionality for file-level backups. Many provide a more robust version of Windows 2000's built-in backup utility, providing the ability to back up across a network, manage the backup of multiple databases across the enterprise, and interface with tape jukebox devices.

Many of these come with an Oracle plug-in, often referred to as the Oracle Agent. The Oracle Agent allows a backup utility the ability to log into the Oracle database and prepare the database for hot backups.

Understanding and Implementing Hot Backups

The glory days of the cold backup are receding quickly into the past, back to a time when a large database was a single gigabyte in size. These days, corporations rely so heavily on their databases that a window for a shutdown and cold backup rarely presents itself. The databases themselves are growing so large that the window for a cold backup would have to extend beyond 24 hours for the entire backup operation to complete. Chances are, you will not be able to plan for cold backups, and therefore need to implement some sort of hot backup strategy.

Backing up the Oracle9*i* database while it is open requires that the database be in archivelog mode. There is no way around this. The redo generation that is saved in the archive logs provides the only means of making sure that every transaction is safe in case of a restore.

The most common type of hot backup utilizes the Oracle capability to mark each datafile as if it is in *backup mode*. The database administrator logs into the database, sets a particular tablespace in backup mode, and then starts an operating system file copy operation on all files that belong to that tablespace.

```
Sqlplus>alter tablespace system begin backup;
```

After all the files in the tablespace are backed up successfully at the OS level, the database administrator must pull the tablespace out of backup mode.

```
Sqlplus>alter tablespace system end backup;
```

When we discussed third-party vendor products previously, we mentioned they used an Oracle Agent to integrate their products with the database. That agent's primary job in life is to issue the commands to start and stop backup mode in coordination with the backup utility's OS file copying.

This method of backup has existed for quite some time in Oracle databases. Here's how it works. When the beginning of a backup is signaled for a tablespace, every datafile in that tablespace has its header modified with a marker that sets the SCN point when the backup begins. The header of the file is frozen at this SCN, and will not advance until an **end backup** command is issued. None of this impedes normal database activity, and all DML continues to be applied in real time to the datafiles that are in backup mode.

However, one other architectural change occurs for files that are in backup mode. If a block is pulled into memory to be modified with DML, the Log Writer (LGWR) process also writes *the entire block to the current log file*. Remember, under normal circumstances, when we change a single row, the log file simply gets a record of that single change, and its SCN. The amount of data recorded in the log file reflects the size of the changed information. Now, Log Writer is dumping the entire block in which that record exists. Instead of writing perhaps 40 bytes of data, Oracle is now writing 4096 bytes (given a 4KB block size).

Obviously, this change in log behavior has a significant impact on the number of redo entries generated while a datafile is in backup mode. So what gives? Why do you need the whole block? Because a file is in backup mode, Oracle assumes an OS process may actively be copying the contents of that file. But Oracle cannot monitor the progress of that OS process, so it does not know if it is in the middle of copying a block it's about to rewrite. If the OS copy is in the middle of a block, and Oracle rewrites that block, then the copied block's first half has one SCN, and the second half has another. This block is known as being *in flight*, and is logically corrupt.

This explains why a hot backup is invalid unless the tablespaces are first put into backup mode. To be able to guarantee that no blocks are in flight when a restore occurs, Oracle dumps the entire block into the redo stream before the change occurs and records the changes in normal fashion. When the restore operation starts, Oracle restores the entire block from the archive logs and overwrites the blocks in the OS file backup before applying the redo changes. Figure 6-1 illustrates this process.

This form of hot backup is extremely popular in the Oracle user base, as it has existed for a long time and has proven its reliability. As long as you have copied the files while they were in backup mode, and all the archive logs since the beginning of the backup are available, then a restore operation will be successful.

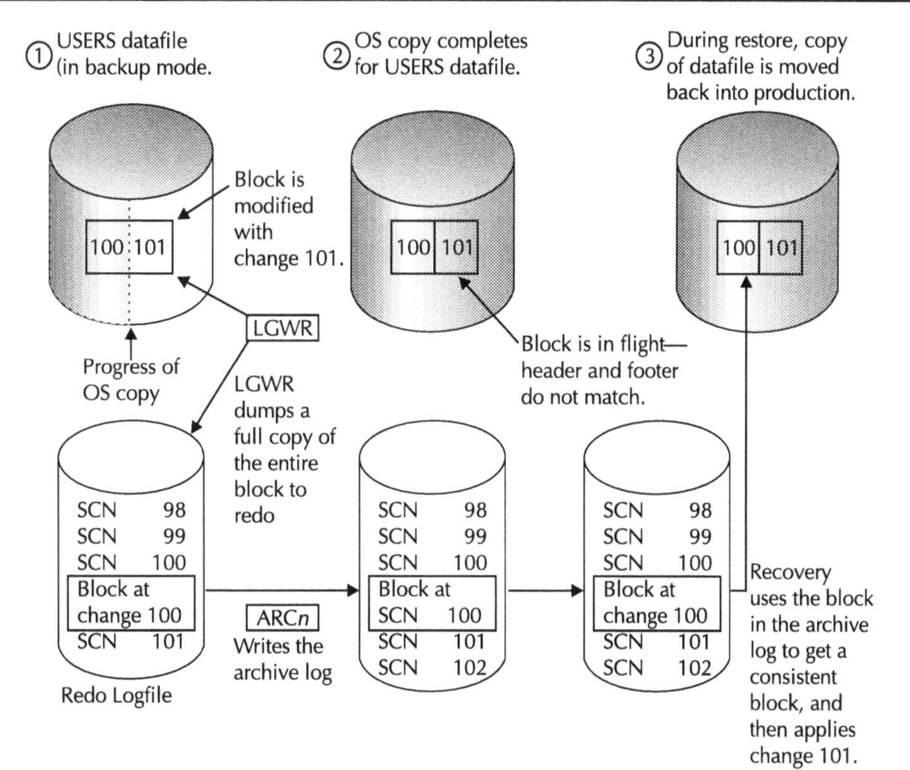

FIGURE 6-1. *Rewriting an in-flight block*

The number one, hands down, most common mistake that occurs when using backup mode to make hot backups is creating a script that puts the files into backup mode, kicks off the **OS copy** command, and then connects back into Oracle and issues the **end backup** command *before the OS copy has completed.* This erroneous script would look something like this:

```
Connect system/manager;
alter tablespace system begin backup;
alter tablespace users begin backup;
alter tablespace data begin backup;
alter tablespace index begin backup;
host
copy d:\oracle\ora9i\oradata   z:\backup
exit
alter tablespace system end backup;
alter tablespace users end backup;
alter tablespace data end backup;
alter tablespace index end backup;
```

This script is perfectly acceptable in all ways, except the most important: the **copy** command kicks off, but will obviously take some time to complete. However, the script just moves on, taking the tablespaces back out of backup mode almost immediately after putting them into backup mode. This causes the backups to be invalid, as there is no protection from in-flight blocks. Backup mode was not in effect for the duration of the copy. To protect yourself from this, use the /wait switch for the **copy** command:

```
copy d:\oracle\ora9i\oradata   z:\backup /wait
```

This tells the script to wait at this command until it completes before moving on to the next command (in this case, an exit).

Leveraging Server Managed Recovery

Oracle introduced a new kind of backup and recovery in version 8.0, referred to as server managed recovery (SMR). SMR is Oracle's ability to back itself up and restore itself using an advanced scripting language that interfaces with built-in kernel code. You interface with SMR using the Oracle Recovery Manager utility, known in the vernacular as RMAN. Allowing the database server to manage its own backups comes with the kinds of benefits that cannot be ignored and, once implemented, become irreplaceable partners in any high-availability environment.

Not that this innovation is without cost. RMAN can be a little unwieldy, as it requires learning a new scripting language all its own. But the benefits far outweigh the trouble that will be encountered at first. That's why we recommend using RMAN for all backup and restore operations, no matter the size or availability concerns of the database. Sooner or later, you'll want something that RMAN offers, and we're proponents of sooner rather than later, especially when it comes to the recoverability of a database.

Understanding the Oracle9*i* Recovery Manager Architecture

Recovery Manager, or RMAN, is a free-standing application that accesses Oracle9*i* database's internal backup and recovery packages. The executable, rman.exe, and its support files, are installed as part of the utilities suite of products during database installation (Export, Import, and Sql*Loader are the other utilities). As such, RMAN can be installed on a client machine and then make a network connection to the database.

We make this point to drive home a common misconception about RMAN: that it does any work. It does not. RMAN is nothing more than a command interpreter, with its own little syntax language. It takes commands you enter and interprets them into PL/SQL blocks that then get passed to and executed at the target database. The important thing to note is that the target database carries the entire load of the backup and restore operations. We use *target database* to refer to the database that you are backing up. Therefore, when you want to look at RMAN performance, you are looking at the target database—the database is backing itself up.

When the rman.exe makes a connection to the target database, it accesses the control file to gather information about the database. From the control file, it can find out everything you will ever need to know about what to back up; to wit, where all the files are located. Whatever it does not discover from the control file it gets out of each data block. But we'll talk about that later. The control file, because of its role as traffic controller for the database, has information about each datafile, each online redo log file, and every archived redo log file. RMAN therefore has access to all this information when it determines what to back up.

In addition to information about the database, the control file also stores information about backups that RMAN makes. So RMAN not only reads from the control file, but after a backup operation it also writes to the control file about where the backups are, how big they are, and when they were taken, as well as SCN information. The control file is the primary repository for information about RMAN backups, and when you must perform a restore operation, the control file information is used to find the proper backups and restore them. Obviously, in this situation, having a valid backup of the control file is imperative to restorability when RMAN is used.

Holding critical backup information in the control file creates a nerve-rattling single point of failure. With the control files so closely linked to the database, what happens when they are lost along with the database files themselves? To increase the robust nature of RMAN, Oracle provides the means for creating a *recovery catalog*.

RMAN and the Rebuilt Control File: A Tragedy

Because RMAN stores all backup information in the control file, we urge you to think twice before re-creating the control file. The operation is quite common among database administrators, and the rebuilt control file is a must for many database problems. But remember this before you use **alter database backup controlfile to trace**: when you rebuild the control file, all backup information is lost. Backups therefore become unusable. There are ways to protect against this, but we thought a warning would be good here.

The recovery catalog is a set of tables, views, and procedures that get created in a second Oracle database. These objects hold a detailed replica of the information in the control file about RMAN backups, as well as datafile and archive log data and anything else it can glean from the control file.

To make use of the recovery catalog, RMAN first connects to the target database. It then makes a second network connection to the database that holds the catalog. After registering the target database in the catalog, RMAN performs a resync operation, which pulls all the control file information into the catalog tables. Thereafter, any backup or recovery operation that is recorded in the control file will be entered into the recovery catalog on every subsequent resync.

The primary reason to keep a catalog is to make sure that the target database control file is not the only repository of information about backups. If the entire database is lost, from datafile to control file to log file, RMAN can still connect to the catalog and restore a control file and then all datafiles. Maintaining a catalog also centralizes backup information for multiple databases, as you can register many target databases in a single recovery catalog, and then run reports about backup operations for all targets at once. But other than ease of enterprise management and control file information redundancy, a catalog is not a necessary component. The control file of the target dictates RMAN's behavior. Burn this into your memory permanently.

When the user issues commands to RMAN, these are interpreted as PL/SQL blocks that are passed to the target database. At the target database, two critical packages share the bulk of work: SYS.DBMS_RCVMAN and SYS.DBMS_BACKUP_RESTORE. SYS.DBMS_RCVMAN is the package that accesses the control file on behalf of RMAN, extracting any necessary data that might be requested. SYS.DBMS_BACKUP_RESTORE is the workhorse package: it performs all backup and restore operations. Figure 6-2 describes these relationships.

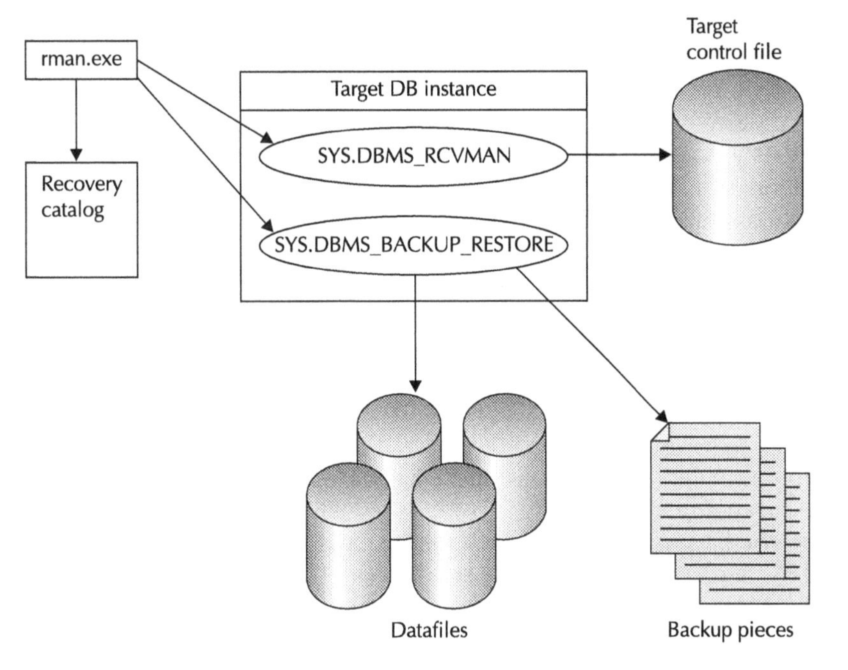

FIGURE 6-2. *RMAN and the target database packages*

RMAN Configuration: A Primer

Initial configuration of RMAN takes only a few moments. But before you perform the initial setup, determine whether your backup environment needs a recovery catalog or not. Essentially, we recommend using a recovery catalog, even though it requires involving a second Oracle database to operate. However, the catalog can be created in the same database that holds your Enterprise Manager (EM) repository, and therefore shouldn't be too much more work. But if you have only one database, skipping the recovery catalog is a legitimate choice. Just make sure you back up that control file early and often. In all of the examples that follow, we assume the use of a recovery catalog.

Target Database Configuration

The target database requires no specific configuration in preparation for RMAN usage. The packages used by RMAN on the target, DBMS_RCVMAN and

DBMS_BACKUP_RESTORE, are created along with all database packages during the running of the CATPROC.SQL script at database creation. They exist on every single Oracle database since version 8.0.3.

Recovery Catalog Configuration

First, decide on a database in which to build the catalog. As stated previously, the same database that houses your EM repository is a logical choice, but any database will do. To fulfill the promise of having a redundant copy of target database control file information, we recommend building the catalog in a database that physically resides on a different computer from the target database. Obviously, this logically rules out putting the recovery catalog in the target database. This will not fail; and for testing purposes, we in the support department do this all the time. However, in a production environment, it makes no sense to go through all the catalog creation steps simply to leave it in the target database. This defeats the purpose by making the catalog reside in the same location as the target database control file. You might as well just use the control file.

Now you have a database chosen for the catalog. Next, log into the database as SYSTEM and create a user whose schema will hold the catalog. This user can have any name, but convention has usually been to create a user with the name of RMAN.

```
Connect system/manager;
create tablespace rcat datafile
'd:\oracle\ora91\oradata\repo\rcat01.dbf' size 50m;
create user rman identified by rman
default tablespace rcat
temporary tablespace temp;
grant connect, resource, recovery_catalog_owner to rman;
```

This final step, granting RECOVERY_CATALOG_OWNER, gives all the system privileges necessary to the RMAN user to own and operate an RMAN recovery catalog. Now the catalog database is prepared. The final step of catalog creation requires you to use RMAN. You log into RMAN from a command prompt, connect to the user RMAN, and issue the command **create catalog**.

```
C:>rman
rman>connect catalog rman/rman@repo
rman>create catalog;
```

The **connect** command tells RMAN that the user specified here will be the catalog owner. If, upon connection to this user, RMAN does not find an existing catalog, it echoes this message:

```
Connected to recovery catalog database
recovery catalog not installed
```

After the create catalog statement is processed, the recovery catalog is built but empty. Your next step is to register your target database in the catalog. You've already connected to the catalog; you need only a target database connection before issuing the **register** command.

Connecting to the target database can be tricky business, but we'll let you in on the secret: RMAN appends the words "AS SYSDBA" to every connection sent to the target. What this means is that you must connect as a sysdba user from within RMAN, or it will reject the connection:

```
Ora-1017: insufficient privileges
Ora-1031: invalid username/password; logon denied
```

To avoid this, be at the target database console when you run any RMAN commands, and logged into Windows 2000 as a user who has sysdba privileges via the ORA_DBA group (see Chapter 4 if you're unfamiliar with this group).

Once RMAN is connected to both the target database and the recovery catalog, a simple **register database** command finishes the deal by populating catalog tables with information drawn from the target database's control file. If you have more than one database that will be registered in your catalog, you need to connect to each target in turn and register them with the **register database** command; the command interprets the currently connected target as the database to perform commands against.

A Note on RMAN Compatibility

RMAN has a checkered past when it comes to compatibility with previous versions of itself. Even as late as versions 8.1.6 and 8.1.7, there existed incompatibilities: you could not register an 8.1.7 database in an 8.1.6 catalog. Oracle9*i* has cleared up most of these problems. For compatibility issues, you should understand and be able to differentiate between the four major components in any RMAN configuration.

- **RMAN executable file** As mentioned previously, the executable file itself has a version. Running RMAN from the same environment that you use to connect to your target database guarantees that the version will be compatible.
- **Target database** The target database version is critical to RMAN usage success. Remember that RMAN translates user commands into PL/SQL calls to packages that exist on the target. Between versions, the composition of these packages can change. Therefore, if RMAN is building calls that were based on package specs from 8.1.6 and then passing them to a package

from 8.0.5, there are inconsistencies that RMAN cannot resolve, and an error results.

- **Recovery catalog** The catalog became much more of a compatibility liability in Oracle8i. Previously, the relationship between the target database and rman.exe was the most problematic. But due to changes in RMAN architecture and its relationship to the catalog, now you need to make sure that the RMAN catalog version matches that of the RMAN executable as well. If it does not match, make sure the RMAN catalog is the latest and greatest.
- **Recovery database** Don't confuse the recovery database with the recovery catalog. The recovery database simply refers to the Oracle database within which the recovery catalog owner resides. The version of this database is the least important piece of the puzzle, and in general isn't worth stressing over. But if you're getting problems, check on the version—a 9i recovery catalog in an 8.0.5 database probably won't work.

Which leads us to an interesting piece of the compatibility puzzle: is it possible to create a 9i catalog in an 8i database? The answer is yes—sort of. To do so, you need to create the RMAN user on the 8i database, granting it the important role of RECOVERY_CATALOG_OWNER. Then, from your 9i installation, fire up RMAN and connect to this user with the **connect** command. The **create catalog** will run, using the scripts built into the 9i RMAN Recover.bsq file, and what gets created in the RMAN user on the 8i database are tables, views, and packages for holding 9i database backup information.

If you think the compatibility issue seems maddening and unreasonable, you're right. The lack of compatibility is inexcusable—and it doesn't end internally with the components mentioned previously. Factor in the piece of third-party code from companies like VERITAS and Legato that allows RMAN to back up to tape, and you have opened a real can of worms. But remember what we said early on: Sweat through this. It's worth it in the long run.

RMAN Integration with Media Management Software

RMAN, as if it weren't bad enough all by itself, has an additional layer that must be configured before you can perform backup and recovery operations using tertiary storage. *Tertiary storage* is a fancy way of saying removable storage devices, the most common being cheap, long, fat tapes. The ability to stream directly to tape is a major selling point for using RMAN—required by anyone whose database gets discussed in sizes larger than just a few gigabytes. Databases are growing into the hundreds of gigabytes in size, and terabyte databases are no longer an object of speculation. However, no one has that much disk storage space just lying around. So tape backups aren't just convenient, they are necessary.

Oracle decided at the onset of RMAN development that trying to build into RMAN code the system calls to access the myriad of different tape devices would seriously hinder the product's development. Besides, a litany of companies sell magnificent products to manage tape devices and the backup operations to those devices. So instead of writing code to back up to tapes, Oracle flexed its market-share muscle and wrote a generic API for issuing commands to tape. This API was then provided to other vendors with the intention that those vendors would then integrate that API into code that could access their existing backup software.

And that is exactly what happens. In its current form, the Oracle SBT API, as it is called, simply makes generic calls to third-party backup software, which must interpret those commands and send them to the appropriate tape device. To enable this communication, you must link the vendor's Media Management Library with the Oracle RDBMS. The Media Management Library, or MML, refers to the DLL that the vendor provides that must interpret RMAN tape commands and send them on to the *Media Management Server*. The Media Management Server, or MMS, is responsible for all tape reads and writes. The MMS also keeps its own catalog, referred to as the Media Management Catalog, which contains data about the names of backups and which tapes they reside on.

Appendix C serves as a quick reference guide for setting up VERITAS NetBackup for tape backups on Windows 2000.

Understanding the Benefits of an RMAN Implementation

Now that we've discussed configuring RMAN, we can begin to think about performing database backups using RMAN. First, let's discuss the exact method by which RMAN backs up the database.

Backup Memory Buffers

Previously, we discussed the basic architecture of the RMAN utility, and how it accesses packages in the target database, which in turn perform the backup operations. When these packages are called by channel processes to perform a backup, they access the control file for a list of datafiles to be backed up, and at the same time they allocate memory buffers that will be used for loading Oracle data blocks for backup.

RMAN allocates two kinds of backup buffers: input buffers and output buffers. RMAN accesses the datafiles and begins to load every data block from the file into an input buffer, where it checks the block header for information. If the block has ever been used, then RMAN does a memory-to-memory buffer write from the input buffer to the output buffer. The output buffer, when full, is written to the backup location (disk or tape).

The number and size of backup buffers is determined by a combination of parameters, some set by the backup operation itself, others by initialization parameters, and others by the OS itself. A *channel process* refers to the process created on the target database for a backup operation. For every file being backed up, RMAN allocates four input buffers. For instance, if the backup operation requires each channel to back up two datafiles, then the process multiplies the number of files by four and creates eight total input buffers. The size of each buffer is the value of the parameter DB_BLOCK_SIZE multiplied by the value of DB_FILE_DIRECT_IO_COUNT. The latter parameter defaults to 64, and represents the total number of blocks that can be used by one I/O operation for backup and restore operations. Therefore you multiply this by your block size, say, 8KB, and you get the size of each input buffer: 52,4288 bytes. The DIRECT_IO_COUNT value can be increased or decreased for performance purposes, but cannot ever exceed the MAX_IO_SIZE for Windows 2000, 512KB.

RMAN creates four output buffers for each backup piece being written to by a channel process. A *backup piece* refers to the physical file created during an RMAN backup operation (see "Backup Sets, Backup Pieces, and Copies" later in this chapter). If there are four pieces being written by a channel process, then sixteen output buffers are created. The size of the output buffer is the same as the input buffer, if the backup is going to disk. For backups to tape, the default size of each buffer on Windows 2000 is 64KB, but the BLKSIZE parameter on the **allocate channel** command can be used to override the default. Be sure to gauge this value based on your Media Manager documentation.

Input and output buffers are built in the Process Global Area (PGA) of the Oracle memory area, meaning they do not compete for space in the System Global Area (SGA). However, if the parameter BACKUP_TAPE_IO_SLAVES is specified to put the process load on I/O slaves for the backup, or DBWR_IO_SLAVES for disk backups, then the buffers exist within the SGA. Within the SGA, these buffers use the Large Pool for allocation, if one is specified by the database administrator. Otherwise, these buffers contend for space in the Shared Pool.

If you are going to use I/O slaves for performance reasons, be sure to create a Large Pool for these memory buffers. Tape I/O slaves better ensure that the flow of data from the channel process to tape is continuous, therefore decreasing expensive tape stops and starts. This is called *tape streaming*. Disk I/O slaves ensure that the input buffers stay full by increasing the amount of calls to disk that happen simultaneously; this also encourages tape streaming and is recommended.

RMAN and Corruption Checking

During the memory-to-memory write that occurs between the input buffer and the output buffer, RMAN checks the block for corruption and reports any discoveries in the data dictionary views V$BACKUP_CORRUPTION and V$COPY_CORRUPTION (depending on whether you are making a backup or making a copy—we discuss the difference later in the sidebar "Backup Sets, Backup Pieces, and Copies"). By default, if a single block is found to be corrupt during a backup, RMAN aborts the operation with a corrupt block error. However, before a backup, you can specify to RMAN to tolerate a certain level of corruption before aborting. This can be useful if you know of corruption in a datafile, but need to preserve in backup form the remainder of the blocks in the datafile. The number of corrupt blocks RMAN tolerates is set during a RUN operation in RMAN:

```
Rman>run {
set maxcorrupt for datafile 8 to 10;
...
backup datafile 8; }
```

RMAN also checks to make sure that any archive log that it backs up is free from corruption. However, there is no way to set RMAN to ignore archive log corruption, as a corrupt archive log would inhibit the ability to roll forward during recovery and therefore cannot be tolerated under any circumstances. The good news is that in Oracle9*i*, RMAN automatically looks at all available copies of an archive log before giving an error reporting archive log corruption.

The Beauty of Block-Level Backups

The primary difference between using RMAN for backups versus an OS utility is the single fact that RMAN is backing up the database at the data block level, not the file level. This granularity provides most of the benefits that come from RMAN backups, and is the reason we recommend all the pain and agony of learning the command interface of RMAN. Think about it for a second: what is the smallest piece of the database that an OS copy utility can understand? It's the file. RMAN, however, utilizes the built-in capabilities of the Oracle9*i* RDBMS, and thus has access to data blocks. When the backup has access to the data block, you can determine more successfully what needs to be backed up versus what does not need to be backed up. For instance, if there is a datafile that is created at 4GB, based on how large you expect certain tables to grow over the next year, chances are that datafile does not start with 4GB of data. Instead, it may start with 50MB and slowly grow by 5- or 10MB each day. With an OS copy, every backup takes a copy of the entire 4GB datafile. However, RMAN knows how many blocks to back up: it looks at each block in the datafile, and if the block has ever held data, RMAN backs it up. If the block is unused, the input buffer simply discards the block instead of passing it to the output buffer, and this block is not backed up.

Two things that cause many misconceptions about RMAN must be clarified. First, every block in the datafile must be read into memory and checked for data. Because RMAN is only backing up used space, there is the perception that RMAN pulls high watermark information about datafiles from the data dictionary. This is simply not the case. RMAN does not access any space management information in the database. This is a design specification, as space management information is only available when the database is open, and RMAN must be able to perform all its functions regardless of whether or not the database is open or closed. Therefore, the only two places RMAN can look for information about the database are the control file and the data block header. Between the two, RMAN knows much more about what to back up than does an OS utility that can read only the datafile header.

Second, because RMAN cannot access space management information, or analyze the internal makeup of a block, it cannot know if a block is empty or full, just if it's been used or remains unused. This means that if a block has been written to in the past, but then all data inside of it is deleted by a user, RMAN still backs this block up. RMAN backs up all used blocks, even if they are currently empty.

Because of its design as a block-level backup utility, RMAN tends to back up less than most OS copy utilities. Block-level information can also be used to perform incremental backups. *Incremental backups* only back up blocks that have changed since the last full or incremental backup. Again, RMAN must read every block into memory, so there is no decrease in the amount of time it takes for RMAN to determine what needs backing up. But based on the SCN number at the time of a previous backup, RMAN then determines whether or not each block needs to be written to the backup file. If the SCN in the block header is higher than that recorded for the previous backup, then the block is moved from the input buffer to the output buffer and written to the backup. If the SCN is equal to or less than the last backup, the block is discarded. In this way, you can decrease the size of your backups even more, as well as possibly increasing the speed of recovery.

Because RMAN has access to the database at the block level, hot backups using RMAN do not require that the files being backed up first be put in backup mode. As RMAN reads the block header, if it shows that the DBWR process is currently writing the block, RMAN simply waits until the Database Writer is finished and then backs up the block. Therefore, you do not have to incur the expense of dumping entire blocks to redo if a single row is updated.

New Feature in Oracle9i

Perhaps one of the most important features of block-level backups did not get introduced until 9i. In this release, RMAN now has the capability to recover a single block. This process, referred to as *block media recovery,* can be used if a single data block is marked as corrupt for some reason. The most common form of corruption is that reported by the infamous error ORA-1578: "data block corrupted." This error can be reported during any form of activity on the database, and will give the file number and block number of the corruption.

```
ORA-1578:ORACLE data block corrupted (file # 4, block # 5678)
```

In the past, this error could only be corrected by restoring the entire datafile and then performing recovery using archive logs. However, RMAN now provides a new way to fix this. Because of its block-level information, a user can now pass to RMAN the file and block number from the ORA-1578 error, and RMAN will restore the single block from a backup and then recover the block using appropriate archive logs. Therefore, MTTR is decreased significantly as the entire file is not offlined for a restore, and other objects in the file remain available to users during the recovery process.

```
run {blockrecover datafile 4 block 5678;}
```


RMAN Backups: Syntax and Usage

So, we finally must get into it: the RMAN command syntax. There is a ruthlessness to it that will fail to surprise only the most cynical of database administrators. However, it is the most efficient and reliable way to work with RMAN. Oracle provides a GUI using Enterprise Manager, but this interface comes with limitations in that it cannot be used for the entirety of RMAN functionality. And when it comes crunch time, when you must recover the database, there will be last-minute alterations in the processes you use to recover the database that cannot be done if the flexibility of the product is stiffened by a flat GUI. Instead of using Enterprise Manager now to set up backups, and then forced to learn the command line interface during a heated recovery, we urge you to take the time to familiarize yourself now with the command line syntax, and then return to the Enterprise Manager interface and decide if it meets your needs.

The RMAN Run Block

We previously discussed connecting to the target database as well as the recovery catalog. These connections must be made prior to running a backup (or restore) operation. After making the connection, you must set the stage within RMAN for the backup. The first step is to allocate channel processes to manage the backup buffers. These processes are created using an **allocate channel** command. However, before you can allocate a channel, you must enclose your entire backup operation so that it runs as a single block. In PL/SQL, for example, the enclosure is the **begin...end** syntax. In RMAN, you begin a run block by using the syntax **run {...}**. All commands that are inside the brackets are run together. In this way, you can allocate channel processes and link them with a backup operation for the life span of the operation, and then release the processes.

```
Rman>run {
      allocate channel ch_1 device type sbt;
      allocate channel ch_2 device type sbt;
      backup database;
      release channel ch_1;
      release channel ch_2;}
```

This operation creates two channel processes that will back up every file in the database to tape. **device type disk** is used to specify a backup to disk. When backing up to disk, it behooves you to specify a format for the backup so that you can choose where you want the backup to reside; otherwise, the backup will be written to the current working directory with a default format. Obviously, choosing the backup format is important for backing up to tape as well, but when you write to tape, you don't need to choose drive locations or directories.

The run block can have multiple backup commands included, so its complexity can mount rather quickly.

```
Rman>run {
      allocate channel ch_1 device type disk format
      'd:\oracle\backup\%U';
      allocate channel ch_2 device type disk format
      'f:\oracle\backup\%U';
      backup datafile 1,2,3,4,5,6;
      backup archivelog all format 'd:\oracle\backup\arch.%U'
      delete input; }
```

This command allocates two channels to write backups to disk; each channel takes a format clause to direct backups to two separate disks. The **backup** command only backs up six files, numbered 1 through 6. RMAN will look at the control file to get the name, location, and size of each of these files, and then load balance so that both channel processes have roughly the same amount of work. After the datafile backup is complete, RMAN then utilizes the same channels to back up all the archive logs. The **format** command attached to the **backup archivelog** command will override that of the channels, so that both channel processes will simultaneously write to the d:\oracle\backup directory. After the successful backup of the archive logs, RMAN deletes them from their location in LOG_ARCHIVE_DEST.

Channel Allocation Guidelines

Deciding on channel allocation can be a tricky business, and we certainly do not have all the answers. The solution that best fits your needs requires looking at the trade-offs involved, as well as the actual benefits of increasing the number of channels for a backup operation.

Disk Channel Allocation

For disk backup operations, there is little benefit from allocating multiple channels if you are writing to a single storage device. For instance, if the entire backup operation will reside on d:\oracle\backup, then having four channels allocated for the operation will mean that there are four processes fighting for access to that disk. Some anecdotal evidence has shown there to be a minor benefit from having two channels writing to the same disk—but the increase is not double; rather, it hovers around a 15 to 20 percent performance increase. Therefore, we recommend at most two channels per disk, if you have the memory resources to spare. Setting DBWR_IO_SLAVES does not affect disk writes with RMAN, only reads into input buffers. Setting this parameter to any non-zero value will flag RMAN to create four I/O slaves to keep input buffers full and blocks flowing steadily to backup pieces. Disk I/O slaves benefit disk and tape backups.

Tape Channel Allocation

Tape channel allocation can be summed up with a blanket statement: only allocate one channel per tape device. If your Media Manager will be streaming backup operations to four tapes simultaneously, then allocate four tape channels to produce the best possible results.

We have seen that some Media Managers will take the stream from four RMAN channels and then serially write them to tape, even if there is more than one tape device available. Also, some Media Managers will take a single RMAN channel stream and break it up into multiple pieces for different tapes. Be sure to check with your Media Manager software documentation to find out what is the best way to handle these sorts of inconsistencies.

Set the parameter BACKUP_TAPE_IO_SLAVES=TRUE in the initialization parameter file. This creates a single I/O slave per process to read from the output buffer and write to tape, which keeps the tape streaming and avoids tape stops and starts.

The Memory Cost of RMAN Channel Processes

Remember that every channel allocated has a memory and CPU cost involved. Therefore, you must balance the importance of backup speed against the cost to the production database. One of the most telling anecdotes we can share came from a dot-com company that called Oracle Support complaining about an RMAN bug. They had tuned the backup operation so that RMAN backed up their 40+ gigabytes of data in little over 30 minutes. However, after getting this set up, they found that when RMAN was running, no users could connect to the database, which is pretty much as big a deal as there is when your entire company relies on a web site for business. After looking at their environment, we discovered that they allocated 64 channels for the backup operation, which maxed out their CPUs and all physical memory for the duration of the backup. Users were, in fact, connecting, but the heavy-duty swapping that occurred to get virtual memory for user process space took so long that the users were simply giving up and aborting the transaction.

CPU utilization is hard to gauge, and relies heavily on what kind of processor is involved and how many there are. However, we can comment on memory consumption. Remember that RMAN allocates input and output buffers for each channel process initiated for backup. Using the math provided previously in the section "Backup Memory Buffers" will give you a nearly exact match for how much memory the backup will take: if you have 20 datafiles in a backupset and you are writing to 5 backup pieces, then you will have 80 input buffers and 20 output buffers, all sized based on the block size multiplied by 64.

The RMAN Backup Command

The **backup** command itself can often seem like a rock of simplicity weathering the storm of configuration that occurs in order to prepare for the backup. But it is important to understand the different kinds of backups and how they are created.

Datafile Backups

The most common backup is a datafile backup. Datafiles are the critical element of a backup: as you know, they contain the data. Datafile backups can be specified for backup either by their datafile number or their name, or by default when the entire database is backed up. The datafile number is found in the V$DATAFILE view:

```
Sqlplus>connect system/manager
sqlplus>select file#, name, status from v$datafile;
```

RMAN has access to this same view, and can thus interpret the number into a file name and location. For the love of carpal tunnels, get used to referring to your datafiles by their control file number: the amount of typing it takes to refer to files by their full directory location and name will be cause for serious HMO griping in

Backup Sets, Backup Pieces, and Copies

It is critical to understand the difference between the terms backup sets, backup pieces, and copies. A *backup set* refers to a logical grouping of files in a backup. A backup set is created when a **backup** command is issued and given a unique number, or key, which is used for internal organization and lookup during restore and recovery operations.

RMAN creates a proprietary output file during a backup operation. This file contains data blocks from one or more datafiles, often intermingled with each other in an unintelligible format. This file is only usable by RMAN during a restore operation, at which point the data blocks are sorted out and placed back in datafile format. These proprietary files are referred to as *backup pieces*. Backup pieces are associated with only one backup set in the same way that a datafile would be associated with only one tablespace.

This proprietary file format can prove to be quite limiting, in the sense that the file cannot simply be moved back into its proper location from a backup location and then recovered. RMAN must manually rebuild the file, and although this process is fast, it is certainly not as fast as simply moving a copy of the actual datafile back into place. In order to satisfy this need for a fast restore, RMAN can perform a datafile copy instead of a backup. A *copy* refers to a backup that RMAN takes by copying each block from the datafile in much the same way as an OS utility might, except that RMAN does not require the file to be placed in backup mode. This copy that RMAN takes can be restored using non-RMAN methods, and is a usable datafile copy.

a few years. However, RMAN understands both; and in certain cases, typing in the full datafile location and name will be critical.

When a full database backup is specified, RMAN backs up every datafile mentioned in the control file, along with a copy of the control file. In fact, RMAN takes a backup of the control file whenever the SYSTEM datafile is backed up. This control file backup will reside in the same backup set as the SYSTEM datafile.

Incremental Datafile Backups

In addition to full backups of datafiles, RMAN can implement an incremental backup strategy that allows the database administrator to only back up blocks that have changed since the last incremental backup. Here's how it works: First, a full backup must be made of each datafile in the database, and this backup must be marked at the time of backup as an incremental level 0 backup. By specifying a backup as a base-level incremental, RMAN records the SCN point of the backup. Then, the next

backup taken has an incremental level greater than zero, and this backup checks the SCN of each block in the datafile and compares it to the SCN of the full level 0 backup. If the SCN has not changed, then the block is not backed up. If the SCN is higher than the level 0 backup, then the block is backed up.

```
Rman>backup incremental level=0 database;
...
rman>backup incremental level=1 database;
```

Incremental backups can be taken up to four levels deep, based on the integer value specified after the INCREMENTAL keyword. These levels allow for deeper and deeper levels of incrementals that can increase the period between full database backups.

There are two kinds of incremental backups: cumulative and noncumulative. Cumulative backups always back up any blocks that have changes since the last *n*-1 backup, where *n* represents the level of incremental specified. For instance, if a level 1 incremental was performed on Tuesday, then on Wednesday, when a level 2 is performed, you only back up blocks that have changed since Tuesday. If on Thursday you perform another level 2 backup, you again back up all blocks that have changed since the level 1 on Tuesday. Figure 6-3 illustrates this.

Noncumulative incremental backups differ only in that they back up blocks that have changed since the last *n* backup, where *n* represents the level of increment specified. Therefore, in the example in Figure 6-3, the noncumulative incremental taken on Thursday would only back up blocks that have changes since the level 2 backup on Wednesday, instead of going back to the level 1 backup on Monday.

RMAN Backups and Disk Utilization

If you are using RMAN to back up datafiles to disk, you may notice a strange behavior concerning how RMAN allocates space on disk for the backup. Regardless of the type of backup (full or incremental), any back up to disk will immediately allocate enough space on disk to back up every datafile in full. That is, if the total size of all datafiles in a database is 800MB, then RMAN immediately creates a file in your backup location of size 800MB. Upon completion of the backup, when only the necessary blocks have been backed up, you will see this file shrink to its final size, which is almost always less than the total of the datafiles. This means that you need to have enough free space on disk to fit the entire size of the database, even if you are only doing an incremental backup that will ultimately only be a few megabytes in size.

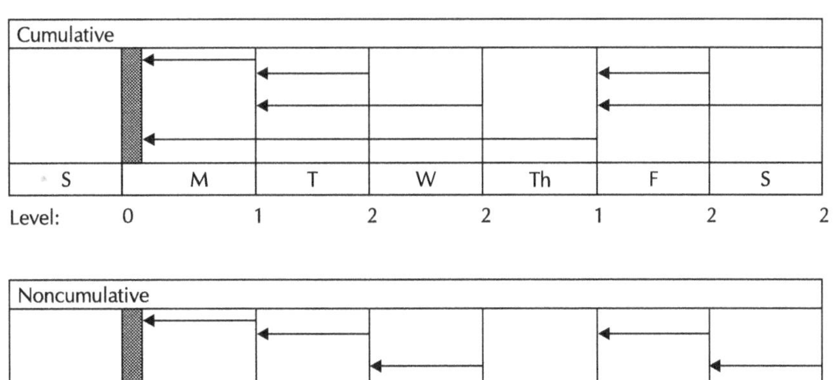

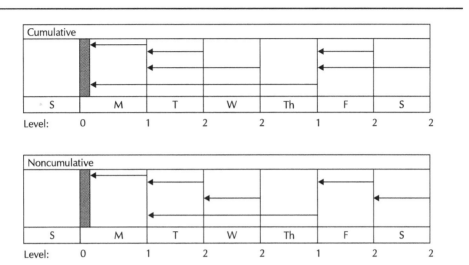

FIGURE 6-3. *Cumulative versus noncumulative incremental backups*

Control File Backup

Because RMAN utilizes the target database control file as the primary repository for backup information, storing a copy of the control file is critical to any backup strategy. If you choose to run RMAN without utilizing a recovery catalog as a backup copy of the repository information in the control file, losing the target database control file can be catastrophic to any recovery. Without a control file, RMAN cannot find the proper backup pieces from which to rebuild the database. Prior to 9i, you could not count on RMAN control file backups for recovery: if you did not have a control file outside of a backup piece, there was no way to access the backup piece that contained a control file backup in order to extract it. Instead, you must take OS backups of the control file using the following command:

```
Sql>alter database backup controlfile
      to 'd:\oracle\backup\cfile_backup.ctl';
```

This binary copy would then be restored in case of disaster and used for RMAN recovery. However, in 9i there is a new control file backup that can be configured. This is referred to as *control file autobackup*; and by switching this on,

RMAN takes a backup of the control file, in its own backup set and using a specific naming convention, whenever any backup operation is performed. In this way, the control file backup is accessible via RMAN, even when an OS copy of the control file is unavailable.

```
RMAN> configure controlfile autobackup on;
```

Archive Log Backup

Perhaps the most complex of operations is the usage of RMAN to back up the archive logs. Archive logs can be produced at a fast pace during heavy DML on the database, and therefore can begin to fill up available disk space quickly. In fact, archive logs account for the largest space management issue faced by database administrators. These files are critical to database recovery in case of any sort of media failure, data block corruption, or other disaster, so you cannot simply delete them.

But how long do you need to keep them? This question has vexed the database administrator since archive logs came into existence. Here, we offer a pragmatist's solution. Archive logs literally provide a timeline of recoverability from the last full database backup (full meaning non-incremental). Therefore, you theoretically only need archive logs to extend back in time to the beginning of the last good backup. However, the last good backup does not necessarily mean the last backup. Perhaps the last backup did not complete successfully, and you have not yet checked the logs to find out. Therefore, the last good backup might be the backup prior to the last backup.

Obviously, the paranoid among us could make this point about every backup, and therefore argue that no archive log should ever be discarded. And to tell you the truth, we've seen this level of paranoia rescue more than one company from complete data loss. However, for the rest of us, we must trust at some level that the backup strategy we have put in place is stable; but just so we can sleep at night, we want some redundancy in the system. Therefore, we propose that keeping archive logs back to the beginning of the backup prior to the last backup—that is, two backups ago—is an appropriate and rational number of archived redo entries to hold onto.

With that settled, we must discuss the more pressing matter of how to get archive logs backed up and moved out of the way for new archive logs. As archive logs pile up in your archive destination, they begin to take a serious toll on disk space. RMAN can assist with this problem, as it can back up archive logs either to an alternate disk location or to tape. The usual problem that is encountered when backing up archive logs using OS utilities is that there is no way to determine, using COPY for example, if a particular archive log is still in the process of being written by the ARC*n* process. If you back up an incomplete archive log and then delete it, you have created a hole in your database recoverability by copying a corrupt archive log and then deleting the complete piece forever. RMAN eliminates this margin of error by coordinating the backups with the RDBMS.

RMAN does not check the archive destination to determine what needs to be backed up. Instead, it checks the V$ARCHIVED_LOG view in the control file. Therefore, it only backs up completed archive logs. This is an important point to remember when working with archive log backups, as you will see soon.

Archive log backups can be specified a number of different ways, all of which serve a different purpose and garner different results. The most common specification is to back up all archive logs:

```
Rman>run { allocate channel ch_1 device type sbt;
     backup archivelog all; }
```

RMAN will back up all archive logs that appear in the view V$ARCHIVED_LOG with an available status (A) in the STATUS column.

```
SQL>col name format a40
SQL>SQL> select name, status, deleted from v$archived_log;

NAME                                       S DEL
----------------------------------------- - ---
D:\ORACLE\ORA90\RDBMS\ARC00002.001         X NO
D:\ORACLE\ORADATA\PROD\ARCH3.1.ARC         A NO
D:\ORACLE\ORADATA\PROD\ARCH4.1.ARC         A NO
D:\ORACLE\ORADATA\PROD\ARCH5.1.ARC         A NO
D:\ORACLE\ORADATA\PROD\ARCH6.1.ARC         A NO
D:\ORACLE\ORADATA\PROD\ARCH7.1.ARC         A NO

6 rows selected.
```

The status of an archive log in this view can only be changed using RMAN techniques. Notice the status of the first archive log is X. This status refers to an archive log that failed a verification check from within RMAN. We moved that archive log to a different directory, and it therefore could not be found during a validation. With a status of X, the archive log is not available for backup.

```
rman>change archivelog all validate;
```

If you choose to have RMAN delete archive logs after backing them up using the **delete input** command, after deleting an archive log, RMAN changes the status of the archive log to deleted (D). Also, the maintenance command **change** can be used to allow RMAN to check the LOG_ARCHIVE_DEST for the existence of archive logs. Any that are currently in V$ARCHIVED_LOG but do not exist in the archive destination will be given a status of deleted. This status can change back to available if at any point archive logs are restored from backup.

```
SQL> select name, status, deleted from v$archived_log;

NAME                                     S DEL
---------------------------------------- - ---
D:\ORACLE\ORA90\RDBMS\ARC00002.001       X NO
D:\ORACLE\ORADATA\PROD\ARCH3.1.ARC       D YES
D:\ORACLE\ORADATA\PROD\ARCH4.1.ARC       D YES
D:\ORACLE\ORADATA\PROD\ARCH5.1.ARC       D YES
D:\ORACLE\ORADATA\PROD\ARCH6.1.ARC       D YES
D:\ORACLE\ORADATA\PROD\ARCH7.1.ARC       D YES
D:\ORACLE\ORADATA\PROD\ARCH8.1.ARC       D YES
7 rows selected.
```

Archive logs can also be specified for backup based on the archive log's LSN or its SCN.

```
Rman>backup archivelog sequence between 100 and 200;
rman>backup archivelog until sequence = 200;
rman>backup archivelog SCN between 10501 and 20501;
```

For a complete listing of all the archive log variations, consult the *Oracle9i Recovery Manager Reference*. The point to take away from this discussion is that all these variations exist whenever an archive log is specified within RMAN for backups, restores, and maintenance commands.

Backup Set Backups

Seems redundant, right? This is a new Oracle9*i* feature in RMAN, and it is quite handy, actually. Often, a backup is made to disk or tape, but at a later point in time, the database administrator needs to move that backup set to a different location, or to tape. For instance, say that you use RMAN to back up the database, and you allocate a disk channel for the backup. However, a few days later you're groping for free space on the system and you need to move those backups. If you manually move them to a different location using OS commands, they will be unusable for recovery until you put them back to the exact location where RMAN backed them up. You can allocate a tape channel, back up the backup set to tape, and then remove the disk version, and the backup is still usable for restore operations. You can move backup sets from disk to tape, and from disk to a new disk location. You cannot move tape backup sets to disk.

Establishing Persistent Backup Parameters

Oracle introduces in 9i the ability to configure persistent settings for backup and recovery using RMAN. In previous versions, every time you ran a backup operation, you had to provide the parameters for the backup in the run block. In 9i, many parameters that are configured identically for all backup operations can be set permanently and, therefore, left out of scripts. Oracle does this by storing the configured settings in the target database control file.

The command **show all** from the RMAN prompt displays the entire list of configurable settings, including the values set by default.

```
RMAN> show all;

RMAN configuration parameters are:
CONFIGURE RETENTION POLICY TO REDUNDANCY 1; # default
CONFIGURE BACKUP OPTIMIZATION OFF; # default
CONFIGURE DEFAULT DEVICE TYPE TO DISK; # default
CONFIGURE CONTROLFILE AUTOBACKUP OFF; # default
CONFIGURE CONTROLFILE AUTOBACKUP FORMAT FOR
  DEVICE TYPE DISK TO '%F'; # default
CONFIGURE DEVICE TYPE DISK PARALLELISM 1; # default
CONFIGURE DATAFILE BACKUP COPIES FOR
   DEVICE TYPE DISK TO 1; # default
CONFIGURE ARCHIVELOG BACKUP COPIES FOR
   DEVICE TYPE DISK TO 1; # default
CONFIGURE MAXSETSIZE TO UNLIMITED; # default
CONFIGURE SNAPSHOT CONTROLFILE NAME TO
   'D:\ORACLE\ORA90\DATABASE\SNCFPROD.ORA'; # default
```

Perhaps most important, the number of channels and their settings can be stored. Rewriting channel allocation code for each backup or restore becomes tedious, especially when you append the environment variables necessary for media management. By configuring these permanently, you avoid the tedium and the increased risk of user error.

```
RMAN> configure default device type to sbt;

new RMAN configuration parameters:
CONFIGURE DEFAULT DEVICE TYPE TO 'SBT_TAPE';
new RMAN configuration parameters are successfully stored
starting full resync of recovery catalog
```

```
full resync complete

RMAN> configure channel 1 device type sbt parms="NB_ORA_CLIENT=ELWAY";

new RMAN configuration parameters:
CONFIGURE CHANNEL 1 DEVICE TYPE 'SBT_TAPE' PARMS  "NB_ORA_CLIENT=ELWAY";
new RMAN configuration parameters are successfully stored
starting full resync of recovery catalog
full resync complete
```

For more information and examples of the **configure** command, refer to *Oracle9i RMAN Reference Guide,* published by Oracle Corporation.

RMAN Restore and Recovery: A Primer

Before we discuss the ways in which RMAN performs recovery, it behooves us to differentiate between a restore operation and a recovery operation. A *restore* refers to the act of bringing the file back into existence in the production environment. If RMAN has been used to back up a datafile, then the term *restore* would refer to the process of rebuilding the datafile from the appropriate backup piece (or pieces). Once the file is back in existence, then we can perform a recovery on the file. *Recovery* is the process of applying the changes saved in the archive logs to the file. This is often referred to as rolling forward through the redo stream.

RMAN can perform both restore and recover operations, but it's not always necessary. Granted, if you used RMAN to create backups, then RMAN must perform the restore. But it will make sense at times to use RMAN for the restore, and then break out of the utility and instead turn to SQL*Plus to perform recovery operations manually. But if you utilize RMAN correctly, letting it take care of all the details of restore and recovery will make more sense.

The RMAN Restore Operation

Using the **restore** command, you can specify to RMAN the file or files that need to be pulled from backup and restored to their location, as specified by the control file.

```
Rman>run { allocate channel ch_1 device type sbt;
     restore datafile 1; }
```

This command will open a channel process that engages the Media Manager and requests the most recent backup of datafile 1. By definition, datafile 1 is always a system tablespace datafile, but every other file number is contingent on its creation time. To obtain a list of datafile numbers, use the following **select** statement:

```
Sqlplus>select file#, name from v$datafile;
```

This list can be used to compile **restore** commands that minimize the amount of typing necessary to specify each file by name. However, the filename can also be specified.

```
Rman>run {allocate channel ch_1 device type sbt;
    restore datafile 'd:\oracle\ora9i\oradata\prod\system01.dbf';
```

More than one datafile can be specified by using the comma as a delimiter:

```
Rman>restore datafile 1,2,3,4;
```

The restore operation also works with two other specifications: **database** and **tablespace**. If the **database** is specified, Oracle restores every datafile listed in V$DATAFILE. If **tablespace** is specified, RMAN restores all datafiles associated with the specified tablespace.

```
Rman> run {allocate channel ch_1 device type sbt;
      restore database;
rman> run {allocate channel ch_1 device type sbt;
      restore tablespace USERS;
```

The restore operation can also be used to restore backed up archive logs to disk. By default, RMAN restores archive logs to the specification of LOG_ARCHIVE_DEST_1. This can be overridden using the SET ARCHIVELOG DESTINATION TO <location> specification to put the archive logs in a new location other than the archive dump destination.

```
Rman> run {allocate channel ch_1 device type sbt;
      restore archivelog all;
RMAN> run {
2> allocate channel ch_1 device type sbt;
3> set archivelog destination to  'd:\oracle\oradata\prod';
4> restore archivelog sequence 2;}
```

Interesting things begin happening when you restore archive logs. As mentioned previously, RMAN interacts directly with the control file, and when RMAN backs up an archive log and then deletes it, the view V$ARCHIVED_LOG is modified to show that the backed up archive log has been deleted (the value in the STATUS column

converts to D). When RMAN restores an archive log, the status of the archive log is changed back to A in the control file. This way, when you issue a **recover** command, the recovery session finds the archive log as available.

Here's the tricky part, so burn this into your memory: when you restore an archive log to a new location using RMAN, the control file is updated with a new entry for the new copy of the archive log in the new location. So, if you ran the run block shown earlier that sets the archive log destination to d:\oracle\oradata\prod, and then restored the archive log with the log sequence number of 2, you would get the following results:

```
SQL> select name, status, deleted from v$archived_log;

NAME                                         S DEL
-------------------------------------------- - ---
D:\ORACLE\ORA90\RDBMS\ARC00002.001           X NO
D:\ORACLE\ORADATA\PROD\ARCH3.1.ARC           D YES
D:\ORACLE\ORADATA\PROD\ARCH4.1.ARC           D YES
D:\ORACLE\ORADATA\PROD\ARCH5.1.ARC           D YES
D:\ORACLE\ORADATA\PROD\ARCH6.1.ARC           D YES
D:\ORACLE\ORADATA\PROD\ARCH7.1.ARC           D YES
D:\ORACLE\ORADATA\PROD\ARCH8.1.ARC           D YES
D:\ORACLE\ORADATA\PROD\2.1.ARC               A NO
8 rows selected.
```

Therefore, the next time RMAN begins to back up archive logs, it checks V$ARCHIVED_LOG and finds a listing of the new archive log and notes that it is available. So RMAN backs it up again. What's the moral of the story? To understand RMAN's relationship with archive logs, keep in mind that everything filters through V$ARCHIVED_LOG. If there is any question about what RMAN is trying to do with archive logs, check the view and see what is happening.

It is worth noting at this juncture that V$ARCHIVED_LOG is a circular reuse section of the control file, and therefore it is possible for entries about archive logs to be aged out of the control file based on the value of CONTROLFILE_RECORD_KEEP_TIME. The default is seven days. This means the default age of records about archive logs may only be seven days old. Usually, this is not the case, as you do not run out of room in the control file in seven days. However, if you have extremely frequent log switches, you may want to change the value of CONTROLFILE_RECORD_KEEP_TIME to a larger value. We recommend you use this alternative approach: simply use a recovery catalog and make sure you resync the catalog at least once in the window of time specified by the CONTROLFILE_RECORD_KEEP_TIME.

RMAN Recovery: Syntax and Usage

Recovery is a tricky term, and its meaning fluidly morphs between vendors and even between product versions. But in the RMAN universe, recovery has a very specific meaning. We stated previously that recovery refers to the process of applying the changes saved in the archive logs to datafiles. This is accurate, but not complete. Recovery is more of a goal than a process. The goal of recovery is to make sure that the Checkpoint SCN in each datafile header matches the Checkpoint SCN in the control file. It's really that simple. Of course, in practice, there are multiple ways to achieve this goal, but keeping the goal in mind will correctly guide you through the recovery process and explain behavior you see along the way.

Manual Recovery Using SQL*Plus

If only restore operations are performed using RMAN, then the act of recovery is left up to the user. This recovery can occur in SQL*Plus using the **recover** command.

```
Sql>recover database;
```

This command would start the *recovery shell*, a subprogram that manages the underlying recovery operations. These operations include checking the control file and datafile headers for SCN information, and determining which datafiles need to have redo applied to them from archived redo log files before they will be in sync with the other datafiles. Then, the recovery shell opens an interactive screen for the user, asking how the user would like to proceed:

```
SQL>recover database;
ORA-00279: change 280425 generated at 07/17/2001 22:16:06
needed for thread 1
ORA-00289: suggestion : D:\ORACLE\ORA90\RDBMS\ARC00009.001
ORA-00280: change 280425 for thread 1 is in sequence #9

Specify log: {<RET>=suggested | filename | AUTO | CANCEL}
```

Entering the return key will apply the suggested archive log. Bear in mind, the recovery session does not actually check first to see if the file exists, so if the archive log file has been deleted, an error will occur. Instead of accepting the default archive log, you can type in the full path and filename of an archive log that may exist in an alternative location. Entering **auto** allows the recovery session to simply check the V$ARCHIVED_LOG view for the necessary archive logs, and apply them automatically

until all datafiles sync up with the control file's last checkpoint SCN. Entering **cancel** will end the recovery session.

Use RMAN to Avoid Manual Restore and Recover Operations

RMAN provides the interface capabilities to avoid issuing manual restore operations, and to avoid using the recovery shell in SQL*Plus to manually operate the recovery process. Instead, it allows the user to simply enter **recover** commands within RMAN, and RMAN will build the internal calls to perform file restoration and recovery. This includes restoring archive logs for the recovery itself. Therefore, if you have configured permanent channel settings, you can simply type the following:

```
Rman>recover database;
```

RMAN will then compile a list of datafiles to restore, and then restore them from the most recent backup. After they are restored, RMAN will begin the recovery process. First, RMAN checks for any incremental backups that will speed up recovery, and restores them. Then RMAN determines if any archive logs need to be restored from backup. If so, RMAN restores these archive logs. After restoring the archive logs, RMAN performs the recovery process of applying changes in the archive logs to the datafiles in order to bring the restored datafiles into sync with the control file.

This ease of recovery is the true payoff of learning and configuring RMAN for backup and recovery. Instead of having a slowdown for searching through backups, then leafing through manuals for commands, searching through tapes for the backups and waiting on the restore, the only time that has to pass between the loss of the database and the startup of your recovered database is literally the time it takes to perform the restore and recovery itself. There is no better way to decrease MTTR than this. Next, we explore the specifics of the RMAN **recover** command and how it functions with the different kinds of recovery.

The Recover Command

The **recover** command can be specified for three different levels of operation. You can recover at the datafile level, the tablespace level, and the database level. All of the following examples assume that you are performing a full recovery. *Full recovery* refers to any recovery that applies all redo entries up to and including the transactions recorded in the online redo logs. We discuss incomplete recovery in the section "Point-in-Time Recovery" later.

Datafile Recovery

In a perfect world, datafile recovery is the only kind of recovery you would need to perform. The datafile recovery allows you to restore and recover a single datafile, or a group of datafiles, without any adverse effect on other datafiles in the same tablespace.

```
Rman>recover datafile 4;
```

When RMAN performs recovery on a datafile, it applies any necessary redo, and then brings the datafile online. This can be issued while the database is open, and is therefore superior to full database recovery, as it allows you to keep the rest of the database available during the recovery process.

Tablespace Recovery

If, for some reason, an entire tablespace has been corrupted or accidentally dropped, RMAN allows for complete tablespace recovery. This allows you to avoid tracking down datafile numbers or datafile names, and instead simply use the logical naming system Oracle uses internally.

```
Rman>recover tablespace USERS;
```

This applies redo entries to every datafile associated with the specified tablespace and then brings the datafiles back online. This command can also be issued when the database is open.

Database Recovery

Instead of specifying which datafiles or tablespace to focus on for recovery, the database recovery checks every datafile in the database to see which file or files need recovery. If there is any question about the status of the database, this command can be run and RMAN will apply the necessary redo entries to each file. For database recovery, the database needs to be mounted but cannot be opened.

```
Rman>recover database;
```

As stated previously, this command can be used to accomplish a complete database restore and recovery, but only if you have a current control file and the appropriate permanent settings have been configured for the channel allocation.

Channel Allocation and Recovery

If the only recovery that must be performed comes from archive logs or online redo logs that already exist on disk, it may seem silly that you still need to allocate a channel to tape to specify where backups exist. But you do this based on the assumption that RMAN may need to restore archive log backups before recovery can be completed, and therefore will have to access tape backups. Likewise, if you are assuming that your **recover** command will perform datafile restore operations prior to recovery, then you need a channel allocated for this restore. As for accessing archive logs in

the archive dump destination, or online redo logs, the default RMAN process that exists on the target database handles this.

Incremental Backups and Recovery

It may have seemed odd that we omitted any discussion of incremental backups during the discussion of the restore operation, but this was done on purpose. An incremental backup cannot be manually restored, as there is no operation for this. Incremental backups can only be restored during an RMAN recover operation.

If you think about this, it makes sense. What is the worth, say, of manually restoring a level 1 incremental backup? Without the level 0 full backup first, the level 1 backup is simply a grouping of a few blocks that may have changed between time A and time B. But they are worthless without a full backup on which to apply the incremental changes. Therefore, the restore operation can only be performed on a full backup, as the full backup is the only backup of every used block in the file.

After the full backup is restored, the recover operation checks the catalog to discover if any incremental backups have been taken since the level 0 backup that was restored. If incrementals do exist, RMAN restores them before applying archive logs; this way, RMAN only has to cycle through archive logs from the date of the incremental backup, and you save significant time during recovery.

Understanding and Using Incomplete Recovery

Often, disasters are the sort that do not allow a full database recovery. Perhaps you have lost the online redo log files, or worse, a user has inadvertently dropped a series of objects from the database. Full recovery will simply drop these objects again, as a drop statement is not a failure. So you must perform an incomplete recovery. An *incomplete recovery* refers to any recovery where the SCN number matches across the datafile headers, but that SCN is lower than the SCN in the control file. In other words, the data is all in sync, but the control file knows for a fact that more changes have occurred—but you are writing those changes off. Incomplete recovery is referred to as *point-in-time recovery*, or PITR. PITR is the process of specifying a specific point in time to which you want to recover, and then stopping the recovery and opening the database. All changes that occurred after the specified point in time are lost.

PITR should be avoided at all costs, and here's why: you cannot recover a single datafile to a point in time in the past. If you have to perform PITR, the entire database must be restored from backup, recovered to the specified time, and then opened. (We'll talk about tablespace point-in-time recovery, or TSPITR, in the next section.) This is extremely costly, obviously, and destroys the availability of the database along with actual data. However, PITR is a fact of life, and being familiar with it will help defray the costs of its use. Even if you never have to perform PITR on a production database, it can be used to take snapshots of production when testing backups (discussed later in this chapter).

Time-Based Recovery

The first and most common form of incomplete recovery requires a user-specified point in time to stop recovery. RMAN takes this point in time and finds the last SCN change that occurred before the time specified, and then applies all redo entries up to that SCN.

```
Rman>run {allocate channel ch_1 device type sbt;
     recover database until time
     "TO_DATE('07/8/01 15:30:00','MM/DD/YY HH24:MI:SS')"; }
```

Note that this example uses a TO_DATE function to provide a date mask for the operation. We recommend using the TO_DATE function every time an incomplete recovery is performed. If you do not, the date must be specified in the format of the target database's NLS_DATE_FORMAT. If this format does not include hours and minutes, then the closest you can get to your time will be midnight of the day specified. For instance, if the target database NLS_DATE_FORMAT is simply MM-DD-RR, then you would specify UNTIL TIME as 07-08-01, and the recovery would end at midnight of July 8, 2001.

The Time Clause and Restore Operations

How does an UNTIL TIME clause affect the restore operation? Well, if RMAN must perform a restore based on a time constraint, the value given in the UNTIL TIME clause provides RMAN with a restriction on how new the backup can be. For instance, if RMAN has a backup of the database on Monday and then another backup on Wednesday, and you specify an UNTIL TIME of Tuesday, then the Wednesday backup is excluded from possible usage in the restore, and RMAN uses the last backup taken prior to the time clause—in this case, Monday's backup. Bear in mind that the backup must have been completed before the UNTIL TIME clause. This means that if you started the backup on Monday, but it didn't finish until Tuesday, and you set the time clause too early on Tuesday, then the backup that was started on Monday will not be available. In this case, you would have to use an even earlier backup, and therefore apply even more archived redo entries to bring the database up to date.

SCN and Log Sequence-Based Recovery

If you know the exact SCN at which a user dropped a table, for instance, you can specify an SCN in your UNTIL clause of the **recover** command. The SCN you specify is not included in the recovery, so if you know **drop table** occurred at change vector 154652, you would specify this in the clause, and the last change applied would be 154651.

```
Rman>run {allocate channel ch_1 device type sbt;
     recover database until scn 154652; }
```

If you are forced to perform an incomplete recovery because you are missing some archive logs necessary for full recovery, you can specify an UNTIL clause that gives the Log Sequence Number of the archive log that is missing. This gives you the upper limit of the recovery. So, if you were missing the archive logs for sequences 1001 through 1020, you could specify that the operation should recover until sequence 1001.

```
Rman>run {allocate channel ch_1 device type sbt;
     recover database until sequence 1001;
```

Resetlogs, Reset Database, and Database Incarnations

If incomplete recovery is performed, then the database cannot be opened unless you issue a **resetlogs** command. The command, **alter database open resetlogs**, performs two actions. First, it restarts the log sequencing of the database at 1. If you had recovered your database until sequence 1001, this sequence number is wiped out of the datafile headers and replace with 1. Second, this command wipes clean the online redo log files of any information they may have previously held. They are now empty, and in V$LOGFILE they will show a status of unused (except for the current log, which shows a sequence number of 1).

Opening a database with **resetlogs** has long-term effects on the status of your backups. Essentially, you've created a wall between any previous backups and any new backups you take after the **resetlogs** operation. This wall is created by the fact that you cannot roll forward using archived redo logs through **resetlogs**, as you have reset the sequence numbering of your redo logs. Whenever a **resetlogs** is performed, our first recommendation is to get a full backup immediately.

The effects of a **resetlogs** within the RMAN catalog are a bit more complicated. When a **resetlogs** operation is performed from within RMAN, RMAN implicitly issues the command **reset database**. If you perform a **resetlogs** outside of RMAN, you will have to manually issue the **reset database** command before you can perform new backups against the target that has been reset.

The **reset database** command tells the RMAN catalog that a **resetlogs** has occurred, and therefore the database has a new incarnation. The *database incarnation* is the means by which RMAN keeps track of database backups that have occurred prior to a **resetlogs**. Therefore, if for some reason a database needs to be restored to a point in time prior to a **resetlogs**, RMAN can be set to the prior incarnation, and then the **recover** command can be issued. Figure 6-4 shows a diagram of how database incarnations can be visualized.

```
Rman>list incarnation of database;
List of Database Incarnations
DB Key  Inc Key DB Name  DB ID            CUR Reset SCN  Reset Time
------- ------- -------- ---------------- --- ---------- ----------
1       2       PROD     4141823660       NO  253462     13-JUL-01
1       55      PROD     4141823660       YES 280426     17-JUL-01
```

The **list incarnation** command gives a listing of every incarnation of every database registered in the recovery catalog, regardless of which target database you are connected to. Make no mistake, though: RMAN can only reset the database incarnation to a database with the same DBID.

The question that must be asked is why would a database administrator ever need to reset a database to a previous incarnation? There are a few different answers, but the most common reason for setting the database incarnation back to a previous

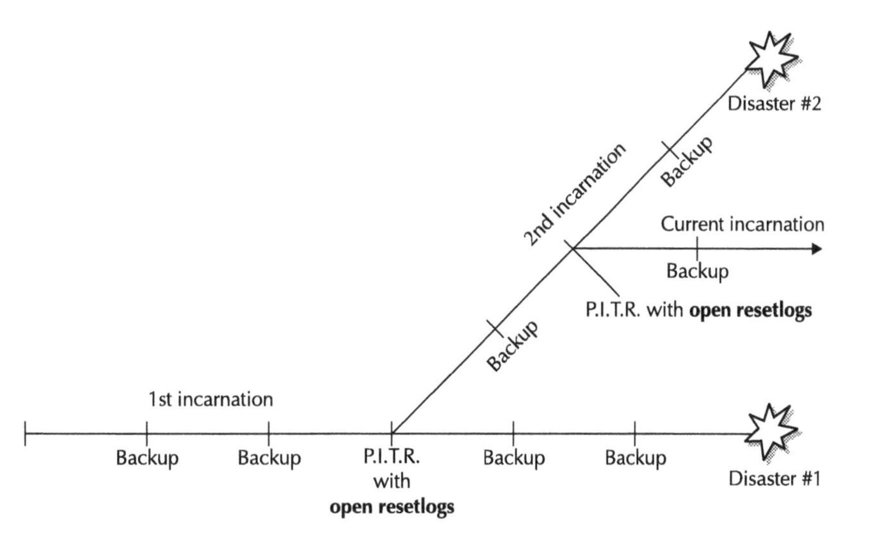

FIGURE 6-4. *Database incarnations*

Resetlogs, Reset Database, and Database Incarnations

incarnation is some error in the recovery process that ended with the **resetlogs** operation. Perhaps the database was recovered too far forward, and the **drop table** command was reissued, so after opening the database with **resetlogs**, the table is still missing. In order to recover to a point in time even earlier, you would need to set the incarnation back and then issue the **recover** command.

```
Rman>reset incarnation to <inc_key>;
Rman>run {allocate channel ch_1 device type sbt;
     recover database until scn 154649; }
```

Using Tablespace Point-in-Time Recovery

Oracle provides granularity for incomplete recovery at only one level—the tablespace. Tablespace point-in-time recovery, or TSPITR (pronounced *tee-spitter*), can be used to recover all the objects in a tablespace to a previous point in time, while leaving the rest of the database at the current time. This process is complicated; RMAN makes it easier than doing it manually, but not much.

Understanding TSPITR Limitations

TSPITR is an effective way to overcome user error, such as a DROP TABLE error or a massive update that has set everyone's salary to the same amount. TSPITR is not the best way to do this. The best way to overcome user error is with logical backups—that is, exports—or by configuring the database for flashback query (see Chapter 5). However, if keeping up-to-date exports is impossible, as is maintaining enough system redo entries for a useful flashback window, then TSPITR may be your only option. Its primary benefit is the simple fact that you already have the backups to do the work; TSPITR uses your RMAN backups and existing archive logs to bring the tablespace to the specified time. Usually, exports are taken nightly, meaning an import operation is only as current as the previous evening. TSPITR can take the point-in-time recovery right up to the second before the user error (or hardware corruption, and so on).

TSITR cannot rebuild a dropped tablespace; if the command **drop tablespace** has been issued, and the tablespace is critical to production, the only option you have is to perform PITR for the entire database. TSPITR cannot rebuild replicated objects, snapshots, or objects created by SYS or SYSTEM. Here's a biggie: RMAN-managed TSPITR cannot work on partitioned tables or indexes; this is a limitation of TSPITR run within RMAN, and will work if you do manual TSPITR. See *Oracle9*i *Recovery Manager's User Guide* for all of the restrictions placed on TSPITR operations; there are simply too many for the confines of this book.

TSPITR Operations

Here's how TSPITR works. From within RMAN, you specify the tablespace you want recovered, and the point in time to which you want it recovered. RMAN then pulls a recovery set from backup. The *recovery set* refers to all the files that need to be restored for TSPITR to work: a backup control file, the system datafiles, any datafiles containing rollback segments, and the tablespace you want recovered.

RMAN then restores this recovery set to an auxiliary database on the same machine as the target database. After the restore is complete, RMAN applies redo up to the point in time specified, and the auxiliary instance is opened.

After opening the auxiliary database, which is now at the point in time you want the tablespace to be on the target, RMAN exports the metadata about the damaged tablespace. The metadata refers to the dictionary information about the tablespace, such as extent information, segment information, and the like.

After the export has finished, RMAN instructs the target database control file to point its datafile specifications for the datafiles associated with your damaged tablespace to the location of those files as they are specified in the auxiliary instance. Essentially, RMAN tells the target database control file, "Stop looking for the datafiles here, and look for them over there."

Finally, RMAN imports the metadata about the tablespace from the auxiliary database into the target database, and the process is complete. The damaged tablespace has been let go, replaced by a copy of the datafiles that were restored in a different database and then transposed into the target database by the TSPITR process.

Configuring the Environment for RMAN TSPITR

To perform TSPITR with RMAN, you must set up the database environment for the auxiliary database first. *Note that the auxiliary database must be on the same machine as the target database.* This poses a few configuration problems that need to be solved. First, the auxiliary instance must have the same DB_NAME as the target instance; however, on Windows 2000, Oracle will not allow two instances with the same DB_NAME open at the same time. To get past this restriction, you add a new parameter to the initaux1.ora file: LOCK_NAME_SPACE=AUX1. This creates the memory segment with a different name, even though our database name is the same.

First, then, you create an auxiliary database parameter file. This should be a copy of the production init.ora file, making sure the value for DB_NAME is the same as the target. Add the parameter LOCK_NAME_SPACE=AUX1, and change the value of the CONTROL_FILES parameter to point to a location other than the production database. The auxiliary init.ora file can also be set up to perform datafile and log filename conversions for any files that are restored (datafiles) or created (log files) during the TSPITR operation. The following parameters do this conversion:

```
DB_FILE_NAME_CONVERT=("/oracle/prod/datafile","/oracle/aux/datafile")
LOG_FILE_NAME_CONVERT=("/oracle/prod/redo_log","/oracle/aux/redo_log")
```

This conversion parameter matches string variables in the first value and converts them to the second value. Each datafile or log file must be configured in a pair, so that in the following example, a file named STRING_A1 is converted to STRING_A2, and file STRING_B1 is converted to STRING_B2:

```
DB_FILE_NAME_CONVERT=("STRING_A1","STRING_A2",
                      "STRING_B1", "STRING_B2")
```

In our following examples, we will leave datafile name conversion in the hands of RMAN using the **configure auxname** command, but we will put log file conversions into the initaux1.ora FILE.

The other way to perform the filename conversion is by using **configure auxname** for each datafile. These persistent values set a new name for each datafile that is used for any auxiliary database operation (such as TSPITR or DUPLICATE, as seen in the next section). By specifying an AUXNAME, you can avoid any internal complications that might arise from reliance on the init.ora parameters of the auxiliary database.

Once the decision for file renaming is complete and you have an auxiliary init.ora file, put it into the ORACLE_HOME/database directory and then build the Oracle Service for the auxiliary instance. Note that the service name must be unique for Windows 2000, so you cannot create an instance with the same name as the target. This does not interfere with the DB_NAME conventions in the init.ora file, which must be identical for both instances.

```
C:>oradim -new -sid aux1 -intpwd oracle
   -startmode manual -pfile c:/oracle/ora9i/database/initaux1.ora
```

The service will be started by default after creating it. If you have any questions about the oradim.exe utility, refer to Chapter 4. Note that we have set the SYS password for the AUX1 instance to "oracle," which you must use when connecting in RMAN. Now start the auxiliary instance in nomount mode.

```
C:>set oracle_sid=aux1
c:>sqlplus
sqlplus>connect sys/oracle as sysdba
sqlplus>startup nomount;
```

After this, you need to create a net alias for the auxiliary database using the Net Configuration Assistant. Fire up Net Configuration Assistant, and run through the steps for creating the alias. After setting up the alias, you will need to manually modify the listener.ora file to register your new instance with the Listener process. Usually, this registration happens automatically, but instance registration with the Listener is done by PMON. You need the Listener to connect to AUX1 before AUX1 has a PMON process. To do this manual configuration, copy and paste the entry for the target instance, and just change the instance name:

```
SID_LIST_LISTENER =
  (SID_LIST =
    (SID_DESC =
      (GLOBAL_DBNAME = PROD90)
      (ORACLE_HOME = D:\oracle\ora90)
      (SID_NAME = PROD90)
    )
    (SID_DESC =
      (GLOBAL_DBNAME = aux1)
      (ORACLE_HOME = D:\oracle\ora90)
      (SID_NAME = aux1)
    )
  )
```

Now, test the alias at the command line.

```
C:>sqlplus /nolog
sql> connect sys/oracle@aux1
```

Next, build the RMAN scripts that will be run for the TSPITR operation. The following example assumes that you want to restore the tablespace USERS to a point in time. Use the **configure auxname** command to rename all datafiles, but set the new log file locations with LOG_FILE_NAME_CONVERT. In the initaux1.ora file, set the following parameters:

```
DB_NAME=prod90
CONTROL_FILES='d:\oracle\ora9i\oradata\aux1\control01.dbf'
LOG_FILE_NAME_CONVERT=('D:\ORACLE\ORADATA\PROD90\REDO01.LOG',
      'D:\ORACLE\ORADATA\AUX1\REDO01.LOG',
      'D:\ORACLE\ORADATA\PROD90\REDO02.LOG',
      'D:\ORACLE\ORADATA\AUX1\REDO02.LOG',
      'D:\ORACLE\ORADATA\PROD90\REDO03.LOG',
      'D:\ORACLE\ORADATA\AUX1\REDO03.LOG')
REMOTE_LOGIN_PASSWORDFILE=EXCLUSIVE
```

After this, you create two scripts. The first script specifies permanent settings that will be stored for longer than the duration of our TSPITR operation, and therefore deserves a separate script. The second script is the actual TSPTIR run itself.

```
###RMAN Configuration Script in Preparation of TSPITR###
### First, connect to the target database ###
connect target system/manager
### Second, configure our default device to tape ###
configure default device type sbt;
### Configure multiple default tape channels ###
configure channel 1 device type sbt
parms="ENV=(NB_ORA_SERV=RM-WGT)";
### Configure the auxiliary channel default to tape ###
configure auxiliary channel device type sbt
parms="ENV=(NB_ORA_SERV=RM-WGT)";
###Finally, configure the auxiliary datafile names ###
configure auxname for datafile 1 to
   'd:\oracle\ora9i\oradata\aux1\system01.dbf';
configure auxname for datafile 2 to
   'd:\oracle\ora9i\oradata\aux1\rbs01.dbf';
configure auxname for datafile 5 to
   'd:\oracle\ora9i\oradata\aux1\users01.dbf';
configure auxname for datafile 12 to
   'd:\oracle\ora9i\oradata\aux1\users02.dbf';
### Where datafile 1 is the system datafile,
### datafile 2 contains all system managed undo,
### datafiles 5 and 12 are all datafiles in
### the USERS tablespace. ###
```

The following is the TSPITR script:

```
###RMAN TSPITR Operation for USERS tablespace
Connect target system/manager
connect catalog rman/rman@repo
connect auxiliary sys/oracle@aux1
RECOVER TABLESPACE users
UNTIL TIME "TO_DATE('JUL 08 2001 16:20:00',
'MON DD YYYY HH24:MI:SS')";
```

After RMAN completes TSPITR, the datafiles of USERS tablespace will need to be brought online before they can be put into production.

```
>alter database datafile
>'d:\oracle\ora9i\oradata\prod\users01.dbf' online;
>alter database datafile
>'d:\oracle\ora9i\oradata\prod\users02.dbf' online;
```

After these have been brought online, the process is complete and the tablespace is available for use again, looking as it did on July 8, 2001, at 4 P.M. The final step in TSPITR is to clean up the auxiliary instance. As the database is open, but currently unusable (it donated its USER datafiles to the prod instance), issue a **shutdown abort** from within SQL*Plus, and then stop the Oracle Service for the AUX1 instance and delete it.

```
SQL>shutdown abort;
SQL>exit;
c:>net stop oracleserviceaux1
c:>oradim -delete -sid aux1
```

Finally, clean up any files that are left behind by the auxiliary database. We recommend holding onto the initaux1.ora file, in case future TSPITR operations need to be performed. But all the datafiles, control files, and log files produced by TSPITR can be removed. In the case of our example, this simply means deleting the d:\oracle\ora9i\oradata\aux1 directory.

Using RMAN Backups to Create Clone Copies of Production Databases

One of the few benefits that come from taking constant and valuable backups of any production database is the ability to use those backups to create a clone version of the production database for testing and development purposes. RMAN has built-in syntax for automating this process using backups that RMAN has taken. This process, using the **duplicate database** command, has the advantage of being able to create a database across platforms. OS backups of datafiles cannot provide this, as the datafiles have proprietary file headers; because RMAN uses the data block as the unit of backup, it re-creates file headers on the new platform, and therefore can convert across platforms.

The other primary advantage is that the process is simple. Really, that's not a typo. Granted, you must familiarize yourself with RMAN's little quirks; but compared to the process of moving a production database to a clone database outside of RMAN, it's not that difficult. Many of the principles were outlined in the section "Using Tablespace Point-in-Time Recovery" earlier: You connect to the target database, the recovery catalog, and an auxiliary instance. You run the **duplicate** command, and RMAN accesses the backups to restore the production data to the auxiliary instance. When complete, RMAN recovers using archive logs from production, and then opens the auxiliary instance with **resetlogs**. In the final step, RMAN changes the auxiliary instance's database ID (DBID) so that the auxiliary is a unique instance that can then be registered for backup in the same recovery catalog as the target from which it was created.

Unlike the TSPITR process, a duplicate database can also be created on a separate server from the target database. There are complications with doing it both ways. When duplicating to the same machine as the target database, the instance

name must be different from production, and the DB_NAME parameter must be the same (just as in TSPITR operations). Also, you have to be careful that all filenames are moved (using CONFIGURE AUXNAME, for instance) so that you don't overwrite production datafiles.

When duplicating to a remote server, you have to make sure that the archive logs from the target are available to the remote server. This means either backing up all necessary archive logs to tape, so that RMAN can restore them to the remote machine, or sharing the LOG_ARCHIVE_DEST directories of the target database on the auxiliary server (making sure you mount them with the identical file structure as appears on the target server). This means if the LOG_ARCHIVE_DEST for the target server is d:\oracle\ora9i\oradata\prod\arch, you must share this drive, and then mount it from the auxiliary server as the exact same directory.

The same concept of sharing directories and mounting them remotely with the same file structure holds true for backups to disk. If you must use disk backups for the **duplicate** command, you must mount the backup directory on the remote server with the same drive letter and directory, or the **duplicate** command will fail. RMAN checks the catalog for the name of backup pieces, and finds the full path encoded for each piece. This backup piece name cannot be modified; therefore, you must obey your original location. Alternatively, instead of sharing drives, you can literally copy the backup pieces from the target server to the auxiliary server, and put them in the same drive and directory location.

Duplicating to the Same Server as the Target Database

For this example, we will again separate the process into two RMAN scripts: the first will set permanent configuration parameters, and the second will house the actual **duplicate** command. But first, you must set up the Windows environment for the duplication process. This is similar in most ways to the setup for TSPITR. You must create an initaux1.ora file, in which you change all directory values that point to the PROD90 environment to point to the AUX1 environment. We suggest copying the production init.ora file to initaux1.ora, and then changing the following list of new values:

```
CONTROL_FILES='d:\oracle\ora9i\oradata\aux1\control01.dbf'
LOG_ARCHIVE_DEST='d:\oracle\ora9i\oradata\aux1\arch'
USER_DUMP_DEST='d:\oracle\ora9i\oradata\aux1\udump'
BACKGROUND_DUMP_DEST='d:\oracle\ora9i\oradata\aux1\bdump'
LOCK_NAME_SPACE=AUX1
REMOTE_LOGIN_PASSWORDFILE=EXCLUSIVE
```

Essentially, you can simply do a find and replace in your production init.ora file and replace any instance of the word PROD90 with AUX1. Make sure that any new directories you specify actually exist! RMAN does not automatically create directories during the duplication process, and if any directory does not exist, the command will fail.

Note that we have left LOG_FILE_NAME_CONVERT out of this list. When running the **duplicate** command itself, you can specify new locations and names for log files. You have also added a passwordfile parameter, which is necessary for connecting to your auxiliary instance remotely when it is only in nomount mode (the passwordfile was created when you ran oradim). Also, DB_NAME must be the same for both instances, but the instance name must be different, so after creating the initaux1.ora file and placing it in the ORACLE_HOME/database directory, you create a service with your AUX1 name.

```
C:>set oracle_sid=aux1
c:>oradim -new -sid aux1 -intpwd oracle -startmode manual
   -pfile d:\oracle\ora9i\database\initaux1.ora
```

As with TSPITR, you must create a net connection alias for the AUX1 database, and manually register AUX1 in the listener.ora file. Then, connect to the AUX1 instance and issue a **startup nomount** command. After this, you are ready to run your RMAN scripts. The first script configures the settings for the renaming of datafiles, as well as setting auxiliary channels. The second script runs the **duplicate** command.

```
###RMAN Configuration Script in Preparation
### for DUPLICATE DATABASE command###
### First, connect to the target database ###
connect target system/manager
### Second, configure our default device to tape ###
configure default device type sbt
parms="ENV=(NB_ORA_SERV=RM-WGT)";
### Configure the auxiliary channel default to tape ###
configure auxiliary channel device type sbt
parms="ENV=(NB_ORA_SERV=RM-WGT)";
###Finally, configure the auxiliary datafile names ###
configure auxname for datafile 1 to
   'd:\oracle\ora9i\oradata\aux1\system01.dbf';
configure auxname for datafile 2 to
   'd:\oracle\ora9i\oradata\aux1\rbs01.dbf';
configure auxname for datafile 3 to
   'd:\oracle\ora9i\oradata\aux1\users01.dbf';
configure auxnmame for datafile 4 to
   'd:\oracle\ora9i\oradata\aux1\tools01.dbf';
...
###List each datafile of the database.  Alternatively,
###FILE_NAME_CONVERT can be used in the init.ora file. ###
```

After the configuration is complete, you can run your actual duplication script.

```
###Connect to the target, catalog, and auxiliary instances ###
connect target /
connect catalog rman/rman@repo
connect auxiliary sys/oracle@aux1
###Issue the Duplicate command ###
duplicate target database to test90
logfile
'd:\oracle\oradata\test90\redo01.log' size 5m reuse,
'd:\oracle\oradata\test90\redo02.log' size 5m reuse,
'd:\oracle\oradata\test90\redo03.log' size 5m reuse;
```

Duplicating to a Remote Server from the Target Database

The benefit of running your duplication to a remote server is that you do not have to change datafile name locations, unless the drives specified on the target do not exist on the auxiliary server. Therefore, your configuration script can be minimized to the simple auxiliary channel configuration.

The one step that is easy to miss is the configuration of your Media Manager client software on the auxiliary server. Contrary to popular belief, when you issue the **duplicate** command and the auxiliary server is on a different machine, all tape access occurs from the auxiliary instance, not the target instance. Figure 6-5 illustrates the relationships in this triangle.

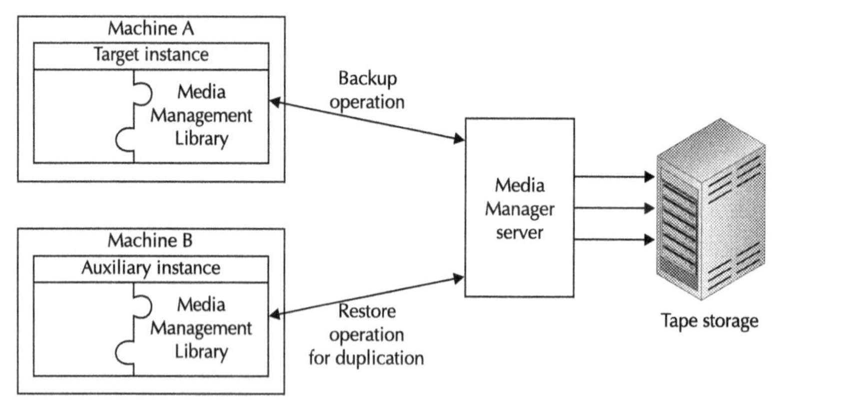

FIGURE 6-5. *Tape access when duplicating to a remote server*

After performing the necessary MML configuration at the auxiliary server, you can configure the Windows environment for the auxiliary instance. All of this configuration occurs at the auxiliary server, not the target server. As before, you need to have an auxiliary init.ora file, but unlike when you duplicate to the same server, you are not compelled to change anything in your production init.ora file. You can simply copy the file from production to the auxiliary server, and then create the service (with the same name as the production service).

```
C:>set oracle_sid=prod90
c:>oradim -new -sid prod90 -intpwd oracle -startmode manual
   -pfile d:\oracle\ora9i\database\initprod.ora
```

Start the instance in nomount mode. Next, create the net alias to the auxiliary server *on the target server, not on the auxiliary server.* Make sure you are modifying the tnsnames.ora file on the target server to point to the auxiliary instance on the auxiliary server. Manually register the auxiliary instance in the listener.ora file on the auxiliary server.

Now you are prepared to run your duplicate scripts. If you have previously used any **configure auxname** commands to set new filenames for TSPITR or otherwise, you must clear these parameters as seen in the following configuration script.

```
###RMAN Configuration Script in Preparation
### for DUPLICATE DATABASE command to a remote server###
### First, connect to the target database ###
connect target system/manager
### Second, configure our default device to tape ###
configure default device type sbt
parms="ENV=(NB_ORA_SERV=RM-WGT)";
### Configure the auxiliary channel default to tape ###
configure auxiliary channel device type sbt
parms="ENV=(NB_ORA_SERV=RM-WGT)";
###Clear auxiliary datafile names, as we want to
### use the same datafile names as production. ###
configure auxname for datafile 1 clear;
configure auxname for datafile 2 clear;
configure auxname for datafile 3 clear;
configure auxname for datafile 4 clear;
...
###List each datafile of the database. ###
```

Next, run your duplicate database script. Notice that you have set an UNTIL TIME clause for this **duplicate** command. Setting a time parameter is essential when duplicating to a remote machine, as you do not have access to any new archive logs that might be created since your last archive log backup. Make sure the time format you use matches the NLS_DATE_FORMAT of your target database.

```
###Connect to Target, Catalog, and Auxiliary Instances ###
connect target /
connect catalog rman/rman@repo
connect auxiliary sys/oracle@aux1
### Run the Duplicate command, with a time clause ###
run {
set until time 'JUL-08-2001';
duplicate target database to test90
logfile
'd:\oracle\oradata\test90\redo01.log' size 5m reuse,
'd:\oracle\oradata\test90\redo02.log' size 5m reuse,
'd:\oracle\oradata\test90\redo03.log' size 5m reuse;}
```

Test All Backups for Recoverability

We said it to start the chapter, and this tip will close the chapter: no backup strategy is worthwhile until it has been tested for recoverability. Some of the operations described to this point should give you some sense of backup stability: a successful TSPITR or **duplicate database** operation proves that the backups not only work, but are recoverable. But neither gives a good sense of actual recoverability of the production database.

In order to prove the viability of backup strategies, we suggest creating a copy of the recovery catalog via export, and then importing this into a second schema on the same database as the original catalog. Next, connect RMAN to this second catalog and use it to test restores to a computer other than the one for production. With a test server, you can restore a backup control file, datafiles, and archive logs. Along the way, you can time different operations (such as datafile restores), perform point-in-time recoveries, and so on. After you have finished, the database you restore can be deleted, and the test catalog schema dropped and refreshed from the production RMAN catalog schema with another export.

Summary

In this chapter, we discussed the importance of having a realistic backup and recovery strategy for your Oracle9*i* Database. We discussed the strength of integrating server managed recovery into your strategies, and how Oracle9*i* Recovery Manager can be used for backups, restores, and recoveries. We explained the benefits and advanced uses of RMAN, from block media recovery to incremental backups. We also gave tips for setting up RMAN for tablespace point-in-time recovery and for setting up RMAN for cloning the production database.

PART III

Windows 2000: The Premiere Enterprise Management Platform

TIPS

&

TECHNIQUES

CHAPTER 7

Oracle Connectivity

Because the majority of Oracle connectivity problems are closely associated with changes in configuration, initial setup, or network issues, it has not traditionally been a major concern for database administrators or even Oracle developers. The network, and connectivity in general, should be seen as a black box in the best of worlds, but the growth of highly available systems that are mission critical or massive revenue producers has brought Oracle connectivity into the spotlight.

Oracle, in keeping with the goal to be *the* Internet database, has matured many of its connectivity features to assist in achieving better scalability and availability. High availability (HA) features such as failover on the client side and load balancing among RAC (short for Real Application Clusters, formerly known as Oracle Parallel Server) database instances on different nodes on the server side are all enabled by Oracle Net technologies. The multithreaded server (MTS), now referred to as the *Shared Server,* has matured massively and is becoming more and more efficient with each release. But with all these great features, a better understanding of the underlying architecture and the intended use of these features is essential to properly tuning your databases to meet application needs for availability, scalability, and performance.

This chapter will give you the overview you need to get *started* on the path to implementing these features properly. In the final section, we offer a large chunk of reference material that will enable you to further understand and tweak your Oracle Net and Windows 2000 configurations to achieve higher availability, scalability, performance, and better pay. (Nudge nudge, wink wink!) Here are the tips we cover in this chapter:

- Resolving Net names
- Connecting to Oracle databases
- Understanding basic client architecture
- Working on dedicated servers
- Understanding the Shared Server
- Using Net Manager
- Configuring clients
- Configuring higher-availability clients
- Configuring Dedicated server
- Configuring the Shared Server
- Controlling and configuring listeners
- Understanding the Virtual Interface Protocol
- Locating reference material on Oracle connectivity

The Oracle Net Architecture

Oracle Net is a layered architecture that works with other layers above and below it. Named layers such as OCI and TNS provide logical functionality found in the OSI model implemented by functions that call down and up the various layers. Examine Figure 7-1 while you follow this somewhat high-level example.

1. You begin by starting SQL*Plus. SQL*Plus is an *Oracle Client Interface* (*OCI*) application that will initialize the OCI environment and run the application. SQL*Plus needs to initiate a connection to a database. To do this, the OCI functions in the SQL*Plus application will call functions in the TTC layer.
2. The *Two Task Common* (*TTC*) layer accepts a function call from OCI and begins its presentation layer negotiation with the server by communicating the client's OS, character set, Oracle version information and more in order to properly synchronize the presentation between the client and the server. This layer is also where differences between OS data types and Oracle's internal data types are resolved. The more well-known character set conversion functionality is also done in this layer. To communicate and negotiate with the server, TTC will call functions in the *Net* (*NI*) layer.
3. The negotiation initiated by the OCI call from SQL*Plus first moves its way first into the Net portion of the stack, and then into the Transparent Network Substrate (TNS) layer. The network interface (NI) layer will call functions in TNS's network routing stack (NR) to decide which address it should route the request to. If you have client-side load balancing turned on, then NR will decide with which address to make the connection. The network interface stack (NI) will also call network name functions (NN) to resolve the alias into an address. If the name requires resolution across a network, it then calls functions lower in the stack to get that information (for example, when using Net naming from an LDAP server).
4. The *Network Session* (*NS*) layer builds the Oracle Net packets that will eventually be managed by TCP and then IP. In this case, the initial negotiation packet is small and simple. When you look at support-level network trace files, this is the layer that will show you the actual Net packets coming and going. In trace files, look for the calls prefixed with nspsend and nsprecv. NS will utilize the Network Authentication (NA) layer to negotiate authorization and other related activities to complete its tasks.
5. The Network Session layer calls functions in the Oracle Protocol Adapter's Network Transport (NT) layer to send packets in the specific format for the protocol and OS. In the NT layer is where hostnames are resolved to IP addresses (look in your trace files for nttbnd2addr) and sockets are created and destroyed (found in your trace files as nttcnp and nttdisc, respectively).

6. The NT layer calls functions at the OS level to perform its duties. These functions reach outside the Oracle Protocol Adapter (OPA) layer into the OS to do things like send packets through the operating system network software and across the wire, where they reach the server and go up through the server's OS network layer to eventually communicate with the database's counterpart to OCI, the Oracle Programmatic Interface (OPI).
7. The server handles the messages and works up the stack within the OPA, TNS, Net, and other layers to respond to the request from the client.

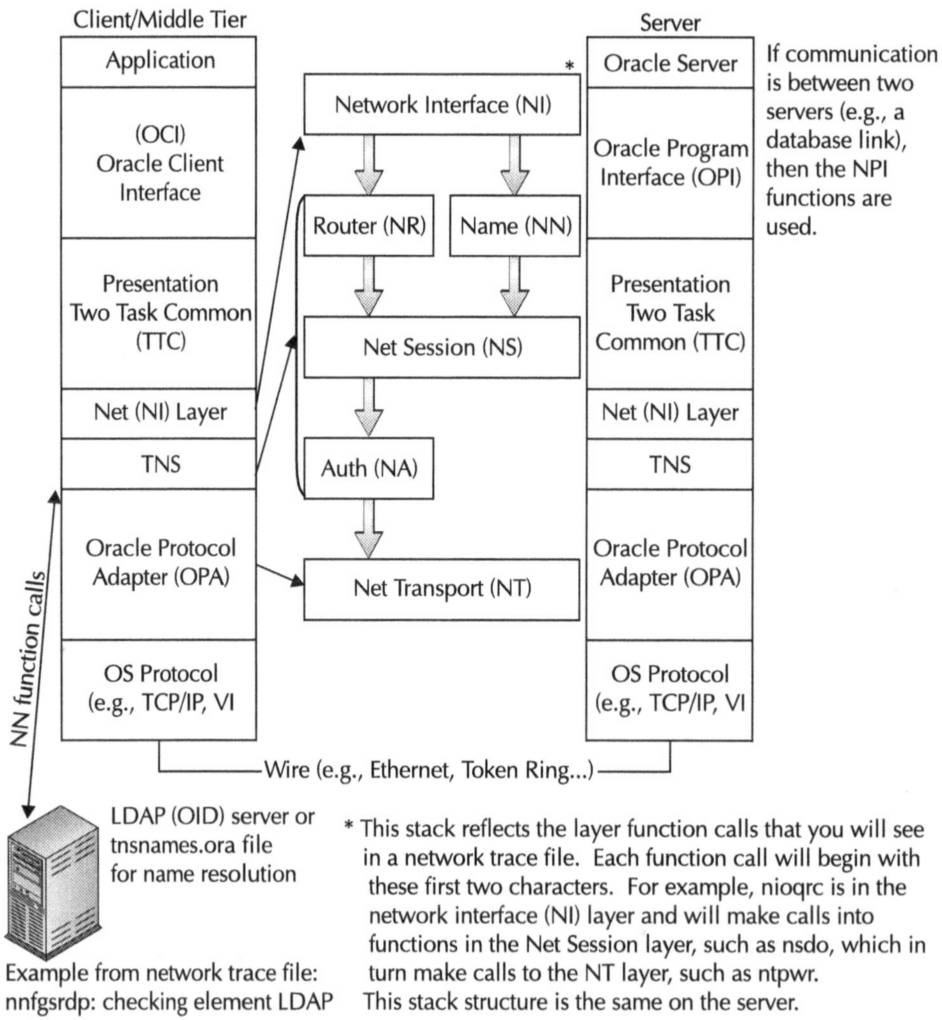

Client/Middle Tier
Application
(OCI)
Oracle Client
Interface
Presentation
Two Task Common
(TTC)
Net (NI) Layer
TNS
Oracle Protocol
Adapter (OPA)
OS Protocol
(e.g., TCP/IP, VI

Network Interface (NI) *
Router (NR)
Name (NN)
Net Session (NS)
Auth (NA)
Net Transport (NT)

Server
Oracle Server
Oracle Program
Interface (OPI)
Presentation
Two Task
Common (TTC)
Net (NI) Layer
TNS
Oracle Protocol
Adapter (OPA)
OS Protocol
(e.g., TCP/IP, VI

If communication is between two servers (e.g., a database link), then the NPI functions are used.

Wire (e.g., Ethernet, Token Ring...)

NN function calls

LDAP (OID) server or
tnsnames.ora file
for name resolution

Example from network trace file:
nnfgsrdp: checking element LDAP

* This stack reflects the layer function calls that you will see in a network trace file. Each function call will begin with these first two characters. For example, nioqrc is in the network interface (NI) layer and will make calls into functions in the Net Session layer, such as nsdo, which in turn make calls to the NT layer, such as ntpwr. This stack structure is the same on the server.

FIGURE 7-1. *Oracle Net and associated layers*

This oversimplification of the process illustrates communication between client and server when viewed in the context of Figure 7-1. Note that client and server need not be on separate boxes. In the case of a local connection, IPC is used instead of TCP. In this case, you will not see much difference in the function calls made until you get into the Network Transport (NT) layer and below. This examination will help you understand the flow of Oracle Net traffic, diagnose errors, and enable you to better read network trace files.

Net Name Resolution

In order to initiate a connection to an Oracle database, the Oracle client software must first determine which alias you want to connect to and retrieve the proper connection information to make that connection in the manner that best fits the application. A simple connection description contains only machine name or IP, protocol, port, and service description (database) to which it should connect. A better-tuned, reliable, and directed connection description will indicate what services should be tried, whether to failover and/or load balance connections, what size the session and transport data units should be, whether to use a dedicated or shared connection, and more. The nondefault information is all contained in the connection *alias*.

This process is in some ways logically similar to the process of connecting to a site via your web browser. When you select a web address (for example, http://www.oracle.com), the browser makes calls to the OS's network layer. The OS must resolve the name you have given to a network address. It does this by querying a DNS server to find out what IP address it should connect to, and returns this information to the OS. The OS initiates the connection and passes information back to the browser, which then interprets that information to display a web page. In the same way, your database application is like a web browser and the DNS server is either an LDAP server or your tnsnames.ora file.

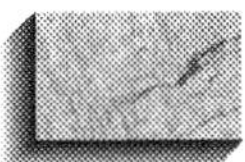

NOTE

If you use hostname resolution, then Oracle Network name resolution uses a hosts file or DNS lookup to determine the IP to connect to. The database global name must be the same as the database service name as well. The port used is assumed to be the default of 1521.

The process of connection requires that the basic details of your connection are resolved before a session can be considered. The connection string of an Oracle database is rather long and drawn out, much more so than just an IP address, and you will typically not want to enter the complete connection information at the command line every time you need to interact with a database.

Your application availability and responsiveness may be enhanced by features such as load balancing, connection failover, or transparent application failover.

Many details of Oracle Net's features are stored in the description of an Oracle database connection used by the Oracle client software. Because you don't want to tie your database server forevermore to a particular box or subnet, you will want to store generic connection information in your application source code and keep the actual details in a location that can be easily altered to meet the needs of a changing IT environment. This will allow you to have an Oracle application that may move from node to node, or subnet to subnet, or even scale up to a Real Application Cluster, without changing any client application code and still allow you to take advantage of all the unique features of Oracle Net.

To solve this problem, Oracle offers the use of what is called a *TNS alias*. A TNS alias describes a connection, including the methodology to make that connection. For example, an alias with an address list and load balancing turned on tells the client software to randomly choose one of the addresses; if that address cannot connect, it will failover to another randomly chosen address and continue this methodology until either the address list is exhausted or the connection is made. TNS aliases are kept in various places. The two most common places for release 9i are the tnsnames.ora file, a text file on your local file system, and a remote LDAP server for the whole enterprise (local versus centralized directory naming).

NOTE

*You can avoid using a connection alias and enter the connection information as you would find it in your tnsnames.ora right where you would otherwise put your TNS alias. For example, to connect via SQL*Plus to the machine msale.oracle.com, using the TCP protocol on port 1526 to the database service prod.oracle.com, you would enter the following on one line at the command line: sqlplus scott/ tiger@(DESCRIPTION= (ADDRESS_LIST=(ADDRESS= (PROTOCOL= TCP) (HOST=msale.oracle.com)(PORT=1521)))(CONNECT_ DATA=(SERVICE_NAME=prod.oracle.com))). As you can see, this is quite cumbersome and should not be used in most situations. However, you can use this method to help troubleshoot connection problems.*

From a simple troubleshooting and performance standpoint, name resolution and connection establishment should be isolated from one another in order to identify bottlenecks or other problems. If a name cannot be resolved, you will typically see an error message like this:

```
ORA-12154: "TNS: could not resolve service name"
```

This means that, for the TNS alias you gave, the network client could not resolve the name to an address. This is normally caused by use of a wrong or missing tnsnames.ora file, a problem with the default domain settings in the sqlnet.ora file, or just fat fingering the alias.

Name Resolution Methodology

Name resolution begs the question, "Where does the Oracle client retrieve this information from?" The answer is via a description repository such as the tnsnames.ora file or an LDAP directory like Oracle Internet Directory (OID). To confirm this answer for a particular client, you must examine the client's *profile* as defined in the sqlnet.ora file.

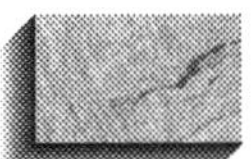

NOTE
It is entirely possible that your client configuration does not contain a sqlnet.ora file. If this is the case, the Oracle client will use the defaults for all elements of the profile.

Your client profile contains a NAMES.DIRECTORY_PATH entry that tells the client how to resolve a TNS alias. This entry is logically similar in function to the resolv.conf file found on many flavors of Unix. If there is no sqlnet.ora file or the sqlnet.ora file has no NAMES.DIRECTORY_PATH entry, then default for this entry is as follows:

```
NAMES.DIRECTORY_PATH=(tnsnames, onames, hostname)
```

This indicates that when an alias is used to connect to a database, it will look for an alias first in tnsnames.ora, search Oracle Names servers listed in sqlnet.ora, and then try hostname resolution. A simple example flow of the name resolution process is shown in Figure 7-2.

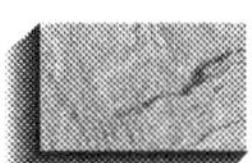

NOTE
If hostname resolution is after tnsnames in the directory path, and the alias is wrong or you cannot contact the LDAP server, you might get a TNS timeout error (ORA-12535) if the alias cannot properly resolve instead of the typical ORA-12154 error. This is because hostname resolution is trying to contact the database on the host with the same name as the alias you entered.

Because Oracle Names is being phased out by Oracle and directories are becoming more and more popular, we have decided to leave out Names server resolution and focus on LDAP and local name resolution (tnsnames.ora) instead.

Oracle client uses OCI to initiate a connection to the database

Search sqlnet.ora to get resolution method and default domain for TNS alias (and other options)

Retrieve the connection description by cycling through naming methods indicated

tnsnames.ora Search for alias (add on default domain in sqlnet.ora)

Found

Initiate the connection process using the connection description resolved

sqlnet.ora content
names.default_domain=oracle.com
names.directory_path=tnsnames,ldap

No

OID or Active Directory Search the directory for the alias

LDAP Query

Use the information in ldap.ora to query the directory for the alias with the default domain

Found

Initiate the connection process using the connection description resolved

No

ORA-12154: TNS could not resolve service name

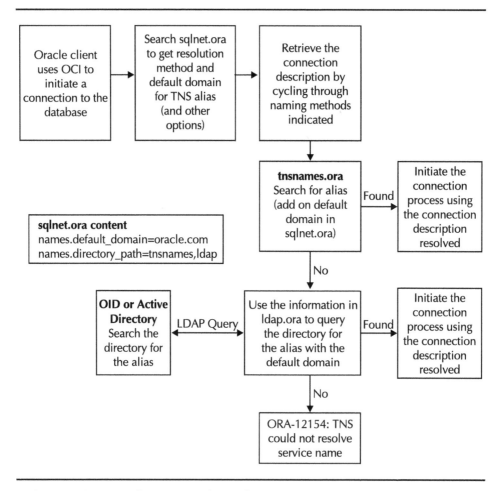

FIGURE 7-2. *Simple name resolution flow*

Local Name Resolution: tnsnames.ora

Local name resolution with the tnsnames.ora file is normally the *fastest* name resolution method. A very large tnsnames.ora file should be avoided because it can slow down resolution due to loading and parsing time. The maximum size of the tnsnames.ora file grew to 640KB in 9i to allow for larger tnsnames.ora files. tnsnames is also the most difficult naming method to maintain in larger environments. It should be used on servers that connect to other servers (that is, database links) as a backup to LDAP, but avoided on clients where multiple versions of the Oracle client software might be installed and the tnsnames.ora text file can easily be corrupted by unknowing users.

In previous versions of Oracle, it was often difficult to determine which tnsnames.ora file you were referring to when trying to connect. A new feature of the tnsping.exe diagnostic tool displays extensive information about the files used to resolve the alias and what the actual alias description is on the command line. See the session replay here for an example:

```
C:\>tnsping OID

TNS Ping Utility for 32-bit Windows: Version 9.0.1.0.0 - Production
on 08-AUG-2001 15:33:47

Copyright (c) 1997 Oracle Corporation. All rights reserved.

Used parameter files:
c:\oracle\901\network\admin\sqlnet.ora
c:\oracle\901\network\admin\tnsnames.ora

Used TNSNAMES adapter to resolve the alias
Attempting to contact (DESCRIPTION = (ADDRESS_LIST = (ADDRESS = (PRO...
<Previous line continues with the complete description>
TNS-12560: TNS:protocol adapter error
```

This example shows that we found the alias but had a problem connecting due to an error making the connection to the network adapter (the network cable was disconnected). Notice that it tells you exactly which tnsnames and sqlnet.ora files it used to make the connection? The example indicates that the tnsnames adapter was used instead of LDAP or hostname resolution—a *vast* improvement over previous versions!

Here is an example of an attempt to tnsping a nonexistent alias:

```
C:\>tnsping nothere

TNS Ping Utility for 32-bit Windows: Version 9.0.1.0.0 - Production
on 08-AUG-2001 15:41:04

Copyright (c) 1997 Oracle Corporation. All rights reserved.
Used parameter files:
c:\oracle\901\network\admin\sqlnet.ora
c:\oracle\901\network\admin\tnsnames.ora

TNS-03505: Failed to resolve name
```

This shows you that we used all the available name resolution methods and found no way to resolve this alias.

Although this new version of tnsping does a great job of telling you how name resolution is attempted for an alias, actual *connectivity* tests should always be performed with SQL*Plus because tnsping does not actually connect to the database.

Directory Naming

The other primary alternative to resolving names through a locally managed list of services in the tnsnames.ora file is to use a directory as a central repository in which to keep names accessible for all clients in an enterprise. From a management perspective, this is a much more scalable option if you have more than just a few instances or more than ten or so clients.

OID Oracle Internet Directory is Oracle's LDAP-compliant directory server. It is highly scalable, highly available because it replicates to multiple nodes, and high performance. If you purchased the Advanced Security Option (ASO) of the database, you actually have a limited-use license to utilize OID for name resolution and enterprise user management (a feature that allows you to have database users kept and managed in OID). OID is being used by more and more Oracle products as a means of storing information needed across applications. OID is also the replacement for Oracle Names. Oracle Names server will not be supported in future versions, and OID has been named the successor. In this chapter, we will show you how to get started with OID for alias name resolution.

OID Installation for Net Naming The first step is to get your OID server up and configured. You can take the easy route for testing and set up OID by using the installer for the Oracle9i database. Just follow these steps:

1. Select the Oracle9i Management and Integration installation option (instead of the database or client) and click Next.
2. On the next screen, select the Custom option and click Next. You can select the Oracle Internet Directory option, but you will need to perform more configuration after the installation is completed that is beyond the scope of this book.
3. Next, you will be given a checklist of the installation options for the Management Server product. Make sure that you have at least Oracle Internet Directory checked and that the Oracle Net Services status appears as Installed, as shown in Figure 7-3, or that it is checked, and then click Next.
4. Assign the OID instance a SID and global name (see Figure 7-4). Alter this value to fit your environment and click Next.
5. The next screen asks you where you want to put files for the OID database. Select the location of your choice that has at least 1.4GB of free space and move on to the next screen.
6. For OID user password encryption, click the Yes radio button and move on to the next screen.
7. Select the password hashing algorithm of your choice and click Next.

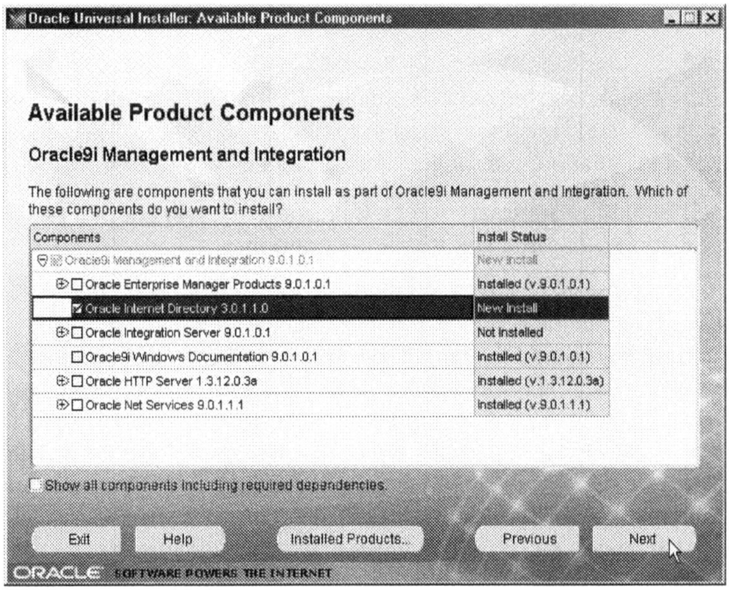

FIGURE 7-3. *Choosing installation options*

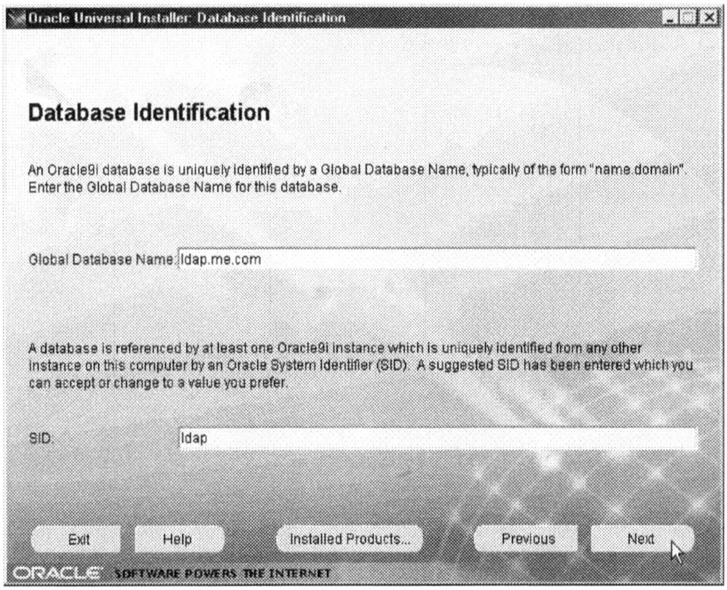

FIGURE 7-4. *Specifying a SID and global name for the OID*

8. Save yourself some heartache and set the password for cn=orcladmin to "welcome" or leave it at the default of "welcome" (see Figure 7-5). Click Next.
9. Figure 7-6 shows that we've configured a relatively small directory server at less than 10,000 entries. In order to minimize unnecessary resource utilization by this installation, we suggest you also select this setting.
10. The Installation Summary screen tells you what will happen next in the installation process. Click Install to continue.
11. After the software has been installed into the Oracle home, the post installation step will create the instance and its associated service, load OID into the database, and create the Directory Service service and start it for you.

Actual planning and implementation of an enterprise directory is not a trivial task that should be performed as a part of a typical database administrator's duties. In a production or development environment where you need and want to experience the scalability and manageability benefits of OID, keep the OID instance on a separate machine with the proper resources as outlined in the OID administration documentation.

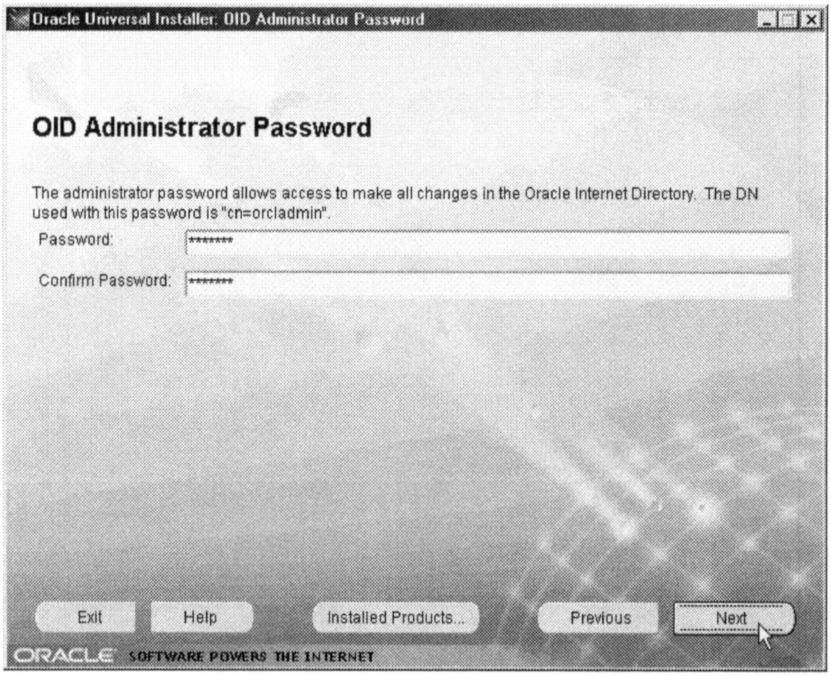

Oracle Universal Installer: OID Administrator Password

OID Administrator Password

The administrator password allows access to make all changes in the Oracle Internet Directory. The DN used with this password is "cn=orcladmin".

Password: *******

Confirm Password: *******

Exit | Help | Installed Products... | Previous | Next

ORACLE SOFTWARE POWERS THE INTERNET

FIGURE 7-5. *Specifying the administrator password*

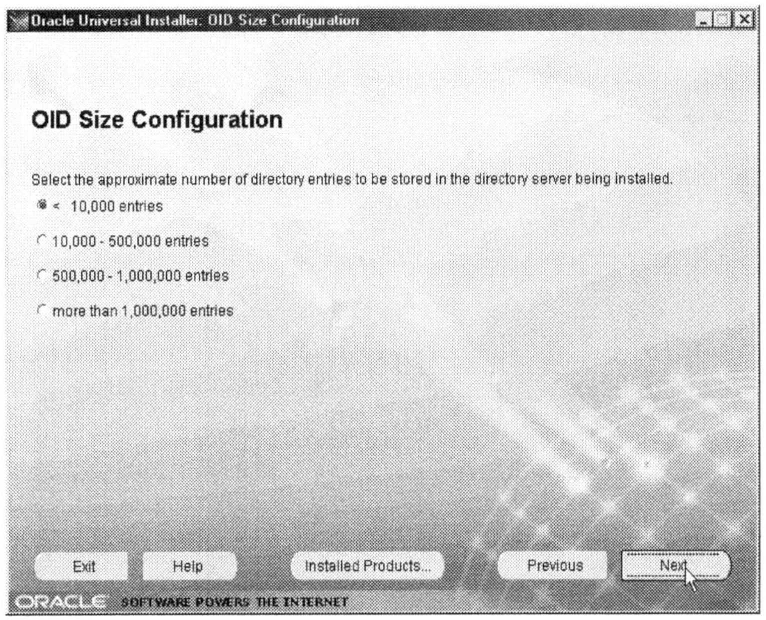

FIGURE 7-6. *Configuring the OID size*

The installation we guide you through will allow you to become familiar with OID for *later* implementation.

Once the installation is completed, you will have an Oracle9i instance dedicated to OID; the instance-related services; and a service that relates to the actual OID process in memory called OracleDirectoryService_<sid>, where <sid> is the SID of the OID 9i database instance.

Once your OID instance and service is up and running, use the Oracle Directory Manager (found in the 9i Oracle Home program menu group under the Integrated Management Tools folder) to connect to OID and create a context for your connections. When you first start the Directory Manager, you will be prompted to add servers. If you accepted the defaults on the installation, leave the port at the LDAP default of 389 and set the hostname to the full qualified name of the node where you have the directory service running. Once this is done, you will see that this server has been selected for your connection and that the username and password are blank.

Log in as the root directory administrator. The *distinguished name* (*dn*) of this user is cn=orcladmin. The initial password is "welcome," unless you changed it during the installation. Figure 7-7 shows what your login screen will look like (except that your server will be different).

Sample OID Configuration for Net Naming Oracle LDAP naming requires a context, referred to as the *Oracle Context,* within the directory tree and a set of

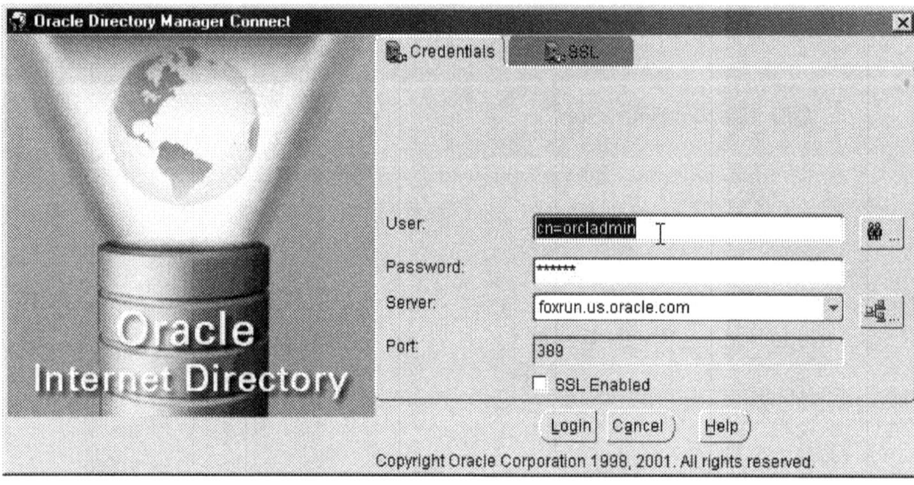

FIGURE 7-7. *OID administrator login*

custom objects to support Net naming and other services. This location, or context, is where all LDAP objects are kept for Net naming. You can have multiple contexts to serve different audiences (for example, users in different regions, developers, and database administrators). The context is installed by default at the root of the directory. This is *not* good practice for reasons beyond the scope of this book, so we will instruct you on how to create a directory information tree (DIT) where you might want to keep your Oracle Context. Once you have successfully logged in as instructed, configure OID for testing:

1. Click the Entry Management node under your OID server (see Figure 7-8).
2. Click the green cube icon with the twinkle on the corner to create a new entity. This will pop up a form that looks like the one in Figure 7-9.
3. Click the Add button to add an object class for this entity. Select the class named "top" from the Super Class Selector list that appears, and then click OK.
4. Repeat step 3, but select domain for the domain class.
5. Enter **dc=com** in the required field, as shown in Figure 7-9.
6. Click OK to save the new entity.
7. Now, while back at the Directory Administrator, right-click the new dc=com entity and select Create Like.
8. Because you selected Create Like, you can just change the dc property and the distinguished name (dn). See Figure 7-10 for proper formatting. When you have finished, click OK.

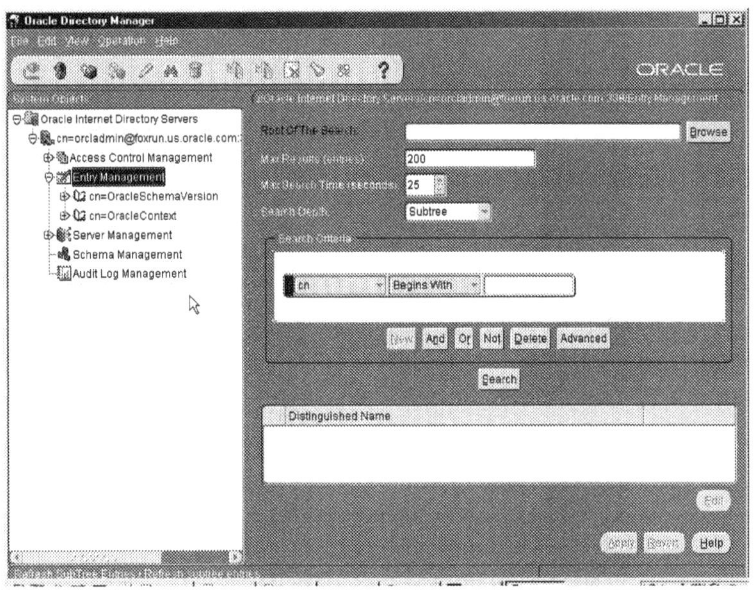

FIGURE 7-8. *Creating objects below the OID Entry Management node*

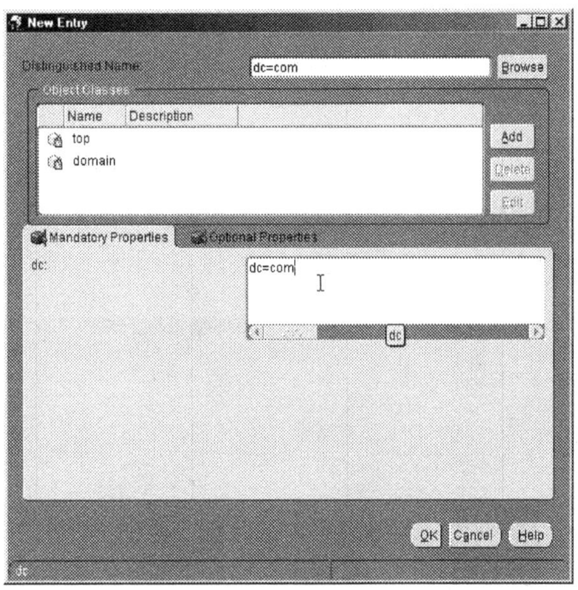

FIGURE 7-9. *New OID Object Creation screen*

9. Back at the Directory Administrator, you should now have a tree that is similar to what appears in Figure 7-11. Go ahead and minimize this application. You will come back to it later to verify configuration.
10. Start the Oracle Net Configuration Assistant found in the Configuration and Migration Tools folder of the Oracle home off the Start menu.
11. Select Directory Usage Configuration and then click Next (see Figure 7-12).
12. Select the option Create additional or upgrade existing Oracle Context (Advanced) and click Next. This will allow you to load the Oracle Context in the directory hierarchy you finished creating in step 9.
13. Make sure that the directory type is set to Oracle Internet Directory and click Next.
14. Enter the hostname where the OracleDirectoryService_<SID> is (in this case, it is the same node as you have installed OID on), and leave the port numbers at their defaults.
15. On the next screen, you will want to add the distinguished name for the tree that you created in step 8 (refer to the distinguished name shown in Figure 7-10), such as dc=oraclecorp,dc=com. See Figure 7-13 for an example that is truncated by the tool.

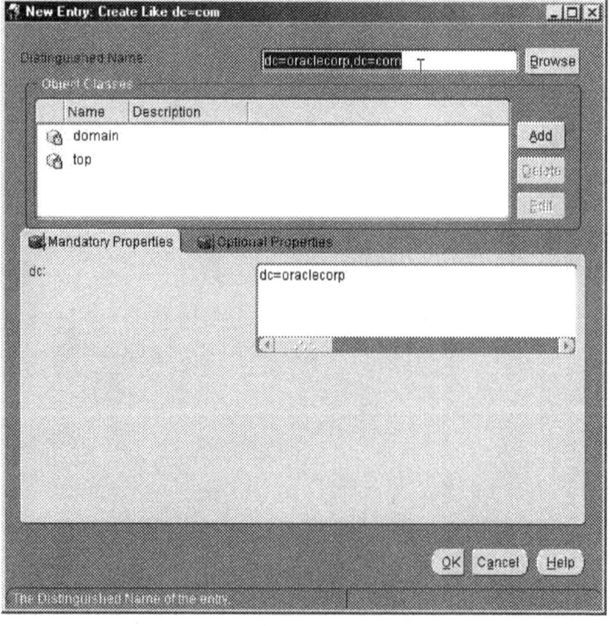

FIGURE 7-10. *Configure the child domain*

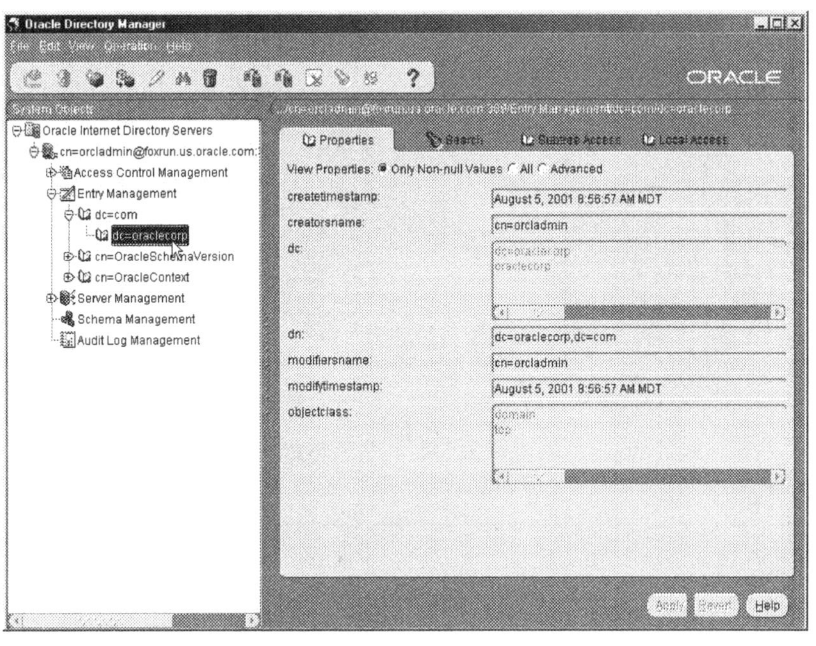

FIGURE 7-11. *Prepared tree for addition of Oracle Context*

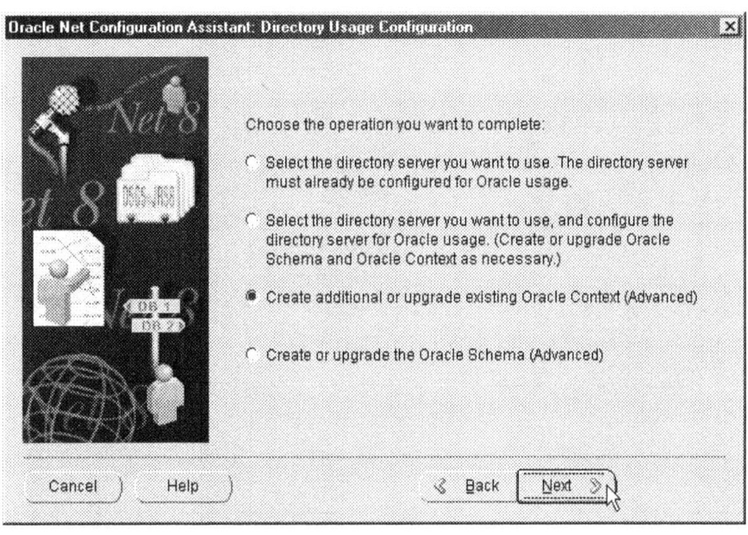

FIGURE 7-12. *Client directory configuration and Oracle Schema load*

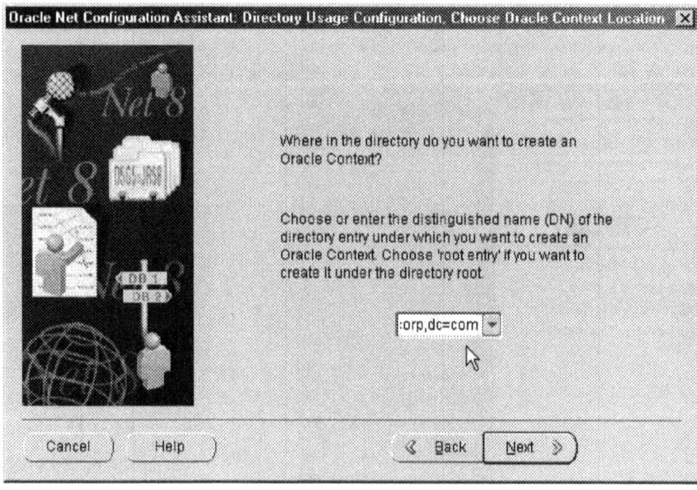

FIGURE 7-13. *Entering the parent directory entry under which the Oracle Context will be installed*

16. For the purpose of our demonstration (that is, don't use this user for production configurations), we will use the root directory administrator to create the context, as shown in Figure 7-14. This step will take a few minutes, as it uses the OID command-line tools to add the context.

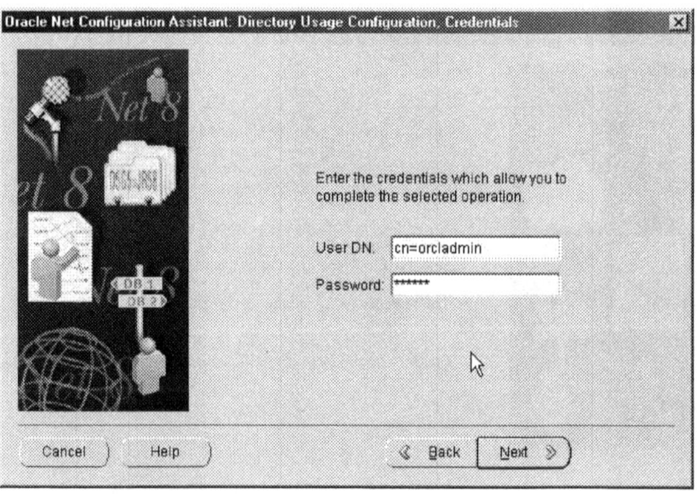

FIGURE 7-14. *Entering the distinguished name (dn) of the administrator to create the entries under the parent directory*

Configure Clients to Use OID's LDAP You will want to configure your clients and add net service names to OID properly, as demonstrated in the steps that follow. To configure *other* clients, use Net Configuration Assistant.

1. Select Directory Usage Configuration and click Next.
2. Select the first option "Select the directory server you want to use. The directory server must already be configured for Oracle usage."
3. Verify that the directory type is Oracle Internet Directory and click Next.
4. Enter the hostname of the machine where the OID service resides, leave the default port settings as they are and click Next. This will take some time as OID is queried for all available Oracle Contexts.
5. A drop-down box with the various Oracle contexts that have been created in your OID instance will appear. Select the one in the appropriate tree (the one with dc=oraclecorp,dc=com in it) and click Next (see Figure 7-15).

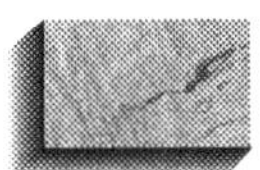

NOTE
If you select the directory root as your Oracle Context, then your pre-Oracle9i clients will not be able to use LDAP for name resolution!

6. Click through the rest of the informational messages and click Finish when it appears on the last screen.

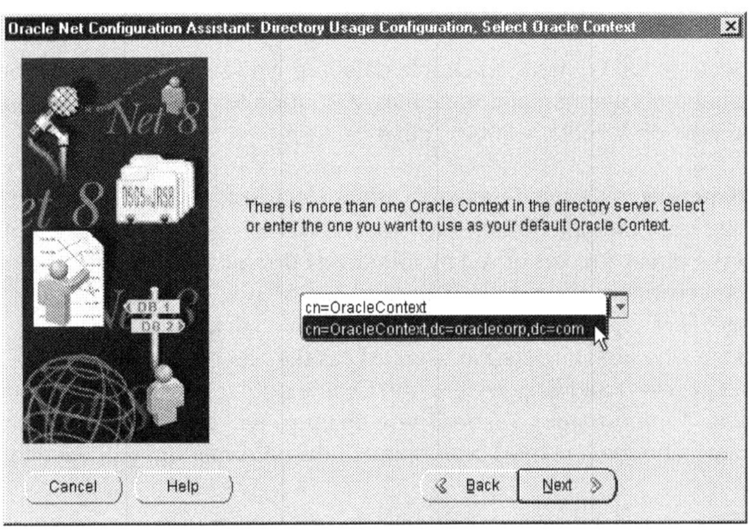

FIGURE 7-15. *Selecting the proper Oracle Context for this client*

Adding Net Services to OID Now that your clients are ready to use LDAP name resolution, you need to add services to the server for resolution. To add net service names, you will use the same tool you should use to add entries to the tnsnames.ora file, Net Manager (found under Configuration and Migration Tools, formerly called Net8 Assistant). Upon opening Net Manager, you will find the first node is titled Directory, with a node beneath it titled Service Naming. If you try to expand the Service Naming node, you will be prompted for a username and password. Enter the OID user as a distinguished name (for example, the root administrator is cn=orcladmin) and the password to continue. Of course, you can use another user that you may have set up with the proper privileges to perform these functions. In a production environment, you should *not* use the directory admin account to create entries.

Troubleshooting and More with OID Although OID troubleshooting is largely outside the realm of this book, we thought we would tell you where to start! Take a look in the %ORACLE_HOME%\ldap\log directory for the log files associated with the OID service processes:

```
c:\oracle>tlist | grep OID
 960 OIDldapd.exe
 972 OIDldapd.exe
1140 OIDservice.exe
```

- Check out the %ORACLE_HOME%\ldap\demo\plsql directory for examples of how to interact with OID from PL/SQL within the database.
- If you are interested in understanding more about how things work in OID, check out the C header files in %ORACLE_HOME%\ldap\public.
- Because OID utilizes an Oracle database, you will want to monitor the database's alert log and trace files. Also monitor the session and process (thread on Windows 2000) activity.

Active Directory Active Directory (AD) is Microsoft's Windows 2000 LDAP directory server. Currently, Oracle Net can use AD to store services and enterprise users, but the direct support of AD by Oracle is currently scheduled to be removed from future versions of the database. For this reason, we suggest that you stay away from using AD as your Oracle object repository and stick with OID.

For those who are interested in using AD as the Net Naming directory, check out Chapter 3 and Chapter 9 of the Oracle online or printed documentation *Net Services Administrator's Guide*. These chapters will give you the Oracle background information you need. To supplement this information, you have to make sure that your AD is properly set up and that the installing user is a member of the Schema Admins group for the whole forest as well as a member of the local machine's Administrators group. For step-by-step instructions and other details, please review the 8.1.6 Metalink document number 111424.1.

Connecting

Connecting to an Oracle database is technically a distinct process from name resolution, as discussed earlier, but it is the next logical integrated step. Most users will never know that name resolution and connecting are separate processes because they are seamless in a properly configured environment. Despite that fact, many misconceptions and troubleshooting difficulties can occur.

The Client Connection

The Oracle Net connection process is essentially always the same on the client despite the possible different server configurations. The client software connectivity profile is determined in the early stages of connection by reading the sqlnet.ora file. You can determine which sqlnet.ora is being used for a connection through the tnsping.exe utility as described previously. Once you know the sqlnet.ora file that is used, you can turn on net tracing. An Oracle network trace file will show you what profile options are chosen, including resolving defaults. Directly following is an example taken from a client net trace file. You can actually review the content to see what you would need to put into your sqlnet.ora.

```
--- PARAMETER SOURCE INFORMATION FOLLOWS ---
Attempted load of system pfile source
c:\oracle\901\network\admin\sqlnet.ora
Parameter source loaded successfully

Attempted load of local pfile source c:\oracle\sqlnet.ora
Parameter source was not loaded

 -> PARAMETER TABLE LOAD RESULTS FOLLOW <-
Successful parameter table load
 -> PARAMETER TABLE HAS THE FOLLOWING CONTENTS <-
  TRACE_DIRECTORY_SERVER = c:\tmp\svr
 TRACE_DIRECTORY_CLIENT = c:\tmp\cli
 NAMES.DIRECTORY_PATH = (TNSNAMES, HOSTNAME, LDAP)
 TRACE_LEVEL_CLIENT = SUPPORT
 TRACE_LEVEL_SERVER = SUPPORT
 SQLNET.AUTHENTICATION_SERVICES = (NTS)
 TRACE_UNIQUE_CLIENT = on
--- PARAMETER SOURCE INFORMATION ENDS ---
```

You can identify what a client does with these parameters by examining the trace file well into the connection process. Here is an example of the connection process checking for client-side encryption settings that must be synchronized with server settings:

```
nam_gnsp: Reading parameter "SQLNET.ENCRYPTION_CLIENT" from parameter file
nam_gnsp: Parameter not found
naequad: Using default value "ACCEPTED"
```

If you examine the options that were in the parameter file (sqlnet.ora), you can see that there is no setting for client encryption. This snippet of the trace file reflects this finding in the calls to NAM_GNSP.

Proper connectivity is often determined by three basic things:

- Profile settings as kept in sqlnet.ora
- Network configuration, availability, and performance
- Server readiness and configuration (including the server-side Listener, server-side profile/sqlnet.ora, and database availability)

In a vanilla configuration without the ASO option in place, you should be able to operate without a sqlnet.ora file for testing purposes. If you are experiencing problems with actual connectivity, check these elements to spot problems and address them.

If you are concerned with client connectivity performance, check the performance using the Performance MMC, as mentioned in Chapter 3, and basic connectivity tools such as tracert, ping, and nslookup. Make sure to separate and quantify the name resolution process using client-side net tracing with timing turned on. To turn net trace timing on, you will have to add the following line to your sqlnet.ora by hand:

```
TRACE_TIMESTAMP_CLIENT = ON
```

Add this entry to the end of the sqlnet.ora on its own line with no spaces or tabs in front of it. This will give you output that looks like the following:

```
  [15-MAR-99 09:20:23] nsopen: opening transport...
  [15-MAR-99 09:20:23] nsoptions: entry
```

This feature is available from the 8.1.6 client and beyond. You can use it to determine where the client connection might be hanging, and it should be used in cooperation with server time-stamped trace files configured as such:

```
TRACE_TIMESTAMP_SERVER = ON
```

Make sure that you specify this in the *server's* sqlnet.ora and that the system clocks on each system are in sync. If the systems are in different time zones, we suggest that you change the client system clock to be in sync with the server's system time. This makes comparing trace files much easier. The other thing you will want to do is compare net packets on the client and the server side by examining the nspsend- and nsprecv-generated packets.

JDBC Thus far, we have discussed client/server connectivity. This is the most common method of connectivity, and all types of connectivity except JDBC thin connectivity eventually boil down to this method of connection. The Oracle JDBC thin driver uses the Java Sockets framework with an emulation of the Oracle Net and TTC layers on top of the Java Sockets implementation. For this reason, you can use the JDBC thin driver on a variety of platforms. It is commonly used in applets, and connections to the server are still the same as client/server connections. The real advantage of the thin driver is that you do not have to install the Oracle client software on the user machine. Instead, the thin driver is designed for Java Applets. The disadvantage is that the thin driver is a bit slower and it must still be downloaded for use.

Server Connection Acceptance

Once the client initiates the connection process, the associated messages travel to the server. The server must be set up to "listen" for connection requests, and then handle those connections appropriately. This architecture is in place whether the client and the server are on the same system or the client is an iMac in another country.

There are two methods for Oracle servers to handle connections, Shared Server (formerly called MTS, or multithreaded server) and Dedicated Server. These *service handlers* inherit their connections from a service called the *Listener* that shows up in your process list as tnslsnr.exe and is controlled either from the OS Services MMC or via the command-line lsnrctl.exe utility.

A listener will service all requests for a set of protocol addresses (host/IP, port, and service/SID) that specify the listening endpoints for the Oracle database. In particular, a listener is exclusively set up to listen on an interface (for example, hostname or IP address) for a discrete port over a particular protocol. For example, there can only be one listener for the host msale.us.oracle.com on port 1521 using TCP. That same listener can also be the sole listener for msale.us.oracle.com on port 1522 on TCP. On a machine with multiple network cards, a single listener may listen for each network card that has its own IP address, or you might have multiple listeners, one or more for each IP.

Once an Oracle Listener is up and running, it services connection requests over those IP/port/protocol combinations for the list of services in listener.ora and those instances that register themselves with the Listener (an 8i+ feature). Once the Listener has a connection request for a service it is configured to listen for,

it immediately either hands off or redirects this connection to the service indicated in the connection request.

New Feature in Oracle9i

Direct handoff for TTC (client/server) connections is a new feature for release 9i. It has been introduced to improve connection performance for WAN connections by reducing the amount of messaging upon connection.

You can implement multiple Listeners to avOID an overloaded Listener or to provide for availability when one Listener goes down by configuring the client address list to contain the multiple Listeners with failover (discussed later in this chapter). We have seen more than 20 Listeners on some boxes used to service particular sets of clients and multiple Listeners to service different networks. You can also use different Listeners in combination with dispatcher connection and session limits to put a form of throttle on the concurrent activity through a particular address.

The Listener configuration is held in the listener.ora file and is best primarily managed by the Java GUI tools Net Manager and Net Configuration Assistant. The Net Configuration Assistant is used primarily for initial setup. Finer control and creation of multiple Listeners is done with Net Manager from the listening node. The 9i version of Net Manager should cover all your Listener configuration needs when used with the lsnrctl utility.

So what does the Listener process hand off or redirect those connections to? Either a dedicated server thread or a dispatcher thread. In the case of a dedicated server configuration, the thread will be spawned via the oraspawn.dll call made by the Listener process.

Dedicated server connections have their own exclusive part of memory allocated where sorting is done and other session-specific information is kept. On a Unix system, this is a separate process with its own User Global Area (UGA) kept in the Process Global Area (PGA); on NT and Windows 2000, the dedicated server thread is a thread with its own PGA memory allocated within the oracle.exe process.

Dedicated server connections are best for long-running, resource-intensive sessions and database links (connections from one server to another). Data warehouses and other applications that use long-running, resource-intensive queries are candidates for dedicated server connections.

Shared Server connections each share a thread similar to the dedicated server thread with other sessions, hence the name "Shared Server." When a session becomes idle and is kicked out of a particular shared server, it can return via the same shared server thread or another without losing the vital session information because it is kept in the SGA. This is called *session migration*. The shared server is used as the working thread to fulfill a session's requests. Shared servers monitor the request queue and fulfill requests on a first in, first out (FIFO) basis.

In a Shared Server configuration, there are threads (processes on all other platforms) called *dispatchers* that manage the actual connections and interaction between the client connection and the shared server. The views V$DISPATCHER and V$DISPATCHER_RATE give good information about the status and statistics, respectively, of the dispatchers. Communication with the database from the dispatcher is maintained through queues. There is a *request queue* located in the SGA that services all dispatchers. You can see stats for this queue in V$QUEUE where the TYPE column is COMMON (for example, **select * from v$queue where type= 'COMMON'**). Each dispatcher has its own response queue, each with its own row in V$QUEUE. Every client connection communicates directly with a dispatcher that works with the shared servers through the request and response queues. The V$SHARED_SERVER and V$SHARED_SERVER_MONITOR views can be used to better understand server thread status and activity.

As an example of connection activity in a shared connection, consider a client that has established a connection and now decides to run a select statement. This statement requires sorting (for example, has an "order by" clause). The client sends this request to the dispatcher, which puts this request on the request queue, where it is picked up by a shared server thread that is either already servicing this session or is monitoring the queue for work to do. Once the request is serviced, the results are placed on that particular dispatcher's response queue, and the dispatcher will usher the results to the client that made the request.

Shared Server connectivity is the preferred method for applications that have short connection lifetimes, are inactive for more than a few seconds regularly, or require a very large number of concurrent, although *relatively* inactive, users.

Basic Client Architecture

Developers and users who are new to Oracle database connectivity usually have a difficult time initiating that first connection. The Oracle client installation and configuration is typically the missing element. In order to connect to an Oracle database, you *must* have the Oracle client software installed first. Even though you may have an Oracle ODBC or OLEDB driver installed on your system, these alone will not enable you to connect to the database. You must have the client software installed.

Figure 7-16 shows a variety of ways that applications may connect to and interact with the Oracle database from the Microsoft operating systems. (Thanks to Geoff Bednarsky for the original diagram from which this was built.) The Oracle client software installation is the key gateway for all but one interface to the database. Eventually, these make calls to the OCI layer, which eventually become calls to the various presentation (TTC, not shown in Figure 7-16) and net layers, to TCP and then IP, and then down to the wire where the application's call meets the server's logical tier.

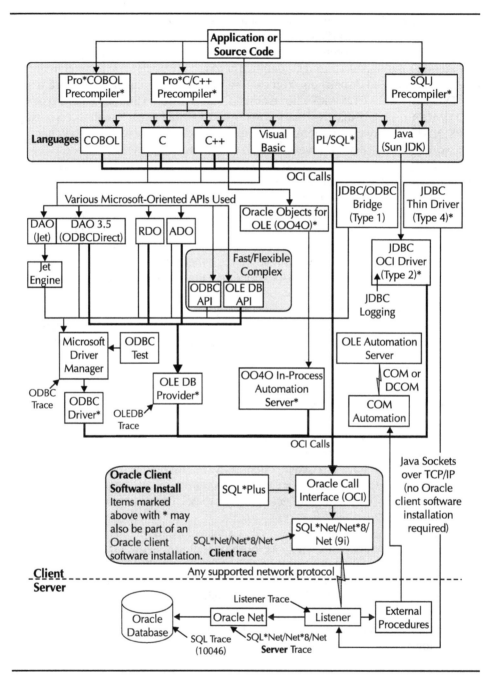

FIGURE 7-16. *Diagram of the different ways you can connect to an Oracle database from a Microsoft platform*

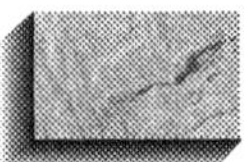

NOTE
There is always an exception to the rule, and that exception in this case is the JDBC thin driver. It emulates the functionality of the client software over Java Sockets to connect and interact with the database. Of course, this lightweight client comes at a cost. The thin driver lacks the functionality and performance of the "thick" JDBC driver that makes calls to the Oracle client software.

As you can see, the developer wishing to use data stored on an Oracle database has myriad choices that enable him or her to completely ignore the network *once* it is properly configured.

Dedicated Server

Windows 2000 and NT use a connectivity process configuration that is different from Unix. On a Unix box, the Listener is a stand-alone process, and connections are implemented in separate processes referred to as *shadow processes*; in a Shared Server configuration on Unix, there are also dispatcher processes, and the connection processes are shared by many connections.

In the Windows architecture, the server-side dedicated server process architecture is implemented as many threads in the Oracle process. For each Listener, you will find a tnslsnr.exe entry in your process list, but the equivalent of all the connection processes and dispatchers on Unix are threads within the oracle.exe process. The Listener calls the system function NTCreateRemoteThread to create the dedicated process in the oracle.exe process. Each dedicated connection is initially allocated 1MB of memory in the oracle.exe process. This can also be influenced by parameters that affect PGA size, as listed here:

MAX_ENABLED_ROLES (4 bytes each)

BITMAP_MERGE_AREA_SIZE

CREATE_BITMAP_AREA_SIZE

HASH_AREA_SIZE

OPEN_CURSORS

SORT_AREA_SIZE

PGA_AGGREGATE_TARGET

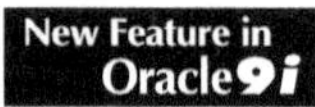

A new parameter and functionality of release 9i, PGA_AGGREGATE_TARGET actually takes the functional place of all of the *_AREA_SIZE and OPEN_CURSORS parameters mentioned by allocating an aggregate amount of memory for all *dedicated* server processes. When PGA_AGGREGATE_TARGET is set, WORK_AREA_SIZE_POLICY is set to auto, and Oracle9i dynamically manages memory allocated to a session according to the total amount of memory to work with as indicated in PGA_AGGREGATE_TARGET, used PGA memory, and the needs of the individual session. Please note that this parameter only works for dedicated server processes because Shared Server processes keep most of their data in the SGA instead of the PGA.

You can get a view of session PGA memory usage by running the following query:

```
SELECT nvl(username,b.name) Consumer, value || ' bytes' "Session PGA memory"
FROM V$SESSION sess, V$SESSTAT stat, V$STATNAME name, v$bgprocess b
WHERE sess.SID = stat.SID
AND sess.paddr = b.paddr(+)
AND stat.STATISTIC# = name.STATISTIC#
AND name.NAME = 'session pga memory';
```

A very similar query allows you to get a look at session UGA memory usage:

```
SELECT nvl(username,b.name) Consumer, value || ' bytes' "Session UGA memory"
FROM V$SESSION sess, V$SESSTAT stat, V$STATNAME name,v$bgprocess b
WHERE sess.SID = stat.SID
AND sess.paddr = b.paddr(+)
AND stat.STATISTIC# = name.STATISTIC#
AND name.NAME = 'session uga memory';
```

In order to see the peak usage, just change the statistic in the last line to

```
AND name.NAME = 'session uga memory max';
```

This will also work for the PGA query.

Using PRIVATE_SGA to Limit Session Memory Usage

We have seen runaway processes that would love to suck all memory in existence into their realm. You can limit session memory usage by setting the user profile resource limit PRIVATE_SGA. Using profiles does add a bit of latency to session activity and should be applied with care in situations where you need to limit users' consumption of particular resources.

First, you will want to create a profile for limiting SGA usage:

```
create profile crazyuser limit
private_sga 10m;
```

Now, create a script to alter the profile of users in the database using a query like this:

```
select DISTINCT 'alter user ' || username || ' profile crazyuser;'
from dba_users
where username not in
(select grantee from dba_role_privs
       where granted_role in ('DBA','OLAP_DBA'));
```

We created this query to exclude those users who were assigned the DBA or OLAP_DBA roles. If you use this query, you will surely want to exclude certain users from the profile. Instead, you may want to change the query to only include application users who have been granted a role you have created. For example:

```
select DISTINCT 'alter user ' || username || ' profile crazyuser;'
from dba_users
where username in
(select grantee from dba_role_privs
       where granted_role in ('APPUSER','DATA_ENTRY'));
```

Now that you have created the profile and assigned it to the appropriate users, you can alter the system to turn resource limitations on like this:

```
Alter system set resource_limit = true;
```

You can also add RESOURCE_LIMIT=TRUE to your init.ora file for the instance to turn it on permanently.

With an application that must handle a very large number of connections concurrently, or where the sessions require large amounts of memory to perform session-specific functions, this architecture can lead to problems that will be addressed by 64-bit Oracle on Windows 2000 when it comes out (see Chapter 3 for details).

Listening for the Masses

You can use one Listener for many databases, even different versions of different databases in different Oracle homes (installations of the RDBMS). In fact, there may be times when you want to use the latest version of a Listener to enable some new feature, increase performance, or get around a problem in the version that exists in your database's installation home. You can create a new Oracle home by using the custom option in the Oracle Universal Installer to install only the network components. Automatic registration will pick up all 8i and above databases running on your system. You can configure the 9i Net Listener service to listen for 8.0.x and 7.3.x databases by adding their configuration information to the Listener via Net Manager.

You can also use a different Listener for each database you have on a computer or have many Listeners for the same database to provide for failover if one Listener dies. You may also decide to do this for management reasons.

One very good reason to set up multiple Listeners is to segment your network traffic onto separate subnets with separate network cards (multihomed node). This can help you improve both performance and security. If you are using replication heavily and you are noticing that your network is being soaked by snapshot refreshes, you can add a network card to your Windows 2000 system on a separate subnet. You then set up your replication source's connection description to point to this new IP address, and by doing so you have segmented the replication traffic and largely relieved the normal user connectivity from network problems related to server-to-server traffic.

Once 64-bit Oracle goes into production on Windows 2000 (it has been available on other 64-bit flavors of Unix for years), a much larger Oracle process size will be possible, thus enabling many more connections as well; multiple Listeners will become more important to balance the load on systems with well over 2000 concurrent connections.

Shared Server

Shared Server (SS) is the new name for multithreaded server (MTS). The name change also changes the associated init.ora parameters. As mentioned previously, Shared Server architecture includes the use of dispatchers that handle sockets handed off from the Listener process or clients redirected to the dispatcher. The dispatcher will use a server thread that holds the PGA for the V$PROCESS entry, but most of the data (for example, the CGA and UGA) is moved into the SGA—in particular the data will be kept in the Large Pool. If there is no Large Pool, then the Shared Pool is used instead. Even if there is a Large Pool configured for SS, then about 10KB per session will be used in the Shared Pool as well.

The dispatchers handle all incoming and outgoing activity through the response and request queues. Dispatchers can be added without bouncing the database by altering the system to change the dispatcher parameter, and dispatchers can be reduced as well. See the SQL reference documentation for details.

The SS architecture is best used in an OLTP environment where connections are relatively inactive. Shared servers should *not* be used for database links, backups, reporting usage, or data warehousing activities—use dedicated servers for these activities instead.

You can have your database configured for Shared Server activity and still have specific users connect via a dedicated server. To do this, you will need to edit the net service (for example, the TNS alias) to force usage to the dedicated server. Do this from Net Manager (see Figure 7-17).

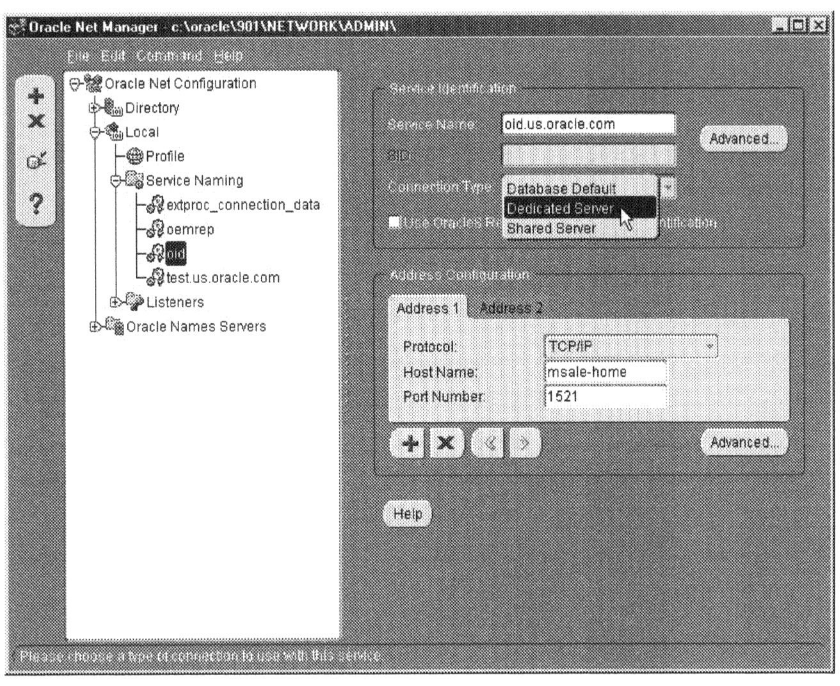

FIGURE 7-17. *Configure a TNS alias to force a dedicated connection.*

Connectivity Configuration

Configuring the proper elements of Oracle to connect to your target databases has been a confusing issue in earlier versions. This section addresses server and client configuration issues in order to help you make informed, intelligent decisions and follow the correct steps.

Net Manager: The Primary Configuration Tool

The Net Manager tool is the Oracle9i incarnation of the Net8 Assistant. The tool has come a long way since its inception and is largely preferable to Net Configuration Assistant.

Figure 7-18 shows the essential tree expanded for working with local TNS alias entries in the tnsnames.ora file. The following numbered list corresponds to the labels in Figure 7-18.

1. To work with the directory server aliases, you should expand Service Naming in the tree. You will be prompted for a directory username and password to add and edit entries under this node. If you have configured

a directory for this client as described earlier, you can use the cn= orcladmin username and "welcome" as the password.

2. To work with any of the local files on both client and server, you do so under the Local node.
3. All editing of sqlnet.ora by the Net Manager tool is done under the Profile node.
4. Editing tnsnames.ora alias entries is done in the leaves beneath the Service Naming node under the Local tree.
5. A server's Listeners can be configured beneath the Listeners node.
6. Names servers may be configured beneath the Oracle Names Servers node.
7. Whenever you have selected a node where a leaf can be added, the Add button becomes active, allowing you to add elements like a new TNS alias or a new Listener. If you have chosen a leaf that can be deleted, then the "X" turns red, allowing you to delete the TNS alias or Listener.
8. The title bar shows you the location of the local configuration files you are editing.
9. You can test connectivity to a TNS alias by clicking this button. It remains grayed out until you have selected an alias leaf in the tree.

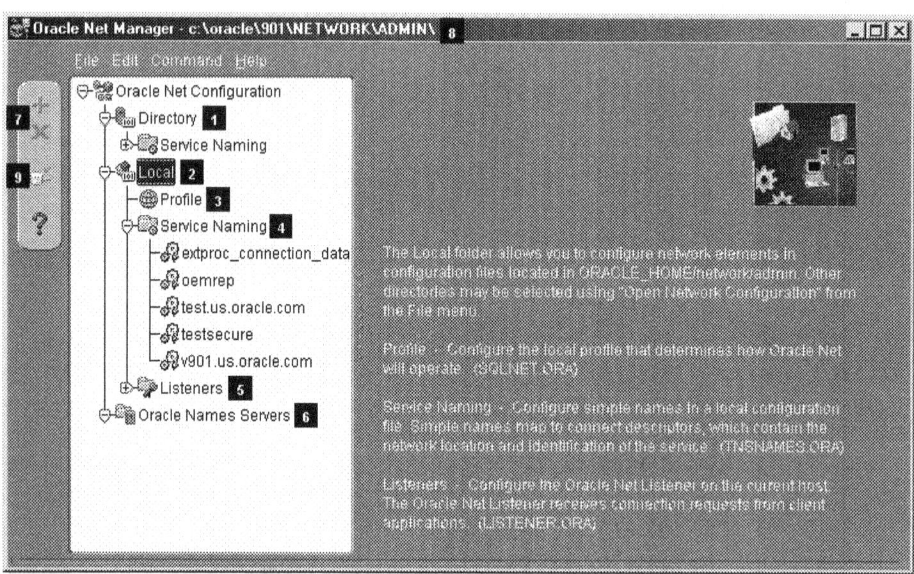

FIGURE 7-18. *Net Manager local configuration*

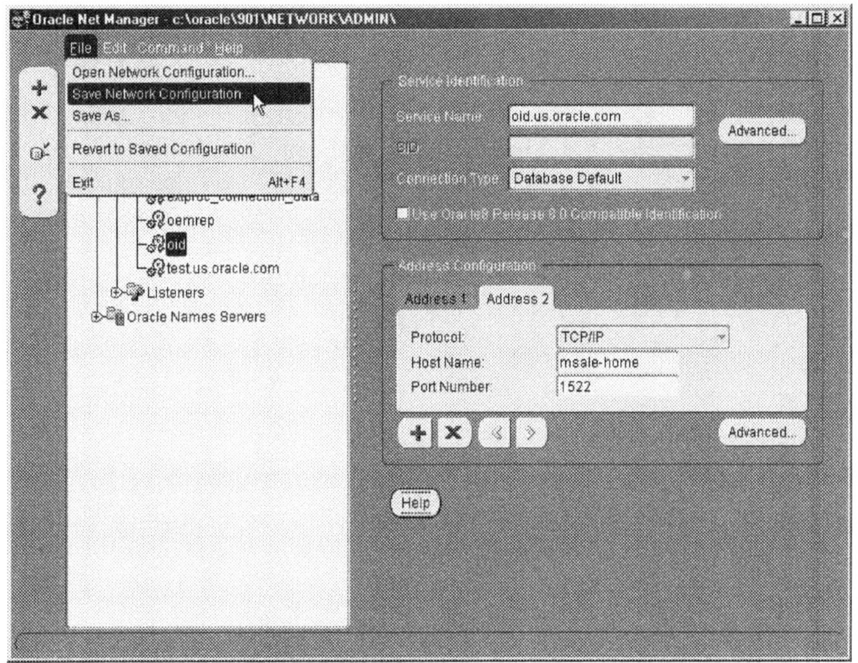

FIGURE 7-19. *Save Net Manager changes*

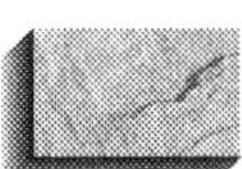

NOTE
Be careful not edit a file by hand until you have closed Net Manager because, when you exit the tool, it will overwrite your changes. Also, do not waste your time editing these files for readability because Net Manager will shuffle everything around in a seemingly nonsensible order.

When you have finished working in Net Manager, make sure that you save your changes, as shown in Figure 7-19.

Client Configuration

The base client configuration includes a number of files that are cryptic and easy to improperly configure when edited by hand. These files are very picky about spaces and tabs (do not ever use tabs in your Net configuration files) as well as being sensitive to special character problems encountered when transferring files from a Unix system to a Microsoft system. For this reason, Oracle provides a couple of tools to manage these files for you.

Net Configuration Assistant is the tool you should use to define directory name resolution. It also allows you to manage most other aspects of Oracle network configuration, but Net Manager is better suited to take advantage of the various options available. Although Net Configuration Assistant is a wizard-style tool that takes you step by step through most activities, Net Manager is available for those administrators that do not need complete hand-holding through the process.

As we stressed earlier, Net Manager is the configuration tool of choice in 9i. You can use this tool to configure the range of client configuration files, as well as your server-side Listeners. Net Manager also allows you to access directory entries and configure your profile (sqlnet.ora) with a simple GUI interface.

There are some parameters that are not yet available from the Net Manager GUI tool; so to enable things like time stamping on your network trace files, you will have to edit the files directly. In these cases, we have the following suggestions:

- Never use tabs.
- Edit right on the machine with a native editor that does not provide formatting functionality (for example, notepad.exe on NT/2000) to avoid special characters being inadvertently included. Avoid editing on your Linux system and ftping the file to your Windows 2000 system at all costs!
- Do not indent new lines. Start with your first character at the first position of a new line.

These hints will help you avoid frustrating encounters with what appear to be your average configuration files.

Profile (sqlnet.ora) Configuration

The first step in configuring your client software is to properly configure your profile. Profile configuration is done from the Net Manager GUI tool. Examine Figure 7-20 and follow the numbered list as it explains the labels in this figure:

1. This pull-down menu contains the various sections for configuration of the profile/sqlnet.ora. When you select an option from this drop-down list, the view of options in Net Manager changes.
2. Tracing should normally be turned off unless you are trying to troubleshoot an issue. If you need to trace an intermittent issue but you know that you only need 10MB worth of trace file content, you can turn on cyclical tracing by adding the following code to your sqlnet.ora by hand at the bottom of the file, each entry on its own line with no tabs. In this example code, the client,

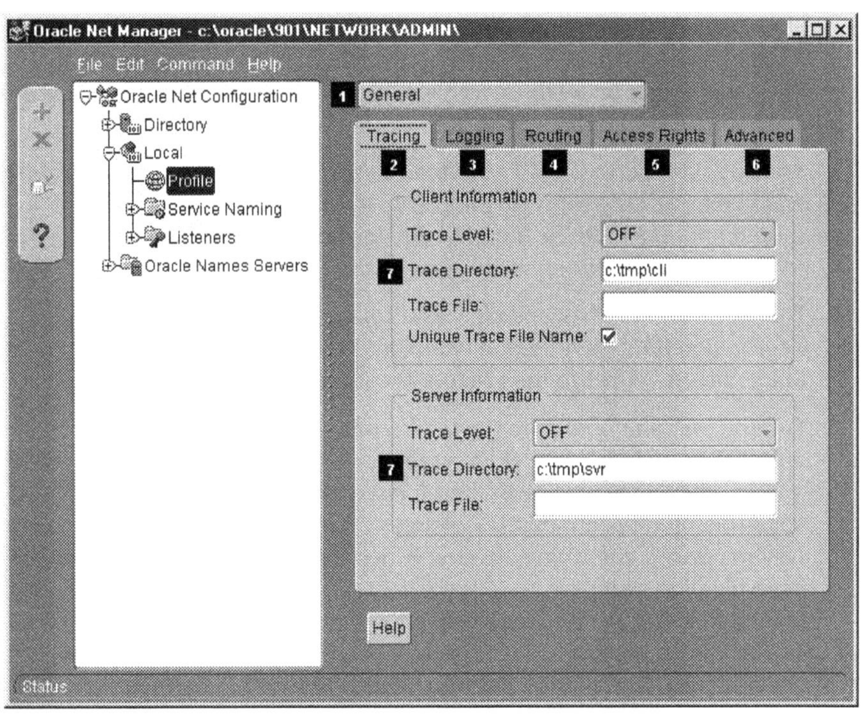

FIGURE 7-20. *Local profile configuration (sqlnet.ora) with Net Manager*

server, and default Listener trace files will not grow beyond 2048KB (2MB). When they do grow to 2MB, they will be copied off and renamed with a digit representing the copy (for example, svr*1*_1676.trc through svr*4*_1676.trc):

```
TRACE_FILELEN_CLIENT = 2048
TRACE_FILENO_CLIENT  = 4
TRACE_FILELEN_SERVER = 2048
TRACE_FILENO_SERVER  = 4
TRACE_FILELEN_LISTENER = 2048
TRACE_FILENO_LISTENER  = 4
```

3. Logging can be configured by editing the elements on the Logging tab. Typically, you will want to use tracing for troubleshooting and logging as a form of auditing.

4. Routing contains the option to force all connections from this client to make a dedicated server connection. Click the check box next to

Always Use Dedicated Server to enable this option. You might use this on a Shared Server–configured server that utilizes database links to avoid having a single connection monopolize a dispatcher to connect. You might also want to set this option on a DBA client machine that performs long-running queries or jobs.

5. You can limit access by IP from the Access Rights tab. We strongly suggest that you avoid using this functionality. If you need this functionality, you should implement IPSec functionality introduced in Windows 2000. This security implementation is far more encompassing and exacting.
6. The Advanced tab has one element of particular interest: the Client Registration ID. Use a unique character string of up to 128 characters to identify the client to the Listener for logging.
7. Turn on, off, and configure tracing from the Tracing tab. Not all tracing options are included in Net Manager yet. See the preceding code example to turn on cyclical tracing to limit the size of your trace files. Locate your traces on a file system that is isolated or quota limited for Oracle to avoid system crashes due to massive trace files. Learn how to manually enable trace file time stamps in the "The Client Connection" section earlier. We suggest that you always have this option enabled along with cyclical tracing, even if tracing is turned off—it prepares you or the next database administrator next time you are in crisis mode and need to turn on tracing. Make sure that you have the Unique Trace File Name option checked in order to distinguish various client connections.

Further client profile configuration for name resolution from Net Manager is displayed in Figure 7-21. The numbered items notate the areas of interest.

1. Notice that we are still in the Local node to configure sqlnet.ora by the path displayed in the title bar (c:\oracle\901\NETWORK\ADMIN in this example).
2. We have changed from the General options to the Naming options for the client profile. Note the changes in content when comparing this figure with Figure 7-20. This screen works with Net name resolution options for the Oracle client software.
3. The Methods tab is similar to resolv.conf in some versions of Unix in that it tells you from where to try and resolve names and in what order. See the previous section, "Net Name Resolution," for more detail.
4. The Selected Methods section tells you the order of attempted resolution from top to bottom.

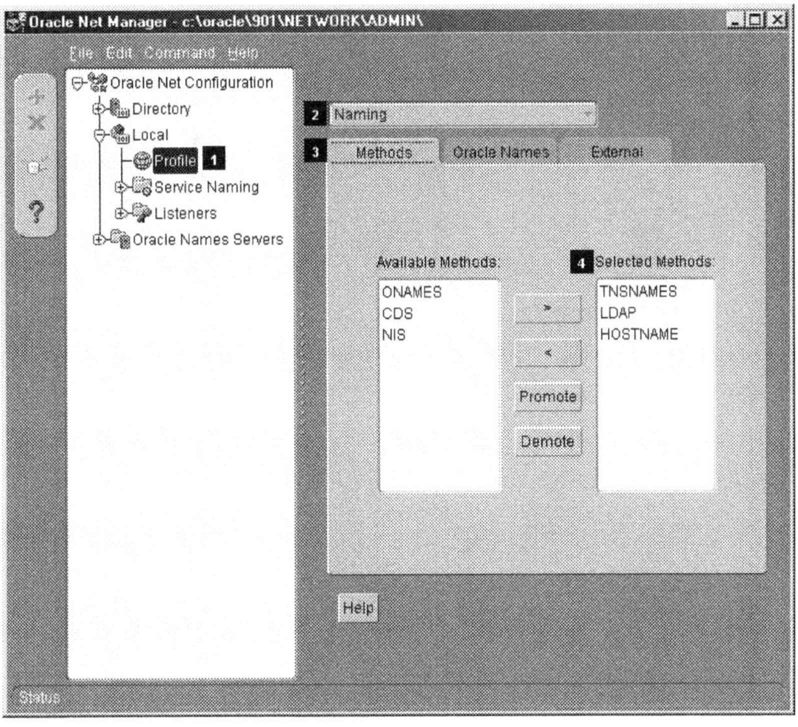

FIGURE 7-21. *Profile naming configuration with Net Manager*

Client Configuration for Higher Availability

Now that we have talked about both basic client network configuration and Shared Server configuration, we can discuss some of the things you can do to configure the connection descriptor to enable greater availability and failover.

Load Balancing

Client load balancing means that the client connection will *randomly* select one of the addresses in the list of the connection alias. This enables you to have the client connect via one of many Listeners, or one of many nodes in a RAC cluster, or one of many nodes in a replicated environment. The key attribute of client-side load balancing is that it forces random selection of an address in the list of addresses in the alias used to connect to the service.

A client TNS alias is configured for load balancing by altering the address portion of the configuration. Turning load balancing on is best done via Net Manager. Load balancing and failover are configured via the Advanced button in the Address Configuration section of the connection alias. This button becomes

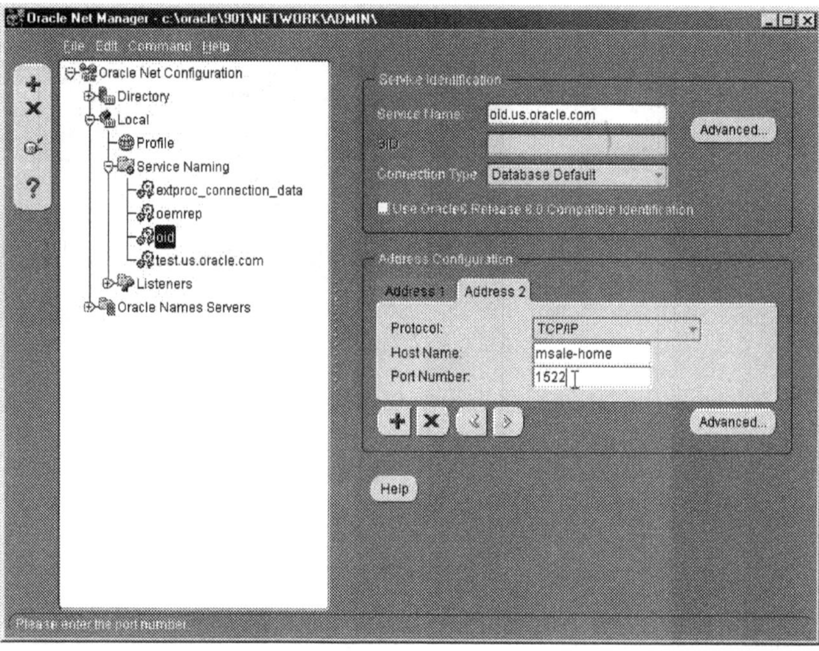

FIGURE 7-22. *Use multiple addresses in an alias to allow for load balancing and failover.*

active in Net Manager when there are multiple addresses for one alias, as shown in Figure 7-22. To turn on load balancing, you need to select either the second or third radio button, as shown in Figure 7-23.

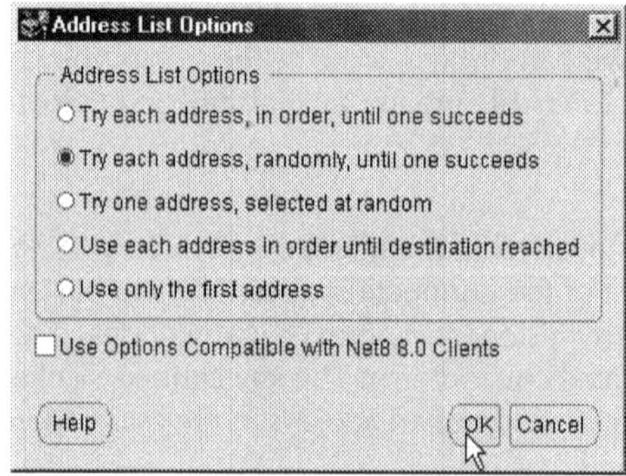

FIGURE 7-23. *Select your load balancing and failover options from the Address List Options dialog box.*

Failover

Client failover does the following: if the client's attempt to connect to one address fails, the client tries the *next* address in the list, unless load balancing is turned on, in which case the *next* address tried is selected randomly from the remaining untried addresses.

Failover is configured by default; it does not need to be enabled. In fact, you must turn off failover explicitly in order to disable the behavior. Why wouldn't you want it turned on? We can think of no good reason. If you don't want failover to occur, then you wouldn't have multiple addresses listed for the alias. If you do want to turn it off, then you can use Net Manager to alter the alias via the Advanced button of the Address Configuration section. Select the radio button option Use only the first address in the Address List Options dialog box and click OK.

Dedicated Server Configuration

There really is no direct configuration needed to enable a dedicated server. It is either requested by the client connection request or enabled by default if no dispatchers are configured. The init.ora parameter PROCESSES limits the maximum number of concurrent dedicated server connections. This parameter actually refers to the maximum number of threads for the instance and as such does not directly relate to the maximum number of connections a dedicated server–configured database can handle. In general, if you expect more than 1,000 connections, then you likely need to move to a Shared Server configuration.

The concern with dedicated server configuration arises because they consume memory in the oracle.exe process. Because the oracle.exe process's addressable memory is shared by servers and the SGA, you run into potential available memory problems. Oracle9i has introduced a new feature implemented by PGA_AGGREGATE_TARGET. See the section "Dedicated Server" earlier in this chapter and documentation to implement this feature. You might also want to limit the size of memory used by a session via the profile feature. Again, look in the "Dedicated Server" section for more information.

Shared Server Configuration

Shared Server configuration is done via database initialization parameters (for example, *initsid.ora*). The parameters that are only related to Shared Server (that is, those that allocate and limit dispatchers and shared servers) are only part of the picture. The more important configuration is that of the Large Pool and the Sessions parameters. The Large Pool gives the Shared Server architecture the primary memory it will utilize in the SGA other than the approximately 10KB in the Shared Pool for each virtual circuit (current connection handled by a dispatcher that is on a queue).

Dispatchers

This parameter is used to allocate and configure dispatchers. Once you create dispatchers, it sets all of the derived shared server parameters in motion. All other parameters, such as SHARED_SERVERS, MAX_DISPATCHERS, and others, will take their defaults only if DISPATCHERS is set. DISPATCHERS is a complex parameter with a variety of permutations. Even so, it can be very simply configured for a configuration that doesn't need much attention. For example, the absolute bare-bones configuration requires only specification of protocol:

```
dispatchers="(protocol=tcp)"
```

This line will configure one dispatcher for database connectivity on a randomly chosen port that registers itself on the Listener listening for port 1521 on the TCP protocol.

For a single-instance database configuration (no RAC enabled) with between 250 and 1,000 concurrent connections at peak usage, this setting is usually sufficient (along with the appropriate SHARED_POOL size). For those who wish to take advantage of all the other elements of shared servers or who are using a RAC system with multiple Listeners on multiple nodes, this is not sufficient.

As a starting point, you can configure one dispatcher for every 250 concurrent connections expected at peak usage. Review statistics from V$DISPATCHER_RATE and status from V$DISPATCHER to help make good decisions regarding the number of dispatchers you might need for your database. You should not configure more than 1,024 connections per dispatcher, the OS maximum; with dispatcher connection pooling, however, you can increase the number of sessions according to the idleness of a typical connection to increase the effective number of connections well into the thousands. When looking at V$DISPATCHER, the Status column values are as shown in Table 7-1.

Status	Description of Dispatcher Activity
WAIT	Idle
SEND	Sending a message
RECEIVE	Receiving a message
CONNECT	Establishing a new connection
DISCONNECT	Disconnecting a session in response to a request
BREAK	Handling a break (for example, CONTROL-C)
TERMINATE	Killing itself
ACCEPT	Accepting connections
REFUSE	No longer able to handle more connections (for example, either the speciied limit or the OS limit for the number of connections has been exceeded)

TABLE 7-1. *Status Column Values in V$DISPATCHER*

You can also run the following query to determine how busy your dispatchers are at the moment:

```
select name, status, ((busy/(busy+idle))*100) as "% time busy", network
from v$dispatcher;
```

If you determine that you do not have enough dispatchers or that you need to alter dispatcher configuration, then you can use the **alter system set dispatchers** syntax to meet your needs. If you want to add dispatchers with the same configuration as an existing dispatcher, you need to know the index of the dispatcher. The index is the number portion of the CONF_INDX column of the V$DISPATCHER view. Here is an example that explicitly sets the address for the first dispatcher:

```
alter system set dispatchers =
'(index=0) (ADDRESS=(PROTOCOL=tcp)(HOST=foxrun)(PORT=50))(dispatchers=2)'
```

If you look at V$DISPATCHER's CONF_INDEX column, you will see that both dispatchers share the same index number. You can increase the number of dispatchers for an existing dispatcher without changing any aspect of the existing configuration, as shown in this example:

```
alter system set dispatchers =
'(index=0)(proto=tcp)(dispatchers=5)'
```

This statement would add four dispatchers if the current number were 1 for that index. In order to add a dispatcher that is not necessarily based on an existing dispatcher, you just use the next unused index number (for example, **select (max(conf_indx)+1) next_index from v$dispatcher**). This statement assumes that the last dispatcher is named *D006*:

```
alter system set dispatchers
'(index=7)(address=(pro=tcp)(host=153.58.52.122)(port=1001))(dispatchers=5)'
```

If you want these settings to persist beyond the shutdown of the database, you must have SPFILE set up properly, then you can add the SCOPE=SPFILE clause to the end of your **alter system** statements. See Chapter 5 for more on using the SPFILE functionality.

When you set up your dispatchers in the init.ora file, you *can* have more than one dispatcher parameter setting, but each setting must be on adjacent lines. You can also keep multiple dispatcher configurations on one line by separating them with a comma. Here are some example dispatcher configurations:

```
dispatchers="(PROTOCOL=TCP)(SER=MODOSE)",
"(PROTOCOL=TCP)(PRE=oracle.aurora.server.GiopServer)",
"(PROTOCOL=TCP)(PRE=oracle.aurora.server.SGiopServer)",
"(ADDRESS=(PRO=TCP)(HOST=152.58.52.122)(PORT=1652)(DISPATCHERS=2)"
```

This listing is all on one line and configures dispatchers for MOD_OSE, the database servlet engine that resides *inside* the database, the database JVM dispatchers for secure (SGiop) and normal (Giop) communication, and two dispatchers for normal connectivity.

The following line will create a single dispatcher and assign it a nonspecified port:

```
Dispatchers = "(ADDRESS=(PRO=TCP)(HOST=foxrun_private))"
```

The next two lines start three dispatchers total:

```
dispatchers="(protocol=tcp)(disp=2)(con=200)(poo=on)(tic=15)(sess=400)"
dispatchers="(index=0)(ADDRESS=(PROTOCOL=tcp)(HOST=foxrun_private)(PORT=55))
(dispatchers=1)(listener=listener2_private)"
```

The first and second dispatcher start up on the default host interface, each on their own database-assigned port. They are *also* set up to pool connections, limit the number of connections per dispatcher to 200, and to wait to allow a connection to be pooled for 15 tics (see the next section for more on dispatcher attribute settings). The third dispatcher is going to serve the private interface on port 55 and register itself with the Listener for that interface on two nondefault listening ports. The reference to Listener2_private is a reference to an alias in tnsnames.ora that might look like the following:

```
LISTENER2_PRIVATE =
  (ADDRESS_LIST =
    (ADDRESS = (PROTOCOL = TCP)(HOST = foxrun_private)(PORT = 1522))
    (address = (pro=tcp)(host=foxrun_private)(port=1523))
  )
```

Dispatcher Parameter Attributes

The dispatcher parameter is very versatile (or confusing, depending on your perspective) if you would like to take advantage of any of the features of Shared Server such as connection pooling, connection limiting, session limiting, and the like. We discuss the various parameters and their related parameters here.

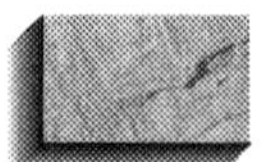

NOTE

We do not address the Connection Manager (CM) multiplexing attributes because very few people will ever need this facility. Do not use CM without doing extensive research and testing to see if it is right for you. For more information, take a look at the Oracle Support web site for various papers relating to multiplexing and CM. In particular, examine the Metalink library document 132729.1.

Dispatcher Listener Registration

A dispatcher will only register itself with the default Listener on port 1521 unless you specify a Listener parameter in the dispatcher notation or you have a LOCAL_LISTENER init.ora parameter set.

init.ora Parameter: LOCAL_LISTENER and REMOTE_LISTENER If you use the LOCAL_LISTENER parameter, then instance registration by the PMON thread and dispatcher instance registration by dispatchers *without* a LISTENER attribute will register themselves with the Listener(s) specified by the LOCAL_ LISTENER's address list. You can configure LOCAL_LISTENER's address list directly in the init.ora file, or you can have it refer to an alias in the tnsnames.ora file for the database Oracle home. The limitation of using the LOCAL_LISTENER init.ora parameter is that it does not allow for different dispatchers to register exclusively with particular Listeners.

There is also a REMOTE_LISTENER parameter for RAC that allows you to register with other Listeners on other nodes in a cluster. REMOTE_LISTENER is configured in the same manner as LOCAL_LISTENER.

Dispatcher Attribute: LISTENER By using the LISTENER attribute of the DISPATCHER parameter, you can set different dispatchers to register themselves with particular Listeners. Make sure that you use an alias that is resolvable through tnsping. Here is an example of a dispatcher configured to register itself with particular Listeners:

```
dispatchers="(address=(pro=tcp)(port=1045))(disp=1)(listener=listener_sales)
```

When the dispatcher tries to register with a Listener, it will attempt to resolve the TNS alias LISTENER_SALES. Here is what the alias might look like:

```
LISTENER_SALES =
  (ADDRESS_LIST =
    (ADDRESS = (PROTOCOL = TCP)(HOST = foxrun)(PORT = 1522))
    (address = (pro=tcp)(host=foxrun)(port=1523))
  )
```

This list may refer to one Listener if it is configured to listen for both ports, or two Listeners if there is a separate Listener for each port. You can use the same alias as is used by the LOCAL_LISTENER or REMOTE_LISTENER init.ora parameters.

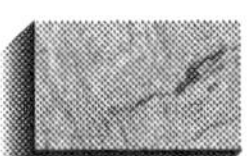

NOTE

You will have to configure the Listener without Net Manager, as it does not support the creation of this type of address list. Once a Listener alias is configured in tnsnames.ora, Net Manager will give you an error message indicating that it cannot retrieve the net service name of the Listener. You can safely ignore this message.

You can use the LOCAL_LISTENER and REMOTE_LISTENER init.ora parameters to tell PMON with which Listeners to register the instance, and then use the LISTENER attribute of the DISPATCHER parameter to tell each dispatcher with which Listeners they should register.

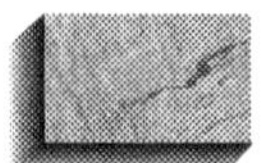

NOTE
Although you can start up the database with an incorrect Listener alias specified, it will not register *with any of the Listeners and* will not receive any connections! *If you try to add a dispatcher with an incorrect Listener specification, you will get an ORA-00101: "Invalid specification for system parameter DISPATCHERS" error message. If you are unsure of your configuration, alter an up-and-running test system to verify proper configuration.*

Dispatcher Connection Pooling

Dispatcher connection pooling allows a session's connection to time out (the TIC parameter) and become available for reuse by another session. This feature allows you to maintain sessions that are relatively inactive without increasing the number of connections. Let's look at an example where the following dispatcher configuration is in place:

```
dispatchers="(pro=tcp)(dispatchers=1)(poo=1)(conn=10)(sess=20)(tic=5)"
```

Sessions connect to the dispatcher until the dispatcher's maximum number of connections, ten in this case, have been reached. The maximum number of connections is determined by the CONNECTIONS attribute used in one of its short forms, (CONN=10). The default number of connections for NT and Windows 2000 is 1,024.

Once the next session's connection is attempted, it will wait until one of the ten connections has been idle for one tic. The attribute (POO=1) sets the timeout to one tic. If the pool attribute was set to (POO=ON), then the timeout defaults to 10 tics. The (TIC=5) attribute defines the length of a tic in seconds, which normally defaults to 15 seconds. You should decrease this value for a fast network connection to as low as 1 second, but in most cases you should keep it around 3 to 4 seconds. Once this timeout has occurred, the idle session's connection will be disconnected but the session will be maintained in the SGA.

Note that the number of sessions is greater than the number of connections. In this case, you could potentially have 10 sessions that don't have a connection, but the sessions are still maintained so that when the idle session makes another call, the connection can be reactivated (given that there is a session that has been idle for one tic). If you don't have sessions set to greater than the number of connections, you will never engage pooling—connections will simply be refused, as **lsnrctl services <Listenername> will show you**.

Setting MAX_DISPATCHERS

MAX_DISPATCHERS is used to limit the number of dispatchers that can be started for an instance. The default, if there is a dispatcher configured, is 5. You should set this parameter in accordance with your expected connection and configuration limitations. As a starting rule of thumb, you can set MAX_DISPATCHERS to the total number of concurrent connections you expect at absolute peak divided by 250. If you expect to have dispatchers configured for more than one interface or in a multiple node RAC configuration, you will need to properly adjust this calculation.

SHARED_SERVERS and MAX_SHARED_SERVERS Configuration

Shared servers are the work horses in a Shared Server configuration. They do the actual work, whereas dispatchers manage the connection and activity. Shared servers are spawned on-the-fly by the database as load dictates until MAX_SHARED_SERVERS is reached. Shared servers are destroyed when the load dictates they are no longer needed. The number of shared servers will be reduced until the number of shared servers reaches the value of the SHARED_SERVERS init parameter. We suggest that your setting for SHARED_SERVERS is equivalent to the normal value of your instance's shared server high-water mark. We suggest this because your system should be configured to handle connections as quickly as they come in, and CPU shouldn't be spent spawning and destroying shared servers, but instead on doing actual user-related work.

MAX_SHARED_SERVERS should be set to the peak number of connections you want to allow. Note that we did not say sessions! A typical system can handle more sessions than it can handle connections. This ability is enabled by the connection pooling attribute of the dispatchers that can manage this dynamic. On a very busy system that lacks memory resources, you may be forced to use fewer shared servers than is ideal in order to limit the size of oracle.exe in memory. This means that you will have to make up for this resource limitation by sacrificing CPU and connection responsiveness. Here are some queries to help you determine shared server load on your system:

```
SELECT maximum_connections, servers_highwater,
servers_started, servers_terminated
FROM V$SHARED_SERVER_MONITOR;
```

This query will show you the high point for connections and shared servers as well as the number of servers started and the number destroyed. The last two columns give you a hint as to what the value of SHARED_SERVERS should be set at.

The next query will show you the number of shared servers that are currently active in an instance:

```
Select count(*) "Number of Active Shared Servers"
FROM v$shared_server
WHERE status <> 'QUIT'
```

This query will show you the activity of each shared server.

```
select name, status, requests,
(busy /(busy + idle)) * 100 "% of time busy" from v$shared_server
```

Here is an example of output from the preceding query:

```
NAME STATUS                 REQUESTS % of time busy
---- ---------------- ---------- --------------
S000 WAIT(SEND)                   46     43.0996998
```

In this case, the shared server is "busy" waiting to send the data to the client. If the status was WAIT(COMMON), very soon after it was likely that the send has completed. You will rarely catch the server executing the SQL when the status shows as EXEC.

The next query shows you how long the average request had to sit on the request queue before being serviced:

```
Select
decode(TOTALQ, 0, 'No Requests',
      (WAIT/TOTALQ) || ' HUNDREDTHS OF SECONDS') as "Avg Wait per Request"
FROM v$queue
WHERE type = 'COMMON'
```

If this number becomes unacceptable, then you should look for the following possible problems:

- The number of shared servers available is lacking.
- The large pool or shared pool is too small.
- System memory or CPU is starving.

LARGE_POOL Configuration

The most important parameter to a well-functioning Shared Server configuration is LARGE_POOL. Shared servers and dispatchers use the Large Pool for most session data kept in the UGA for processing statements. Be careful to properly allow the other options that use the large pool, such as RMAN and Parallel Query, enough memory to function in the manner they should without starving the shared server connections. To effectively size the Large Pool for connections, you must first understand how much memory a typical connections is going to use. If you are unable to simulate or monitor a typical session, then you can start with about 300KB for each concurrently active connection. If you can simulate a typical session or monitor existing sessions for typical activity, then you should examine the V$SESSSTAT view in a manner such as this:

```
select
sid,
decode(statistic#,15,'session uga memory',16,'session uga memory max') stat,
value/1024 K
from v$sesstat
where statistic# in (15,16)
order by sid,statistic#
```

You can also look at the UGA memory usage of all sessions by running the following query:

```
select
decode(statistic#,15,'session uga memory',16,'session uga memory max') stat,
sum(value)/1023 K
from v$sesstat
where statistic# in (15,16)
group by
decode(statistic#,15,'session uga memory',16,'session uga memory max')
```

This will show you the total kilobytes used by all sessions in the current instance:

```
select
decode(statistic#,15,'session uga memory',16,'session uga memory max') stat,
sum(value)/1023 K
FROM
v$sesstat s, v$process p, v$session ses
WHERE
s.sid=ses.sid and
ses.paddr=p.addr and
p.addr not in (select paddr from v$bgprocess) and
s.statistic# in (15,16)
GROUP BY
decode(statistic#,15,'session uga memory',16,'session uga memory max')
```

Note that we made sure to remove background processes for our calculations.

We cannot stress enough that proper sizing of the Large Pool is critical to a successful implementation of a Shared Server configuration. To illustrate, let's look at an example case of a business that depends on large numbers of orders taken over the phone.

We have a database that maintains about 1,000 concurrent connections at its daily peak. Business needs require that there is little or no lack of tolerance for a drop in performance, and we have no idea what the typical UGA memory usage will be. We will initially configure the Large Pool at 307,200,000 bytes (1000×300KB). Yup, that's right, about 293MB. This number does *not* include any usage by Parallel Query (because heavy use of the Parallel Query feature is not likely on a dedicated order entry system during business hours) or RMAN because business hours allow us to make backups during late hours of the night when the number of sessions drops. Before backups are run, an **alter system** command is run to lower the number of shared servers and dispatchers, and connections are made to populate a data mart via dedicated servers.

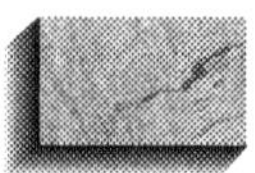

NOTE
Make sure that there is about 10KB per concurrent session available in the Shared Pool when using the Large Pool for shared server configurations.

Listener Control and Configuration

The Listener is a process of its own dedicated to handling incoming connections. You can stop a Listener without causing current connections to disconnect because all Listener connections are handed off or redirected to either a dispatcher or dedicated server thread in oracle.exe.

There are two ways to control a Listener on Windows NT and 2000. The first is through the Services MMC (see Chapter 3), and the next is from the command line. The Listener as a service is useful because it can run without anyone logged in to the server and can be started automatically. The command line is useful if you are experiencing trouble and want a more interactive interface to tell you what is going wrong. There is also a good amount of informative information to be found by running a **status** or **services** command against a Listener when you cannot quite tell what is not working properly. Here is sample output from an **lsnrctl status** command:

```
c:\oracle>lsnrctl status

LSNRCTL for 32-bit Windows: Version 9.0.1.1.1 - Production on 07-AUG-2001
12:12:27
```

```
Copyright (c) 1991, 2001, Oracle Corporation.  All rights reserved.

Connecting to (DESCRIPTION=(ADDRESS=(PROTOCOL=IPC)(KEY=EXTPROC1)))
STATUS of the LISTENER
------------------------
Alias                     LISTENER
Version                   TNSLSNR for 32-bit Windows: Version 9.0.1.1.1 -
Production
Start Date                07-AUG-2001 12:08:00
Uptime                    0 days 0 hr. 4 min. 28 sec
Trace Level               off
Security                  ON
SNMP                      OFF
Listener Parameter File   c:\oracle\901\network\admin\listener.ora
Listener Log File         c:\oracle\901\network\log\listener.log
Listening Endpoints Summary...
  (DESCRIPTION=(ADDRESS=(PROTOCOL=ipc)(PIPENAME=\\.\pipe\EXTPROC1ipc)))
  (DESCRIPTION=(ADDRESS=(PROTOCOL=tcp)(HOST=foxrun)(PORT=1521)))

Services Summary...
Service "PLSExtProc" has 1 instance(s).
  Instance "PLSExtProc", status UNKNOWN, has 1 handler(s) for this
service...
Service "ldap.me.com" has 2 instance(s).
  Instance "ldap", status UNKNOWN, has 1 handler(s) for this service...
  Instance "ldap", status READY, has 2 handler(s) for this service...
Service "oltp.us.oracle.com" has 1 instance(s).
  Instance "oltp", status UNKNOWN, has 1 handler(s) for this service...
The command completed successfully
```

This command has shown you the following:

Alias—the name of the listener. If this was a nondefault listener name, such as list2, we would have to use the syntax **lsnrctl status list2**.

Listener configuration, like what the listener.ora file gets its definition from, security (whether it has a password), and status of tracing and logging.

What endpoints this listener will hear connection requests on, a summary of the services it is listening for, and the listener's view of the service status.

Although this status gives you some good information as far as the general listener configuration, it does not tell you how it is handling connections, and how many connections have been services and how many have not. If you run the command **lsnrctl services** from a command line, an excerpt of your output would look like this:

```
  Instance "ldap", status READY, has 2 handler(s) for this service...
    Handler(s):
```

```
"DEDICATED" established:4 refused:0 state:ready
   LOCAL SERVER
"D000" established:1 refused:0 current:1 max:400 state:ready
   DISPATCHER <machine: FOXRUN, pid: 1324>
   (ADDRESS=(PROTOCOL=tcp)(HOST=foxrun)(PORT=1364))
```

This tells you that four dedicated server connections have been made since the Listener has been up, and that no connections have been refused. It also tells you that the dispatcher D000 is currently servicing one connection and that it is set to take 400 maximum. You can see that this is set by the dispatcher because the default on Windows is 1,024. The output also indicates on what interface (foxrun) and port (1364) the service is listening, as well as the thread ID (1324) of the dispatcher. One possible reason for a refused connection is that your PROCESSES init.ora parameter is too low, or the CONNECTIONS or SESSIONS parameters have been exceeded. Check the listener.log for more information if needed.

Creating a New Listener

To create a new Listener, you must first configure the Listener for a different listening endpoint. This means that the address it is listening on must not be configured for an existing Listener. For example, if you have a listener listening for TCP on port 1521, you cannot create another TCP listening endpoint that uses port 1521 on that IP address. The combination of host, port, and protocol must be unique.

The easiest way to configure a new Listener is from the Net Manager tool. Under the Local node, click Listeners (item labeled 5 in Figure 7-18), and then click the plus sign (+) to add a new Listener (item labeled 7 in Figure 7-18). Give the Listener an appropriate name, and then add an address for the first listening location. Select General Configuration from the drop-down list that starts as Listening Locations, click the Authorization tab, and enable and set the password for the new Listener. Quit and save your changes.

A new Listener on Windows 2000 requires more than just adding the configuration information to the listener.ora file via Net Manager. You must also start the Listener from the command line for the first time in order to have the new Listener service created. Once you have the Listener named listener2 configured in listener.ora, use LSNRCTL to start it like this:

```
lsnrctl start listener2
```

When you run this command, you will see an error message like this:

```
Failed to open service <OracleOraHome901TNSListenerlistener2>, error 1060.
```

You can ignore this message because the Listener process will create this service for you. From this point forward, you can start the new Listener from the Services MMC or the command line.

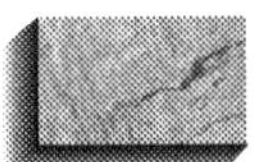

NOTE
If you remove the Listener from the configuration, it will no longer be available to start, but the service will remain. You can safely remove the service by using the Windows 2000/NT tool regedit.exe. Do take extreme care not to remove the wrong Registry key, as you can easily and completely disable your system.

Queue Size

If you have a system that needs to be able to handle a burst of connections, you may need to increase the Listener queue size to avOID the load-related error message TNS-12203: "Unable to connect to destination."

The default for QUEUESIZE on the Windows platform in release 9i is 50. If you experience "unable to connect" error messages, add the QUEUESIZE parameter to the Listener address configuration for which you are experiencing problems. Here is an example:

```
LISTENER2 =
  (DESCRIPTION =
    (ADDRESS = (PROTOCOL = TCP)(HOST = foxrun)(PORT = 1522)(queuesize=100))
  )
```

Listener Monitoring and Logging

You can use the Listener log to identify issues, and track automatic instance registration and dispatcher registration with a Listener. You can find the Listener log at %ORACLE_HOME%\network\log\<listenername>.log.

You can use the command line to view the services and their current status. Here are a couple of examples:

```
lsnrctl status
```

or

```
lsnrctl <listener_name> status
```

These commands will give you the Listener configuration, the listening endpoints, and a summary of the services the Listener is listening for.

If you are interested in the services specifically, for example how many current connections are being managed by the dispatchers, then you can examine the output of this lsnrctl.exe command:

```
lsnrctl services
```

This command spits out extensive information regarding the current state, connections accepted and refused, and more.

General Network Tuning and Configuration

Oracle network tuning is largely not Oracle related. Instead, it relies heavily upon your network infrastructure's performance and configuration as well as the OS and hardware layers. Actual tuning of the Oracle net layer is related to configuring Oracle Net to match up with these other elements of your network.

Many database administrators and system administrators do not seem to connect the value of a highly available and high-performance network to application performance, although they understand the effect of high performance and high availability on a single node. On the other hand, system administrators and DBAs that have dealt with older clusters very much understand the importance of high performance and available network segments because most clusters implement some form of high-performance network. This perception is also largely changing due to the rise of the Storage Area Network (SAN) where storage methods such as disk and tape are kept on a high-performance network, available to nodes for utilizing the storage assets on the SAN.

The Virtual Interface Protocol

Oracle 9i provides support for a relatively new protocol, the Virtual Interface (VI) protocol, designed to provide much lower network latency (time delay due to network round-trip time) and is coupled with a wire topology, sometimes referred to as a fabric, that provides greater bandwidth (throughput capacity of the network). In fact, VI was designed with cluster internode communication in mind. The ideal place for you and Oracle to use this protocol is between application and database servers or between databases that use database links or replication. In these environments, you want communication between nodes as fast and fat as possible. For example, if you have an application server that is connecting to multiple databases and have a very fast (gigabit) network topology between them, you can increase performance by using VI (see Figure 7-24 as an example).

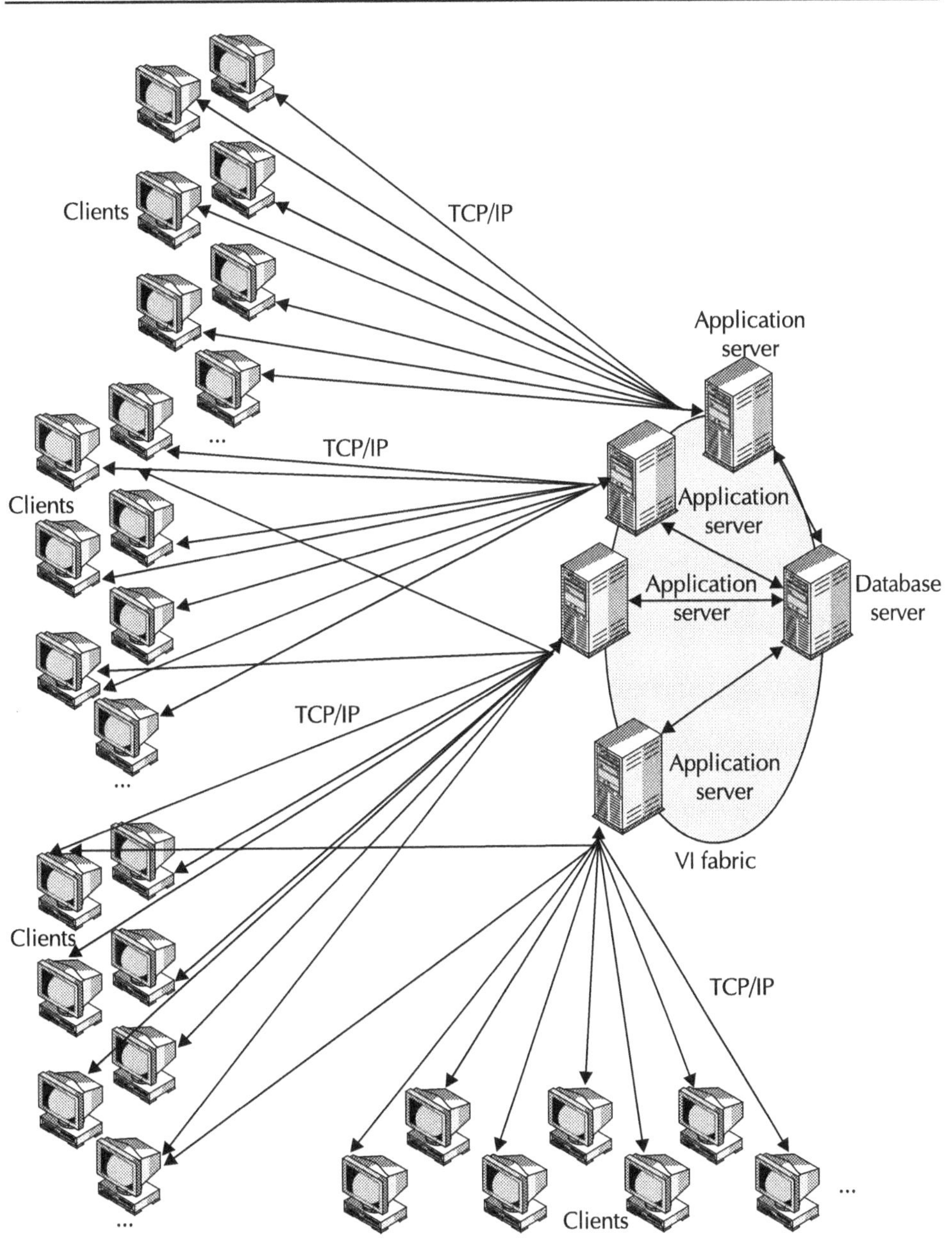

FIGURE 7-24. *Possible VI implementation*

So why isn't VI for everyone? VI uses a special host bus adapter that allows the VI-enabled card to connect directly to process memory. This adapter also has much more processing power than a typical network adapter. The card offloads work that would normally be handled by the CPU. It also works only on high-bandwidth topologies that require expensive connectivity equipment. For these reasons, cost is a factor.

To tune your use of the VI protocol, you size the session data unit (SDU) and configure the VI_SEND_BUFFERS and VI_RECEIVE_BUFFERS parameters in sqlnet.ora on the application and database servers connecting to one another. The memory requirements for the application server and the database server are different. In particular, VI_SEND_BUFFERS represents the number of buffers of the SDU size designated for queuing up send requests. The default mapping is named "medium" and indicates that 15 send buffers are allocated.

For more general information on the VI protocol, check out the Oracle Net documentation and the VI Architecture site at http://www.viarch.org.

Resources

Oracle networking options are expansive and flexible. In this section, we provide some resources that you can use to go beyond the content of this chapter.

Reference Material

Complete information on networking and Oracle requires more space than is available, so we thought we would include a limited number of valuable references to help you with various tasks. Access to some of these do require that you have a support agreement with Oracle and can access the Oracle Support web site. Check this site for updated articles that address specific issues with Oracle9i that we may not mention here. In addition, most of the material in the notes on the Oracle Support web site can be found in the documentation set at Oracle TechNet (http://otn.oracle.com).

Networking-Related Articles on Metalink

In order to get directly to any of the network-related articles on Metalink, perform an advanced search by document ID. A general search on the document ID will also show forum response to documents that may be a little bit confusing, a nice help sometimes when articles are beyond comprehension without context. To learn more generally or to check out the latest alerts and other information, be sure to check out the technical libraries on the Oracle Support web site, listed in Table 7-2, as well. Table 7-3 contains articles that feature links to other articles of interest to the topic mentioned.

Technical Library Title	Comments	Doc ID
Security and Authentication Library	Check here for the latest articles, white papers, and alerts on security and authentication.	132857.1
Connection Manager and Firewalls Library	Go to this library for the latest articles, white papers, and alerts on CM and firewalls.	132729.1
Connection Models Library	Check here for the latest articles, white papers, and alerts on topics like Database Links and MTS.	132839.1
Networking Tools and Configuration Library	Check here for the latest articles, white papers, and alerts on networking tools and configuration.	132800.1
Failover and Load Balancing Library	Go to this library for articles on Transparent Application Failover.	132831.1
HTTP Server Library	Vital resource for configuring the Apache HTTP server that comes with Oracle. Check out the articles on using MOD_PLSQL to generate Excel documents!	132323.1
Oracle Internet Directory Library	Learn more about setup and configuration of Oracle's LDAP-compliant directory server.	137335.1
DBA Architecture Library	Check this library out for Large Pool and Shared Pool information. Also includes a script index for a variety of uses. The Platforms section has specific architecture information on NT/2000.	133405
Transparent Gateway Library	Check this library out to find information on configuring Oracle's generic connectivity to other databases such as SQL Server, or a database that has an ODBC or OLEDB driver with the level of support needed.	132692.1

TABLE 7-2. *Technical Libraries on the Oracle Support Web Site*

Article Title	Comments	Doc ID
Configuring Enterprise User Security	Learn how to use LDAP for single sign-on.	114544.1
What is LDAP?	Need somewhere to start? Try here.	90691.1
Configuring NET8 TCP/IP via SSL	Learn how to encrypt your network traffic.	112490.1
Troubleshooting TNS-12500 on Microsoft Windows NT		2064864.102
Net8 Hostname Naming Adapter—No Client Configuration Files	This article is older, but it explains the concept well and still applies today.	47369.1
Database Links: An Overview		117278.1
Database Link Troubleshooting		117759.1
Troubleshooting Database Links in a Replicated Environment		121716.1
Dead Connection Detection Explained		151972.1
Windows NT Settings for TCP/IP Timeouts		119249.1
Disabling Automatic Registration of the Database with the Default Listener	This information is especially useful in 9i if you need to turn off direct connection handoff.	130574.1
Firewalls, Windows NT, and Redirections		2064550.102
New SQL*Net Tracing Parameters	Parameters for cyclical trace files of a specific size and timestamps on your net trace files make this article a gem reference.	69042.1

TABLE 7-3. *Oracle's Miscellaneous Network-Related Articles*

Microsoft OS–Related Networking Articles

Table 7-4 presents a number of articles that are key to understanding the issues facing networking on Windows 2000. Even before you dig into these articles, we suggest that you obtain a paper copy of the Resource Kit and investigate the "Network Configuration and Management" section. The "Core TCP/IP Networking Guide" that comes with the 2000 Server Resource Kit has some great information as well. You can check these books out online at http://www.microsoft.com/windows2000/techinfo/reskit/en/default.asp.

ID Number	Title
Q224829	Description of Windows 2000 TCP Features
Q120642	TCP/IP & NBT Configuration Parameters for Windows NT and Windows 2000
Q140375	Default MTU Size for Different Network Topology
Q169292	The Basics of Reading TCP/IP Traces
Q170359	How to Modify the TCP/IP Maximum Retransmission Timeout
Q294769	Data Transfer to "Localhost" or Loopback Address Is Slow
Q159168	Multiple Default Gateways Can Cause Connectivity Problems
Q230082	How to Enable TCP/IP Forwarding in Windows 2000
Q236869	How to Install Microsoft Loopback Adapter in Windows 2000
Q239924	How to Disable Media Sense for TCP/IP in Windows 2000
Q254031	Multiple IP Addresses Registered to Multiple Domains Under Dynamic DNS
Q268781	Description of the Netset.exe Tool from the Windows 2000 Resource Kit
Q259922	DNS Request for blackhole.isi.edu
Q281962	Documentation on Maximum Transmission Unit Incorrectly States Registry Location
Q169789	High Rate of Collisions on 100-MB Networks
Q159211	Diagnoses and Treatment of Black Hole Routers

TABLE 7-4. *Microsoft OS–Related Networking Articles*

Summary

Oracle database connections are often one of the more misunderstood elements of database applications. This chapter has been designed to give you both the understanding and the essential elements of configuration and implementation of Oracle networking. We also talked about some of the things you can do to provide greater availability and stability through both client and server configuration.

The GUI network configuration tools in Oracle9i have expanded capability and ease of use. Net Manager, the Oracle9i incarnation of the Net8 Assistant, almost completely replaces the use of the old Net8 Easy Configuration and Net8 Configuration Assistant tools from Oracle8 and Oracle8i. Despite these improvements, there are still many times that you will need to edit the networking configuration files by hand to take advantage of advanced features.

The Oracle networking components have been improved for performance and scalability for Windows NT and Windows 2000 specifically. The Shared Server

architecture, formerly called multithreaded server (MTS), is moving toward being the default configuration for Oracle databases, unlike the bleeding edge technology that it was in Oracle7.

Oracle9i provides new levels of manageability and scalability through the Oracle Internet Directory. This LDAP-compatible hierarchical database allows you to centrally manage users and client networking configurations. We have opened the door for you to explore this application with step-by-step instructions for a tutorial-oriented installation.

CHAPTER 8

Oracle Enterprise Manager

How do you manage more work, in less time, with greater accuracy and efficiency? Oracle's Enterprise Manager addresses these problems with a variety of tools for taking care of general administration issues, such as reacting to events, and specific Oracle database needs, such as tablespace management. The combination of these tools in a common framework allows you to accomplish more with less from remote terminals across platforms.

This chapter is dedicated to a candid discussion of Enterprise Manager (EM), from configuring it for the enterprise down to the nuts and bolts of its different pieces. We supply tips to maximize EM's usage for enterprise-wide database administration. EM allows powerful, productive management of Oracle databases on any platform that has the Agent from a Windows 2000 client machine. In this chapter, we look at the following tips and techniques:

- Understanding Enterprise Manager functionality
- Working in the Enterprise Manager Framework
- Understanding the EM agent
- Monitoring changes through the EM Event system
- Managing jobs through the EM Job system
- Essential EM database administration
- Understanding the Oracle Management Server (OMS)
- Generating reports through the EM Reporting system
- Configuring EM to work with firewalls
- Getting more information through EM references

EM Functionality

Oracle's Enterprise Manager (EM) is designed to help database administrators manage a number of *targets,* which are EM-managed entities. The primary targets are listed here:

- Node
- Database
- Listener
- HTTP Server

There are also other targets of interest to Windows DBAs such as SQL Server (if you happen to be so handicapped). A target is identified and managed through the EM Agent that runs on a node. An *Agent* is an executable that acts as an intermediary between the *Oracle Management Server* (*OMS*) and the target. EM provides services to help you manage these targets; jobs, events, reporting, notification, EM security and tools, and management packs are just some of the functions that EM can provide for your shop.

Jobs

Jobs are the execution of scripts managed by an Agent. They are monitored by the Agent, and notifications of the various stages of jobs, including edits and job assignments, are communicated to the console user or users who are specified as recipients of notification for that job. If advanced notification is properly set up, then notifications can be sent out via e-mail or pager upon job start, assignment change, completion, and deletion. You can create custom jobs that leverage scripts already part of your own script repository. When you migrate your personal job scripts into the EM Job facility, you gain these benefits:

- Job notification of job state change
- Job history
- Security to manage who can run, alter, delete, and receive notification of a job for a particular node
- The ability to submit the job, your script, to multiple targets at one time
- Access to easy and flexible OMS scheduling facilities.
- The ability to run your script as a particular user easily (as opposed to using the Runas Service on Windows 2000)
- Composite jobs for running multiple job tasks as one with cascading dependencies you can configure
- Quick implementation of new jobs across many different targets
- Quick-and easy creation of fix-it jobs that respond to an event.
- Use of the web-based EM, reporting of job status and history

The Job system is a flexible component of the EM infrastructure that allows mundane and complex tasks, performed in reaction to predictable events or on a regular schedule, to be managed from a central location with less human interaction.

The key message here is that EM Jobs can be used to *enhance* as opposed to *replace* the scripts you use today to perform repeated tasks or react to events that occur and need a specific, predictable response.

Events

An EM Event is the occurance of one or more event tests at a user-defined interval performed by either the Agent or the OMS. Event tests are checks for occurrences of a condition as defined by a list of available event tests for the various target types. For example, you can test for database listener response with the standard ListenerUpDown event test. Event tests are performed at an interval that you set when defining the event. When an event is triggered, it will perform the configured notification and, if so configured, engage an assigned fix-it job.

If you have the Diagnostic Pack, your can create your own tests to trigger events. This functionality allows you to do a wide variety of testing that may not be available through the EM system, but for which you have already created scripts to test for this condition.

The Diagnostic Pack also adds a number of specialized events related to performance and conditions other than the simple UpDown events for each target. These metric-oriented events allow you to trigger events at four different user-defined levels of severity: script failure, clear, warning, and critical. You can configure notification for each EM user's notification filters so that the notification system will react differently according to the severity of the event. For example, you may want to only be paged upon the trigger of a critical or node down event and receive e-mail for all other events. Configure EM user preferences under the Preferences option of the Configuration pull-down menu on the EM console.

Notification

The EM notification system reacts to changes in job or event status. Without special notification, configuration changes in job and event status will *only* be communicated through the console. Events triggered show up on the first tab of the Event leaf of the tree on the left of the console. You can view the history of Event notifications via the third and final History tab.

You can configure notifications to send e-mail or utilize a paging server to page administrators with chunks of information that you can select and configure. You can further define how notification is performed for events and jobs with filters based on event status and job status.

Reporting

EM Reporting in release 9i is HTML based and either viewed independently via a browser from the file system at a client installation if generated, or via the EM web site run by the Oracle HTTP Server. There is large number of predefined reports you can use right out of the box or edit to match your needs. These reports are also great examples of the proper way to accomplish your reporting goals.

EM Reporting is designed to give you an overall view of the state of your systems and allow you to drill down to detail according to your needs. Its flexibility enables you to incorporate reports that meet your specific needs.

A limited number of reports for database targets can be generated from a stand-alone console. Once these are generated, you will find them under the %ORACLE_HOME%\sysman\report directory.

Security

With the EM and its repository, you can configure a management infrastructure that isolates administrators from the targets for which they are responsible. Multiple administrators can be assigned to the same target. One of the more confusing elements of this security system is that the EM logins are in no way related to a database login. The equivalent of the OS Administrator user or the SYS database user in the EM security system is sysman. The default initial password for sysman is oem_temp; and upon sysman's first login, he or she will be prompted to change that password. Super administrators should be restricted to DBA managers in cases where the highest level of access to all managed targets is not a security risk. We suggest that two accounts should be maintained for those that require super administrator access: one for day-to-day administration and notification, and the other for security, target discovery, and other OMS configuration functions.

The EM security subsystem allows multiple administrators to work from a common management system that provides flexible, reportable, and quick management of systems without compromising security or causing confusion as to who is responsible for what.

Database Administration

EM allows administrators a database toolkit that makes many tasks that are difficult to issue from a command line simple. It provides tools that can advise you of current possible problems as well as potential problems.

Just because you can do many things with the EM database tools does not mean that you should not understand what is happening at the command-line level when you perform an action. Use the Show SQL option available with most commands to identify what is actually going to occur. It is important that you understand *what* you are doing before you decide to use a feature or alter an object.

Danger Ahead

Many people think that the various functionalities available via the GUI makes Oracle software more and more accessible and easy to use. We would prefer to say that it can make Oracle database administrators more and more productive instead. If you do not understand the underlying principle of what you are doing with the GUI interface, you are likely going to cause more problems than you solve. We have seen GUI-focused database administrators create items with functionality they do not understand, but their cursory reading of the description makes it sound like a good idea (for example, index-organized tables, clustered tables, and so on).

Be aware the power of the GUI is also its weakness in that it gives those who do not understand a function the ability to abuse that function without knowing that they are abusing it.

We also suggest that you create an independent method (for example, a script) to check on OMS availability and generate independent notification from a node not involved in the EM infrastructure in case of failure. In other words, we suggest that you use redundant systems to verify system availability.

EM: How, When, and Where

Enterprise Manager is a maturing product that does not do *everything* you need in order to manage all aspects of Oracle software and its supporting software and hardware. It has come a very long way in its product lifetime, and future plans for EM will continue to make it more and more encompassing of all the functions you need in a complete enterprise management tool.

Oracle as a company is moving with clear purpose in the direction of making Oracle software self-tuning and easily managed. EM is a key part of that vision. The database has more functionality than most people will ever venture to use. Now is the time for Oracle to lower the cost of operation through attention to manageability, availability, performance, and overall ease of use.

EM today has a complex, 3-tier infrastructure that can be difficult to troubleshoot and maintain. Database administrators who have been around for quite some time likely have a clearly defined and easily implemented methodology for getting work done without using EM. For these people, EM can be a frustrating and annoying addition if it is thrust upon them without a plan to integrate their proven methods with the reporting, job, and event functionality EM provides. If the reporting, job, and event functions do not interest you, then we suggest that you stick to using the Standalone Console. Otherwise, we suggest that you learn about EM and implement the features incrementally in a test environment.

For example, your DBA team may have scripts that they use to report on the health of the database and notify the owner of the database if problems are detected. First, try replacing simple notification scripts with the NodeUpDown event and other basic events. Fine-tune issues with notification and security, and then expand implementation or mandate new event tracking through the EM event system. Use the relevant EM packaged report or customize a report to your own needs. Over time, you can replace most scripts on each computer in your enterprise with the centralized event system that EM provides.

EM Framework

In order to effectively use EM, it is important that you have an understanding of the architecture. There are essentially two distinct architectures: stand-alone and 3-tier. The stand-alone architecture is quite limited in functionality. For example, the Standalone Console does not include the job, event, or reporting systems, and you can only use it to manage database targets. The EM framework, because it is 3-tier, enables the job, event, and reporting systems, and incorporates much more functionality that requires elements of the 3-tier architecture.

Jobs, Events, and Reports

The Jobs, Events, and Reporting web site elements are created and managed from the OMS. Examine Figure 8-1 as an example of EM Console interaction with the OMS for report, job, and event submission. Database administrators and their managers work from the EM Console, through the Oracle Management Server (OMS). The OMS connects to the OMS Repository. This repository contains definitions of jobs, events, reports, the various EM user rights and privileges, the times and methods of notification of events or job stages, information regarding historical performance data for targets, and much more.

The OMS communicates with *discovered* Agents. There is one Agent running per node that uses a methodology to discover potential targets for management. The Agent and the OMS work independent of one another to ensure that management of targets continues in a temporarily disconnected environment.

For example, a database administrator submits a job, say, an export operation, to be run every night at 11 P.M. on four database targets on four different nodes. The OMS will communicate this to the Agent on the four nodes. The Agent will then take the command and run the scheduled job at the proper interval. Once it starts the job, the Agent will queue up a message to be sent to the OMS that the job has been started. If the OMS is available, the message will be accepted and notification of the interested parties by the assigned methods will begin. Once the Agent finishes the job, it will communicate this to the OMS and notify you as configured, and that particular run of the job's detail will be archived. The archived version of the job's detail can be reviewed from the History tab within the EM Console.

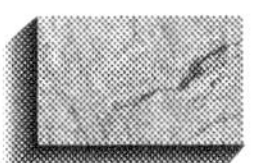

NOTE
Be careful to keep times on the various nodes synchronized with the management servers; otherwise, there could possibly be problems. The effect is exacerbated if you are using multiple management servers.

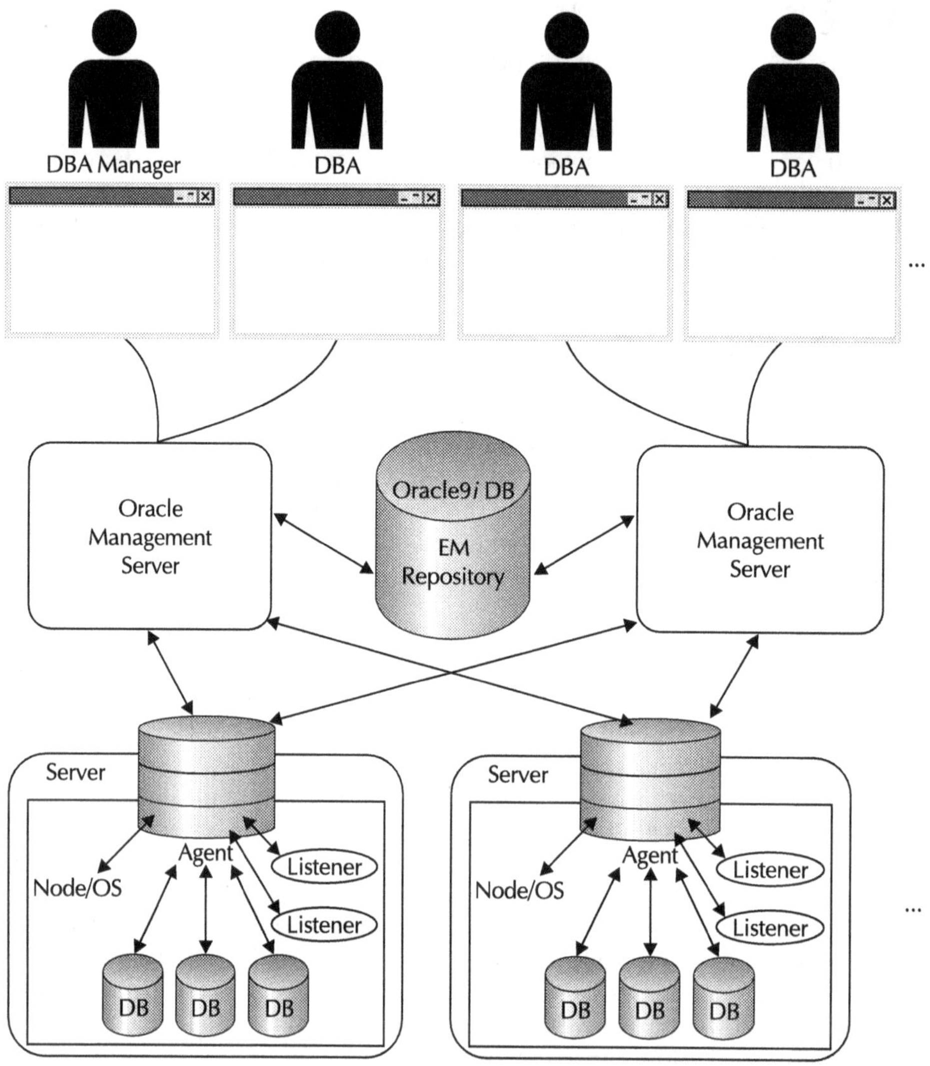

FIGURE 8-1. *EM tier interaction*

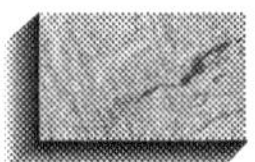

NOTE
Consoles connecting to perform database administration directly do not connect through the OMS, but instead get their connection information from the OMS and make the connection themselves. This is important to understand when identifying network security and connectivity issues.

EM Users

Before you can utilize the 3-tier EM Console, you must have a login. Security rights determine your access to particular targets. There is one super administrator, similar to the database user SYS, who first sets up new users and manages rights for a repository. This user is sysman. The default password for sysman is oem_temp. Upon first login via the EM Console, you will be prompted to change the sysman password to avoid security problems. Once logged in as sysman, you should create at least one user for each database administrator.

Notification Configuration

Notification setup is one of the initial tasks you should perform before implementation. E-mail notification is simple to configure, whereas paging is a bit more work. There are two steps in initializing e-mail notification: the first is to set up the e-mail server configuration, and the second is to configure the EM users' e-mail address and delivery options.

E-mail notification requires access to a Simple Mail Transfer Protocol (SMTP) server that the OMS can use to deliver mail. You can typically use the same SMTP server that your corporate e-mail infrastructure offers for personal e-mail. Some companies may require a username and password to access the corporate e-mail SMTP services. In this case, you will want to obtain an account for the EM e-mail notification (as opposed to using your username and password). This account will *not need* a mailbox (that is, an IMAP or POP server account) because the OMS never reads mail, it only sends mail. The advantage to having a mailbox is that returned mail can be identified in the case of failed delivery.

Initial notification setup is done through the Configure Paging/Email property sheet found under the Configuration pull-down menu in the OMS-connected console (see Figure 8-2). Once this property sheet is up, you need to give it two values. The first

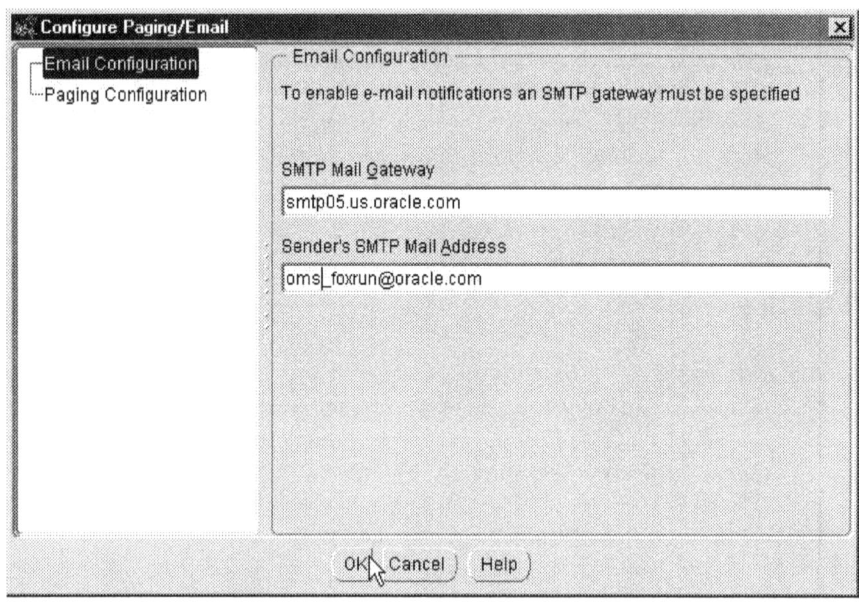

FIGURE 8-2. *OMS e-mail configuration options*

is the host that runs the SMTP server, and the second is the e-mail address of the sender. Click OK, and you are finished. Although this configures e-mail notification, it does not verify anything about the validity of the configuration. You can test this from EM user e-mail notification setup by clicking the Test button, as shown in Figure 8-3.

User e-mail notification in Oracle9i EM is versatile and can be configured to send the full text of various items of interest in a job or event notification. You configure EM user notification through the Notification tab of the Edit Administrator Preferences property sheet, accessible by selecting the Preferences option from the Configuration pull-down menu. Once you click the Email node of the tree on the left of the property sheet (see Figure 8-3), you can view and/or configure the following items.

Receiver's Email The EM user's e-mail address to be used for notifying the user. This can be an e-mail addressable pager or text-messaging phone that is e-mail capable (for example, an AT&T text-messaging–enabled cell phone number of 650-555-1212 will display text messages sent to 6505551212@mobile.att.net).

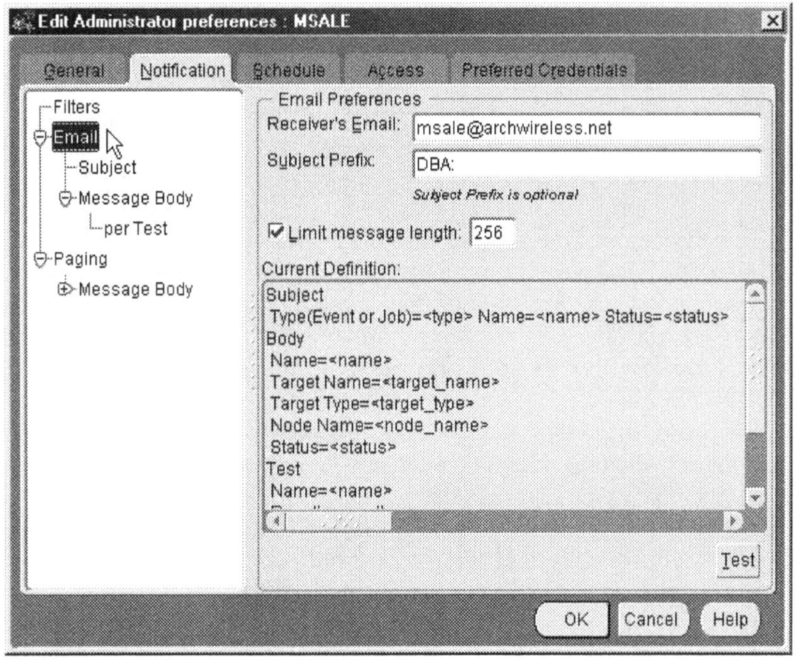

FIGURE 8-3. *EM user e-mail notification preferences*

Subject Prefix An optional field that can help the EM user quickly identify e-mail sent from this OMS.

Limit Message Length Most text message capable devices have a relatively small capacity for a single message; and longer messages can cause the whole message to become garbled, making the message ambiguous and thus requiring the highest level of response. Use this field to limit the length of the notification sent to your text messaging device. If you are sending notification to a typical e-mail account, then you need to set the value to greater than the default length of 256 characters, especially if you configure job output to be appended to your notification!

Current Definition This shows you the content and structure of any notification that will go out. If there are multiple tests that have been triggered, and you have configured the definition to send event test information, then each event test for the event that is not clear at the time of the notification will still be included in the notification. For example,

> if you have an event that does two CPU utilization tests, and only one of them fires, then this notification will only include information regarding the fired event test. If both event tests are fired at the same time (as per the check interval settings for that event), then the data for both event tests will be sent in the notification. If only one event clears three minutes later, the event notification for the change in status to clear will still include data for both tests.

Just below the Current Definition section in the lower right of the window is a button labeled Test. Once you have entered the e-mail of the notification recipient on this page, you can test your SMTP server configuration and the recipient configuration by clicking this button. If you do not like the format sent in the test, you can customize your notification to use abbreviations, add and remove information, set timestamp display options (for example, we typically don't need to know what day or date it is when we are paged, so we only include hours and minutes in our alpha pager e-mail notification format). Perform multiple tests to fine-tune message content and form until you find the right format for your notification needs.

Table 8-1 explains options for the e-mail subject line and message body. In general, keep the subject line concise and make sure it only contains data that prompts you to properly prioritize your reaction to various notifications. For example, in an environment where you manage all production systems that have a service-level agreement for uptime, you likely do not care as much if a machine is notifying you of a completed job, but instead, which machine has fired a node down or database down event. In this case, you want the subject line to contain only the node name and status. With the node name you can identify the source of the notification, and from the status you can tell if the problem involves a job or an event because jobs and events have mutually exclusive statuses. From this point, *you* determine the level of reaction required. If the SLA for these production systems demands a rapid time to resolution, you may also want to put the hours, minutes timestamp format in the subject. The message body should then contain as much relevant, but concise, data related to the source of the notification as your notification receiving device can handle.

Table 8-2 delimits the per-test item options. Per-test selections are contained within the message body. Per-test items included in the definition can be redundant and actually cause confusion, so be sure to test out the best definition for your notification target devices.

Option	Description
Name	The title of the event or job.
Node Name	The name of the node that shows up under the node list that contains the relevant target. If your event does not span nodes, then you might just want to include an abbreviated node name in the event or job title.
Owner	The EM username that owns the event or job.
Status	One of the list of standard statuses: critical, warning, clear, error, and unknown. Most notifications will include only the first three statuses. You can use the abbreviated format by checking the box when the item is selected. (See Table 8-3 for the abbreviations.)
Target Name	Name of the target as shown in the property sheet of the event or job. Only needed if the event or job is assigned multiple targets.
Target Type	Indicates target type of database, listener, or node. Not often needed if the event is narrowly defined. If it is needed then use the abbreviated form by clicking the check box (DB=database, LSR=listener, N=node).
Timestamp	Because most alpha pagers and text messages include delivery time, you should not need highly detailed timestamps, especially in the subject line. We suggest that you set the timestamp format to <hours>:<minutes> AM/PM in the message body. Keep it short and succinct.
Type (Event or Job)	If you need this item in the subject line, then use the abbreviated form.
Append Job Output (Message Body Only)	If the notification is from a job, you can include the output from the job in your notification. Be careful with length if you are notifying a per-message capacity-limited alpha pager or text message–enabled phone!

TABLE 8-1. *E-mail Notification Subject and Message Body Options*

Option	Description
Name	The title of the event test. For user-defined events, remember to keep the name short enough to be effective in your notifications.
Result	The result portion of an event test based on a metric. For example, for an event test that measures packets per second on a network interface, this field will show the actual number of packets per second at the time of the last event test.
Status	Status of the event test (see Table 8-3 for event statuses and their abbreviations).
Timestamp	Time notification is issued. Keep this to the most terse format you can handle to keep things more readable.

TABLE 8-2. *E-mail Notification Per-Test Options*

Once you have refined a standard for notification definition, you will need to pass this configuration on to your other administrators because there is no supported way to propagate your customized defaults to new or existing users. The customization options available to each administrator allows them to change their notification definition, but you cannot initiate or propagate standards to new or existing EM users.

Abbreviation	Notification Status
ST	Started
C	Completed
F	Failed
D	Deleted
W	Warning
CR	Critical
CL	Cleared
NU	Node Unreachable
AC	Assignee Changed

TABLE 8-3. *Notification Status Abbreviations*

Notification Filtering

You likely do not want to receive a page every time a job starts or when an event is edited by one of your fellow administrators. For this reason, notification configuration allows you to filter which possible changes in event status or definition, or in job state or definition, trigger a notification. Unfortunately, these notification filter settings cannot be initially set as desired upon creation or propagated to existing users. You configure notification filters for job and event statuses to be either turned on or off for e-mail and paging (see Figure 8-4).

Use Multiple EM User Accounts to Address Different Notification Needs

You might find that you wish to be notified differently according to the event or job. Unfortunately, notification filters and the notification definition are universal for each EM user. That is, you cannot decide that for one set of jobs you want to be notified of changes in ownership, starts, and stops, and for another set of jobs you just want

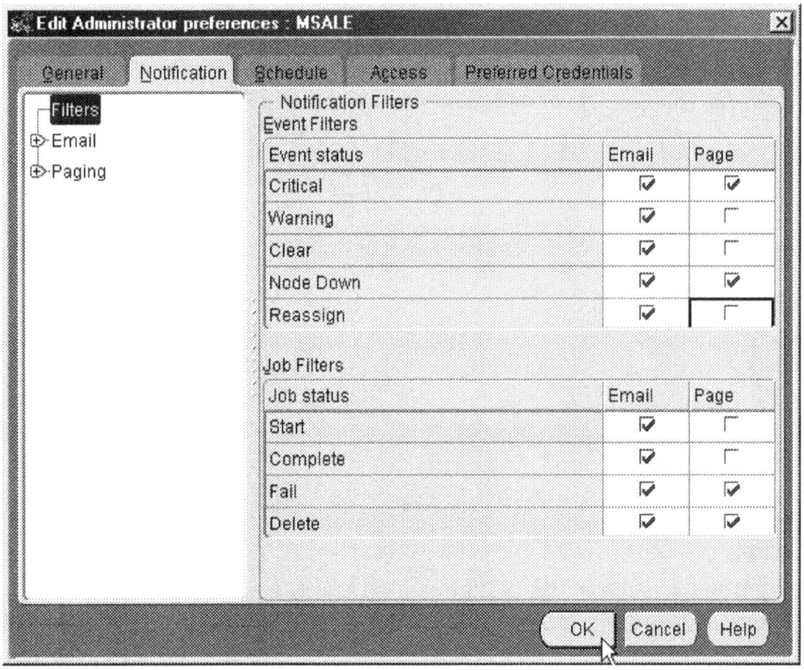

FIGURE 8-4. *Event notification filters*

to be notified upon failure. You may also want to receive an e-mail with all job output appended to the end of the e-mail to review the job output, but want to receive only notifications of job failure in a terse format on your alpha pager. The way to get around these limitations is to create multiple EM accounts for each unique notification configuration you desire.

For example, your database administrators may each have an alpha pager, an e-mail account, and a cell phone with text messaging. You have found that your pager carrier is much more reliable and quicker to complete notification than your cell phone text-message system. The administrators' standard cell phone configuration is to be silent on receipt of a text message. You have decided as the DBA manager that you will use the pager for urgent notifications, standard e-mail inbox for detailed notifications of all kinds, and the cell phone for terse notifications of events that you wish to be notified of, but do not need to react to. Create four accounts for each actual DBA with the appropriate notification filters and definitions. When you configure job or event notification, you will select multiple administrators for each actual database administrator.

Here's another situation you may run into; suppose you have list of people who all need the same notification and filter setup. You do not want to configure details for each person that needs to receive notification, and some of them may be unprivileged owners of the application that is running on your system. In this case, you can minimize work by creating one EM user whose e-mail address is actually the distribution mailing list to which all of the interested parties are members.

Paging

Paging notification is a service that must be set up on an NT or 2000 box that can be used by an OMS on any other platform. The paging service requires that you have a modem installed, and can provide the modem connection number to your paging system provider and the proper PIN to send a page. Once you have a paging server up and running, all you need to do is add the hostname of the machine with the paging service to the list of paging systems (done from the same location as e-mail notification, the Configure Paging/Email property dialog box). For more details, check out the *Oracle Enterprise Manager Configuration Guide* in your online documentation or from http://docs.oracle.com.

Discovery

Discovery is the process of the OMS initiating communication with Agents on nodes that you specify as a super administrator. When an Agent starts up, it examines the system, in particular, the Registry and the network configuration files (tnsnames.ora and listener.ora) found in the Oracle homes defined in the Registry. The Agent then adds service information it has found to its configuration files. The resulting files are as follows:

The services.ora file, found in the %ORACLE_HOME%\network\agent directory.

The snmp_ro.ora and snmp_rw.ora files, found in the same location as your sqlnet.ora file. To add tracing and other options to your Agent configuration, you will directly change snmp_rw.ora.

You can use the command-line utility tnsping to identify the current network home as described in Chapter 7.

From the console, select the Discover Nodes option from the Navigator drop-down menu. When you initiate discovery from the EM Console, the OMS will communicate with the Agent. The Agent will communicate the services it found on its last startup by sending the services.ora file content to the OMS. The OMS will then add these targets to the super administrator's tree. If you add services and recycle the Agent, you must refresh the OMS by rediscovery. Choose the option Refresh All Nodes under the Navigator drop-down menu, and, if you don't want to refresh all nodes, select certain nodes to refresh by clicking the Skip radio button.

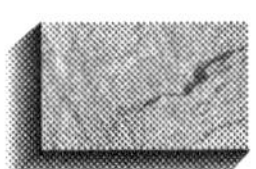

NOTE
If you add a potential target, for example, a new listener or database, and do not recycle the Agent, it will not be found in the discovery process. You need to restart the Agent after every target addition.

The Discovery Name Game

You can get around this problIf your database targets have the same name as another database target on another node, you will receive an error message when attempting to discover the node (Discovery Failed: VD-420: "Targets with the same name have already been discovered"). em by making sure that you have a tnsnames.ora file on each system with a database target and that the TNS aliases are unique across all nodes. (For example, you might want to append the hostname to the dbname for each alias.) If you run into this problem and you need to address it immediately, you should make the alterations to your tnsnames.ora file, and then recycle the Agent and verify that the new target name will be used by examining the contents of the services.ora file in OH\network\agent. This will *not* work if the listener on the node you are attempting to change the discovered name of is configured with the GLOBAL_DBNAME parameter. Instead, change the value of this parameter or remove it if feasible to allow discovery to accept the TNS alias name.

Although you can "discover" a node manually and lose the capability of interacting with the Agent for the job, event, and reporting functions, this practice is generally discouraged because it can make it difficult to add the node later on.

Management Regions

You can assign users to a region that defines a particular set of targets that are managed by a distinct set of Agents. A target cannot exist in more than one region. Regions allow you to segregate traffic between OMSs that are on separate nodes and preferably on separate network subnets. It also allows you to have targets segregated by a firewall. To use this functionality, you need at least one OMS for each region. For more on firewalls and EM, see the section "EM 3-Tier Infrastructure and Firewalls" later in this chapter.

Connecting to a Target

Once a database administrator is connected to the OMS via the console, he or she is presented with a list of targets to attempt connection to in order to manage them. In essence, the repository stores targets and information about connecting to these targets. When you connect to the OMS with your EM user, you are presented only those targets for your region that you have been granted the right to manage. Once provided with these targets, you must learn to properly connect to them. These are the steps that occur if you attempt to connect to a database target by clicking on the target's plus sign (+) in the tree:

1. The EM Console looks for preferred credentials for the target. You can verify that there are credentials from the Preferences dialog box by the green check mark to the right of the target's type notation. You can sort by column by clicking the column header if you are trying to find a target by type, name, or credential type. If the OMS finds credentials, it sends them to the console, and the console attempts the connection with this username and password to the target. If the connection fails, you will prompted for connection details with the option of setting these as your preferred credentials for this target.
2. If there are no preferred credentials for this target, then the OMS will send the default credentials for the target type you have specified *if* you have set the defaults for that type. You can tell the default is set if there is a grayed-out check mark indicating that the OMS will attempt to use the target type default credentials to connect. The connection is made directly by the console to the database via its listener.
3. If there are no preferred or default credentials for the target and its type, then you will be prompted for credentials with the option of saving them as the default credentials for this EM user.

Some key things to note:

- The connection to a database is made directly from the console to the database via the listener. *The Agent plays no part in this connection.*
- The credentials are encrypted and stored in the repository.
- Credentials are specific to the EM user (for example, sysman) and cannot be used by others. The exception to this is that default credentials for the target type are inherited in the beginning from the super administrator.
- If you do not want to attempt the connection with the preferred credentials, you can right-click the target name and then select Connect. You will then be presented with the Connection dialog box. From here, you can enter the connection credentials you wish to use for this particular session. You can also opt to change your Preferred Credential setting to the new connection information you enter.

Standalone Console

The Standalone Console can be used to manage database targets you identify and configure manually. It is the replacement for the Oracle 8i DBA Studio tool. Typically, you will only want to use this console to work with a database on a node where the Agent is not available. The Standalone Console is very limited in what it can do, and virtually all functionality provided by the Standalone Console can be accomplished from the command line, whereas this is not true of the OMS-connected console. Why use the Standalone Console? Here are a list of reasons:

- You need to manage a database on a node where the Agent is not available.
- You only need to manage a very small environment where you already have job and event functionality via other methods.
- The complexity of maintaining the Management Server's repository is beyond the DBA staff's capability.
- You only want to use certain GUI functionality that is otherwise difficult to understand and manage from the command line (for example, SPFILE management, session monitoring and management, lock management, undo management, and space management).
- You have not purchased the Enterprise Edition of the Oracle database.

It is important to note that the Standalone Console cannot use the configurations you have saved in the OMS and that the inverse is true as well; you cannot use the

connection/configuration you have for the Standalone Console in an OMS-connected console.

Ultimately, if you have no desire to use the extensive functionality provided by the OMS and its repository, you can use the Standalone Console as a tool in your kit to manage databases in an environment where other enterprise management tools are in place.

The Agent

The Agent is the workhorse of the EM architecture. It runs job tasks and event tests on a node, interacts with the OMS to communicate job status, and event triggers fired, and registers new events and jobs. Whenever the Agent starts, it searches the system for new services that EM can monitor and manage. The foundation for completing these functions is TCL, a scripting language available on all Oracle platforms.

Because an Agent functions for the node, or machine, that it runs upon, there should only be one Agent per node. If you have other Oracle homes that have Agents configured in the Services MMC, then you should edit the service to disable it.

The 9i Agent

New Feature in Oracle9i

The 9i Agent is very much improved over previous versions. New in 9i, the Agent will try and restart itself if it encounters a catastrophic failure. If the Agent believes that its attempts to restart are failing repeatedly, it will stop retrying to avoid thrashing the CPU.

The previous implementation of the Agent required that you also start the Data Gatherer to utilize much of the performance-related monitoring functionality. In release 9i, this functionality has been incorporated in the Agent.

As in previous versions of the Agent, you can start the Agent from the Services MMC, but in Oracle9i you can control it from the command line as well:

```
c:\oracle>agentctl

Usage:
          agentctl start|stop|status|restart [agent]
          agentctl start|stop|status         blackout [<target>]
                   [-d/uration <timefmt>] [-s/ubsystem <subsystems>]

        The following are valid options for blackouts
         <target>    name of the target. Defaults to node target.
         <timefmt>   is specified as [days] hh:mm
         <subsystem> is specified as [jobs events collections]
                     defaults to all subsystems
```

Whereas in previous versions of the Agent command-line control was unsupported on Windows platforms, with the 9i Agent you can start, stop, monitor, and configure the Agent from the command line safely.

Agent Processes

You might want to identify the Agent processes to track the impact of the Agent and its associated work on your system or to identify the processes you need to kill in case of an unclean death of one or more of the other associated processes:

agntcrvc.exe

dbsnmp.exe

dbsnmpj.exe

You can identify specific job impact by tracking resource utilization by the dbsnmpj.exe process.

Agent Blackouts

You can see from the previous listing that you can also "black out" Agent functionality for a specified time period. If you have scheduled downtime where you need to take down the database to apply a patch, you do not want the DatabaseUpDown event test firing and running a fix-it job that starts up the database. You could just shut down the Agent for the time being, but you also have other targets that have jobs to be run and event tests that need to occur. In this case, you can black out the Agent activity for a particular target:

```
c:\oracle>agentctl start blackout PROD
```

This causes the Agent to stop all activity for the PROD target until you end the blackout with the following command:

```
c:\oracle>agentctl stop blackout PROD
```

You may also want to just black out the target for a period of time, like this:

```
c:>agentctl start blackout PROD -d 0:30
```

This command will start a blackout on the PROD target for 30 minutes. You can identify current blackouts with the following Agent command line:

```
c:>agentctl status blackout
Target=PROD,ORACLE_DATABASE  Subsystem=All Endtime=Indefinite duration
```

You also have the capacity to black out a particular EM subsystem on the Agent:

```
c:>agentctl start blackout -d 0:45 -s jobs events
```

This command will not execute any jobs or event tests for the next 45 minutes.

If you want to identify all of the targets that are available for blackout, you can look at the services.ora file in the OH\network\agent directory. The value before the equal sign in services.ora indicates the discovered target name.

Isolate the Agent

Because the Agent is used to monitor and manage all Oracle products, old and new, as well as other targets such as the operating system it functions on top of and SQL Server installations, it is always a good idea to keep the Agent in its own Oracle home. This allows you to isolate updates and upgrades of the Agent from the day-to-day functioning of your databases, listeners, and web application servers running on the same node. To take advantage of many of the new 9i features, you will be required to use the 9i Agent. You can then use most of these new features to manage databases from versions 7.3 through 9i.

Agent Configuration

There are three primary Agent configuration files: snmp_ro.ora, snmp_rw.ora, and services.ora. Of these, typically only the snmp_rw.ora file should be edited by hand.

The services.ora File

The services.ora file is regenerated on every Agent startup, so editing this file is an exercise in futility. Whenever the Agent is started, it examines the Registry, listener.ora, tnsnames.ora, and nmxw.ora, to determine what services/targets it will interact with. The nmxw.ora file is only available if the HTTP extensions have been installed in the Agent home. It is used to identify Apache HTTP Servers and should be edited by hand if you have an HTTP Server other than the one installed in the Agent home. Once the Agent has finished the auto-discovery phase during startup, it will generate the services.ora file. If there is a problem with this generation, check the nmiconf.log file (typically found in OH\network\agent\log) for problems, address those problems, and restart the Agent to regenerate a proper services.ora.

The snmp_ro.ora File

This file is generated by the first Agent startup and should only be edited when specifically needed. If you delete it, the Agent will re-create it upon its next startup. If you are having trouble with connectivity to a particular target, verify the information here.

The snmp_rw.ora File

This is the primary user-configured file for the Agent. You typically do not need to make any changes to this file. In Table 8-4, we present some of the parameters that will likely be of interest to you. Check the Agent readme file and Appendix A of the *Oracle Intelligent Agent User's Guide* for more information.

Parameter	Description
DBSNMP.POLLTIME=<NUMBER OF SECONDS>	The number of seconds between Agent tests for database availability. The default is 30 seconds.
DBSNMP.LOG_DIRECTORY= <DIRECTORY PATH>	Indicates where the dbnsnmp log file will go. Typically, set this to OH\network\agent\log.
DBSNMP.LOG_UNIQUE=<TRUE/FALSE>	If this is left at the default of FALSE, then the dbsnmp log file will be overwritten on every Agent startup.
DBSNMP.HOSTNAME=<HOSTNAME OR IP>	If you have multiple NICs, and this is left at its default setting of the default hostname, then the Agent will interact with all the NICs on the machine. The better option is to bind it to a particular NIC by specifying the IP address for a more secure, less traveled NIC.

TABLE 8-4. *Agent Configuration Parameters for snmp_rw.ora*

Events

The EM Event subsystem allows you to monitor for important changes in the condition of the targets you manage. An Agent can respond to the event by sending a notification to the OMS, which will decide who to notify and how to notify them, and the Agent can respond immediately with a fix-it job if so configured.

The Base Events

The EM event system without the Diagnostic Pack only comes with five event tests to test the UpDown status of each type of target:

Database This test checks the availability of the database via the Agent. If the Agent is pre-8.0.5, then this test will also fail when the listener is down. If the Agent is version 8.0.5 or higher, then this test will *not* fail if the listener is down and the database is up and running.

Node This test is initiated by the OMS instead of the Agent. It tests for both Agent and node availability. If either are down, then the event is triggered.

Listener This tests for listener availability. If the database is down and the listener is up, this test will not fire the event.

Data Gatherer This test is *not* a valid test against a 9i Agent because the Data Gatherer functionality is incorporated in the Agent, and the Agent is tested by the Node UpDown event.

HTTP Server This test simply checks for any response from the web server.

Advanced Events

With the Diagnostics Pack, you gain a large number of additional events beyond the UpDown event tests provided with the vanilla EM product. These additional events allow you to incorporate tests for excessive resource use, declining performance, and other problems. Good descriptions of these events can be found in the *Oracle Enterprise Manager Event Test Reference Manual.*

User-Defined Events: Leverage Your Current Scripts

User-defined events allow you to extend the base and advanced events to include tests that you develop with your own scripts. These scripts can use any runtime facility that is available on the node that you will test for the condition.

The standard installation of the Agent comes with the HTTP Server. The HTTP Server includes Perl version 5.005_03. The installation also puts Perl in your system path and can therefore be used in the creation of user-defined events as well as custom jobs. You can use Perl with its installed package modules to accomplish a variety of tasks. If you have Perl skills, you can add .pm packages specific to Win32 administration to expand functionality and increase ease of administration. (Take a look at CPAN at http://www.cpan.org, and ActiveState at http://www.activestate.com, for Win32-specific modules to meet your administrative needs.)

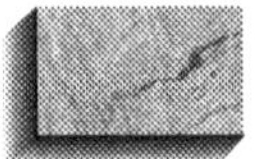

NOTE
User-defined events require the Diagnostics Pack.

Event Creation

The process to create an event is actually very simple if you understand the choices you need to make and how events interact with the job, security, and notification systems. Pressing CTRL-E will bring up the Create Event property sheet for a new event. The first tab of the sheet (see Figure 8-5) contains the target type, which

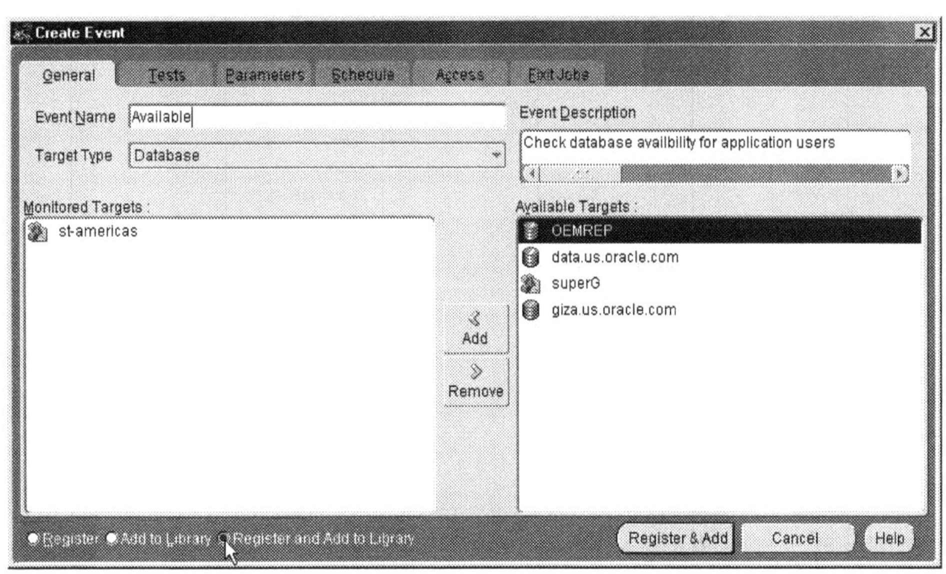

FIGURE 8-5. *Create Event property sheet*

determines the available tests later on and the selection of targets, as well as the name and description of the event. It is important to keep the name terse and relevant to your notification needs. Remember not to include redundant information in the name. The target type and target name are already available as content for notification and all these properties show in the Alert, Registered, and History tabs on the console. If a group is one of the monitored targets, then the event will register with all the targets of the event type that are in that group.

From the Test tab (see Figure 8-6), you will select one or more event tests. Each event test will have its own characteristics. If you have the Diagnostics Pack, you will have a much larger collection of event tests. For node events, the Diagnostics Pack provides OS-specific events that read from the same data that the Windows 2000 Perfmon tool does. If you do not have the Diagnostics Pack, you are limited to the UpDown events. Most of the events in the listing have a tool tip description that appears when you hover your mouse over the event test name; you can also check out the *Oracle Enterprise Manager Event Test Reference Manual* for detailed descriptions.

The Parameters tab allows you to configure event test parameters (see Figure 8-7). If you are using your own event test, you will set the script name for a node test or import the SQL script and identify the thresholds for metric-based tests (see Figure 8-8).

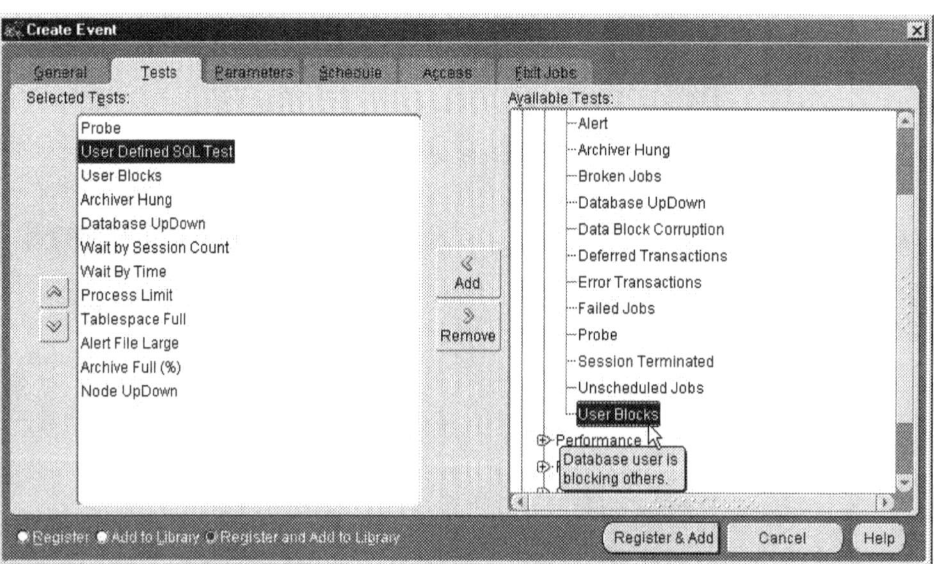

FIGURE 8-6. *Tests for an event*

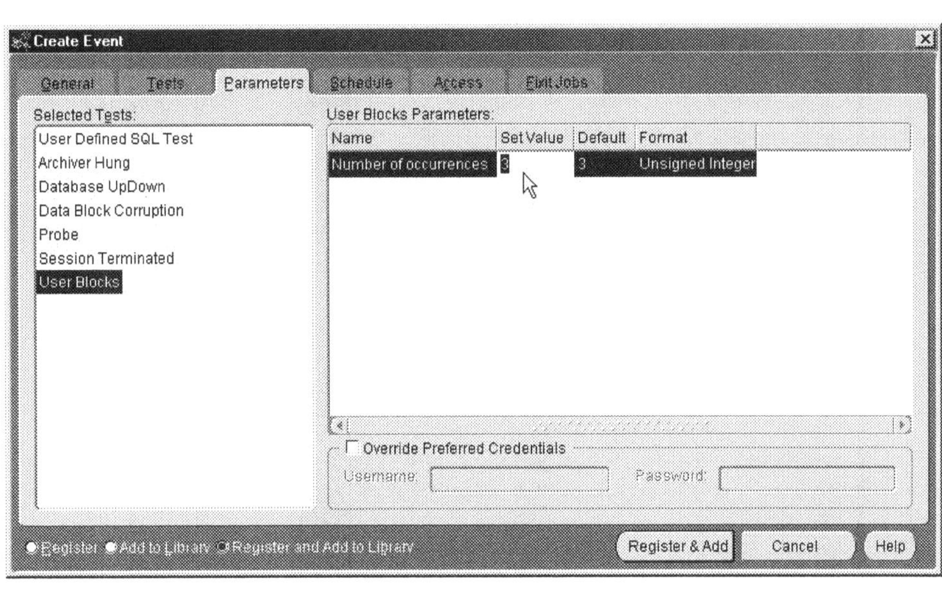

FIGURE 8-7. *Event test parameter configuration*

Create Event
General
Tests
Parameters
Schedule
Access
Fixit Jobs
Selected Tests:
User Defined SQL Test
Archiver Hung
Database UpDown
Data Block Corruption
Probe
Session Terminated
User Blocks
User Defined SQL Test Parameters:
SQL:
select bytes from v$sgastat where pool='shared pool' and name='free memory'
Import
Operator: <
Critical threshold: 1048576
Warning Threshold: 4194304
Occurrences Preceding Notification: 3
Override Preferred Credentials
Username:
Password:
Register
Add to Library
Register and Add to Library
Register & Add
Cancel
Help

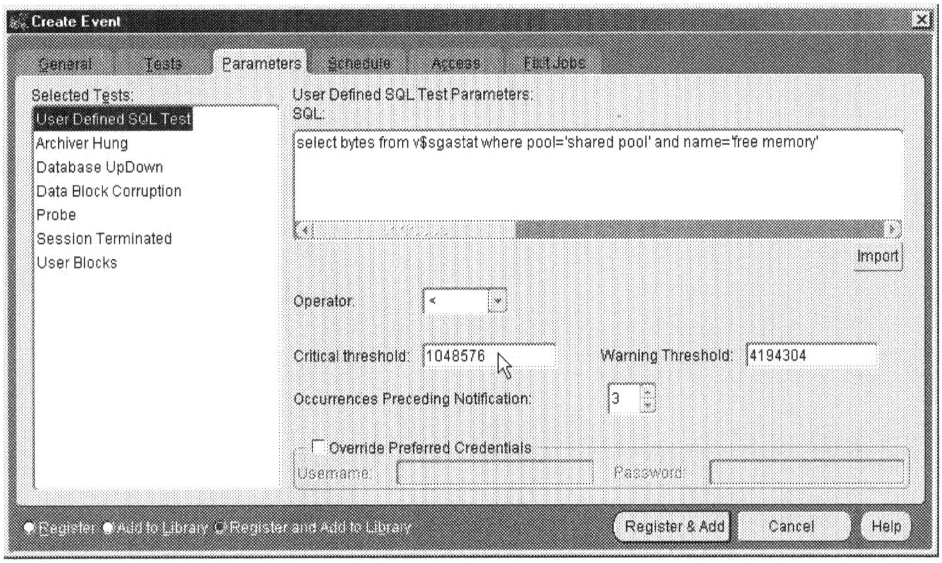

FIGURE 8-8. *User-defined event test parameter configuration*

From the Parameters tab, you can identify how many iterations of this event test must be triggered consecutively before the event itself is considered triggered—three times in this case.

The Schedule tab allows you to configure when the tests will be performed. The On Interval option runs all of the tests on the Test tab at the appointed time interval. In Figure 8-9, the tests will be performed once every five minutes starting immediately. You could also delay implementation to correspond with a go-live date or other milestone-related date where acceptable event states change in the future. Instead of performing an event test based on an interval of days, hours, minutes, and seconds, between each test you can use the On Day of Week or On Day of Month options to run the test only on certain days of the week or certain days of the month. These should only be used for tests that will be performed once per day though, as you cannot specify anything other than the time of day for the Day of Week and Day of Month schedules.

The Access tab allows you to grant varying levels of access to EM users and notify them if the event is triggered (see Figure 8-10). You cannot restrict super administrators from any level of access by nature of their level of privilege. Event filters set for the EM users indicated here determine how and on what changes in status they will get notified.

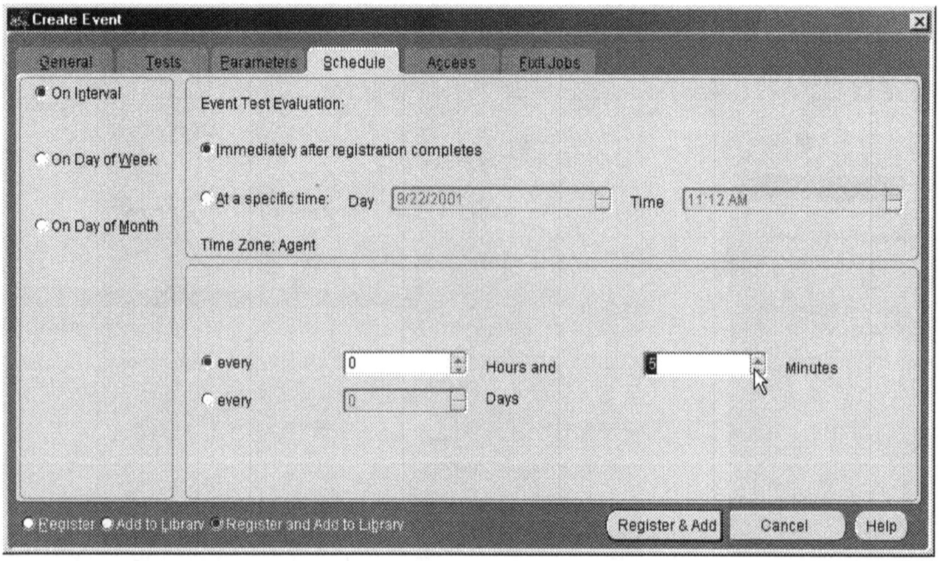

FIGURE 8-9. *Event test interval schedule*

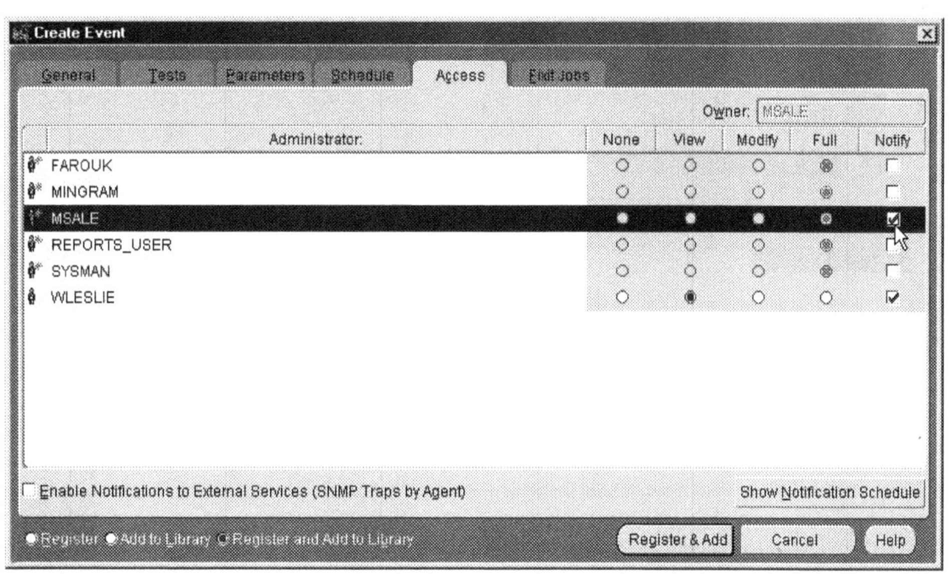

FIGURE 8-10. *Event notification settings*

The Fixit Jobs tab allows you to assign *one* fix-it job if *any* of the event tests fails (see Figure 8-11). If you decide to create a fix-it job on-the-fly, you need to make sure that once the job is registered with the relevant targets (must be at least all of the targets identified in the event), it shows up in your list of available fix-it jobs. Just switch to a different tab and back. If you cannot wait until the new fix-it job finishes registering with all the targets, you can always edit the job later to assign a fix-it job to an event.

Event Library

Once you have an event configured or created, you can add it to the Event Library. This allows you to keep the event as a template for use on other targets where you might need slightly different configurations. It also allows you to keep standards for event tests that other administrators can use as guides.

Event Registration

Once an event has been created, or when it has been edited to add new targets, the OMS communicates the job to the Agent on the target's node. Before the event has been registered with the targets, the event status will show as Registration Pending.

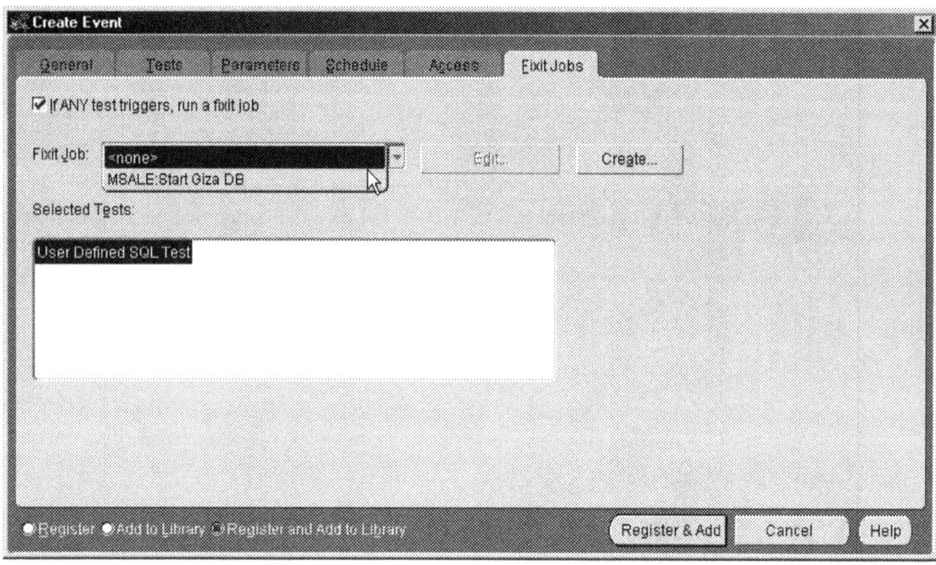

FIGURE 8-11. *Event fix-it configuration*

You can view this registration status from the Status column of the event under the Registered tab. If registration fails, it is most often due to improper preparation of the node or target for interaction with the OMS's attempt to register the job. Here are some of the most common reasons for the failure of an event registration:

Preferred credentials on the node are not correct or not privileged enough to allow the Agent to complete registration.

The Agent is not up and running on the target node.

The Agent running on the target node is not the Agent that the OMS knows about. This might happen if you install a new Oracle product in a separate home that also installs and starts an Agent from the software in its own home.

Responding to Events

Once an event has been triggered, you can decide what to do. When an event is initially triggered, or the event status changes from warning to critical, then the flag icon indicating the status will have an eyeglasses icon overlaying it. This eyeglass icon indicates that no one has edited or acknowledged the event occurrence since the last change in its status. One of the options an administrator has is to acknowledge the event occurrence by right-clicking the event and selecting Acknowledge Event (or selecting this same option from the Event pull-down menu). If an administrator edits the job, the eyeglasses go away as well. In an environment where there are multiple administrators for the same targets, it might be useful to assign ownership of an event by editing it as well. These two features, the eyeglasses icon overlay and event ownership, can foster clear communication between administrators and prevent duplication of work.

Another feature that your shop can use to track the progress of an event is the logging feature. An administrator with the Modify privilege can add log entries to the event by editing the event. Next, on the Log tab of the Event property sheet, add your log entry in the Type Entry field and click Apply to continue on the property sheet, or save and close right away by clicking OK. After saving, there will be a time-stamped, EM user–identified entry in the Event Log list under the Author tab.

You can track the event notifications under the Notification Details tab. Entries here include the administer notified, the time of notification, and the method of notification—e-mail and/or pager. If you need to identify response times of administrators to events, you can compare the Log tab data with the Notification Details tab. You can also investigate the repository content to write an EM report to show response times for events. Here is a query to get you started on that path:

```
select eid, ROUND(1440*(max(timestamp)-min(timestamp)),2) minutes_to_close
from
( select entry, author, timestamp, event_occurrence_id eid
   from smp_vde_event_log
  UNION
  select method entry, owner author, time_stamp timestamp, execnum eid
   from smp_vdm_notification_details) e
group by eid
```

This query returns the number of minutes between the first notification and the last log entry for each event. This is obviously not accurate and does not reflect time zone differences, notifications not received, and much more. It is a starting place for helping you begin developing your own reports on metrics that are interesting to you.

Here is a list of some essential characteristics of events you should know when deciding how to use them in your overall management strategy:

- Events are triggered upon the conditions of a test.
- An event can be configured for only one target type (for example, database, node, listener, or HTTP Server).
- An event can be configured for multiple targets of the same target type.
- Each event can have multiple tests.

An event will change its status to cleared once the condition that caused the event to trigger has been altered back to a condition that would no longer cause the event to be triggered.

Any environment associated with a node's preferred credentials is *not* effective during the execution of an event test. This is especially important to note when implementing user-defined events.

Event History

Event occurrences are found in History either if an administrator has moved them there by hand or if the Agent has cleared the event. For example, if a monitored listener goes down, an Agent in turn fires the ListenerUpDown event and notifies the OMS. The OMS uses the relevant notification systems. An event occurrence shows up under the Alerts tab. In our example, there is also a fix-it job associated with the ListenerUpDown event that is registered with the node. This fix-it job is executed and the listener started. Once the Agent has determined that the listener is back up and running, it will set the event occurrence to cleared, and the OMS will move the event occurrence to History.

Because events may be moved into history if the tests return to a cleared status before administrators identify them, it is important to initiate some form of notification of event occurrences that can be assigned and addressed. The other option is that all events in the history that are unassigned must be addressed with a log entry and assigned.

You can examine the progressive history of an event in the History by selecting the event in the right-hand pane, and then select Edit Event Occurrence from the Edit pull-down menu. Once the Event Occurrence properties page is up, you can look at the list of event tests, the timestamp of the test's last change in status, and the associated message. From this Event Occurrence properties page, you can click the test's title and then the Advice button to view associated advice describing the test. This feature will only work for those tests where it is enabled and the Diagnostics Pack is installed. You can also view the *current* status of the event-monitored element with a Performance Manager chart, if available, by clicking the View Chart button that will appear if available.

You can view the changes in status and the associated messages by examining the elements of the log entries under the Log tab. Once an event has occurred, you can still add entries to the log if you have the Modify privilege for that event. You might use this functionality to explain event occurrences and resolution explanation. Other database administrators can examine the history for previous event log entries to find out how previous occurrences of this event were addressed.

Jobs

The EM Job subsystem is designed to let multiple users run jobs unattended at scheduled times and intervals. The appropriate administrators can then be notified of the status and results of those jobs in the console or via pager and e-mail. Jobs allow you to take the scripts you run now on your nodes and place them under EM Job subsystem management. The caveat is that your jobs do not necessarily inherit the environment of the user's credentials you use to run the job. For this reason, you need to make sure that you set your environment properly within the job to avoid problems.

Job Tasks

Every job is made up of one or more job tasks. Job tasks, other than the first job in the list of tasks, can be conditionally run according to the previous job completion status. You can decide to run a subsequent job task only if the previous task completed successfully or if the previous task failed. For example, if you have a fix-it job that responds to a listener down event by attempting to start the listener, you may want to respond to a failure to start the listener by running an OS script, and then try to shut down the listener and attempt to start the listener upon the success of the listener shut down.

Jobs on Windows 2000 and NT require that you set up a user account to run the job and that you set that user up with preferred credentials for the node. That user needs to have the ability to write to the %ORACLE_HOME%\network directory, as well as ability to write to either the %ORACLE_HOME% or the %TEMP% directory. Once you have created the user, you need to assign that user the "Log in as a batch job" privilege via the Local Security Settings tool. You can find the Local Security Settings tool in the Administrative Tools section of the OS Control Panel. If you don't assign this user the proper privilege, you will get an access error when the Agent attempts to execute any job.

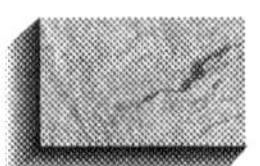

NOTE
Node permissions as well as target credentials are required to run any job.

Already Available Job Tasks

Many tasks that can be run from the various tools EM provides can be scheduled to run as jobs. You can schedule these tasks to run one time only so that you avoid running the job during peak use times, or you can schedule a task to run as a job on a regular interval or schedule. You can schedule a job to do exports for your development system that then get imported into the test system. If you have a load that you run regularly, you can use the Job system to do the load for you on the scheduled day of the week at the appropriate time. The notification system can inform you of progress and outcome.

If you are monitoring Oracle Application Server or HTTP Server installations, you can run a log analysis report that provides you with an overview of Apache listener activity. Although this is not a WebTrends quality product by any stretch of the imagination, it does provide a bare-bones overview that can be useful.

As the Oracle database progresses in features and performance, the effective use of the Cost-Based Optimizer (CBO) has become more and more important. The foundation of the CBO is the statistics that are gathered for database objects and used in determining the optimal execution plan for your SQL. If you do not generate statistics for an object and the CBO must be used, a set of typically unrealistic assumptions are made about the data. To avoid these assumptions, you need to develop a statistics generation methodology.

There are two ways to generate statistics, the first by using the analyze table syntax for objects. The second method, the DBMS_STATS package, is newer and generally better at gathering statistics that are more useful to the Cost Based Optimizer. It is also less intrusive (that is, it does not require a table lock for the duration of the analysis as does the analyze table statement). You can use the Job system to gather statistics on a schedule. You can tailor the gathering to run as you configure it (for example, 18% Estimate for schema X objects, Compute for Schema Y, use DBMS_STATS package for both, and so on).

Tools such as the Reorg Wizard and others allow you to schedule implementation of a change with the Job system. Check out Figure 8-9 for a typical Schedule properties tab.

SQL*Plus Script as a Job Element

One of the most useful functions of the EM Job system is that you can leverage the use of your existing scripts to complete activities unattended, yet properly monitored for proper completion. In order to properly exit from a SQL script, you need to return a nonzero value to indicate failure; otherwise, jobs will succeed even when they actually may have failed. The first approach to this is to use this line at the beginning of the script:

```
WHENEVER SQLERROR EXIT SQL.SQLCODE
```

This line will cause the script to exit with an error if any SQL error is encountered.

This is all well and good for many scripts, but what about those scripts where you know you will likely encounter errors? An example of this situation is where you might try and drop a nonexistent table. This will cause an ORA-942 error message that you wish to ignore. One option is to put all statements where you expect

SQL errors to occur before the whenever statement. The other is to use a number variable set in your script that will return a zero when the script has completed and its job has completed successfully. If you return a nonzero value, the job will show as failed. Here is an example of the essentials of using a SQL*Plus variable as a return value:

```
variable ret_code number
begin
if (1=1) then
 :ret_code:=0;
else
 :ret_code:=1;
end if;
end;
/
exit :ret_code
```

If 1=1 is true, then this script implemented as a job will complete with success. If 1!=1, then the script implemented as a job will fail.

Fix-It Jobs

Fix-it jobs are used by Agents to respond to an event trigger. If you have a standard response to one or more events, you should create a fix-it job that implements that fix. There are some restrictions that you need to know before implementing fix-it jobs:

- Fix-it jobs must be assigned to the same target type as the associated event.
- Fix-it jobs must be preregistered with *all* the targets assigned to an event before it can be assigned as the fix-it job for that event.
- You *can* run an OS script job in a fix-it job that is of the types Database, Listener, or HTTP Server, but you *cannot* run a SQL*Plus script directly from a fix-it job of the type Node. Instead, you will need to run the SQL*Plus script from an OS script.

Job Output Limit Configuration

Some jobs you create may have extensive output that extends beyond the default limit of 128KB. You can increase this limit in the OH\sysman\config\omsconfig.properties file in either kilobytes (KB) or megabytes (MB), as shown here:

```
oms.vdg.joboutput.maxsize=256K
```

Database Administration

The EM Console, stand-alone and management server connected, can be utilized to manage most aspects of your database instances. We want to stress that it is *vitally* important to your stress level and your job that you understand the underlying changes that you are making when using the console to manage your instances. The advantage of using EM to manage your databases is that there are aspects of a database that are often more easily grasped when in a graphic format. Also, many of the real-time monitoring and managing capacities allow rapid assessment and response to systems in danger.

Navigating Objects

For database administration, there are a few things to know that can increase your productivity and help you become at ease with the tool much more quickly:

The Object pull-down menu will contain activities you can perform related to the objects selected in the left-hand pane. This same content is also available by right-clicking the selected object.

The Related Tools menu off of the Object menu can be helpful in identifying helper applications for an object you are working with.

The Navigator pull-down menu allows you to change the perspective of the tree, either object-type focused (View by Object) or user focused, (View by Schema). If you are interested only in a particular schema's objects, then View by Schema is the appropriate choice. Try the different views and discover which paradigm works best for which tasks.

If you are looking for a particular object, you use the Find Database Object option under the Object pull-down menu. This search allows you to use wild cards for the object name, restrict the search to one or more chosen schemas, and restrict the search to a particular object type.

Use the ALT-ENTER keystroke to edit the details of any selected object (for example, tablespace, package, datafile, user, role, and more).

You can use the Create Like option by pressing CTRL-L to create a new database object (for example, tablespace, datafile, user, package, redo, rollback segment, and more) based on the definition of the currently selected object.

Most lists of objects that you can find in the right-hand pane of the console can be saved in an HTML or CSV format. The CSV format is easily imported into Microsoft Excel for analysis and incorporation into presentations or loaded into a table in a database. The HTML format allows you to publish this information statically to a web site for reference purposes. Choose the Save List option from the Object menu when one or more objects are selected. You will be prompted for format and location for generated report storage. The default storage area is found under %ORACLE_HOME%\sysman\report.

Space Management

The management of datafiles, tablespaces, and extents can be tough for most people to keep all in their heads. The space management facilities of EM allow those of us who are more visual to see space usage in a visual representation. You can quickly and easily see those datafiles that have auto-extend turned on, identified by the yellow triangle arrowhead at the end of the datafile graphic in the right-hand pane. You can edit a tablespace by selecting the tablespace and then pressing ALT-ENTER. From here, you can also drill down to edit the datafiles as well.

Have you ever wanted to drop a tablespace and needed to know what database objects depend on that tablespace? Identify and select the tablespace in the left-hand pane, and then select the Show Dependencies option from the Object pull-down menu. From here, you can identify those objects you will need to move, re-create, or delete. If the number of objects is too great, you can generate a report of the dependencies in either an HTML file or a comma-separated listing (easily imported into Microsoft Excel). This functionality is not limited to tablespaces. If you want to drop a procedure or a package, you can identify other packages, triggers, functions, and procedures that are dependent on the object of interest. You can generate static reports from the list of datafiles to keep for historical purposes, analysis, or presentations (see Figure 8-12).

Security Management

User management from the command line can be a hassle. EM's database tools allow you to drop, alter, and create users from a GUI that makes it simple to find information about a user's rights. If you were doing this from the command line, you would need to craft a script (still not a bad idea) that will show you the particular rights and privileges granted to a user in a text format.

You can quickly and easily lock, unlock, and expire passwords by selecting the associated options from the Object pull-down menu when the user of interest is selected in either the right or left panes of the console. If you want to see the DDL statement that would be used to create a user, select the Show Object DDL option from the Object drop-down list or by right-clicking and selecting the option from the pop-up menu.

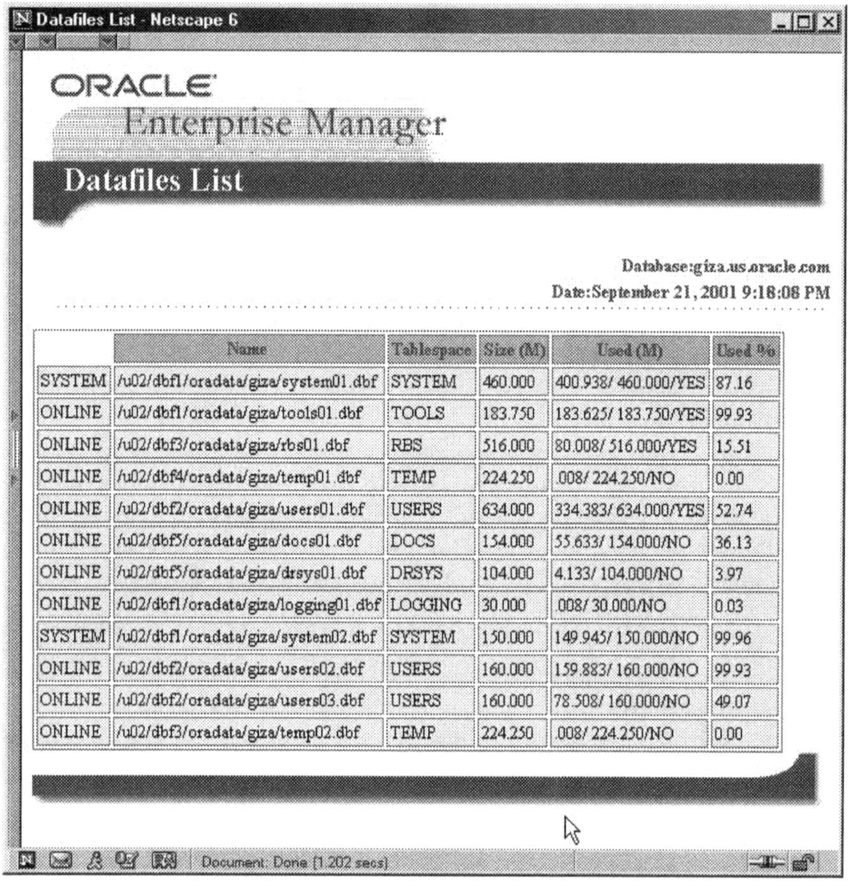

	Name	Tablespace	Size (M)	Used (M)	Used %
SYSTEM	/u02/dbf1/oradata/giza/system01.dbf	SYSTEM	460.000	400.938/ 460.000/YES	87.16
ONLINE	/u02/dbf1/oradata/giza/tools01.dbf	TOOLS	183.750	183.625/ 183.750/YES	99.93
ONLINE	/u02/dbf3/oradata/giza/rbs01.dbf	RBS	516.000	80.008/ 516.000/YES	15.51
ONLINE	/u02/dbf4/oradata/giza/temp01.dbf	TEMP	224.250	.008/ 224.250/NO	0.00
ONLINE	/u02/dbf2/oradata/giza/users01.dbf	USERS	634.000	334.383/ 634.000/YES	52.74
ONLINE	/u02/dbf5/oradata/giza/docs01.dbf	DOCS	154.000	55.633/ 154.000/NO	36.13
ONLINE	/u02/dbf5/oradata/giza/drsys01.dbf	DRSYS	104.000	4.133/ 104.000/NO	3.97
ONLINE	/u02/dbf1/oradata/giza/logging01.dbf	LOGGING	30.000	.008/ 30.000/NO	0.03
SYSTEM	/u02/dbf1/oradata/giza/system02.dbf	SYSTEM	150.000	149.945/ 150.000/NO	99.96
ONLINE	/u02/dbf2/oradata/giza/users02.dbf	USERS	160.000	159.883/ 160.000/NO	99.93
ONLINE	/u02/dbf2/oradata/giza/users03.dbf	USERS	160.000	78.508/ 160.000/NO	49.07
ONLINE	/u02/dbf3/oradata/giza/temp02.dbf	TEMP	224.250	.008/ 224.250/NO	0.00

FIGURE 8-12. *Manual datafile HTML report output*

Configuration Management

EM allows you to quickly and easily identify and alter a variety of configuration options associated with an instance. You can identify SGA memory use from a pie chart; if the database is in archive log mode, instance state (open, mounted, nomount, or closed) in the form of a stop light; and other items in useful metaphors that communicate instance state and configuration. This does *not* mean that you should not be very familiar with how to configure the system without EM; however, this feature allows administrators that already understand the essentials of configuration management to quickly and easily ascertain and alter instance state and configuration. You can use EM as we do, to identify issues, and use the command line to alter state and configuration to address those issues.

Determine Configured and Running Initialization Parameters

If you click on the Instance Configuration leaf (found in the left pane of the console) for a database you are connected to, you can view the configuration file that was used to start the database. In the example shown in Figure 8-13, you can tell that the file was an SPFILE named spfiletest.ora (given that in this case we know the SID and the DB name are the same) by looking at the last line of the Database and Instance Information section of the General tab.

If you are interested in determining the current running configuration, including instance altered initialization (init) parameters or the SPFILE configuration, click the All Initialization Parameters button shown in Figure 8-13. This will display the

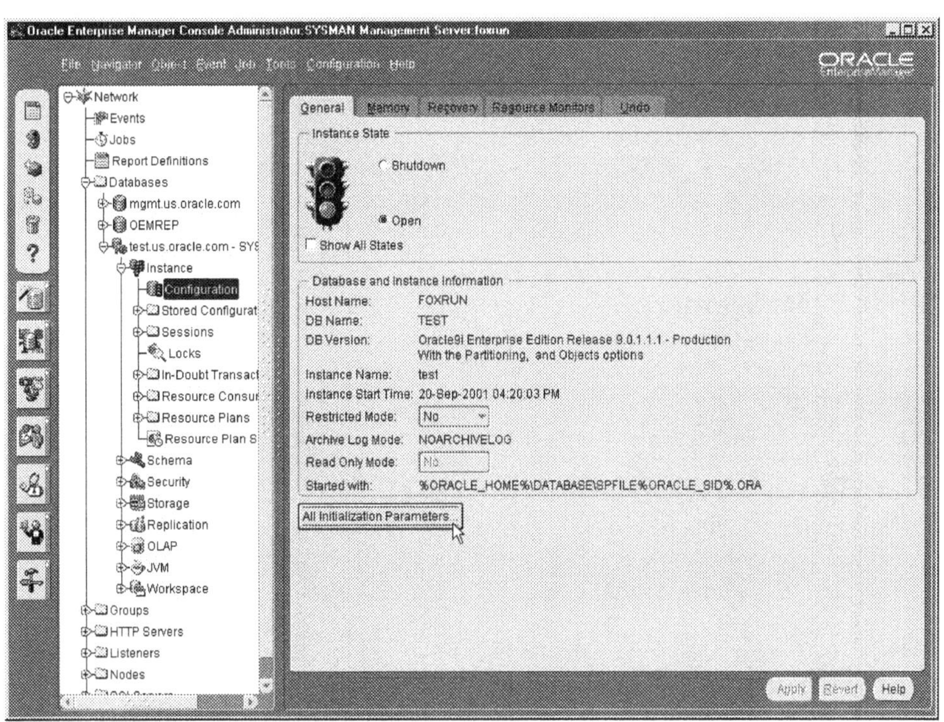

FIGURE 8-13. *Database instance status connected as SYSDBA*

contents of V$PARAMETER when the Running radio button is selected, and when the Configured radio button is selected, you can view the SPFILE configuration. The Configured view is the EM perspective and is based on the V$SPPARAMETER view.

You can make changes to the parameters *only if* you are connected to the instance as SYSDBA. Changes made to running dynamic parameters will alter the current state of the instance. Changes to running static parameters will require you to restart the database in order to apply the changes. In most cases, you will *not* want to do this. This is one of the advantages of using an SPFILE. If you make changes to configured dynamic parameters, these changes are implemented right away.

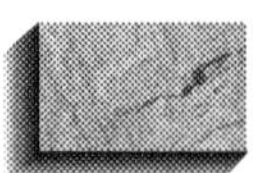

NOTE
If you are connected to a pre-9i database, then you will not find the Configured option because the SPFILE functionality is new to release 9i.

Stored Configurations

You can use EM to start up an instance with a configuration you have stored in the repository using the GUI. This might be useful for a situation where you have infrequent, massive batch jobs that can be done in scheduled, intermittent downtime with an altered init.ora optimized to the need of your batches.

You can export stored configurations as an init.ora file on the local machine (default location is %ORACLE_HOME%\sysman\ifiles) or on the OMS machine. If you want to use an existing stored configuration as the base for another, save it under another name with the Save As button or menu option.

SPFILE Management

EM allows you to take an existing configuration and save is as an SPFILE (see Chapter 5 for more information on SPFILEs) or generate an init.ora file from the existing SPFILE.

Real Time Session Management

The Diagnostics Pack allows you to look at sessions in real time (at an interval you specify) in a sort order you identify. If one of your instances appears to be unresponsive to users, you can connect locally as a privileged user such as SYS or SYSTEM.

Real Time Lock Management

If you have the Diagnostics Pack, you can monitor locks on your system in real time. You can filter these locks by user locks (that is, TX, TM, and UL locks) or filter to show only those locks that are blocking other sessions and those that are waiting for other sessions to release locks.

Once you find a lock you are interested in, you can drill down to the Edit Session property sheet or kill the session. To get to the session edit option, you must first select the lock of interest in the right-hand pane, and then click the Details button below the list of locks. From this view, you can see the SQL for the session, session statistics, and other details related to the session. You can also kill the session from the property sheet.

The Oracle Management Server

The Oracle Management Server (OMS) is the foundation for centralization and all of the management subsystems such as security, jobs, events, collection, and notification.

The Repository

The OMS needs persistent storage of data for a variety of functionality. For example, the EM repository stores data for the following purposes:

- Notification schedules and configuration
- Discovered target metadata (for example, connection strings, default target credentials, and so on)
- OMS security information for EM users, targets, regions, and more
- Metadata for jobs and events
- Report definitions
- Group definitions
- Job and event historical data
- Collection data (if you configure and enable collections from the Diagnostics Pack tool)

As you can see, the OMS uses the repository to perform most of its functions. For this reason, it is important to ensure the availability of the repository. Without the repository, your EM management system is no longer reliable for notification of events, thus it becomes a point of failure. The message: The availability of the repository is as important as the most important notification you depend upon! Back it up and keep it on a machine you can depend on. Monitor and tune the repository as you would any other critically important database.

Because the repository is a single point of failure, you may want to use a hot standby (see Chapter 13), or be prepared to restore from backup to another node and reconfigure each of your OMSs using the Enterprise Manager Configuration

Assistant in case of failure. Depend on the latter option only if you are not concerned about historical data, job, and event history, and changes to configuration since the last backup of the repository. If you use a TNS alias to configure your OMS instead of the service specification used by JDBC (<host>:<port>:<sid>), then you can configure your TNS alias to use failover (see Chapter 7 for details) to an activated standby database without administrator intervention.

The repository can be shared by a number of different OMSs to distribute the OMS process and network workloads. To create a new OMS that uses an existing repository, just use the Enterprise Manager Configuration Assistant on the node where you want to create the OMS service and follow the path for using an existing repository. You will need to know the EM repository schema name and password.

If you use the default setup of the OMS and you did not happen to take down the generated schema password, or you change the schema password, you will have to run the Enterprise Manager Configuration Assistant again to reset your configuration. In the case of a forgotten schema password, you will need to log in as a database administrator to the database containing the repository and change the password as in the following example:

```
Alter user OEM_FOXRUN_OEMREP identified by oem0nf8xrnIs;
```

This changes the password for the repository and allows you to reconfigure your OMS to use this repository connection information.

OMS Performance and Configuration

The OMS provides a good chunk of management functionality and can become overloaded if given too much to do. It can also help to saturate a network with all that it does to monitor node and Agent availability. OMS configuration files are found in %ORACLE_HOME%\ sysman\config. Particular files of interest are listed here:

omsconfig.properties This is the general OMS configuration file.

dbappscfg.properties Use this file to configure variables for the database applications of the console. If you need to alter the SQL worksheet NLS parameters, this is the starting point.

reporting.properties Examine the properties generated by the **oemctl configure rws** command.

If you have an OMS monitoring more than 64 nodes, then you may want to look at adding additional OMSs or altering the ping interval. By default, all nodes and Agents are pinged every two minutes. You can alter this interval by setting the following parameter in your omsconfig.properties file:

```
oms.vpd.ping_interval=<number of minutes between pings>
```

If you have an unreliable network, you can alter the number of retries to connect to the Agent in the omsconfig.properties file with the following parameter:

```
oms.vgd.conn_retries=<number>
oms.vgd.conn_retries_delay=<number of seconds between retries>
```

The CONN_RETRIES number represents the maximum number of attempts to connect to the Agent. CONN_RETRIES_DELAY indicates the time between retries. CONN_RETRIES_DELAY defaults to 5. By default, the OMS will not even try to reconnect before firing the NodeUpDown event. (Once the node has been seen as up again at the next ping, the NodeUpDown event will be cleared.) In essence, only set CONN_RETRIES to avoid false NodeUpDown events. For unreliable networks, you might want to set this parameter as high as 3. If you use the default ping interval of 2 minutes, set CONN_RETRIES to 3, and leave the delay at the default of 5 seconds, the NodeUpDown event will allow for up to 2 minutes and 15 seconds of network problems before being triggered.

You can limit the number of simultaneous connections (default limit of 64) from the OMS to remote Agents via this parameter in the omsconfig.properties file:

```
oms.vgd.max_out_cons=<max number of simultaneous outgoing connections>
```

Ultimately this should specify at least the number of managed nodes.

As events occur and job status changes on a node, the Agent is tasked with communicating this information to the OMS so that it can, in turn, notify the proper authorities. In an environment where the OMS may be overloaded, you can alter the maximum number of incoming connections from the Agent. The default maximum number of incoming connections is 32. In order to maintain performance, you should keep this parameter set to less than half the maximum number of outgoing connections. Set this parameter in your omsconfig.properties file as such:

```
oms.vgd.max_in_cons=<max number of simultaneous incoming connections>
```

If the OMS loses connectivity to the repository, then there are attempts to reestablish the connection. The properties of this methodology are configured by the following parameters in the omsconfig.properties file:

```
oms.repository.connect_timeout=<number of seconds>
oms.repository.connect_numTries=<max number of connection attempts>
```

The interval between connection establishment attempts is CONNECT_TIMEOUT divided by CONNECT_NUMTRIES. If you use the defaults of timeout at 120 and numTries at 12, then the interval between connection attempts is 10 seconds (120/12=10).

Preparing Instances to Be Managed

Before you can use much of the database functionality in reporting and collecting performance data, you need to create a role that is granted to the user indicated in the connection to a database, usually in your preferred credentials. This role is created in any database version by running the catsnmp.sql script from an Oracle9i home. You can find this file under %ORACLE_HOME%\rdbms\admin. It is important that you run the latest version of catsnmp.sql to properly create the role to interact with the Oracle9i version of EM. You need to run this script as the sys user. After you have created the OEM_MONITOR role with this script, you need to grant it to the database user identified in your preferred credentials. For example, if your preferred credentials to connect to the prod.us.oracle.com database target are em_mon/em4me, then you need to run something like the following:

```
SQL> connect /as sysdba
SQL> grant oem_monitor to em_mon;
Grant succeeded.
```

The other more obvious step is to make sure that you have the 9i Agent installed and running. The 9i Agent is needed to enable much of the new functionality. You can verify the availability of the Agent from the command line as follows:

```
c:\oracle>agentctl status

DBSNMP for 32-bit Windows: Version 9.0.1.0.1 - Production on 20-SEP-2001
14:56:35

Copyright (c) 2001 Oracle Corporation.  All rights reserved.

Version              : DBSNMP for 32-bit Windows: Version 9.0.1.0.1 -
Production
Oracle Home          : c:\oracle\901
Started by user      : SYSTEM
agent is running since 09/18/01 19:07:56
```

If you do not have the Agent on the node you wish to manage targets on, and you will not be able to install the Agent, you can gain *very* limited functionality by adding the database as a target manually during discovery (select Discover Nodes from the Navigator pull-down menu). The Standalone Console also allows you to add database targets by looking at your tnsnames.ora file.

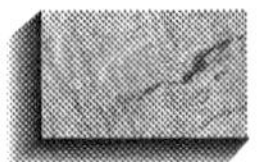

NOTE
Functionality without the Agent on a node is restricted to limited functions only on a database target with an up-and-running listener. If you do not plan on using the Agent, you should not plan on using EM as the be-all end-all tool for managing your database because it has no understanding of your box, listener, or other targets on the same box as your database.

Directory Structure

You can learn a good bit just by roaming around the directory structure of the OMS by looking under the %ORACLE_HOME%\sysman directory. For more detailed information, check out Appendix A of the *Oracle Enterprise Manager Configuration Guide,* downloadable from http://docs.oracle.com. Following is discussion of some of the interesting directory structures and some of their files.

OH\sysman\admin

This directory contains OMS migration scripts and files used to create the OMS and its repository. If you are interested in using more information from the repository in your reports, you will likely want to familiarize yourself with some of these files. Some of the SQL scripts do have helpful commenting. If you are interested in the innards of the reports, check out the agent_reports.tar file.

OH\sysman\config

This is the directory where you will find configuration files for the OMS, console, and the Reporting web site. The omsconfig.properties file is the primary OMS configuration file you will be interested in. See the previous information under "OMS Performance and Configuration" for details on OMS configuration.

OH\sysman\log

If you are having trouble diagnosing what is wrong with your OMS, check out the oms.nohup file for problems. This is the log of output from the running OMS and is appended to OMS recycling. Hopefully, you will find the statement "The OMS is now started and ready" at the bottom of your oms.nohup file.

OH\sysman\report and OH\sysman\reporting

Any reports that you generate from the locally installed console (as opposed to from the web console) will be found under the report directory structure. The foundational images used to generate saved reports are found under the reporting\gif structure.

Tracing, Logging, and Troubleshooting the OMS

If you experience problems with the OMS that are not identified by the oms.nohup file in the OH\sysman\log directory, you can add greater logging of events in the omsconfig.properties file:

```
logging.enabled=true
logging.dir=C:\\oracle\\myomslogs
logging.filename=myomslog
logging.max_size=5
logging.max_file_cnt=4
logging.save_previous_log=true
```

Note the double backslashes for the directory. If you do not specify the directory, the log will be writing to the same location as the oms.nohup file, OH\sysman\log. The MAX_SIZE parameter is in megabytes. Once the maximum size is reached, more logging will prompt the system to move the current log to myomslog.1. This cycling will occur up to four times before data is deleted as per the MAX_FILE_CNT parameter setting. The SAVE_PREVIOUS_LOG setting keeps the logs from being deleted upon restart of the OMS. By default, the previous OMS session's logs are deleted upon startup of a new session. For more details, check out Appendix B in the *Oracle Enterprise Manager Configuration Guide*, which you can download from http://docs.oracle.com as an Adobe Acrobat file.

EM Web Reporting

As we mentioned previously, EM reporting is built upon the Oracle HTTP Server. The Oracle HTTP Server is in turn built upon the Apache web server with Jserv and Oracle's JSP container. The EM reporting feature is driven by services that generate the reports from the OMS and the web server where those reports are published. Each report has a definition that the OMS will use to build the report. A report definition is made up of report elements. Example elements are listed here:

HTML Free-form custom HTML you can add for notation or look and feel (LAF)

Queries SQL that you enter that will be transformed into results in a table

Service levels Time-based statistics for services that are monitored (only available with the Diagnostics Pack)

You can set up reports to be run at an interval, reducing load on the managed systems, the OMS, and the Servlet engine, or dynamically, such that each hit on a page reruns the services needed to build the report as defined. There are a wide variety of standard reports that act as a great starting point and as exemplars for your own reports.

Although the initial page can be found quickly on your system at port 3339, you will need to do a bit of configuration before you can effectively use any of the features. If you do not do this configuration, the EM web site will generate the following error message: "No OMS location specified for the Servlet to connect to. Make sure that reporting has been successfully configured for this web server." Here is a recipe for the Reports web site configuration:

1. Make sure that the Oracle Apache HTTP Server is up and running (either the start the Command Console from the Programs menu or the check that the OracleHTTPServer_<oracle_home_name> service is up and running).
2. Once you have an up-and-running Management Server with repository (OMS), log in to the console as a super administrator (for example, sysman/oem_temp).
3. Select the Manage Administrators option from the Configuration pull-down menu. This option will not be available if the user you are logged in as is not a super administrator.
4. You will notice that even right after initial creation of the OMS, there is a REPORTS_USER. From the console's list of report definitions, you will also see that the majority of reports are owned by REPORTS_USER. Click Edit to change this user's password.
5. From the resulting dialog box, set the password to something secure that you will use in a later step to configure your EM web site and click OK. The password *must* be different from the default oem_temp.
6. Start a command line (select Start | Run and enter **cmd**).
7. Enter the following line:

   ```
   C:\> oemctl configure rws
   ```

8. This will prompt you for the hostname of the OMS, as well as the Reporting web site and the REPORTS_USER password. Here is an example session:

   ```
   c:\oracle>oemctl configure rws
   Configuring the reporting web server...

   This command line utility configures a web server on this machine so that
   it can be used for Enterprise Manager reporting.  Answer each prompt and
   hit return.  After you answer each prompt, you will be asked for
   confirmation
   ```

Tracing, Logging, and Troubleshooting the OMS

```
before the web server is configured.

To quit this utility, hit CTRL-C.
For Help, see EM_ReportingConfig.HTML.

Webserver Name [default is foxrun]:
Port number [default is 3339]:
Oracle Management Server [default is foxrun]:
Password for the REPORTS_USER Administrator : oracle_rocks

You have provided all of the information required to configure the web
server.
Configure the web server now? [Y/N, default is Y]: y

CONFIGURATION COMPLETED: The webserver has been successfully configured.
You can now access the Enterprise Manager Reporting Home Page using the URL
http://foxrun:3339/em/OEMNavigationServlet.
You can also access the Reporting Home page using the View Published Reports
menu command in the Enterprise Manager Console.
```

9. If your OMS and web server are on two or more machines, then you will need to follow steps 6 through 8 for each web site–OMS pair.

Check again to ensure that you have things properly configured by returning to http://<webhostname>:3339/em/OEMGenerationServlet?reportName=EM_REPORTING_HOMEPAGE. If you get an error connecting to the OMS, make sure that your OMS is on a static IP machine. Other possible problems are listed here:

The hostname cannot be resolved (DNS setup).

The OMS is not up and running.

The EM web site is not yet properly configured.

There is a firewall between the OMS and the EM web site.

You can do a quick check if you do an nslookup operation on both the IP and the hostname of the OMS *from the web server*. For example, run an nslookup from the web server (**nslookup foxrun**). This command returns an IP address for the hostname if the host is properly configured in DNS. Next, run nslookup on the returned IP nslookup 138.2.85.44.

One of the problems mentioned previously is the proper configuration of the EM web site. If you have installed the web site along with the Oracle HTTP Server, then usually this configuration should be fine. To check configuration, look at the Apache configuration files in the Apache home located under %ORACLE_HOME%\Apache\Apache\conf. In this directory, you will find the main httpd.conf Apache configuration file. Near the end of this file, you will find an include (ifile=.) for the oracle_apache.conf file also found in the same location as the httpd.conf file. In the oracle_apache.conf file, you (hopefully) will find the EM web site configuration file included. The EM configuration file is %ORACLE_HOME%\oem_webstage\oem.conf, and its contents should look something like this:

```
Listen 3339
<VirtualHost _default_:3339>

ServerName foxrun
DocumentRoot "c:\oracle\901/oem_webstage/"
<Directory "c:\oracle\901/oem_webstage/">
    Options Indexes FollowSymLinks
    AllowOverride None
    Order allow,deny
    Allow from all
</Directory>

DirectoryIndex emwebsite.html
ScriptAlias /cgi-bin/ "c:\oracle\901/oem_webstage/cgi-bin/"
ScriptAlias /oem_webstage/cgi-bin/ "c:\oracle\901/oem_webstage/cgi-bin/"
Alias /oem_webstage/ "c:\oracle\901/oem_webstage/"

<Directory "c:\oracle\901/oem_webstage/cgi-bin/">
    AllowOverride all
    Allow from all
</Directory>

ApJServMount /em /oemreporting

</VirtualHost>
```

If this is not similar to your configuration, alter it to conform and bounce the HTTP Server to effect the changes.

Another thing to check for is the existence of another web server running on the same box. Microsoft's IIS and Oracle's HTTP Server installed in another home are the more common perpetrators of this problem. Disable these additional services in the meantime to prevent problems from the Services MMC (see Chapter 3 for more information on the MMC options).

Using the Reporting Web Site

The EM Reporting web site comes with a large number of prepackaged reports you can review the definitions of from the OMS-connected console under Report Definitions, as shown in Figure 8-14. These reports are published if there is a plus sign (+) appended to the icon in the first column, and unpublished reports have a small red *X* appended to the icon in the first column. In this example, Reporting Home Page is not published and Jobs In Library is published.

The Reporting home page is an overview of the current status of all managed systems in your OMS (see Figure 8-15). This page has a matrix of all target types (first column), with the number of targets for each event status in that category populating each row. You can use this home page as a one-stop availability status for your shop's systems.

Every report includes the category and subcategory as part of its definition. The category refers to the tabs for a target's set of reports. The General tab is the initial

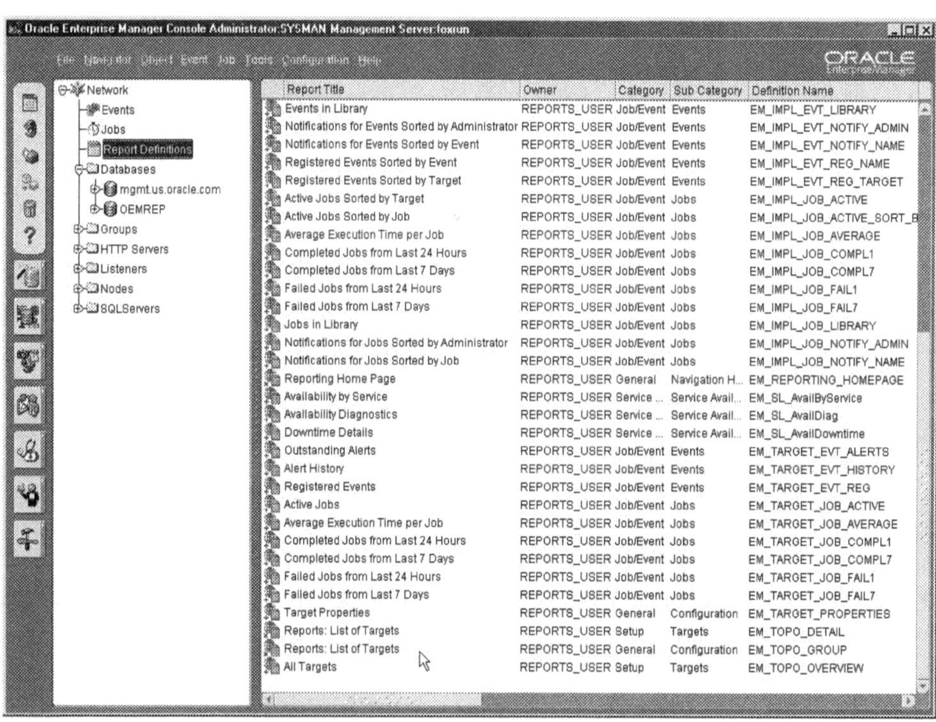

FIGURE 8-14. *Report definitions in the console*

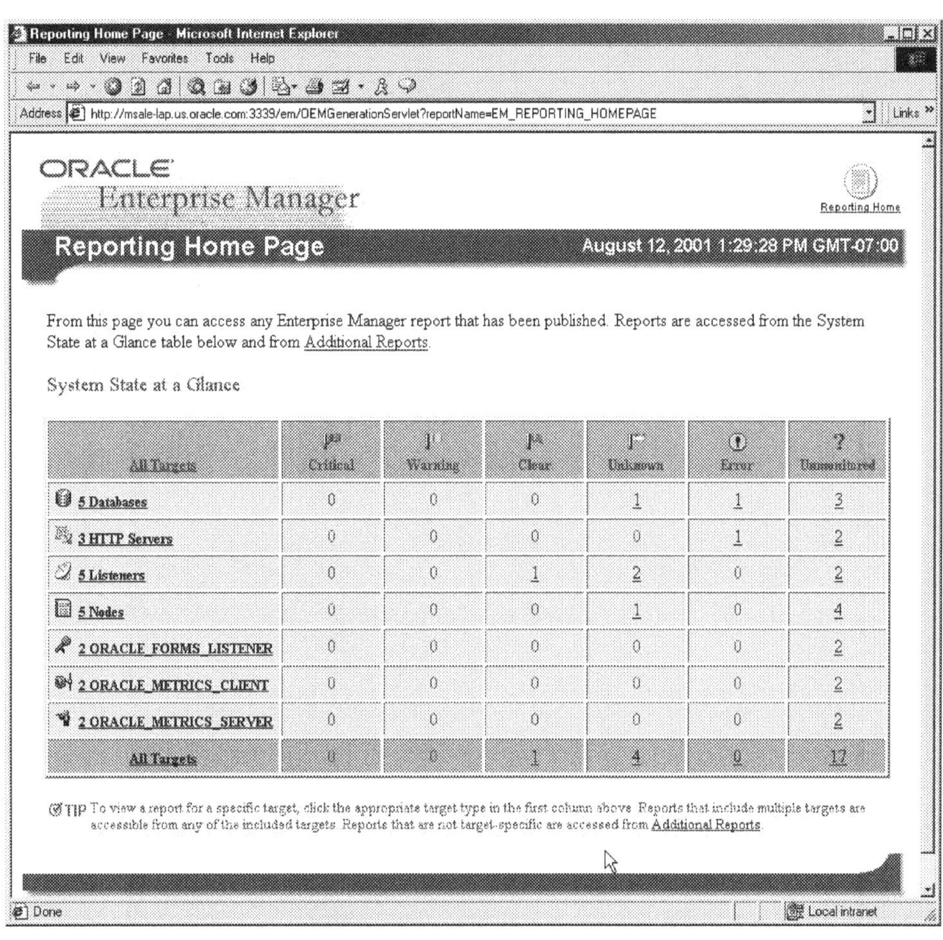

FIGURE 8-15. *EM Reporting home page*

tab that appears for each target's set of reports, and it corresponds to the General category. The subcategory corresponds to the column running down the left of the target's reporting page for that category. From Figure 8-14, you can see that the Target Properties report is going to be found on the General tab when the Configuration subcategory is selected from the left column as a report available to run. If you edit the report (right-click the report and select Edit), you can see that this report is published for All Managed Targets so you know that you will find this report as part of any target's set of reports (see Figure 8-16). If you view the last tab of the report definition, you can also see that this report is generated every time the report is selected for viewing (see Figure 8-17).

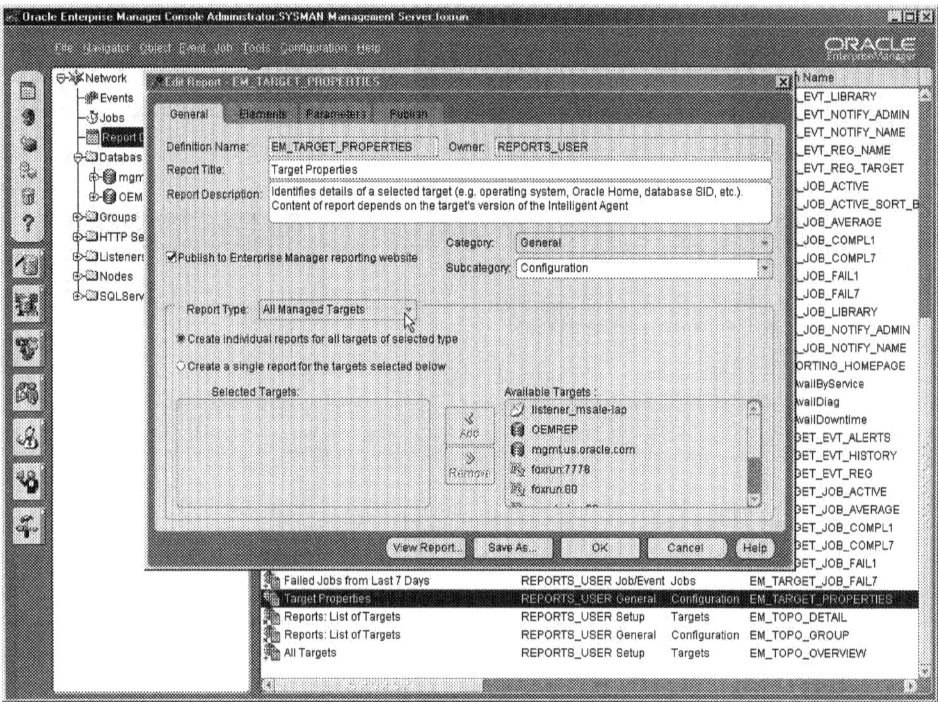

FIGURE 8-16. *EM report definition*

Custom Reports

If you find that the existing reports do not meet your needs, you can alter existing reports, create new reports based on existing reports, or create your own reports from scratch. The existing reports offer a great collection of reports you can use as exemplars. Reports created by REPORTS_USERS can display data derived from the repository database in your custom reports. Therefore, you can log in as the EM repository database user, and create tables and other objects that you can use in your own custom reports. Even better, create your new objects in a separate schema and grant explicit rights to the EM schema directly.

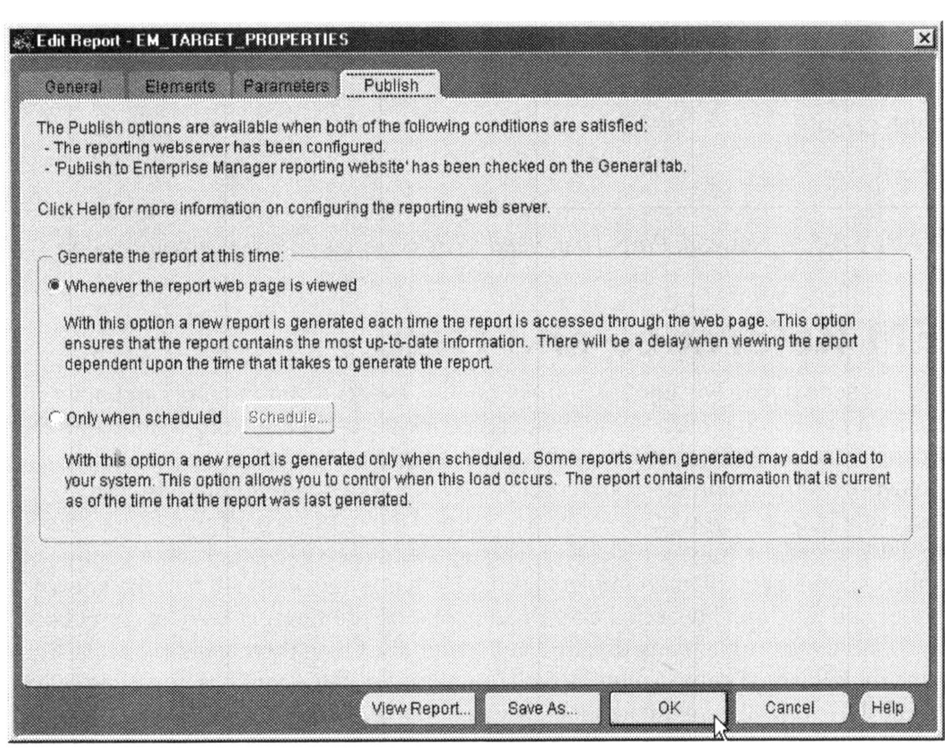

FIGURE 8-17. *EM report publishing options*

EM 3-Tier Infrastructure and Firewalls

Previous versions of EM made working with elements of the 3-tier architecture that were separated by firewalls very difficult to manage. Oracle has a technical white paper titled *Using Oracle Enterprise Manager with Firewalls and VPNs* to clarify the things you need to do to allow EM to work across these secure boundaries. The matrix in Table 8-5 comes from that white paper and is only meant to act as a reference of the essentials you need to know. The ports used need to be open between the hosts. For example, if you have a firewall between your OMS and the Agent, you need to open up ports 1748, 1754, 7772, and 7773 for bidirectional communication between the node running the OMS and the node running the Agent. Make sure that you understand the ramifications of opening up ports in your firewall. Work with your network security people to develop a solution that doesn't jeopardize the security of all of your systems.

	Management Server (OMS)
EM Console	7771–7777
Web Console	7771–7777 and 3339
Agent	1748, 1754, 7772, 7773

TABLE 8-5. *Network Ports That Need to Be Opened for EM Communication*

EM Reference and Help

EM has such a massive amount of functionality, events it can monitor, and other things it can do, that making the right choice means using the Help system and documentation. You can find constantly updated information at Oracle Technology Network (http://otn.oracle.com) and the Oracle9i documentation set at http://docs.oracle.com. If you haven't already learned the hard way, let me advise you to always read the release notes and readme files of *every* Oracle product and subcomponent you plan on implementing. Here is where you will find the known issues and functionality added after documentation printings, as well as corrections and clarifications of already documented materials. Often there will be a release note for individual components as well (for example, the Agent has a readme in %ORACLE_HOME%\network\doc). If you find that there is a known issue that keeps you from implementing EM or any other Oracle product, let Oracle know. *It does make a difference!* The more Oracle understands your needs and priorities, the more it will respond to them. In essence, keeping up with the release notes is almost more important than reading the documentation!

Oracle Enterprise Manager Concepts Guide

The *Oracle Enterprise Manager Concepts Guide* gives an overview of the functionality and purpose of EM. Use it to get a deeper understanding of particular components and their intended functionality. This chapter provides much of the information you need to get started with an implementation or improve your existing EM implementation, but the guide will give you the greater detail you need to make key implementation decisions.

Oracle Enterprise Manager Configuration Guide

The *Oracle Enterprise Manager Configuration Guide* lays out the details of implementing and tuning the 3-tier architecture as well as the details of the Standalone Console. This guide will likely be heavily used when you actually start testing and implementing EM features.

Oracle Enterprise Manager Administrator's Guide

Once you have EM up and running, you will use this guide to best understand and utilize the various functions of the EM system. The details and caveats of various job types are spelled out here. A detailed explanation of setting up the paging functionality is found in its first chapter. If you want to use EM's RMAN interface, the *Oracle Enterprise Manager Administrator's Guide* is the place to start.

Oracle Intelligent Agent User's Guide

The *Oracle Intelligent Agent User's Guide* provides you with exacting details of the discovery process. It explains upgrading and migrating configurations from previous Agents to the 9i Agent. Here is where you will find a guide to creating your own jobs and events with OraTCL. However, we suggest that you use the Diagnostic Pack's functionality that allows you to use any scripting language hosted by the OS that leverages your shop's existing scripting skills and scripts. Appendix A in this guide is devoted to the configuration files related to the Agent, and therefore to service discovery, logging, and tracing. It also has information on troubleshooting, advice on configuration, and more.

The Management Packs

The *Getting Started...* guides provide an overview of the functions the Management Packs add to the EM system. If you only implement one pack, we suggest it be the Diagnostic Pack. This pack provides more value in the long term with the Capacity Planner, Advanced Events, and Performance Manager features. With Advanced Events, you can leverage the monitoring scripts already in your arsenal in the EM framework, ensuring greater productivity and availability.

Oracle Enterprise Manager Event Test Reference Manual

This document is just what is says, a copious reference to the various events you can test for and respond to with the job system. Each operating system's events are spelled out and explained. Much of this can also be found in the Help system explained next, but an independent printed reference is always nice!

EM Help

The help accessible from the EM console is actually rather extensive and can be accessed from the web client or locally. You can use the context-sensitive help to explore and increase your knowledge over time. With the Performance and Diagnostic Packs, you can use the context-sensitive help and the advice to address areas of weakness in your understanding of the database. On a system where the

EM client is installed, you can find the documentation in the following locations for direct access:

Oracle Database %ORACLE_HOME%\doc\EM\Webhelp\dba\dba.htm

Windows %ORACLE_HOME%\doc\EM\Webhelp\nt_os\NT_OS.htm

Oracle Applications %ORACLE_HOME%\doc\EM\Webhelp\oafnd\OAFND.htm

You can also find the documentation for Solaris, AIX, HP-UX, Tru64, and SAP under the Webhelp directory. There is a wealth of information to be found in the Help system, and the web interface includes a search function.

Oracle's Support Web Site

Make sure to frequent Oracle's Support web site (currently http://metalink.oracle.com) for bug fixes for the Agent and the OMS. EM patches are not included with database patches. EM patches may be specific to the OMS (and its repository), a particular tool, or the Agent. Make sure you understand how and when to apply a patch before you implement it, and test it before you roll it out into production. Do not apply a patch unless you are experiencing a problem addressed by that patch or when a security issue is addressed by the patch.

Use the EM Technical Library and Forums to do research and find out more about what others may be doing. Search for examples and solutions to issues you may be encountering. Finally, enjoy the time regained by a proper EM implementation by taking the authors of this book out to dinner!

Summary

We have examined the capabilities of the EM system and given you methods for usage. Remember that EM is ultimately only a tool to add to your toolkit to address complex issues. We suggest that you use independent verification and have backup plans for any management system you put into place no matter what enterprise management solution you choose to use.

CHAPTER 9

Advanced Management, Tools, and Analysis

Chapter 9 picks up where Chapter 8 left off: after essential Oracle EM, what else can we do? This chapter provides an overview of other tools and techniques available for enterprise management on Window 2000. We will introduce pieces of a good database administrator's toolkit and then provide examples of how to use all those tools to create and run a hot backup from within the database. In this chapter, we review the following tools, tips, and techniques:

- Using iSQL*Plus to run SQL scripts with only a web browser
- Reading from and writing to files on Windows 2000 file systems with UTL_FILE
- Sending e-mail from within the database via UTL_SMTP
- Using the database job facility with DBMS_JOB
- Leveraging Java stored procedures
- Sending e-mail from the command line or within your batch files with Blat
- Using Perl to manage your database and the operating system environment
- Using CVS for version control
- Understanding Statspack
- Accessing flat files totally outside database control with standard SQL
- Using the Oracle-supplied PL/SQL packages

Techniques with Tools

In this section, we introduce you to a number of tools new in Oracle9i and show you how to use them to accomplish the task of dynamically creating a backup script and running the script on a schedule managed by the Oracle database job subsystem. Use these tools and techniques as a starting point for more effective system and database management.

iSQL*Plus: SQL from a Browser

One of the great new features of Oracle9i is the introduction of a new incarnation of SQL*Plus that allows you to run most scripts from a web browser. iSQL*Plus is a module that is installed as part of the Oracle HTTP Server. Figure 9-1 shows the initial login screen you will receive at the URL http://<Oracle HTTP Server hostname>/isqlplus. From here you can either leave the Connection Identifier field blank to connect to the default database local to the machine and the Oracle home hosting the Oracle HTTP Server. If you would like to connect to a database other than the iSQL*Plus Oracle home's default database, you must use a valid connection descriptor. In addition, you can use a TNS alias that can be resolved from the local tnsnames.ora file, or you can enter the complete address string (see Chapter 3 for more details).

Once you have made the connection to the database, you can enter SQL statements freehand or you can load a SQL script from your local file system. If your SQL script uses prompts, you will be forwarded to a web page that asks you to enter values for each of the variables in your script when you execute your script. Once you fill these values in, you submit the script for execution, and the results are returned to your browser (see Figure 9-2).

Often, you may want to save the results to a file or display the results in a separate window that you can then save as an HTML file for later display or publishing to your internal administrative web site. To change the output, you only need to select the alternative File or Window, and execute the statement as shown in Figure 9-3. If you choose Window, a new browser window will pop up with the results (see Figure 9-3). If you select the File output option, you will be prompted for a location where you want to save the results. The resulting HTML file is equivalent to the HTML generated with the Window option. The File option is valuable for very

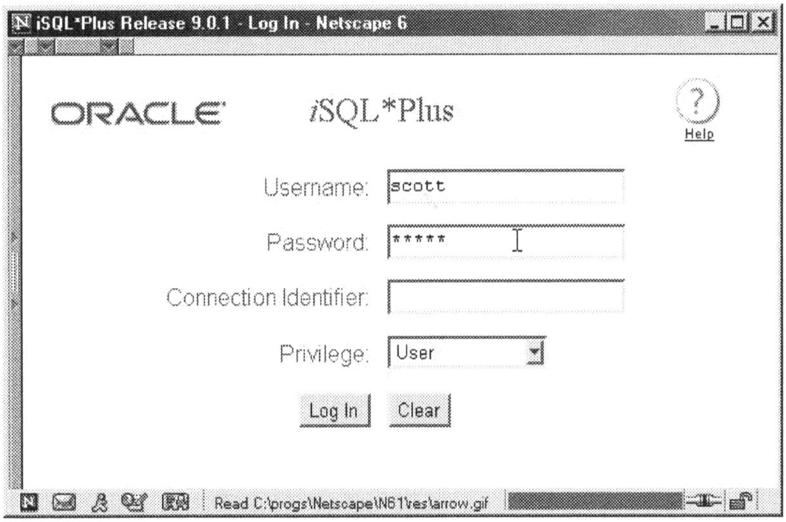

FIGURE 9-1. *iSQL*Plus login screen*

iSQL*Plus Release 9.0.1 Report - Netscape 6

EMPNO	ENAME	JOB	MGR	HIREDATE	SAL	COMM	DEPTNO
7369	SMITH	CLERK	7902	17-DEC-80	800	0	20
7499	ALLEN	SALESMAN	7698	20-FEB-81	1600	0	30
7521	WARD	SALESMAN	7698	22-FEB-81	1250	0	30
7566	JONES	MANAGER	7839	02-APR-81	2975	0	20
7654	MARTIN	SALESMAN	7698	28-SEP-81	1250	0	30
7698	BLAKE	MANAGER	7839	01-MAY-81	2850	0	30
7782	CLARK	MANAGER	7839	09-JUN-81	2450	0	10
7788	SCOTT	ANALYST	7566	19-APR-87	3000	0	20
7839	KING	PRESIDENT		17-NOV-81	5000	0	10
7844	TURNER	SALESMAN	7698	08-SEP-81	1500	0	30
7876	ADAMS	CLERK	7788	23-MAY-87	1100	0	20
7900	JAMES	CLERK	7698	03-DEC-81	950	0	30
7902	FORD	ANALYST	7566	03-DEC-81	3000	0	20
7934	MILLER	CLERK	7782	23-JAN-82	1300	0	10

14 rows selected.

Document: Done (4.396 secs)

FIGURE 9-2. *iSQL*Plus Query Results*

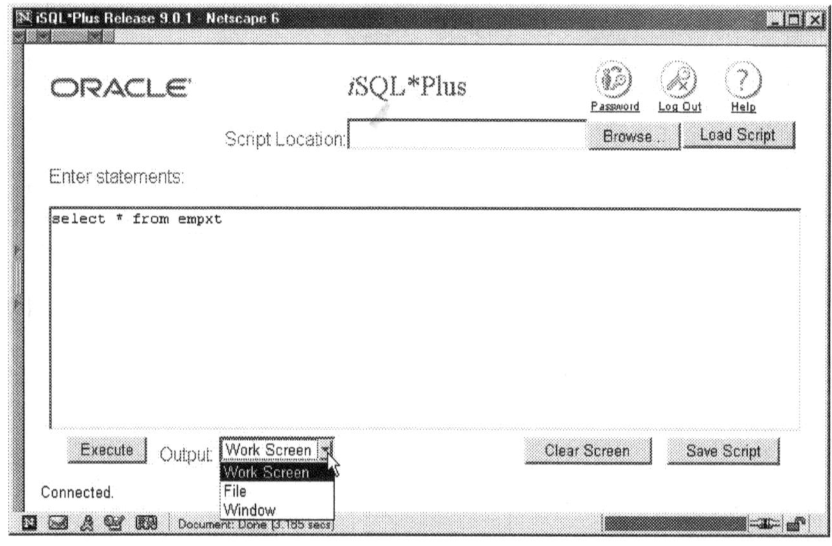

FIGURE 9-3. *Selecting iSQL*Plus output*

large result sets. Every time you use the Window option, it spawns a new browser window. This feature is useful if you want to keep a set of data available for reference to make other queries (for example, identifying session activity from the SID value of V$SESSION to make queries against VSQL, VTRANSACTION, V$SESSTAT, and other session statistic tables).

iSQL*Plus Configuration

iSQL*Plus configuration depends on a chain of configuration related to the Oracle HTTP Server. The server is started from the Programs menu under the Oracle HTTP Server menu of the Oracle9i home or as a service titled OracleService <OHomeName> HTTPServer. If you cannot get the login screen from the http://<host>/isqlplus URL, then check these configuration details:

Look in the %ORACLE_HOME%\Apache\Apache\conf\httpd.conf file for an include statement that looks similar to this one near the end of the file:

```
# Include the Oracle configuration file for custom settings
include "c:\oracle\901\Apache\Apache\conf\oracle_apache.conf"
```

If the previous include statement is present, make sure that the indicated file is there, and then examine oracle_apache.conf for the following line:

```
include "c:\oracle\901\sqlplus\admin\isqlplus.conf"
```

If the isqlplus.conf inclusion is present, follow the path to review the content of the file. In particular, look within the Directory tag for Allow and Deny declarations.

```
<Directory "c:\oracle\901\sqlplus\admin\iplus">
   AllowOverride None
   Options None
   Order deny,allow
   Deny from all
   Allow from localhost
</Directory>
```

If your system is only set to Deny All, then you will not be able to access even the login screen. In the case of a tool this powerful, which is essentially anonymous in use, you will want to restrict access in most cases. If you are having trouble connecting because you are prompted for a password that you do not have, you likely need to initialize the password file iplusdba.pw or iplus.pw in %ORACLE_ HOME%\sqlplus\admin.

In most cases, you will want to enable some basic form of security in addition to the Allow/Deny host capability. The Oracle HTTP Server provides for many forms of

authentication. We talk about the basic authentication method here, but you can use one of many other more complex methods.

To initialize the password file, use the htpasswd.exe utility found in %ORACLE_HOME%\Apache\Apache\bin. Here is an example that generates the password file that allows you to connect as sysdba from iSQL*Plus:

```
htpasswd -b iplusdba.pw <username> <password>
```

Once you have added an entry to the password file, you need to make sure that basic authentication is properly configured in the isqlplus.conf file mentioned earlier. The standard installation is set up to force basic authentication. The Location tag should look like this:

```
<Location /isqlplusdba>
  SetHandler iplus-handler
  Order deny,allow
  AuthType Basic
  AuthName 'iSQL*Plus DBA'
  AuthUserFile c:\oracle\901\sqlplus\admin\iplusdba.pw
  Require valid-user
</Location>
```

The key things to copy from this configuration are the last four lines inside the tag. AuthUserFile should point to your modified or generated password file.

You should be very careful when granting the sysdba right because a user with this capability can shut down any database that allows remote sysdba connections and access passwords used in database links to other databases stored in the data dictionary. In general, avoid granting this right on a node outside your corporate firewall.

Use the UTL_FILE Package to Access the Windows 2000 File System

How do you access information in operating system files from the Oracle database? The UTL_FILE package provides this functionality. Because this opens up a gigantic security hole, you need to be careful how you implement this functionality.

UTL_FILE_DIR and File Permissions

Before you can use the UTL_FILE package, you need to do some initial setup. In your init.ora or your SPFILE, add at least one value for UTL_FILE_DIR. This initialization parameter indicates where UTL_FILE will be enabled for activity. If you set this parameter to "*", it completely opens up all directories for access by the UTL_FILE package. Well, not really—each of these file systems also need to be accessible by the user who starts the RDBMS Service. Upon service creation, this user is set to the local OS user SYSTEM. You may have changed this to enable Oracle Service access to remote file systems or to tighten up security. You can check this by examining the Log On As column of the Services MMC. If it displays LocalSystem, then the special user SYSTEM accesses the file system as directed by UTL_FILE. In order to tighten security, you should do the following:

Remove the special Everyone user from the list of users who can access the directories indicated in UTL_FILE_DIR.

Add the user that runs the Oracle Service (defaults to the special user SYSTEM) to the list of users who can access the directory and the files contained and make sure that this user has at least the Modify privilege.

You can set the allowable location or locations in a parameter file or in the SPFILE. Here is an example of setting that parameter in the SPFILE in an up-and-running instance that had an SPFILE specified at startup:

```
alter system set utl_file_dir='c:\utl_file' scope=spfile;
```

Repeating this command for each directory will only replace the previous value. If you want to use multiple UTL_FILE_DIR settings with an SPFILE, then save your SPFILE as an init.ora file, add the multiple UTL_FILE_DIR lines, and create a new SPFILE from that init.ora file. Because UTL_FILE_DIR is a static parameter, this change will not take place until you restart the instance. If you decide to use the parameter file instead (we would actually suggest that you always back up your SPFILE to a parameter file), then add a line for each directory to be used by UTL_FILE. If the directory includes a space in the name, you can either use the 8-character equivalent of the long name or enclose the value in double quotes in the init.ora, as shown here:

```
UTL_FILE_DIR=c:\utl_file
UTL_FILE_DIR="c:\Program File\Oracle"
```

If these entries are not on consecutive lines, then only the last one listed will be in effect after startup with that PFILE. If you have set up the Oracle Services to access remote drives with the share mechanism, then you can specify the remote location with UNC notation:

```
UTL_FILE_DIR=c:\utl_file
UTL_FILE_DIR="c:\Program File\Oracle"
UTL_FILE_DIR="\\pager-pc\logging\oralogs"
```

In this last line, pager-pc is the NetBios name of the computer, typically the hostname, followed by the remote share name, and finally the path from the root of the share, the oralogs directory in this case.

After you have set the init.ora parameter and file system permissions and restarted the instance, you can identify the value of the parameter from SQL*Plus using the following command:

```
SQL> show parameter file_dir
```

Creating a Stored Procedure That Uses UTL_FILE

Once you have properly configured UTL_FILE_DIR and the underlying directory permissions, you can create a procedure or anonymous PL/SQL block that works in these directories. Here is a simple anonymous block example you can use to test your setup:

```
set serveroutput on
DECLARE
  fd utl_file.file_type;
  v_incoming varchar2(100);
BEGIN
  fd := utl_file.fopen ('c:\temp','touch.txt','w');
  utl_file.put_line (fd, 'Success');
  utl_file.fclose(fd);
  fd := utl_file.fopen ('c:\temp','touch.txt','r');
  utl_file.get_line(fd,v_incoming);
  dbms_output.put_line(v_incoming);
  utl_file.fclose(fd);
EXCEPTION
WHEN UTL_FILE.INVALID_PATH THEN
   UTL_FILE.FCLOSE(fd);
   RAISE_APPLICATION_ERROR(-20000,'Invalid Path');
WHEN UTL_FILE.INVALID_MODE THEN
   UTL_FILE.FCLOSE(fd);
   RAISE_APPLICATION_ERROR(-20001,'Invalid Mode');
WHEN UTL_FILE.INVALID_OPERATION THEN
   UTL_FILE.FCLOSE(fd);
   RAISE_APPLICATION_ERROR(-20002,'Invalid Operation');
WHEN UTL_FILE.INVALID_FILEHANDLE THEN
   UTL_FILE.FCLOSE(fd);
   RAISE_APPLICATION_ERROR(-20003,'Invalid Filehandle');
WHEN UTL_FILE.WRITE_ERROR THEN
   UTL_FILE.FCLOSE(fd);
   RAISE_APPLICATION_ERROR(-20004,'Write Error');
WHEN UTL_FILE.READ_ERROR THEN
   UTL_FILE.FCLOSE(fd);
   RAISE_APPLICATION_ERROR(-20005,'Read Error');
WHEN UTL_FILE.INTERNAL_ERROR THEN
   UTL_FILE.FCLOSE(fd);
   RAISE_APPLICATION_ERROR(-20006,'Internal Error');
```

```
WHEN OTHERS THEN
   UTL_FILE.FCLOSE(fd);
END;
```

You will need to alter the first parameter of the fopen procedure to match one of your UTL_FILE_DIR directories. If you succeed, you will find the touch.txt file that contains the word "Success," and when you run the procedure, it will echo "Success" to the screen. If you need to write a line longer than 1,022 characters, then you will need to add another parameter, an integer, to specify the maximum line length.

Once you have a working, tested configuration, you can create procedures to perform read, write, or append actions on a file. If you want to append to an existing log file, just set the fopen procedure's third argument to "a." If the file does not exist, then append mode will create the file.

Generate Your Hot Backup Script Automatically

Now that you know how to write a file to disk, you can read the appropriate pieces of the data dictionary to create a script that will be used to run a hot backup. Because you read the dictionary just before you actually run the backup, you avoid the issues of moved or added datafiles.

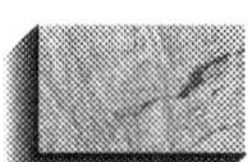

NOTE

To perform this function, you will need to use some procedural logic, and this dictates the use of PL/SQL. We do not feign to teach PL/SQL here, but instead point you to the Oracle Press books by Scott Urman. If you want more trick and tips like these, look to the releases of other Oracle Press books on SQL and PL/SQL.

```
CREATE OR REPLACE procedure cre_backup_script
(p_backup in varchar2 default 'C:\Oracle\backup' ) is
  fd utl_file.file_type;  -- file descriptor
  cursor c_ts is select t.name tablespace, d.name datafile from
          sys.v_$tablespace t, sys.v_$datafile d
          where t.ts#=d.ts# order by t.name;
  v_ts varchar2(30) := '1'; -- create a variable initialized
                            -- to an invalid tablespace name
BEGIN
  fd := utl_file.fopen ('c:\oracle\scripts','hotbackup.sql','w');
  utl_file.put_line(fd,'connect system/manager');
  utl_file.put_line(fd,'alter system switch logfile;');
  -- Loop through tablespaces and datafiles
  for r_ts in c_ts loop
    if v_ts='1' then
```

```
      utl_file.put_line(fd,'alter tablespace '||r_ts.tablespace||
                           ' begin backup;');
      v_ts := r_ts.tablespace;
    elsif v_ts != r_ts.tablespace then
      utl_file.put_line(fd,'alter tablespace '||v_ts||' end backup;');
      utl_file.put_line(fd,'alter tablespace '||r_ts.tablespace||
                           ' begin backup;');
      v_ts := r_ts.tablespace;
    end if;
    utl_file.put_line(fd,'host ocopy '||r_ts.datafile||' '||p_backup);
  end loop;
  utl_file.put_line(fd,'alter tablespace '||v_ts||' end backup;');
  -- add any post datafile sql activities here.
  utl_file.put_line(fd,'exit');
  utl_file.fclose(fd);
  fd := utl_file.fopen('c:\oracle\scripts','hotbackup.cmd','w');
  utl_file.put_line(fd,'sqlplus /nolog
@c:\oracle\scripts\hotbackup.sql');
  utl_file.fclose(fd);
EXCEPTION
    WHEN UTL_FILE.INVALID_PATH THEN
       UTL_FILE.FCLOSE(fd);
       RAISE_APPLICATION_ERROR(-20000,'Invalid Path');
    WHEN UTL_FILE.INVALID_MODE THEN
       UTL_FILE.FCLOSE(fd);
       RAISE_APPLICATION_ERROR(-20001,'Invalid Mode');
    WHEN UTL_FILE.INVALID_OPERATION THEN
       UTL_FILE.FCLOSE(fd);
       RAISE_APPLICATION_ERROR(-20002,'Invalid Operation');
    WHEN UTL_FILE.INVALID_FILEHANDLE THEN
       UTL_FILE.FCLOSE(fd);
       RAISE_APPLICATION_ERROR(-20003,'Invalid Filehandle');
    WHEN UTL_FILE.WRITE_ERROR THEN
       UTL_FILE.FCLOSE(fd);
       RAISE_APPLICATION_ERROR(-20004,'Write Error');
    WHEN UTL_FILE.READ_ERROR THEN
       UTL_FILE.FCLOSE(fd);
       RAISE_APPLICATION_ERROR(-20005,'Read Error');
    WHEN UTL_FILE.INTERNAL_ERROR THEN
       UTL_FILE.FCLOSE(fd);
       RAISE_APPLICATION_ERROR(-20006,'Internal Error');
    WHEN OTHERS THEN
       UTL_FILE.FCLOSE(fd);
END;
/
```

This script creates a PL/SQL procedure that you can run to generate the foundation of a hot backup. The procedure generates two files, the command file you actually run at the OS level and the SQL script that puts a tablespace into backup mode. The procedure then copies the associated datafiles to the backup location, takes the tablespace out of backup mode, and repeats these steps for each process. Here is an example of the generated hotbackup.sql script:

```
connect system/manager
alter system switch logfile;
alter tablespace SYSTEM begin backup;
host ocopy C:\ORACLE\ORADATA\OEMREP\SYSTEM01.DBF C:\Oracle\backup
alter tablespace SYSTEM end backup;
alter tablespace UNDOTBS begin backup;
host ocopy C:\ORACLE\ORADATA\OEMREP\UNDOTBS01.DBF C:\Oracle\backup
alter tablespace UNDOTBS end backup;
alter tablespace CWMLITE begin backup;
host ocopy C:\ORACLE\ORADATA\OEMREP\CWMLITE01.DBF C:\Oracle\backup
alter tablespace CWMLITE end backup;
alter tablespace DRSYS begin backup;
host ocopy C:\ORACLE\ORADATA\OEMREP\DRSYS01.DBF C:\Oracle\backup
alter tablespace DRSYS end backup;
alter tablespace EXAMPLE begin backup;
host ocopy C:\ORACLE\ORADATA\OEMREP\EXAMPLE01.DBF C:\Oracle\backup
alter tablespace EXAMPLE end backup;
alter tablespace INDX begin backup;
host ocopy C:\ORACLE\ORADATA\OEMREP\INDX01.DBF C:\Oracle\backup
alter tablespace INDX end backup;
alter tablespace TOOLS begin backup;
host ocopy C:\ORACLE\ORADATA\OEMREP\TOOLS01.DBF C:\Oracle\backup
alter tablespace TOOLS end backup;
alter tablespace USERS begin backup;
host ocopy C:\ORACLE\ORADATA\OEMREP\USERS01.DBF C:\Oracle\backup
alter tablespace USERS end backup;
exit
```

The procedure also generates the command file that runs this SQL script. Here is the generated output:

```
sqlplus /nolog @c:\oracle\scripts\hotbackup.sql
```

You can add a task via the operating system task scheduler that runs the hotbackup.cmd command file to back up your database. Do *not* just take this script, drop it in, and expect it to complete your backup solution. It is incomplete in that it does not address control files, SPFILEs, password files, and archive and redo logs (V$LOGFILE and V$CONTROLFILE). This version is also sorely lacking error handling and logging of what you actually accomplished. Use it as a foundation to build on as opposed to the final product.

UTL_SMTP: Send Mail from Stored Procedures

UTL_SMTP is the Oracle-supplied package that uses Java Sockets from the UTL_TCP package to send e-mail through your SMTP server. Now you can quickly and easily send e-mail from within the database. For example, if you have an application that keeps user information (such as a web application), including e-mail addresses and passwords, stored in the database, and someone forgets his or her password, you can use UTL_ SMTP to send the user the old password, or you can run a procedure to randomly generate a new password and send that instead. Here is an example of a simple but versatile procedure you can use to send a simple e-mail by passing it the information you would normally provide to your e-mail client software:

```
CREATE OR REPLACE PROCEDURE send_email (
     p_recipient IN VARCHAR2,
     p_message   IN VARCHAR2,
     p_subject in varchar2 default '',
     p_sender IN VARCHAR2 default 'dba@mydomain.com')
IS
    crlf varchar2(2) := chr(13) || chr(10);
    -- make sure you set the proper smtp server for your org here
    v_mailhost     VARCHAR2(30) := 'mysmtpserver.com';
    mail_conn  utl_smtp.connection;
    msg varchar2(4000) := 'Date: ' ||
      TO_CHAR( SYSDATE, 'dd Mon yy hh24:mi:ss' ) || crlf ||
      'From: ' || p_sender || ' <' || p_sender || '>' || crlf ||
      'Subject: ' || p_subject || crlf||
      'To: '|| p_recipient|| ' <' || p_recipient || '>' ||crlf||
      p_message;
BEGIN
    mail_conn := utl_smtp.open_connection(v_mailhost, 25);
    utl_smtp.helo(mail_conn, v_mailhost);
    utl_smtp.mail(mail_conn, p_sender);
    utl_smtp.rcpt(mail_conn, p_recipient);
    utl_smtp.data(mail_conn, msg);
    utl_smtp.quit(mail_conn);
EXCEPTION
    WHEN OTHERS THEN
      -- add your exception handling here. The following lines
      -- are useful for debugging but should NOT be in your
      -- customer facing code!!
      dbms_output.put_line(dbms_utility.format_error_stack);
      dbms_output.put_line(dbms_utility.format_call_stack);
END;
/
```

Once this procedure is created, you can send an e-mail from SQL*Plus on-the-fly like this:

```
SQL> exec send_email('me@mydomain.com','Test','Test Message');
```

This call will attempt to send an e-mail to me@mydomain.com with the subject "Test Message" and the body of the message containing the single word "Test." You may now want to put an ON INSERT trigger on the user registration table for your web site that calls this procedure to confirm and thank users for their registration. This trigger might look like this:

```
Create or replace trigger trg_newuser
before insert on web_users for each row
DECLARE
  v_msg varchar2(400);
  crlf varchar2(2) := chr(13) || chr(10);
BEGIN
v_msg := 'Welcome '|| :new.firstname || ',' || crlf ||
         'We are glad to have you join our team of really ' ||
         'silly people that have nothing better to do! ' || crlf ||
         'Here is your newly assigned password:'|| :new.password
||crlf ||
         'Regards,'||crlf ||
         'The Management';
send_email( p_recipient => :new.email,
            p_message => v_msg,
            p_subject => 'Welcome to Goofy.com!' );
EXCEPTION
  WHEN OTHERS THEN
    --add exception handling code here
    dbms_output.put_line(dbms_utility.format_error_stack);
    dbms_output.put_line(dbms_utility.format_call_stack);
END;
/
```

Now every time your new user process inserts a record into the WEB_USERS table, it will send users an e-mail with their password. You can use UTL_SMTP to help manage your database by sending an alpha page via e-mail as well. There are countless uses for this package.

Using DBMS_JOB to Get Things Done Regularly

DBMS_JOB is the facility that the Oracle database uses to run stored procedures just once at a specified time or at a predetermined interval. For example, you can run a procedure that checks on the health of your database (or another database via a database link) and uses UTL_SMTP to send an e-mail message to your alpha pager. The job facility is also used by Materialized Views to run its refresh at the interval you have specified. There are some minor preliminary steps that must be taken to enable the job system. You must set the initialization parameter JOB_ QUEUE_ PROCESSES to greater than zero. This parameter indicates the maximum

number of job processes (threads in the case of NT/2000) that can be spawned by the database instance. You can set this parameter dynamically (that is, without shutting down the database) by using the alter system syntax:

```
Alter system set job_queue_processes = 5;
```

If you are *not* using an SPFILE to start your database, then you need to add the following line to your init.ora file:

```
job_queue_processes=5
```

Of course, the value of 5 is ambiguously chosen here. Set this parameter according to the maximum load that you want from concurrent jobs running. If you are using an SPFILE, you just need to add the scope clause to the previous alter statement like this:

```
alter system set job_queue_processes = 5 scope=spfile;
```

Now this value will persist across database shutdowns in your SPFILE-enabled startups.

When you create a job as a schema user, that user is the only user who can run or alter the job. The job is truly owned by the schema that submitted it. For this reason, you will have problems trying to run a job that is owned by another user.

As a case study, we will use DBMS_JOB to run a stored procedure that sends an e-mail if the number of processes (the measurement of the number of threads in NT and Windows 2000) is coming close to the process limit of the instance. First, you need to create the procedure that checks for this condition:

```
Create or replace procedure check_status as
v_plimit number;
v_processes_now number;
v_instance varchar2(512);
v_msg varchar2(200);
BEGIN
select to_number(value) into v_plimit from v$parameter
  where name = 'processes';
select count(*) into v_processes_now from v$process;
select global_name into v_instance from global_name;
IF v_processes_now > (v_plimit - 20) THEN
  v_msg := 'The database '||v_instance||
           ' is nearing its process limit at '||v_processes_now;
  send_email('dba@mydomain.com',
             v_msg,
             'Process limit warning from '||v_instance);
END IF;
END;
/
```

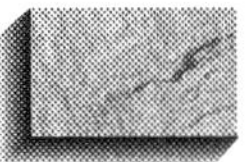

NOTE
In order to have a schema other than SYS compile this properly (even SYSTEM), you must explicitly grant select on SYS.V_$PROCESS and SYS.V_$PARAMETER to that user while connected as SYS.

After creation, you can run this procedure any time to e-mail you when you come within 20 threads of your database instance limit. This isn't much good to you unless it can be run unattended. So now submit a job that runs this procedure every thirty minutes:

```
SQL> set serveroutput on
SQL> declare
  2  v_jno pls_integer;
  3  begin
  4
dbms_job.submit(v_jno,'CHECK_STATUS;',sysdate+5/1440,'sysdate+30/1440');
  5  dbms_output.put_line('The Job Number is: '||v_jno);
  6  end;
  7  /
The Job Number is: 2

PL/SQL procedure successfully completed.
```

You now have a job number of 2 that will first run in five minutes and will be run again every 30 minutes. If you wanted to run this job outside of the schedule, you can execute it any time in SQL*Plus with the following command:

```
exec dbms_job.run(2);
```

If you later decide that you want to remove the job, you can do so with this command:

```
exec dbms_job.remove(2);
```

If you happen to forget the job number, but you remember what the job actually runs, you can run the following statement while connected as the user that submitted the job:

```
SQL> column what format a50
SQL> select job, what from user_jobs;
       JOB WHAT
---------- -------------------------
         2 CHECK_STATUS;
```

You can then use the number in the DBMS_JOB.REMOVE procedure. If your job attempts execution and fails sixteen times, it gets marked as broken and execution will no longer be attempted. To "fix" the job, you need to run the following command:

```
exec dbms_job.broken(2,FALSE);
```

You can also "fix" the job when you force the job to run with the DBMS_JOB.RUN procedure. In this case, the job will attempt execution again and "fix" the job as part of the process.

Java Stored Procedure to Run Commands

One of the common desires of many database administrators is to run an OS command called from within the database. If you have an Oracle database that has the Oracle JVM installed, then you can use this tip to create a Java stored procedure that will allow you to run an OS command from a stored procedure you can call within a PL/SQL stored procedure, package, or function. You can then run this command on a schedule by using the DBMS_JOB package. You can also use UTL_ FILE to generate an OS command script, and then run that script using this functionality.

Create a text file and rename it DoCmd.java, and then edit the file to contain the following code:

```
import java.lang.Runtime;
import java.lang.Process;
import java.io.IOException;
import java.lang.InterruptedException;
class DoCmd {
     public static void main(String args[]) {
          System.out.println("In main");
          try {
               Process p = Runtime.getRuntime().exec(args[0]);
               try {
                  p.waitFor();
               }
               catch(InterruptedException intexc) {
                  System.out.println("InterruptedException on waitFor: " +
                                     intexc.getMessage());
               }
               System.out.println("Return Code:"+ p.exitValue());
          }
          catch (IOException e) {
                System.out.println("IO Exception from exec : " +
                                     e.getMessage());
                System.out.println("Print Stack Dump");
```

```
                    e.printStackTrace();
            }
    }
}
```

Save and close this file. Now make sure that you have the JDK binary directory in your path. If you do not have a JDK installed, but you do have the Oracle HTTP Server installed, you can use the HTTP Server's JDK. To use the HTTP Server's JDK, add the %ORACLE_HOME%\Apache\jdk\bin directory to your path:

```
C:\>set PATH=C:\ORACLE\901\Apache\jdk\bin;%PATH%
```

You can now compile the DoCmd.java file into a class file with the following command:

```
javac DoCmd.java
```

Next, grant JAVASYSPRIV to a user, say, SCOTT, while connected as SYS:

```
SQL> grant javasyspriv to scott;
```

Now SCOTT will be able to execute the procedure once you load the class. Load the class into the database with the following code:

```
C:\src\javacmd> loadjava -resolve -user scott/tiger -v DoCmd.class
arguments: '-resolve' '-user' 'scott/tiger' '-v' 'DoCmd.class'
creating : class DoCmd
loading  : class DoCmd
resolving: class DoCmd
```

The class is now loaded into the database in the SCOTT schema. Now you need to create a wrapper class so that you can call the Java stored procedure from SQL*Plus:

```
SQL> connect scott/tiger
SQL> create or replace procedure runcommand (P_COMMAND VARCHAR2)
  2    AS LANGUAGE JAVA name 'DoCmd.main(java.lang.String[])';
  3  /
Procedure created.
```

To see the output from the command, you need to change the SQL*Plus environment:

```
SQL> set serverout on
SQL> exec dbms_java.set_output(1000);
PL/SQL procedure successfully completed.
```

Now you can see the output from the System.out.println calls in the loaded class. You are ready to run the procedure. Before you do that, however, there is one important thing to note about running programs. You will run any command as the same user that started the Oracle database service. You also need to be careful to specify that the service is allowed to interact with the desktop, in case you call a command that needs to interact with the desktop.

Run a command from within the database:

```
SQL> exec runcommand('c:\oracle\scripts\hotbackup.cmd');
```

This command will run the command file you created previously with UTL_FILE. You could add this call to a procedure that first generates your hot backup file. It might look something like this:

```
create or replace procedure run_backup as
BEGIN
  cre_backup_script('c:\oracle\scripts');
  runcommand('c:\oracle\scripts\hotbackup.cmd');
END;
/
```

This script first runs a procedure that reads the dictionary views and uses the UTL_FILE package to write the proper commands to a file. The next call runs the command file you previously created from the runcommand call.

Next, you will likely want to schedule a time to run the backup, as follows:

```
set serveroutput on
declare
    v_jno pls_integer;
begin
dbms_job.submit(v_jno,'run_backup;',sysdate+5/1440,'sysdate+30/1440');
dbms_output.put_line('The Job Number is: '||v_jno);
end;
/
```

You now have the shell of a job that will run backups for you that automatically compensate for new and removed datafiles. How can you tell what you actually did? Use the next hint to generate an e-mail message that sends a log of the output to your e-mail and pages you if an exception is encountered.

E-mail Notification from the Command Line

One of the key database administrator tasks is to respond to new conditions on a computer, network, database listener, or database that endangers continued database/application availability. So how does a database administrator know if one of these conditions exist? One solution is to use Oracle Enterprise Manager, BMC, HP OpenView, or some other management tool. All these solutions are nice, and in bigger shops where you will have to manage a large number of systems, these more scalable solutions are imperative to effective management—but what about when those systems are not functioning? What about when you need an independent verification of their availability? What if these solutions cost more than your management is willing to spend (and you have plenty of free time on your hands to write and test the scripts they implemented in their systems)? For these situations, you will need to use a very basic, yet functional, tool to send notifications of an actual or potential problem to the responsible database administrators and other responsible or interested parties. On Windows NT or Windows 2000, the tool Blat (http:// www.blat.net) allows you to send e-mail from the command line—it even allows you to attach files to your message. There are other alternatives (for example, Microsoft's Sendmail port at ftp://ftp.microsoft.com/developr/drg/unix-to-windows/ ports/sendmail), but Blat is simple, flexible, and powerful.

Blat is both simple in usage and complex in capability. This program lets you attach files; set the content type (for example, HTML); carbon copy (CC) and blind carbon copy (BCC) recipients; use text files that contain the e-mail addresses for direct, CCed, and BCCed recipients; set the various "from" elements as described in RFCs 821 and 822; and create a log file of Blat actions. Here is a simple example that e-mails the alert log:

```
C:\> blat c:\oracle\admin\prod\bdump\alertprod.log -to dba@yours.com
```

This simple usage requires that you have installed Blat by running Blat with the -install option:

```
C:\> blat -install <server addr> <sender>
```

The <server addr> should be the host name or IP address of your SMTP server and the <sender> is the sender's address known to the SMTP server. You can also identify these elements on the command line:

```
C:\> blat alertprod.log -to dba@yours.com -f admin@yours.com -server
smtp.yours.com
```

You could use this utility to send the contents of files you prepare earlier in a batch file and execute the batch file from within the database with DBMS_JOB and a Java stored procedure as described previously.

Tools for Holistic Database Management

In this section, we introduce you to new Oracle features, and tools and utilities not part of Oracle. In particular, we show you how to use external tables to view structured files as tables from SQL within Oracle9i and how to look at data from a point in time in the past with the DBMS_FLASHBACK package. We also introduce the essentials of Statspack to help you understand the activity and health of your database over time.

We also felt that it is important to introduce you to tools such as Perl and CVS to assist you with the overall management and productivity problems that face database administrators. These tools are free, and the skills developed using them translate well to many other tasks outside of database administration.

Use Perl for Database and System Administration

Perl is one of the gems in your administration toolbox. It is not just a web CGI scripting tool—Perl can be used to manage files, and it more than makes up for the lack of GNU tools for parsing text files. The most difficult part of the Perl learning curve for most people is learning how to use regular expressions effectively.

Perl on the Database Server

If you have completed the 8.1.7 or 9.0.x Enterprise Edition default database installation, then you have also installed Perl version 5.005_03. You can verify this installation at the command line with the following command:

```
c:> perl -version
```

When you install the Oracle HTTP Server, the installation process puts the following path in your Windows 2000 System Path setting: OH\Apache \Perl\ 5.00503\bin\mswin32-x86, where OH represents the Oracle home directory of the installation of the Oracle HTTP Server (or Oracle iAS, for that matter). With just this functionality in place, you can use the following command to check any trace or log file for an ORA- error message or "err" and print that line:

```
perl -ne "print if /ora-/i || /err/i" testALRT.LOG
```

The "i" causes the pattern match to be case insensitive. The double bars (||) force a Boolean OR. This will print any line in testalrt.log that contains "ora-" or "err" regardless of case.

Although Perl originated on Unix, the Windows platform has a benefactor in the Perl world that packages and distributes a version of Perl for the Win32 platform, ActiveState. ActiveState also creates additional development tools that allow you to quickly develop and distribute Perl applications. There are a number of modules that ActiveState packages together as a set of extensions that provides access to the OS through the Windows APIs. These extensions allow you to access and alter the Registry, users, file system, network, event logs, and more. If you decide not to use ActiveState's build of Perl, you can get this same functionality by installing the equivalent modules manually.

Perl is an incredibly powerful tool for processing text. Perl's primary strength on the NT and Windows 2000 platforms is the modules available that allow you to use Perl to access and manipulate many of the services exposed by the operating system without using GUI tools or writing C++ code. Most Perl modules are freely available from CPAN (search.cpan.org) and are easy to find via the search engine. Search Distribution for "win32" to get a good idea of all the Windows-specific modules available to you. Table 9-1 lists some of these modules.

Perl Module	**Description**
Win32::EventLog	Processes the three primary event logs.
Win32::Process	Manages and creates processes.
Win32::TieRegistry	Accesses and alters Registry entries.
Win32::Service	Manages services.
Win32::ODBC	Uses Perl to get database access through an ODBC driver.
Win32::Internet	Accesses Internet resources.
Win32::PerfLib	Accesses the same performance counters as the Perfmon tool from Perl.
Win32::API	Makes calls to the Win32 API from Perl.
DBI	Constitutes the Perl interface to databases. The Oracle database driver is written in OCI code, ensuring fast, efficient access. A search of CPAN for DBI modules also brings up a large number of associated helper modules.

TABLE 9-1. *Useful Perl Modules*

You might want to check a remote system for the existence of trace files on a regular basis. If this system has an FTP server, you can use the Win32::Internet module to check that system and list the files in a directory for you:

```
use Win32::Internet;
$INET = new Win32::Internet();
$INET->FTP($Session, "test.yours.com", "administrator", "password");
$Session->Ascii();
print "BDump Directory\n";
$Session->Cd("/oracle/admin/test/bdump");
@myfiles = $Session->List();
foreach $file (@myfiles) {
print $file, "\n";
$Session->Close();
print "\n\nHit Enter to continue\n";
$wait = <STDIN>;
```

You might also want to create a process that starts up another process from Perl. You can do this with the Win32::Process module, as shown in this script, which starts up an instance of SQL*Plus:

```
use Win32::Process;
#use Win32::FormatMessage;
sub ErrorReport{
                print Win32::FormatMessage( Win32::GetLastError() );
        }
        Win32::Process::Create($ProcessObj,
                                " C:\\oracle\\901\\bin\\sqlplus.exe",
                                " system/manager",
                                0,
                                NORMAL_PRIORITY_CLASS,
                                ".")|| die ErrorReport();
        $ProcessObj->Suspend();
        $ProcessObj->Resume();
        $ProcessObj->Wait(INFINITE);
```

These simple examples give you an idea of the capability of Perl. The other nice thing about Perl is that you can take the skills and scripts you develop in Perl and leverage them on Linux and other flavors of Unix where you may have other Oracle instances. To take this to the next level, start at the ActiveState homepage at http://www.activestate.com.

Tracking Changes: Version Control with CVS and Wincvs

One of the problems with scripts and the edits you make to them over time is that once in a while you want to return to a previous version of a script. When you develop a script library, and you build scripts that call other scripts, if you make a change to one of the underlying scripts, all of the scripts that used to work are now not functional. Although keeping backups helps with this problem, backups do not address situations where you do not discover this problem until after the backup with the needed version has aged out. Version control software is better suited for these purposes (although you want to make sure that you back up the version control system). The open source product Concurrent Versions System (CVS) allows you to do either simple check-in, check-out of your scripts or complex branching, version tags, merging, and many other things.

Wincvs is a GUI front end to CVS on the Windows platform. If you are used to the command-line interface in Linux, you can use the command line on Windows once you install Wincvs, but the GUI makes those same functions easily available. You can also run command-line commands from within the GUI as well.

Comprehensive information on implementing, using, and configuring CVS for your system is not possible here. Instead, we provide you with the essential resources to get started:

The CVS home page can be found at http://www.cvshome.org.

The WinCvs site is at http://www.cvsgui.org.

Although large CVS repositories are designed for and usually best hosted on a Linux/Unix platform, you can create and maintain a repository on Windows without encountering problems. Once you have Wincvs installed, you can create a repository for local use via the GUI under the Create a new repository selection of the Create pull-down menu. You can also run the following command from the command line if cvs.exe is in your path:

```
cvs -d :local:c:\temp\cvsroot init
```

Once you have a repository created, you can import files into the repository as a project with a vendor tag indicating the purpose/cause of the project. For example, you might have a set of application-specific scripts that you want to keep in a separate project for your functional applications DBAs, and another project for your system administrators, and yet another project for your Oracle generic DBAs (that is, those who are not specifically assigned to an application).

Once you have these files checked into the repository, you can check them out at any time and indicate where you want them to be generated. You should *not* use the same scripts as you did for the import, as these files are not under source control. Instead, when you have imported the files, check them out to a different location than the location from which you checked them in. Once you have verified that the newly checked out files are okay, you should delete or archive the old files that are not under source control.

When you have made changes that you would like to ensure are saved, you should commit your changes for the file or for the directory that contains the file. If you commit a directory that is part of a checkout operation, then a commit performed on the directory will recurse through the contents of the directory and its subdirectories and commit all changes to all the files found that have changed since the last checkout.

You will experience problems with files that have spaces in the name of the file, so avoid using file and directory names that have spaces in them. This is good general practice anyway to ensure portability between platforms. Keep things simple—they are complex enough!

If you are working with other database administrators who are using the same repository to store their scripts, and they have told you that they have found and fixed bugs in the xyz.sql script, you can use the CVS **update** command to bring your local version of the xyz.sql script up to date with the version in the repository.

If you have a number of different teams, you might include a script branch for each team and do a frequent review of changes at a higher level to bring work together by merging branches back into the main branch and begin the team customization process all over again. Only merge in the changes and new scripts you feel are relevant to the group as a whole.

Source control is a useful tool for database administrators, just as it is for developers. With the open source tools that are available on Windows and other platforms, there is no reason not to evaluate the value of a version control system implementation for your database administrators. If you deal with development instances, you may instead want to work with the development management to ask about integrating your work into its product release process.

Statspack: A New Approach to Performance

Basic performance tuning of an up-and-running application on an up and running application requires that you understand the changes that occur in the database over a period of time. You can use Statspack resources to get a good idea of how your database is being utilized over time.

New Feature in Oracle9*i*

In Oracle 9i, Statspack replaces utlbstat/utlestat reports (also known as bstat/estat reports). Statspack uses a point-in-time snapshot of primary performance-related views in the database. Once you have two or more snapshots, you can run a report that informs you of the difference in cumulative database statistics and SQL run in the database between the beginning and ending snapshots. Because much of the gathered data is cumulative for the uptime of the instance, then a standard report that spans a database shutdown is not possible. Oracle Press has an excellent book on using the captured data beyond the standard report called *High Performance Tuning with STATSPACK*, if you wish to go deeper than what we offer here.

All of the relevant files to set up Statspack are in the %ORACLE_ HOME%\rdbms\admin directory. If you run a directory listing for files that begin with "sp*", then you can view the various files associated with Statspack. The starting point is the documentation file, spdoc.txt. This documenting file explains the essentials of initializing Statspack snapshot captures. Over time, snapshots can take a substantial amount of space. For this reason, Statspack needs to be managed like any other database schema that grows over time. The basic minimum space requirement is 64MB megabytes.

Statspack Installation

Statspack keeps historical data in a database schema. In this way, it is distinct from the bstat/estat reports because these reports did not require any storage in the database. Keeping report.txt from older versions of Oracle bstat/estat reports taken from a well-performing system is always important to establish a proper baseline for later tuning efforts. The actual Statspack installation requires that you log into the database using SQL*Plus as SYSDBA and run the spcreate.sql script:

```
SQL> connect / as sysdba
SQL> @%ORACLE_HOME%\rdbms\admin\spcreate
```

When you run this script, it calls three other scripts (spcusr.sql, spctab.sql, and spcpkg.sql) to create the perfstat user and install the necessary schema objects. Once you run the create script, you should check the resulting corresponding "lis" files for problems. Please make sure that you set the default tablespace to either a dedicated tablespace or a nonvital tablespace to avoid space problems. If you do experience problems with the installation, you can drop Statspack with the spdrop .sql script run as sysdba.

Once you have "installed" Statspack, you need to change the schema password for PERFSTAT for security reasons. If your database is outside your corporate firewall, you should install Statspack as a different user, as well as changing the schema password. To install with a different username, first back up the current versions of the four SQL scripts used to create the user (spcreate, spcusr, spcpkg, and spctab). After you have backed up these files, alter the spcusr.sql script starting at line 131 in the initial production 9.0.1 version of the spcreate.sql script and then the subsequent use of the schema name. Then change the spcreate.sql script's connect statements from perfstat/perfstat to your new username/password combination.

Gathering Statspack Snapshots

Once you have Statspack installed, you need to gather snapshots to create reports of value. How often you gather snapshots is really dependent upon your database, its activity, and your needs. The first thing you need to do if you have a properly functioning system is gather a number of snapshots from that system to establish a baseline for future comparison. You will want to do this frequently (for example, monthly) in order to establish changes in usage patterns. You should also gather snapshots just before and after changes to applications that use a database.

To gather a snapshot, you only need to run the snap procedure in the Statspack package while logged into the database as the perfstat user:

```
SQL> connect perfstat/perfstat
SQL> exec statspack.snap;
```

This procedure gathers data from V$ and X$ views and inserts the data into PERFSTAT tables with a SNAP_ID to identify the data gathered for the statspack.snap procedure execution. Table 9-2 is a listing of the tables that contain this data. Watch data growth in these tables for space reasons.

Statspack Reporting

Once you have gathered at least two snapshots, you can run the spreport.sql script to generate the default report of activity between two snapshots. Remember that you cannot run a report between snapshots that span a database shutdown. When

STATS$BG_EVENT_SUMMARY	STATS$BUFFER_POOL_STATISTICS
STATS$DATABASE_INSTANCE	STATS$DB_CACHE_ADVICE
STATS$DLM_MISC	STATS$ENQUEUE_STAT
STATS$FILESTATXS	STATS$IDLE_EVENT
STATS$INSTANCE_RECOVERY	STATS$LATCH
STATS$LATCH_CHILDREN	STATS$LATCH_MISSES_SUMMARY
STATS$LATCH_PARENT	STATS$LEVEL_DESCRIPTION
STATS$LIBRARYCACHE	STATS$PARAMETER
STATS$PGASTAT	STATS$RESOURCE_LIMIT
STATS$ROLLSTAT	STATS$ROWCACHE_SUMMARY
STATS$SESSION_EVENT	STATS$SESSTAT
STATS$SGA	STATS$SGASTAT
STATS$SNAPSHOT	STATS$SQLTEXT
STATS$SQL_PLAN	STATS$SQL_PLAN_USAGE
STATS$SQL_STATISTICS	STATS$SQL_SUMMARY
STATS$STATSPACK_PARAMETER	STATS$SYSSTAT
STATS$SYSTEM_EVENT	STATS$TEMPSTATXS
STATS$UNDOSTAT	STATS$WAITSTAT

TABLE 9-2. *Statspack Tables*

you run the report script, it will present you with a list of the available snapshots for reporting and ask you to specify the number of the begin and end snapshot IDs:

```
Instances in this Statspack schema
~~~~~~~~~~~~~~~~~~~~~~~~~~~~~~~~~~

   DB Id    Inst Num DB Name      Instance     Host
----------- -------- ------------ ------------ ------------
 3132690149        1 OEMREP       oemrep       FOXRUN

Using 3132690149 for database Id
Using          1 for instance number

Completed Snapshots
                                   Snap                     Snap
Instance     DB Name                 Id   Snap Started     Level Comment
------------ ------------ ----- ----------------- ----- -------
oemrep       OEMREP                   1 05 Sep 2001 01:57     5
                                      2 05 Sep 2001 02:09     5

Specify the Begin and End Snapshot Ids
~~~~~~~~~~~~~~~~~~~~~~~~~~~~~~~~~~~~~~
Enter value for begin_snap:1
Begin Snapshot Id specified: 1

Enter value for end_snap: 2
End   Snapshot Id specified: 2

Specify the Report Name
~~~~~~~~~~~~~~~~~~~~~~~
The default report file name is sp_1_2.  To use this name,
press <return> to continue, otherwise enter an alternative.
Enter value for report_name:
```

This (unrealistic) example of a Statspack report session will generate a report that you can use to identify key issues for the system activity between the snapshots used. One of the new features of Statspack (not available in bstat/estat reports) is the report of SQL in the Shared Pool with statistical data. Once you have determined that one or more SQL statements appear to be the culprit of a performance issue, you can use the sprepsql.sql script to report on the particular SQL statement. When you run this script, you will be prompted for the SQL's hash value, as well as the start and end snapshot IDs. You can get the SQL hash value from the last column of the spreport.sql report. If you determine that you have a problem with one or more sessions, you can gather snapshots for those particular session statitistics. To gather wait events and other session data, execute the snap procedure while connected as perfstat like this:

```
SQL>  execute statspack.snap(i_session_id=>131);
```

Once you have a regular strategy for collecting snapshots, you can use the DBMS_JOB package to gather snapshots at a regular interval. The spauto.sql script provides you with an example of this practice, but this script is only an example and not the correct interval for all systems. Make sure that you choose the correct interval to match your system activity and needs.

You will want to analyze the report data once you have it. A thorough analysis of this data requires solid knowledge of the database. Check out the Oracle Press performance tuning volumes, and in particular, *High Performance Tuning with STATSPACK*. You can also go to the web site http://www.oraperf.com to upload your bstat/estat and Statspack reports for a formulaic analysis of your reports. We cannot stress enough that to properly act on information in Statspack reports, you must have a good understanding of the database. Take the time and make the effort to understand the database through reading and running your own tests.

Managing Statspack Data

Once you have collected data for a period of time, and you wish to archive this data or move it to a separate instance used for reporting purposes, you can use the spuexp.par export parameter file to export data that can then be shared:

```
C:\> exp perfstat/perfstat parfile=spuexp.par
```

Once you have the export datafile, you can import the data into a separate user in a reporting instance by using the FROMUSER and TOUSER import parameters:

```
C:\> imp oemrep_perf/password fromuser=perfstat touser=t
file=spuexp.dmp
```

After this data is imported into the new user, you can use the default reporting scripts, while logged in as this new user, to generate reports and drill down into the data from various databases. You could also grant select rights across schemas to allow you to write custom queries that compare statistics across databases.

Once your reporting data grows to a point where you no longer want to keep a portion of the historical data, you can use the spurge.sql script to select a snapshot range to remove from the historical data. If you decide to archive your data to an export file regularly, you can use the sptrunc.sql file to remove *all* Statspack historical data.

Upgrading Statspack from Previous Database Versions

If you have been using Statspack in Oracle versions 8.1.6 or 8.1.7, then you will need to run a script to upgrade the snapshot data to be compatible with the improved Oracle9i version of Statspack. The spup816.sql and spup817.sql scripts upgrade performance data from 8.1.6 and 8.1.7 databases, respectively. Once you upgrade this data, you can then use the reporting capabilities of the Oracle9i scripts and continue to gather historical snapshot data for the upgraded release Oracle9i database. When you do upgrade with these scripts, you will *not* be able to downgrade.

New Feature in Oracle9i

External Tables

External tables are a new feature for 9i that allow you to access formatted text files on your file system with SQL. You can use this for loading instead of SQL*Loader. Like SQL*Loader, external tables allow you to take advantage of parallel loading capabilities if you have many CPUs. You might want to look at external tables as an extension to the capabilities of SQL*Loader. It can accomplish the same thing with added capability. It allows you to avoid actually loading data that you may only need for a very short period of time. You might have older legacy data stored on optical or other read-only media that you just need temporarily for particular analysis.

External tables open up many doors that external tables open up for DBAs and application integration. We will walk you through a simple example here to familiarize you with the essential details. External tables are very flexible and allow you to do much more than work with the file format we deal with in this technique. Examine the documentation for more details and case studies.

Generating Sample Data for External Tables

The first step in this example is to generate a simple comma-separated data file. You can do this from SQL*Plus using the **spool** command and a quick edit:

```
Set head off feed off
spool c:\oracle\load\employees.dat
select empno||','||deptno||','||ename from scott.emp;
spool off
```

Edit the output to get rid of blank lines, trailing spaces, and lines from the actual SQL statement to end up with something that looks like this:

```
7369,20,SMITH
7499,30,ALLEN
7521,30,WARD
```

Now you will need to create the constructs in the data dictionary to generate the external table while connected as a database administrator (for example, as the system user):

```
create directory load_dir as 'c:\oracle\load';
grant read on directory load_dir to scott;
grant write on directory load_dir to scott;
```

After these commands have been successfully completed, you are ready to create your external table on top of employees.dat:

```
Create table emp_external
(empno number, deptno number, ename varchar2(10))
  ORGANIZATION EXTERNAL
  (TYPE ORACLE_LOADER
    DEFAULT DIRECTORY load_dir
    ACCESS PARAMETERS(
      records delimited by newline
      badfile load_dir:'employees.bad'
      discardfile load_dir:'employees.discard'
      logfile load_dir:'employees.log'
      fields terminated by ','
      missing field values are null
      (empno, deptno, ename))
   LOCATION ('employees.dat')
  );
```

This statement will create an external table you can only read by using SQL. In fact, you can join it to other tables to form a query or perform a CTAS (create table as select) operation for a newly transformed table. You will find a log of access to the table in the c:\oracle\load directory, which does includes selects. You can remove logging by replacing the logfile clause with the single word nologfile without any trailing information.

Although you can do all kinds of querying and use the data in external tables in your queries and to build other tables, you cannot perform DML (insert, update, or delete) on the external table. You will get an ORA-30657: "Operation not supported on external organized table" error message if you try to perform DML on an external table.

If you do not remove trailing spaces, you will get an error when you attempt to query. If you look in the employees.log file, you will find the error message ORA-01401: "Inserted value too large for column."

If you happen to try and query the table from SQL*Plus while the file is not available, you will get an error message that looks like the following:

```
ERROR at line 1:
ORA-29913: error in executing ODCIEXTTABLEOPEN callout
ORA-29400: data cartridge error
KUP-04040: file emp.csv in LOAD_DIR not found
ORA-06512: at "SYS.ORACLE_LOADER", line 14
ORA-06512: at line 1
```

Do not worry too much about this. Once the file is available again, it will recover gracefully and read the contents without blinking.

This flexible architecture allows you to load data from a variety of legacy sources or even from the output of a Microsoft Excel spreadsheet gathered from users while disconnected. In essence, you can use it to transparently read and load data kept in a flat-file format using standard SQL.

DBMS_FLASHBACK

Oracle9i features a new procedure to help recover from user error. User error is an error perpetrated by a user. For example, suppose your new junior DBA database administrator forgets the where clause on that delete statement for the order management schema's orders table. With previous versions of Oracle, you had to recover from a physical or logical backup; typically, you would recover from an export operation if the table is fairly static, or if the data is both very important and changes quickly, and then you would have to restore the database to a particular point in time. Tablespace point-in-time recovery (TSPITR pronounced Tee-Spitter) made this process of user error recovery less time consuming, but much more complex.

DBMS_FLASHBACK and Automatic Undo Management (AUM) help fix this problem by enabling you to roll back a session to a particular point in time. You can then query data from that point in time and, by using PL/SQL, you can put the needed data into a PL/SQL table. With the PL/SQL table populated, you roll forward and apply the changes from the data in the PL/SQL table.

There are some limitations in this release, however:

- Only the data in tables is flashed back to a point in time in the past—the state of the data dictionary from the present is in effect when the database is flashed back. For this reason, user errors that perform most DDL (for example, truncate, drop table, drop column, move table, drop partition) are not recoverable by flashing back in this version.
- In this first release, you can only retain up to five days of data (43,200 seconds).
- You cannot nest flashbacks.
- You cannot perform flashbacks on tables across database links.
- A flashback query may fail if it uses an index that is created or rebuilt after the effective SCN of the flashback. In this case, you will need to add a hint to your query in the flashback state that forces a full table scan:

```
Select /* full(emp) */ from emp;
```

User Error Recovery

There are a few preliminary steps you need to take to keep the data from the past available to DBMS_FLASHBACK. First, you *must* make sure that your database is configured for AUM:

Set the init.ora parameter UNDO_RETENTION to the number of seconds you wish to be able to query back into the past. You can alter this value while the database is up and running with the alter system syntax, but this will only increase the retention capacity for the future UNDO—the operation cannot reach back into time to make past data previously unretained available. The default value is 900 seconds, or 15 minutes. The more retention you have, the larger your undo tablespace needs to be.

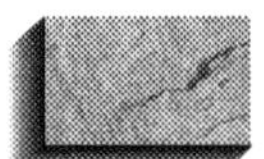

NOTE
If you use the ENABLE_AT_TIME procedure, you will not go back to the exact time, but instead times are mapped to SCNs every five minutes. To avoid this problem, you must use SCN instead.

To show you the basics of how to use this feature, follow this example session that flashes back five minutes to recover from a delete statement:

```
SQL> select count(*) from test_flash where ename = 'BLAKE';
  COUNT(*)
----------
      1024
1 row selected.

SQL> delete from test_flash where ename = 'BLAKE';
1024 rows deleted.

SQL> commit;
Commit complete.

SQL> select count(*) from test_flash where ename = 'BLAKE';
  COUNT(*)
----------
         0
1 row selected.

SQL> begin
     DBMS_FLASHBACK.ENABLE_AT_TIME(SYSDATE - 5/1440);
     -- The FOR loop is examining data values from the past.
     FOR c in (SELECT EMPNO,ENAME,JOB,MGR,HIREDATE,
                           SAL, COMM, DEPTNO
                  FROM  test_flash WHERE ename='BLAKE')
     LOOP
```

```
DBMS_FLASHBACK.DISABLE;
-- Because flashback is disabled within the loop body, we can access
-- the present state of the data, and issue DML statements to undo the
-- changes or store the old data.
INSERT INTO test_flash values (c.EMPNO,c.ENAME,c.JOB,c.MGR,c.HIREDATE,
c.SAL, c.COMM, c.DEPTNO);
END LOOP;
COMMIT;
end;
/
PL/SQL procedure successfully completed.

SQL> select count(*) from test_flash where ename = 'BLAKE';
  COUNT(*)
----------
      1024
1 row selected.
```

You can begin to utilize this new feature, but do not depend on it for all user errors due to the current limitations. You should still continue logical backups (for example, exports) to allow you to recover relatively static data and serve as a platform to perform TSPITR for vital, dynamic data. All in all this functionality allows you to recover from the majority of user errors quickly and efficiently.

Oracle-Supplied PL/SQL Packages

Throughout this chapter, we have shown you how to use some of the DBMS packages to perform advanced tasks. Become familiar with the DBMS packages by exploring *Oracle9i Supplied PL/SQL Packages and Types Reference,* which is part of the Oracle documentation. If you are familiar with these packages, you will know how to use them when you encounter problems in the future. Here is a list of other packages you might want to investigate:

DBMS_ALERT

DBMS_DDL

DBMS_IOT

DBMS_LOB

DBMS_OBFUSCATION_TOOLKIT

DBMS_RANDOM

DBMS_REPAIR

DBMS_STATS

DBMS_UTILITY

DBMS_XMLGEN, DBMS_XML_QUERY, and XML_SAVE

UTL_HTTP

In particular, become familiar with DBMS_STATs. This package is the replacement for the **analyze** command. It generates and manages Optimizer statistics using a new methodology that is less intrusive and does not hold locks as long or as restrictively as the **analyze** command.

Summary

In this chapter, we have reviewed the use of procedural languages such as PL/SQL, Java, and Perl to manage your system and your database. This introduction to these languages needs to be supplemented by other materials and practice. The Oracle Press books on PL/SQL programming are more than sufficient to address PL/SQL programming for database administrators. There are too many good Java and Perl books to mention here. For Java, start at Sun's Java web site (http://java.sun.com). For Perl, there are two web sites with Perl information, one specific to Perl on Windows (http://www.activestate.com), and one that addresses generic Perl programming (http://www.perl.com).

CHAPTER 10

Change Management

This chapter provides a frank discussion about the techniques all professional database administrators should employ when managing the inevitable evolution of the database. We begin by discussing upgrading the operating system, and the impact this has on an existing Oracle installation. We also discuss tips for migrating from Oracle7 to Oracle9i, and upgrading from Oracle8 releases to Oracle9i. We conclude by discussing how upgrades affect various different environments, such as Failsafe, RAC, and standby databases. The following tips and techniques will be discussed:

- Upgrading the operating system
- Reinstalling Oracle after a clean OS installation
- Changes to service packs on Windows 2000
- Performing rolling upgrades in an MSCS setting
- Migrating versus upgrading Oracle RDBMS
- Performing premigration steps
- Migrating from Oracle7
- Upgrading from Oracle8
- Re-creating services as part of migration or upgrade
- Performing post-migration steps
- Patching in an Oracle environment
- Making rolling upgrades of Failsafe and the RDBMS in a Failsafe environment
- Upgrading in a RAC environment
- Upgrading and migrating in a standby environment

Upgrading the Operating System

We begin with a discussion of upgrading the operating system, including upgrading a major release, such as NT 4.0 to Windows 2000, or applying a Service Pack or hotfix from Microsoft, with a focus on how this affects the Oracle RDBMS. The first thing to realize when embarking on an upgrade of any type is that bad things can and do happen. Without backups, you are toast. Therefore, any upgrade advice dispensed in this chapter is done so with the assumption that you have first made a valid backup, and are prepared to use this backup should anything go wrong.

Impact of an Operating System Upgrade

The term *upgrade,* when referring to an operating system upgrade, is used in place of the term *clean installation.* A straightforward upgrade of the operating system will, in fact, preserve the Registry entries for Oracle. As such, it is possible to go from Windows NT 4.0 to Windows 2000 without affecting your Oracle installation. However, this is only possible if you are upgrading to an equivalent OS version—that is, going from Windows NT 4.0 Standard Server to Windows 2000 Standard Server, or going from Windows NT 4.0 Enterprise Edition to Windows 2000 Advanced Server. Notice in Figure 10-1 that the option to upgrade is grayed out, because the version of Windows NT is not equivalent to the version of Windows 2000. Thus, a clean installation is necessary if you intend to do any type of upgrade of the operating system along those lines.

Upgrading the Operating System

If you do proceed with an upgrade of the operating system, with the intent of preserving the current Oracle installation, you should make sure that the database

FIGURE 10-1. *Upgrade or clean installation?*

is cleanly shut down, and set all Oracle services to manual startup. Be sure that you have a full backup before proceeding. Also, make sure that the version of the database you are running is certified with both the original version and the new version of the operating system. This is critical if you are currently running an older version of the database. For example, no versions prior to 8.1.6 are certified to run on Windows 2000. So, if you are currently running 8.1.5 or older, you cannot upgrade directly to Windows 2000. You must first upgrade the database (to Oracle9i, presumably) and then upgrade to Windows 2000. This is a supported process because the initial release of Oracle9i (9i Release 1) is supported and certified under both Windows 2000 and Windows NT 4.0. We will be discussing database versioning and database upgrades/migrations later in this chapter in the section "Migrating or Upgrading the Oracle Database."

A Clean Installation of the Operating System

A clean installation of the operating system will also require a clean installation of Oracle. You may be tempted to try a shortcut of backing up all Oracle components, Registry keys, and so on, and then simply restoring them once the OS has been reinstalled. We strongly advise that you do not do this. As you have seen with our discussion of installation in Chapter 4, there are many Registry keys and multiple directories related to the Oracle installation to back up, not to mention environment settings, groups such as ORA_DBA, and members of these groups that would have to be re-created. If you unwittingly miss any of these pieces, you can spend hours trying to figure out what went wrong, and you will ultimately end up reinstalling Oracle anyway.

Reinstalling Oracle After a Clean OS Installation Instead, if you intend to do a clean installation of the operating system, we recommend that you shut down and back up any and all databases. In addition, back up any configuration and networking files, such as the parameter file, and files such as tnsnames.ora, listener.ora, and sqlnet.ora. Once these are backed up, proceed with the clean installation of the OS. When the OS has been set up and configured as necessary, follow the steps outlined in Chapter 4 for a new installation of Oracle.

A simple way to get the database back up is to go ahead and allow the Database Assistant to create and run a database of the same name as your previous database. You can then simply shut down that shell database and copy your datafiles back into place, including the parameter file (or SPFILE), datafiles, log files, and control files. This method has the advantage of creating the directory structure and services and configuring the listener and tnsname.ora files for you. Alternatively, you can allow the Oracle installation to run without creating a database at all. After the new installation, you can manually create the directory structure for the database and copy all appropriate files into place (including the listener.ora and tnsnames.ora files). You will then need to re-create the services for the instance by running the **oradim** command, as documented in Chapter 4.

A note on doing new installations: you do not necessarily have to reformat the drive to do a clean installation; however, we recommend it in most cases. Otherwise, you will be forced to define the base installation directory (or SystemRoot) as something other than \WINNT (since that directory will already be in use by your prior installation). This implies that you are using your server in a dual-boot configuration. Doing so has the potential to lead to confusion, especially if you choose the same drive letter for the new SystemRoot. In such a case, you will end up with both versions of the operating system writing to the same \Program Files directory. Since Oracle writes to this directory to install the JRE and also to keep track of inventory of installed products, this can wreak havoc on current and future installations. Therefore, it is much simpler to do a clean installation into the same directory as before, necessitating that you format the OS drive during the installation. For this reason and others, we do not recommend running a dual-boot configuration in a production environment. (Dual-boot servers are only recommended for support organizations with very limited purchasing power, who have to support multiple versions of products on multiple operating systems, all with one server.)

Windows 2000 Service Packs

There is nothing wrong being the first kid on the block to download the new service pack for Windows 2000. If you are one of those types who constantly surf the Internet to make sure that you are the one who tells everyone else that the latest service pack has been made available, that's great. You can even install it that very night, if you wish. Just don't do it on the production box where your Oracle database is running.

On Windows NT 4.0, Oracle9i requires that you be on Service Pack 5 or higher—if you are not, the installation will not continue. However, there is not a service pack requirement currently being enforced for Windows 2000 with the initial release of Oracle9i. Oracle does recommend that you run on the latest service pack available that is known to be stable. We recommend implementation of a policy that facilitates the testing of service packs as soon as possible after their release, and the migration of the production system to the latest service pack as soon as adequate testing has been done.

Service Pack Requirements for Oracle

The service pack installation itself is not complicated—simply run update.exe from whatever location the service pack is staged. Of course, we recommend that in a new environment, you make an Uninstall directory, from which you can run **spuninst** if necessary. Nothing real complicated or earth-shattering there. However, there are a couple of things to take note of on Windows 2000.

Service Pack Changes in Windows 2000 It is no longer necessary to reinstall service packs any time you make driver changes or install other applications. It used to be true that under Windows NT 4.0, any time a new application, new driver or driver update was installed, it was recommended that the service pack be reinstalled. Windows 2000 does away with this requirement by adding a file called, for example, sp2.cab into the \WINNT\Driver Cache\I386 directory. This does not replace the existing driver.cab, but a new driver index file is copied over, which points to the new .cab file for any driver installation information.

In addition, Windows 2000 supports the concept of integrated installation, which allows you to do a fresh installation that includes the latest service pack. Gone are the days when you had to install Windows NT 4.0, and then install Service Pack 3 just to make your system partially functional (that is, make it recognize network settings), and then, once you were able to get onto the network, follow that up with another service pack installation to get yourself the latest and greatest. With integrated installation, you can stage the Windows 2000 base release, apply the service pack to the staging area, and then proceed to doing your OS installations from the staging area. The end result is that all subsequent installations that you do from the staging area will include the service pack.

To set up an integrated installation, you must first copy the contents of the i386 directory from the base Windows 2000 release to a staging area. Next, run the update from your service pack using the -s switch, specifying the staged area. For example, assume that you have copied the contents to X:\W2k_I386. Now, go to the directory where you have extracted the service pack and run the following command:

```
D:\SP2_Stage\i386\update>update -s X:\W2k_I386
```

Once you have updated the files in the staging area in X:\W2k_i386, you can copy this back out to a CD-ROM, or use it as a staging area from which to run installations remotely. This method is a convenient time-saver if you have to install multiple machines, or if there may be a need to reinstall the OS with the current service pack at a future time.

MSCS and Rolling Upgrades of the Operating System

In this section, we will discuss the steps in performing a rolling upgrade of the operating system in a Microsoft Cluster Server (MSCS) environment. (If you are not familiar with MSCS, please refer to Chapter 11, where we discuss MSCS and Oracle Failsafe.) Later in this chapter, we will discuss a rolling upgrade of the database itself.

Rolling upgrades are supported in an MSCS environment both for upgrades of the OS (from Windows NT 4.0 to Windows 2000) and to apply a service pack. However, if you are upgrading from Windows NT 4.0, you must start out on at least

Service Pack 4. A rolling upgrade allows you to keep groups created in MSCS online and accessible on one of the nodes while the other node is being upgraded, limiting the amount of downtime during the upgrade. The only downtime that should be incurred is the time needed to move groups back and forth between nodes to allow them to be upgraded. The alternative is to have all groups offline during the course of the upgrade.

To begin a rolling upgrade, you must determine which node will be the first to upgrade. Identify any groups on that node by highlighting the group itself in Cluster Administrator and viewing the Owner column in the right-hand pane. Move any active groups off that node by right-clicking the group and selecting Move Group. Once all groups have been moved to the other node, you need to pause the cluster service on the node to be upgraded. Identify the node at the bottom of the left-hand pane in Cluster Administrator, right-click the node, and choose Pause Node from the pop-up menu. Once the status of the node has changed to Paused, you can proceed with the upgrade or service pack installation. The node will remain paused, even after a reboot.

When the upgrade has completed, right-click the node again and choose Start Cluster Service, and the node should rejoin the cluster, at a higher revision than the other node(s). You will now repeat the process by moving all groups over to the higher level node that has just been upgraded. Once all groups have been moved, choose the lower version node in Cluster Administrator and pause the Cluster Service on that node, in the same fashion as before. Complete the upgrade or service pack installation and reboot the second node, restarting the Cluster Service and confirming that the node rejoins the cluster. If there are more than two nodes in the cluster, repeat this process on any remaining nodes. Once all nodes have been upgraded, move any groups back to their preferred nodes to resume normal activity.

Migrating or Upgrading the Oracle Database

Assuming that you have upgraded the operating system to an adequate version, or are already satisfied with the current version you are on, you may now want to focus your attention to upgrades of the database. The next section will be devoted to upgrades, migrations, patchsets, and patchset exceptions on the Oracle database on the Windows 2000 platform.

Migration and *upgrade* are terms that are often used interchangeably, and for the most part this poses no concern. However, the terms do have specific meanings in an Oracle context. For our purposes, migration refers to the process of moving from Oracle7 to Oracle9i. This process requires specific use of the mig utility to convert data blocks within the database from Oracle7 format to Oracle8+ format. However,

if you are already on a version of Oracle8 or later, this migration process, and use of the mig utility, is not necessary; we refer to such a case as an upgrade.

Migrating from Oracle7 to Oracle9i

Officially, Oracle recommends you migrate from a supported release. Since the last supported release of Oracle7 is release 7.3.4, you should upgrade to that version prior to migrating to Oracle9i. Although migration from a previous release may work, it is impractical to test migrations from all prior releases; so if you encounter a problem, there is no recourse.

Premigration Steps

Aside from upgrading the database to the latest Oracle7 release, some other basic steps should be taken prior to migrating to Oracle9i. One of these involves checking for corruption in the data dictionary. Starting with release 8.1.6, there is a flag set to enable block checking on the system tablespace. If any block in the system tablespace is detected as corrupted, the header will be zeroed out and the data in the block is lost. To prevent this from happening, objects such as tables and clusters in the SYS schema should be analyzed prior to upgrading. The simplest way to accomplish this is to generate a script, such as the one shown here, which will then do the work for you:

```
set head off feedback off pagesize 500 echo off termout off
spool C:\TEMP\analyze_premig.sql
select 'ANALYZE '||object_type||' '||object_name||' VALIDATE STRUCTURE
CASCADE;'
from dba_objects
where owner='SYS'
and object_type in ('TABLE','CLUSTER');
```

The resultant script, called analyze_premig.sql, should then be run as user SYS. Otherwise, you may need to preface the object names with the owner name (that is, sys.obj$). The validate structure cascade syntax will check all indexes on the objects as well as the objects themselves. It is very possible that your database may have been running fine, in spite of the fact that there are one or more corrupt blocks in the data dictionary. If any errors arise during any of these **analyze** commands, you cannot proceed with the migration, because the corrupt block will be zeroed out. Should an error occur, contact Oracle Support. Alternatively, you may want to consider migrating by means of a full database export operation and importing into a newly created database in the newer version.

It is important to reiterate that we recommend this check on objects in the *system* tablespace because, starting with 8.1.6 and higher, block checking is enabled on the system tablespace by default, but not on other tablespaces. However, this should not preclude you from checking for problems on other objects in other tablespaces.

The preceding script can easily be customized to check for objects in any schema or in any tablespace.

Additional Premigration Checks

Besides checking the SYS objects, you should take additional measures. First, make sure that you have adequate free space in the system tablespace and that the SYS account has its default tablespace set to system tablespace. We recommend at least 100MB. The following query will tell you how much free space you have:

```
select sum(bytes) from dba_free_space where tablespace_name = 'SYSTEM';
```

Summing the bytes will give you the total free space of all chunks in the tablespace. If this number is not adequate, you should then resize the existing file:

```
SQL> select file_name, bytes from dba_data_files
   where tablespace_name = 'SYSTEM';
FILE_NAME                              BYTES
D:\ORANT\DATABASE\SYSV734.ORA    104857600

1 row selected.

SQL> alter database datafile 'D:\ORANT\DATABASE\SYSV734.ORA'
  resize 225m;
Database altered.
```

In addition, you should ensure that your system rollback segment is adequately sized for the migration, and make sure that optimal is set to NULL. You can reset storage on the system rollback segment as follows:

```
SQL> ALTER ROLLBACK SEGMENT SYSTEM SHRINK TO 1M;

Rollback segment altered.

SQL>ALTER ROLLBACK SEGMENT SYSTEM STORAGE (NEXT 1M MAXEXTENTS 121
OPTIMAL NULL);

Rollback segment altered.
```

Finally, make sure that you know the DB_BLOCK_SIZE and CHARACTERSET of the database. During the migration, Oracle creates a user called MIGRATE, and in the MIGRATE schema a copy of the data dictionary will be created. Storage for these objects is calculated using an internal multiplier. The default value for this multiplier is 15. If your database block size is 4KB (4,192 bytes), you should specify a multiplier value of 30 to ensure that the storage clauses are adequate for the objects created in the MIGRATE schema. As for the character set, you must set the NLS_ LANG value in the environment to match the database character set (we will show you how to do this in the next section). The following commands will answer these two questions for you:

```
SVRMGR> show parameter db_block_size
NAME                                TYPE    VALUE
----------------------------------- ------- ------------------------------
db_block_size                       integer 2048
SVRMGR> select name, value$ from sys.props$ where name = 'NLS_CHARACTERSET';
NAME                           VALUE$
------------------------------ ----------------------------------------
NLS_CHARACTERSET               US7ASCII
```

Embarking on the Migration

Once you have followed the recommended premigration steps and you have taken a full backup, you are ready to proceed with the migration. Of course, Oracle provides a GUI Data Migration Assistant, which can be launched from Program Tools | Oracle OraHome90 | Configuration and Management Tools. However, we will focus here on running the migration from the command line. Even if you do not do it this way, this discussion will give you an idea of what the Data Migration Assistant is doing behind the scenes. If the Data Migration Assistant encounters any errors, you may be able to pick up where the assistant left off and manually complete the migration on your own.

First, ensure that the service for the Oracle7 instance is running, but make sure that the database is shut down cleanly by simply connecting in Server Manager (SVRMGR23) and issuing a **shutdown immediate** command. Exit from Server Manager, and set the NLS_LANG value from a command prompt. The mig utility is then run from within that command prompt, specifying the parameter file used to start up the Oracle7 database. The example that follows shows a multiplier value of 30 being specified, and the output spooled to a file called mig.log (run **mig /?** for a full list of command-line switches):

```
C:\>set NLS_LANG=AMERICAN_AMERICA.US7ASCII
C:\>mig pfile=d:\orant\database\initv734.ora multiplier=30 SPOOL=MIG.LOG
starting up database ...
```

If NLS_LANG is not properly set to match the database, you will receive an error here. If you run the migration using the GUI Data Migration Assistant, then you must make this setting in the Registry, under HKLM\Software\Oracle. Also, if using the GUI Data Migration Assistant, you will be given an opportunity to specify a multiplier value, as shown in Figure 10-2, if you choose to do a custom migration.

The mig utility will start the database, create and populate the migrate schema, scrolling information across the screen on what is being done, and ultimately shut

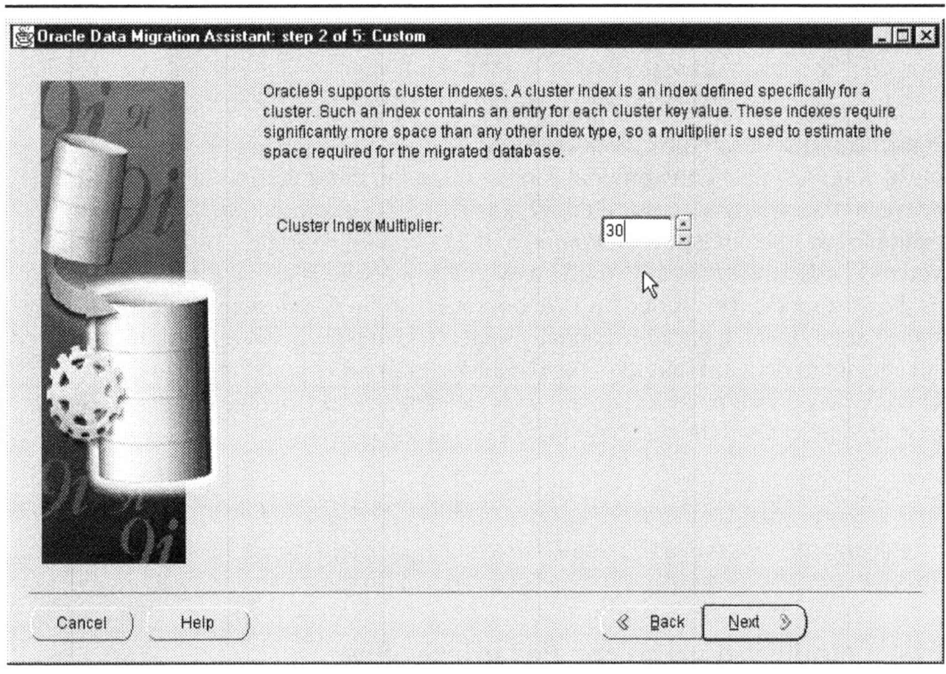

FIGURE 10-2. *Setting the multiplier with the Data Migration Assistant*

the database back down when it completes. If errors occur at this point, these errors can be addressed (based on what you see in the mig.log), and then the **mig** command can be rerun. Once this command has run successfully, a file called convert.ora will be created in the Oracle9i ORACLE_HOME\rdbms directory. This file will be used momentarily to re-create the control files.

Once the mig utility has run successfully, you should stop the Oracle7 service, and immediately rename or delete the control files for the V7 instance at the operating system level:

```
D:\ORANT\DATABASE>net stop oracleserviceV734
The OracleServiceV734 service is stopping.
The OracleServiceV734 service was stopped successfully.

D:\ORANT\DATABASE>rename ctl* *.bak
D:\ORANT\DATABASE>dir *.bak
 Volume in drive D has no label.
 Volume Serial Number is 385C-C703

 Directory of D:\ORANT\DATABASE
```

```
10/04/01  08:30p                159,232 CTL1V734.bak
10/04/01  08:30p                159,232 CTL2V734.bak
               2 File(s)          318,464 bytes
```

Re-create the Oracle Services

Next, you must delete the original service using the older version of oradim, and re-create the new service using the Oracle9i version of oradim. In the following example, we specify a new SID name and a new parameter file. To accomplish this, you must copy the old init file to the new filename. Note also that we specify manual as the start mode. This is because we do not want the database to be automatically started at this point. It must be manually started with the nomount option and converted. An attempt to do a full startup of the database at this point could result in corruption. This is why we recommended renaming or deleting the control files earlier—to prevent any attempt to open the database from succeeding.

```
D:\ORANT\DATABASE>oradim73 -delete -sid V734

D:\ORANT\DATABASE>oradim -new -sid V901 -intpwd Remember911 -startmode
manual -pfile d:\oracle\ora90\database\initv901.ora
```

Make Modifications to the Parameter File

After creating the service, ensure that the parameter file has been copied to the correct location. You must also set the COMPATIBLE parameter to 9.0.1.0.0 in the new init.ora file, as well as change any parameters for BACKGROUND_DUMP_DEST, USER_DUMP_DEST, and LOG_ARCHIVE_DEST, if so desired. Be sure that you create the directories at this point. We recommend a directory structure as outlined in Chapter 4. To change the control files to appear in a different directory, you can also specify the new location now in the modified init.ora. We recommend that you make any changes to DB_NAME and locations of the datafiles and log files themselves *after* the migration has been completed.

Last, we recommend setting the following event in the init.ora:

```
EVENT="10619 trace name context forever, Level 1"
_SYSTEM_TRIG_ENABLED = false
```

This event must be included to allow you to successfully open the database with COMPATIBLE set to 9.0.x. We mention _SYSTEM_TRIG_ENABLED in case you are upgrading from an Oracle8i release (which we discuss in the section "Upgrading the Database from Oracle8.x to Oracle9i" later in this chapter).

Starting the Instance

The time has now come to start the instance up. Since we changed the instance name in our example, we must set ORACLE_SID to the new value. We then connect and issue a **startup nomount** command. Remember that you must now use SQL*Plus, and connect as sysdba:

```
D:\ORANT\DATABASE>set oracle_sid=V901
D:\ORANT\DATABASE>sqlplus

SQL*Plus: Release 9.0.1.0.1 - Production on Tue Sep 11 08:48:00 2001
(c) Copyright 2001 Oracle Corporation.  All rights reserved.
Enter user-name: / as sysdba
Connected to an idle instance.

SQL> startup nomount
ORA-32004: obsolete and/or deprecated parameter(s) specified
ORACLE instance started.
```

Note that in spite of the ORA-32004 error indicating that obsolete parameters have been specified, the instance will still start. A listing of the obsolete parameters will be placed in the alert log. That list in the alert log may look something like this:

```
Obsolete system parameters with specified values:
  sequence_cache_entries
  sequence_cache_hash_buckets
  distributed_lock_timeout
  text_enable
  job_queue_interval
  job_queue_keep_connections
  snapshot_refresh_processes
  snapshot_refresh_interval
  snapshot_refresh_keep_connections
End of obsolete system parameter listing
```

Check the alert log for an entry similar to this one, and then remove the listed parameters from the init.ora file at your first opportunity.

Converting the Database

Once the instance is started with the **startup nomount** command, you are ready to run the **convert** command:

```
SQL> alter database convert;

Database altered.
```

We mentioned earlier that running the mig utility creates a file called convert.ora. The **alter database convert** command reads this file and creates new Oracle9i-compatible control files, placing the control files in the new location specified in the modified init.ora file. If the convert.ora file is not found at this point, this indicates the mig utility failed and should be rerun as described earlier. After a successful convert operation, you are ready to open the database with the RESETLOGS option:

```
SQL>alter database open resetlogs;
```

Once the database has successfully opened, the migration portion of the process has completed.

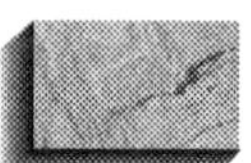

NOTE

If ***open resetlogs*** *fails with an ORA-01092: "ORACLE instance terminated. Disconnection forced" error, refer to the earlier section "Make Modifications to the Parameter File." Make sure that you have set Event 10619. If you have not, you can set it in the init.ora file now, and restart the database.*

Upgrading the Database from Oracle8.x to Oracle9i

As noted earlier, a migration, which we have just detailed, differs from an upgrade, because with an upgrade there is no need to run the mig utility to convert the data blocks to the new format. As such, believe it or not, upgrading a database from Oracle8.x to Oracle9i is a considerably simpler process than migrating. If you have followed the steps earlier in regard to a migration, then you are ready to complete the process by upgrading the data dictionary. Since there are similarities in this process to a regular upgrade, we will diverge for a moment here and outline how to get to this same point in a simple upgrade process.

Delete and Re-create Services

Of course, there is no need to run the mig utility upgrade from Oracle8x to Oracle9i. The similarities begin in deleting and re-creating the services. This must be done as part of an upgrade or migration. Bear in mind that to delete the services for an Oracle 8.0 instance, you will have to run oradim80 instead of oradim73. Of course, make sure that you shut down the Oracle8x database cleanly prior to deleting services. Services should be re-created using the Oracle9i version of oradim. In the case of an upgrade from Oracle8i, where the oradim executable has the same name in both releases, you must ensure that you are using the correct version of oradim. Do this by running the Oracle Home Selector to set the Oracle9i home as first in the path (as noted in Chapter 5), or by running the **oradim** command directly from the Oracle9i

ORACLE_HOME\bin directory. To verify that the new service was created pointing to the correct executable, check the path in the Registry in the following location:

```
HKLM\System\CurrentControlSet\Services\OracleServiceV901
```

On the right-hand side there will be an ImagePath value. Check the path and make sure that it points to the Oracle9i executable (see Figure 10-3).

Modifying the Parameter File for Upgrade

Once the services are re-created (again, specifying a start mode of manual), you will want to follow the steps given earlier for modifying the parameter file. If you have chosen to use a new instance name, rename the parameter file appropriately, and move it to the appropriate directory. When making modifications to the init file, bear in mind that you will not be issuing a **convert** command, and therefore will not be re-creating new control files. If you want the control files to be relocated, you can physically move them to the new directory, and then simply modify the path that is

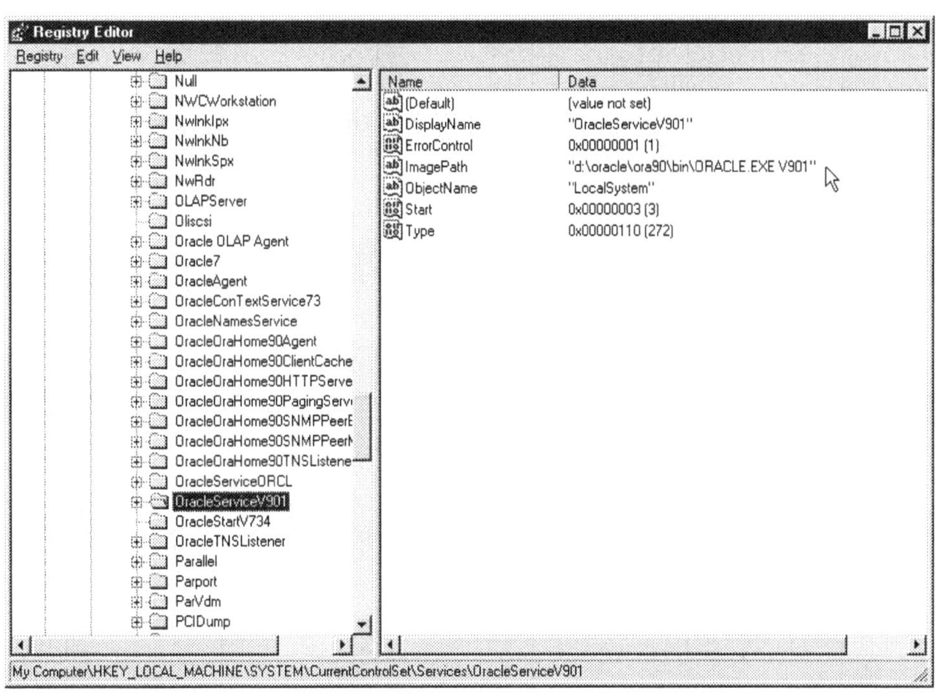

FIGURE 10-3. *ImagePath for Registry key*

listed in the control file. As with a migration, you should set the COMPATIBLE parameter to 9.0.1.0.0, and also set these two parameters:

```
EVENT="10619 trace name context forever, Level 1"
_SYSTEM_TRIG_ENABLED = false
```

Once these values are set, go ahead and set the ORACLE_SID, connect in SQL*Plus, and issue a **startup** command. Again, make sure that you are running the correct version of SQL*Plus by setting the directory path first with the Oracle Home Selector or by running it directly from the Oracle9i ORACLE_HOME\bin directory. With an upgrade, there is no need for an interim step of doing a startup nomount operation, and no need to issue an **alter database open resetlogs** command—simply issue a normal **startup** command.

Upgrading the Data Dictionary

Once the database is opened, you are at the same point as where we left off with the migration. In either case, you must now update the data dictionary views and packages to make them compatible with the Oracle9i executables. There are several scripts that must be run to incorporate the various changes that have been made to different versions of the database along the way. Depending on the version you are upgrading from, you will have to run different subsets of these scripts.

This is simplified by having one main calling script for each supported version from which you may be upgrading or migrating. This script will call the various minor upgrade scripts needed for incorporating changes made in releases between your current release and Oracle9i. It will then call catalog.sql and catproc.sql. These upgrade scripts are located in the Oracle9i ORACLE_HOME\rdbms\admin directory. Table 10-1 shows the supported releases to migrate/upgrade from, and the appropriate script to run, depending on which version you are coming from.

Choose the appropriate script from Table 10-1, and then run it as shown next.

Version Prior to Migration/Upgrade	Run This Script
7.3.4.x	u0703040.sql
8.0.6.x	u0800060.sql
8.1.5.x	u0801050.sql
8.1.6.x	u0801060.sql
8.1.7.x	u0801070.sql

TABLE 10-1. *Supported Releases and Scripts for Migration/Upgrade to Oracle9i*

```
SQL> spool upgrade.log
SQL> @d:\oracle\ora90\rdbms\admin\u0703040.sql
```

Upon completion of this script, you can check the spool file for critical errors. The script will run for some time, and the spool file will be very large. Most of the errors will be innocuous, such as ORA-00942 or other errors indicating an object does not exist or already exists. Search for critical errors such as space errors, starting with ORA-015x or ORA-016x, and critical errors, such as ORA-006x. This is not a comprehensive list, but gives you an idea what to search for.

Recompile Invalid Packages

Once the script completes, it is normal to have a high number of invalid objects. Any time catalog.sql and catproc.sql are run, the STANDARD package is re-created, invalidating all PL/SQL objects in the database. In addition, views whose base tables have been re-created will also show as invalid. During the normal course of activity, as these objects are accessed, they will be automatically recompiled. However, to save this performance hit at runtime, and to uncover any potential problems, you will want to recompile all objects after running the upgrade scripts. Do this by running the utlrp.sql script:

```
SQL> @d:\oracle\ora90\rdbms\admin\utlrp.sql
```

Once the recompile script has completed, check for invalid objects by spooling the output from the following query:

```
SQL> select object_name, object_type, owner from DBA_OBJECTS
where status = 'INVALID';
```

If there are still invalid objects, try compiling them manually. Find errors for troubleshooting by querying the USER_ERRORS view.

Block Conversion After a Migration

The migration process itself does not change the formatting of all Oracle data blocks to the new block format originally introduced with Oracle8. Once the migration has completed, data blocks within the database are converted as they are accessed and used. Of course, the migration "touches" all blocks in the data dictionary, so these blocks are the first to be converted to the new format. Your application data, however, will remain untouched and unconverted until the first time the data is accessed. This may result in a slight performance hit the first time data is scanned after a migration.

Post-Migration/Post-Upgrade Steps

Once the migration or upgrade has completed, you should remove these parameters from the init.ora file and restart the instance:

```
EVENT="10619 trace name context forever, Level 1"
_SYSTEM_TRIG_ENABLED = false
```

Also remove any parameters that were listed as obsolete in the alert log at the last startup. If you want to take advantage of new features such as system managed undo, the default temporary tablespace, and/or the SPFILE, refer to Chapter 5 for information on enabling these features after the database has been created. At this point, once the migration has succeeded, you should also immediately take a full backup.

Adding Features After Migration or Upgrade

If you are using additional features such as advanced replication, Oracle Context (Intermedia), the Java Virtual Machine, and so on, you need to run additional scripts. Refer to the *Oracle9i Migration Manual* for more information on steps for migrating these add-on features. If you want to add features to the database after migration, run the Database Configuration Assistant and select the option Configure database options in a database.

Moving Datafiles After a Migration

When migrating from Oracle7 or Oracle8.0, it is likely that the datafiles were in a non-OFA-compliant directory structure, since OFA was not implemented on the NT platform until Oracle8i (refer to Chapter 4 for more details and a description of OFA). If you want to move your datafiles to an OFA-compliant directory structure, we recommend doing so *after* the migration or upgrade process has completed successfully, for the simple reason that trying to do too much at once can lead to confusion and errors.

After the migration, the most straightforward method to move datafiles is to re-create the control file. To accomplish this, you must first get an ASCII copy of the control file. The database must be mounted or open, and then the following command should be issued:

```
SQL> alter database backup controlfile to trace;
```

This will generate a trace file in the udump directory. The trace filename will contain the SPID of the session that issued the command, but the simplest way to find it is to look for the most recent file in the udump directory. The file will have a section similar to this:

```
# The following commands will create a new control file and use it
# to open the database.
# No data other than log history will be lost. Additional logs may
# be required for media recovery of offline data files. Use this
# only if the current version of all online logs are available.
STARTUP NOMOUNT
CREATE CONTROLFILE REUSE DATABASE "TEST" NORESETLOGS NOARCHIVELOG
    MAXLOGFILES 32
    MAXLOGMEMBERS 2
    MAXDATAFILES 32
    MAXINSTANCES 16
    MAXLOGHISTORY 1600
LOGFILE
  GROUP 1 'D:\ORANT\DATABASE\LOG1TEST.ORA'  SIZE 200K,
  GROUP 2 'D:\ORANT\DATABASE\LOG2TEST.ORA'  SIZE 200K
DATAFILE
  'D:\ORANT\DATABASE\SYSTEST.ORA',
  'D:\ORANT\DATABASE\RBS1TEST.ORA'
;
# Recovery is required if any of the datafiles are restored backups,
# or if the last shutdown was not normal or immediate.
RECOVER DATABASE

# Database can now be opened normally.
ALTER DATABASE OPEN;
```


This is a simplified version of the control file, as we only list two datafiles. The concepts are the same, though, regardless of how many files you have.

The database should be shut down cleanly, the service for the instance stopped, and the files moved to their new locations. The resultant trace file can then be modified with the new path information for the new location of your files. Save this as a script, beginning with the STARTUP NOMOUNT section of the file. The modified file will then look similar to this:

```
STARTUP NOMOUNT
CREATE CONTROLFILE REUSE DATABASE "TEST" NORESETLOGS ARCHIVELOG
    MAXLOGFILES 32
    MAXLOGMEMBERS 4
    MAXDATAFILES 1024
    MAXINSTANCES 16
    MAXLOGHISTORY 1600
LOGFILE
  GROUP 1 'D:\ORACLE\ORADATA\PROD90\LOG1TEST.ORA'  SIZE 200K,
  GROUP 2 'D:\ORACLE\ORADATA\PROD90\LOG2TEST.ORA'  SIZE 200K
DATAFILE
  'D:\ORACLE\ORADATA\PROD90\SYSTEST.ORA',
  'D:\ORACLE\ORADATA\PROD90\RBS1TEST.ORA'
```

```
;
RECOVER DATABASE;
ALTER DATABASE OPEN;
```

If you have not already done so, set the start mode of the database to manual by setting the Registry value of ORA_<sidname>_AUTOSTART to FALSE, and restart the service. This will allow the service to be started without starting the database. We advise that you also rename the existing control files. Connect in SQL*Plus and run the newly saved script. This should re-create the control file with information on the new locations of the files.

Note that we have also changed the value for MAXDATAFILES and MAXLOGMEMBERS. This allows for more files to be created within the database, which is one reason why we advise renaming the control files prior to re-creating them. Even though we specify the word REUSE, there are times when the existing file cannot be reused if the size of the control file changes from that of the original file. Changing MAXDATAFILES and other settings can cause the control file size to grow, so renaming the existing control file will prevent any problems along these lines.

If you want to change the database name, you will have to change the first line of the create control file statement as such:

```
CREATE CONTROLFILE SET DATABASE "PROD90" RESETLOGS ARCHIVELOG
```

Note that the word REUSE has been changed to SET, and the new database name is included within quotes. We also *must* specify resetlogs, meaning that the recover statement and open statement at the end needs to be changed:

```
RECOVER DATABASE UNTIL CANCEL;
ALTER DATABASE OPEN RESETLOGS;
```

For this reason, it is critical that the database be shut down cleanly prior to recreating the control file.

Applying Patchsets to the Oracle RDBMS

A *patchset* is an installable subset of fixes that does not involve either a migration or an upgrade. Patchsets are generally downloaded from the Internet and installed over the top of an existing release, usually changing the fourth digit of the version. Patches and patchsets do not require that services be deleted and re-created, because the ImagePath of the service in the Registry points to the same directory and file. This file is simply overwritten with a new version. After applying a patchset, the database is restarted, and scripts are run per the instructions in the readme file (usually suggesting that catalog.sql and catproc.sql be run). We advise that whenever possible you run on the latest patchset for your platform. Again, we advise caution, though, on applying patchsets that are brand new, and, of course, we recommend applying patchsets on a test system first, whenever possible.

Backing Out of a Patchset

One of the critical things to be aware of is that, once installed, a patchset cannot be removed. If you uninstall a patched component, the base component is uninstalled with it, and must then be reinstalled from the original media. If an error occurs during the installation of a patchset, the inventory files may be updated, indicating that the patch was installed, yet in reality the patch did not go on successfully. The most common errors to occur during the installation of a patchset are write errors on a DLL that may be in use by Oracle or another program. Make sure that all Oracle Services are stopped during the patch installation, and also stop the Distributed Transaction Coordinator, which is a Microsoft Service. If you receive a write error during a patch installation, do not choose Ignore. Choosing Ignore and continuing with the installation will result in the inventory being updated with the patch information so you cannot reinstall it, yet not all of the files will have been successfully copied over. If you see a write error, leave the screen up, and try to find the program that is using the DLL named on the screen. The tlist utility provides an ideal method of doing this (tlist is described in more detail in Chapter 5):

```
C:\>tlist -m ociw32.dll
ociw32.dll -   684 msdtc.exe
```

To avoid running into a scenario where you cannot reinstall a patch, you may want to prepare by backing up the ORACLE_HOME directory, as well as the \Program Files\Oracle directory. This second directory is necessary because this is where the inventory information is located. Even if you restore a backup of the ORACLE_HOME from prior to patching, unless the inventory information is also restored, the Oracle Universal Installer will still think that patch has been applied, and will not let you install that patch again.

Apply Patches After Migration or Upgrade

We advise that any patches be applied after you have migrated or upgraded to the base release. Oracle does not support migrations or upgrades to a patched release that is not the original media release. In the case of Oracle9i Release 1 on Windows NT/2000, the media release is 9.0.1.1.1. Migration or upgrade to this release is fully tested and supported from the previously documented releases, but once you have patched, migration or upgrade from an earlier release is not supported.

Upgrading in a Clustered or Standby Environment

The steps that we have described previously are the same essential steps no matter what the environment. However, when running in a clustered environment or a standby environment, there are some additional considerations to be aware of. In this section, we will discuss upgrades and migrations in a Failsafe environment, RAC environment, and standby environment. We discuss this information here, even though we have not yet covered these topics, because it fits well into the change management theme of this chapter. This section assumes that you are already familiar with these various features. If not, please refer to the appropriate chapters for more detail.

Upgrading/Migrating in a Failsafe Environment

To upgrade the database in a Failsafe environment, it is recommended that the database be taken out of the Failsafe group and made stand-alone first. This is true whether we are discussing an upgrade or a migration. Thus, you should follow the steps in Chapter 11 for making the database stand-alone, and then proceed with the steps outlined previously for upgrading and migration. Once the upgrade is complete, add the database back into the Failsafe group.

Patching and Rolling Upgrades in a Failsafe Environment

Since applying a patch to the database does not change the major release, you can apply a patch to the database while the database is still in a group. This is referred to as a *rolling upgrade*. To do this, you will have to patch both nodes, one at a time. First, determine which node you want to patch first. For the sake of this example, assume that you are patching node 1 first. Next, move all groups off that node, and change the group properties to Prevent Failback (to keep the group from moving back over automatically if you need to reboot). Finally, stop the Cluster Service on node 1, and then stop any remaining Oracle services for any stand-alone products.

You are now ready to apply the patch to node 1. In the meantime, the database group is online and accessible on node 2. After installing the patch on node 1, restart the Cluster Service on that node. You can now move the database group back to node 1. Be aware that as soon as the group is moved back over to node 1 and the database is brought online, you must immediately connect in SQL*Plus and run the upgrade scripts required for the patch installation. If there are multiple databases involved (that is, multiple groups or multiple databases in the same group), you must run the scripts against *each* database. During this time, even though the database is online, users should not be accessing it, so you may want to bring the listener offline in Failsafe Manager to prevent users from connecting.

While the scripts are running against the database(s) on node 1, you can install the patch on node 2. Follow the same procedures as described previously: after moving all groups back over to node 1, stop the Cluster Service on node 2 and then stop any Oracle Services still running. Once the services are stopped, install the patch on node 2. Once the patch has been installed on node 2, restart the Cluster Service and any stand-alone Oracle Services on that node. When the scripts have completed running on node 1, the patch installation is complete. Change the failback properties of the group(s) back to their original settings, and if desired, move the group(s) back to the preferred node. Run the verify group operation on all of the groups, and also run the verify cluster operation to ensure that everything is in good working order.

Rolling Upgrade of the Failsafe Software

A rolling upgrade of the Failsafe software can also be accomplished without having to remove resources from groups or re-create groups. As a first step, you must ensure that the new release of Failsafe that you are upgrading to will support the version of the database that you are on. In most cases, you will want to upgrade the Failsafe release to a newer version *prior* to upgrading the database, as the most current release of Failsafe is generally compatible with the current RDBMS release as well as older terminal releases of the RDBMS. However, if you are running an older release of the database that is not a terminal release (that is, release 8.0.5 or 7.3.3), your version of the database may not be compatible with the newer release of Failsafe. If this is the case, you must upgrade the database to a supported release first.

To upgrade the Failsafe release, assume that you are starting with node 1. Again, move all groups over to node 2, and change the group properties to Prevent Failback. However, you should *not* stop the Cluster Service for a Failsafe upgrade. The Cluster Service must be running while installing Failsafe.

Uninstalling the Previous Failsafe Release Generally speaking, it is not necessary to uninstall the previous Failsafe release. If you are satisfied with the current location (directory) of the Failsafe home, you can install the newer release of Failsafe into the same directory. The older Failsafe release will be uninstalled automatically, as long as it is at least version 3.x. However, if you want to change the directory or home name, or if you are running Failsafe 2.x, you *must* uninstall the older release first. When uninstalling Failsafe, you will be asked if you want to unregister the resource DLL. Say no to this option. The new release of Failsafe will unregister and reregister a newer version of the resource DLL once the installation completes on all nodes and you have run the verify cluster operation.

If you uninstall Failsafe, you should do this on node 1 after having moved the groups over to node 2, and then reboot the node. You will then install the newer release of Failsafe and reboot node 1 again. Remember that the Cluster Service must be running during a Failsafe installation. Once Failsafe has been installed on node 1, and that node has been rebooted, move the groups from node 2 back over to node 1. Now, repeat the process on node 2. If uninstalling the older release, reboot node 2 prior to installing the new release of Failsafe. After installing the new release, reboot node 2 again. Once the installation has been completed on all nodes, you must run the verify cluster operation to ensure that the new version of the resource DLL is registered with the cluster. Do not run this operation until the installation has completed on all nodes and all nodes have been rebooted. You should also run this operation on each group. Finally, reset the failback properties to their original settings, and move any groups back to their preferred nodes.

Upgrade Considerations in a RAC Environment

Rolling upgrades are not supported in a RAC environment. As such, all instances should be shut down prior to embarking on any type of installation of a new release for a migration or upgrade. Once the installation has been completed, the migration or upgrade should be done with only one instance running. All other instances should be shut down. However, it is critical that when you reach the point of deleting and re-creating services that you remember to do this on all nodes. By the same token, any changes to the parameter file should be done on all nodes (with the exception of events or parameters that are set only during the upgrade).

If applying a patch to a database in a RAC environment, the patch installation should also be done with all instances shut down. The patch installation should recognize that it is being done in a clustered environment, and the installation will be distributed to all nodes. Once the patch installation has been completed, start up one instance and run the scripts, after which the other instances can be brought back online.

Migration in a Standby Environment

Depending on the size of your database, you may decide to simply re-create a standby database after the production database has been migrated. However, this is not absolutely necessary. It is possible to migrate the standby database from Oracle7 to Oracle9i without completely re-creating it.

To do this, you must make sure that you keep separate the logs generated while the database is still under Oracle7 from the new logs generated after the database has become an Oracle9i database. Once the process of running the mig utility has completed, you should transfer those logs to the standby database and apply all of the log files as part of the normal standby recovery process (see Chapter 13). It is critical that you apply *all* logs generated under the primary Oracle7 to the standby while the standby database is still running under Oracle7.

Next, shut the standby database down and ensure that Oracle9i has been installed in its own home. The services on the standby database should then be re-created using the Oracle9i version of oradim. Again, make sure that you specify a start mode of manual. Leave the database down until you have completed the rest of the migration on the primary database.

Once you have completed all of the scripts on the primary database and the migration is complete, you must create a new standby control file. Issue the following command on the primary database:

```
SQL> alter database create standby controlfile as
'C:\TEMP\Standby.ctl';
```

Next, shut the primary database down and make a new copy of all datafiles associated with the system tablespace. Copy these files and the new standby control file to the standby server and put them in place there. In addition, on the standby site, make any necessary changes to the init.ora file for the standby instance.

Once these new files are in place on the standby, you can do a startup nomount operation with the modified parameter file, and then mount the standby database using the new control file. Issue the **recover** command, this time applying all of the new archived logs generated under Oracle9i on the primary site. These logs will be new logs, generated *after* **open resetlogs** was issued on the primary site:

```
SQL> startup nomount
ORACLE instance started.
....
SQL>alter database mount standby database;
SQL>Recover standby database
```

Once all files from the primary site have been applied, you can put the database in managed recovery mode, if desired, by following the steps in Chapter 13.

Upgrading and Patching in a Standby Environment

Upgrades and patches are much simpler than a migration, because they don't require you to re-create the control file or copy new system datafiles. Simply make sure that all logs have been applied to the standby, and then shut both instances down. For an upgrade, you will need to follow the steps noted previously for upgrading in a stand-alone environment, including deleting and re-creating the services on *both* the primary and the standby site. After running the upgrade scripts on the primary site, simply transfer the logs to the standby site and make any necessary modifications to the init.ora file on the standby site. Finally, mount the standby site again as noted earlier, and apply the redo logs to the standby. When applying a patch, the steps are the same, but there is no need to re-create the services, and likely no need to change the parameter file.

Rolling Upgrades in a Data Guard Environment

It is often tempting to think that a rolling upgrade can be done in a Data Guard environment by simply executing a switchover, patching one of the databases, and then doing a switchback and patching the other. Unfortunately, this process is not supported at this time. When patching in a Data Guard environment, you should follow the same steps outlined earlier, which will incur some downtime, as both instances are down during the patch installation.

Open the Standby Database in Read-Only Mode During Upgrade or Patch Installation

If you are on Oracle8i or higher to begin with, you should be able to get by with having the standby database open in read-only mode while an upgrade or patch installation is taking place on the primary database.

With a patch installation, this would simply involve recovering the standby database as far as possible prior to patching the primary. Then, open the standby in read-only mode. While the standby is open, no logs are being applied, so continue with the installation and run the necessary scripts on the primary site. Once this is done, the primary site is brought back online and is accessible to users. Now, shut the standby site down, apply the patch, and then apply any new logs generated from the primary site.

If upgrading from Oracle8i to Oracle9i, shut the primary Oracle8i instance down, ship all remaining logs to the standby site, and complete the recovery on the standby, ensuring again that all Oracle8i logs are applied to the standby prior to opening in read-only. With the standby Oracle8i instance open in read-only mode, complete the upgrade on the primary site. Once completed, open the primary database back up to users, and shut the standby database back down. Re-create the services and make needed modifications to init.ora on the standby, and mount it as an Oracle9i instance. Recover by applying all logs generated during the upgrade of the primary site.

Summary

Maintaining an Oracle database necessarily involves an inevitable evolution, as new features evolve, and current features are made more stable through fixes and patches. This chapter has given insights into some of the nuances of database version evolution on the Windows 2000 platform. In addition, insights were provided on managing database change in various environments, such as an Oracle Failsafe environment, a Real Application Clusters environment, and a standby environment. We go into more detail on these high-availability solutions in Part IV.

PART IV

Clustering and High Availability

TIPS & TECHNIQUES

CHAPTER 11

Oracle Fail Safe

This section is dedicated to giving the Oracle DBA the tools to maximize uptime and availability of the Oracle database in a Windows 2000 environment. In this chapter, we introduce the first of our high-availability and clustering solutions— Oracle Failsafe. In the following chapter, we discuss Real Application Clusters (the next generation of Oracle Parallel Server), followed by chapters on standby database implementation and replication. In the final chapter, we introduce a new product called Real Application Cluster Guard, and we provide a case study scenario combining the best of these solutions into the ultimate in high availability.

As mentioned in the preceding paragraph, this chapter is devoted to Oracle Failsafe. In this chapter, we will disseminate tips and advice on the following topics:

- Understanding Oracle Failsafe
- Crash recovery versus disaster recovery concepts
- Understanding virtual servers and groups
- Defining resources and resource monitoring
- Understanding MSCS concepts and architecture
- Planning an Oracle Failsafe solution
- Determining numbers of disks and groups
- Understanding active/active versus active/passive setup
- N-node clusters
- Configuring shared disks
- Configuring network cards
- Installing Microsoft Cluster Server
- Installing cluster administrator on a client machine
- Installing Oracle Failsafe
- Configuring security setup for Oracle Services for MSCS
- Creating groups
- Making the database failsafe
- Troubleshooting and maintaining a failsafe database

Oracle Failsafe Concepts

Before deciding on Oracle Failsafe as the clustering solution for your needs, you need to understand some of the key concepts behind Microsoft Cluster Server and Oracle Failsafe, and also the difference between Oracle Failsafe and Real Application Clusters (RAC). This section is devoted to clarifying these issues for you.

Understanding Failsafe and MSCS Concepts

Oracle Failsafe (OFS) provides a relatively inexpensive, yet reliable methodology for maintaining the uptime and availability of your database. Because it makes use of the *Microsoft Cluster Server (MSCS)* infrastructure, OFS can be run on a wide variety of available hardware, provided the hardware is on Microsoft's Hardware Compatibility List (HCL) for Microsoft Cluster Server. Support for Oracle9i is included in Failsafe 3.2.1 and higher. In addition, the 3.2.1 release of Failsafe provides support for earlier releases of Oracle RDBMS, including 8.1.7 and 8.0.6. Currently, there is no additional charge for OFS itself. The cost factor comes into play in that you *must* have Windows 2000 Advanced Server or Windows 2000 Datacenter Server in order to run MSCS and take advantage of the clustering infrastructure required for Oracle Failsafe.

The benefit of Oracle Failsafe and MSCS is essentially the ability to provide redundancy of the hardware, operating system software, and database software, by having two or more nodes in a cluster with identical hardware and software setups. All nodes have access to the same shared storage device (though not concurrently, as we discuss later on). Therefore, should one of these components fail, or should a need for maintenance arise, the downtime can be mitigated.

Crash Recovery Versus Disaster Recovery

It is important to distinguish the difference between *crash recovery* and *disaster recovery*. Crash recovery implies that you have the ability to recover when just one node becomes inaccessible, due to some type of hardware or software problem specific to that particular node. Disaster recovery implies that you have the ability to recover from a problem affecting an entire geographic site or area. Accordingly, in order to provide disaster recovery, the nodes in the cluster must be located great distances from each other. The geographic separation is usually limited by the fact that both nodes need access to the disk drive, and even if that separation can be achieved, the shared disk drive is still in a single location. There are continuous improvements in fibre channel technologies that are constantly allowing nodes further geographic separation from the disk storage itself. In addition, technologies

such as geomirroring can allow geographical separation of disks within an array, providing disaster recovery capability should a site housing your disk storage go offline. Some examples of technology along these lines are EMC's GeoSpan clusters or Compaq Stretch Clusters. Thus, the ultimate answer as to whether Failsafe and MSCS can be used for disaster recovery purposes has to be addressed by your hardware vendor—some vendors have technology available now to provide disaster recovery capability in a clustered environment. For the most part, without this hardware capability, Failsafe is generally used for crash recovery purposes, not disaster recovery. Technologies such as standby databases and replication can be combined with a Failsafe or RAC environment for disaster recovery purposes, as we will discuss in Chapter 15.

Lessen the Impact of Normal Maintenance Operations

In addition to providing crash recovery capability, the impact of normal activities such as hardware repairs or maintenance is lessened, as repairs can be done on one node, while the database is running on the other node, just as operating system patches can be applied on one node while the other node is fully operational. When the maintenance operation is finished, the database can be manually moved to the other node, and if necessary, the maintenance/repairs can be repeated on the original node. Oracle requires you to install the database and Failsafe software on the private drive as well, providing redundancy of the Oracle software, and the ability to perform rolling upgrades under certain circumstances.

Shared Drive Redundancy

The one component that is not duplicated between the nodes is the shared drive. For this reason, it is common that the shared drives be part of an array, which is then striped into a RAID 5 volume, thereby providing protection at the disk level as well. This striping and volume configuration should be done at the hardware level, as a hardware RAID is generally more reliable and efficient than a software RAID. You should avoid the temptation to stripe all available drives into one large volume, because this severely limits your flexibility when it comes to locating data files and assigning drives to groups.

Virtual Servers and Groups

The basic concept behind Microsoft Cluster Server (MSCS) is the idea of providing multiple server systems, or nodes, access to the same shared disk array. While only one node can access the disk array, MSCS uses the concept of *virtual servers,* with their own independent IP addresses, in a grouping of logical resources, to provide basic high availability. Should a failure or other problem arise with one node in the cluster, the virtual *group* will fail over to the other node, along with the IP address, making the transition nearly seamless to clients that are connecting via the virtual server's IP address.

One of these key concepts behind MSCS and Oracle Failsafe is the concept of the *virtual server.* A virtual server is essentially defined as a *group* containing logically associated *resources,* including a network name and IP address combination, which makes the group/virtual server appear to be an independent machine on the network. The group floats between the nodes in the cluster, depending on which node(s) are up and which node is determined to be the preferred owner. While the group resides on a given cluster node, it is consuming memory and CPU resources on that owning node, but clients on the network will essentially see it as a separate machine, because it has its own network name and IP address. The advantage of this configuration is that client connections to the virtual server/group will always use the same IP address or network name. So, regardless of which node owns the group, clients will always connect in the same fashion, to the same "virtual" machine.

Resources

Simply put, resources are the reason for running MSCS. You want to make something highly available. What is that "something"? In our case, it is the Oracle database, but it may be a shared disk drive, or some other type of application executable—all of these are examples of resources. In order to make the main resource, the Oracle database, function properly, you must also have supporting resources. In order to connect to the database resource in a group, you must have a listener in the group, which is also a resource. The listener requires an IP address resource and a network name resource to facilitate that connection. In addition, your database files reside on disks, and the disks are considered resources as well.

Dependencies between resources are created to ensure that everything works together smoothly. The Listener service depends on the network name, which in turn depends on the IP address, so the IP address must be online and accessible first, before either of the other two resources can be utilized. By the same token, the disks must come online prior to any attempt to bring the database online. If a given resource fails, any resources that are dependent on that resource will fail as well. The Oracle Failsafe Manager sets these dependencies up for you when adding a database to a group. In earlier releases of OFS, the database was also made to depend on the listener, but starting with the 3.1 release, it was determined that this dependency was not needed, and thus it was removed. Therefore, if the listener fails, it can be restarted on the same node without necessarily impacting the database. We will discuss viewing and manually creating dependencies later in this chapter.

A resource can, of course, belong to only one group. As such, two different databases with files on the same disk must both belong to the same group, as it is not possible for a resource (in this case, the database) to have a dependency on another resource (the disk) that is in a different group. It is important to note also that MSCS considers a disk to be a resource at the physical level. So, regardless of how many partitions you carve the physical drive into, MSCS will view this as one resource, and all logical partitions on that disk will move in tandem.

Resource Monitoring

MSCS uses a *resource DLL* called clusres.dll, which contains monitoring information for the predefined resource types that come with Microsoft Cluster Server. These resource types include an IP Address, Network Name, Physical Disk, File Share, and Generic Service, among others. In addition, Oracle Failsafe registers a resource type for the Oracle database and a resource type for the Oracle TNS Listener. Oracle provides a resource DLL called FsResOdbs.dll, which MSCS uses to poll these resources at a predetermined interval, verifying that the database and listener are functional. If the polling detects a failure of some sort, then the resource is automatically restarted or moved to an alternate node in the cluster, with no manual intervention required.

Cluster Software

In an Oracle Failsafe environment, Microsoft Cluster Server is the cluster software responsible for maintaining communications between cluster nodes, polling resources, and ensuring the health and stability of the cluster as a whole. Accordingly, Oracle Failsafe must subscribe to the limitations of the cluster software itself. For example, on Windows 2000 Advanced Server, MSCS supports two nodes as the maximum number of nodes in a cluster. With Datacenter Server, the number of supported nodes jumps to four. This may be increased further in future releases of MSCS, but this limitation is a function of the clustering software, not a Failsafe limitation. Additionally, MSCS requires that shared drives be formatted as NTFS volumes.

As you will see in Chapter 12, when we discuss Real Application Clusters, MSCS is not required in a RAC environment. Instead, Oracle provides its own clustering software for RAC on Windows 2000, and Oracle requires hardware vendors to certify their individual RAC configurations with Oracle directly. Thus, the number of supported nodes in a RAC environment varies by the vendor, and, due to stringent requirements for RAC certification, the list of supported hardware for a RAC environment is considerably shorter than the hardware compatibility list for MSCS. In addition, the shared drives in a RAC environment must be left *raw* (unformatted). We discuss this in detail in Chapter 12.

Shared Nothing Architecture

Another of the key precepts of the MSCS architecture is that it is a shared-nothing architecture. This means that a resource, be it a disk, a database, or whatever, can be accessed through only one node at a time. If a node fails, the group must be failed over and brought online on an alternate node before its resources can be accessible through that node. This is another key difference between Failsafe and Real Application Clusters, as RAC utilizes a shared-everything architecture. It implies that Failsafe is geared toward high availability, rather than scalability, since, at any given time, only one node's processing power, memory, I/O capability, and networking horsepower can be utilized by the resources in a group. We will discuss Active/Active and Active/Passive scenarios, and how to maximize the resources that you have in a Failsafe environment, in the next section of this chapter.

Designing an Oracle Failsafe Solution

Once you have decided that Failsafe is the solution that fits your needs, time needs to be spent in determining how to design your cluster. Before you embark on what should be a three-hour tour, and instead find yourself stranded on a desert isle, you should know the answers to these questions:

- How many databases do I expect to run on the cluster?
- Is the horsepower of one node adequate to handle all databases in the event that one node fails?
- Are there other applications besides the database that need high availability on the same cluster?
- How many disk devices do I need for acceptable I/O throughput?

Answers to these questions will provide insight into how the cluster should be set up before Oracle or Failsafe is installed.

How Many Groups Do I Need?

The number of groups directly correlates with how many databases or additional resources you plan to have on the cluster. The way the Failsafe polling mechanism works, if a database is determined to be inaccessible (because, for instance, media recovery is needed or a background process [thread] keeps dying), then a failover can be initiated. There are many perfectly legitimate reasons why a resource such as the database may fail, even though the node on which it resides is perfectly healthy.

By default, a group is configured such that a database failure would warrant an attempt to move to the other node, so you must bear in mind that all resources in the group must go to the other node in concert. Thus, if you have two or more databases in the *same* group, a failure of any one database could potentially lead to the failure and subsequent migration of the entire group.

For this reason, it is advantageous to create separate groups for separate databases. By doing so, you ensure that a failure specific to one instance in Group A will not cause the failure of another instance residing in Group B. As each group will require its own IP address, this necessitates some forethought. At a minimum, to install a cluster running Oracle Failsafe with just one Failsafe group, you will need to have a total of four IP addresses that are valid on your network and accessible by clients— one IP address for each node, one for the Cluster Group, and one for the first Failsafe group. The Cluster Group *cannot* be used for your database, so at a minimum, you will *always* create at least one group for Failsafe. Each subsequent Failsafe group created must be assigned its own IP address and network name as well. These IP addresses should be registered in DNS or in the local HOSTS file. In large companies, with entrenched IT bureaucracies, it can often take days to get a single IP address, much less four or five IPs, so planning ahead here can avoid delays when it comes time to implement.

Groups and Shared Disks

If you decide that you will have multiple databases running in distinct groups, you must also be aware of the placement of the files for each database. As noted previously, a physical disk resource can be assigned to only one group. Thus, files for two databases that are slated for different groups cannot share the same physical drive. Making sure that you have enough shared disks available to handle multiple instances, and also to load balance different files for a single instance, is a key to your cluster design. So, often we have seen cases where the sysadmin will stripe all of the available shared drives together into a single, very large volume. Microsoft Cluster Server now views this volume as a single physical drive resource, and you, the DBA, are destined to manage a cluster with unfulfilled potential.

Active/Active Configuration

An Active/Active configuration is defined as a cluster in which both nodes have active groups. When all is well in the world, each group is running on its assigned node, and never the twain shall meet. However, in the event of a failure of one of the nodes, the other will act as a backup. Since both nodes are actively working and own groups that are consuming CPU cycles and memory, a failure of the other node can cause a strain on resources. For this reason, Failsafe allows the init.ora file to be stored on the private drive of each node. Thus, in case the group owning database A on node A fails over to node B, you may decide that the init file for database A on the other node should have smaller values for memory-related parameters, so as not to crowd out the existing database already running on node B. When node A comes back online, database A will return to that node and will use the original parameter file, with processing returning to normal on all nodes.

Multitiered Solutions

In addition to having multiple databases on your cluster, you may also have an Active/Active scenario where one node in the cluster hosts an application tier, and the other node hosts a database tier. Oracle Failsafe supports cluster configuration of application software such as Oracle 9iAS, Oracle WebDB, and Oracle Applications 11i. If you are running in an environment such as this, consideration must be given to the configuration of these applications in the event that the database fails over to the application server, or vice versa. However, it is beyond the scope of this book to detail those configurations—our focus here will be on the database and related supporting resources. Please refer to the "Oracle Failsafe Concepts and Administration Guide" for details on configuration of these additional products in an MSCS environment.

Active/Passive Cluster Configuration

The counterpoint to an Active/Active setup is an Active/Passive configuration. This implies that one node in the cluster has no active groups assigned to it but instead waits patiently for the other node to fail. This is an ideal setup, because of the fact that there is no loss in horsepower in the event of a failure—the passive node is normally decked out identically to the active node. The drawback, of course, is that for the majority of the time these hardware resources are wasted—the passive node spends most of its time holding a clipboard on the sidelines, drawing a paycheck, and just waiting for the starting quarterback to go down.

N-Node Clusters

Perhaps a solution to the conundrum of Active/Active versus Active/Passive is having a cluster with more than two nodes. For example, assume that you have a cluster with an application tier and a database tier. If you run your application tier on one node and the database tier on another node, you can add a third node, which remains idle, waiting for either of the other nodes to fail. Your cluster can be configured such that if the database fails, it will fail over to the passive node first. The same with the application tier—in the event of a failure, rather than using cycles on your database server, the application software will fail over to the passive node, leaving the database node untouched. If you require more than two active nodes, you can take this to the next

logical step by adding yet a fourth node, with three nodes actively running groups, and having the fourth as the sole passive/standby node. In this situation, your standby node will have to have all of the necessary software installed to support either the database or the application in the event of a failure.

Achieving Economies of Scale

On the surface, this may seem to be an expensive solution. However, compare this to a situation where you have three separate clusters, each in an Active/Passive environment. In this situation, you would actually have six nodes instead of four. With a four-node cluster, you are achieving a similar level of reliability and performance, but with an economy of scale that allows you to expend only two-thirds of the cost of running three separate clusters. The potential downside, which must be factored in, is that if two nodes can fail at once, the remaining node(s) will be under added strain. An additional upside is that you can have multiple backup nodes by allowing a group to fail over to any or all of the other nodes if the need arises.

Preparing to Install MSCS

Prior to installing MSCS, you should ensure that the hardware is properly configured. Specifically, you must configure the shared disks in preparation for making them accessible as resources to the cluster. Additionally, in most clusters, you will have at least two network cards. Therefore, you must ensure that all cards are bound in the correct order. Finally, you must ensure that all network names and IP addresses to be used have been properly configured in DNS or the hosts files on each node.

Configure Disks

Pick a node from which to configure the disks, and open the Disk Management console from that node. Disks need only be configured from one node. Do not attempt to write to the disks from multiple nodes until the clustering software has been installed. Avoid creating software volumes—any striping or RAID configuration should be done at the hardware level, prior to configuring the disks in the Disk Management console, as this will provide you better performance.

Quorum Disk

MSCS requires that one of your shared disks be assigned as the quorum disk, to assist in handling certain clustering functions. The quorum disk is critical to resolving ownership of resources should the interconnect go down; in addition, it provides an area of physical storage that all nodes can access. The quorum disk currently does not require much space, so you should choose the smallest drive possible. Microsoft recommends a minimum drive size of 500MB, but these requirements may increase in future releases. Bear in mind also that if the quorum disk fails, the cluster fails, so you may want the quorum disk to be a RAID 5 volume. While it is possible in some versions to place Oracle datafiles on the same drive as the quorum disk, Oracle and Microsoft recommend that the quorum disk be kept separate from any other resource disks.

Configure the disks on the shared array, keeping in mind that a physical drive with multiple partitions still behaves as a single cluster resource. Format all shared drives as NTFS volumes, assigning drive letters as appropriate.

Configure Network Cards

As mentioned previously, you will likely have at least two network cards in each node of the cluster. One network card is generally used for public communication with clients and other servers on the network, while the second network card is generally reserved for cluster communications only. If there are only two nodes in the cluster, these cards can be connected directly to each other via a crossover cable, or you can go through a hub if you have more than two nodes. It is possible to have the cluster communications go through the public network, but this is not recommended, as the cluster communication involves polling of resources on a regular basis. Not only can this result in a large amount of traffic, but also a network glitch could be incorrectly interpreted as a resource failure, resulting in a restart or failover of a healthy resource. Thus, it is better to have a dedicated network for the resource polling.

Since the card dedicated for cluster communication is likely talking only to other nodes in the cluster, the IP address assigned does not have to be valid on your network. Thus, when we mentioned earlier that you would need at least four IP addresses to install MSCS and Oracle Failsafe on a cluster, we did not include IP addresses assigned to the private interconnect, since those can be drummed up at a moment's notice. It is common to use IP addresses such as 10.10.10.1 for node 1 and 10.10.10.2 for node 2, and so on, or something along those lines.

Binding Order

With a network card dedicated to the interconnect, and a second card dedicated to the public network, it is important to ensure that the bindings are set up correctly. Any public cards, which will be communicating with client machines, should always be bound first, leaving the network card for the interconnect bound last of all. This is critical in ensuring that name resolution works correctly, particularly when nodes are communicating with each other. If the binding order is incorrect, you may see that a ping of the public host name resolves to the private IP address. In addition, the listener may end up resolving the host name to the private IP address, meaning incoming connections on the public IP address would fail to find the listener. To check the bindings, right-click My Network Places and choose Properties. From the Advanced drop-down menu, choose Advanced Settings. Under the Adapters and Bindings tab, ensure that the card with your public IP address is first in the list. If not, move it up. Follow the same steps on all nodes.

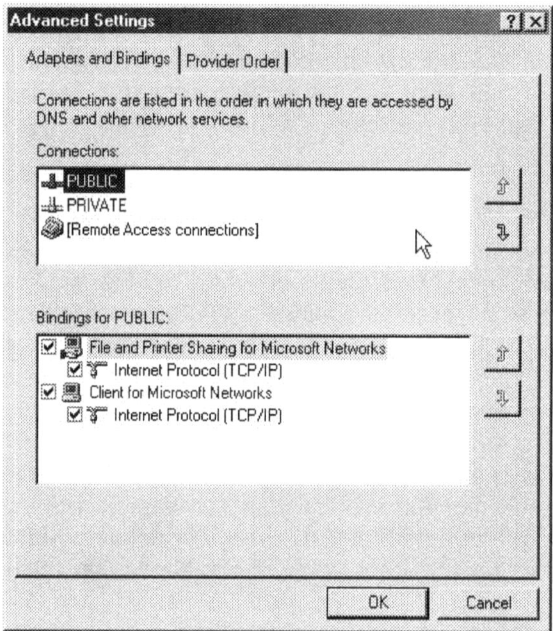

Disabling WINS on Interconnect

You also want to ensure that the WINS address is left empty for the private card. Right-click the private network connection in Network and Dial-up Connections, choose Properties, and then select Properties again for the Internet Protocol (TCP/IP). Choose the Advanced button and then select the WINS tab. If there is a WINS address defined, remove it. This will prevent the Cluster Service from becoming confused when attempting to communicate with the Domain Controller (all cluster nodes must be members of a domain).

Use DNS or HOSTS for Name Resolution

Finally, make sure that all public IP and host name combinations have been registered in DNS. This includes IP addresses and host names for groups that you intend to create for the cluster itself and for any Failsafe groups. In addition, you may want to assign a network name to the cards on the private interconnect. Since these cards usually are not going to be connected to a DNS server, you should add entries into the hosts file (found in the \WINNT\System32\drivers\etc directory). A popular convention is to append ".SAN" to the end of the actual node name, and use that as the host name assigned to the private card. This convention indicates clearly that this hostname is on its own subnet, using the private interconnect. Thus, if you have two nodes called RMNTOFS1 and RMNTOFS2, your host file entries for the private cards might look like so:

```
10.10.10.1      RMNTOFS1.SAN
10.10.10.2      RMNTOFS2.SAN
```

Double-check the setup by pinging the public and private names of all nodes in the cluster, including pinging each node from itself, and verify that a ping of the public name always returns the public IP address, and a ping of the private name returns the private IP address:

```
C:\>ping rmntofs1
Pinging rmntofs1.US.ORACLE.COM [138.1.144.108] with 32 bytes of data:

Reply from 138.1.144.108: bytes=32 time<10ms TTL=128
..
C:\>ping rmntofs1.san
Pinging RMNTOFS1.SAN [10.10.10.1] with 32 bytes of data:

Reply from 10.10.10.1: bytes=32 time<10ms TTL=128
..
```


Installing Microsoft Cluster Server

Okay—so you have made your decision to go with Oracle Failsafe, and you have planned out the cluster accordingly. You know how many nodes you will need, and you have all of the hardware in place. Your disks are partitioned such that you have enough physical drives to support the appropriate number of groups, and at the same time allow you to balance I/O across multiple devices. And, finally, you have asked for, and received, all of the necessary host names and IP addresses from your internal IT department, had them registered in DNS, and configured your network cards appropriately. You are now ready to install Microsoft Cluster Server.

Installing the First Node

Open up the Windows 2000 Control Panel on one of your cluster nodes, and choose Add/Remove Programs. In the dialog window that opens up, choose Add/Remove Windows Components. Place a check box next to Cluster Service and choose Next. You will be prompted for the Windows 2000 Advanced Server CD-ROM, and then the Cluster Configuration Wizard will be started. Choose Next on the welcome screen, and the next page will display a link to the Microsoft Hardware Compatibility List, with a disclaimer that hardware not on that list is not supported. Click the button indicating "I Understand" (if you do—otherwise, do not pass Go—instead go directly to jail), and choose Next again. Since this is the first node in the cluster, indicate this on the next screen and continue. On the next screen, you are prompted for the Cluster Name. Type in the network name that you have chosen for the Cluster Group. Remember, this network name and cluster IP combination should have already been registered in DNS or in the hosts file. If not, this step will fail. (You will be prompted for the IP address later on in the install.)

User Account for Running Cluster Service

On the next screen, you will be prompted for a username under which the Cluster Service will run. This is a Domain Account, and the domain name that the cluster node is a member of should show up in the bottom box. Type in the correct username and password and continue on to the next screen. Here, you should see the listing of shared drives that you previously configured in the Disk Management console. Ensure that all of the drives you intend to use are listed on the right-hand side, under Managed Disks. Continue to the next screen, where you will choose which drive will be the quorum disk.

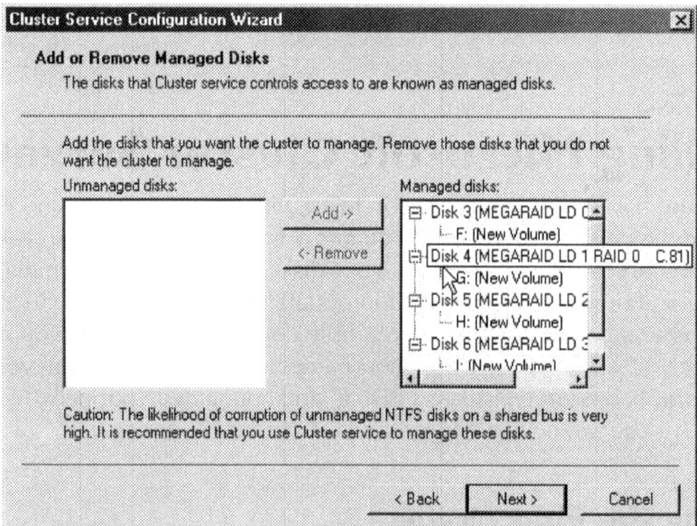

Defining Networks

After selecting the quorum disk, you will be presented with a screen on which you will define the networks. You can name them whatever you choose here—generally, we keep it simple and call them "Public" and "Private." For the Private network, you should ensure that you select the radio button to enable the network for Internal Cluster Communications Only. For the public network, you should probably select All Communications, to provide a certain amount of redundancy. On the next screen, you will determine which network should be used first for cluster communications, assuming that both networks are functioning. Be sure that the Private network is first, so that as long as it is functional, the public network will be configured only as a fallback. It is also fairly common at some sites to have three or four network cards in each node, so =redundancy. If you have more than two cards in each node, configure the networks according to which order you want cluster communications to fall back in the event of a failure.

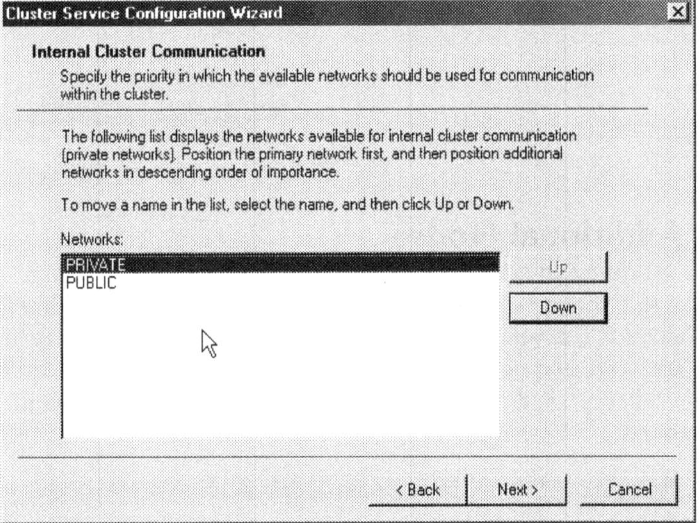

For the final step, you will be prompted to enter the IP address that you have reserved for the virtual Cluster Group. As we mentioned previously, this IP address is the same that was registered in DNS or hosts with the cluster's Network name, which was specified at the outset of the MSCS install. Type in the IP and ensure that the correct network is chosen. Most times, this is going to be the public network— however, this is not technically a requirement. You can select an IP address that is on the private network and registered in the hosts file. However, this will render the actual Cluster Group inaccessible to clients, making it more difficult to manage remotely, so generally, this is an IP address on the public network. On the final screen, be sure to click Finish to complete the cluster installation.

Cluster Service Configuration Wizard

Cluster IP Address
The IP address identifies the cluster to the network.

Type the IP address for management of the cluster. The subnet mask may be supplied automatically.

IP address: 138 . 1 . 144 . 117
Subnet mask: 255 . 255 . 252 . 0

Select the public network from which clients gain access to the cluster.

Network: PUBLIC

< Back | Next > | Cancel

Adding Additional Nodes

The process of adding an additional node to the cluster is much quicker. On the second node, start the install in the same fashion as before, but this time, select the radio button for The Second Or Next Node In The Cluster. Provide the same username, password, and domain information as in the initial install, and then finish the cluster installation on the second node. This node has now joined the cluster as an equal member.

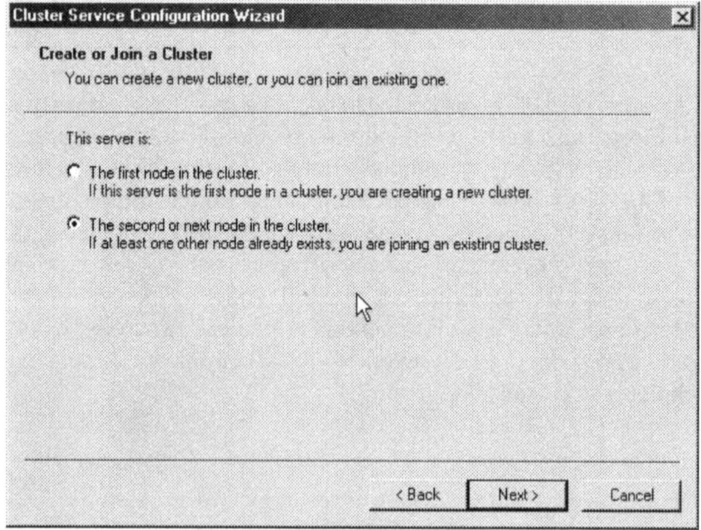

Using Cluster Administrator

Once you have installed Microsoft Cluster Server, you will be able to run the Microsoft Cluster Administrator to view the nodes, groups, and resources in your cluster. Start Cluster Administrator by clicking Start | Programs | Administrative Tools | Cluster Administrator. Refer to Figure 11-1, which is an expanded view of Cluster Administrator. Initially, after a fresh install, you will have a group called Cluster Group, which contains as resources the Cluster IP Address, the Cluster Name, and the quorum disk. This is the first virtual server group that has been created as part of your cluster. You cannot add an Oracle database or other resources to this group—you must create a second group. However, the install of Failsafe later on will add the Oracle Services for MSCS into the Cluster Group. We discuss this in the upcoming section on Failsafe installation.

Disk Groups

In addition to the Cluster Group, you see in Figure 11-1 that you will have a Disk Group for each additional shared disk besides the quorum disk. These Disk Groups are simply placeholders for the disk resources—they are not true virtual groups, as they do not have network names and IP addresses associated. However, ownership

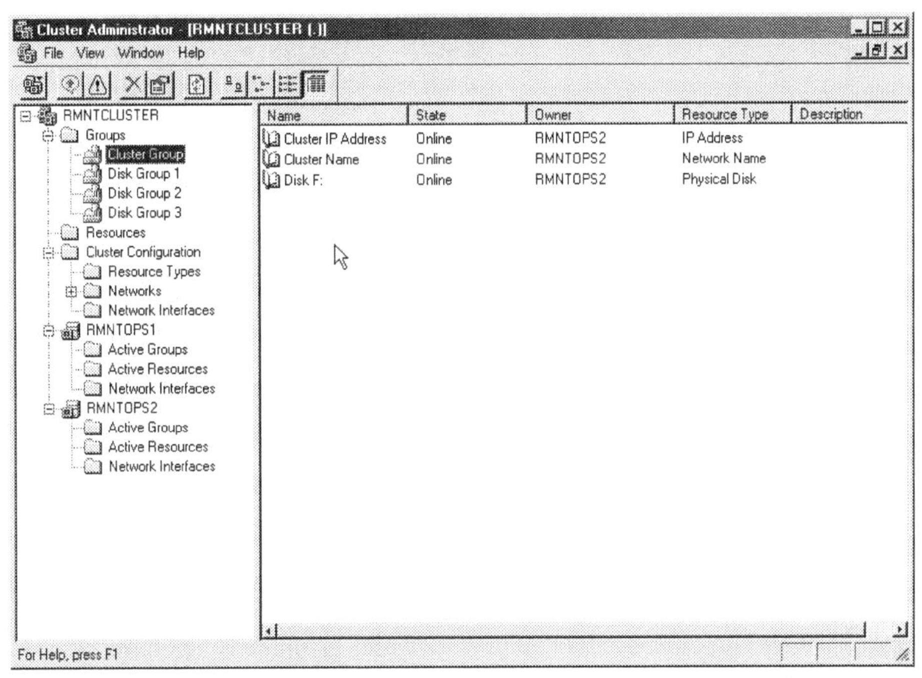

FIGURE 11-1. *Expanded Cluster Administrator view*

of the disk groups can still be transferred back and forth between the nodes. When a database with files residing on one of these disks is added to a new group, the disk resource associated will be removed from the temporary disk group and placed into the database group. At this time, you will be able to delete the disk group, if you so desire.

Resources and Resource Types

Refer again to Figure 11-1, showing the Cluster Administrator. You will also see a folder called Resources. When this is highlighted, it will list all cluster resources, the group in which each resource resides, and the current owning node. In addition, under Cluster Configuration you should see a Resource Types folder. When highlighted, this will list each of the resource types and the Resource DLL used to monitor that type of resource. Once Oracle is installed and configured, you should see a resource type of Oracle Database listed here.

Installing Cluster Administrator on a Client Machine

You may find it useful to install the Cluster Administrator by itself on a desktop machine, or another server outside of the cluster, to enable management of the cluster from a remote location. To do this, you must install the Administrative Tools from the Windows 2000 CD-ROM. Navigate to the \I386 directory on either the standard Windows 2000 Server CD-ROM or the Windows 2000 Advanced Server CD-ROM, and execute the file called ADMINPAK.MSI. This will start the Windows 2000 Administration Tools Setup Wizard. This wizard will install many server administration tools on your local system, including the Cluster Administrator, which you can then use to connect to any cluster on your network, provided you have the proper privileges.

Installing Oracle Failsafe

As mentioned earlier, Oracle software must be installed on the private drive on each node of the cluster. This includes the database software, any Oracle application software (such as Forms, Reports, or 9iAs) and Oracle Failsafe itself. As such, this also requires proper planning prior to embarking on the install. First, you must ensure that you have enough space available on the private drives of all nodes in the cluster. Second, you must determine which nodes in the cluster are meant to run which software. This is primarily a consideration in clusters with multiple nodes. If you are, in fact, planning an architecture with three or four nodes, comprising different tiers, you may not want or need all of the software on all of the nodes in the cluster. Determine which nodes should be able to run the database and which nodes should be able to run the application software, and plan accordingly. We recommend that you install the Failsafe software last. During the install of Failsafe, the Cluster Service *must* be running.

Match Home Names on All Nodes

Since our focus is on making the database itself highly available, we will assume for our purposes here that you will be installing the Oracle9i RDBMS on all nodes in the cluster. You should ensure, at the very least, that home names for the database software and the Failsafe software, respectively, are identical on each node—this is required. Thus, on node 1 if the database software is installed in a home called OraHome90, and Failsafe itself is installed in a home called OFSHome, you *must* make sure that the home names match identically for each of these products on all nodes in the cluster. We also recommend that you match the directory names and orders of install on all nodes when possible. Though this is not strictly required, it prevents confusion and simplifies administration. Once you have decided on the Oracle product choices, home names, and directories, you are ready to begin the actual install of the product.

Again, the install must be done as a user account with Local Administrator privileges on each node. After selecting the home name and directory, when installing Failsafe 3.2 (the first release to be certified with Oracle9i), you will be prompted to select either Oracle Failsafe or Real Application Cluster Guard. Select Oracle Failsafe (we discuss Real Application Cluster Guard in Chapter 15). Choosing a Typical install will give you the components necessary to make the database highly available. Prior to the actual beginning of the installation, you will be cautioned that a reboot is required after the installation completes.

Oracle Services for MSCS Security Setup

At the end of the installation, you will be prompted for another domain name, username, and password combination. This is the account that will be used to run the OracleMSCSServices. (In prior releases, this service was named the Oracle Fail Safe service.) This can be the same account information that you provided earlier for the MS Cluster Server installation, but it does not have to be. The account that you specify must be a Domain User on the same domain as MSCS uses, and must also have Local Administrator privileges on all nodes of the cluster. You should use the same account for all nodes. The Security setup will configure the OracleMSCSServices service to be started and run as the user that you specify.

DCOM Security

In addition to configuring the service logon, the security setup will configure DCOM access by calling the configuration tool and adding the local SYSTEM account to the default access permissions list for Distributed COM security. You can view this by running **dcomcnfg** at a command prompt, choosing Default Security, and editing Default Access Permissions. In earlier releases of Oracle Failsafe, the default access permissions were left untouched. This is normally empty, and thus the

SYSTEM and INTERACTIVE accounts are assumed to have privileges. However, some third-party applications may add user accounts to the default access list, nullifying any default permissions. If default permissions are modified, you may see a hang when running the Verify Cluster tool (discussed later in this chapter) unless SYSTEM is explicitly added to the default access permissions, so starting with the 3.2 release, the Oracle Services for MSCS Security Setup has been modified to always add the SYSTEM account.

Running the Security Setup Post Install

Should the need arise to change passwords after an install, or to update the security, the Oracle Services for MSCS Security Setup can be run after the install by choosing Start | Programs | Oracle – <OFS Homename> | Oracle Services for MSCS Security Setup. Any post-installation changes that you make with this tool will not take effect until after the OracleMSCSServices service is restarted.

Reboot Each Node After Install

After Failsafe has been installed on the first node, it must be rebooted. Wait until the reboot completes and the node has rejoined the cluster prior to beginning the install on the second node. Then, repeat the preceding steps on each node of the cluster, rebooting each node after the Failsafe install completes.

Registry Keys Updated

The Oracle Failsafe install will add a Registry key as a subkey of the normal Oracle key, at HKLM\Software\Oracle\Failsafe. In addition, an Oracle key is created under the cluster key at HKLM\Cluster\Oracle. Once the Oracle Database and Oracle TNS Listener resource types are registered, you will be able to view this under HKLM\Cluster\Resource Types. If you ever need to remove Failsafe from a cluster, you should uninstall it if possible, so that the resource types are unregistered and removed from the Registry. Uninstalling Cluster Server will remove the HKLM\Cluster key, forcing you to reregister the Failsafe resource types after you reinstall MSCS. This can be accomplished by rerunning Verify Cluster, discussed in the next section.

Managing Your Failsafe Environment

As noted previously, the install of Oracle Failsafe creates a service called OracleMSCSServices. This service is a resource that gets added to the Cluster Group, which was created when you initially installed Microsoft Cluster Server. This is the only Oracle resource that should be added to the Cluster Group, and the install will do this for you. Though the service exists on each node, it will be actively running only on the node that owns the Cluster Group. This is the process that Failsafe Manager attaches to when it is run, so failure of this service will lead to a failure when logging in to Failsafe Manager.

Logging in to Failsafe Manager

So, what is Oracle Failsafe Manager (OFSM)? Failsafe Manager is the interface provided by Oracle to interact with the cluster. Failsafe Manager duplicates some of the things that you see in Cluster Administrator. It can be used to monitor the location and ownership of resources, change dependencies and failover policies, and so on, and it can be used to create new virtual groups. All of these operations can be done through Cluster Administrator as well. However, Failsafe Manager must be used to add an Oracle database or other supported Oracle resources into a Failsafe group. In addition, Failsafe Manager provides invaluable troubleshooting tools to verify the cluster setup and resource configuration prior to adding resources to a group, and to verify the integrity of a group after it has been created.

When logging in to Failsafe Manager, you must provide an operating system account that is a member of the cluster's domain, and that also has local administrative privileges. The Cluster name and Domain name are, of course, the same as specified when installing the cluster.

Like Cluster Administrator, Failsafe Manager can be installed on a client machine to allow you remote management access to the cluster. Previous releases of Oracle Failsafe required that the Failsafe Manager client be the same version as the Failsafe Server running on the cluster. However, beginning with the 3.2 release of OFS, the Failsafe Manager can be used to manage clusters running Failsafe version 3.1.1 or later. Thus, in an environment with multiple clusters, you do not have to upgrade all at once, nor do you need to sacrifice the manageability of using Failsafe Manager to manage multiple clusters. Simply ensure that you have the latest version of Failsafe Manager on your desktop, and it will work with the 3.1.x clusters and 3.2.x clusters.

Running Verify Cluster

Run OFSM by choosing Start | Programs | Oracle – <OFS Homename> | Oracle Fail Safe Manager. As you can see in Figure 11-2, the first time that it is run on a new cluster, you will be given the choice to run the Verify Cluster tool or exit. Verify Cluster is the first of the "Verify *xxx*" operations provided by Failsafe Manager to assist in configuration and assurance of the integrity of the database. This tool *must* be run to register the Oracle Resource DLL and Oracle Resource Types for use by the cluster. However, in addition to doing this, Verify Cluster checks the cluster configuration to make sure that all of the networking components are properly configured, and also to confirm that the Oracle install was done properly (i.e., the home names and products installed match on each node).

Heed Warnings in Verify Cluster

Because Verify Cluster must complete in order to register the Resource DLL, you will not get an absolute failure message—you will almost always read that the operation completed successfully. However, you may get warnings. You should save the output from the clusterwide operation to a text file and check this file

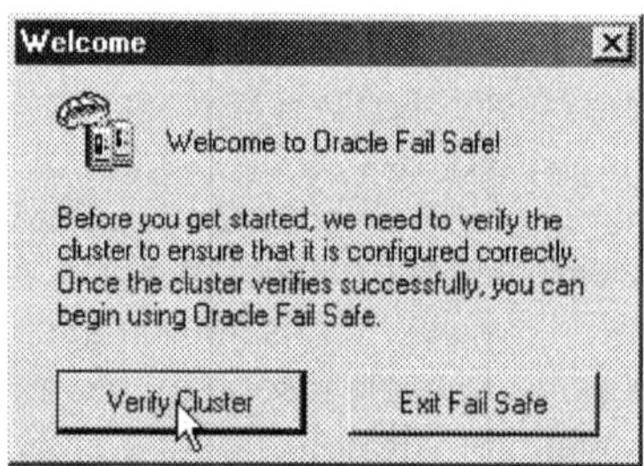

FIGURE 11-2. *Verify cluster at first Failsafe logon*

closely for any errors. Some errors/warnings are only informative in nature, indicating that certain software components are not installed. However, if you see errors indicating an IP address mismatch, this is an indication that the binding order of your cards is incorrect, a condition that may lead to name resolution problems and resource failures down the road. Refer to the earlier section on cluster configuration to resolve these problems, and then rerun the Verify Cluster operation. You should also pay close attention to any errors reporting a mismatch in the names of the ORACLE_HOMEs on the respective nodes. If you mistakenly name the Failsafe home or the database home incorrectly on one of the nodes, you will need to reinstall in order to get Failsafe to work properly. Once the Verify Cluster operation completes, you should be able to see the Oracle Database and Oracle TNS Listener resource types listed in Cluster Administrator.

Making the Database Failsafe

Once Failsafe has been successfully installed and the cluster setup has been verified, you are now ready to create the Failsafe group and add a database. Essentially, these are the steps that you will follow:

- Create the database
- Verify the stand-alone database
- Create the Virtual Group
- Add the database to the group

In this section, we detail each of these steps.

Creating the Database

If you have not yet created the database, you can do so via the Database Configuration Assistant, as described in Chapter 4, or you can create a database manually. In addition, Oracle Failsafe provides a template for a sample database, which you can create through Failsafe Manager itself. To do this, choose Create Sample Database from the Resource menu in Failsafe Manager. However, this is meant more for demonstration purposes than as a template for your production instance. So while you can use this to quickly create a database to show the concept works, we recommend that you use the DBCA or your own scripts to create the true database.

You should create the database on one node only, but be sure when creating the database that all files associated with the database are on a shared drive. This includes control files, log files, datafiles, and any local archive destinations that you define in the init.ora. While it is not required to have the background_dump_dest and the user_dump_dest on shared drives, we strongly recommend it. Having an alert log that is written to the private drive can lead to gaps in the log file if the group moves to another node in the cluster. Move all drives where files will ultimately reside, so that they are all owned by the same node, and create the database from that node.

Placement of Parameter File

In addition to placement of trace files, you must also determine if you are going to have the init file or spfile reside on the private drive or on the shared drive. Having the parameter file on the shared drive will ease administration, since you do not have to be concerned with maintaining multiple copies of init.ora on all nodes. However, this reduces the flexibility to have differences in certain parameters, depending on which node the database resides on. As a general rule, if you have an Active/Active configuration, you may need to consider having different parameter files, placed on the private drive of each node. With an Active/Passive scenario, you should put the parameter file on the shared drive. In a three- or four-node cluster, you will have to determine which nodes the database will reside on, and what resources would be available to the database on each node in event of a failure. Place the parameter file accordingly, depending on your needs and the available resources.

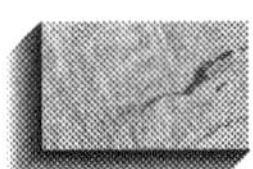

NOTE
If using an spfile, you will have to have a normal init file with the line spfile=xxxx as discussed in Chapter 5. You cannot pass the spfile directly to Failsafe when adding the database to a group.

Verifying the Stand-Alone Database Configuration

Once the database has been created, you should be able to discover it as a stand-alone resource on the node on which it was created. Failsafe Manager will list the nodes in the left-hand pane. Expand the node on which the database exists, and you will see a folder for Groups on that node, and another folder for Standalone Resources. Under Standalone Resources, you will see a message that Failsafe is "Discovering Standalone Resources" on the node, and then you should see a listing of Oracle resources on that machine that are supported in a Failsafe environment. An existing database will be discovered as a resource on the node where it resides, providing there is a service for the instance on that node (OracleService<sid>), *and* there is a valid TNSNAMES.ORA entry on the node, which connects to the same SID name or SERVICE_NAME, using the Host name or IP address of the node.

Once you identify your database, right-click it and choose Verify Standalone Database. You will be prompted for the instance name, parameter file location, and whether you want to connect using OS Authentication or you want to provide a password. If you choose OS authentication, Failsafe will create a local OS group called ORA_<sidname>_DBA and add the accounts that were specified for the Cluster Service and the OracleMSCSServices. Recall that this allows members to connect *only* to this particular instance—Failsafe will not automatically create the more generic ORA_DBA group, but it will work if you manually add the accounts to this group instead of a group specific to your SID.

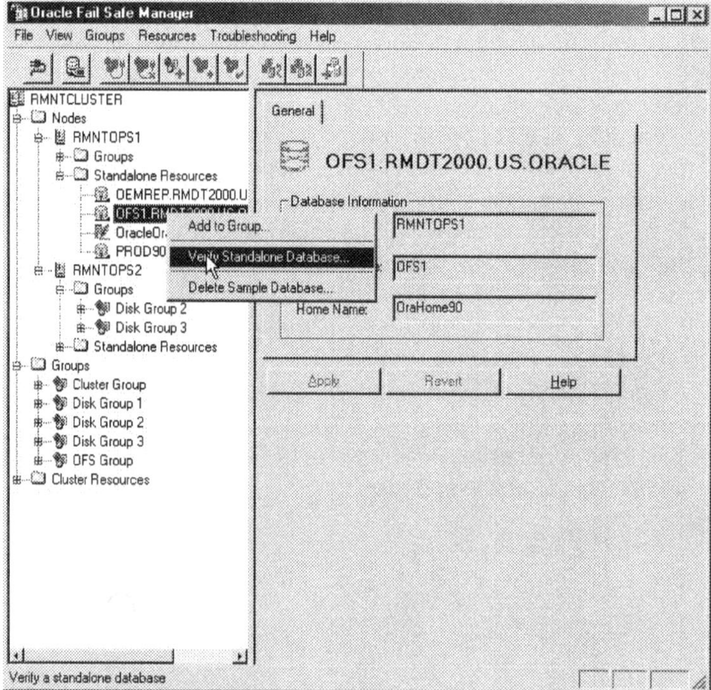

Why Run Verify Standalone?

The Verify Standalone Database will check the configuration of the database and prepare it to be added into a Failsafe Group. It will check that all drives being used by the database are shared drives. If the database is configured for Automatic Startup or Shutdown (refer to Chapter 4), those features will be disabled, because once in the group, the Cluster Service will be responsible for bringing the database offline and online. The Verify Standalone Database operation will also check to ensure that the services for the instance exist on only one node. At this point, since the database is still a stand-alone database, the services for the instance should not yet exist on the second node—if they do, you will be prompted for the correct node, and the services will be deleted from the other node(s).

In addition, the Verify Standalone Database operation will check the tnsnames.ora and listener.ora files and ensure that they are configured correctly, in order to allow them to be parsed by Failsafe when it comes time to add the database to a group. This is critical, because when the database is ultimately added to the group, these files must be reconfigured on each node to account for the virtual server connect information. Failures in parsing these sqlnet configuration files is one of the most common reasons that an operation to add the database to a group will fail, so running Verify Standalone Database is an important step in ensuring these files are set up correctly and ready for the impending Add to Group operation.

Creating a Group

At the risk of sounding repetitive, we will reiterate that you cannot add the database into the Cluster Group—you must create a separate group for the database, and you must have a host name and IP address combination ready. Even though you can use MS Cluster Administrator to create the group, we recommend that you create it through Failsafe Manager, as it provides an interface to add a host name and IP address into the group. In Failsafe Manager, right-click the Groups folder and choose Create. You will be prompted for a name for the group—this can be any name that you decide on; it need not match the host name. Type in the name and an optional description and choose Next.

Defining a Failback Policy and a Preferred Node

On Page 2 of the Create Group Wizard, you will be prompted to define a Failback Policy for the group. If the group fails over to the other node, and the original node then comes back online, do you want this group to go back to the original node automatically? If so, how quickly? Should it happen immediately, or should it happen only during specific hours? If you choose the Prevent Failback option, then the group will not fail back automatically—you will need to manually move the group back to the preferred node if so desired.

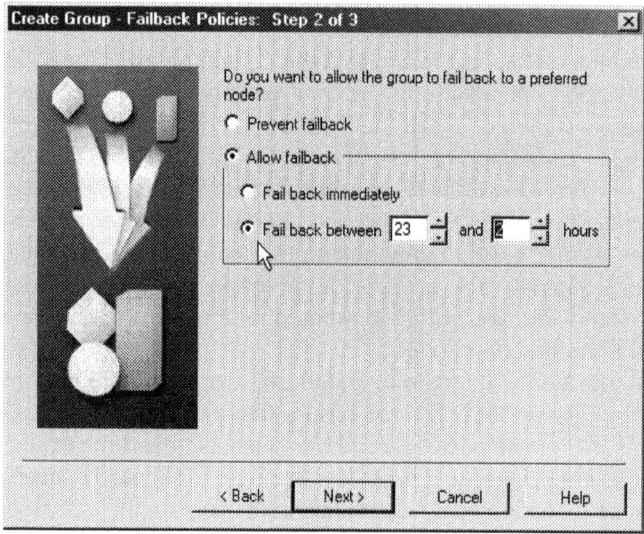

A Failback Policy does not have any meaning if there is not a preferred node, because the failback is triggered when the preferred node rejoins the cluster. Accordingly, if you choose Fail Back Immediately, this failback event will be triggered as soon as the preferred node comes back online. Choosing Prevent Failback on Page 2 implies that there is no preferred node, so you will not see Page 3 of the Create Group Wizard, which is where the preferred node for the group is selected.

Adding Virtual Addresses to a Group

Once the group is created, you will be immediately prompted to add a *virtual address* to the group. A virtual address is simply an IP address and network name combination that will be assigned to the group that you have just created. Think of this process as like adding an entirely new server to your network. In order to bring up a new server on your network, you must have an IP address and network name that are valid for your network, and you must configure the server with that information. Adding a virtual address to the group accomplishes the same thing for your virtual server, which is associated with your newly created group—the wizard configures the group with that address, and then MSCS is responsible for registering that address with the gateway and directing all network communications to the appropriate owning node. This virtual address then becomes the means by which your clients connect to the virtual server and communicate with the rest of the resources that will ultimately be added to this group. As such, this network name and IP address combination must be unique on your network, even among other virtual addresses that already exist, and it must resolve successfully and be accessible by any clients that wish to access the database.

Choose Yes in answer to the Add Virtual Address question, and the Add Resource Wizard will be initialized. You will be prompted to select which network you want to add the virtual address from. In most cases, you will be choosing the public network, which allows your clients to access the network. Theoretically, though, if the only client is an application tier, which runs on one of the other cluster nodes, you could select the private cluster network.

The network name and address that you supply must be valid on one of the subnets tied to a physical card. As an aside, it is possible to have multiple IP address and network name combinations existing in a single group, and it is also possible to have these IPs be on different subnets, to provide further redundancy and load balancing. However, a virtual IP address must always be on the same subnet as at least one physical card within the cluster. Thus, having two IP addresses in a group that are on different subnets would require two different physical network cards, each with an IP address on the respective subnets used by the virtual IP.

Choose the appropriate network for the initial virtual IP, and then put in the host name that you have predefined in DNS or your hosts file. If this is set up correctly, the IP address should be filled in automatically. If not, you will get an error indicating that the host name does not resolve to an IP address. Another common error here is to put in the existing host name of the Cluster Group. If you do so, this will fail with an FS-11221 error, indicating that this network name is already in use. Duplicate network names, of course, are not allowed. The group will still be created, but it will not have a virtual address assigned. You must then go back to Failsafe Manager, right-click the empty group, and choose Add Resource to Group.... The Add Resource Wizard will be initiated again, and you can choose Virtual Address from the list of available Resource Types, this time selecting a new network name and IP address combination not currently in use anywhere on your network.

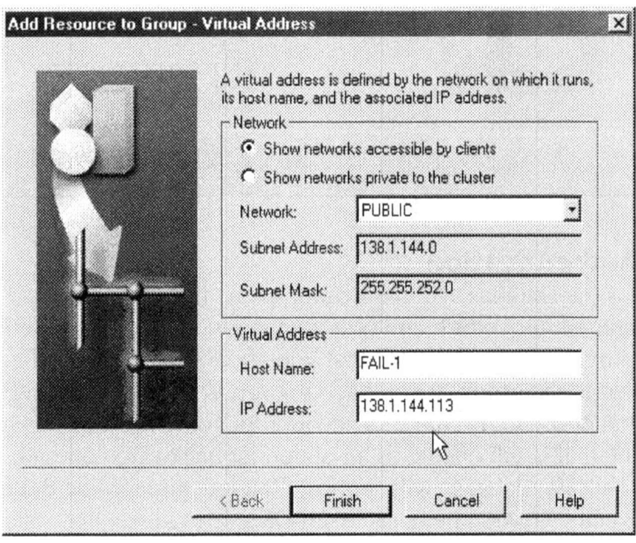

Adding the Database to a Group

Once you have completed the steps of successfully verifying the cluster setup, creating and verifying a stand-alone database, and creating a group with a virtual IP address and host name combo, you are ready to add your database into the group. You can do this in a couple of ways—by right-clicking the database itself, under Standalone Resources on the given node, or by right-clicking the newly created group, choosing Add Resource to Group…and then selecting Oracle Database for the Resource Type. However you start the process, the steps will be the same—be sure the appropriate Resource Type (Oracle Database) and group name are highlighted on the first page of the Add to Group Wizard, and continue on to the next screen. Here, you will define the network service name, the instance name, the database name (as defined by DB_NAME in the init file), and the location of the parameter file that you wish to use.

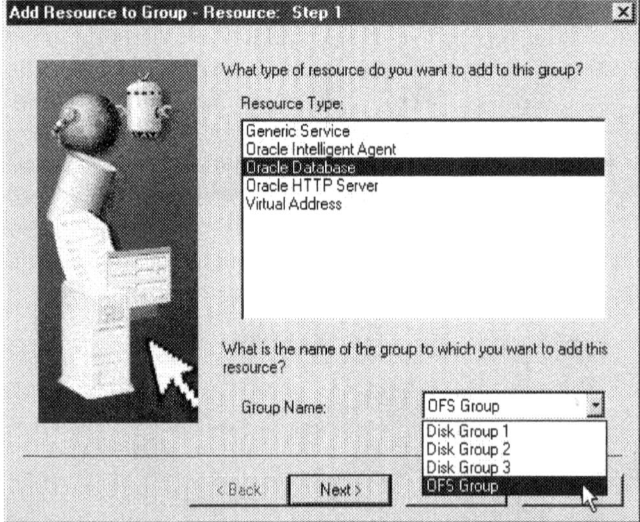

Database Authentication

The next page is the Database Authentication page. If you previously ran the Verify Standalone Database procedure and specified that you wanted to use OS authentication at that time, then it is assumed that you are doing so again when the database is actually added to the group. If you have not run Verify Standalone Database previously, or if you chose to use the SYS account for authentication, then you will be asked again. (Internal is still offered as an option for backward compatibility, because this release of Failsafe Manager will support Oracle8i and Oracle 8.0 databases.) If you choose OS authentication here, again, an OS group called ORA_<sidname>_DBA will be created, and the logon accounts for both the Cluster Service and the OracleMSCSServices will be added to this group. If you had done this during the Verify Standalone Database operation (see Figure 11-3), this group will already exist.

Next, you will still be asked if you want to maintain a password file on all nodes of the cluster. This is recommended if you want to allow access via the password file, but you do not want to add certain OS users to the ORA_DBA group. (Refer to Chapter 4 for more information on using a password file.) The key thing to realize here is that if you do not use OS authentication, then you must ensure that any changes to the password file are propagated to all nodes in the cluster. The polling that is done by the Cluster Service uses this information to connect, and if the password is wrong on one of the nodes, the polling may fail, or the database may not be able to come online at all.

Behind the Scenes When Adding a DB to a Group

Once you have answered the questions on database configuration and authentication, the process to add the database to the group will begin. The service for your instance (i.e., OracleServicePROD90) will be set to manual start, if it is not already, and a second listener will be added to listener.ora. The listener name will be FSL*xxxx*, where xxxx is the virtual host name associated with the group. This will cause a second listener service to be created on the current node, which will be set to manual start also. In addition, the tnsnames.ora file will be updated to reflect the virtual host

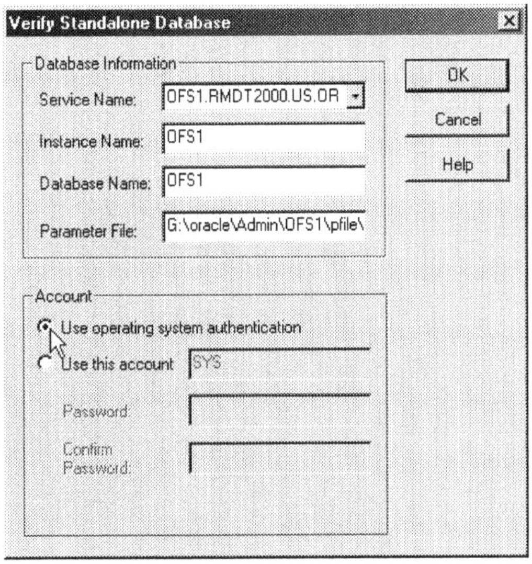

FIGURE 11-3. *Using OS authentication for database resource polling*

information for the group. Once these changes are made, the entire group will be brought offline and moved to the other node(s) defined as possible owners. Failsafe will create a service for the instance (OracleServicePROD90) and configure the tnsnames.ora and listener.ora files on the subsequent node; it will then actually bring the database online on that node, to confirm that all is configured correctly. Once this is done, the group will be returned to reside on the preferred node, or it will go back to the original node if a preferred node is not defined for the group. When this operation is complete, the database will be running in a Failsafe environment.

Behind the Scenes with a Failsafe Database

Once a database has been made Failsafe, we can begin to explore some of the resource properties to determine just exactly what is going on. Expand the group in Failsafe Manager and select the recently added database. On the right, choose the Policies tab (See Figure 11-4). The Looks Alive interval is the shorter period of time; this is the interval at which the service for the instance is checked, to ensure that it is still running. The "Is Alive" interval is a more thorough check. By default, every

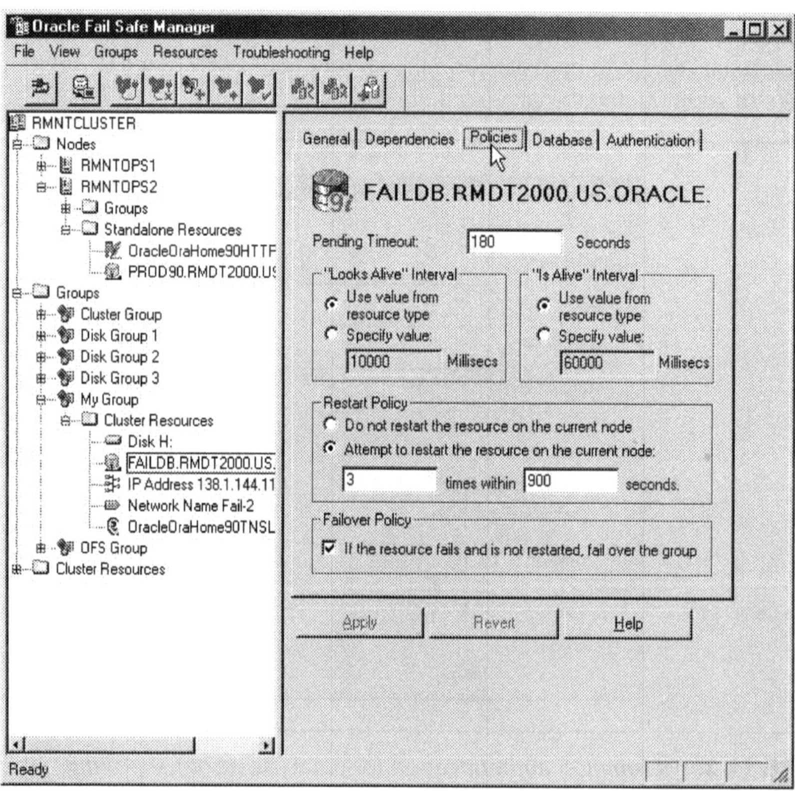

FIGURE 11-4. *Database resource policies*

60 seconds a login to the database is completed and a query is run. These checks are actually performed by the Microsoft Cluster Service, using information provided to it by the Oracle Database Resource DLL. The Cluster Service will actually log on to the database using a sqlnet connect string. If the logon fails, it is directed to retry using a local bequeath connection. Once connected, the following query is run:

```
Select NAME from TS$ where TS$.NAME='SYSTEM';
```

This is just a basic check to verify that the database is running. Should the connect attempt fail, or the query fail, then an error is logged in the Application Log in the Windows 2000 Event Viewer. An internal retry is executed three more times before the resource is officially considered to have failed. These retries after an error are normally executed within 15 seconds or less—this interval is internal and not configurable.

If four attempts to log on and run the query have failed, then the Restart Policy defined for the database will kick in. By default, Failsafe will attempt to stop and then restart the database on the same node, as seen in Figure 11-4. If the restart fails three times, then a failover to another node is initiated because the Failover Policy has determined that if this resource fails, the entire group should be affected. If this check box is not selected, then once the resource has failed to restart the specified number of times, it will be marked as Failed and will be left alone.

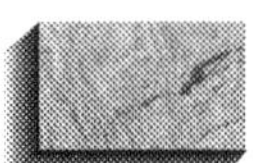

NOTE
If you are forced to run both production and test databases in the same group, due to a lack of disk resources or other limitations, you may want to remove the check from the Failover Policy box for your test database, so that a failure of a test instance will not affect the entire group.

The same information can be viewed in the same manner for all of the other resources in the group. Note that since there is no longer a dependency between the database and the listener, you should ensure that the properties of the listener are set such that if it fails and cannot be restarted, it will affect the entire group. Otherwise, the polling may continue on successfully using a bequeath connection, yet no clients may be able to connect. The removal of this dependency, however, has helped to reduce a false failover that may occur if the listener is temporarily unable to handle connections, yet the database is unaffected.

Removing a Database from a Failsafe Group

Once a database has been added to a group, it can be made stand-alone again by simply right-clicking the database resource itself and choosing the option Remove from Group. Failsafe Manager will automate the process of reconfiguring services,

so that the service for the instance exists on only one node. By the same token, the listener.ora and tnsnames.ora files will be reconfigured so that they are pointing to the stand-alone node's IP address, instead of the virtual group's IP address, and the listener for the group will be deleted if this was the last database in the group.

Manually Removing a Database from a Group If the Remove from Group process fails for any reason, perhaps because the cluster is not functioning properly, or the Failsafe install has become damaged in any way, you can manually make a database into a stand-alone database fairly easily. Resources in a group can be deleted using Cluster Administrator by simply right-clicking the resource and choosing Delete. This deletes the logical resource but does not affect the actual database itself. You should delete the Database resource and the Listener resource from the group, to prevent MSCS from attempting to do any polling or initiate any failures of these resources. The IP address and network name can be left in the group, or deleted, depending on your needs. The disk resources should be left in the group, as we still need to be able to manage the disks and ensure that the proper node owns the disks.

Next, determine which node should be the owning node for the database, and move the group with the disks to that node in Cluster Administrator. Right-click the group and choose Move Group from the pop-up menu. Delete the services for the instance from the *other* node(s) using the **oradim** command (as documented in Chapter 4). Finally, on the node that owns the database, you will need to manually reconfigure listener.ora and tnsnames.ora so that the connections are directed to the stand-alone server IP address instead of the virtual server IP address. Also change tnsnames.ora on any client machines that will connect to the database. The Net Manager tool, discussed in Chapter 7, is an ideal way to accomplish this task.

Troubleshooting in a Failsafe/MSCS Environment

Failsafe introduces some unique situations when attempting to troubleshoot problems. The next section is devoted to ways of uncovering some common problems in a Failsafe environment.

Troubleshooting Tools in a Clustered Environment

Because Failsafe is intertwined so tightly with MSCS, it is often difficult to ascertain the source of a problem. Therefore, Oracle Failsafe provides several troubleshooting tools to help determine the cause of problems, and often, if the problem is an Oracle issue, these troubleshooting tools will also serve as a means of correcting uncovered problems.

Verify Operations

We have already discussed the Verify Cluster operation and the Verify Standalone Database operation as tools provided by Failsafe to help uncover problems with the cluster or the database. In addition, Failsafe provides a Verify Group utility, which can be run against a given group to check for problems specific to the group configuration. For example, if a datafile is placed on a shared disk that was not previously part of the group, you can run the Verify Group operation and the disk resource will be added to the group. If dependencies were modified somehow, Verify Group can be used to repair the problem. If a node goes offline or software needs to be reinstalled, Verify Group can be used to help reconfigure services and sqlnet configuration files on the node once it comes back online, or on an alternate node that may not have been designated as a possible owner in the past.

Before any changes are made by the Verify Group operation, you will be prompted to accept or reject changes. In some cases, these changes will require that the database be brought down and restarted. You will be warned if this is the case.

Dump Cluster

From the Troubleshooting menu in Failsafe Manager, you can also choose to issue a Dump Cluster command. This will write information to the familiar clusterwide operation window, which you can then save as a text file for further diagnosis. This Dump Cluster output will delineate all cluster groups and resources, as well as information on group policies and individual resource polling intervals, restart policies, and dependencies. In addition, all subnets on the cluster will be listed together with ORACLE_HOME information for each node. This Dump Cluster output is invaluable for determining the setup of a cluster and determining any configuration problems with group policies and the like that may heretofore have gone unnoticed.

Event Viewer

Any time an error occurs with a Failsafe resource, an error should be logged to the Application Log of the node on which the group was residing. If an unexplained failover occurs, the Application Log, as well as the instance's Alert Log, should be one of the first items checked to discover the source of the problem. If there is a hardware or OS problem, information should be written to the System Log of the owning node.

Cluster Logging

Starting with Windows 2000, clusterlogging at the operating system level is set up and enabled by default when MSCS is installed. The location of the clusterlog file is determined by an environment variable set as a system variable. To view this location, simply type the following from a command prompt on a cluster node:

```
C:\>set clusterlog
ClusterLog=C:\WINNT\cluster\cluster.log
```

This clusterlog can be used to help determine causes and problems whose solutions are not readily available by checking the System Log. Clusterlogging is not enabled by default on Windows NT 4.0, so this environment variable would need to be set manually and the Cluster Service restarted in order to gather this information.

Listener Log

Because the Cluster Service logs on so frequently, it is possible for the listener log for a group's listener to become very large in a short period of time, since, by default, every connection attempt is written to the listener log file. This is a cause for concern because if the log becomes too large, connections may fail with an ORA-12500 because the listener times out or runs out of resources as it tries to append connect information to the log. To prevent this, you need to regularly delete this log file—it will be re-created automatically when written to. The log file will be located by default in the ORACLE_HOME\Network\Log directory. Keep in mind that the Failsafe listener log will not be called Listener.log, because the listener in the group is not the default, so look for a log file called FSL<Groupname>.Log. You may need to stop the listener in order to delete the log file. Alternatively, you can disable listener logging by setting the parameter LOGGING_<listener_name>=OFF in listener.ora on each node. For example, assume the listener name is FSLFAIL-1. Set the following in each listener.ora file on the cluster:

```
LOGGING_FSLFAIL-1=OFF
```

This will take effect the next time the listener is restarted.

Maintenance in a Failsafe Environment

Once the database is in a Failsafe group, it is considered a highly available resource. Thus, maintenance issues such as cold backups or media recovery must be viewed in a different light. If you simply connect in SQL*Plus to a Failsafe database and issue a shutdown immediate command, Failsafe will detect very quickly that the database is down and will restart it almost immediately. If you have a backup script that shuts down the database in this fashion prior to copying files, you will soon find that these backups are not valid, because after your script does a shutdown, it may proceed to copy files for a database that is expected to be closed. In the meantime, Failsafe has restarted the database and you are now copying open files.

Backups in a Failsafe Environment

To avoid this, if you want to shut down a database and not have it restart, you must do so within the Failsafe structure. In Failsafe Manager, you can right-click the database resource itself and choose Take Offline. Failsafe is now aware that you want the database shut down, and no attempts will be made to restart it until you specifically go back and choose Place Online to make the database Failsafe again. This can be scripted using the FSCMD command-line interface. Here is an example of using FSCMD to take the database offline and back online again:

```
D:\>D:\Oracle\ofs\fs\fsmgr\bin\fscmd offlineresource
faildb.rmdt2000.us.oracle.com /cluster=RMNTCLUSTER /DOMAIN=RMDT2000
/USER=ADMINISTRATOR /PWD=Broncos /offline=immediate

D:\>D:\Oracle\ofs\fs\fsmgr\bin\fscmd onlineresource
faildb.rmdt2000.us.oracle.com /cluster=RMNTCLUSTER /DOMAIN=RMDT2000
/USER=ADMINISTRATOR /PWD=Broncos
```

Recovery in a Failsafe Environment

If you are in a situation where you need to do media recovery on a file, it is probable that the database has already been taken offline, due to repeated failures. Checking the Application Log will confirm this, with errors such as an ORA-1113, or an ORA-1157, or something similar. Once a resource has been marked as failed, the cluster will stop attempting to bring it online. The Failover Threshold, viewed by selecting the group in question in Failsafe Manager and selecting the Failover tab, determines how soon this occurs. By default, if a resource fails ten times over a six-hour period, all attempts to bring it back online are stopped. If a media failure occurs, or a file needs recovery, chances are that these ten failures will actually occur within a very short period of time—normally, a few minutes.

To recover the database, you must first determine which node owns the group. Do this by highlighting the group either in Cluster Administrator or Failsafe Manager. The owning node appears in the right-hand window, under the General tab in Failsafe, or under the Owner column in Cluster Administrator. Once the owner is determined, you must manually start the service for the instance on that node.

```
C:\>net start OracleServicePROD90
```

Once the service is started, manually set the ORACLE_SID and then launch SQL*Plus. From here, you can issue a startup mount command and begin the database recovery. If using RMAN for backup and restore operations, as recommended in Chapter 6, you may also need to manually start the listener service for the group, so that you can connect with RMAN if you are running it remotely.

Upgrading in a Failsafe Environment

Failsafe supports rolling upgrades in a couple of different instances. First, a rolling upgrade is supported when upgrading the Oracle Failsafe software itself. Second, a rolling upgrade of the database software is supported in regard to applying patches to the database. When upgrading a database from one major release to another, you should remove the database from the Failsafe group, perform the upgrade/migration,

and then add the database back into the group once the process is finished. Refer to the section in Chapter 10 on "Upgrading/Migrating in a Failsafe Environment," and/or the Oracle Failsafe Installation Guide, for further instructions on upgrading in a Failsafe environment.

Removing Failsafe Components

The best way to remove Failsafe cleanly from your environment is to run the Oracle Universal Installer and choose the option to Deinstall Products. Select the ORACLE_HOME where Failsafe is installed, check the Oracle Failsafe product, and then choose Remove. You will be asked if you want to unregister the resource DLL. If you intend to permanently remove Failsafe, or if you are attempting to get a truly clean environment, then you should choose yes.

If you are unable to successfully uninstall Failsafe, you can follow the instructions in Chapter 4 for "Removing Oracle Altogether" from a machine. Add to that, however, the need to remove the Oracle key Database and Oracle TNS Listener Resource Types from the Cluster section of the Registry. The Oracle key is located under HKLM\Cluster and the Resource Types are located under HKLM\Cluster\Resource Types. If you successfully uninstall Failsafe and choose to unregister the resource DLL, then these entries are removed, but if you clean the machine manually, you need to manually delete the keys for the Oracle Database and Oracle TNS Listener. By the same token, if you uninstall Microsoft Cluster Server, with Oracle Failsafe already installed, you will be warned with a dialog box that these Resource Types will be lost, because the entire Cluster key under HKLM will be removed. Thus, if you reinstall MSCS, you will need to rerun Verify Cluster to ensure that the Oracle Resource Types are reregistered.

Summary

This chapter has been devoted to Microsoft Cluster Server and Oracle Failsafe. We have discussed how to determine if Failsafe and MSCS will work for you. Once that decision is made, we discussed the design of a Failsafe solution, including hardware and software, the installation of Microsoft Cluster Server, and the installation of the Failsafe software. This was followed by steps needed to create a Failsafe Group and successfully add your database to the group. Finally, we discussed certain aspects of troubleshooting and maintaining your database once it has been made Failsafe. In the next chapter, we move on to discuss Oracle Real Applications Clusters.

CHAPTER 12

Oracle Real Application Clusters

This chapter in the high availability section is devoted to the discussion of Oracle Real Application Clusters. Real Application Clusters (RACs) constitute the next generation of Oracle Parallel Server—it is technology that has expanded beyond the original capability of Parallel Server to allow easier shipment of blocks between instances, reducing the additional I/O normally associated with Parallel Server. At the same time, RAC maintains the *cache coherency* needed for multiple nodes to be able to read the most current data. It is beyond the scope of this book to go into a full description of Real Application Cluster architecture—the Oracle9*i* documentation set has a total of six different books devoted to various RAC-related topics. This chapter essentially presents a cookbook approach to RAC to allow you to get up and running as quickly as possible in a RAC environment on Windows 2000. We will disseminate the following tips:

- Understanding the RAC environment
- Using the interconnect
- Discovering scalability advantages in a RAC environment
- Configuring network cards
- Configuring the interconnect
- Creating and managing raw partitions for your files
- Using the clustercheck tool
- Manually installing Object Link Manager prior to cluster setup
- Creating symbolic links
- Exporting and importing link definitions
- Initiating the Cluster Setup Wizard
- Defining symbolic links within the cluster setup
- Installing Oracle RAC software
- Creating a RAC database
- Maintaining a RAC database
- Using system managed undo in a RAC database
- Using multiple redo threads
- Adding additional instances
- Adding additional datafiles and log groups

The RAC Environment

The hardware setup used for Real Application Clusters on Windows 2000 is similar to what you would use for Oracle Failsafe—it consists of two or more nodes, is connected to the same shared disk array, and includes an interconnect for private communications between the nodes. Like Failsafe, this interconnect normally consists of a private, dedicated network between the nodes. However, there are differences in the way the shared drives are accessed, how the interconnect is used, and in the clustering software.

Shared Everything in the RAC Environment

Because of the shared-everything concept, a RAC setup differs from an Oracle Failsafe setup in many ways. To begin with, a RAC environment puts a much greater load on the interconnect. In addition to checking the status of each node, the interconnect is used for shipping data blocks between nodes for cache coherency. Oracle's term for this mechanism is *cache fusion*. This essentially means that, whenever possible, data blocks move between each instance's cache without needing to be written to disk, with the key being to avoid additional I/O being necessary to synchronize the buffer caches of multiple instances.

Importance of the Interconnect

This traffic is directed to go through the interconnect, with the expectation that this will be significantly faster than going to disk. To meet this expectation, you must ensure that the hardware you have dedicated to your private network is capable of meeting the demands for throughput that will be placed upon it. A gigabit Ethernet connection is recommended. Also, since the interconnect provides an even more crucial role, you are more likely to require redundancy in this area. In addition, new methodologies for maintaining cache coherency are evolving. One such methodology is VIA, or Virtual Interface Architecture (discussed in Chapter 7), which is essentially a technology standard that has evolved specifically for clustered environments. This standard calls for a simple hardware implementation for reading data structures in a user's memory space and moving them directly to the user memory space on another node. Oracle9*i* Real Application Clusters provides support for VIA, but you must contact your hardware vendor for configuration and certification information. This chapter will focus on the more common Ethernet connection for the private network.

Availability and Scalability in a RAC Environment

Because there are multiple nodes, RAC still gives you crash recovery and Transparent Application Failover (TAF) capabilities, similar to what you have in an Oracle Failsafe environment: when one node goes down, the other node continues processing. (We discuss TAF in more detail in Chapter 15.) As discussed in the previous chapter, disaster

recovery capability is still a function of the hardware and how much separation you can attain between nodes and disks and disk mirrors. In addition to crash recovery or disaster recovery capability, a RAC environment also affords scalability. This is because all nodes are simultaneously accessing the shared disk, which contains the database. With this shared-everything architecture, the horsepower of multiple nodes, in terms of memory, processing power, and networking capacity, can all be put into play all at once, vastly increasing throughput and the number of concurrent users. This is one solution to the per-process memory limitations mentioned in Chapter 5.

Use Raw Partitions

Aside from differences in how the private network is used, the shared-everything architecture requires you to view the shared drives in a totally different light. Because all nodes are accessing the disk concurrently, you cannot rely on a normal file system such as NTFS to maintain access to these drives and avoid disk or data corruption. Instead, this is accomplished by leaving the drives unformatted, or raw. This allows the *distributed lock manager (DLM)* within the Oracle RDBMS to control access to the data blocks, ensuring that only one node is writing a given block at any given time.

Since there is no file system on a raw partition, there can only be *one* file per partition, and all database files must be on a raw device—including datafiles, control files, redo logs, and even the SPFILE. An exception to this is the archive logs, which must be written to a file system. This need for all files to be on their own raw partition results in the necessity to spend much forethought and time in laying out and partitioning the disks for all of the various files required by the database. Once the disks are partitioned, Oracle accesses the raw partition by virtue of a symbolic link, mapping a link name to a physical disk number and partition number. This work must be done prior to the installation of the cluster software, which in turn must be completed before RAC can be installed.

RAC Cluster Software

Which brings us to the next topic—the cluster software. The cluster software for a RAC environment must be installed and running prior to installing Oracle Enterprise Edition. Otherwise, the Real Application Clusters option will not be available for installation. Here, we will discuss tips regarding the RAC software requirements to be aware of when planning your setup. Later in this chapter, we will discuss the actual installation of the cluster software itself.

No Virtual Groups

As we noted in the previous chapter, Real Application Clusters do not use the MSCS software, except in the case of Real Application Clusters Guard, discussed in Chapter 15. As such, unless you are using Real Application Clusters Guard, there is no concept of a virtual server or virtual groups. Since both nodes are accessing the disks, and hence the database, simultaneously, a virtual group is not needed—connections can be made to either node. Also in Chapter 15, we will discuss Transparent Application Failover, or TAF, which is a method of configuring SQLNET files so that a client can connect to any node in the cluster or cause failover to any node in the cluster transparently (that is, with no end-user intervention required).

Vendor-Provided Versus Oracle-Provided OSD Software

In releases prior to Oracle9*i* on the Windows NT/2000 platform, sites that used Oracle Parallel Server relied on the hardware vendors of certified platforms to provide and support the cluster, or OSD, software. This is no longer the case with Oracle9*i*—Oracle now provides the OSD software on the 9i CD-ROM, and Oracle also provides the necessary support. However, the certification requirements are not changed. Even though you have ready access to the clustering software, you must still ensure that you are running RAC on a hardware platform that your vendor has certified for the version of RAC and the version of the OS that you are running on. Oracle may still support third-party OSD software, but it will have to be certified to run Real Application Clusters, and in the case of third-party OSD software, Oracle will not support the cluster configuration. To obtain the latest list of certified hardware and software combinations, you should contact Oracle Support or your hardware vendor.

Voting Disk

Similar to the quorum disk used by MSCS, the RAC cluster software requires that one of the shared drives be configured as a voting disk. This is needed to resolve any conflicts between nodes, as an alternate communication means that all nodes can access should the interconnect fail. In addition, this disk contains information on the instances and nodes for each database in your cluster, as well as the ORACLE_HOME for the database. This information is read by the DBCA, Enterprise Manager, and other Oracle tools.

Preparing for the Cluster Installation

Configuring the operating system environment consists of a couple of different steps that must be taken before you even begin to install the clustering software or the RAC option. First, you must ensure that the interconnect is configured correctly. Second, you must partition disks according to how they will be laid out for your database, keeping in mind that each file requires its own partition. Finally, you must define the links for these raw partitions. This last step of configuring the symbolic links can be done prior to the cluster installation using the Oracle Object Link Manager, or it can be done during the cluster installation using the Cluster Setup Wizard. We will discuss both methods in detail in this chapter.

Configuring the Interconnect

Configuring the interconnect in a RAC environment is almost identical to what we described in Chapter 11 for Oracle Failsafe. You will most likely have at least two network cards on each node. Again, you will want to ensure that the card you assign the *public* IP address to is the card that is bound first, and the card with the *private* IP address is bound last. (Refer to the sections "Configuring Network Cards" and "Binding Order" in Chapter 11 for more details on this setup.) Since there is the potential for high traffic going across the interconnect in a RAC environment, you want to ensure that you provide the fastest possible connection, as noted previously. Also, since the private network card is usually not connected to a DNS server, you should define a network name for the private IP in the HOSTS file of each node (the HOSTS file is found in \WINNT\system32\drivers\etc, as discussed in Chapter 11). Again, use the convention of <nodename>.SAN for the private host name:

```
127.0.0.1         localhost
10.10.10.1         RMNTOPS1.SAN
10.10.10.2         RMNTOPS2.SAN
```

Configuring the Raw Partitions

As in the case of Oracle Failsafe, you will also need to configure the shared drives and partition the drives according to your needs. However, there is a huge difference in how many partitions you configure, since you must have one shared partition for each file. First, you must determine how many shared physical devices you have available. Next, determine how many of them can be used for the RAC database that you intend to create. In Figure 12-1, you see that we have Disks 0 through 8, for a total of nine physical drives. Of these, three have been labeled as private, and three have been labeled as shared, but they are already formatted NTFS (this is not required—we have it configured thus because we intend to install Microsoft Cluster Server and Real Application Cluster Guard later). That leaves us with three additional shared drives on which we can place datafiles for our RAC database.

Link Names and Partitions Required by the Database Assistant

Recall from the previous section that all datafiles, control files, online redo logs, and even the SPFILE must be on the shared drive, and each one must have its own partition. If you use the DBCA (which will be kicked off automatically after the installation), the Database Assistant will expect a certain number of partitions to have been created already. In addition, it will also anticipate that certain link names have been defined

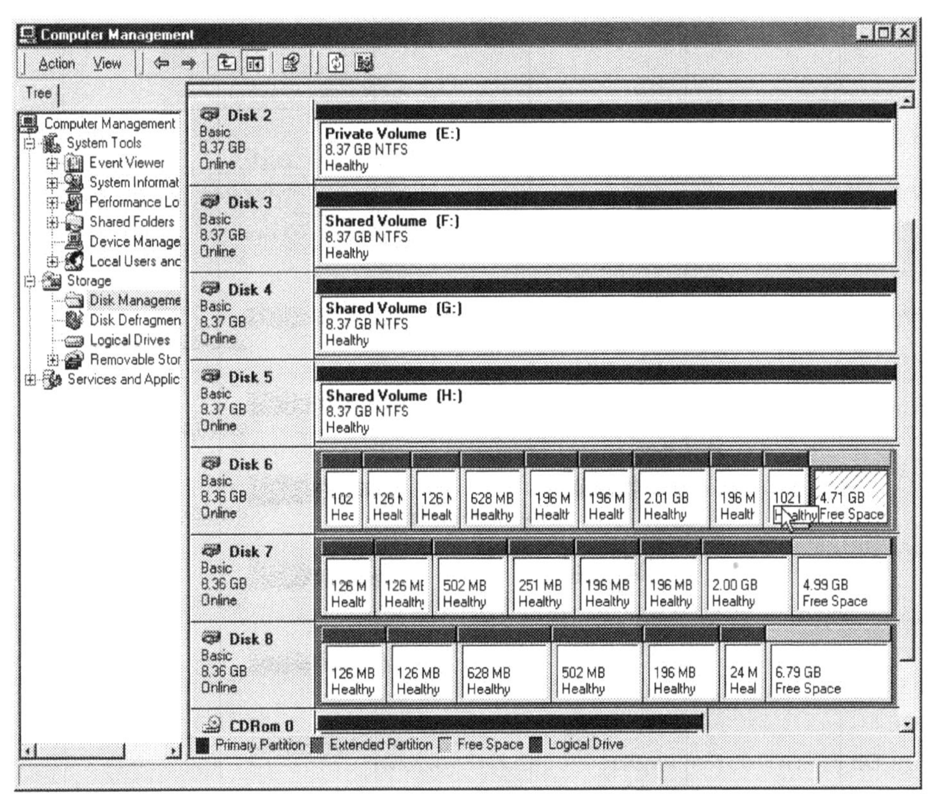

FIGURE 12-1. *Disk Manager view of available drives*

for each partition. The link name should always be prefaced with the global database name of the database you are creating. We recommend that you lay out a table similar to Table 12-1 to help you determine how many partitions to create, and on which devices they should go. In Table 12-1, you see that the DBCA anticipates at least 17 partitions. One partition is for the SPFILE, and two partitions are for control files. Each instance must have its own online redo log group, so there are a total of four online logs (we have only two nodes). In addition, if you are using system managed undo, each instance requires its own undo tablespace. Finally, you have these tablespaces: system, temporary, drsys, cwmlite, example, users, index, and tools. An eighteenth partition is required as a voting disk, or quorum disk, to allow the cluster to resolve ownership of the disks in case the interconnect should fail.

So, assuming that you are creating a database with the name RACDB, you would need partitions of the names and sizes shown in Table 12-1.

Link Name	File Type	Min Size	Disk Number	Partition Number
SRVCFG	Voting disk	100MB		
RACDB_SPFILE1	SPFILE	25MB		
RACDB_CONTROL1	Control file 1	125MB		
RACDB_CONTROL2	Control file 2	125MB		
RACDB_REDO1_1	Instance 1 redo 1	125MB		
RACDB_REDO1_2	Instance 1 redo 2	125MB		
RACDB_REDO2_2	Instance 2 redo 1	125MB		
RACDB_REDO2_1	Instance 2 redo 2	125MB		
RACDB_SYSTEM1	System tablespace	500MB		
RACDB_UNDOTBS1	Instance 1 undo tablespace	625MB		
RACDB_UNDOTBS2	Instance 2 undo tablespace	625MB		
RACDB_TEMP1	Temporary tablespace	500MB		
RACDB_USERS1	Users tablespace	100MB		
RACDB_INDX1	Index tablespace	50MB		
RACDB_DRSYS1	Intermedia tablespace	250MB		
RACDB_TOOLS1	Tools tablespace	50MB		
RACDB_CWMLITE1	OLAP tablespace	200MB		
RACDB_EXAMPLE1	Example schemas tablespace	150MB		

TABLE 12-1. *Determining Numbers and Sizes of Partitions to Create*

These values in Table 12-1 are minimum sizes for using the Data Warehousing template. Other templates used by the DBCA will work with the same links, but you can get by with a smaller temporary tablespace and a smaller undo tablespace. On the other hand, you may decide that you want to create larger partitions for your temporary or undo tablespaces, and/or larger partitions for the online redo logs. It makes life easier to plan for these things up front. To expand these tablespaces later, or to add additional online redo logs, you will have to create a new partition, and a new link, so that you can then add a second datafile to a tablespace. In addition to the partitions we've just outlined, you will want to include partitions for any additional tablespaces that you require for your own application, and any additional redo log groups that you need.

Mapping Link Names to Devices

Once you have determined the number and sizes of partitions that you will need, you must determine next how you are going to spread them across the available shared disks. Using Table 12-1, fill in disk numbers first to give yourself an idea of what types and numbers of files will be on each disk. Next, go back and assign the partition numbers of the partitions that you will create, starting with number 1 on each disk.

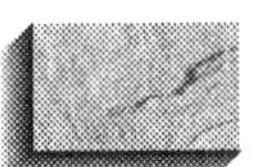

CAUTION
Never assign a symbolic link name to partition 0. Partition 0 is used by Windows 2000 to write the signature on the disk. Always start counting at partition number 1.

The result of this exercise will end up looking something like what we have in Table 12-2 (note that this table has been sorted by the disk number).

Link Name	File Type	Min Size	Disk Number	Partition Number
SRVCFG	Voting disk	100MB	6	1
RACDB_REDO1_1	Instance 1 redo 1	125MB	6	2
RACDB_REDO2_1	Instance 2 redo 2	125MB	6	3
RACDB_USERS1	Users tablespace	100MB	6	4
RACDB_INDX1	Index tablespace	50MB	6	5
RACDB_UNDOTBS2	Instance 2 undo tablespace	625MB	6	6

TABLE 12-2. *Determining Locations of Partitions*

Link Name	File Type	Min Size	Disk Number	Partition Number
RACDB_REDO1_2	Instance 1 redo 2	125MB	7	1
RACDB_SYSTEM1	System tablespace	500MB	7	2
RACDB_DRSYS1	Intermedia tablespace	250MB	7	3
RACDB_TOOLS1	Tools tablespace	50MB	7	4
RACDB_CONTROL1	Control file 1	125MB	7	5
RACDB_CWMLITE1	OLAP tablespace	200MB	7	6
RACDB_CONTROL2	Control file 2	125MB	8	1
RACDB_REDO2_2	Instance 2 redo 1	125MB	8	2
RACDB_UNDOTBS1	Instance 1 undo tablespace	625MB	8	3
RACDB_TEMP1	Temporary tablespace	500MB	8	4
RACDB_EXAMPLE1	Example schemas tablespace	150MB	8	5
RACDB_SPFILE1	SPFILE	25MB	8	6

TABLE 12-2. *Determining Locations of Partitions* (continued)

Creating the Actual Partitions

You are now ready to create the actual partitions. Go to Disk Management in the Computer Management Console and highlight the first shared drive to be partitioned. In our case, this is disk number 6. Be sure that each disk that you intend to use is defined as a basic disk. Dynamic disks are not supported in a RAC environment. For each shared disk, create an extended partition that is equal to the entire size of the disk (do not create primary partitions, as you are limited to how many primary partitions you can have on a machine). Do this by right-clicking the disk itself, and choosing Create Partition. When prompted for the partition type, choose Extended Partition and then use all of the available space. Do this for each disk listed in the Disk Number column.

Creating Logical Drives

Once you have created an extended partition on the disk, go back and right-click the disk again. This time, choose Create Logical Drive (see Figure 12-2). Enter the size that you want for the first partition (corresponding to the Partition Number column in Table 12-2). On the next screen, choose the option Do not assign a drive letter or

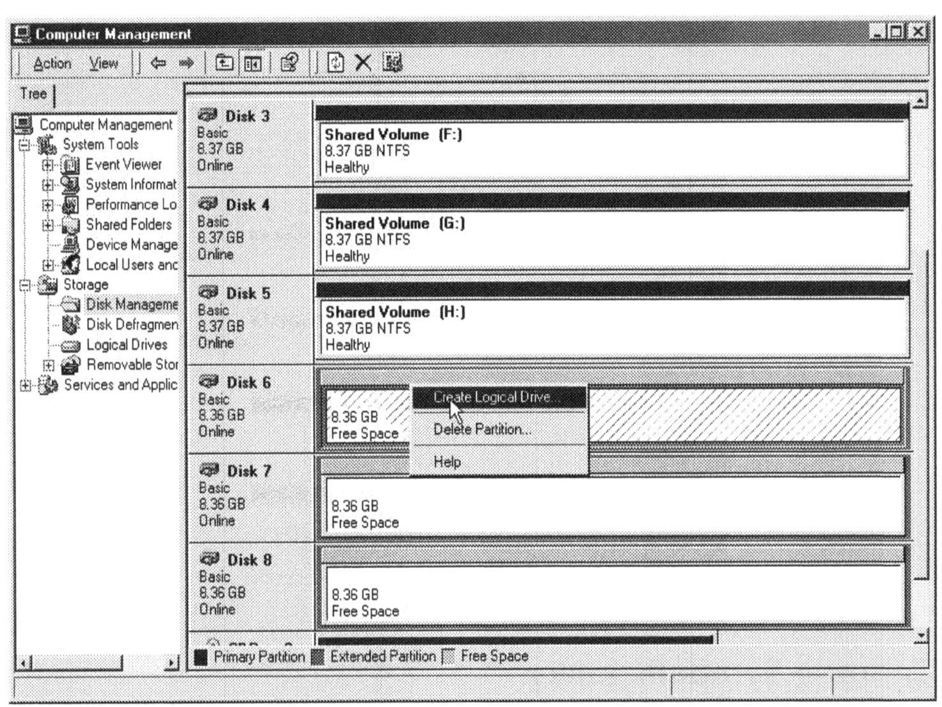

FIGURE 12-2. *Creating a logical drive*

path. Next, choose the option Do not format this partition, and finally click Finish on the last screen. Repeat these steps for each of the partitions listed in Table 12-2.

Removing Drive Letters The steps in the preceding section should be performed from one node only. You will find that once these partitions are created, even though you elected not to assign a drive letter, drive letters will have been assigned on the additional nodes. You can remove these drive letters on the other nodes through Disk Manager by right-clicking each drive, choosing Change Drive Letter and Path, and then choosing Remove. This is very cumbersome, however. To ease this process, Oracle provides a utility called LetterDelete, which can be run on each node to remove drive letters on all raw partitions. This utility will be found on Disk 1 of the Oracle9*i* CD-ROM set, located in the subdirectory Disk1\preinstall_rac\olm. Simply run the utility from a command prompt as follows:

```
C:\preinstall_rac\olm>letterdelete
Letter Delete: About to delete all drive letters on Oracle Partitions.
 Are you sure (y/n)?y
```

```
Deleted J:\ on \Device\Harddisk6\Partition1
Deleted K:\ on \Device\Harddisk6\Partition2
Deleted L:\ on \Device\Harddisk6\Partition3
Deleted M:\ on \Device\Harddisk6\Partition4
Deleted N:\ on \Device\Harddisk6\Partition5
Deleted O:\ on \Device\Harddisk6\Partition6
Deleted P:\ on \Device\Harddisk6\Partition7
Deleted Q:\ on \Device\Harddisk7\Partition1
Deleted R:\ on \Device\Harddisk7\Partition2
Deleted S:\ on \Device\Harddisk7\Partition3
Deleted T:\ on \Device\Harddisk7\Partition4
Deleted U:\ on \Device\Harddisk7\Partition5
```

NOTE
As evidenced by the preceding warning, all drive letters will be removed from any unformatted (raw) partitions. If you determine that you need a drive letter on one of these partitions, you can reassign the drive letter afterward to the partition individually after running LetterDelete.

Creating Symbolic Links

Symbolic links are the method by which Oracle accesses the raw partition. Without a drive letter and a file system allowing you to track directory names and filenames, you must somehow be able to tell the database where to find its files. This is done by creating a symbolic link with a name that, in translation, says something like, "Go to hard drive number 6, partition number 3, to find my data." Symbolic links are referenced within Oracle as \\.\<link_name>. In the next section, we will show you how to create these link names.

Manually Installing the Object Link Manager

For the example in the previous section, we have copied the contents of the preinstall_rac\olm directory to the local hard drive. Aside from the LetterDelete utility, there are several other useful utilities in this directory. One of these utilities is the GUI Object Link Manager, run by the executable GUIOracleOBJManager.exe. Once your drives are partitioned, this is the utility you use to create the symbolic links, telling Oracle how to access the files on these partitions. Before you can use this utility, you must install the Oracle Object Service by running the following command on each node of the cluster:

```
C:\ preinstall_rac\olm> oracleobjservice /install
```

After installing the service, ensure that it is started on each node by checking the Services Console, and start it on each node if necessary. Once you have started the service, you will be able to proceed to the next step, creating symbolic links from one node and syncing them automatically on all nodes.

NOTE
This command is run prior to the installation of the cluster software. With this method, we are defining the links prior to installing the cluster software. If you do not run this command now, the Object Link Manager Service is installed automatically when the cluster server is installed. This will require that you define the links during the cluster setup. We will discuss how to do so later in this chapter. The Oracle Object Service can be removed by running the command ***oracleobjservice /remove****.*

Creating the Links

Once the service is running, you can now run the Link Manager. Do this by double-clicking GUIOracleOBJManager.exe in the preinstall_rac\olm directory. You will see a screen similar to the one shown in Figure 12-3, which displays the hard disk number, partition number, and partition size of the shared partitions it has found on the cluster. To assign a link name, right-click under the column called New Link Name. Referring back to Table 12-2, enter the link name assigned to that particular hard drive and partition. Remember that you must have a link called srvcfg for the voting disk, and the rest of the links must be prefaced with the global name of your database. Once you have entered all of the link names under the New Link Name column, choose Commit from the Options menu, and then choose Sync Nodes. You should now be able to see all links under the Oracle Link Name column, on all nodes.

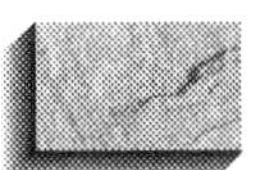

CAUTION
Placing a check mark in the box next to a link name will result in the link name being deleted once you perform a commit operation.

Exporting and Importing Links

Once the links have been created, you should export them to a file as a backup. Again, there is a utility in \preinstall_rac\olm to allow you to do this—the ExportSymLinks utility. Export symbolic links to a file with a .tbl extension using the /F: switch, as in

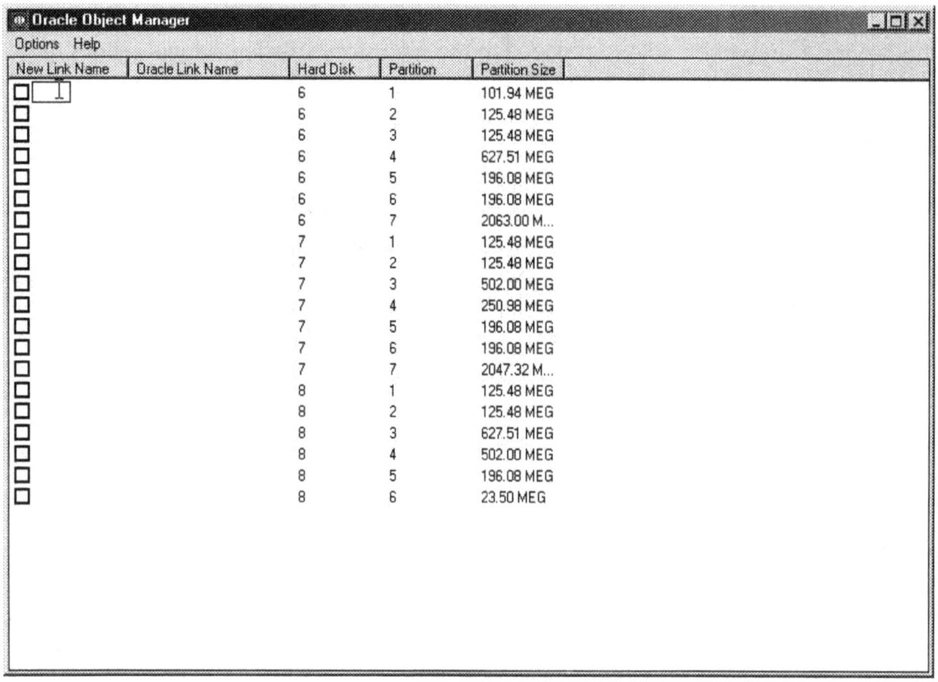

Oracle Object Manager

Options Help

New Link Name	Oracle Link Name	Hard Disk	Partition	Partition Size
		6	1	101.94 MEG
		6	2	125.48 MEG
		6	3	125.48 MEG
		6	4	627.51 MEG
		6	5	196.08 MEG
		6	6	196.08 MEG
		6	7	2063.00 M...
		7	1	125.48 MEG
		7	2	125.48 MEG
		7	3	502.00 MEG
		7	4	250.98 MEG
		7	5	196.08 MEG
		7	6	196.08 MEG
		7	7	2047.32 M...
		8	1	125.48 MEG
		8	2	125.48 MEG
		8	3	627.51 MEG
		8	4	502.00 MEG
		8	5	196.08 MEG
		8	6	23.50 MEG

FIGURE 12-3. *Creating links in Object Link Manager*

the following example (note that /F: does *not* refer to a drive letter—this is a required switch indicating a filename follows):

```
C:\preinstall_rac\olm>exportsymlinks /F:D:\backups\racdblinks.tbl
Symbolic Link Exporter
Version 2.0.1
Copyright 1989-2001 Oracle Corporation. All rights reserved.

 Links exported to file D:\backups\racdblinks.tbl
 ExportSYMLinks completed successfully
```

If you should ever need to import the links back to reassign names to partitions, rather than retyping everything in the Object Link Manager window, you can now run the ImportSymlinks utility:

```
C:\preinstall_rac\olm>importsymlinks /F:D:\backups\racdblinks.tbl
```

Additional Utilities for Managing Raw Partitions

As you can see, there is a plethora of handy little utilities in the preinstall_rac\olm directory. A couple of other utilities that are now available are crlogdr and logpartformat. Once an extended partition has been created, crlogdr can be used from the command line to create logical drives on a given physical drive number (as opposed to using the Disk Management console). For usage, simply run crlogdr.exe by itself from a command prompt. The logpartformat utility is used to "format" a raw partition. Obviously, it does not truly format the partition with a file system, but it does clean up any stray bytes on the partition. If you are testing and end up deleting and re-creating files on these partitions on a regular basis, it is recommended that you run the logpartformat utility to clear the partition of any junk that may have been on there previously, prior to placing files for your production system. To run logpartformat, simply pass the link name of the partition you wish to format:

```
C:\preinstall_rac\olm>logpartformat racdb_junk
Logical Partition Formatter
Version 2.0
Copyright 1989-2001 Oracle Corporation. All rights reserved.

The logical drive racdb_junk will be formatted.

Formatting the logical drive WILL result in loss of ALL data.
Are you sure you want to continue?...(Y/N) y
```

Running the RAC Clustercheck

One final check should be run on your cluster prior to installing the cluster software. This is done with the clustercheck utility, found on the CD-ROM in the \DISK1\preinstall_rac\Clustercheck directory. This utility is similar in concept to the Verify Cluster tool that we use in a Failsafe environment, in that it is checking the health of the cluster components involved, including the interconnect and the available shared drives. However, it differs in that it is run *prior* to installation, and is therefore not meant to check the health of Oracle installation itself. Kick it off by running clustercheck.exe:

```
C:\preinstall_rac\clustercheck>clustercheck
```

Defining Public and Private Node Names for Clustercheck

You will be prompted for the number of nodes that are in the cluster and the public names of those nodes, as you see in Figure 12-4. Notice that the utility asks for the host name for node 1 and then for node 2. The host name that you specify for node 1 should be the host from which you eventually run the Cluster Setup Wizard and the Oracle installation. Clustercheck will then verify that the host name given can be successfully resolved to an IP address, and you will be asked to confirm the results.

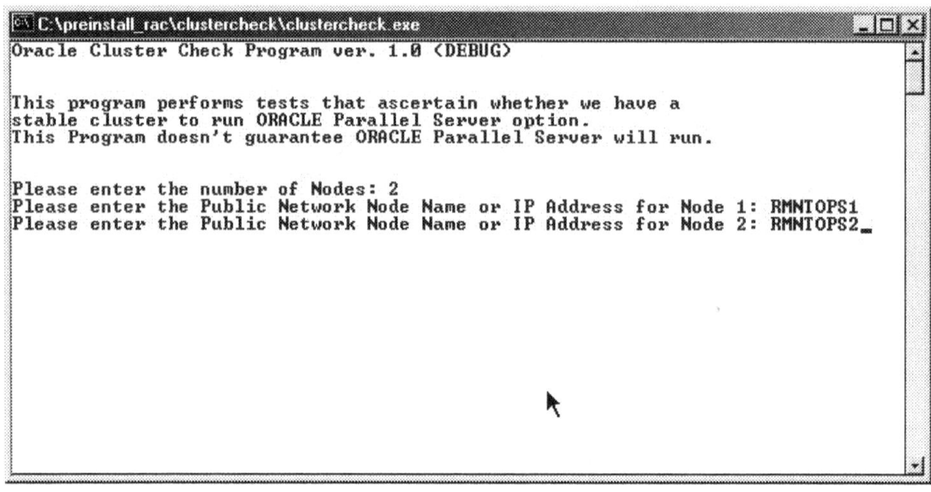

FIGURE 12-4. *Public node names in clustercheck*

Next, you are prompted for information on the private interconnect. Put in the private network names, as defined in the host's file in the earlier section "Configuring the Interconnect." In our example, these names are RMNTOPS1.SAN and RMNTOPS2.SAN (see Figure 12-5). You will then be asked to confirm the IP information for the private interconnect as well.

Clustercheck Log Files

During the clustercheck run, a service called InfoGatherer will be created on each node—this service will write log files into your temp directory, and then it will be deleted as quickly as it was created. The log files left behind by the InfoGatherer Service hold the key to determining if the clustercheck operation was successful. To find these logs, you must determine what Temp is set to. Right-click My Computer on the desktop, and choose Properties | Advanced | Environment Variables. Look under User Variables. By default, you will see something like C:\Documents and Settings\Administrator\Local Settings\Temp, where Administrator is the name of the user account you are logged in under. In this directory will be a subdirectory called OPSM, which is where the log files from the InfoGatherer Service are located.

The clustercheck utility will make sure that it has permissions to write to drives on all nodes and open Registry keys on all nodes. It will also verify access and check the health of the shared drives. Check these logs carefully for any indication of a problem. If you see a message similar to this at the bottom of OraInfoCoord.log,

```
ORACLE CLUSTER CHECK WAS SUCCESSFUL
```

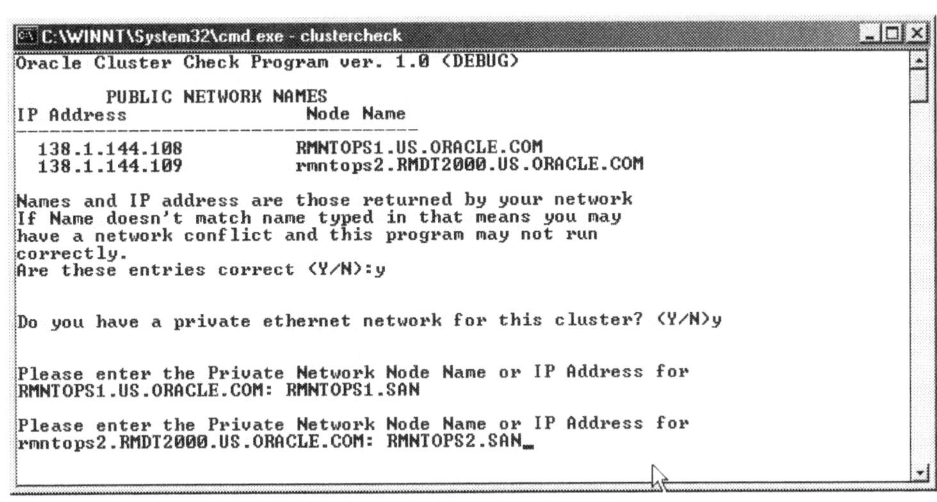

FIGURE 12-5. *Defining the private network in clustercheck*

then chances are good that you can proceed with the cluster setup. Otherwise, troubleshoot any permissions problems or problems with the shared drives, and then rerun the clustercheck utility.

Installing the Cluster Software and Oracle9*i* RDBMS

Once you have completed all of the necessary preinstallation work for the cluster, now comes the moment you have been waiting for—the installation of the cluster software for Real Application Clusters. Drumroll please! Okay, forget the pomp and circumstance. This next section will cover the final preinstallation piece necessary prior to installing the actual Oracle RDBMS. As noted previously, Oracle may support clustering software from other third-party vendors in order to run RAC, but it will not support the installation and configuration of another vendor's product. Thus, this section is devoted to the installation and configuration of the Oracle-provided cluster software only.

Running the Cluster Setup Wizard

Like just about everything else we have discussed so far in this chapter, the Cluster Setup Wizard is found in the \preinstall_rac directory, in a subdirectory named, appropriately enough, clustersetup. Previously, we showed you how to run many of the utilities by simply copying the contents of the preinstall_rac directory to the local machine, and kicking off everything from there. You will find, however, that the Cluster Setup Wizard must be run from the actual CD-ROM or staging area because it makes use of the Oracle Universal Installer. Therefore, unless you run it from the CD-ROM or staging area, it will not be able to kick off. If you run Cluster Setup Wizard and briefly see a command prompt window and then nothing, verify that you are running it from the CD-ROM or the staging area.

Creating the Cluster

When you first run the Cluster Setup Wizard, the second screen of the Oracle Cluster Setup Wizard will only give you the option to create a cluster. On subsequent runs of the wizard, you will have the option to add additional nodes. It will be necessary to run this wizard again if you expand in the future. With the Create A Cluster option selected, click Next and continue on. If you have not yet partitioned any drives, you will not be able to continue past this point; instead, you will see the error in Figure 12-6. This is because you must have at a minimum one shared partition to be used for the voting disk. If you receive this error, you must exit and revisit the section "Creating Logical Drives," earlier in this chapter.

Assuming you make it to the next screen, you must now select the partition you want to represent the voting disk. Highlight the correct partition. In our example, shown in Figure 12-7, all of the link names and partitions are already filled in because we installed the Oracle Object Link Manager and defined them as described in the previous section. If you have not done this, the next section will walk you through defining the symbolic links using the Cluster Setup Wizard.

Defining Links in Cluster Setup Back up for just a moment and assume that we did not have the links predefined. If this were the case, the Symbolic Link column will be blank in the Cluster Setup Wizard. In such a scenario, you would click the Create Oracle Symbolic Links button. This actually calls the Oracle Object Link Manager,

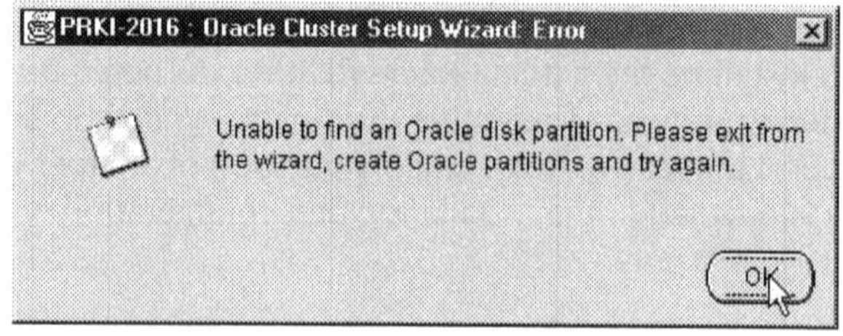

FIGURE 12-6. *Cluster Manager error generated if no raw partitions exist*

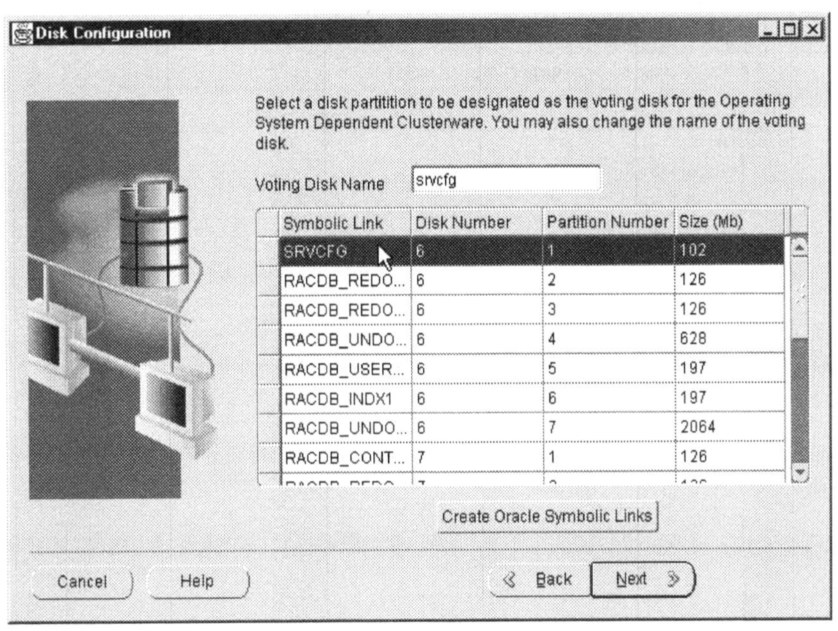

FIGURE 12-7. *Cluster Manager with symbolic links predefined*

with a slightly different interface. A screen like Figure 12-8 will appear. Simply enter the link names from Table 12-2, based on the disk and partition number associated. Once you have typed in all of the names, click Apply, and then close the window.

Defining the Network for the Interconnect

On the next screen, Oracle will check for the existence of VIA. If it is detected, you will be prompted to use that for the interconnect. If not, the setup will continue, and you will be asked which network you want to use for the interconnect. Choose the Private option and continue on. You will now be prompted for the public and private names assigned to each node. Fill them in as shown in Figure 12-9, using the same names defined in the local hosts file for the private name as were used when running the clustercheck utility. If you are using the convention of <nodename>.san, the private names will be filled in for you automatically. Once you have filled in the names, click Next. Note that the default location to install the files is not in the ORACLE_BASE directory structure; instead, the files will go in \WINNT\System32\osd9i. We recommend that you accept this default location and finish the installation.

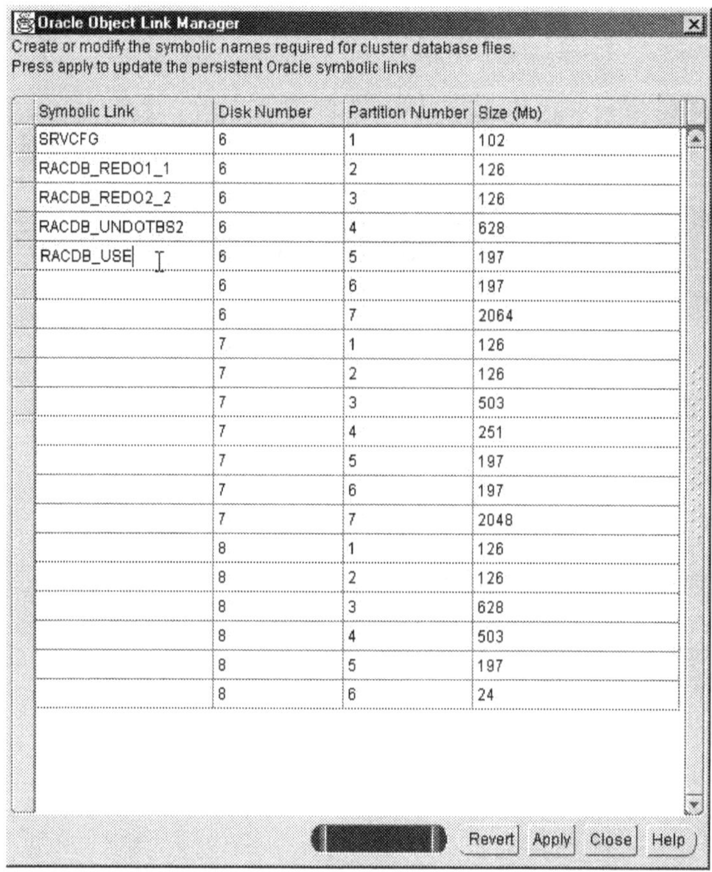
Oracle Object Link Manager
Create or modify the symbolic names required for cluster database files.
Press apply to update the persistent Oracle symbolic links
Revert
Apply
Close
Help

Symbolic Link	Disk Number	Partition Number	Size (Mb)
SRVCFG	6	1	102
RACDB_REDO1_1	6	2	126
RACDB_REDO2_2	6	3	126
RACDB_UNDOTBS2	6	4	628
RACDB_USE	6	5	197
	6	6	197
	6	7	2064
	7	1	126
	7	2	126
	7	3	503
	7	4	251
	7	5	197
	7	6	197
	7	7	2048
	8	1	126
	8	2	126
	8	3	628
	8	4	503
	8	5	197
	8	6	24

FIGURE 12-8. *Oracle Object Link Manager as seen during cluster setup*

What Just Happened?

When the installation is complete, you may want to investigate the changes made to your system. Recall that we recommended you run the Cluster Setup Wizard from what you defined as node 1 when you ran clustercheck. You only need to run the setup from this node. It will use the interconnect to write to the Registry and copy files over

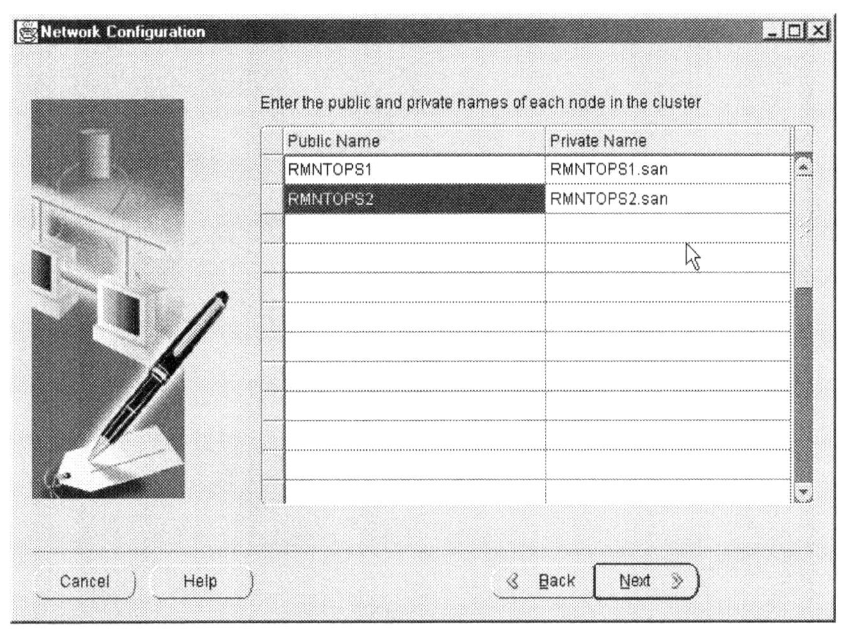

FIGURE 12-9. *Defining the public and private names in cluster setup*

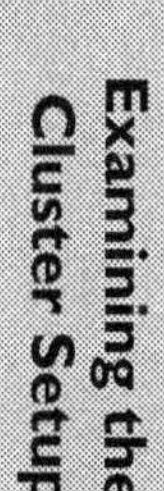

to all nodes defined during the installation. You will see that on each node, an OSD9i Registry key has been created under HKLM\Software\Oracle\osd9i. When highlighted, the subkey called CM will display the current host name, all public node names, all private node names, and the voting disk (as defined by the value for CMDiskFile). In addition, services are created for the Cluster Manager and the Object Link Manager (OracleCMService9i and Oracle Object Service, respectively). Last, observe that the osd9i directory, created in \WINNT\System32 during the installation, is also created on all nodes of the cluster. The log file for the CM server will be located in this directory for troubleshooting purposes. In addition, all of the utilities from the \preinstall_rac\olm directory will be copied to \WINNT\System32\osd9i\olm, as shown next.

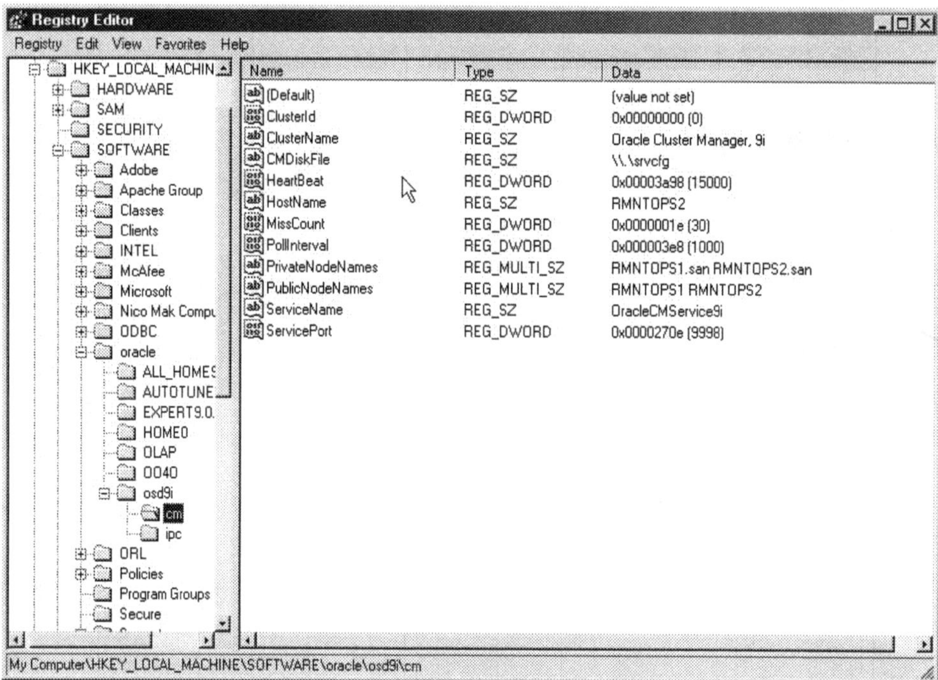

Removing or Reinstalling the Cluster Software

If you find that you need to reinstall the cluster software for some reason, you will want to clean up the previous installation first. If instances are running on the machines, you should stop all services for the instances and set them to manual, as you may need to reboot. Next, delete the OSD9i key under HKLM\Software\Oracle, and also delete the services under HKLM\System\CurrentControlSet\Services, OracleCMService9i and OracleGSDService. Last, remove the osd9i directory under \WINNT\System32. After you reinstall the cluster software, you may need to manually re-create the OracleGSDService (which is created initially during the database creation, after the Oracle install completes). Change to the ORACLE_HOME\bin directory and run the following command on each node. If the service does not exist, this command will re-create it:

```
D:\oracle\ora90\BIN>gsdservice -start

OracleGSDService
Version 9.0.1

Copyright 1989-2001 Oracle Corporation. All rights reserved.
The service OracleGSDService has been started
```

Installing the Oracle Software

As noted previously, if the cluster software is not installed ahead of time, you will not be given the option to install the option for Real Application Clusters. So, once the cluster software has been successfully installed, you are ready to install Oracle. Be sure that OracleCMService9i is running during the installation, and follow the installation procedures outlined in Chapter 4 when performing the installation from node 1.

Installing from One Location

Choose your ORACLE_HOME with the understanding that the installation is going to copy files to the same location on all nodes. On the Available Products screen, choose the Oracle9*i* Database, and then choose Enterprise Edition for the installation type. Pick the type of database that you want on the Database Configuration screen. Remember that the previously defined links will allow you to create any type of database listed. Even the custom configuration will use the same links unless you specifically modify the link names. The custom configuration has the advantage of allowing you to deselect some of the options, therefore you may not need all of the links and partitions defined earlier. Remember that the global database name that you specify must match the symbolic link names you have defined (in this example, RACDB). You will know that the cluster software is recognized when you go to the next screen after the Database Configuration screen. Here, you should see your public node names listed on the Cluster Node Selection screen, as shown in Figure 12-10. As the wizard states, the current node will always be selected, but you need to ensure that you manually highlight any additional nodes that you want the installation propagated to. From here, go to the Summary screen, and then proceed with the installation.

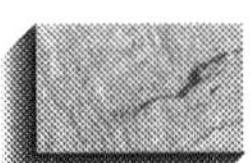

NOTE
When the installation reaches 100 percent, it will sit there for quite some time, and it will appear to be hung. Do not kill the installer. This is normal behavior, and is due to the fact that the installation is being pushed to the additional nodes in the cluster. How long the installation actually sits at this stage is dependent on the speed of the system. If installing to a cluster with more than two nodes, please obtain the patch for BUG#2031489 from Oracle Support before beginning the install.

Creating the Database During the Installation

At the end of the installation, the Database Configuration Assistant will be started and immediately begin to create the database, using the predefined link names it is programmed to anticipate. If there was a problem creating any of these links, or if

Oracle Universal Installer: Cluster Node Selection

Cluster Node Selection

The local node : RMNTOPS1 will always be selected. Please select any additional nodes:

RMNTOPS1

rmntops2

Exit Help Installed Products... Previous Next

ORACLE SOFTWARE POWERS THE INTERNET

FIGURE 12-10. *Cluster node selection showing all nodes in the cluster*

they were not created, you will see an error during the validation stage, as noted in Figure 12-11.

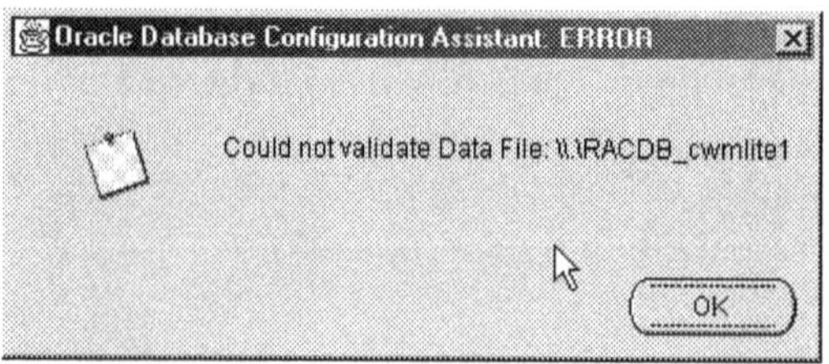

FIGURE 12-11. *Error during file validation phase*

If you receive an error such as this, you can leave the Configuration Tools screen on the installer up, and go back to the Object Link Manager, correcting any mistakes that were made in the link names. Then, go back to the Configuration Tools screen, highlight the Oracle Database Configuration Assistant line, and choose Retry.

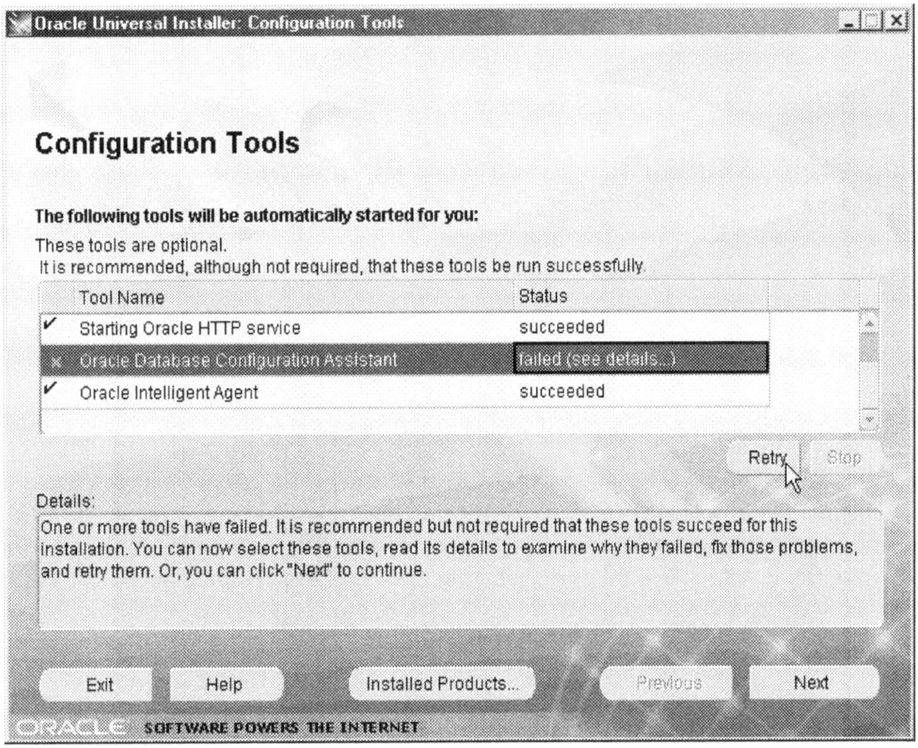

Updating the Path on Secondary Nodes

Once the installation is complete, you should be able to observe that all program groups, services, Registry keys, and so on, have been updated on all nodes that were selected for the installation. The path will be updated too; however, we have found that the secondary nodes do not recognize this path change. It is not necessary to reboot the secondary nodes; instead, simply right-click the My Computer icon on the desktop and choose Properties | Advanced. Select Environment Variables, and then you can observe that the path, as defined in System Variables, will have the appropriate Oracle directories already defined. Simply choose OK on this screen, and the path will be updated to reflect the changes previously made by the Oracle Universal Installer.

Creating the Database After the Installation

It is not necessary to create the database during the installation. The Database Assistant can be run at any time. When your cluster software is running, it will be detected and you will be given the option to create either a cluster database or a single instance database. It is possible to have more than one cluster database running, as long as you have properly defined the necessary links using the global database name of the second database. Oracle also supports creation of a nonclustered, or single-instance, database on one or all of the nodes in the cluster.

Additional Considerations in a RAC Environment

Once the database has been created, the view V$ACTIVE_INSTANCES can be queried to determine what instances are currently running. If you want to know which instance you are currently connected to, simply query the V$INSTANCE view. The command-line utility lsnodes can be used at a command prompt to determine which nodes the cluster is active on.

Maintaining a RAC Instance

Just as Oracle Failsafe introduces some vagaries when it comes to maintenance operations, Real Application Clusters provides some twists that one needs to be aware of when operating in a RAC environment. As mentioned previously, the Oracle9*i* documentation set has a total of six separate books on Real Application Clusters, so we cannot be comprehensive here by any stretch. However, we will touch on some of the essentials of which you should be aware.

Services for Multiple Instances

First, be aware that even though the global database name is RACDB (in our example), the instance names on each node will have the node number appended. Thus, node 1 will have an instance name of RACDB1 and a service will be created called OracleServiceRACDB1. Node 2 will have an instance name of RACDB2, with a service name of OracleServiceRACDB2. On node 1, the ORACLE_SID will be set in the Registry to RACDB1, and of course it will be set to RACDB2 on node 2. Likewise, the Listener will be configured differently on each node, with the SID_LIST section containing either RACDB1 or RACDB2, respectively. If you find that you need to manually re-create any of these services or files, be aware of these differences.

Configuration Files

By the same token, the password file in the ORACLE_HOME\Database directory will be named either pwdracdb1.ora or pwdracdb2.ora. This is contrary to a Failsafe setup, where Failsafe maintains an identical password file for each instance. Of course, if you are using OS authentication, this is not an issue.

SPFILE in a RAC Environment The init file is an interesting story as well. If you chose to use the SPFILE during database creation (which is the default), you will find that the initracdb1.ora file, which exists in the ORACLE_HOME\Database directory, will have only one entry, as we recommended in Chapter 5. That entry points to the link name for the SPFILE:

```
SPFILE='\\.\RACDB_spfile1'
```

In prior releases, before the SPFILE came into existence, it was common practice to keep separate parameter files, which included instance-specific configuration information. Then another, common parameter file was maintained that contained parameters that had to be the same across all instances. The SPFILE does away with this, because each instance points to the same logical partition—both instances point to \\.\RACDB_spfile1. There is still the need for instance-specific parameters, but this problem is resolved by prefacing these parameters with instance_name. Here are some example parameters from our SPFILE:

```
cluster_database_instances=2
cluster_database=true
RACDB1.instance_name=RACDB1
RACDB2.instance_name=RACDB2
RACDB1.instance_number=1
RACDB2.instance_number=2
RACDB1.thread=1
RACDB2.thread=2
RACDB1.undo_tablespace=UNDOTBS
RACDB2.undo_tablespace=UNDOTBS2
```

We want to point out a couple of things here. First, notice that the filenames are prefaced with the \\.\<link_name> convention. All files on the raw partitions are referenced in this manner (notice the CONTROL_FILES parameter). Second, observe that the parameter to define a parallel database has changed. In previous releases, this was defined by specifying PARALLEL_SERVER=TRUE. Now, the parameter is CLUSTER_DATABASE=TRUE. In addition, note that the instance name prefaces certain parameters. Last, you should be aware that the initial release of RAC on Oracle9*i* does not support dynamic changes to memory parameters, or the Dynamic SGA, as described in Chapter 5. Therefore, changes to memory parameters must be written to the SPFILE alone, rather than specifying a scope of memory, and the instance must be restarted before changes will take effect.

You can create an init file that can easily be viewed by issuing the **create pfile** command, as discussed in Chapter 5. For example,

```
SQL> create pfile='D:\Oracle\admin\racdb\pfile\initbak.ora' from spfile;
```

Since the SPFILE is on a raw partition, you will need to run this command in order to view its contents.

System-Managed UNDO and/or Rollback in a RAC Environment

As mentioned earlier, each instance must have its own undo tablespace when using system managed undo, so you can see in the previous example that RACDB1 is using UNDOTBS, and RACDB2 is using UNDTOBS2. If you prefer to use the older method of defining standard rollback segments, you can get by with only one tablespace for rollback. However, each instance must define its own rollback segments in the SPFILE or init.ora.

Redo Log Groups

As with system managed undo, each instance must have its own separate set of Redo Log groups, with a minimum of two per instance. With two instances, you will need a total of four groups. When creating groups, thread numbers are assigned to the groups, and those threads are then picked up based on the THREAD=X parameter in the init.ora file. If the need arises to drop these log groups, say, if you were to manually remove a node, you would need to disable the thread:

```
SQL> alter database disable thread 2;
```

Alternatively, a thread must be enabled if adding another node, using the **enable** command.

Even though the redo log groups are assigned to a particular instance, they still must be on a raw device, accessible by any instance. In the case of an instance crash, the redo logs for the downed instance will be read by one of the surviving instances, and the automatic instance recovery that would normally occur at startup will instead take place while the surviving instance(s) are running. If this happens, you will notice a pause in the surviving instance(s) during instance recovery.

Archiving with Multiple Threads of Redo

Having multiple redo streams adds some complexity to running in archivelog mode. We discuss this in more detail in Chapter 15; but for our purposes here, you should be aware of a couple of things. First, all archived redo logs must go to a file system; so, generally, archiving is done to the private drives. It is possible to map a network drive to the other node(s) in the cluster, so that a single node is archiving its own private drive, and to the private drive of the other node. Another point of note is that the thread number must always be part of LOG_ARCHIVE_FORMAT, ensuring that each archived redo log will always be created with a unique name. Again, we discuss these issues in more detail in Chapter 15.

Adding Additional Instances

The Database Configuration Assistant simplifies the process of adding additional nodes and instances by providing additional functionality in a RAC environment. Aside from the option to create a clustered database, the DBCA adds an Instance Management feature. You would use this if you have added a node after the installation. Recall that a third or fourth node can be added to an existing cluster by running the Cluster Setup Wizard and choosing the option to add a node. If you add a node to the cluster, you should also run the DBCA, and after choosing the Oracle Cluster Database option, select the option for Instance Management. This will walk you through the process of defining an instance on your new node. If you were adding a third node, it would create an instance named RACDB3, with the associated services and so on, create and enable the thread for the additional instance, and create the undo tablespace for the additional instance. Of course, you must prepare for this by first creating the partitions and assigning the link names using the Oracle Object Link Manager. The Instance Management option also gives you the choice to delete an instance, should the need arise.

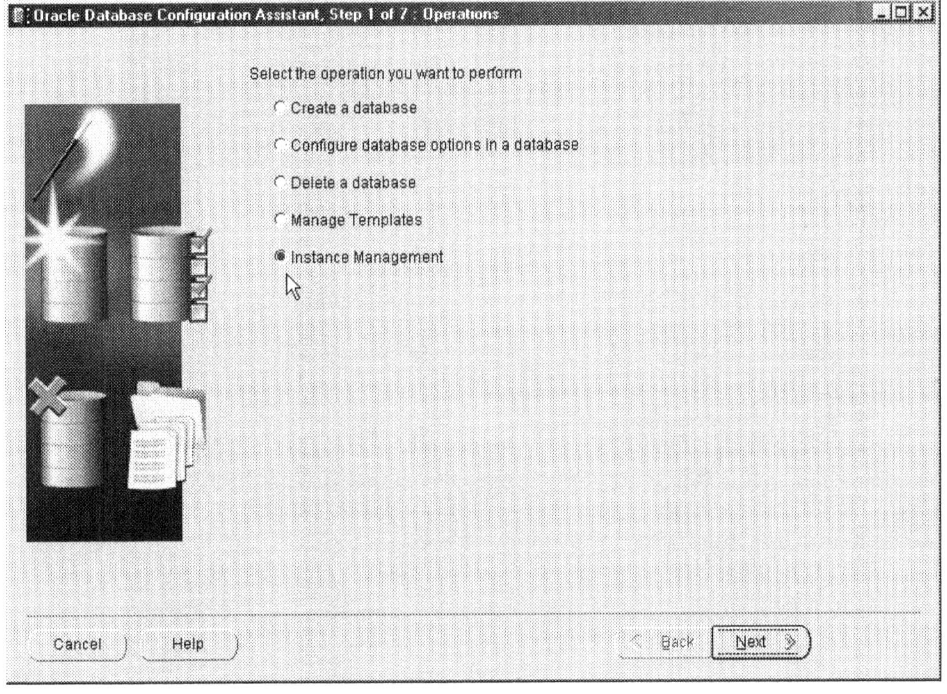

Adding Datafiles and Creating Additional Tablespaces

Creating additional tablespaces is a simple enough prospect, now that you are a veteran with the Disk Management Console and the Oracle Object Link Manager. You need to know in advance the size of the partition to create, and carve it out as a logical drive using Disk Management. Remember to delete the drive letter from the additional nodes using the LetterDelete utility. Run the Oracle Object Link Manager (remember that this was installed in the \WINNT\System32\osd9i\olm directory), and define the link name for the partition you have created. Next, simply use the syntax of \\.\<linkname> to add the file to your tablespace (or create the new tablespace):

```
SQL> alter tablespace users add datafile '\\.\RACDB_JUNK' size 100m;
```

Remember that the size you specify must be slightly smaller (by at least 1MB) than the actual size of the partition that you have created.

Using the ocopy Command to Back Up Files on Raw Partitions

Since files cannot be copied from a raw partition using a conventional copy command, and tape devices do not copy directly from a raw device, it is common to use RMAN as the primary backup mechanism of a RAC database. RMAN does not care what type of file system the datafiles are on, since it strictly backs up data blocks. However, if you need to copy files from a raw partition, either for backup purposes (perhaps to create a clone database) or just to be able to view the SPFILE, you can use the **ocopy** command. The syntax for this command is shown here:

```
ocopy from_file [to_file [a | size_1 [size_n]]]
```

In order to copy the SPFILE, for example, the following syntax, using the link name for the SPFILE, will copy it to drive D:

```
D:\oracle\ora90\bin>ocopy \\.\racdb_spfile1 d:\backups\spfile1.ora
```

This will now create a file on drive D: that can be viewed using Wordpad, as a regular SPFILE can. Note that **ocopy** copies the entire raw partition, regardless of how much data is actually used. The rest of the file is just empty filler. Also, be aware that **ocopy** does not copy to tape—if you want to back up files to tape, you must first copy them to a drive on a file system as a staging area, and then back up the files to tape from there.

Summary

This chapter has provided a cookbook approach to implementing Real Application Clusters on a Windows 2000 Cluster. After reading through this chapter, you should have a solid and thorough understanding of how to set up and implement RAC in your environment, from defining your partitions to creating the symbolic links, installing and configuring the cluster software, and installing and creating the database. In Chapter 15, we will discuss further strategies on backing up a RAC database using RMAN, and combining this with a standby environment to provide further levels of availability. In addition, we will discuss combining a RAC setup with the clustering capability of Microsoft Cluster Services, using Real Application Cluster Guard.

CHAPTER 13

The Standby Database

At its heart, the concept of the Oracle Standby Database is simple. If you already journal every change in the database by running in archivelog mode, what's to stop you from applying those archive logs to a second database? That way, if the production database is lost to a disaster, you can redirect users to the second database, and you will only have lost the final changes in the production database's online redo logs. You would have disaster recovery that is complete and only takes a few minutes.

From this simple idea, the Oracle Standby Database was born. As an afterthought in early versions, the Standby Database has evolved significantly over the years, with no end in sight. What started out as a process that required significant user administration in versions 7 and 8.0 became an automated process in 8i, where the production database could be configured to automatically apply the archive logs to the standby database with no user intervention. In 9i, Oracle Standby Database has evolved into a product that can apply redo entries to the standby at the same time as the primary database, allowing for even smaller data loss scenarios. And in 9i, the Standby Database feature has been integrated into the new Data Guard product, with the ability to switch back and forth between the standby database and the production database.

In this chapter, the following tips and techniques are discussed:

- Implementing Standby Database recovery modes
- Opening a standby database in read-only mode
- Creating sort space for long-running queries on the standby database
- Knowing standby database limitations and restrictions
- Creating a traditional standby database: a test case
- Using Oracle9i Log Transport Services
- Using Oracle9i Data Guard for standby database management
- Configuring a standby database through RMAN
- RMAN: Backing up archive logs on the standby database

Standby Database Architecture

As we said, the concept of the standby database is very simple. With a specialized copy of the production control file, you build a second instance on a different server. Backups of the production datafiles are put in place on the standby database server, and the standby database is mounted in standby mode. As redo logs fill up with changes on the production server, archive logs are produced, and these archive logs from the production server are moved to the standby server. With the Standby Database mounted, a recovery session is started, and the archive logs from the production database are applied to the Standby Database. In case of a failure on the production database, the standby database is opened with **resetlogs**, and users can be redirected to the standby database. Figure 13-1 displays this relationship.

There are a few key operating pieces to the Standby Database model. The first is the creation of the *Standby control file*. This is a specific control file backup used to mount the Standby Database. It is created at the production database with this command:

```
SQL> ALTER DATABASE CREATE STANDBY CONTROLFILE AS
    'd:\oracle\oradata\prod90\standby01.ctl';
```

This binary file is then moved to the standby server and renamed to fit the location and name specified in the CONTROL_FILES parameter of the standby init.ora file.

The second piece of the model is the Standby Database initialization parameter file. This is merely a copy of the init.ora file used to build the production instance, with a few minor changes. The primary parameter that is needed is STANDBY_ARCHIVE_DEST, which is where archive logs moved from the production database will be placed, if the Standby Database is running in managed recovery mode (which we'll discuss in a moment). All other destination parameters, such as USER_DUMP_DEST, should be changed to reflect a new location, if it changes from the production server to the standby server. The same goes for using the parameters DATA_FILE_NAME_CONVERT and LOG_FILE_NAME_CONVERT, which we saw briefly in

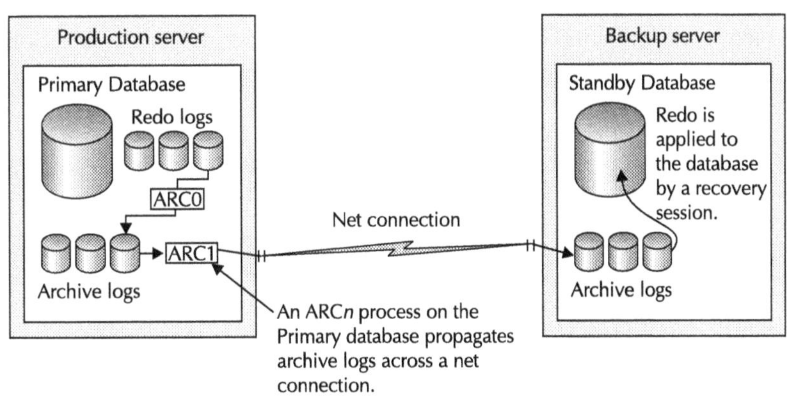

FIGURE 13-1. *Standby Database architecture*

Chapter 6. These only need to be used if the file locations will change, or if the Standby Database will be on the same machine as the production database.

Putting the Standby Database on the same server as production database has severe limitations, and can be too much work for too little payoff. The Standby architecture was created to provide a disaster recovery solution; if the Standby Database is on the same computer as the Production database, you've reduced the solution back to a single point of failure. The only reason to put them on the same computer is for testing purposes, or if you will be setting up more than one standby database, and the second (or third) database is on a different server. Remember, if you have the standby database on the same computer as the production database, you will have to use the parameter LOCK_NAME_SPACE, so that two instances with the same name can run simultaneously. This parameter renames the database in memory, so that applications can differentiate between the standby and the primary databases. The value you give to this parameter is inconsequential, as long as it does not match the name of any running databases on the computer. Convention tells you to keep it similar to the primary database:

```
LOCK_NAME_SPACE=_PROD90
```

On the production database, you need to make parameter changes in the init.ora file so that you can automatically archive redo logs to the standby database. You do this by modifying the LOG_ARCHIVE_DEST_*n* parameters. In Oracle9i, you can set up as many as ten different destinations for archive logs to be created when you switch log files. This allows you to duplex archive creation to multiple disks to protect against hardware failure. It also allows you to specify a net service name as the destination, which tells the database to make a net connection to a remote database and create an archive log in the location specified by STANDBY_ARCHIVE_DEST in the init.ora file of the standby database. For example, on the production server, you would create a net service name, called STBY, that points to your standby instance. Therefore, your archive destination setup would look something like this:

```
LOG_ARCHIVE_DEST_1='LOCATION=d:\oracle\oradata\prod90\arch'
LOG_ARCHIVE_DEST_2='LOCATION=e:\oracle\oradata\prod90\arch'
LOG_ARCHIVE_DEST_3='SERVICE=STBY'
```

This would cause the ARC*n* processes on the primary database to write three archive logs for each redo log switch: one to the destination on drive D:, another to drive E:, and the third to the database specified by the STBY net service.

In addition to a location, you can specify if archiving is *mandatory* before you overwrite an online redo log file. By doing so, Oracle will confirm the successful write of the archive log before allowing the online redo log file to be overwritten. If you specify a destination as MANDATORY, then the database will hang until you have written the specified archive log. If you specify a destination as OPTIONAL, then Oracle will signal an archival failure in the alert log, but move on with normal operations. In addition, the parameter LOG_ARCHIVE_MIN_SUCCEED_DEST can be used to specify the number of archive destinations that must succeed for the redo log file to be overwritten. This parameter, set to a number value between one and ten, overrides an optional setting. For instance, say you have two archive destinations, one set to **mandatory** and the other to **optional**. If you then set LOG_ARCHIVE_MIN_SUCCEED_DEST=2, then both sites must succeed before you can move on, functionally ignoring the optional setting.

OPTIONAL is the default for every destination except for the first local disk destination. Oracle requires there be at least one destination to disk, and this destination will always be mandatory. For standby destinations, we recommend a setting of OPTIONAL, as there is more likelihood of failure due to network outages and the like. And if an archive operation fails, you can manually copy an archive log from the production destination to the standby destination at a later time. The parameter for mandatory archiving is set in the archive destination parameter:

```
LOG_ARCHIVE_DEST_1='LOCATION=d:\oracle\oradata\prod90\arch MANDATORY'
LOG_ARCHIVE_DEST_2='LOCATION=e:\oracle\oradata\prod90\arch OPTIONAL'
LOG_ARCHIVE_DEST_3='SERVICE=STBY OPTIONAL'
```

For each destination, there is also a parameter to specify the state of an archive destination. This parameter can be set dynamically, and thus can be changed without affecting the production database. The destination state indicates to Oracle if it should attempt to write to that destination or not. There are two values available: ENABLE and DEFER. If enabled, Oracle attempts to write to this location. If the value is set to DEFER, Oracle will not attempt to write to that location. The state has a parameter that corresponds to a LOG_ARCHIVE_DEST number:

```
LOG_ARCHIVE_DEST_STATE_1=ENABLE
LOG_ARCHIVE_DEST_STATE_2=DEFER
```

Altering an archive destination state to defer will thus stop Oracle from attempting to write to that location. This is useful if you are having network problems and cannot access the standby database for a period of time. All of the current settings for the archive destinations of the production database can be viewed by logging into the production database as sysdba and issuing a **show parameter** command:

```
SQL>connect / as sysdba
SQL> show parameter log_archive
```

```
NAME                                 TYPE        VALUE
------------------------------------ ----------- ----------------
log_archive_dest                     string
log_archive_dest_1                   string
                   LOCATION=c:\oracle\oradata\prod90\arch MANDATORY
 log_archive_dest_2                   string
                   LOCATION=c:\oracle\admin\prod90\arch OPTIONAL
log_archive_dest_3                   string
...
log_archive_dest_state_1             string      enable
log_archive_dest_state_2             string      DEFER
log_archive_dest_state_3             string      enable
...
```

After you have created a Standby control file and made the appropriate modifications to the initialization parameter files for both the production instance and the standby instance, you can move the backup copies of the datafiles to the standby database location and mount the standby database. Before mounting the standby database, you will first need to use the oradim.exe utility to create a standby service. The service name must be different from that used by the primary database if you are creating the standby on the same server as the primary, as shown in this example:

```
Oradim -new -sid standby -intpwd oracle -startmode manual -pfile
c:\oracle\admin\standby\pfile\initstandby.ora
```

Now you can start the standby instance and mount it. You must specify that this will be a standby instance at the mount stage:

```
SQL>startup nomount
pfile= c:\oracle\admin\standby\pfile\initstandby.ora
SQL>alter database mount standby database;
```

After mounting the standby instance in this way, you can begin recovery of the standby to bring it up to date with the production instance. After modifying the production instance to automatically archive to the standby instance, you may still need to manually copy any earlier archive logs to the standby database. The recover operation will tell you which archive log is needed, and you can track it down and put it in the LOG_ARCHIVE_DEST_N parameter of the standby database, as follows:

```
SQL>recover standby database;
ORA-00279: change 280783 generated at 08/07/2001 16:15:27 needed
for thread 1
```

```
ORA-00289: suggestion : C:\ORACLE\ORADATA\STANDBY\ARCH\ARCH.11.1\
ORA-00280: change 280783 for thread 1 is in sequence #11

Specify log: {<RET>=suggested | filename | AUTO | CANCEL}
```

Standby Database Recovery Modes

The Standby Database runs in one of two recovery modes: manual or managed. Manual recovery is performed by the means described previously: the database administrator logs into the Standby Database, issues a **recover standby database** command, and then applies the archive logs that have been produced by the production database.

Alternatively, the Standby Database can be put into managed standby mode. In managed standby mode, the archive logs are automatically applied to the standby database as they are produced. To enter managed recovery mode, the following command is used on the Standby instance:

```
SQL>recover managed standby database;
```

When this is initiated, Oracle immediately looks for the next necessary archive log in its archive destination, and applies it to the standby database datafiles. This way, no manual intervention is required. However, Oracle looks only for the next necessary archive log, so it assumes that if the primary database is at sequence number 10, then the Standby database is at sequence number 9. Thus, all of the accumulated logs must be manually applied *before* starting a managed recovery session.

In addition, the keyword TIMEOUT can be added to the managed standby command. The TIMEOUT specification tells the standby database how many minutes to wait for the next archive log to be generated by the production database before canceling recovery. This can be used to stop recovery if no archive logs are being produced by the standby database. Thus, the following statement would put the standby database in recovery mode, and tell it to wait an hour before canceling recovery:

```
SQL>recover managed standby database timeout 60;
```

The SQL*Plus session you use to start recovery will appear to hang without returning a prompt. This is normal. To cancel managed recovery, you will need to open a second session, log in as sysdba, and issue the following command:

```
SQL>recover managed standby database cancel;
```

Opening the Standby Database in Read-Only Mode

In addition to its role as a disaster recovery solution, the Standby Database can be used for reporting purposes. The Standby Database can be opened in read-only mode, which allows queries against the database, but no DML operations (updates, inserts, and deletes) can be performed. In this way, long-running reports that can suck valuable resources away from the production database can be offloaded to the standby database.

If you open the database in read-only mode, you cannot simultaneously perform recovery. This means that any queries against the standby database will only be as current as the last archive log that was applied before it was opened.

To open the standby database in read-only mode, you need to cancel recovery first. If you are performing manual recovery, use the following command:

```
SQL>recover cancel;
```

If you are running in managed recovery mode, enter the following:

```
SQL>recover managed standby database cancel;
```

Next, open the database in read-only mode:

```
SQL>alter database open read only;
```

Creating Sort Space for Long-Running Queries on the Standby Database

The single biggest problem for running queries against a standby database is that you cannot do anything that would cause a write operation to the data dictionary. This includes creating temporary segment information, meaning that you cannot do any disk sorts.

The easiest way to get past this restriction would be to make the value for SORT_AREA_SIZE in the initstandby.ora file be greater than any possible sort that could occur. But this has severe limitations, as you have limited memory, and some sorts can grow to gigabytes in size. In addition, if you need to activate the standby database for production data entry, you would need to shut down the instance, set SORT_AREA_SIZE to a reasonable value, and then start it back up; this could waste valuable time at the point of catastrophe.

Instead, the standby database can use temporary tablespaces for sorts. Do not confuse this with a tablespace set up to hold temporary segments. A temporary tablespace is literally temporary: if you shut down the instance and restart, the temporary tablespace is gone. The difference can be seen in the V$VIEWS: permanent datafiles for tablespaces appear in V$DATAFILE, and temporary datafiles for temporary tablespaces appear in V$TEMPFILE. The important aspect of temporary tablespaces is that they exist for the instance itself, and therefore can be used for sort operations to disk because they do not write any information to the data dictionary. The following is an example statement for creating a temporary tablespace for sort operations:

```
SQL>create temporary tablespace sort_temp
datafile 'd:\oracle\oradata\prod90\sort_temp01.dbf'
extent management local uniform size 1m;
```

Standby Database Limitations and Restrictions

Standby Database Limitations and Restrictions

The pure simplicity of the Standby configuration also gives it severe limitations over other versions of disaster recovery. Most important, the Standby Database cannot guarantee 100 percent data recovery. Because the standby database is dependent on the archiving process of the production server, there is the possibility that changes in the production redo logs do not get archived and moved to the Standby before a loss occurs. This limitation is eliminated if you use the Log Transport Services for guaranteed zero data loss (discussed in the section "Utilizing Oracle9i Log Transport Services" later in this chapter), but Log Transport Services come with heavy performance costs.

Second, the standby database must reside on the same type of computer system as the Production Database. Technically, this only means that the operating system is the same, but Oracle Corporation recommends that you make the standby server identical in all ways to the production server, and we agree. Because failover to the standby database turns it into the primary database, if the server is not equipped with the same hardware as the production server, it can only hobble along until production is restored and you move production operations back to the original server. This process could take days, or even weeks, and your standby configuration has bought you nothing.

Standby activation is one-way and irreversible. If a standby database is activated (that is, taken from a mounted status to an open status), it cannot be shut down and then have more archive logs applied from the production database. Once opened, it has its own online redo log files, and therefore its own redo stream, which will be incompatible with the redo stream of the other computer. For all practical purposes, the standby database *is* the production database.

An example will help illustrate. We have a production database running on server WEBPD and a standby database running on server STBY01. Users connect to the database on WEBPD and make updates to the application tables, and the changes are recorded in the redo logs. We use Oracle9i capabilities to automatically

archive the redo logs to the standby database on STBY01. At some point, the WEBPD server's power supply gets fried by a power surge, leaving the server inoperable until a new power supply arrives in two days. So, we activate the standby database on STBY01, and open it up.

From this point forward, the database on STBY01 is not the standby database, it is the production database. We connect users to the machine, and new data is added. Two days later, WEBPD gets a new power supply and comes back online. In order for us to get the database back onto WEBPD, we must take a backup of the production database on STBY01 and move the files over to WEBPD. We then take a standby backup of the control file on STBY01 and move it to WEBPD, and mount the standby database there. We now have reversed the roles of our two servers: STBY01 is the production server, and our standby database runs on WEBPD. In order to move production data entry back to WEBPD, we need to shut down the production on STBY01 and activate our standby database. And then the process repeats itself.

To sum up, when you activate a standby database, be prepared for it to be your production database for at least a few days. If this is unacceptable, then the Standby Database feature is not for you.

Traditional Standby Configuration: A Test Case

The following is a test case that demonstrates setting up the standby database using traditional (that is, Oracle8i) methods. It assumes that the production datafiles have been backed up using an OS **copy** command. In this test case, the production server is named WEBPD, and the standby server is named STBY01, as in our example in the preceding section. The production instance name is PROD90, and the standby instance will be called STANDBY. The ORACLE_HOME on WEBPD is on drive C:, but on STBY01, Oracle has been installed on drive D:. Therefore, you will have to convert file names.

1. Move the copies of the production datafiles from WEBPD to STBY01. First, you mount the drive of STBY01 from WEBPD and then copy the files over.
2. Modify the initprod90.ora file with the following changes. These changes assume you have created a net service name that points at the standby instance, and that service name is called STBY.

```
log_archive_dest_1='LOCATION=c:\oracle\oradata\prod90\arch
MANDATORY'
log_archive_dest_2='SERVICE=STBY OPTIONAL'
log_archive_dest_state_2=DEFER
```

This creates a second optional destination for archive logs on the remote database. Setting this destination to a state of DEFER suppresses the ARC*n* attempt to write to this location immediately. You can alter this state dynamically later on. After making these changes, you will need to restart the instance. If an instance outage is impossible, make the changes to the init.ora file, but then use **alter system** to change the parameters dynamically. Making the change dynamically but failing to make permanent changes in the init.ora file can lead to mix-ups down the road when the instance is bounced for some reason. If you are using the new Oracle9i SPFILE for storing initialization parameters, be sure to set the SCOPE to BOTH when altering the parameters.

3. Make a copy of initprod90.ora, rename it initstandby.ora, and move it to STBY01. Place it in the d:\oracle\admin\standby\pfile directory, and make the following changes:

```
#log_archive_dest_1=
#'LOCATION=d:\oracle\oradata\prod90\arch MANDATORY'
#log_archive_dest_2='SERVICE=STBY OPTIONAL'
#log_archive_dest_state_2=DEFER
db_file_name_convert = ('C:\ORACLE\ORADATA\PROD90\SYSTEM01.DBF',
'D:\ORACLE\ORADATA\STANDBY\SYSTEM01.DBF',
'C:\ORACLE\ORADATA\PROD90\UNDOTBS01.DB',
'D:\ORACLE\ORADATA\STANDBY\UNDOTBS01.DB',
'C:\ORACLE\ORADATA\PROD90\CWMLITE01.DB',
'D:\ORACLE\ORADATA\STANDBY\CWMLITE01.DB',
'C:\ORACLE\ORADATA\PROD90\DRSYS01.DBF',
'D:\ORACLE\ORADATA\STANDBY\DRSYS01.DBF',
'C:\ORACLE\ORADATA\PROD90\EXAMPLE01.DB',
'D:\ORACLE\ORADATA\STANDBY\EXAMPLE01.DB',
'C:\ORACLE\ORADATA\PROD90\INDX01.DBF',
'D:\ORACLE\ORADATA\STANDBY\INDX01.DBF',
'C:\ORACLE\ORADATA\PROD90\TOOLS01.DBF',
'D:\ORACLE\ORADATA\STANDBY\TOOLS01.DBF',
'C:\ORACLE\ORADATA\PROD90\USERS01.DBF',
'D:\ORACLE\ORADATA\STANDBY\USERS01.DBF')
log_file_name_convert = ('C:\ORACLE\ORADATA\PROD90\REDO03.LOG',
'D:\ORACLE\ORADATA\STANDBY\REDO03.LOG',
'C:\ORACLE\ORADATA\PROD90\REDO02.LOG',
'D:\ORACLE\ORADATA\STANDBY\REDO02.LOG',
'C:\ORACLE\ORADATA\PROD90\REDO01.LOG',
'D:\ORACLE\ORADATA\STANDBY\REDO01.LOG')
standby_archive_dest = d:\oracle\oradata\standby\arch
log_archive_dest = d:\oracle\oradata\standby\arch
```

After making these changes, also make sure any destination parameters, such as USER_DUMP_DEST and BACKGROUND_DUMP_DEST, have been modified to reflect the drive change as well.

4. On STBY01, create the Windows Service for the standby database:

```
d:>oradim -new -sid STANDBY -intpwd oracle -startmode manual
   -pfile d:\oracle\admin\standby\pfile\initstandby.ora
```

5. Log into the production database as sysdba and create the Standby control file:

```
SQL> ALTER DATABASE CREATE STANDBY CONTROLFILE AS
'c:\oracle\admin\prod90\standby.ctl';
```

6. Move this file into the control file destination specified in the initstandby.ora file. If you have more than one location for control files in the initstandby.ora file, then make copies of this Standby control file and replicate them to the locations specified by the CONTROL_FILES parameter.

7. Mount the standby database:

```
SQL>startup nomount
pfile=d:\oracle\admin\standby\pfile\initstandby.ora
SQL>alter database mount standby database;
```

8. Begin the process of automatically creating archive logs on the standby database by changing the state of LOG_ARCHIVE_DEST_2 on the production database:

```
SQL>connect /@prod90 as sysdba
SQL>alter system set log_archive_dest_state_2=enable
```

To test to make sure that the archive log is being pushed to the standby instance, force a log switch, and then check STANDBY_ARCHIVE_DEST on STBY01:

```
SQL>alter system switch logfile;
```

Operating the Standby Database in Manual Recovery Mode

Manual recovery mode refers to the process of monitoring each archive log as it is applied to the standby database, similar in all ways to monitoring a normal recovery session in SQL*Plus. Begin the process of applying archive logs to the standby database by connecting to the standby database and issuing the **recover** command:

```
SQL>connect /@stby as sysdba
SQL> recover standby database;
ORA-00279: change 278218 generated at 08/07/2001 10:11:58 needed
for thread 1
ORA-00289: suggestion : D:\ORACLE\ORADATA\STANDBY\ARCH\ARCH.3.1
ORA-00280: change 278218 for thread 1 is in sequence #3

Specify log: {<RET>=suggested | filename | AUTO | CANCEL}
```

If the archive log requested is not already in the standby destination specified, you will need to manually copy any necessary archive logs from the production database and put them in the suggested location, as specified by the ORA-289 message shown in the preceding code. This lag time between the creation of the standby control file and the **recover standby database** command is called the *gap sequence*. The gap sequence requires a manual process of moving the archive logs from the production database to the standby database.

After all the necessary archive logs exist on the standby server, you can simply enter **auto** and press ENTER, and all the available archived redo logs will be applied. Or, you can use the ENTER key after each archive log is applied to apply the next archive log in order to monitor the recovery process. Your standby database is now currently running in manual recovery mode.

Setting Up the Standby Database in Managed Recovery Mode

The switch from manual to managed standby mode takes a little work. First, make sure that you have set up LOG_ARCHIVE_DEST_N in the initprod90.ora file to be a service that points to your standby instance:

```
SQL>connect /@prod90 as sysdba
Alter system set log_archive_dest_2='SERVICE=STBY';
```

Next, cancel your manual recovery session, and then set it to managed mode:

```
SQL>connect sys/oracle@stby
SQL> connect /@stby as sysdba
SQL>recover managed standby database;
```

You will notice that this SQL*Plus session seems to hang after this **recover** command. This is normal; if you need to cancel a managed recovery session, you will have to create a second session to the standby database and issue the **cancel** command:

```
SQL>connect /@stby as sysdba
SQL>recover managed standby database cancel;
```

Alternatively, use the **disconnect** option of the **recover** command, as demonstrated in the code that follows. This will create a detached thread in the background for managed recovery, and return control of the SQL session to the user. This is recommended for the sake of a clean desktop, but it masks the managed recovery thread, and you will not know it is running unless you check the V$MANAGED_STANDBY view.

```
SQL>recover managed standby database disconnect;
Media recovery complete.
SQL>select process, status, sequence# from v$managed_standby;
```

To confirm that the standby database is automatically applying archive logs as they appear on the standby site, check the standby alert log. The following is an excerpt of the messages displayed as Oracle automatically applies archive logs:

```
ALTER DATABASE RECOVER  managed standby database
Tue Aug 07 12:31:06 2001
Media Recovery Start: Managed Standby Recovery
Successfully started datafile 1 media recovery
Datafile #1: 'C:\ORACLE\ORADATA\STANDBY\SYSTEM01.DBF'
Successfully started datafile 2 media recovery
Datafile #2: 'C:\ORACLE\ORADATA\STANDBY\UNDOTBS01.DBF'
Successfully started datafile 3 media recovery
...
Datafile #7: 'C:\ORACLE\ORADATA\STANDBY\TOOLS01.DBF'
Successfully started datafile 8 media recovery
Datafile #8: 'C:\ORACLE\ORADATA\STANDBY\USERS01.DBF'
Media Recovery Log
Media Recovery Waiting for thread 1 seq# 7
Tue Aug 07 12:31:22 2001
Media Recovery Log C:\ORACLE\ORADATA\STANDBY\ARCH\ARCH.7.1
Media Recovery Waiting for thread 1 seq# 8
Tue Aug 07 12:31:53 2001
Media Recovery Log C:\ORACLE\ORADATA\STANDBY\ARCH\ARCH.8.1
Media Recovery Waiting for thread 1 seq# 9
```

Utilizing Oracle9i Log Transport Services

Log Transport Services refer to processes already discussed in this chapter: the automatic creation of archive logs on the Standby database as they are created on the primary database. However, Oracle9i has introduced an enhancement to this process that allows changes to be propagated to the standby database as they occur on the primary database. It's a subtle but critical difference. Prior to 9i, the only way to propagate changes to the standby database meant configuring the ARC*n* process on the primary database to make a copy of the archive log on the Standby server. Thus, database updates are only available in batches that are controlled by the size of the redo log file, or how often the redo log file switches. If a disaster struck and the online redo log file was lost before it was archived, those changes would be gone forever.

In 9i, Log Transport Services can be configured so that instead of depending on the ARC*n* process to propagate changes, you can utilize the LGWR to write all database updates to the primary online redo log files and the standby archive log files simultaneously. In this way, you get changes recorded at the standby site as they occur, instead of when a redo log switch occurs. Figure 13-2 illustrates this process. The upside: you now have the ability to guarantee that every transaction is recorded at the standby database, thus achieving a *no data loss* solution. The downside: this is remarkably expensive, if you consider the network chat that it promulgates.

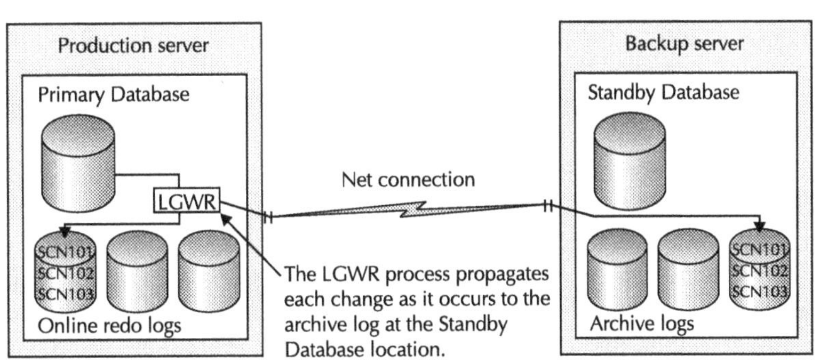

FIGURE 13-2. *LGWR control of log transport*

Configuring LGWR for Log Transport

The LGWR process is configured to be responsible for log transport by configuring the LOG_ARCHIVE_DEST_N parameter. Instead of simply specifying the service name of your standby database, you also specify LGWR:

```
log_archive_dest_2='service=standby LGWR'
```

Oracle9i allows for manipulation of the two primary variables of log transport: how often you push changes to the archive log of the standby database, and the degree of importance placed on a successful push to the standby database. The first parameter is specified in the LOG_ARCHIVE_DEST_N parameter as either SYNC or ASYNC. When SYNC is specified, LGWR writes to the online redo log file of the primary database and the archive redo log file simultaneously. Sync mode is required if you want to guarantee that every transaction is propagated to the standby database, and you specify this mode like this:

```
log_archive_dest_2='service=standby LGWR SYNC'
```

Alternatively, ASYNC can be specified for the log destination. In async mode, LGWR fills an SGA buffer with changes that are being recorded in the primary redo log. When the buffer is full, LGWR pushes the changes to the standby database. The buffer size is specified in a number of OS blocks. If ASYNC=500, as shown in the example, the buffer size is 500 multiplied by the OS block size (see Chapter 2 for an overview of the Windows 2000 block size).

```
log_archive_dest_2='service=standby LGWR ASYNC=500'
```

In addition to setting the propagation mode, you can also determine if the actual I/O operation of recording the changes on the standby database must occur before control is returned to the user at the primary database. This differs mildly from the SYNC/ASYNC setting: SYNC/ASYNC sets the network transmission priority. AFFIRM/NOAFFIRM controls, demonstrated in the code that follows, the actual write operations to the standby database archive log. If AFFIRM is set in addition to SYNC, then every transaction that is written to the primary database redo log must also be successfully written to the standby database archive log before transaction processing can continue. This obviously can significantly delay production operations, so you must be extremely committed to zero data loss to operate in this mode. NOAFFIRM is the default, and does not need to be specified. NOAFFIRM does not require that the primary database receive affirmation that the changes were successfully written to the standby database. Specify AFFIRM/NOAFFIRM as shown here:

```
log_archive_dest_2='service=standby LGWR SYNC AFFIRM'
log_archive_dest_2='service=standby LGWR ASYNC=500 NOAFFIRM'
```

Remember that these parameters can be changed on-the-fly using an **alter system set** command. So you can change the value to SYNC AFFIRM and gauge the performance hit, and then set it back without having to restart the instance.

Using Oracle9i Data Guard for Standby Database Management

New in Oracle9i, Data Guard represents the next evolutionary step in standby databases. It allows for more fine-grained control of the relationship between the primary database and multiple Standby databases. It does so by introducing a management interface called the Data Guard Broker for the entire standby configuration. The Broker can be used via a command-line interface, using the utility dgmgrl.exe, or via the GUI Data Guard Manager. In addition, a new database process, DMON, monitors all Standby communication and maintains configuration-wide parameters between all standby sites.

We thought about showcasing Data Guard when writing this chapter, but instead decided to include a smaller section on its principles and configuration. Data Guard is a build-on to the Standby Database architecture, and is not a necessary component for a standby database configuration. Everything we have shown you up to this point concerning the standby database can be put in place with or without Data Guard. Data Guard is really just a name for a suite of new feature add-ons to the Standby Database architecture, which includes the management interface (Broker) and features we have already discussed: Log Transport Services and Log Apply Services.

The usage of Data Guard gives you an intriguing new feature: the ability to perform switchover and switchback between the primary and standby databases without being forced to reinstantiate the primary database. Remember, in a traditional standby environment, the failover to the standby database makes the primary database invalid, and you have to rebuild it from scratch. With Data Guard, this is still the case for failover. However, Data Guard also has the ability to gracefully switch over the primary database role to a standby database and then switch back, without having to restore and rebuild the original database. Switchover can be used for rolling upgrades of hardware and operating system patches, but cannot be used for rolling upgrades of Oracle software.

Other than graceful switchover, familiarity with Data Guard comes in handy when you are configuring more than one standby database for your primary database, and you need a way to manage the increased level of complexity that comes when the Standby configuration expands beyond a one-to-one relationship. It also provides a central management location for handling the tangled web of archive logs and their multitude of locations, including setting up FAL servers and clients. FAL (Fetch Archive Log) server refers to the database that will be used to distribute archive logs to all Standby sites. By default, the FAL server is the primary database, but this can be switched to one of the standby databases in order to perform the work of archive log distribution offline, away from the production server.

Data Guard Configuration

Data Guard can be configured via a command-line utility, dgmgrl.exe, or via the Data Guard Manager, which comes bundled as part of Enterprise Manager (a management server must be configured for Data Guard Manager to be available). By far the best approach to configuration is with the GUI Data Guard Manager. Using this utility, a brand-new standby database can be configured from scratch, if you are using RMAN to back up the primary database. By clicking the green gleaming box on the left-hand side of the Enterprise Manager Console, the Create Configuration Wizard will walk through the configuration steps. You will need to name the Data Guard configuration; in the following examples, the configuration is named DG_TEST.

If you have previously created a standby database using conventional means, as outlined previously in this chapter, the wizard will find your previous standby database and ask if you would like to use it instead of creating a new one. Note that a warning box tells you that any previously configured log archiving parameters will be cleared and re-created by Data Guard Manager. Thus, this is a good time to back up your standby and primary init.ora files.

After using the wizard, the Data Guard Manager will show all your resources, as seen in Figure 13-3. By default, a new Data Guard configuration is disabled. Right-click your new configuration and choose Enable/Disable; this will bring up a splash window asking you if you want to enable the configuration. By choosing yes, you are enabling the DMON process to monitor log transference between the primary and Standby databases. For DMON to run, the parameter DRS_START=TRUE must be set at all sites. The Data Guard Manager will do this for you dynamically, so if you use an SPFILE it will be set permanently. If you do not use an SPFILE, you will need to set DRS_START=TRUE in your init.ora file for each database in the Data Guard Configuration.

Graceful Switchover and Switchback

Unfortunately, the Data Guard Manager does not provide an interface for performing the switchover operation, one of the most important functions of a Data Guard configuration. Instead, you will need to revert to a SQL session, first connecting to the primary database and then to the standby database, which will now become the primary database. In fact, you will have to delete the configuration information from the Data Guard Manager, and then add it back when the switchover is complete. To do so, simply right-click the configuration resource (in our example, DG_TEST) and

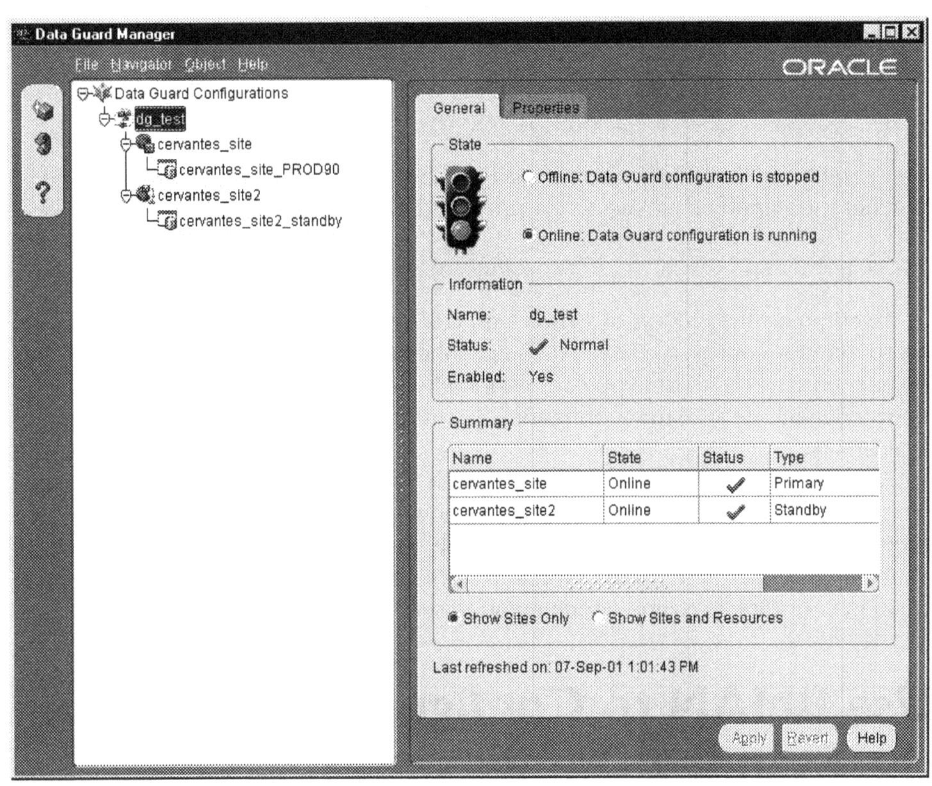

FIGURE 13-3. *Data Guard Manager's resources*

choose Delete. After promptly ignoring the warning, you can choose OK. Deleting the configuration does not undo any of the configuration, it simply removes any memory of the configuration from Data Guard Manager. You will have to add it back after you perform the switchover.

Before engaging the switchover process, you also must stop the DMON process on both the primary and Standby site:

```
ALTER SYSTEM SET DRS_START=FALSE;
```

You must then ensure that no user processes are connected to the primary and standby databases. It is critical that you disconnect all users, including any sessions created by jobs in the job queue, the EM Intelligent Agent, and all user connections. It may be necessary to shut down the production and standby instances, and then

bring them back up and reenable the managed recovery mode on the standby. In this way, you ensure all sessions have ended. Next, while connected to the primary database, the following command begins the switchover process:

```
ALTER DATABASE COMMIT TO SWITCHOVER TO STANDBY;
```

After confirming that this has completed in the alert log, the following command switches the standby database to the primary database:

```
ALTER DATABASE COMMIT TO SWITCHOVER TO PRIMARY;
```

To complete the process of switchover, it is necessary to shut down all databases in your standby configuration, and then open the new primary database. After opening the new primary database, you can mount all your Standby databases and begin recovery again. Be sure to reconfigure your archive log destinations and FAL server, if necessary.

After making the switchover, you will need to log back into Data Guard Manager and rebuild your configuration, which will now reflect a new primary site. For more information about the logistics, and especially the extended functionality of the Data Guard Broker, refer to the *Oracle9i Data Guard Concepts and Administration,* found in your Oracle online documentation set.

Use RMAN to Configure the Standby Database

If you took our advice in Chapter 6 and set up a backup and recovery strategy that utilizes Oracle9i Recovery Manager, then you can use RMAN to configure the standby database. RMAN utilizes the **duplicate** command to create the datafiles for the Standby instance. There is additional syntax for creating the standby database using RMAN.

To use RMAN for standby database creation, first refresh your understanding of the **duplicate** command discussed in Chapter 6. This is the basis for creating the standby database, and all rules and stipulations that apply to the **duplicate** command apply here. Remember as well to create the Windows 2000 Service for the standby database using the oradim utility. RMAN will not complete this step for you.

Next, configure the initialization parameter files for both the production and Standby databases as noted previously in this chapter. Note that from RMAN's perspective, the production database is the target, and the Standby database is the auxiliary. Make the appropriate net service name changes, and start up the auxiliary (standby) instance in nomount mode.

Next, create a standby control file available to RMAN. After connecting to the target, auxiliary, and catalog, enter the following:

```
Rman>backup current controlfile for standby;
```

This will use the default target channels to back up a copy of the control file with a standby configuration. This file is the same as that produced by **alter database backup standby controlfile to 'location'**. After these steps, in addition to the steps for running a **duplicate** command, the following syntax builds the standby database from RMAN backups:

```
rman>run {set until time = 'sysdate-(1/24)';
duplicate target database for standby; }
```

It is critical to set an UNTIL TIME parameter for the duplicate. Because of the standby nature of this duplication command, you cannot assume that you will be doing a full recovery and then opening the new database, so you must set a time frame for the restore operation. The only other restriction above and beyond the regular **duplicate** command is that you cannot put a LOGFILES parameter into the command. If the log files need to be in a new location, you will need to use the init.ora parameter LOG_FILE_NAME_CONVERT.

The **duplicate...for standby** operation does not perform any recovery by default, meaning any archive logs that have been backed up using RMAN will need to be restored manually, and then recovered from SQL*Plus. Alternatively, you can append the keyword DORECOVER to the **duplicate** command. This will tell RMAN to use its archive log backups in order to recover the standby database. If you use the DORECOVER keyword, you will need to set an UNTIL TIME clause as well in order to satisfy the condition that any **duplicate** command that connects to an auxiliary instance on a different computer have a time clause:

```
Rman>run {set until time 'SYSDATE-(1/24)';
 duplicate target database for standby dorecover;}
```

RMAN cannot be used for managed recovery on the standby instance. Instead, after the standby database has been created, you will need to log into the standby database and issue the **recover managed standby database** command.

Use the Standby Database for RMAN Backups of the Production Database

Often, one of the largest obstacles to overcome with a backup and recovery strategy is trying to find a time to perform the backup in a way that does not adversely effect the production application that runs against the database. But in high-availability situations, where the application runs against the database nonstop, there is no good time to perform backups. Every backup operation interrupts the flow of production usage.

The standby database can be used to fix this problem. If you have set up a standby database, RMAN can connect to the Standby database to perform backup operations of production data. In a recovery situation, these backups seamlessly restore to the production database. Essentially, the backed up files from the standby database are interchangeable with the database files of the production. The only file that cannot be used interchangeably is the control file. The standby database control file cannot be restored to the primary database and used to mount the database.

The key to successfully using the Standby database to backup the production database is one of perception. When connecting to the standby database in RMAN, it is essential that you perceive the standby database as the production database, not the standby. This means connecting to the standby database as the target in RMAN, not the auxiliary, and then connecting to the catalog normally. In this fashion, the Recovery Catalog cannot differentiate between the Standby and the production databases, and when a backup is performed, the Catalog registers the backups as those of the production database.

You must be connected to a Recovery Catalog in order for RMAN to take production backups from the standby database. If you are not connected to a Catalog, the only record of the backups is the Standby control file. When you need to restore those backups at the production database, the production control file has no record of the backups, and will not be able to find them.

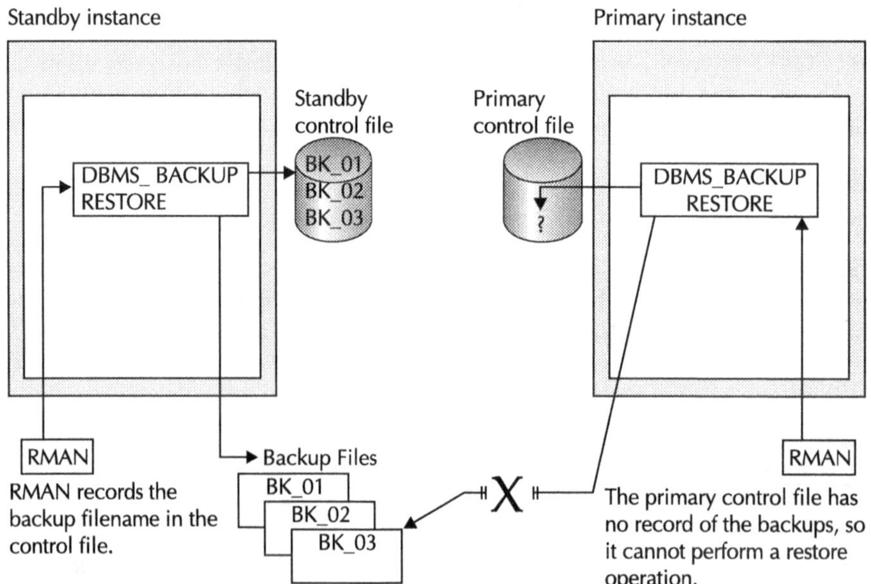

Archive log backups are a bit more complicated, but the same rules apply: you must be connected to the Standby Database as the target database, and connected to a catalog for the backups to be available to production.

Here's the complicated part: RMAN uses the view V$ARCHIVED_LOG in the control file of the target database to determine which archive logs need to be backed up. This is an essential component of RMAN operations, but when you want to take a backup of the archive logs from the Standby Database, it can lead to problems. The control file of the standby instance may not have a complete listing of all the archive logs that need to be backed up. This disparity occurs when archive logs are moved to the Standby instance using any method other than managed standby mode. In a managed standby database, the archive logs arrive at the Standby Database via a net connection from the primary database, and the Standby control file is updated to reflect any new archive logs. However, if a gap occurs for any reason, and archive logs are manually moved to the Standby instance, these archive logs will not be recorded in V$ARCHIVED_LOG, and therefore RMAN will not back them up.

So here's the tip: before using RMAN to back up the archive logs from a standby database, make sure you have the managed standby mode set up and running smoothly. This way, you will minimize the possibility of any archive log gaps being created. If you will be operating in an environment where sequence gaps are simply a fact of life, do the archive log backups from the production server. The datafiles can still be backed up from the standby, but the administrative headaches of keeping track of where your archive logs are is simply too great. If for some reason a gap is created in the archive logs at the standby, make sure you immediately create a backup of those archive logs from production before you put the standby back in managed mode.

Summary

In this chapter, we discussed the architecture of the standby database, as well as standby database modes. These modes included different recovery modes, as well as how to open the standby database for read-only access. We gave techniques for creating sort space on the Standby Database when it is open for read-only, and long-running queries are expected. After giving a few restrictions and limitations, we built a test case of a standby environment. We then moved on to new Standby features in 9i, from Log Transport Services to the management interface of Data Guard. Finally, we discussed using your RMAN backups to create the standby, as well as using the standby database for subsequent backups of the primary database.

CHAPTER 14

Oracle9*i* Advanced Replication

In the preceding chapters, you have seen three different paths that can be taken in order to achieve a level of availability that matches your business needs: Real Application Clusters, Oracle Failsafe, and Standby Databases. None of these, however, invoke dread quite like Oracle's Advanced Replication feature.

Medusa's hair seems like the most vivid visual metaphor for this feature, or perhaps the song of the sirens, luring you down a path that seems simple and luxurious, and that can solve all of your problems. Here in Oracle Support, we thoroughly enjoy the myth of Sysyphus, the existential hero cursed to forever push the rock up the hill, only to watch it tumble down and have to push it back up. However, the most realistic metaphor, when it comes to replication, is that of the Hydra: a beast that, upon having one head cut off, grew two new heads in its place. So if you fight and fight and fight, you only create more and more snapping, biting maws to fend off.

This gives rise to the question of why we might venture into the lair of the beast, when we've already covered most of the more common forms of availability. In short, we could not in good conscience omit replication in the course of any realistic discussion of high availability. Despite the hardships of setting up and administering replication, it remains to date one of the best solutions for making data available across large geographic areas. Replication is also one of the only methods of allowing multiple databases to have the same records at each site and allow them to independently update that data.

So, put on your best gladiator garb. In this chapter, we will discuss the following tips and techniques for Advanced Replication:

- Replication: load balancing, disaster recovery, and distributed offline transaction processing
- Getting to know the advanced replication architecture
- Understanding n-way master replication
- Looking at materialized views
- Understanding replication in relation to database performance
- Comparing Replication Manager and the Replication API
- Setting up and configuring n-way masters
- Understanding the basics of conflict resolution
- Performing offline instantiation
- Starting and stopping replication
- Monitoring replication processes
- Conclusions and advice for the replication database administrator

Replication: Load Balancing, Disaster Recovery, and Distributed Offline Transaction Processing

There are a number of critical needs that replication can address in modern data availability models. And while you can draw your own conclusions about what you might use replication for, at this point it behooves us to generalize the implementations so that you get a sense of its usefulness.

Load Balancing

Perhaps the most important implementation of replication is its ability to load balance user connections and data updates across multiple physical sites. Unlike RAC, where the nodes of the cluster are by definition connected by hardware, replication allows users connected to two different databases to see the same data, even if the two databases physically reside in Tokyo and Chicago. The only connection necessary is the Internet.

The load balancing ethos is clear: if you have two or more servers residing in different locations, you can connect half the users to one server and half to the other, thus increasing the number of simultaneous users connecting. Using replication, all of the users are inserting, updating, and deleting from tables that are logically identical. However, don't let us sell this too quickly; the performance hit that replication incurs may offset any benefit you might get out of distributing users across multiple databases.

More realistically, replication works best for load balancing when there is a subset of application data that is the same across multiple sites, but each site is also maintaining independent data. For instance, perhaps each hardware store in a chain maintains its own inventory of wood screws. However, if they need to order more wood screws from the centralized location, every other site needs to know about the order so that the central warehouse does not run short on wood screws. So tables holding warehouse orders for wood screws, along with wood screw fulfillment tables, get replicated across all sites.

Disaster Recovery

With the onset of new zero data-loss solutions provided by Oracle Standby Database and Data Guard, the use of replication for disaster recovery will probably begin to taper off. However, replication still provides the ability to keep a full, nearly synchronous copy of production data available and online in case the production database goes offline for some reason. Unlike with RAC, replication is a bit safer in the case of a natural disaster because replicated database sites do not necessarily have to live in the same location, as do RAC nodes. And, unlike Standby Databases, the secondary database in a replicated environment is always online for reporting and for updating. In a disaster situation, users can be rerouted to a different master site, and production moves on. Perhaps the finest selling point of replication is that it works across different operating systems, because it is a solution that exists fully within the Oracle RDBMS structure.

Distributed Offline Transaction Processing

One of the most powerful implementations of replication is to use it for distributed offline transaction processing. This refers to the necessity in many lines of business to have salespeople out in the field who have access to database information, and who need to update that database, but may not always be connected to the database. Thus, you may have hundreds of users who are simultaneously updating the database, but none of them are online. Using materialized views (formerly known as snapshots), these users can update copies of production data that they carry on their laptops. At regular intervals, they can then connect to the master database and sync up by pushing their changes up to the master and then refreshing the copy on their laptops. Application and replication logic take care of inconsistencies that might arise from so many users changing data.

Distributed Offline Transaction Processing (DOTP), while powerful, is not explicitly a high-availability solution. Although it provides large benefits over other forms of data entry for hundreds of offline users, it cannot be used to prevent data loss or data outages in the case of a disaster. Therefore, we will not spend much time in this chapter discussing its configuration or administration. For more information on using materialized views, refer to the *Oracle9i Replication Guide*.

The Advanced Replication Architecture

In reality, the beastly nature of replication is mostly an image problem: it suffers from a lack of an elegant, simple architectural model. Instead, even replication oversimplifications (such as the one you are reading) look like huge IF-THEN-ELSE nested programmatical flow charts. Yet it is worth your time to explore the architecture to understand the benefits you can reap for your highly available database. There are two distinct forms that replication takes: n-way master replication and materialized views.

N-Way Master Replication

N-way master replication refers to the ability to keep two or more sites (thus the *n* in n-way, where *n* is the variable number of masters) simultaneously updating the same set of tables, as well as refreshing the changes from the other masters.

All things must have an origin, and the site of origin for the tables, and thus where the bulk of administrative work first takes place, is known as the *master definition site*. This is the site where your base tables exist. *Base tables* refers to the tables prior to their incarnation as replication objects. At the master definition site, you create a *replication group*, which is a logical grouping of all objects that need to be replicated together (for purposes of referential integrity), and then you add your objects to the group. After adding the objects to the group, you generate replication support for these objects. *Replication support* refers to the row-level triggers that get engaged for the objects, so that whenever DML occurs on the table, the transaction is recorded and moved to the deferred transaction queue.

The Deferred Transaction Queue

The *deferred transaction queue* is the heart and soul of replication. It is responsible for recording every transactional change that occurs to replicated objects, and then pushing them across a database link to every other database that needs to receive the transaction and have it applied to a copy of the tables at that site.

Any database other than the master definition site that is set up for n-way replication is referred to as a *master*. At the master sites, you have replication groups full of replication objects that match those of the master definition site. When the transactions are pushed from the master definition site across the database link to the master site, these transactions are placed in the local deferred transaction queue, and then applied to the replicated tables of the master site.

This process can work both ways: if a transaction is entered on a table at the master site, a trigger fires and places a copy of the transaction in the deferred transaction queue of the master. At the push interval, these transactions are then moved via a database link to the master definition site's transaction queue, and ultimately applied to the replicated table there. The primary difference between the master definition site and the master sites is administrative: most administrative tasks necessary for replication upkeep must originate at the master definition site.

The Deferred Error Queue

If there is any sort of problem getting a transaction applied at a remote site, the transaction is moved from the deferred transaction queue to the deferred error queue. The transaction remains applied to the site where the transaction originated, but the deferred call to the remote database lands in the deferred error queue, where it sits and waits for user intervention to either delete the error or fix the problem that caused the error. Here's the stickler: if there is even one error in the deferred error queue, no transactions can be pushed. None. Zero. Replication is completely halted. Either you delete the transaction or you fix the problem. To view transactions that have moved to the deferred error queue, you can look at the DEFERROR view, which any user with DBA privileges can access.

So you have transactions that originate at two sites, both of which have a deferred error queue. So what gives? If a transaction fails, which deferred error queue do you look at? Well, it depends on the nature of the failure. If the remote procedure call fails due to site failure (for instance, if the other site has a network outage), then the error goes to the local deferred error queue. But if you make a successful connection, but the error occurs due to a primary key constraint or a value conflict, then the transaction will remain in the remote site's deferred error queue.

That's n-way master replication, in a nutshell: two or more sites, with tables that reside in replication groups, fill up deferred queues and push them to other sites to be applied to the same table at the other site. Ah, if only it were that simple.

Materialized View (Snapshot) Replication

During the transition from Oracle8 to Oracle8i, someone had the brainstorm to rename the erstwhile snapshot as the new and improved *materialized view (mview)*. This was done to reflect a change in the code for the overall functionality of the snapshot: no longer solely a component of replication, the materialized view used much of the same underlying constructs, but now could be used for the purposes for data warehousing and the like. Prior to mviews, if you wanted to create a view for a table, all you really constructed was a hidden query that executed against the base tables every time you selected against it. This caused performance heartbreak for data warehousing folks, who wanted queries to run faster than they could on select operations against their enormous base tables. So, using snapshot architecture, Oracle created materialized views, which were refreshable subsets of data in the base tables.

From a replication perspective, the name changed but the song remains the same: materialized views provide the means to create a replicated copy of production data that could be refreshed via a database link.

Snapshots provide the ability to perform Distributed Offline Transaction Processing (DOTP). Unlike a master replication environment, a snapshot does not require that it be constantly in connection with the master site. All local updates to a snapshot are placed in a specialized table. Based on a time specification or user intervention, the snapshot makes a database link connection to the master site and pushes its transactions up. After they are applied to the master table, the snapshot then pulls a refreshed copy of the table back down.

There are no such things as conflicts for snapshots: if there is a disparity between the snapshot and the master, the master always wins, period. This can lead to some baffling experiences: imagine updating a materialized view, and then forcing a refresh from the master site. Without any errors being returned, you run a query against your mview and find that your most recent work has vanished. You check the master table, and your work is not there either. This is because a failure in the update at the master does not signal an error for the refresh mechanism, so the new copy of the master table that you pull down does not have your newly minted rows—they are deleted from the mview.

We could go on and on about mviews, but they do not provide a proficient or guaranteed form of data availability. They do provide excellent benefits in other arenas, which are outside the scope of this book. Therefore, we will concentrate solely on n-way master replication from this point onward.

Replication and Database Performance

Not that we haven't already painted a cautionary tale about replication, but here is more fuel for the fire. With the addition of triggers being fired and deferred queue tables being populated with values, all the internal work Oracle does means one thing: every transaction against a replicated table takes longer than the same transaction would on a nonreplicated table.

Results may vary, but in the old-school days of replication (back in release 8.0), here in Oracle Support we had a mantra for replication performance: it takes six times as long as a usual transaction would. Do we live by that number? Absolutely not. It was a way to frame the performance conversation with customers by highlighting one simple fact: replication slows things down significantly. The only way to know how replication will actually affect your environment is to test. With each update occurring, and then a trigger firing, and then a DEFTRAN entry being made, you can expect a significant slowdown in all DML activity. The silver lining is that query statements are unaffected by all the machinery in the background.

Outside of the database itself, replication relies on a solid, interruption-free network connection between the masters. Network drop-offs do not cause replication to fall to its knees, but an on-and-off network is not a candidate for replicated environments. Likewise, make sure you have a very fat pipe between your masters—replication is quite the bandwidth hog. Not only is it sending transactions both directions, but it also sends back confirmation of transactions being received, as well as chatty administrative requests. All in all, it makes for heavy network utilization. So give it what it needs, and keep your masters connected on a megabyte-per-second network.

Replication Manager vs. Replication API

Now, to the setup steps themselves. Bear in mind, what we will attempt to show you is the most basic of replication tasks: replication for two master sites, one replicated table. We will not discuss the replication of user-defined types, LOBs, triggers, or procedural replication. Again, this chapter is an introduction. If you want more advanced information, you'll have to pull out the Oracle replication documentation. Better yet, attend one of Oracle's replication courses (you'll get your money's worth from this one). But most importantly, test replication in a nonproduction environment, one that mimics production in terms of transaction load and network bandwidth. Otherwise, you will be surprised. And we don't mean in a pleasant way.

As with all things Oracle, there are two ways to set up replication: you can use the API interface, meaning a direct execution of Oracle-supplied DBMS packages at the database level, or you can use the GUI Replication Manager, which is now tied up neatly with OEM. By all estimations, using the Replication Manager utility is far easier than executing the packages at the command line. And Replication Manager provides a nice interface for troubleshooting errors and even looking at the transactional values for remote procedure calls. However, usage depends on one important thing: that you have successfully set up and configured Enterprise Manager, including the Management Server. The Standalone EM does not allow you to use Replication Manager.

Making a decision about which direction to choose, command line or GUI, will most likely be decided by your background in the technology industry, and where you feel more comfortable. The bottom line is there is no right or wrong way to configure replication. That being said, if you are serious about replication, you'd better learn the command-line API calls. Sooner or later, that is where you end up, as there are certain functions and programmatic subtleties that get left out of the GUI. On the other hand, the GUI simplifies some pretty advanced monitoring queries that would otherwise have to be written in SQL.

For the purpose of this chapter, we will primarily focus on the API calls to be made, and mention how these same things are accomplished from the GUI.

N-Way Setup and Configuration

The setup example we walk you through in this section includes only two masters, PROD90 and REPO. PROD90 will be the master definition site. Here, only a single table, TESTITOUT, will be replicated from the user JIBBER. The following is the setup for the JIBBER user on both PROD90 and REPO. You will only create the TESTITOUT table on the master definition site, PROD90. The process of configuring replication will build the table at the master site.

```
connect system/manager@prod90
create user jibber identified by jabber
default tablespace users
temporary tablespace temp;
grant connect, resource to jibber;

connect system/manager@repo
create user jibber identified by jabber
default tablespace users
temporary tablespace temp;
grant connect, resource to jibber;

connect jibber/jabber@prod90
 create table testitout (
 col1 number (10) primary key,
 col2 varchar2(10));
```

```
declare
v_loopcounter binary_integer :=1;
begin
loop
insert into testitout
     values (v_loopcounter, 'GOT REP?');
v_loopcounter := v_loopcounter +1;
exit when v_loopcounter >500;
end loop;
end;
/
commit;
```

Preparing the Oracle Databases for Replication

First, you need to prepare two Oracle instances for replication. This involves system parameter changes, and possibly data dictionary work. The parameters are as follows:

```
GLOBAL_NAMES=TRUE
JOB_QUEUE_PROCESSES=3
```

These are the only changes you need. Prior to 9i, JOB_QUEUE_INTERVAL had to be set, but this is no longer necessary in 9i. These system parameters can be set with an **alter system** command if you are using an SPFILE. If not, you will need to specify them in the init.ora file so they are permanently set.

After making the parameter changes, you need to make sure that you have the proper data dictionary setup for replication. This involves running the supplied catalog script catrep.sql. However, this is run by default on most databases created using the Database Configuration Assistant. An easy query will determine if you have the right objects:

```
DESC DEFTRAN;
```

If this returns a table description, catrep.sql has been run. There may be invalid objects, so you can always run the script utlrp.sql to revalidate all database objects. Both catrep.sql and utlrp.sql can be found in the %ORACLE_HOME%\RDBMS\ADMIN directory.

Building the Users and Configuring Connectivity

After configuring the database, you need to build your Replication Administrator user. In a more advanced replication environment that adheres to strict security rules, you would also create separate users for the Replication Propagator and the Receiver. These users would be responsible for pushing and applying changes from the deferred transaction queue, respectively. However, in this oversimplified example, the Replication Administrator will be performing all duties. Call this user REPADMIN.

```
create user repadmin identified by repadmin
default tablespace users
temporary tablespace temp;
grant connect, resource to repadmin;
execute dbms_repcat_admin.grant_admin_any_schema('repadmin');
grant comment any table to repadmin;
grant lock any table to repadmin;
execute dbms_defer_sys.register_propagator('repadmin');
```

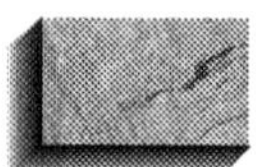

NOTE
Remember, you must create this user and run all these grant and execute operations on both databases.

TIP
If you are using the API to set up replication, open two command prompt windows on your desktop, and perform operations for each master site in a different window. Always be cognizant of which database you are logged in to. There is no worse mistake than issuing a command at the wrong database, and the likelihood of this error is only exacerbated by a replication environment, where you are working with identical users and objects at both sites.

If you are using Replication Manager, you will need to log into the OEM Console as an OEM administrator (the default is SYSMAN/OEM_TEMP—see Chapter 8 for more information), and then expand the folder marked Databases. If you expand one of the databases, one of the options underneath the database is Replication; expand Replication, and three options appear: Administration, Multimaster Replication, and Materialized View Replication. Select Multimaster Replication, and two links will appear in the right pane, as shown in Figure 14-1.

Choosing Setup Master Sites will open a wizard that will guide you through the steps of adding master sites (selecting from a list of discovered nodes) and creating the REPADMIN user.

Back at the API, the next step is to set up the replication communication environment. You must build the secure database links that will connect your two databases. Because you specified GLOBAL_NAMES=TRUE (a necessity for replication), the database link name must match the GLOBAL_NAME of each database.

```
SQL> select * from global_name;
GLOBAL_NAME
-----------------------------------
PROD90.US.ORACLE.COM
```

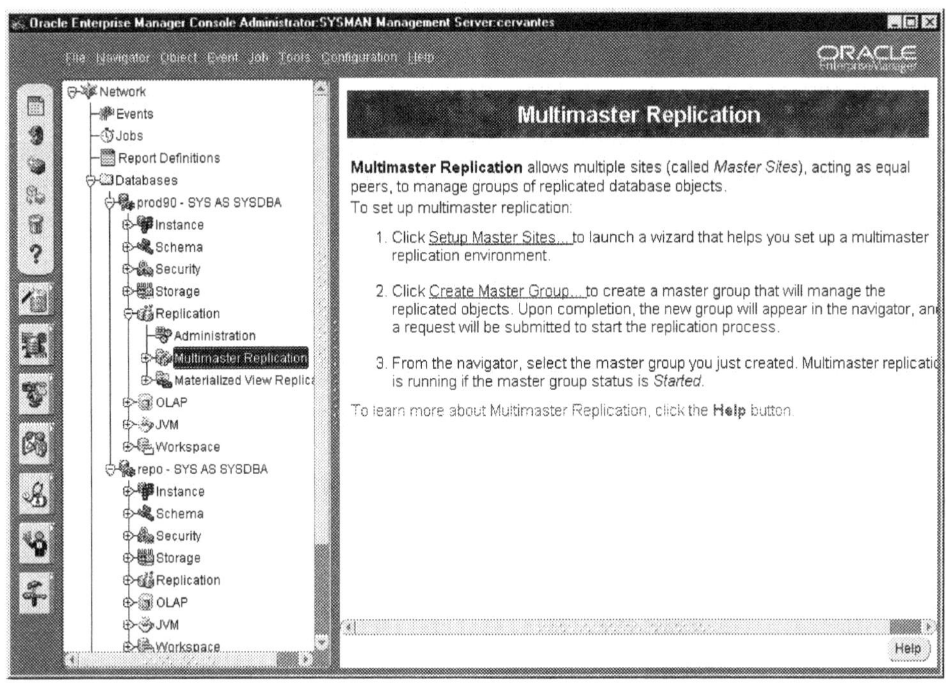

FIGURE 14-1. *Replication Manager setup, Step 1*

Database links can be tricky, but only because they are created on one instance but must point to another instance; in this example, when you are connected to PROD90, you build a database link named REPO.US.ORACLE.COM that references the REPO database.

Database links for replication become even more confusing, and here's why: to create a secure environment, and one that is ultimately manageable, you will actually create two database links that will be used simultaneously for your connection to the remote database. Here's how this works: Normally, when a database link is created, you have to pass two critical pieces of information to Oracle in order for the link to operate: a net service name and a username/password combination. The net service is the layer that allows the database link to make the remote connection. The username and password tells the new net connection which user is connecting. The net service must match an actual service that is listed in the tnsnames.ora file, as well as the remote listener.ora file (for more details, see Chapter 7). The username and password must match an actual user that exists on the remote database.

To maintain security and manageability, in a replication environment you break out these two pieces of information into two separate database links with the same name. The first one, created as a public database link (usable by all database users), contains only the net service information. The second link, created as a private link, contains only the username and password. This way, when you use the database link as REPADMIN, for instance, Oracle pulls the Net Name from the public link and the username/password combination from the private link. Between these two items, you have sufficient information to make a successful connection to the remote database.

Why do we instruct you to do this? By associating the net name with a public link, the database administrator can alter the link to point to a different server, and not have to change every individual user's database link. By associating the private link only with a username and password, individual schemas are protected from being accessible by all users. With all this in mind, the following shows the database link creation, starting with PROD90:

```
SQL> create public database link repo.us.oracle.com using 'repo';
Database link created.
SQL> connect repadmin/repadmin@prod90
Connected.
SQL> create database link repo.us.oracle.com connect to repadmin
  2  identified by repadmin;
Database link created.
SQL> select sysdate from dual@repo.us.oracle.com;
SYSDATE
---------
20-AUG-01
```

Then, on the REPO database, add the following code:

```
SQL> create public database link prod90.us.oracle.com using 'prod90';
Database link created.
SQL> connect repadmin/repadmin@repo
Connected.
SQL> create database link prod90.us.oracle.com connect to repadmin
  2  identified by repadmin;
Database link created.
```

Building Automated Push and Purge Jobs

After your database links are created, the final configuration step before diving into the actual replication setup is to create automatic jobs for pushing transactions from the local DEFTRAN and for purging transactions from the DEFTRAN after they have been successfully pushed.

The push procedure that you set up in the following step does one thing: it sets an interval for how often a job process wakes up and checks the DEFTRAN to see if there are any transactions that need to be pushed to the remote site, and if so, it pushes them. After a transaction is successfully pushed, it is marked as such in the local DEFTRAN. To remove the successfully pushed transactions from DEFTRAN, a purge job must be run. So you need to schedule a second job to do this work. (The reason you don't automatically purge transactions is really a performance gain: by offlining this work to scheduled intervals, there are less likely to be enqueue problems in the DEFTRAN.)

```
connect repadmin/repadmin@prod90
begin
dbms_defer_sys.schedule_push(
     destination =>     'repo.us.oracle.com',
     interval =>'/*three minutes*/ sysdate + 5/(60*24)',
     next_date =>      sysdate,
     stop_on_error =>FALSE,
     delay_seconds =>0,
     parallelism =>    1);
end;
/
begin
dbms_defer_sys.schedule_purge(
     next_date => sysdate,
     interval =>'/*30 minutes*/ sysdate +30/(60*24)',
     delay_seconds =>0,
     rollback_segment => '');
end;
/
connect repadmin/repadmin@repo
begin
dbms_defer_sys.schedule_push(
     destination =>     'prod90.us.oracle.com',
     interval =>'/*three minutes*/ sysdate + 5/(60*24)',
     next_date =>      sysdate,
     stop_on_error =>FALSE,
     delay_seconds =>0,
     parallelism =>    1);
end;
/
begin
dbms_defer_sys.schedule_purge(
     next_date => sysdate,
     interval =>'/*30 minutes*/ sysdate +30/(60*24)',
     delay_seconds =>0,
```

```
    rollback_segment => '');
end;
/
```

In an actual replication environment, you would have to do all of these previous steps at each master site. Likewise, you have to create a separate push job for each remote master that will be in the n-way configuration. To check on these jobs, you can look at the view DBA_JOBS:

```
SQL> select job, what from dba_jobs;
       JOB
----------
WHAT
------------------------------------
         1
declare rc binary_integer; begin rc :=
sys.dbms_defer_sys.push(destination=>'REPO.US.ORACLE.COM',
stop_on_error=>FALSE, delay_seconds=>0, parallelism=>1); end;
         2
declare rc binary_integer; begin rc := sys.dbms_defer_sys.purge(
delay_seconds=>0); end;
```

Keep your eyes on the view DBA_JOBS. In the event of a problem in the replication environment, one of the first places to check is the push job, to see if there has been a failure in the actual job itself. The job mechanism works using the snp background processes, the total number of which is controlled by the parameter set earlier, JOB_QUEUE_PROCESSES. The following query is an example of what you might look for:

```
SQL> column interval format a40
SQL> select job, next_date, broken, interval, failures from dba_jobs;
    JOB NEXT_DATE B INTERVAL                                 FAILURES
------- --------- - ------------------------------------ -----
      1 20-AUG-01 N /*three minutes*/ sysdate + 5/(60*24)
      2 20-AUG-01 N /*30 minutes*/ sysdate +30/(60*24)
```

Building Replication Groups and Objects

Now that you have your replication environments established, you can move to the process of enabling transactional propagation for specific tables. This involves a few steps: creating a replication group, adding masters to the group, adding replication objects, generating replication support (read: enabling internal triggers), and then begin replication.

```
connect repadmin/repadmin@prod90
execute dbms_repcat.create_master_repgroup (gname => 'JIBBER_REP');
execute dbms_repcat.create_master_repobject ( -
sname => 'JIBBER',-
oname => 'TESTITOUT',-
type  => 'TABLE',-
gname => 'JIBBER_REP');
execute dbms_repcat.generate_replication_support( -
sname => 'JIBBER', -
oname => 'TESTITOUT', -
type  => 'TABLE');
execute dbms_repcat.add_master_database( -
gname => 'JIBBER_REP',-
master=> 'REPO.US.ORACLE.COM');
```

At any point during the execution of these steps, you can check on the progress by using the view DBA_REPGROUP:

```
SQL> select gname, master, status from dba_repgroup;
GNAME                          M STATUS
------------------------------ - ---------
JIBBER_REP                     Y QUIESCED
```

In addition, take a look at DBA_JOBS, and you'll notice another job has been added to your list:

```
SQL> column job format 99
SQL> column what format a40
SQL> select job, what from dba_jobs;
JOB WHAT
--- ----------------------------------------
  ...
  3 dbms_repcat.do_deferred_repcat_admin('"JIBBER_REP"', FALSE);
```

This new job is required to push administrative work back and forth between the two masters. If you connect to REPO and run the same query, you'll see the same results.

Finally, you can perform the final step, which is to take the replication group from quiesced to normal. This means that you can now update the replicated table at either site, and the updates will be pushed across the remote site based on the interval you built into the push job.

```
execute dbms_repcat.resume_master_activity(gname => 'JIBBER_REP');
```

After this, you can check dba_repgroup and see that our status has changed again:

```
SQL> select gname, master, status from dba_repgroup;
GNAME                          M STATUS
------------------------------ - ---------
JIBBER_REP                     Y NORMAL
```

Congratulations! You have now set up a replicated environment. Admittedly, this is an extremely weak and powerless replication environment, but it displays the principles involved. To check to see if it is working, you can insert more rows into the table JIBBER.TESTIOUT and see if they get replicated:

```
connect jibber/jabber@prod90
declare
v_loopcounter binary_integer :=501;
begin
loop
insert into testitout
     values (v_loopcounter, 'YOU BET!');
v_loopcounter := v_loopcounter +1;
exit when v_loopcounter >1000;
end loop;
end;
/
commit;
```

After this, you can log back in as REPADMIN, and check the DEFTRAN view to see your transaction sitting there, waiting to be pushed:

```
SQL>connect repadmin/repadmin@prod90
SQL>select * from deftran;
DEFERRED_TRAN_ID               DELIVERY_ORDER D START_TIM
------------------------------ -------------- - ---------
7.18.561                               312189 R 20-AUG-01
```

At this point, you can wait for your push job to fire off, or you can write a little PL/SQL to manually push the transaction to the remote site.

```
Declare
p binary_integer;
begin
p := dbms_defer_sys.push('REPO.US.ORACLE.COM');
end;
/
```

Finally, you can confirm the replication by checking the row count of the remote TESTITOUT table on the REPO database:

```
SQL> connect jibber/jabber@repo
SQL> select count(*) from testitout;
  COUNT(*)
----------
      1000
```

Using Replication Manager for Master Group Setup

If you are using Replication Manager, navigate in OEM to the master definition site node (in this example, PROD90.US.ORACLE.COM). You need to expand the Multimaster Replication view and right-click the Master Groups folder and choose Create. But wait! You will need to right-click the database name again, choose Connect, and then specify the REPADMIN user and password. The user you have connected as will appear next to the database name, as shown in Figure 14-2.

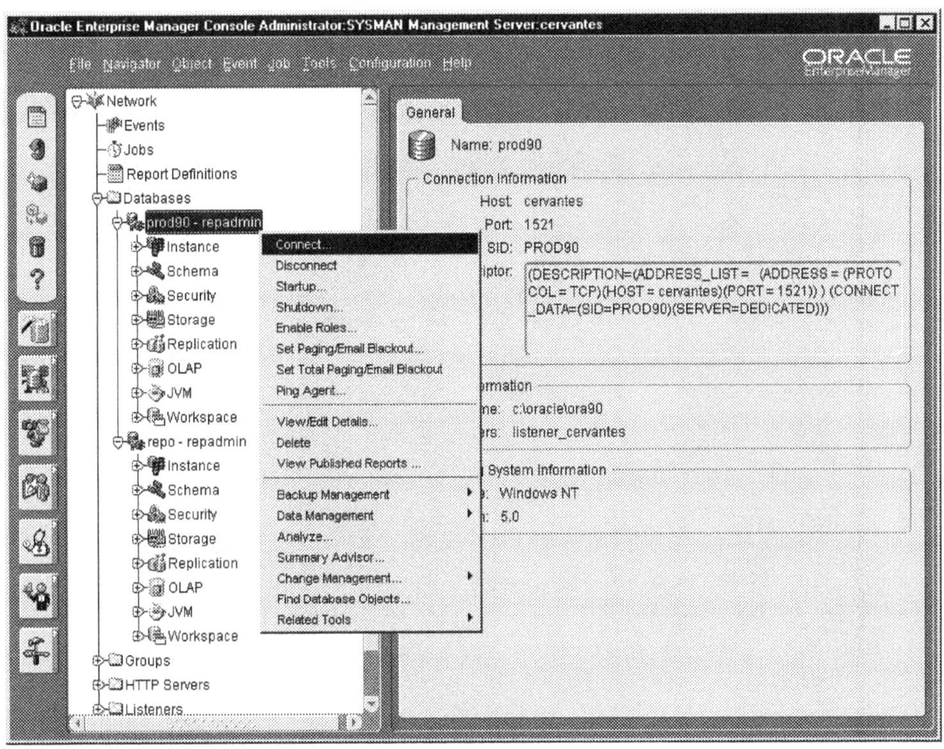

FIGURE 14-2. *Connect as REPADMIN*

For the name of the Master Group, specify JIBBER_REP, and leave the Connection Qualifier blank. Click the Objects tab and then click the Add button. From the window that appears, choose the JIBBER schema, click the Tables radio button, and then choose the TESTITOUT table, as shown in Figure 14-3.

Next, click the Master Sites tab, and click the Add button. You will be prompted to enter the type of database link you will be using. If you have not already created a database link to your other master site, you will need to follow the steps outlined in the API instructions for doing so. There is an option to manually enter the database link name, but we recommend creating the database links manually.

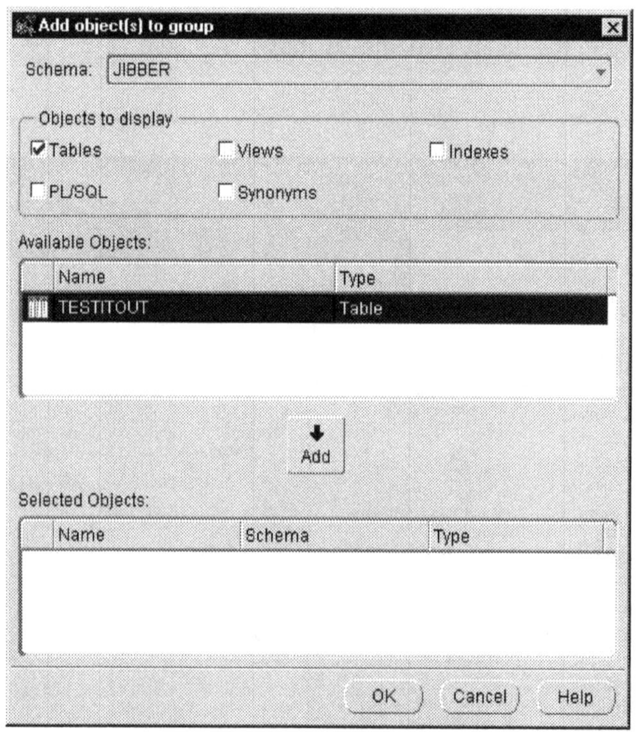

FIGURE 14-3. *Adding objects to the replication group*

Click the button that reads Show SQL, and you will see an output that echoes the API steps outlined previously for creating your group. After reviewing the output, you can click the Create button, which will execute the PL/SQL in the SQL window. After this completes, you will be returned to the Oracle Enterprise Manager screen, with Master Groups highlighted, and showing the new group JIBBER_REP in a quiesced state (see Figure 14-4).

If you move back to the navigation pane, the Masters Group now has a + (plus sign) to its left, which, when expanded, shows the group JIBBER_REP. When this is highlighted, you get your administrative options for the group.

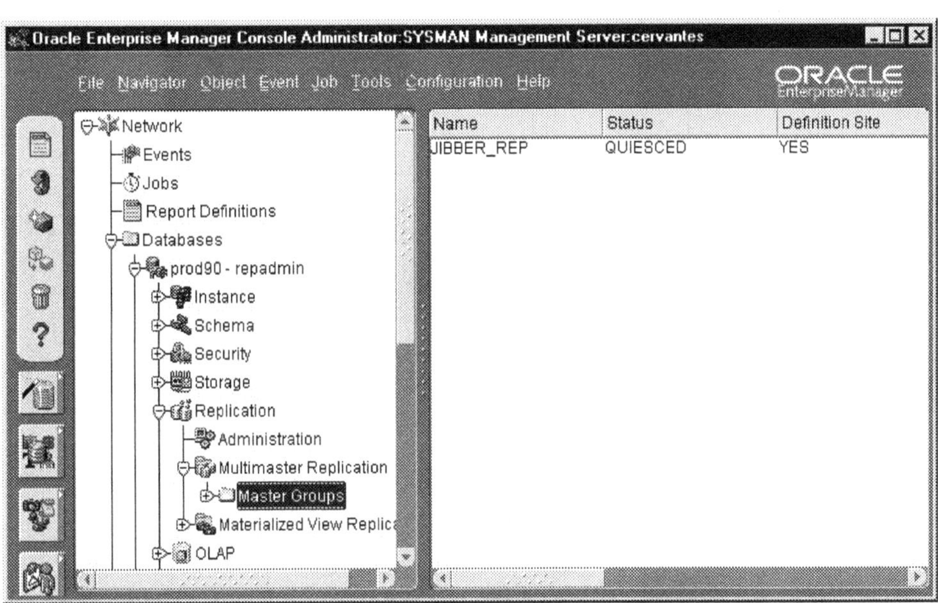

FIGURE 14-4. *Master group JIBBER_REP is currently quiesced.*

Figure 14-5 shows that the master group is currently stopped (quiesced), but notice that there is an administrative request still pending. If you click View Administrative Request, you see that you're in the middle of resuming activity. After these administrative jobs complete, the replication environment is set up.

Finally, from the Administration tree under Replication, you can look at errors, transactions, and other administrative information that might be useful (see Figure 14-6). Of most importance to this utility, and one of the best reasons to labor through the GUI interface, is the use of the Errors and Transactions screens. By clicking a transaction in either of these screens, you can actually get the values being passed by the transaction, broken down by each call. A *call* refers to the atomic unit replication uses to pass information within a transaction. Essentially, each row change is a separate call, so if you updated every row in the table TESTITOUT in a single transaction, you would have over 500 calls in one transaction. Prior to this, trying to find the actual data in the calls would be nearly impossible.

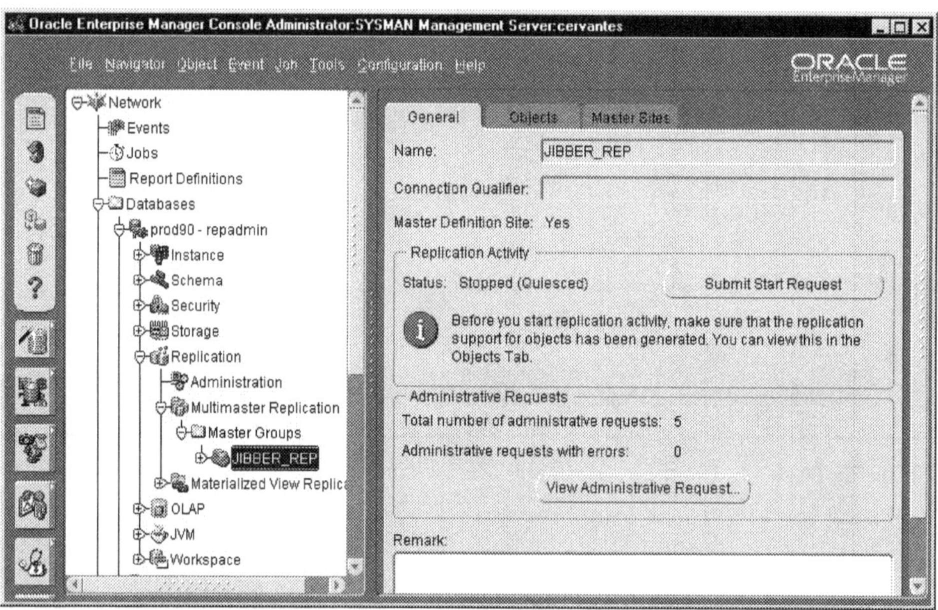

FIGURE 14-5. *The Replication Manager options for the master group*

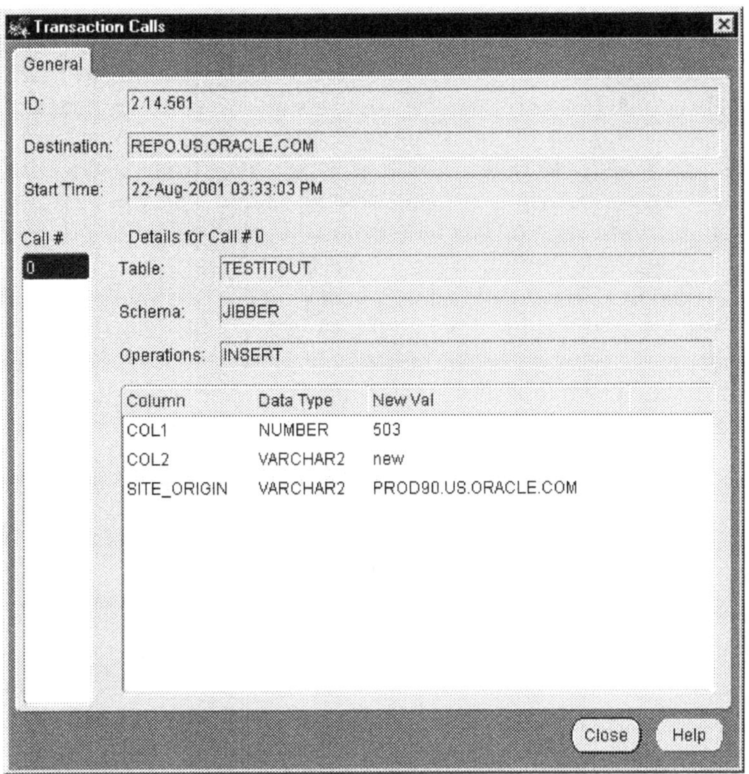

FIGURE 14-6. *Looking at the values in a transaction using Replication Manager*

Conflict Resolution Techniques

Congratulations on your successful configuration. However, you have not actually completed replication setup. It may look like it works, and it may act like it works, but the replication example we just walked you through is fundamentally flawed. We have not shown you how to set up any protection from the inevitability of having a conflict between your two sites.

We know, we know. After years here in Oracle Support assisting customers who have failed to do this step, let us just preempt the argument: *there's no way you'll ever have a conflict. You only allow users to update one site, and the other is simply for failover.* As true as this may be, conflicts always happen. Somewhere, somehow, if you do not specifically set up protection against the possibility of a conflict, then you are risking an expensive offline resynchronization process.

Types of Conflicts

The three types of conflicts that can possibly occur correspond to the three forms of DML: update conflicts, which arise from updates at different master sites of the same row; uniqueness conflicts, which usually arise from inserts that create new primary key values at each site; and delete conflicts, which come from simultaneous delete operations. There are many forms that conflict resolution takes, but it boils down to functions that perform certain tasks when conflicts are detected.

But how does Oracle detect conflicts? When a user issues DML against a replicated table, the remote procedural call that gets built contains two values that it passes to the remote site: the "before" image of the change, and the new, or "after" image. At the remote site, Oracle checks the "before" image against the local table, and when it finds it, replaces it with the "after" image of the row. However, if Oracle cannot match the "before" image against any row (due to a delete or an update operation), then it signals an error and fails to make the change. This error is ORA-1403: "No data found," and might possibly take the prize for most worthless message for any error. Regardless of the message, this error can mean only one thing when you find it in your DEFERROR view: a delete or update conflict. If the transaction is an insert, then there is no "before" image, and Oracle passes a null in the RPC. However, if Oracle then finds the new value in the table, you get a uniqueness constraint error (ORA-00001).

If there is no conflict resolution set up, then these errors halt all transference of deferred transactions to the other sites. Transactions can continue to be created at each site, but the deferred transaction queue cannot be cleared until the error is fixed, so transactions continually build up.

Many of the most useful forms of conflict resolution that should be implemented in a production environment require a strong understanding of PL/SQL, and are therefore outside the scope of this chapter.

Offline Instantiation

Our little test case is extremely small and somewhat unrealistic about the amount of data that most production databases handle, and how many tables must be simultaneously kept up to date in a real replication environment. Those type of situations (that is, any situation you might actually face in the real world) require more advanced forms of getting the data synced up before replication begins.

Indeed, one of the largest challenges of replication is the requirement that the production tables that are going to be replicated be read-only for the duration of the data move from the production table to the replicated table. In the preceding example, replication was allowed to create the table at the REPO database and then move the rows across. However, allowing replication to move rows over is the least efficient way to get data to the replicated site. Granted, it is the ultimate goal, but we assume that using replication to move data will be incremental in nature. Letting replication move millions of rows at once can take days.

More likely, you will use a process known as offline instantiation to make the initial copy of production data to the replicated table. Offline instantiation is the process of using nonreplication means to create the initial copy of the production database, and then enabling replication on top of this copy. Offline Instantiation can be tricky business: you cannot use any means that cannot guarantee a perfect copy of the original table. Therefore, simply exporting the table while it is in production is alone insufficient. New rows can be added while the export occurs, as there is no DML lock on the table during export.

In release 9i, perhaps the most provocative new form of offline instantiation is the use of transportable tablespaces. To transport a tablespace, it must be set to read-only mode, which satisfies your need for getting an exact copy. However, unlike other methods of moving the data, making an OS copy of the datafiles in which the tables are located is perhaps the fastest method of getting the data moved. The only exception would be the file transfer across the network—if the bandwidth is low, the file copy may not be any faster than any other method. However, if you listened to us earlier and established a fat pipe between your masters, then you should have no problem blasting the file across the network. Remember, of course, that your master sites must run the same OS for transportable tablespaces to work. (Refer to Chapter 5 for the ins and outs of transportable tablespaces.)

The only catch to using this for moving data between two sites is that the tablespace that gets transported must be brought back to read-write mode before you can run through the steps of creating the replication group and objects, and generating support. This means there is a window of time during which the data at the production site will be available for updates prior to replication setup. If a user were to log in and make changes, then all your efforts would be in vain. Make sure that you leave the tablespace in read-only mode up to the moment when you will run your replication scripts.

Other than that, the other change comes when you issue the command to create repobjects:

```
execute dbms_repcat.create_master_repobject ( -
sname => 'TRANSTEST',-
oname => 'TRANS',-
type  => 'TABLE',-
copy_rows => FALSE,-
gname => 'TRANS_REP');
```

The new parameter you pass is COPY_ROWS, which tells replication to forgo the process of manually pushing rows to the master site, and instead accept the rows that already exist on the remote site.

Offline Instantiation for Resolving Conflicts

Transportable tablespaces will not work for resolving conflicts between two masters, as one of the primary limitations of transportable tablespaces is that you cannot transport replicated objects. So it works for moving data prior to setting up replication, but if replication is already set up, you have to revert to exports or other means of resynchronizing data between two sites.

The best situation to be in is to have successfully tested and implemented a conflict resolution methodology that is airtight, and it is impossible for your replicated tables to be out of sync. However, in the off chance that it occurs, there are ways to fix the situation. All of these fixes require taking the table out of production updates, as you must manually fix the tables, meaning you cannot leave replication running. And if replication is not running, then the data is quiesced, and updates are disallowed.

If you run into a situation where you have tables out of sync, there are many ways to clear up the inconsistencies between the two tables. Oracle9i comes with the package DBMS_RECTIFIER_DIFF, which can be used to check the difference between two tables and then used to rectify the situation. You can also determine the difference by using your own means, and then turn replication off on one of the sites using the DBMS_REPUTL package. DBMS_REPUTL allows you to turn off the replication triggers for a site. Without triggers firing, you can make changes at one site without those changes being replicated to your other masters.

It's outside the scope of this humble little chapter to go into depth about synchronizing tables, but it's important that you be familiar with the concepts and practices before you put replicated objects into production use. Refer to the *Oracle9i Replication Management API Reference* for more information; the notes on the subject on the Oracle Support Web site, http://www.metalink.oracle.com, are also extremely useful when you are testing offline instantiation.

Administration of the Replication Environment

It may have already become clear to you throughout this chapter, but we'll say it again: it is occasionally necessary to suspend replication activity for a number of different reasons. Essentially, any administrative task that might affect the replication environment requires that you quiesce your master replication groups.

Suspending replication is simple using the DBMS_REPCAT package:

```
execute dbms_repcat.suspend_master_activity('JIBBER_REP');
```

However, this will return you to the prompt, indicating to you that the master group JIBBER_REP is successfully quiesced. However, this may not be the case. In order to determine that you have successfully quiesced the replication group, you need to be familiar with the views you can use to check the status.

Monitoring Replication

To check the status of your master sites, you can use the view DBA_REPGROUP:

```
select gname, master, status from dba_repgroup;
GNAME                          M STATUS
------------------------------ - ---------
JIBBER_REP                     Y NORMAL
```

The status column may also show you a status of QUIESCED or even QUIESCING. If you have issued a command to suspend replication activity, but are not moving to a quiesced state, there a few possible explanations. The most common reason is the existence of transactions in the deferred transaction queue that have not been committed. Check the view DEFTRAN to determine if this is the case.

```
Select * from deftran;
```

However, you may see rows in here that reflect transactions that have been pushed, but have not yet been purged. We suggest running a manual push, and then purge, of the deferred transaction queue before checking the DEFTRAN view for possible transactions that still need to be pushed:

```
Declare
p binary_integer;
begin
p := dbms_defer_sys.push('REPO.US.ORACLE.COM');
end;
/
declare
p binary_integer;
begin
p := dbms_defer_sys.purge( delay_seconds => 0);
end;
/
```

Do this at all master sites. If you still get values returned in DEFTRAN, it is time to check the DEFERROR view:

```
Select error_number, error_msg from deferror;
```

If even one row exists in DEFERROR, your replication environment might be stuck. The previous SQL will give the Oracle error number and its corresponding message. You will need to either fix the underlying problem that caused the error, or if necessary delete the error. Note that if you delete an error, you are deleting the underlying transaction. Only do this if you can afford to lose the transaction that failed. From the DEFERROR view, identify the DEFERRED_TRANSACTION_ID, and then submit it to the DBMS_DEFER_SYS package:

```
Select deferred_tran_id from deferror;
DEFERRED_TRAN_ID
----------------
9.9.552
execute dbms_defer_sys.delete_error('9.9.552');
```

Another view of vital importance is DBA_REPCATLOG. This view resembles the DEFTRAN view, except the queue in repcatlog refers to pending administrative requests. So, for instance, you might issue the SUSPEND_MASTER_ACTIVITY command, but it does not immediately go through. You can check the DBA_REPCATLOG view for errors:

```
Select errnum, message from dba_recatlog;
```

For a complete listing of replication catalog views, refer again to the *Oracle9i Replication Management API Reference.*

Conclusions and Advice for the Replication DBA

So, after all these warnings, you still want to pursue replication as your method of availability. We applaud your decision. As such, we want to leave you with the advice that only comes from support analysts.

Test, Test, Then Retest

Think we're a little paranoid about this? Although that might be the case, we want to reiterate the saying, "Just because you're paranoid doesn't mean they're not out to get you." When it comes to replication, there is no substitute for going over every single step of not only establishing the replication environment, but also putting it under the same transactional duress you would expect in your production environment. See if the performance will hold up. Force conflicts between two sites and see if your conflict resolution techniques capture and resolve it. Work out techniques for performing manual resynchronization.

The alternative to thorough testing is to be caught off guard by just how interruptive a replication outage can be to your production environment. Remember, unlike a standby database, you must treat every master site in a replication group as a production database. If it goes down, it will not immediately take down the other masters, but you will begin to build up transactions in the deferred transaction queue that could negatively affect performance to clear out.

Keep All Database Staff Informed

Replication, even when implemented correctly, introduces multiple points of failure due to its distributed nature. And more likely than not, the different master sites are geographically located in different places. As such, if you have database staff that have access to the database at each location, you must be very vocal and very clear about the replicated objects that exist at each site. Recovering from a user error on a replicated table, such as any DDL, can seriously impede production processing.

Keep an Eye on Things

Replication is not a database option that you can test, implement, and then walk away from. You need to build into your daily tasks a look at the different views associated with replication. If you use Enterprise Manager, you can check replication from the GUI interface. But you may want to implement any number of notification services that will alert you whenever a transaction is moved to the DEFERROR view. As soon as one error occurs, replication is impeded, and the transactional buildup behind the error can take days to clear out. If you have pager services configured for events on your database, a good event to add to your pager list is a simple row count select from the DEFERROR view. If the value of the select is not zero, you should be checking your replication environment for problems.

Summary

In this chapter, we discussed the different uses of Oracle advanced replication: load balancing, disaster recovery, and offline distributed transaction processing. We gave a brief overview of the replication architecture, concentrating on n-way master replication, as this is the only option that provides availability solutions. We briefly warned you about the performance hit caused by replication before going into a test case setup for a single table across two master sites. We gave the usage for both the API user and the GUI Replication Manager user. We then provided an overview of conflict resolution and offline instantiation before finishing up with some advice for any would-be replication administrators.

CHAPTER 15

Maximizing Availability

In the previous chapters of Part IV, we introduced various ways in which you can increase the availability and uptime of your database, including Oracle Failsafe, Real Application Clusters, and Standby Databases. In this chapter, we take this one step further by combining these methods into an overall comprehensive solution. By combining solutions, you can take advantage of the unique features and strengths of differing methods of high availability, allowing you to maximize the availability and performance of your database. In this chapter, we begin with a discussion of Transparent Application Failover, and then discuss a new product called Real Application Clusters Guard, which combines the virtual group concept of MSCS with Real Application Clusters. Finally, we discuss the use of a single-instance standby environment in conjunction with a Real Application Clusters setup. Intertwined throughout is an emphasis on the use of RMAN as a means to strengthen your backup strategy, as well as minimize the impact that backups have on your production environment. In this chapter, we introduce the following tips and techniques:

- Introducing Transparent Application Failover (TAF) and load balancing
- Understanding Real Application Clusters Guard
- Configuring a database in a RACG environment
- Defining termination and restart policies
- Defining a hang detection policy
- Understanding a primary/secondary configuration
- Using the oracgcmd command-line interface
- Backing up a RAC database using RMAN
- Taking datafile and control file backups
- Taking archive log backups
- Restoring in a clustered environment
- Setting up a single-instance standby
- Backing up from the standby
- Restoring from your standby backup

Transparent Application Failover

We begin this chapter with a discussion of Transparent Application Failover, or TAF, for short. TAF is the means by which client connections continue on, uninterrupted, even if a failure of some type occurs on the server side. The ability for a failure to go unnoticed, or to provide minimal disruption, is a key to success in a high-availability environment. TAF can be useful in many situations. The most common is in a clustered environment, using Real Applications Clusters or Oracle Failsafe, but it also can be implemented in the case of a standby or replication environment. TAF can be utilized to continue a select statement that is in progress when a disconnect happens, and in addition, when TAF is used in a RAC environment, it provides the additional benefit of being able to automatically load balance connections across instances.

Understanding Transparent Application Failover

Transparent Application Failover (TAF), Connect-Time Failover, and Connection Load-Balancing are all means of configuring your client, via parameters in your tnsnames.ora file for a single alias, to be able to connect to multiple hosts/instances if the need arises. TAF and Connect-Time Failover are terms describing how the client can reconnect automatically should your connection fail, either after you have already been connected, or during the actual connect process itself. Connection Load-Balancing, on the other hand, describes the process of having client connections randomly connect to any of a list of hosts. To best illustrate how these configurations work, let's first dissect a sample tnsnames.ora file:

```
RACDB1 =
    (DESCRIPTION =
      (LOAD_BALANCE=OFF)
      (FAILOVER=ON)
      (ADDRESS_LIST =
        (ADDRESS = (PROTOCOL = TCP)(HOST = RMNTOPS1)(PORT = 1521))
        (ADDRESS = (PROTOCOL = TCP)(HOST = RMNTOPS2)(PORT = 1521))
      )
      (CONNECT_DATA =
        (SERVICE_NAME = racdb)
        (FAILOVER_MODE=
          (BACKUP=RACDB2)
          (TYPE=SELECT)
          (METHOD=PRECONNECT)
        )
      )
    )
```

Here we have a TNS alias called RACDB1. The first thing to note is that there are multiple address entries in the ADDRESS_LIST section. In our example, LOAD_BALANCE is set to OFF, so when a connect attempt is made, the first address in the address list will always be tried first. If a connection is not possible to that host, then the second address in the list will be tried, and so on; if you have more than two nodes in a cluster, you can simply add additional address entries to the address list. If LOAD_BALANCE were set to ON, then it would not matter which is the first or second entry in the list—addresses are picked from the address list at random until one succeeds.

The fact that failover is set to ON indicates that should the database fail in the middle of a connection, then Oracle will fail over to an alternate address in the address list. In the CONNECT_DATA section, we have a FAILOVER_MODE entry, with type set to SELECT. This means that should a failure occur in the middle

of a query, the failover will be transparent to the user, and, after a slight pause for the failover, the query should pick back up where it left off. This is accomplished by keeping track of the row number that the original query was on when it died. After the failover, the same query will be reissued behind the scenes, but the rows that have already been returned to the application will be discarded. The application will pause while this is going on in the background, and then continue uninterrupted as soon as the first new row is encountered. If type is set to SESSION, then a query that is in progress will not pick back up, but the session will still automatically reconnect to the next address in the list.

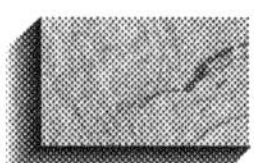

NOTE
It is still the case that any uncommitted inserts, updates, or deletes will have to be rolled back after a connection failure, and then manually reissued by the user, no matter what TYPE is set to.

Setting the method to PRECONNECT implies that we actually spawn two sessions—the first connection is to the appropriate address in the address list, and a second connection is spawned within the instance defined by the backup entry. This entry (RACDB2 in our example) is another TNS alias that should exist in the same tnsnames.ora file as the original RACDB1. The prespawning of connections in this manner decreases greatly the time to failover. The drawback is that even though the connection is sitting idle on the backup server, it still counts as a connection, and therefore still consumes memory on the backup server by simply creating the thread (as discussed in Chapter 5), and counts against the processes allowed in the instance. Setting the method to BASIC directs the client to connect only to one instance at a time, and should a failover occur, a new connection will have to be made to the backup or to the next address in the address list.

The view V$SESSION contains columns that allow you to see what settings are in effect for your connected clients. Following is a sample query that can be run after the user SCOTT has connected with our TNSNAMES entry show previously:

```
SQL> select schemaname, failover_type, failover_method, failed_over
  2  from v$session where schemaname = 'SCOTT';

SCHEMANAME FAILOVER_TYPE FAILOVER_METHOD FAILED_OVER
---------- ------------- --------------- ------------
SCOTT      SELECT        PRECONNECT      NO
```

Real Application Clusters Guard

In the first section of this chapter, we began with a brief discussion of Transparent Application Failover. Our focus now shifts to a new product for Oracle9i called Real Application Clusters Guard (RACG). RACG uses Microsoft Cluster Server technology and the virtual server concepts used in Failsafe to enhance connect-time failover and availability of your RAC instances. The following section will illustrate why you may want to use this feature, and how to configure it.

How Real Application Clusters Guard Works

As noted, RACG works by use of a virtual server, as defined in MSCS. When the Real Application Clusters Guard wizard is used to configure a RAC database, a separate virtual group is created for each instance. So, in a two-node cluster, you will have two separate virtual groups created, one on each node. (For a full discussion and explanation of virtual groups, refer to Chapter 11.)

In a traditional RAC environment, clients generally connect to a given instance by specifying the IP address or host name of one of the owning nodes in a cluster. However, once a database has been configured with the RAC Guard, the instances will be reconfigured to listen on the virtual IP address of each node's associated virtual group. Your clients should be reconfigured to connect to this virtual group's IP address, instead of the IP address of the individual node.

Rapid Connect-Time Failover

You are now surely asking yourself, "What is the benefit of doing this?" The main benefits are the rapid reduction in time that it takes for a client to fail over, or for an initial connection using the first address in the address list to time out, and then try the next address in the list. Consider the example of our tnsnames.ora entry in the previous section on TAF. Take a look again at just the ADDRESS_LIST portion:

```
(ADDRESS_LIST =
        (ADDRESS = (PROTOCOL = TCP)(HOST = RMNTOPS1)(PORT = 1521))
        (ADDRESS = (PROTOCOL = TCP)(HOST = RMNTOPS2)(PORT = 1521))
```

What happens if the node RMNTOPS1 is down? The client still tries to connect to it first, but since the entire node is down, it could take a considerable amount of time for the host lookup to timeout and return an error. Once the timeout is received, the client is then freed up to go to the next address in the list. When using Real Application Clusters Guard, the node is added to a virtual group, whose virtual IP address comes online on the node where the instance is running. If that node fails, the instance itself does *not* fail over. It does not need to, because the other node already has a running instance. However, the IP address and network name do fail over with the group. Since the virtual IP address is still online, when the client connects, it gets an immediate response back from that host, indicating no listener is available there. The next address on the list is then attempted almost immediately, and there is no delay when connecting.

Resource Monitoring

Aside from the more rapid connect-time failover, an additional benefit provided by Real Application Clusters Guard is the ability afforded by MSCS to monitor resources. Recall from Chapter 11 that Failsafe provides a resource DLL that is registered with Microsoft Cluster Server to monitor specific resource types. RACG uses the same resource DLL, but with slightly different resource definitions. Since you are configuring the instances as resources in a virtual group, you will have the same ability as with Failsafe to define polling intervals and restart properties should a resource fail.

Hang Detection

Another benefit of running RACG is the ability to set up a hang detection policy, whereby a hung instance can be restarted automatically if prescribed. The hang detection policy is initiated if the "Is Alive" polling does not get a response. It takes into account the possibility of a logon storm or a parse storm, in which many users can be logging on all at once or many parse calls are made within a short amount of time. It will also check that instance recovery for another instance is not underway, or that the locks are not being remastered, or that you are not waiting on an archive problem. If these possibilities are ruled out as the cause of the hang, then the termination policy will kick in, whereby an instance or multiple instances are killed and then restarted. We will discuss setting up a hang detection policy and a termination policy in the next section.

Installing MSCS

In order to take advantage of this feature on Windows 2000, you must first install Microsoft Cluster Server. The steps for doing so are the same as outlined in Chapter 11. The key point to account for when installing MSCS in a RAC environment is that you must have a shared drive, which is formatted NTFS, available for the quorum disk for use by MSCS. This is in addition to any drives you have used for your raw partitions, and the MSCS quorum disk must be on a *separate* physical disk from any raw partitions that are being used by your RAC instances. You will, of course, need to provide a virtual group network name and IP address for the cluster group that is formed when installing MSCS.

Installing Real Application Clusters Guard

The steps for installing Real Application Clusters Guard are also very similar to installing Failsafe. However, be aware that if you are already running Oracle Failsafe, you must install Real Application Clusters Guard into the same ORACLE_HOME. As such, the versions must match. Therefore, if you are currently running Oracle Failsafe 3.1.x, and want to continue to run Failsafe, you must first upgrade it to version 3.2 (or whatever the current RACG version is that you are installing). Once the Failsafe version is upgraded, you can proceed to install the matching version of Real Application Clusters Guard software.

Prior to installing, we recommend that you stop the following services on each node, and set them to manual startup:

- OracleGSDServices
- OracleCMService9i
- OracleService<sid1> or OracleService<sid2>

The installation for RACG is identical to the installation for Failsafe, except that you choose the option for Oracle Real Application Clusters Guard on the Available Products screen. After installing on the first node, you again must reboot. Wait for the first node to boot back up completely, and continue with the installation on the second node, followed by a reboot of that node. Repeat this process on any additional nodes. Since RACG uses the Microsoft Cluster Server architecture, you will again be limited as to the total number of nodes that RACG can support—two nodes for Windows 2000 Advanced Server, and four nodes for Windows 2000 Datacenter Server.

Oracle Services for MSCS Security Setup

Just as with Oracle Failsafe, the setup for Real Application Clusters Guard creates a service called OracleMSCSServices—this is the same service used for Oracle Failsafe. The security setup is identical to what was discussed in Chapter 11, so if Failsafe is not already installed, you will need to go through the security setup, providing a domain username and password for an account that also has Local Administrator privileges on each node. Refer to Chapter 11 for more details.

Verifying the Cluster

Real Application Clusters Guard provides a management tool very similar to Oracle Failsafe, called the Real Application Clusters Guard Manager. When this tool is started for the first time, you will see a Welcome screen similar to what was shown in Failsafe Manager, prompting you to run the verify cluster operation. Again, this is required for dual purposes—to check the setup of the cluster itself and also to register the resource DLL and the resource type Oracle Real Application Clusters Instance. After running the verify cluster operation, you should see this resource type in the Microsoft Cluster Manager, under Cluster Configuration in the Resource Types folder, as shown in Figure 15-1.

Once the verify cluster operation has completed, you can view the services in the Services applet and confirm that the proper dependencies are in place. Do this by right-clicking OracleCMService9i and choosing Properties | Dependencies. The OracleCMService9i will have been made to depend on the Cluster Service, meaning that if the Cluster Service does not start, the OracleCMService9i will not start. Since the service for the instance (OracleServiceRACDBx) depends on the OracleCMService9i, a failure of the Cluster Service to start will lead to a failure of your instance to start. After verifying that the dependencies are in place, you can

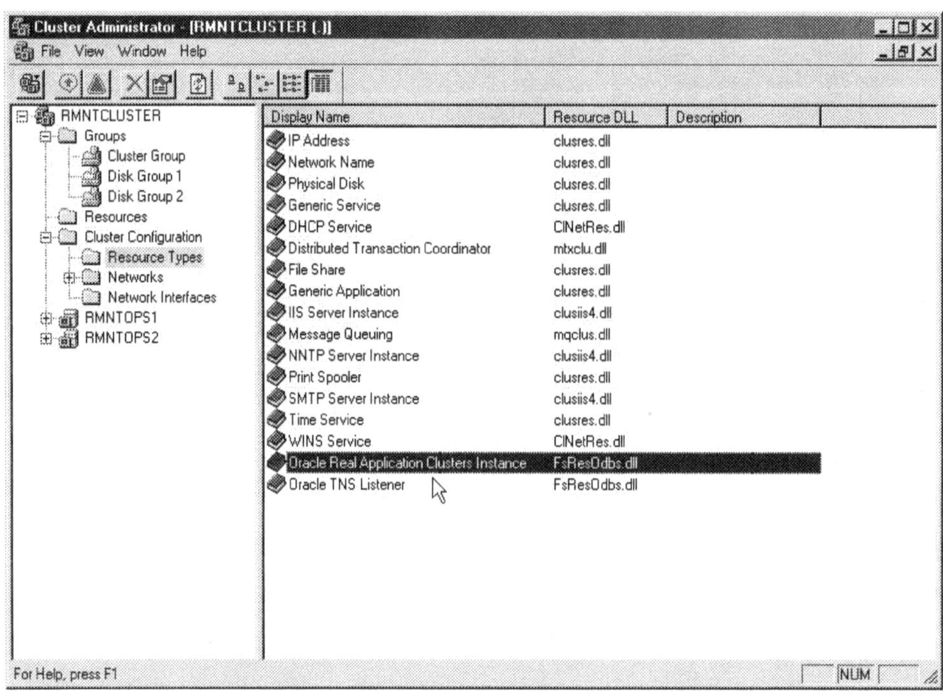

FIGURE 15-1. *Resource type register for Real Application Clusters*

restart OracleCMService9i, OracleGSDService, and OracleServiceRACDBx. Verify that both instances start up successfully and everything is in working order.

Configuring the Database

Now that you are in the Real Application Clusters Guard Manager, you should see a split screen with your cluster name in the upper-left corner (see Figure 15-2). Below it you will see the nodes and a folder for configured databases and one for unconfigured databases. Prior to configuring the databases in a cluster guard configuration, we recommend that you shut each instance down. Next, expand the Unconfigured Databases folder and select your database. Right-click the database and choose Configure Database from the pop-up menu to bring up the Configure Database Wizard.

Defining the Groups

To successfully configure the database, you will need to be prepared for the Real Application Clusters Guard Manager to create two more virtual groups—one for each node in the cluster. If there are more than two nodes, this will require more

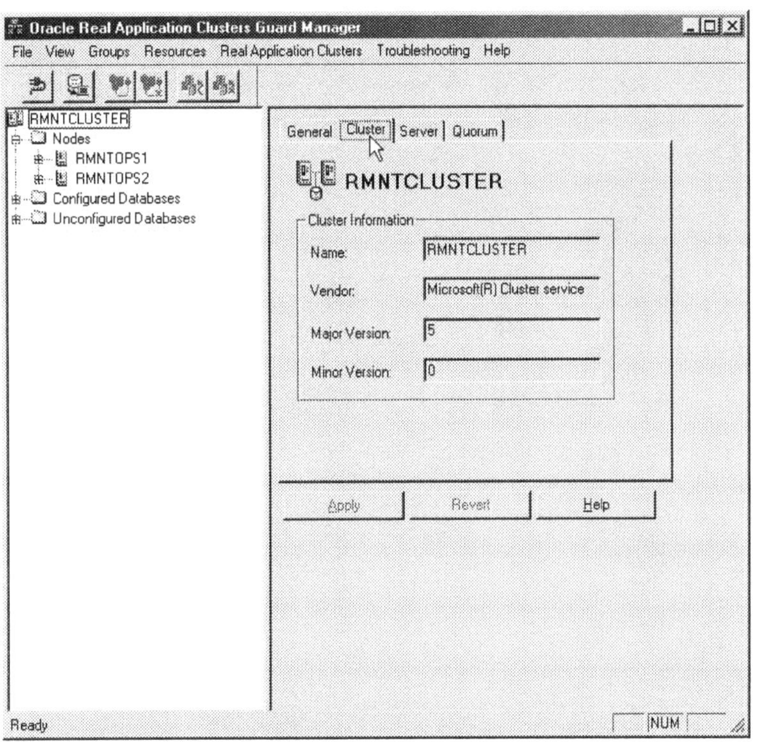

FIGURE 15-2. *Real Application Clusters Guard Manager*

groups. Preparing for this feat involves defining a new network name and IP address combination in DNS or in the host's file prior to configuring the database. You will be prompted for this information as the database is configured, and the groups will be created for you. For a more complete discussion on setup prior to group creation, refer to Chapter 11.

When you are prepared to create these additional groups, proceed with configuring the database via the Configure Database Wizard. The first screen will ask you for the database name, service name (connect string), and port number, as shown in Figure 15-3. Fill in the appropriate information and click Next.

On the following page, you will be prompted for the type of authentication that you prefer to use. If you choose OS authentication, you will be advised that a group will be created on each node for the respective instance. Otherwise, enter the SYS password and continue to the next screen. Next, you will be prompted for the base group name. When the Configure Database Wizard completes the database configuration, you will actually end up with one group on each node, called <BASEGROUP>_<NODENAME>. In our example, we chose CGUARD for the group name, as you can see in Figure 15-4, so when the process completes,

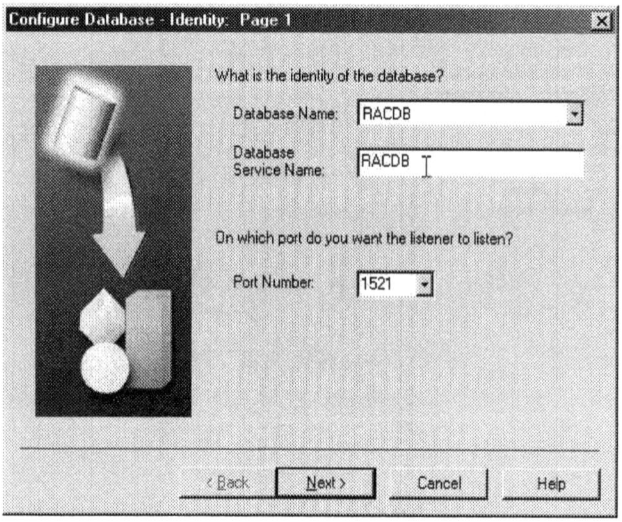

Configure Database - Identity: Page 1

What is the identity of the database?

Database Name: RACDB

Database Service Name: RACDB

On which port do you want the listener to listen?

Port Number: 1521

< Back | Next > | Cancel | Help

FIGURE 15-3. *Configure Database Wizard—Identity screen*

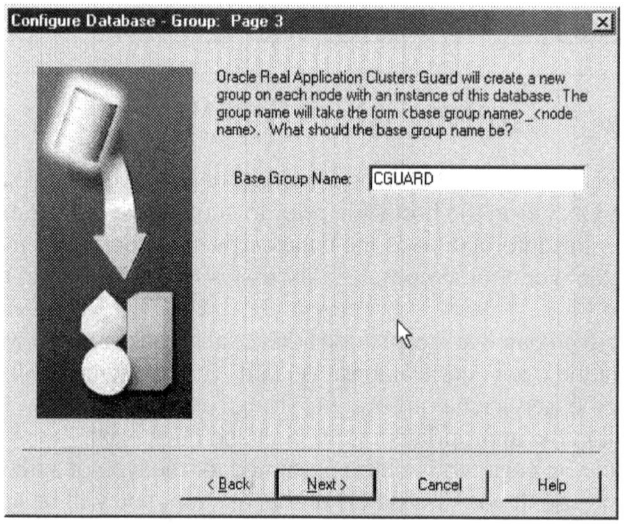

FIGURE 15-4. *Defining the base group name*

we will have a group called CGUARD_RMNTOPS1 on node 1 and a group called CGUARD_RMNTOPS2 on node 2.

On the next screen, you will be advised of what we have already told you—at least one virtual address is required for each node. In our example, since we have two instances, we will need to have at least two virtual addresses ready to be added to groups. Click Next to continue with this process. On the fifth screen of the wizard, you will be asked to define the first virtual address for the first instance. Click New on this screen and the Create Virtual Address dialog box will display. Here you will enter the network name setup for the first virtual group. If it is configured correctly on your network, the IP address field should be filled in automatically. See Chapter 11 for more details on this.

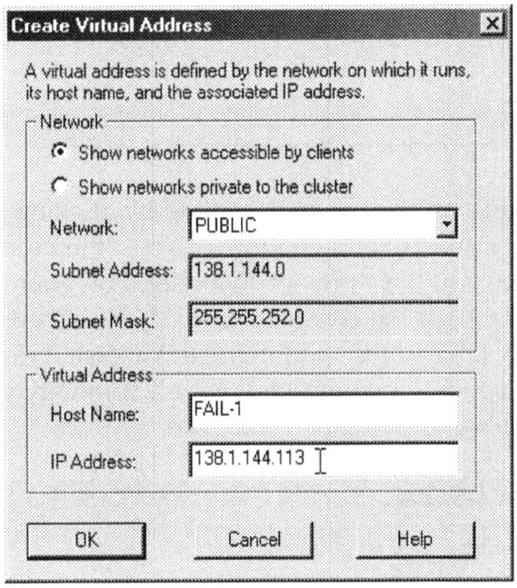

Create Virtual Address

A virtual address is defined by the network on which it runs, its host name, and the associated IP address.

Network
- (•) Show networks accessible by clients
- ( ) Show networks private to the cluster

Network: PUBLIC
Subnet Address: 138.1.144.0
Subnet Mask: 255.255.252.0

Virtual Address
Host Name: FAIL-1
IP Address: 138.1.144.113

OK | Cancel | Help

Once you have created the virtual address, click OK. This will put you back into the Virtual Address dialog box for the first instance. Do not add your second virtual address on this screen, because this is still defining the group for the first instance only. Instead, verify that the path to the parameter file is correct. Your SPFILE cannot be listed here, but it is okay to have an init.ora file defined whose only entry is

```
SPFILE='\\.\RACBD_SPFILE1'
```

The default for the first instance will be something similar to 'D:\oracle\ora90\database\initRACDB1.ora'. Once you have verified that this is the correct init file for the first instance, click Next. Now, you will see a similar Virtual Addresses screen, but this time for the second instance.

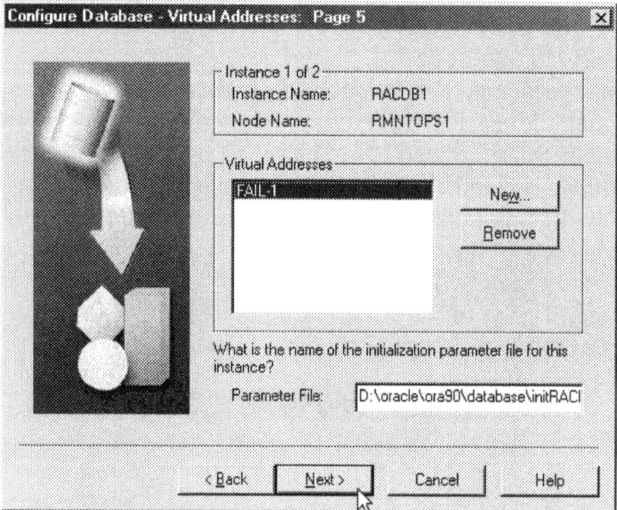

Repeat the same steps as previously described by clicking New to add a virtual address for the second instance, and go through the same process with the next virtual name and IP that you have previously defined on your network. Again, confirm that the init.ora file is the correct one for this instance (that is, 'D:\oracle\ora90\databae\initRACDB2.ORA'), and then click Finish. Prior to the configuration process being started, you will be presented with a Summary screen, delineating your choices on the various screens of the wizard.

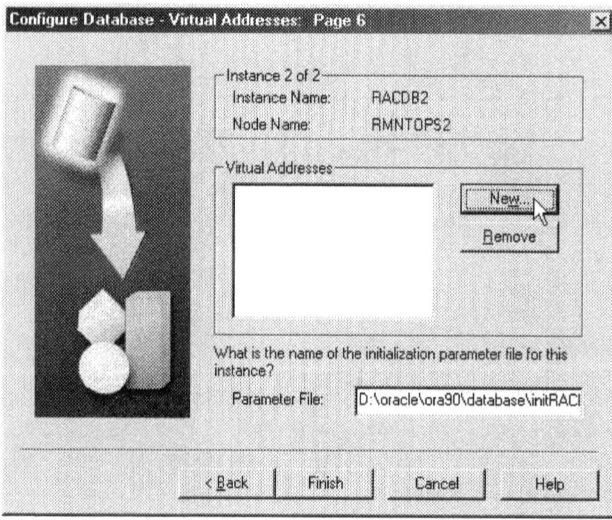

The actual process to configure the database will run for several minutes. The progress will be displayed in the Clusterwide Operation status box. Should any errors be encountered, you will see a pop-up box in the Clusterwide Operation window listing those errors. If this does not provide enough information to resolve the problem, check the following sources for information on troubleshooting and resolving these errors:

- Application log on each node
- System log on each node
- Alert log for each instance
- LMON trace file for each instance
- Any other pertinent trace files in the BACKGROUND_DUMP_DEST directory

If an error is encountered, the process should be rolled back, putting everything back in its previous state. This will give you the opportunity to resolve any issues and then rerun the Configure Database Wizard.

What Configuring the Database Does

When the Configure Database Wizard completes, and the dust settles, you can take a look around and determine what exactly was done. You will observe in Cluster Manager that two new groups besides the cluster group have been created, combining the base group name you provided and the node name for each node. Each group will have its own unique IP address and network name, as well as a RACDB resource and a new TNSListener resource, which will listen on the virtual IP address in the group. As such, each node will have a new listener.ora file, which will have added a new listener name called FSL<virtualhostname>. This process will also create a new Listener Service called OracleTNSListenerFSL<virtualhostname>. Since this is a new service, if you follow our advice later in this chapter and change the logon IDs for the instance and listener (in order to allow remote archiving to a mapped drive), then you will have to remember to change the logon ID for this new service.

In addition to the creation of a new listener for each virtual group, the tnsnames.ora on each node will be reconfigured so that the aliases are connecting to the virtual group's IP address rather than the IP address of the node. You will have to make the same changes to tnsnames.ora on any client machines that will be connecting to the instances.

Initially, each group will reside on its prospective node, and that node will be defined as the preferred owner. However, each group will have the ability to fail over to the other node in the cluster. If this happens, though, *only* the IP address and network name will come online. The instance and the listener will fail to come online on any other node besides the preferred owner node. Again, this is to facilitate the connect-time failover discussed earlier in the chapter. Once the preferred owner rejoins the cluster, the group can be configured to fail back to the preferred node immediately or during a defined time period, or you can prevent failback altogether and move it manually at your leisure. Refer to Chapter 11 for more insights on the failback policy.

Defining a Termination Policy

Once the database has been configured, you will see a screen similar to Figure 15-5, in the Real Application Clusters Guard Manager. Highlight the database at the top-most level under Configured Databases. In our example, this is RACDB, not one of the

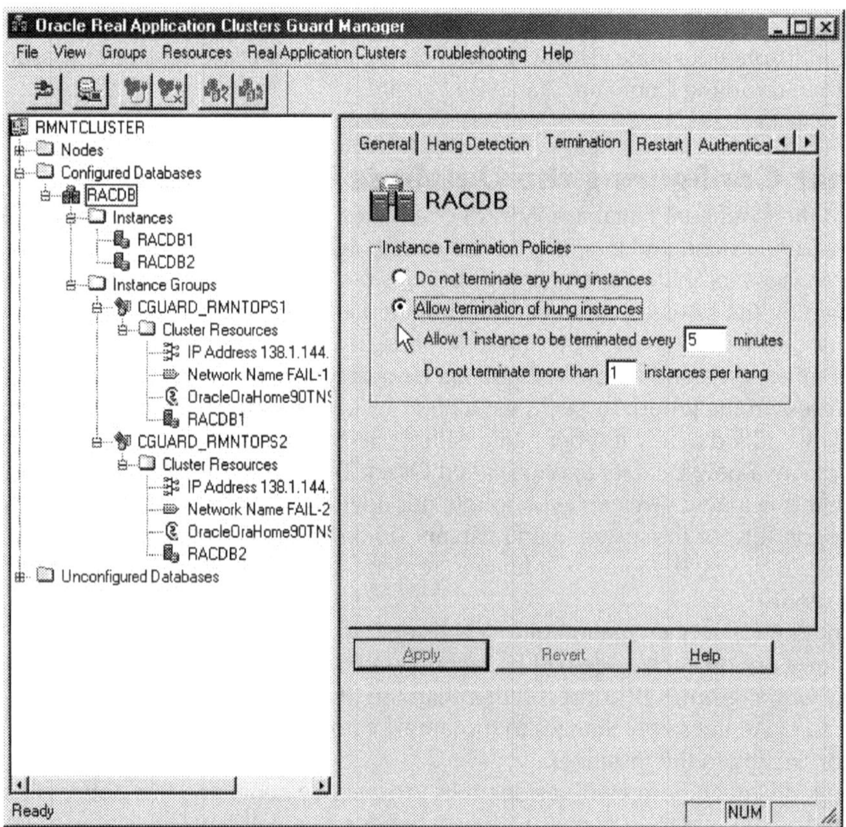

FIGURE 15-5. *Defining database policies*

instances under it. On the right-hand side, you will see tabs allowing you to define a hang detection policy, a termination policy, and a restart policy, among other things.

A termination policy essentially defines whether you are monitoring for a hang or not. If you do not allow instances to be terminated for a hang, then the hang detection policy is essentially a moot point. If you allow instances to be terminated, realize that only one instance is terminated at a time, even if multiple instances appear to be hung. Sometimes terminating a hung instance can result in the other instance(s) being freed up. If not, then additional instances will be terminated based on the maximum number of instances you allow to be terminated.

Instance Restart Policy

When an instance is terminated, this does not mean it goes away forever, nor does it mean a failover of the group is initiated. You define what happens to an instance after termination by choosing the Restart tab and setting up the policies you want to have enforced. By default, if an instance is terminated by RACG, the instance will not be restarted unless it was the last instance online. You may want to change this by unselecting this box; alternatively, you may want to define a delay time, advising RACG to wait *x* number of minutes before it tries to restart, giving the surviving instances time to remaster locks and finish any rollback begun when the instance was initially terminated. If you specify a restart threshold (such as "Restart 3 times within 30 minutes"), then once the threshold is exceeded, the group will fail over. Again, keep in mind that when the group fails over, only the IP address and network name come online on the alternate node. However, a restart on the same node will attempt to bring all resources in the group back online on the current node.

Hang Detection Policy

The hang detection policy helps you define what is a true hang, and how to avoid incorrect termination of an instance that is not truly hung. See Figure 15-6 for the options under the Hang Detection tab. Here you define what constitutes a logon storm and a parse storm by inputting values based on your understanding of the day-to-day operations of your business.

Logon Storms and Parse Storms

If a group of users all log on at the same time, the instance may appear to be hung, when it is really just undergoing an unusual amount of logon activity. You define what determines a logon storm, and if Real Application Clusters Guard detects a hang, it will check to see if that threshold is exceeded. If so, the instance will not be

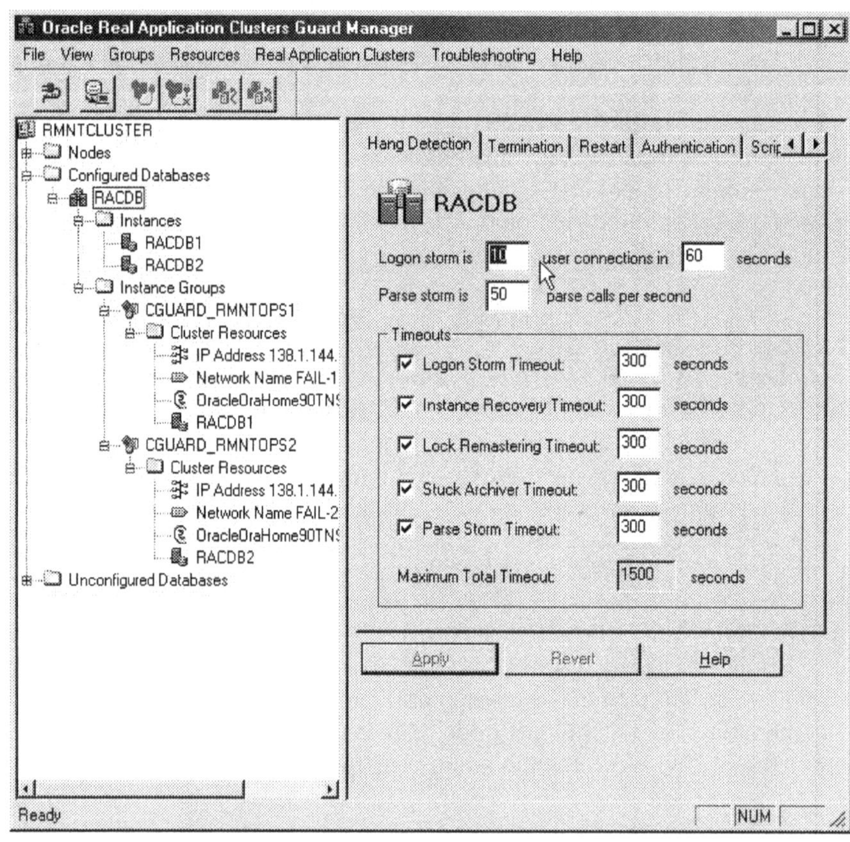

FIGURE 15-6. *Hang Detection tab*

terminated, but the polling will continue. By the same token, if an instance appears to be hung, Real Application Clusters Guard will check for a parse storm as you have defined it. If a parse storm is detected, the instance will not be terminated, and the RACG will wait the storm out.

Hang Detection Timeouts

Timeouts are where you determine whether Real Application Clusters Guard even bothers to check for a particular event that could cause the hang. By default, all options are checked. What this means is that in the event an instance appears to be hung, Real Application Clusters Guard will first check for a logon storm by querying the database for the number of logons over the specified interval. If the query responds and indicates a logon storm has occurred, then no termination occurs. If the query does not respond within the specified timeout period, then Real Application Clusters Guard moves on to the next event—a parse storm. Again, if the query for this event does not respond within the specified timeout period, Real Application Clusters Guard moves on to the next event, until all options have been exhausted. If none of these queries pinpoints the source of the problem, or if none return within the specified timeout, then a termination of the instance occurs. The drawback of having all of the options enabled is that it could take longer to detect a true hang. As you can see, with the default settings, it may take up to 25 minutes (1,500 seconds) before a hang is signaled. On the other hand, not checking all of the possibilities could result in a bogus termination of the instance.

Additional Options

Aside from defining the policies for hang detection, termination, and restarts, there are other options you may need to change on the Authentication tab and the Script tab (see Figure 15-6). The Authentication tab is important if you chose to use the SYS account instead of using operating system authentication when the group was initially created. If you change the sysdba password for the instance, you must also change it in the Authentication tab for the instance. Otherwise, the Real Application Clusters Guard will continue to try logging in with the original password, and that login will fail with an ORA-1031 error. This will cause the restart policy to kick in, and eventually the group will fail over to the other node.

Aside from the Authentication tab, the Script tab will allow you to provide the path to a user-created script that you want run in the event an instance has to be restarted. The script must complete within the specified timeout period, or else the script will be terminated. The maximum timeout period for the script is 10 minutes (600 seconds).

Policies for Individual Instances

Refer to Figure 15-6 again, and note the Instances folder, directly underneath the RACDB database itself. By highlighting one of the individual instances, a Policies tab will appear, through which you have the ability to determine the individual values for the Pending Timeout, Is Alive, and Looks Alive interval settings. By default, these values come from the properties of the actual resource type itself. In this case, the resource type is Oracle Real Application Clusters Instance, as seen on the General tab. To view these default values for Is Alive and Looks Alive intervals, you will need to go back to Cluster Administrator. Under Cluster Configuration on the left-hand side, select Resource Types. In the right-hand pane, select Oracle Real Application Clusters Instance, and right-click and choose Properties. This will give you a look at what the default polling intervals are for this particular resource type, and afford you the opportunity to change those defaults from here.

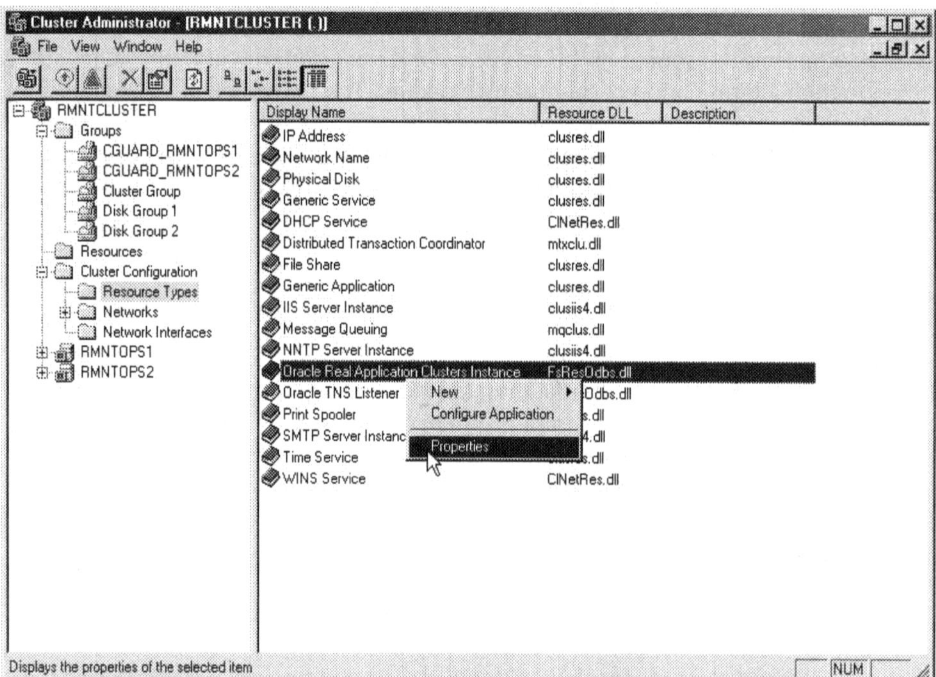

Primary vs. Secondary Instances

Neglected so far has been a discussion of the instance role. Check this by again selecting the database itself, RACDB in our example, and choosing the General tab. Here you will see each instance's name, node, state, and role. By default, each instance has a role status of primary, meaning that each instance is active and available for user connections. This default configuration is referred to as an *n-node configuration*, because multiple nodes are online and accessible. In a 2-node cluster, you can define the cluster such that only one node is active at a time. The active node assumes the role of the primary node, and the other node assumes the role of a secondary node.

Setting the init.ora parameter ACTIVE_INSTANCE_COUNT to a value of 1 on each cluster node will define the cluster with a Primary/Secondary configuration. Setting ACTIVE_INSTANCE_COUNT means that the first instance to come online becomes the primary instance, and the second instance to start up will take on the role of secondary instance. Should the primary instance fail, or be shut down, the secondary instance will automatically assume the primary role.

Connecting to a Secondary Instance

A normal TNS alias will not allow a user to connect to the secondary instance. However, you may need to connect to the secondary instance to perform maintenance or run reports, and so on. To do this, you must define the INSTANCE_ROLE parameter in the TNS alias description. Here is our earlier example, with the necessary modifications:

```
RACDB_SEC =
    (DESCRIPTION =
      (LOAD_BALANCE=OFF)
      (ADDRESS_LIST =
        (ADDRESS = (PROTOCOL = TCP)(HOST = RMNTOPS2)(PORT = 1521))
        (ADDRESS = (PROTOCOL = TCP)(HOST = RMNTOPS1)(PORT = 1521))
      )
      (CONNECT_DATA =
        (SERVICE_NAME = racdb)
        (INSTANCE_ROLE=SECONDARY)
       )
    )
```

If the secondary instance is unavailable, your connection will not go to the primary instance, because you have set the INSTANCE_ROLE. Instead, you will see the following error:

```
ORA-12522: TNS:listener could not find available instance with given
INSTANCE_ROLE
```

Hang Detection and Termination in a Primary/Secondary Environment

Very little changes in this regard from that of the default n-node, except that if a hang is detected, the terminated instance will always be the primary instance. Once the primary instance is terminated, or if it in fact fails for any reason or is simply shut down, the secondary instance will automatically assume the primary role. If and when the original primary instance is restarted, it will now become the secondary instance.

Changing Instance Roles

Real Application Clusters Guard provides a simple method of changing the roles of an instance, by providing a pop-up menu that allows you to take the primary offline, move it, or switch roles of the instances (refer to Figure 15-7).

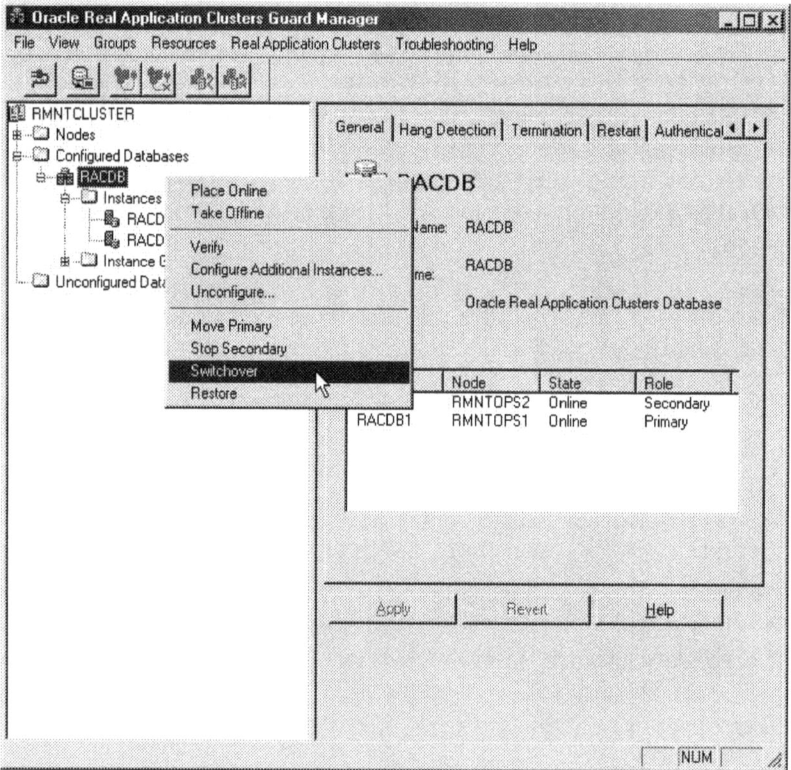

FIGURE 15-7. *Changing instance roles*

The following options are available from the pop-up menu:

- **Take Offline** By default, this will take all instances offline, but you will be prompted first for which instances to bring down.
- **Move Primary** This shuts down the primary instance and leaves it down, with the result being that the role of primary moves to the other instance.
- **Switchover** This option causes the primary instance to be shut down and then restarted, with the end result being a role reversal.
- **Stop Secondary** This stops the secondary instance.
- **Restore** This restarts the secondary instance, if needed.
- **Unconfigure** This option removes the RAC database from the RACG configuration by deleting the groups and reconfiguring SQLNet files for connection via the actual node names instead of virtual addresses.

Manual Shutdowns and oracgcmd

We close this section out with one final note on maintenance of instances in a Real Application Clusters Guard. Recall from our discussion of Oracle Failsafe in Chapter 11 that if you manually shut down a database, it is detected as a failure of a resource and the database is automatically restarted. The same applies with Real Application Clusters Guard. If you manually shut down an instance that has been configured into a group, RACG will detect this as a failure and restart the instance. To avoid this, you should take the instances offline through the Real Application Clusters Guard Manager interface. If you need to script this, or if you simply detest GUI tools, the **oracgcmd** utility is provided so that this can be done from the command line. As you can see from the following example, the syntax is similar o the **fscmd** utility:

```
D:\oracle\RACG\fs\fsmgr\bin>ORACGCMD offlineorac racdb /CLUSTER=RMNTCLUSTER
/USER=administrator /PWD=Back2Back /DOMAIN=rmdt2000 /OFFLINE=immediate
```

In addition, the oracgcmd utility can be used to disable and reenable the Is Alive polling using the DISABLEISALIVE and ENABLEISALIVE switches. Other actions include dumping the cluster, moving a group, verifying the cluster, and so on. For a full list of options for running the oracgcmd utility, refer to Chapter 5 of the *Oracle Real Application Clusters Guard Concepts and Administration Guide.*

Backing Up a RAC Database Using RMAN

We now shift our focus from the RACG setup to backups and a standby configuration. Even with the peace of mind offered by the Real Application Cluster configuration, backups are still necessary and imminent. For recovery from corruption, massive hardware failure, and user errors, a solid backup strategy must still be in place. As you may have suspected, we encourage the use of Oracle9i Recovery Manager in any backup strategy. However, RMAN takes on added importance when datafiles and control files exist on raw devices. Most OS utilities, such as the copy utility, cannot access raw devices, and therefore cannot back up your files. As mentioned in Chapter 12, Oracle provides a copy utility called ocopy, which will in fact serve to copy files to and from a raw partition. RMAN, however, has no limitations in regard to accessing files on a raw partition. This is because it gains access to the data through the memory buffer of the Oracle RDBMS. Therefore, RMAN does not care how the data is physically stored—RMAN backs up database blocks only, not files.

So now is a good time to review Chapter 6 and refamiliarize yourself with the ins and outs of RMAN. In addition, we will in the following sections discuss

the particular challenges of successfully backing up a multinode database. To understand these challenges, you must remember the unique nature of the clustered database: you share datafiles and control files, but each node maintains its own redo log files.

Datafile and Control File Backups

In a RAC database, you have two or more instances reading from and writing to a single set of datafiles and control files. RMAN, of course, can only connect to a single instance, and therefore is blind in many ways to the RAC configuration. For this reason, we recommend setting a business rule that RMAN will always connect to the same node for backups. This simplifies the configuration at your end, and does not affect the backup process. If that node is lost, and a recovery operation must be performed, you can always restore from a different node. Remember: RMAN stores its information in the control file, which is shared by all nodes, and therefore is independent of the instance. We recommend setting a single backup node for ease of use only. It also can provide performance gains: if you have backups always running from one place, you can load balance your user connections and application work appropriately by placing the bulk of such work on the nodes not involved in backups.

However, just because RMAN can only connect to a single instance does not mean that only a single instance can perform a backup. RMAN provides the means for configuring channels to make connections to different instances in the RAC configuration. Thus, if you have two nodes in your cluster, you can configure two default channels, each of which connects to a different instance:

```
Configure default device type to sbt;
configure device type sbt parallelism 2;
configure channel 1 device type sbt connect  'sys/sys_pwd@racdb1'
      parms "ENV=(NB_ORA_SERV=rm-wgt)";
configure channel 2 device type sbt connect  'sys/sys_pwd@racdb2'
      parms "ENV=(NB_ORA_SERV=rm-wgt)";
```

When a **backup** command is issued, RMAN opens a channel on each node and distributes the backup load across both nodes. Keep in mind that having multiple channels running in parallel only gives you performance gains if you are backing up to multiple tape devices. If both channels write to the same tape device, these channels will have serial access to the tape, and you will actually increase the backup time (and significantly impede the time to restore as well). After storing the previous configuration information, the **backup** commands for the database and control file do not differ from those used by single-instance databases:

```
Rman>backup database;
rman>backup current controlfile;
```

Archive Log Backups

The means by which we successfully back up all archive logs in a RAC configuration is a bit more complicated. This is due to the fact that each node maintains an independent redo log stream, but the control file knows about each stream. If the control file catalogs an archive log, then RMAN must back it up. But here is where RMAN has problems: because it can only connect to a single instance, it only has access to the archive logs from that thread. RMAN checks the control file, and discovers that there are archive logs that need to be backed up from two different threads, but when it checks the local system, it only finds archive logs from one of those threads. RMAN fails, telling you it cannot identify a necessary archive log.

Using Network Drives for Archiving Threads to Each Node

There are two methods of successfully backing up the archive logs of every node in your cluster. The first method provides for a simpler backup model, but requires a bit more configuration at the onset of the strategy. This method requires that you mount as network drives on each node the archive destination of each other node. After mounting these folders, you then set up LOG_ARCHIVE_DEST_N parameters at each node to write archive logs to the mounted archive destinations of each other node. By doing so, you create an environment where each node's archive destination has a full set of archive logs from all threads. Figure 15-8 illustrates this method in a 2-node cluster.

Before this methodology can be implemented, you must configure the OracleService<sid> for each instance in your cluster to log on as a domain administrator who has full disk privileges on all nodes in the cluster. Don't forget to change the listener on each node as well! See Chapter 4 for the exact steps.

With the services set up so that Oracle can read and write to mounted network drives, you can concentrate on the archive log destination setup. Before you can take any other steps, the clustered database must be in archivelog mode. If you have already performed this step, kudos. If you are unsure, check by connecting to each node as a sysdba user and issue the command **archive log list**. If you are not in archivelog mode, the following steps apply to you.

The database cannot be placed in archivelog mode if you currently have the parameter CLUSTER_DATABASE set to TRUE. So you will need to set this to FALSE, and then shut down the database and mount each instance in exclusive mode before you can alter the mode. In the following example, we assume you are using an SPFILE.

```
alter system set cluster_database=false scope=spfile;
shutdown immediate;
connect /@racdb1 as sysdba
startup mount exclusive
```

```
alter database archivelog;
alter system set cluster_database=true scope=spfile;
shutdown immediate
startup
```

Repeat this procedure for the second instance.

After getting your database into archivelog mode, concentrate on the archival destinations. For this archive log backup method to work, the local destination for archive logs *must be the same on each node*. For example, both nodes in our ongoing example in this chapter have Oracle installed on drive D:. We therefore created a directory on each node named d:\oracle\oradata\racdb\arch, and then we specified this directory as LOG_ARCHIVE_DEST_1 at each node:

```
Connect system/manager@racdb1
alter system set log_archive_dest_1=
'location=d:\oracle\oradata\racdb\arch mandatory';
connect system/manager@racdb2
alter system set log_archive_dest_1=
'location=d:\oracle\oradata\racdb\arch mandatory';
```

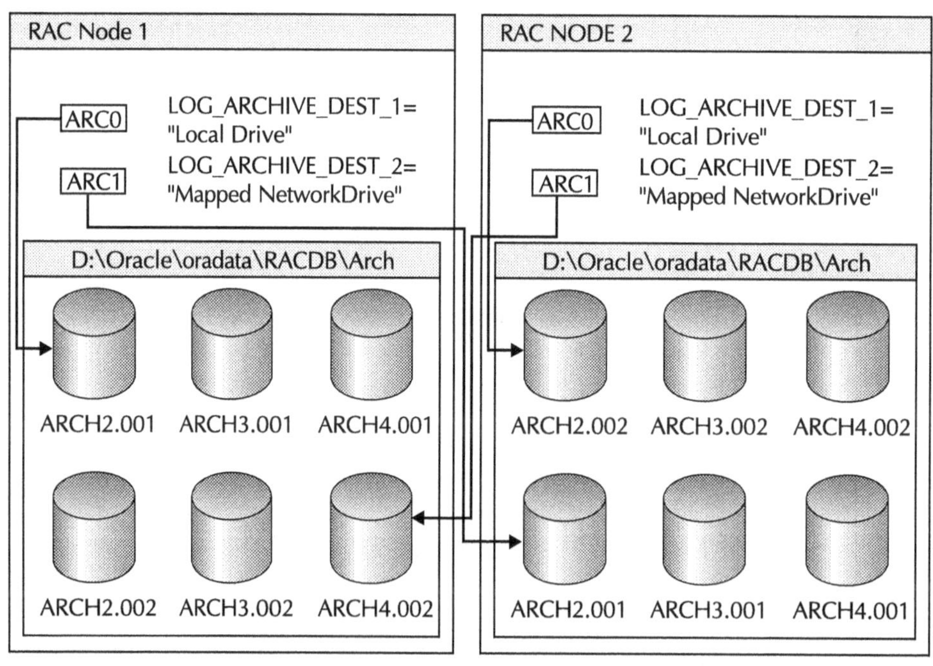

FIGURE 15-8. *Archiving each thread's logs to the archive destinations of both nodes*

Now that you have set up your first archive destination at each site, you need to map the drive at the remote site, and then set up your second archive destination (LOG_ARCHIVE_DEST_2) for each instance. Before you can map the directory, you must first share the folder. We have shared the oradata subdirectory at both nodes in our example, and will map drive T: to the oradata directory at each node. After doing so, we can set the second archival destination as such:

```
Connect system/manager@racdb1
alter system set log_archive_dest_2=
'location=t:\racdb\arch mandatory';
connect system/manager@racdb2
alter system set log_archive_dest_2=
'location=t:\racdb\arch mandatory';
alter system switch logfile;
```

This LOGFILE switch at the end is unnecessary, but it allows us to view the new behavior we have just enforced: when a log is switched at node RACDB2, an archive log is simultaneously produced in the d:\oracle\oradata\racdb\arch directory on both nodes.

Now you can begin the archive log backup. Connect RMAN to the first instance as the target instance, and then connect to your catalog and back up the archive logs. For this method, you do not need to specify a connect string for your channels.

```
Connect target /@racdb1
connect catalog rman/rman@repo
configure channel 1 device type sbt
parms "ENV=(NB_ORA_SERV=rm-wgt)";
backup archivelog like 'D:\ORACLE\ORADATA\RACDB%' delete input;
```

You will notice immediately that we did not use **backup archivelog all**. This syntax is perfectly acceptable, but you will be making a duplicate copy of each archive log if you use the ALL qualifier; it will back up the copy made to LOG_ARCHIVE_DEST_2. To avoid such duplication, the LIKE qualifier is used. We have also enlisted the delete input option, which will delete the archive logs after confirmation has been received that the backup succeeded. Be warned, though, that this will not delete the archive logs on the second node. You will need to create a manual OS task to clean up backed up archive logs on the second node.

There are many different variations to this method of archive backups. For instance, if you are uncomfortable with producing twice as many archive logs by archiving to two destinations at each node, consider setting up node 1 to archive locally, and having node 2 only archive to the mounted destination on node 1. In this model, you would always have to back up from node 1, but you minimize the number of archived redo entries you produce. This mode is also less fault tolerant, but if you had three or four nodes, it might make sense to hedge your bets and only have one or two nodes with full copies of every thread of archived redo. But if you wanted to hedge your bets, would you still be reading this book?

Using Node-Specific Channels to Back Up Archive Logs

The other method for backing up archive logs is to specify connect strings for multiple channels so that at least one channel connects to each node. You can then specify a **backup** command for each node's archive logs. For this method, *the archive log destination of each node must be different.* Remember, if you use the network drive method, the destinations need to be the same. But for this method, they must be uniquely named. You need unique names so that you can use the LIKE qualifier in the **backup** command to differentiate the work for the RMAN channels at each node. For the following example, we set up LOG_ARCHIVE_DEST_1 on both nodes to reflect the instance name: on the first node, d:\oracle\oradata\racdb1\arch; on the second, d:\oracle\oradata\racdb2\arch.

```
configure device type sbt parallelism 2;
configure channel 1 device type sbt connect  'sys/sys_pwd@racdb1'
      parms "ENV=(NB_ORA_SERV=rm-wgt)";
configure channel 2 device type sbt connect  'sys/sys_pwd@racdb2'
      parms "ENV=(NB_ORA_SERV=rm-wgt)";
backup
(archivelog like 'D:\ORACLE\ORADATA\RACDB1\%' channel ORA_SBT_TAPE_1)
(archivelog like 'D:\ORACLE\ORADATA\RACDB2\%' channel ORA_SBT_TAPE_2);
```

Restoring Files in a Cluster Environment

Performing a restore operation in a clustered environment is no different than a restore that occurs for a single-instance database. RMAN connects to the target and the catalog, and performs its duties as asked. If you have used the RMAN **configure** command, you will not even have to worry about channel allocation.

If you have taken the backup from one node, but due to an outage need to restore from a different node, RMAN behaves no differently, as the control file is shared by all nodes. However, you may run into interesting behavior from your media management product. VERITAS NetBackup, for instance, tracks which client has performed a backup, and requires this same client to perform the restore. If a different client attempts to perform the restore, you will see an RMAN error stack like this:

```
RMAN-10035: exception raised in RPC: ORA-19507: failed to retrieve
sequential file, handle="0dd4bela_1_1", parms=""
ORA-27029: skgfrtrv: sbtrestore returned error
ORA-19511: Error received from media manager layer, error text:
sbtrestore: Backup file not found.
RMAN-10031: ORA-19624 occurred during call to
DBMS_BACKUP_RESTORE.RESTOREBACKUPPIECE
```

To overcome this, you need to pass the parameter NB_ORA_CLIENT when you allocate the sbt channel for backup. Specify this parameter as the name of the client that performed the backup. For instance, if you have backed up from node RMNTOPS1, but are currently connected to RMNTOPS2 for the restore operation, your channel would need to specify RMNTOPS1 as the client:

```
configure channel 1 device type sbt connect  'sys/sys_pwd@racdb1'
     parms "ENV=(NB_ORA_SERV=rm-wgt,NB_ORA_CLIENT=rmntops1)";
```

Also, by default, NetBackup does not allow clients to restore backups taken from other clients. This is a security design so that your backups cannot by default be pulled down to someone else's computer and viewed. NetBackup provides the means of overcoming this design feature. Go to the Program Files directory of your system disk, and you will find the Veritas installation directory. Navigate to \Veritas\NetBackup\db\altnames. If there is no altnames directory, create it yourself. Next, build an empty ASCII file in the altnames directory named No.Restrictions. The presence of this file allows you to specify the NB_ORA_CLIENT parameter in order to restore to an alternate client machine.

Creating a Single Instance Standby Database from a Cluster Database

Standby databases provide incredible disaster protection for any database. However, the cost of maintaining a second clustered computer system that may never be used may be restrictive to many shops. Fortunately, there is a method for creating a standby database in a single instance based on a clustered primary database. This method gives you a cost-to-performance compromise: should you ever fail over to the standby database, your data processing will necessarily be slower than that on the clustered database, but you've saved yourself the cost of a second multinode cluster.

There is no particular difference in creating this standby database as opposed to those outlined in Chapter 13. Using RMAN to create the standby database, you may run into issues if you specify the DORECOVER clause of the **duplicate...for standby** command, but only if you are using an archive log backup methodology in which all nodes back up their own archive logs (versus the network drive method). Our recommendation is to omit DORECOVER, and then manually move the necessary archive logs to the standby database for the initial recovery.

Before beginning manual recovery of the standby database, perform a final log switch at all nodes in your cluster. This confirms that all current redo entries, through

the backup and up to the recovery, have been archived. Next, move the files to the standby site and issue the **recover** command. The command **recover standby database** will request archive logs from both nodes based on the chronological order of the redo operation. This is based on SCN information, not log sequence information. Therefore, it is feasible that there are six or seven archive logs from node A that will be applied before the recovery session ever asks for an archive log from node B. It simply depends on the activity of each node in the cluster.

After applying these changes, you can place the standby database in managed recovery mode as specified in Chapter 13. The alert log will reflect that it is waiting on two threads of archive logs (if you have two nodes).

Putting Your Standby Database to Use

Contrary to popular belief, the standby database no longer must sit idly by and simply wait for the worst-case scenario to catch up to it. Now, you can put that computer to work doing tasks that otherwise would be required of the primary database.

For the sake of an ultimate high-availability solution, the primary task you can give to the standby database is the creation of your backups. As mentioned in Chapter 6, it is both possible and agreeable to connect RMAN to the standby database as the target and perform your backups. The fact that the primary database is in a RAC configuration and the standby database is a single-node database does not interfere with this backup solution. Remember: RMAN checks the control file for information about where files are located, then records that information to the control file (and the catalog). The standby database does a filename conversion based on memory parameters, so in theory the files you back up from the standby database still map to the raw devices on the shared disks at the primary site. This is how Oracle preserves file integrity so that the backups can be restored to the primary site at a later point.

When connecting to the standby database to take backups for the primary RAC database, make sure you connect to the standby database as the target, and not as the auxiliary. There is no need to connect to the actual primary database in RMAN. However, connection to the catalog is required. For the backup operations, you will need to allocate manual channels for the backup. You cannot change RMAN configuration parameters at the standby database, otherwise you will receive the following error:

```
RMAN-03013: command type: configure
RMAN-06003: ORACLE error from target database: ORA-01649: operation
not allowed with a backup controlfile
ORA-06512: at "SYS.X$DBMS_BACKUP_RESTORE", line 3132
ORA-06512: at line 1
```

Reasons for not using your preexisting channel configurations have everything to do with your media management product. As you remember from our example earlier, we configured our channels with the NB_ORA_CLIENT parameter set to RMNTOPS1. However, now we are backing up from the standby database, which in our example is named RMNW2, and NetBackup will fail to perform a backup if it is passed an erroneous NB_ORA_CLIENT parameter at the time of backup. Instead of passing an error to RMAN, however, NetBackup simply records the error in its server logs and leaves RMAN hanging indefinitely. If you see RMAN hanging for an unusually long period during a backup, check your NB_ORA_CLIENT parameters and make sure they match the name of the machine you are actually backing up from:

```
run {allocate channel ch1 device type sbt
parms "ENV=(NB_ORA_SERV=rm-wgt,NB_ORA_CLIENT=rmnw2)";
backup datafile 8;}
```

The log output from this backup operation will indicate that a file with the specified name at the standby site is being backed up, not the file of the same name on the RAC database. Obviously, these are markedly different: the standby database exists on a file system, and therefore has a drive letter and directory structure; the primary database's files all exist on raw partitions and therefore map to symbolic links, denoted by the *//./* symbols. Don't be alarmed by this. As mentioned earlier, the real location of the files is safely recorded in the standby control file, and therefore passed to the catalog.

Before you finish your backup operations at the standby database, we recommend that you perform a manual resync of the catalog. A resync does not occur by default after every backup, and therefore your backup records may only get stored in the standby control file and not be passed to the recovery catalog. These backups will not be available to the primary database unless their records are propagated to the catalog.

Restoring to the Primary RAC Database from a Standby Database Backup

After backing up datafiles from the standby database, there is little difference between the restore operation to the primary database versus a restore operation to the standby database. The recovery catalog does not differentiate between the standby and the primary databases when connecting to them as the target database. Remember, the catalog identifies a database by its DBID, which is the same for the primary and standby databases. When the backups are taken at the standby database, and you resync with the catalog, the records of those backups propagate to the catalog.

Next, you connect to the primary database as the target, connect to the catalog, and then issue a **restore** or **recover** command.

Be aware of the channel configuration that is required for the restore operation to the primary database. Because you backed up using the NB_ORA_CLIENT setting of the standby server, you will need to specify that same NB_ORA_CLIENT when restoring to the primary server. In effect, now that you have successfully set up your standby database, you will never again be connecting to any of the RAC nodes for backup. We recommend, therefore, that once you have established the standby database for RMAN backups, connect RMAN to the primary RAC database as the target, connect to your catalog, and configure your permanent channel settings with an NB_ORA_CLIENT setting of your standby node (in our example, this means changing NB_ORA_CLIENT from RMNTOPS1 to RMNW2).

Summary

In this chapter, we take the concept of high availability a step further by combining multiple methods into an overall comprehensive solution. We introduced the concepts of load balancing and Transparent Application Failover. In addition, we discussed a new product called Real Application Clusters Guard, which combines the virtual group concept of MSCS with Real Application Clusters to speed up reconnections in the event of a failure. Finally, we discussed the use of a single-instance standby environment in conjunction with a Real Application Clusters setup, using RMAN as the main backup strategy, both for creation of the standby database and backups of the cluster database.

PART V

Appendices

TIPS & TECHNIQUES

APPENDIX A

Media Management Configuration for RMAN Backups to Tape

As most database administrators and system administrators know, backing up to tape provides an inexpensive place to store files that by all accounts are not used very frequently. By performing these backups with RMAN, you can then harness the power of the database for streamlined backups that rely on Oracle's data block structure. These tape backups can then be used to create duplicate databases for testing purposes and create standby databases for disaster recovery.

Although there are many different products that integrate with RMAN, this book uses VERITAS NetBackup for its tape backup examples (see Chapters 6 and 15). The following instructions for setting up VERITAS assume you have obtained all of the appropriate VERITAS software and will be using NetBackup as the primary means of writing Oracle database backups to tape.

VERITAS NetBackup

A complete guide to using VERITAS NetBackup as your partner in database backup is certainly beyond the scope of this book—it would be a book in itself. The following brief guide is simply meant to be the criminally abridged version of that book.

NetBackup is a backup product produced by VERITAS to aid in the administration and management of storage devices. It can be roughly broken into two separate pieces: NetBackup Server and NetBackup Client. The NetBackup Server product is installed on the computer that operates the media devices themselves, and is responsible for reading, writing, and managing the tapes in the tape drives. The server is where NetBackup keeps its Media Catalog, the storage database for information about all backups taken on that server.

The NetBackup Client software resides on all computers that need to write backups to the NetBackup Server computer. The client is registered at the server, and can connect to it based on policies implemented at the server. In addition to the client software, NetBackup has an individually priced (and therefore individually installed) product called NetBackup for Oracle. This is the key piece for integration with RMAN. NetBackup for Oracle installs the necessary SBT_API integration files and places them in a searchable path in the Windows 2000 computer so that RMAN finds NetBackup when a tape channel is allocated.

NetBackup Configuration for RMAN Backups

VERITAS NetBackup Client software must first be installed on the machine that holds the target database. After making a client software installation, NetBackup for Oracle needs to be installed. No further configuration is necessary at the client machine.

On the NetBackup Server, you need to first set up an Oracle class for backup. This is done using the Backup Policy Management GUI. Right-click <servername> classes and choose New. Name the class Oracle, specify the class type as MS-Windows-NT, and change the Class Storage Unit setting to the appropriate tape device.

After class setup, you need to register the client so that it can access the server. From the Backup Policy Management utility, right-click Clients and choose New. The client name should be the name of the server on which your target database resides (where you installed NetBackup for Oracle). The Hardware and Operating System option should be set to PC, Windows NT. Click OK.

And that is all the configuration that is needed. Next, you move back to the client machine (in our examples, the client and server are on the same computer) and run RMAN backup to test for proper integration.

```
RMAN>run {
allocate channel c1 device type sbt;
send 'NB_ORA_SERV=rm-wgt';
backup database; }
```

Notice the **send** command. The **send** command must be used to establish within the RMAN environment the name of the Media Management Server to connect to in order to find a tape device. This information is not for RMAN's sake, but rather for the NetBackup Client software that needs to make the network connection.

If the NetBackup configuration is correct, you will see RMAN echo information about the NetBackup Software when it allocates the channels:

```
Allocated channel: c1
channel c1: sid=12 devtype=SBT_TAPE
channel c1: VERITAS NetBackup for Oracle8 - Release 3.4GA (030800)
```

This tells you that RMAN is seeing the Media Management Library correctly, and any problems you have from here on out will be either in your environment or at the NetBackup Server. By environment, we refer to the environment variables that are sent from within RMAN to NetBackup. Table A-1 covers the different variables briefly.

Variable	Description
NB_ORA_SERV	Specifies the name of the Media Management Server.
NB_ORA_CLIENT	Specifies the name of the client computer where NetBackup for Oracle is installed. This is necessary if you are restoring to a computer that is different from the one that was backed up.
NB_ORA_CLASS	Names the class used for this particular backup.
NB_ORA_SCHED	Names the Backup Policy schedule set up at the server.

TABLE A-1. *RMAN Environment Variables Sent to the NetBackup Server*

Monitoring Backups from the NetBackup Server

Any usage of NetBackup is logged at the server, and you can monitor the usage with the NetBackup Device Monitor. This GUI is available on the server, and shows current device usage:

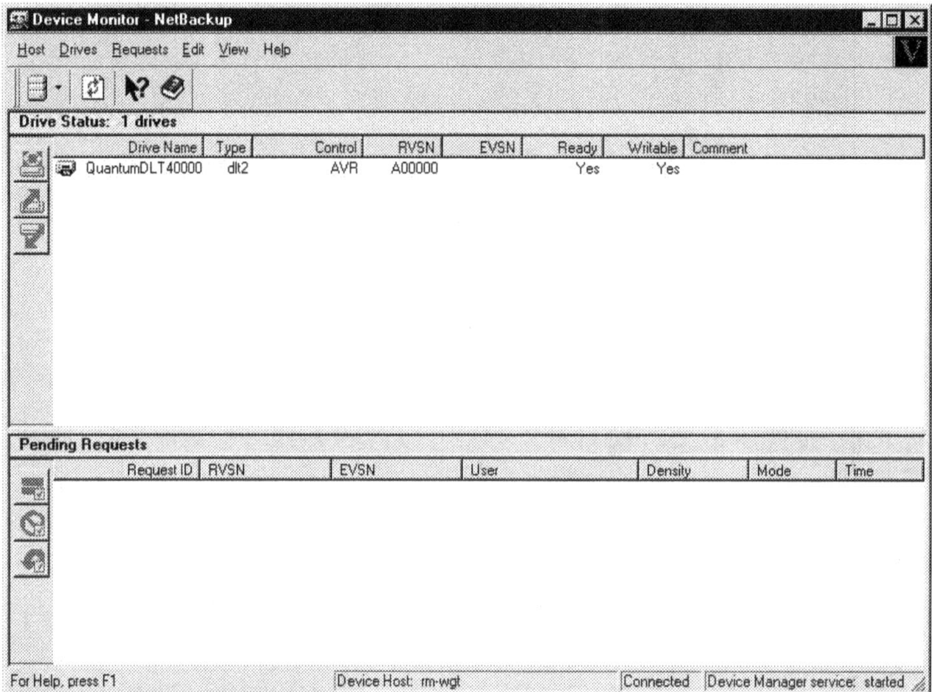

If you need to look at historical backup and restore information, use NetBackup Reports, shown next. This can be passed variables based on the sort of activity you need to view, and a window of time in which that activity occurred.

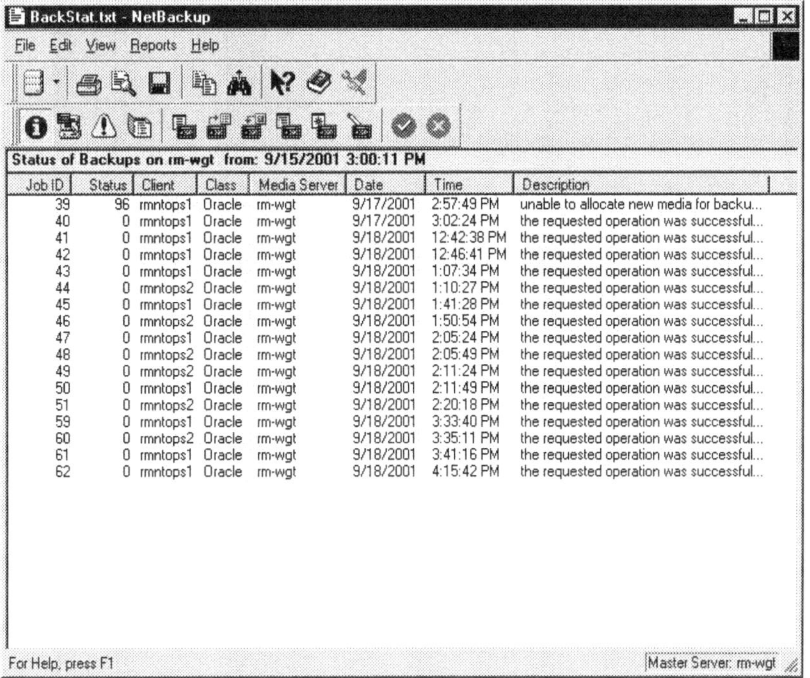

APPENDIX B

Generating and Finding Diagnostic Information for Oracle 9*i*

In this appendix, we provide you with the tools Oracle Support typically uses to diagnose issues that are not easily determined by looking in just the alert log or by using the Enterprise Manager tools. This appendix is to help you if you are much more interested in learning more about Oracle than you typically need to know. While all of this information is publicly available on the Oracle Support web site, you may find it useful as a quick reference to a number of different resources. Typically, if you *need* this information, you should engage Oracle Support. For example, reading a system state dump is not of much use to most people, but it is important to understand what it is, what it can be useful for, and how to get the output to Oracle Support in the case of a TAR that requires one or more state dumps.

One of the more recent DBMS packages, DBMS_SUPPORT, has the capability to do much of what Oradebug does that a typical customer would be interested in. I opted not to add that information here, because DBMS_SUPPORT is described in Oracle documentation and in documents found at the Oracle Support web site.

Setting events is designed to be a very temporary activity. Events can have an undesirable impact on the system because events are often used to resolve unforeseeable issues. Many times, we find customers have events that are set in their production system, but they have no idea why.

The events that we directly discuss here are for dumping trace files that contain valuable information for experts. You *can* learn quite a bit from these trace files if you are patient and understand the essential concepts of Oracle's implementation of the relational database. With that said, we open the door for you to completely annihilate your database due to lack of understanding. Understand what you are doing! Search the Internet (we found all things discussed here except the explain plan trace file using Google's search engine) and Oracle's support web site for more information. To understand more about events, read the Oracle Support document number 75713.1.

Oradebug

Oradebug is a tool that is used to access the innards of the database to gather information that can be used to analyze the state of the database as a whole, a particular process or session, or a particular activity for a session. Oradebug can be used to provide specific tracing information and to alter the behavior of the database through the use of events. Oradebug can even be used to modify areas of internal memory via the **poke** command. This latter functionality is usually used only at the request of Oracle Development. Changing internal memory structures will normally only corrupt the database and its data forever. You typically should not use Oradebug unless otherwise directed by Oracle Support analysts. If you are very careful, you can get interesting, sometimes even valuable, information from Oradebug trace files. Oradebug is a dangerous tool as well as a helpful one. It is *not* designed for customer use and is not "supported."

Oradebug is accessed through SQL*Plus. Any commands you find in this appendix require that you start SQL*Plus and are connected as SYSDBA. You can get a listing of the basic commands from a SQL*Plus command prompt by typing **oradebug help**. From here, you can get further help regarding the number and types of arguments by typing **oradebug help <command>**. For example:

```
SQL> oradebug help dump
DUMP      <dump_name> <level>     Invoke named dump
```

To get a list of the various things that you can dump, you can type this command from SQL*Plus:

```
SQL> oradebug dumplist
```

This command spits out a list of all the different facilities you can dump to a trace file. Some, if not many, of the dump names in the list will not work for you. Some of the more common commands appear in the following table. These commands do not change the system but only dump information about the system.

FILE_HDRS	CONTROLF	ERRORSTACK
HEAPDUMP	SYSTEMSTATE	REDOHDR
HANGANALYZE	HANGANALYZE_PROC	PROCESSSTATE

Oradebug Context

One of the most popular trace files generated is the result of a SQL_TRACE=TRUE setting for your session. What if you want to trace a session other than your own and you do not want to trace all of the SQL executions in a database? This is a common case with web applications or with any application that has more than two tiers where you cannot instrument the code due to restrictions or impacts. You may also want to trace the activity of a background process like SMON, PMON, or a Job process. In these cases, you need to use Oradebug to set the Oracle PID of the Oradebug session context. You determine the Oracle PID from the PID column of the V$PROCESS view. This PID is the internal Oracle process identifier.

```
SQL> oradebug setorapid 6
Windows thread id: 236, image: ORACLE.EXE
SQL> oradebug unlimit
Statement processed.
```

```
SQL> oradebug event 10046 trace name context forever, level 12
Statement processed.
SQL> oradebug event 10046 trace name context off
Statement processed.
```

There is one more way to set the Oracle thread context for your Oradebug session. If you care to set the context for only the current session in order to get system-level dumps (file headers, system state, and so on), then you can use the following syntax:

```
SQL> oradebug setmypid
Statement processed.
SQL> oradebug unlimit
Statement processed.
SQL> oradebug dump systemstate 10
```

This command will set the Oradebug session-specific commands to examine the current thread ID's information. This is not much help in diagnosing most session-specific problems, because the Oradebug user must be connected as SYSDBA. However, for getting quick-and-dirty system state or other dumps, it is quick and easy.

NOTE
You do need to make sure that you set the "unlimit" switch to enable full dumping of information. If you cannot dump the whole trace file, it is usually not worth the time and effort to get the trace file.

Dumping Information to Trace Files

In Oracle9i, the capability to get greater information about a thread's current state was added to aid in problem diagnostics. The core dump functionality in 9i has been improved. A log file with more information regarding a process is generated without destroying the process. The syntax is simple:

```
SQL> oradebug core
```

This functionality is available only from Oradebug. You can also dump the content of file headers, redo logs, and other items of interest in a difficult-to-diagnose situation with or without Oradebug. You can use the ALTER SESSION and ALTER SYSTEM statements to set specific events and dump diagnostic information to the file system.

Which Trace File?

Sometimes it is difficult to determine which trace files are the product of your Oradebug actions. At the time you set your PID with Oradebug, the resulting output indicates the naming nomenclature of the trace file. For example, if I **setorapid** to 16, it will then spit out the "Windows thread id" that makes up the latter part of the filename. The extension will almost always be "TRC" for trace files. A trace file generated by a background processes is often indicated in the alert log with the cause, trace file name, and location. You should always check your alert log if you are interested in the cause of a particular trace file, as well as to determine trace file location. The alert log will give you a context to help understand the ultimate reason that a trace file was generated. There is a new feature that allows sessions to set a trace file identifier string that will be appended to the trace file name. This feature can be changed dynamically:

```
alter session set tracefile_identifier='MySession';
```

If your Windows thread (spid column value in v$process) is 263, then the resulting trace file after running this command would be ORA00263_MySession.TRC.

If a trace file is generated by a background process (e.g., SMON or PMON), you will find the resulting process's trace file in the BACKGROUND_DUMP_DEST locations. You can determine this and the other database trace file locations with the following command from SQL*Plus connected as SYSDBA:

```
SQL> show parameter dump
```

This command will show you all the initialization parameters with the pattern "dump" in them. If you find that you need to send dump files to a different location on-the-fly, you can do that with the following command:

```
SQL> alter system set user_dump_dest='c:\oracle\trace\testing';
```

This command will also change the location of *new* trace files to this directory for user process generated traces to the indicated directory. If you want to change the core or background dump locations, then just substitute "core" and/or "background" for the word "user" in the preceding statement.

State Dumps

The system state dump is a picture of the state of the objects in the Oracle threads during the period of the dump generation. It is important to note what this is *not*. It is not a snapshot in time of the state of database objects. The state dump process has to

cycle through all of the processes involved and loop through all of its state objects and their child state objects. For this reason, it is normal to find inconsistencies in a system state dump. This is the syntax for obtaining a system state dump:

```
Alter session set events 'immediate trace name systemstate level 10';
```

or from Oradebug:

```
SQL> oradebug setmypid
SQL> oradebug dump systemstate 10
```

There is also a dump that is a subset of the system state dump, the process state dump. This dump will dump only the state objects of the interesting process. It is almost always better to get a system state dump, but sometimes they can take too long to complete or generate too large a file on very large and active systems. If you find that a system state dump is too intrusive, you may need to run one or more process state dumps instead. To do this, you need to use the Oradebug facility after you have identified the processes you are interested in. For each process, you must set the PID or OSPID before running the DUMP command. In this example, we are going to dump Oracle PIDs 445 and 28:

```
SQL> oradebug unlimit
SQL> oradebug setorapid 445
SQL> oradebug dump processstate 10
SQL> oradebug setorapid 28
SQL> oradebug dump processstate 10
```

State objects are a representation of a structure that refers to resources that are accounted for by the database. For example, there is a process state object that contains information about the process:

```
PROCESS 6:
  ----------------------------------------
  SO: 7AD9198C, type: 2, owner: 00000000, flag: INIT/-/-/0x00
  (process) Oracle pid=6, calls cur/top: 7AE14C98/7AE14C98, flag:
  (16) SYSTEM
            int error: 0, call error: 0, sess error: 0, txn error 0
  (post info) last post received: 0 0 67
             last post received-location: ktmchg
             last process to post me: 7ad930d8 2 0
             last post sent: 177 0 15
             last post sent-location: ksasnd
             last process posted by me: 7ad912e4 1 6
    (latch info) wait_event=0 bits=0
    Process Group: DEFAULT, pseudo proc: 7ADAF8E0
    O/S info: user: SYSTEM, term: FOXRUN, ospid: 1168
    OSD pid info: 1168
```

In this case, we are looking at the Oracle Process number 6. This relates to the PID column of the V$PROCESS table. This is repeated in the "Oracle pid=6" on line 4. The "SO: 7AD9198C" refers to the address in memory of the process state object. This is important because it will enable us to identify objects that might be waiting for a resource held by this process or one of its children.

There are three basic things that a state dump can be used for: first, determining change, lack of change, and other patterns across state dumps; second, to get a better idea of what a process, session, or user was doing at the time of the state dump; and third, to spot weirdness (errors and the like). A complete book could be written about reading and interpreting the content of a system state dump, but it would be useful to no one outside of Oracle Support and Development. Typically, you will only want to pass on the system state dumps to Oracle Support for analysis in the case of a hanging process. You can use them to become more familiar with what exists in an Oracle thread or to put you to sleep at night.

Tracing SQL

If you are interested in getting more information about the SQL that is actually being run on your system at a given time, you can use the simple ALTER SESSION syntax:

```
SQL> alter session set sql_trace=true;
```

This will give you the lowest level of SQL tracing available. This statement is equivalent to setting the following event:

```
SQL> alter session set events '10046 trace name context forever, level 1';
```

It will not provide you with the actual bind variable values or waits that occurred. You can set the SQL trace level higher by using this last ALTER statement and changing the level to one of those indicated in the following table.

1	Same as setting SQL_TRACE to true for the session of interest
4	Adds the values actually bound for a SQL statement to level 1 tracing
8	Adds Wait information to level 1 tracing
12	Combines levels 1, 4, and 8 into one trace file

You can also set event 10046 on a different session than your own with Oradebug. You first need to determine the thread that is running the session you are interested in and then use Oradebug to connect to that thread:

```
SQL> select paddr from v$session where username = 'SCOTT';
PADDR
--------
```

```
7AD9342C
SQL> select pid from v$process where addr='7AD9342C';
      PID
----------
       14
SQL> oradebug unlimit
SQL> oradebug setorapid 14
Windows thread id: 1780, image: ORACLE.EXE
SQL> oradebug event 10046 trace name context forever, level 12
```

This will start tracing the user's session logged into the SCOTT schema with all waits and variable bindings. Once you have gathered the amount of data you need, you can turn it off from Oradebug as well:

```
SQL> oradebug event 10046 trace name context off
```

This will halt SQL trace for that session. You do not have to turn off the tracing from the same user session that began the tracing. Just use Oradebug to set the PID to the correct session (14, in this case) and turn it off from there.

If you need to trace all SQL activity in the database, you can set the event in your init.ora file or the SPFILE. This can be very resource-intensive and cause thousands of files to be generated in a very short period of time. Here is the change you would make to the init.ora:

```
Event="10046 trace name context forever, level 12"
MAX_DUMP_FILE_SIZE = UNLIMITED
```

Oradebug is a very powerful, versatile, and flexible tool. However, what if you are simply trying to dump SQL TRACE information for either your session or another database session? The DBMS_SUPPORT package comes in handy in these cases. To create the package, you must log in as SYSDBA and execute $OH/rdbms/admin/dbmssupp.sql. DBMS_SUPPORT contains four procedures that can be used to start/stop tracing in your own session, and also to start/stop tracing another user's session. The great thing about the package is that it can also be used to trace bind variables and even wait events recorded during the execution of the SQL statement, just like Oradebug. This use of this package is much simpler than Oradebug. You need to look at V$SESSION to get the SID and SERIAL# of the session you want to trace. For example, to trace session 10, serial# 25, showing waits but not bind variables, you would execute this statement:

```
SQL> exec dbms_support.start_trace_in_session(10,25,true,false)
```

If you are using row-level security (virtual private databases) and you are receiving wrong results, you may need to set another event to get basic information about the predicate added onto the SQL statement altered by the policy:

```
Alter session set events '10730 trace name context forever, level 1';
```

If you are tracing a session other than your own, you can set this event from Oradebug:

```
SQL> oradebug event 10730 trace name context forever, level 1
```

The output will give you the logged-in user, the policy name and function, the table or view, and the SQL predicate.

TKPROF

If you are starting to lose your mind while trying to interpret the activity in your 10046 trace, you may want to use the tkprof.exe tool to generate a nicely formatted summary of the trace. In Oracle9i, this utility has also added the capability to show wait statistics by default, as well as a large number of other options. To use the utility, simply use the command line to navigate to the location of the trace file and use this syntax:

```
C:\oracle\admin\prod\udump> tkprof tracefile outputfile
```

If you want to learn more about the options available, then simply run tkprof on the command line without parameters. To interpret the output, check out the Oracle Support web site for numerous notes on tkprof interpretation.

New Explain Plan Event: 10132

Oracle9i introduced a new event that generates an explain plan in a trace file. The nice thing about this event is that it is able to generate a plan without the plan table. You can set this event for a session other than your own using Oradebug. This makes it easy for you to get an explain plan for SQL being run from a middle-tier application or in a situation where you are unable to create a plan table but can connect as SYSDBA:

```
SQL> oradebug event 10132 trace name context forever
```

And to turn it off:

```
SQL> oradebug event 10132 trace name context off
```

Why Do All the Elapsed Times Show Zero?

Most people forget to enable timed_statistics when running a SQL trace. If you want to understand why something is taking so long, you must turn it on. You can alter your system to turn it on, then turn it back off when you have finished if you do not need it. If you are using Statspack, then you really should leave it on to get valuable numbers for timing with Statspack. Here is the syntax to turn it on:

```
Alter system set timed_statistics=true;
```

And to turn it off:

```
Alter system set timed_statistics=false;
```

Dumping Datafile, Redo, and Control File Headers

If you are interested in the state of datafiles or the range of content in a redo log, you can dump just the headers of these files to determine which files are of interest and the next step to take in those situations.

FILE_HDRS

When you dump file headers, you cycle through the datafiles, as listed in v$datafile, and dump out information related to the state of the datafiles. This is typically an important dump in the case of an unrecoverable database. There are two ways you can dump file headers from SQL*Plus:

```
SQL> alter Session Set Events 'immediate trace name file_hdrs level 10';
```

or

```
SQL> oradebug setmypid
SQL> oradebug dump file_hdrs 10
```

Both of these methods generate the same trace file.

REDOHDR

The need to dump redo headers is relatively rare, but you may want to do so in some cases of a botched recovery or just to determine quickly on a down database the time range of the logs and the equivalent SCNs. As with the file_hdrs dump, you can perform this function two ways:

```
SQL> alter Session Set Events 'immediate trace name redohdr level 10';
```

or

```
SQL> oradebug setmypid
SQL> oradebug dump redohdr 10
```

CONTROLF

Control file header dumps allow you to understand what that control file identifies as a part of your database. They also enable you to check for things like database name and DBID and to identify other problems that can be caused by bad or mixed-up restores.

```
SQL> alter Session Set Events 'immediate trace name controlf level 10';
```

or

```
SQL> ordebug setmypid
SQL> oradebug dump controlf 10
```

Dumping Redo Log Files

If you have a situation that requires that you examine redo, you can most often access it through the support Oracle tool Log Miner, but there are situations where Log Miner may not help. For these situations, you can often get more information by dumping the redo. Once you have determined that something has gone seriously wrong and you need to determine absolutely what the data looked like previously, you can dump the formatted content of a redo or archived log file:

```
alter system dump logfile
'g:\oracle\oradata\test\archive\arch1_76.log';
```

This will dump the log file content with all of the activity for that log's actions. It is not easy to interpret the actual goings-on from a formatted log file dump, but you can use it to target specific needs. The much more friendly tool to do this kind of work is Log Miner. Log Miner looks at your log files for a time in history and enables you to search for interesting data for your situation. Dumping the log file in this manner is more useful for those situations where Log Miner is not sufficient or you have a corrupted log. Even in the case of a corrupted log, this dump is not sufficient and you will likely have to use a hex editor to view the content of the file directly. This is not a process that is supported or easy for anyone to do, but it can be done with many hours of work.

Dumping Blocks in Datafiles

Oracle9i is moving closer to a more and more formatted block dump and less impactful ways to recover from a block corruption, whether caused by Oracle or not. If you have a corrupted block, you can review the contents of this block by dumping its contents from the command line:

```
SQL> alter system dump datafile 1 block 5586;
```

This statement dumps the content of one block in datafile number 1. The statement "select file#, name from v$datafile" will show you the name and datafile numbers in your database. If you are experiencing corruption, it is most often more useful to dump blocks around the corruption as well as the actual corrupted block. This allows your analysis to determine what an uncorrupted block should look like and enables you to check for undetected corruption in the body of the surrounding blocks. You can dump a range of blocks with the following command:

```
SQL> alter system dump datafile 1 block min 5585 block max 5586;
```

If you are interested in dumping a block from a datafile that is not part of a database, you can use the following statement:

```
SQL> alter system dump datafile '/u01/oradata/mydb/system01.dbf' block 98;
```

Formatted data block dumps can easily be converted by Oracle Support into readable data if only the data block metadata has been corrupted. Even if the data itself has been corrupted, you can still get most of the data from the formatted dump.

Error Stack Dumps

Sometimes you will run into an error that causes more havoc than it should. Because Oracle may provide only minimal information for this error, it will not necessarily generate all the information you need (e.g., a trace file) to diagnose a problem. In cases like these, you can cause an error occurrence to trigger more trace information upon each occurrence. If you set the errorstack event for the event of interest, you can get extensive information about the session and its process at the time of the error. You can set this event in the init.ora file or the SPFILE. Here is the syntax to set it for an ORA-942 (no such table on operation error) for all sessions:

```
event = "942 trace name ERRORSTACK level 10"
```

If you are interested in generating a trace file for another error, then add another line with that event. If you want to set this event for your session when it encounters an ORA-3113 error, you can use the ALTER SESSION syntax:

```
alter session set events '3113 trace name errorstack level 10';
```

Once you have a resulting trace file, you can search for the phrase "Current SQL statement for this session:" to identify the problem SQL. Then try executing it yourself from SQL*Plus to help identify what the problem might be. There should also be a process state dump, as well as a good chunk of other information related to the session's process at the time of the error. Set the level appropriate to your needs.

See the following table for information on the differences between the levels. Once you have this information, you can get a better understanding of what the process is doing and diagnose the problem yourself.

0	Error stack only
1	Error stack and function call stack with the current SQL
2	Level one plus the process state
3	Level two plus all cursors

More to Explore

As Oracle grows and matures, it is becoming more and more diagnosable and controllable where it counts, while it removes controls where they can only cause harm. One of the new features available to Oracle Support analysts is the Flashfreeze feature, which allows you to stop the database, or processes within the database, upon an event or prompting. This then allows Support and Development to analyze the actual state of the system at the time of the interesting event. This allows Oracle to identify intermittent problems much more quickly than it ever could before.

If you are really interested in knowing more, make sure to search the Oracle Support web site frequently for new articles. Oracle is trying to enable customers to serve themselves where it is not detrimental to their continued success.

Index

A

B

C

D

E

F

G

J

K

L

M

N

P

Q

R

S

T

U

W

INTERNATIONAL CONTACT INFORMATION

AUSTRALIA
McGraw-Hill Book Company Australia Pty. Ltd.
TEL +61-2-9417-9899
FAX +61-2-9417-5687
http://www.mcgraw-hill.com.au
books-it_sydney@mcgraw-hill.com

CANADA
McGraw-Hill Ryerson Ltd.
TEL +905-430-5000
FAX +905-430-5020
http://www.mcgrawhill.ca

GREECE, MIDDLE EAST, NORTHERN AFRICA
McGraw-Hill Hellas
TEL +30-1-656-0990-3-4
FAX +30-1-654-5525

MEXICO (Also serving Latin America)
McGraw-Hill Interamericana Editores S.A. de C.V.
TEL +525-117-1583
FAX +525-117-1589
http://www.mcgraw-hill.com.mx
fernando_castellanos@mcgraw-hill.com

SINGAPORE (Serving Asia)
McGraw-Hill Book Company
TEL +65-863-1580
FAX +65-862-3354
http://www.mcgraw-hill.com.sg
mghasia@mcgraw-hill.com

SOUTH AFRICA
McGraw-Hill South Africa
TEL +27-11-622-7512
FAX +27-11-622-9045
robyn_swanepoel@mcgraw-hill.com

UNITED KINGDOM & EUROPE (Excluding Southern Europe)
McGraw-Hill Education Europe
TEL +44-1-628-502500
FAX +44-1-628-770224
http://www.mcgraw-hill.co.uk
computing_neurope@mcgraw-hill.com

ALL OTHER INQUIRIES Contact:
Osborne/McGraw-Hill
TEL +1-510-549-6600
FAX +1-510-883-7600
http://www.osborne.com
omg_international@mcgraw-hill.com

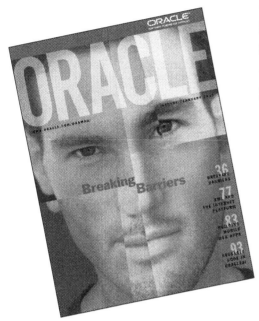

☐ YES! Please send me a FREE subscription to *Oracle Magazine*. ☐ NO

To receive a free bimonthly subscription to *Oracle Magazine*, you must fill out the entire card, sign it, and date it (incomplete cards cannot be processed or acknowledged). You can also fax your application to **+1.847.647.9735. Or subscribe at our Web site at www.oracle.com/oramag/**

SIGNATURE (REQUIRED) X ______ **DATE** ______

NAME ______ TITLE ______

COMPANY ______ TELEPHONE ______

ADDRESS ______ FAX NUMBER ______

CITY ______ STATE ______ POSTAL CODE/ZIP CODE ______

COUNTRY ______ E-MAIL ADDRESS ______

☐ From time to time, Oracle Publishing allows our partners exclusive access to our e-mail addresses for special promotions and announcements. To be included in this program, please check this box.

You must answer all eight questions below.

1 What is the primary business activity of your firm at this location? *(check only one)*

- ☐ 03 Communications
- ☐ 04 Consulting, Training
- ☐ 06 Data Processing
- ☐ 07 Education
- ☐ 08 Engineering
- ☐ 09 Financial Services
- ☐ 10 Government—Federal, Local, State, Other
- ☐ 11 Government—Military
- ☐ 12 Health Care
- ☐ 13 Manufacturing—Aerospace, Defense
- ☐ 14 Manufacturing—Computer Hardware
- ☐ 15 Manufacturing—Noncomputer Products
- ☐ 17 Research & Development
- ☐ 19 Retailing, Wholesaling, Distribution
- ☐ 20 Software Development
- ☐ 21 Systems Integration, VAR, VAD, OEM
- ☐ 22 Transportation
- ☐ 23 Utilities (Electric, Gas, Sanitation)
- ☐ 98 Other Business and Services ______

2 Which of the following best describes your job function? *(check only one)*

CORPORATE MANAGEMENT/STAFF

- ☐ 01 Executive Management (President, Chair, CEO, CFO, Owner, Partner, Principal)
- ☐ 02 Finance/Administrative Management (VP/Director/ Manager/Controller, Purchasing, Administration)
- ☐ 03 Sales/Marketing Management (VP/Director/Manager)
- ☐ 04 Computer Systems/Operations Management (CIO/VP/Director/ Manager MIS, Operations)

IS/IT STAFF

- ☐ 07 Systems Development/ Programming Management
- ☐ 08 Systems Development/ Programming Staff
- ☐ 09 Consulting
- ☐ 10 DBA/Systems Administrator
- ☐ 11 Education/Training
- ☐ 14 Technical Support Director/ Manager
- ☐ 16 Other Technical Management/Staff
- ☐ 98 Other ______

3 What is your current primary operating platform? *(check all that apply)*

- ☐ 01 DEC UNIX
- ☐ 02 DEC VAX VMS
- ☐ 03 Java
- ☐ 04 HP UNIX
- ☐ 05 IBM AIX
- ☐ 06 IBM UNIX
- ☐ 07 Macintosh
- ☐ 09 MS-DOS
- ☐ 10 MVS
- ☐ 11 NetWare
- ☐ 12 Network Computing
- ☐ 13 OpenVMS
- ☐ 14 SCO UNIX
- ☐ 24 Sequent DYNIX/ptx
- ☐ 15 Sun Solaris/SunOS
- ☐ 16 SVR4
- ☐ 18 UnixWare
- ☐ 20 Windows
- ☐ 21 Windows NT
- ☐ 23 Other UNIX ______
- ☐ 98 Other ______
- 99 ☐ **None of the above**

4 Do you evaluate, specify, recommend, or authorize the purchase of any of the following? *(check all that apply)*

- ☐ 01 Hardware
- ☐ 02 Software
- ☐ 03 Application Development Tools
- ☐ 04 Database Products
- ☐ 05 Internet or Intranet Products
- 99 ☐ **None of the above**

5 In your job, do you use or plan to purchase any of the following products or services? *(check all that apply)*

SOFTWARE

- ☐ 01 Business Graphics
- ☐ 02 CAD/CAE/CAM
- ☐ 03 CASE
- ☐ 05 Communications
- ☐ 06 Database Management
- ☐ 07 File Management
- ☐ 08 Finance
- ☐ 09 Java
- ☐ 10 Materials Resource Planning
- ☐ 11 Multimedia Authoring
- ☐ 12 Networking
- ☐ 13 Office Automation
- ☐ 14 Order Entry/Inventory Control
- ☐ 15 Programming
- ☐ 16 Project Management
- ☐ 17 Scientific and Engineering
- ☐ 18 Spreadsheets
- ☐ 19 Systems Management
- ☐ 20 Workflow

HARDWARE

- ☐ 21 Macintosh
- ☐ 22 Mainframe
- ☐ 23 Massively Parallel Processing
- ☐ 24 Minicomputer
- ☐ 25 PC
- ☐ 26 Network Computer
- ☐ 28 Symmetric Multiprocessing
- ☐ 29 Workstation

PERIPHERALS

- ☐ 30 Bridges/Routers/Hubs/Gateways
- ☐ 31 CD-ROM Drives
- ☐ 32 Disk Drives/Subsystems
- ☐ 33 Modems
- ☐ 34 Tape Drives/Subsystems
- ☐ 35 Video Boards/Multimedia

SERVICES

- ☐ 37 Consulting
- ☐ 38 Education/Training
- ☐ 39 Maintenance
- ☐ 40 Online Database Services
- ☐ 41 Support
- ☐ 36 Technology-Based Training
- ☐ 98 Other ______
- 99 ☐ **None of the above**

6 What Oracle products are in use at your site? *(check all that apply)*

SERVER/SOFTWARE

- ☐ 01 Oracle8
- ☐ 30 Oracle8*i*
- ☐ 31 Oracle8*i* Lite
- ☐ 02 Oracle7
- ☐ 03 Oracle Application Server
- ☐ 04 Oracle Data Mart Suites
- ☐ 05 Oracle Internet Commerce Server
- ☐ 32 Oracle *inter*Media
- ☐ 33 Oracle JServer
- ☐ 07 Oracle Lite
- ☐ 08 Oracle Payment Server
- ☐ 11 Oracle Video Server

TOOLS

- ☐ 13 Oracle Designer
- ☐ 14 Oracle Developer
- ☐ 54 Oracle Discoverer
- ☐ 53 Oracle Express
- ☐ 51 Oracle JDeveloper
- ☐ 52 Oracle Reports
- ☐ 50 Oracle WebDB
- ☐ 55 Oracle Workflow

ORACLE APPLICATIONS

- ☐ 17 Oracle Automotive
- ☐ 35 Oracle Business Intelligence System
- ☐ 19 Oracle Consumer Packaged Goods
- ☐ 39 Oracle E-Commerce
- ☐ 18 Oracle Energy
- ☐ 20 Oracle Financials
- ☐ 28 Oracle Front Office
- ☐ 21 Oracle Human Resources
- ☐ 37 Oracle Internet Procurement
- ☐ 22 Oracle Manufacturing
- ☐ 40 Oracle Process Manufacturing
- ☐ 23 Oracle Projects
- ☐ 34 Oracle Retail
- ☐ 29 Oracle Self-Service Web Applications
- ☐ 38 Oracle Strategic Enterprise Management
- ☐ 25 Oracle Supply Chain Management
- ☐ 36 Oracle Tutor
- ☐ 41 Oracle Travel Management

ORACLE SERVICES

- ☐ 61 Oracle Consulting
- ☐ 62 Oracle Education
- ☐ 60 Oracle Support
- ☐ 98 Other ______
- 99 ☐ **None of the above**

7 What other database products are in use at your site? *(check all that apply)*

- ☐ 01 Access
- ☐ 02 Baan
- ☐ 03 dbase
- ☐ 04 Gupta
- ☐ 05 IBM DB2
- ☐ 06 Informix
- ☐ 07 Ingres
- ☐ 08 Microsoft Access
- ☐ 09 Microsoft SQL Server
- ☐ 98 Other ______
- ☐ 10 PeopleSoft
- ☐ 11 Progress
- ☐ 12 SAP
- ☐ 13 Sybase
- ☐ 14 VSAM
- 99 ☐ **None of the above**

8 During the next 12 months, how much do you anticipate your organization will spend on computer hardware, software, peripherals, and services for your location? *(check only one)*

- ☐ 01 Less than $10,000
- ☐ 02 $10,000 to $49,999
- ☐ 03 $50,000 to $99,999
- ☐ 04 $100,000 to $499,999
- ☐ 05 $500,000 to $999,999
- ☐ 06 $1,000,000 and over

If there are other Oracle users at your location who would like to receive a free subscription to *Oracle Magazine*, please photocopy this form and pass it along, or contact Customer Service at +1.847.647.9630

Form 5

OPRESS